Dreams
of
Everyday

The Poetry Guild

Dreams of Everyday
Copyright © 1997 by The Poetry Guild

Library of Congress
Cataloging in Publication Data

ISBN 1–888680–21–0

Printed in the United States of America by
The Poetry Guild
Finalist Publishing Center
3687 Ira Road · Bath, OH 44210

Editor's Acknowledgment

In conducting its poetry competitions, The Poetry Guild has received and evaluated poems written by poets from all walks of life. The collected works of *Dreams of Everyday* consist of a wide range of sounds and styles: free verse, traditional verse, narrative, lyric, dramatic, avant-garde and even experimental.

As the Editor of this book, the hardest part of my job was going through all the poems and making choices about which ones to use. All of the poems featured in this anthology deserve to be celebrated in the form of publication. And all beginning poets should especially be cheered.

Of course, our panel of judges assumed the most difficult task in choosing the prize winners. Because so many of the poems exhibited a powerful voice, it was even harder to pick the Grand Prize Winner. But one poem did succeed. You will find this poem, entitled "Comparison," by Edna Horvath Hansen featured on page 3.

One of the traits that makes this anthology unique is that it gives newcomers a chance to write and be read, and by doing so brings poetry back to the people. After all, art is meant to be appreciated.

The real beauty of this anthology is its inspiration. In some ways, all of us can relate to the topics and themes expressed in these poems, which address important and often timely issues that we might otherwise ignore or suppress. Each poem conveys its own message, and provides a vehicle of expression for diverse attitudes and fresh insights.

I would like to congratulate each and every poet on their inclusion in this special anthology. In addition, I am grateful to the editors, book designers, production assistants and countless others for their efforts in creating this important work. Most of all, a special thanks goes out to those of you who chose to share your poetry with us and the world!

Terence Troon, Editor

"Poetry is life distilled."

–Gwendolyn Brooks

Welcome to the Poetry Guild's heralded edition of *Dreams of Everyday!* This unique anthology contains a collection of selected poems composed by a variety of individuals.

When the idea for this anthology surfaced, its main purpose was to create an ongoing resource for those interested in publishing their own poetry and, more than anything else, to showcase the best original work.

Members of our staff have been hard at work creating this special edition. Our judges vigorously critiqued thousands of poems in order to select only the most praiseworthy of verse. Each poem in this prize anthology has been chosen based on its merit.

You will find featured the work of 1,834 contributors whose poems deal with a wide range of subjects. The selected poems focus on the reflective power of words to inform the public and create awareness about significant issues through frequently meaningful observations and vastly different poetic styles.

We are happy to say that we have a number of prize winning poems featured in the book as well, including the Grand Prize Winner and a number of honourable mention awards. (The winning entries are presented in Chapter One.) We are also delighted to publish those poets who were not prize recipients, but whose work we feel is definitely worthy of publication.

As communicators in the literary field, we all want to reach the widest possible audience. This anthology appeals to a broad spectrum of poetry lovers. By having a poem published in this anthology, you will be gaining exposure and sharing your work with many others in the poetry community.

In addition to poems, this anthology also features special dedications and a most interesting chapter of "Personal Profiles." This book encourages you to browse. In reading it, we hope that you will come away with new understandings and shared realizations of our world and experiences.

Table of Contents

Chapter One   **The Winners' Forum**   1

Winners' Announcement Page   2

The Winning Poems   3

Chapter Two   **Noteworthy Works**   21

The Anthology of Poems   22

Chapter Three   **Personal Profiles**   323

The Biographies   324

Appendix   **Index of Poets**   339

CHAPTER ONE

The Winners' Forum

It is with great pleasure that we proudly present to you this year's National Poetry Competition winners.

The poems featured in this chapter are notable not only for the masterful way in which they convey the poets' ideas, but also because they challenge the reader to reinterpret significant subject matters. It is truly amazing to see the variety of styles among the poems submitted. All have received honourable mentions from our judges. Edna Horvath Hansen's "Comparison" stands out with its superb style, craft and the poet's ability to make her poem "live and breathe."

EDITOR'S NOTE: *You will find that some of the works represented in this and the following chapter are dedicated to people who perhaps influenced or inspired the individual authors. All special dedications are composed by the poets at their personal request.*

Grand Prize

"Comparison"
– Edna Horvath Hansen

Honourable Mention

Elise and Ryan Alcorn–*Bedtime*

Susan Allen–*The Blessing*

Roberta Anselmi–*Brief Interlude*

S. John Arber–*My Dream*

David Atkinson–*Untitled*

Ted L. Barnes–*The Transfiguration*

Angelia O. Bell–*Kisses From God*

Sheila Bettney–*Dunblane*

Christopher Billing–*Untitled*

Denny Boyce–*The Fax Me, E–mail, Internet Blues*

L. E. Brouse–*Untitled*

Julia Brown–*Untitled*

Rosina Brown–*Village Stores*

Sharon Bryant–*Corn Cat*

Andrea Marie Chenoweth–*Majestic Madness*

Cassie Chester–*Snow*

Christopher Chivers–*Shyness*

L. A. Churchill–*So Many Songs*

Keith J. Coleman–*Lost Sheep*

Cynthia D'Adamo–*Melody*

Karen Davies–*Count Your Blessings*

William Davies, Jr.–*Indian Summer*

Emilia DeLisa–*The Hudson River*

Kevin Dittrich–*Life's Journey*

Robert Dye–*More To Say*

G. Thom Edwards–*Grandma's Spring*

Emily Ferrill–*Alone*

Susan Ann Fleckney–*The Wind*

Deborah Fowles–*Don't Cry For Me*

Matthew Dodge Gewirtz–*A Midnight Rose*

Elizabeth Gibson–*Awakening*

E. S. Gould–*Alternative Modes*

Megan Guest–*Atmospherics*

Christi A. Hart–*Unrequited*

Karen Hatcher–*Morning Coffee*

Michelle Hoffman–*Father Time*

Lorraine Horry–*Outside The Window*

Wes Hyde–*The Bridge*

R. J. James–*Broken Toys – Broken Hearts*

Beth Jarzomski–*A Mother's Silent Thoughts*

Jean Jones–*The Sea Sprite*

Epi Juarez–*I Ran*

Amy B. Kehrli–DeDeaux–*Frank's Rainbow*

John W. Knight–*Lepidoptera*

John Leighton–*The Mermaid Queen*

Kathleen Linhardt–*Single*

Elizabeth Lyulkin–*Sappho's Fire*

Chau Mai–*The Master's Touch*

Adelle Manning–*Foreign Boy*

Jason M. Mass–*Be An Are!*

Edith McGrail–*My Mother's Hands*

Bobbi McLendon–*Parental Rights*

Marion R. McManamy–*Maritime September*

Micheal McParland–*Hot And Cold*

Mary Christina Meadows–*Mama's Walk*

Norvell A. Molex, Jr.–*A Jazzman's Dream*

Elizabeth Morris–Pierce–*A Day In May*

Diana Mowat–*The Bonnie Braes O' Fair Kinoull*

Sandy Mudger–*My Room*

Michael J. Murray–*The Forgotten*

Laurie A. Nicholson–*Sunday Morning*

Tracy Phipps–*War Cemetery*

Donna Pilch–*Rocky Road Cake*

Jim Ploss–*Autumn Sonnet To A Sugar Maple*

Robin Leigh Portune–*Summer Night*

Marguerite Pratt–*The Dropped Bottom Brigade*

T. Pratt–*Last Mile*

George H. Randall–*Mama's Rocking Chair*

Jonathan Rew–Dixon–*Eden*

David Riemenschneider–*Cool Nights In Town*

Debra Lynn Robinson–*Is It Really Failure?*

Sara Roegge–*Little Girl Dancing*

D. I. Ross–*Blind*

Zoe Murphy Rudolph–*What's Next?*

C. Rushton–*The Magic Of Life*

Sharon T. Salter–*In The Key Of C*

Laurie Woods Sanders–*What You Took Away*

Kenneth Scarff–*Springtime*

John Schultz–*Meeting Again*

Ramona Seitzinger–*Christina*

P. J. Selby–*Santa Didn't Come*

G. Shankly–*Iron Horses*

Joan Slatalla–*Final Pages*

Gilbert T. Smith–*The Willow Tree*

K. Spinks–*Disillusion*

Philip Stickley–*Girl In The Chip Shop*

Lora Sutterfield–*Three Wishes*

Jared Terwilliger–*Mom And Dad Are Aliens*

Wendy Thompson–*Lover's Secret*

John Tierney–*Daydreams*

Ivan Wampler–*Climbing The Wind*

Carl Warmann–*The Flood*

Bernice Wenzel–*Lilacs After Rain*

Judi Westgate–*The Doorway*

Jo Wightman–*The One Within*

Elwyn Williams–*Fate*

Christina L. Yard–*Visions Of Greece*

Erika Zettl–*Last Rite*

Comparison

by Edna Horvath Hansen

Loneliness is gray.
Not the lush, velvet gray of the pussy willow,
But the dull, leaden gray of a snow–heavy sky.
Not the wild, electric gray of a summer storm.
But the cold, drab gray of a wet March rain.
Not the soft, pink gray of a spring evening,
But the sunless gray of winter twilight
Without joy and love.

Aloneness is green.
A deep, emerald green of sweet summer peas
With reminiscence in sugar taste and snapping pod.
A vibrant, blue–green of the crashing sea
With sea gulls calling from a cheerful past.
A pale, green promise of new spring leaves
With remembrances of happy days of youth,
With quiet joy and love

Loneliness can be alone or in a crowd
Without peace in the heart
Aloneness is being by oneself, but
Surrounded by the peace of God.

Broken Toys – Broken Hearts
R. J. James
There are two empty rooms at the top of the stairs
gone are my little boys whose lives I once shared

They are grown up now into fine young men
their lives are so busy, will I see them again

I'm lonely without them now they're not here
there's no noise and laughter just a sad atmosphere

The house is filled with their memories, old junk and toys
we're a close family no longer, I'm not "one of the boys"

I know that I'm selfish and must let them go
but how much I'll miss them they'll never know

I'll put on a brave act and pretend its all right
then pace up and down cry through the night

Maybe they'll visit once in a while
I must make an effort and put a smile

I hope they find happiness in their new start
and know how I love them although we're apart

If ever you should need us, in good times or sad
we're here for you always, your mum and dad

The Fax Me, E–mail, Internet Blues
Denny Boyce
I now, without apology,
Will introduce technology
In bringing up to date
The way to find a mate.

If you're without a female,
Try getting one by e–mail;
Should that not bring you content,
find one from each continent.

If you prefer your love platonic,
as to keep it electronic.

Please don't ignore these facts,
Just get yourself a fax.
Communication's quick and sure
and surfing has its own allure.

You'll be surprised how far you get
While courting on the Internet.
There is no doubt that you will meet
someone who'll make your life complete.

But if you are married why then, of course,
The search may lead to your divorce.

Corn Cat
Sharon Bryant
Cat and Corn
yellow–eyed, yellow–eared
Silk.
Against a black field
Stark!
Like thoughts at night.

A Mother's Silent Thoughts
Beth Jarzomski
Summer has ended
it's the 1st school night of the year,
as I sit alone in my yard
on my cheek I find a tear.

The kids are sleeping
the pool is still
the crickets are chirping
it's lonely on the hill.

Hey! There's a basketball
it's not put away
and just like me
it waits for someone to play.

There's a paper plate in the bushes
a napkin in the tree
remnants of summer
no more stings from a bee.

And now it's time
for school to start
my memories of summer
I'll hold close to my heart.
Dedication: Erika and Justin

Blind
D. I. Ross
A blind woman at the bookstall.
Every morning as I pass.
Seeing more than we?
Seeing more than me.

See the light...second sight.

Living on pin sharp perception.
Sound, smell, touch.
Aided only by canine eyes.
A golden dog loved much.

People pause to stimulate conversation.
Her most immediate sensation.
Though neither dog nor master seek attention.

Pat the hound.
Hiatus in their morning round.
Conscience salve.

I'm not brave enough to stop.
Not brave enough to talk.

Are you?

Disability is mine.
Life darkened by taboo.

Meeting Again
John Schultz
Your voice burns
my cheeks with a smile.
Approaching to embrace, our eyes meet.
We shy our heads
– as marionettes –
fearful we might kiss
as if we had never been lovers.

The Willow Tree
Gilbert T. Smith
I have seen the willow turning green
The willow weep as willows will
Dripping in dampness in springtime chill.

I have played in the willow's shade
The willow wild in summer storm.
The willow wilted in August warm.

I behold the willow turning gold
The willow wane when its leaves are lost
The willow weak in September's frost.

I awake to watch the willow greet the dawn
With snow upon the lawn.
The willow's beauty lingers on
Even though its leaves are gone.

The sunset's burning embers glow
Casting crimson upon the snow
Silhouetting the ruler of the hill below!

The willow was there when I was born
Oh willow be there when I am gone!
And if ever the woodsman sets his saw to thee
He will answer to God or by God he will answer to me!

War Cemetery
Tracy Phipps
A breeze gently stirs the leaves,

Dead on the ground.

Rank upon rank of chalk white crosses,
Loom above the grass, cold and unnatural.
A widow weeping,
Kneels and touches a cross,
Which to her has special meaning,
But all she feels,

Is cold, wet stone.

Somewhere a gardener works,
Quietly trimming the eager grass,
Keeping the ranks more uniform,
Than life could ever make them.

Row upon row of shattered lives.

Not remembered as a son,
Husband, father or brother,
But as a soldier,
Whose life "FOR HIS COUNTRY",
Was taken "WITH HONOUR",

And swept under a carpet of leaves.

Lover's Secret
Wendy Thompson
They build a boat
From little pink helicopter leaves
Stems embracing
Downy white feather for a sail.
Launched in the quiet eddy
By the river stone and fallen birch
To cast away their dreams.

In The Key Of C
Sharon T. Salter
fallen leaves
pirouetting in graceful symphony

orchestrations of nature
mark October's debut
in scenic song
the night's sleep long and
wearily

except the evergreen
does not perform
this seasonal ballet

so sweetly sung
the swan song of the green
the hibernating scream
of floral majesty

the ardent breeze
retreats
replete
with summer's sweet cuisine

i dreamed
i conducted it all

A Jazzman's Dream
Norvell A. Molex, Jr.
A Lick hit on diamond–like keys.
A melodic little melody
Fairy tales of a world unseen

That's a Jazzman's Dream

Little notes dance through his dreams
While moon lit nights and candlelight set
The scene.
Smoke filled rooms and piano keys hitting licks
You've never seen.

That's a Jazzman's Dream

Notes are hanging in a tree picked
Like apples off a tree.

That's a Jazzman's Dream

River Flowing full of melodies
Take a sip and sing a certain key.

Water falls in a certain
Way like a band playing a romantic
Melody.

In a Jazzman's Dream.

The Flood
Carl Warmann
Like a battering ram...

The river shoves against the levee,
and then it soon recedes.
But again its thrust is heavy,
and brings the levee to its knees.

From woods, the bucks and doe escape
to dry ground they had sped
Soon the highway looks a painted red
where deer were hit and left for dead.

Next, the river's victims
are the houses for its prey
...life's memories washed away.

In one–hundred–degree heat
we sandbaggers kept the beat
the rising flood we did defeat. Yea!

Then the cunning mighty river
...a whirlpool it would make
As it burrowed 'neath the levee
to ooze out another lake,
...behind us.

Lepidoptera
John W. Knight
Although its flight is quite erratic
This tiny insect soars ecstatic
And though it seems to have no power
It effortlessly gains each flower
On wings so fragile and exquisite
Every blossom begs its visit
And we entreat the question why
God created the Butterfly

The Bonnie Braes O' Fair Kinoull
Diana Mowat
As I wandered o'er the bonnie braes o' fair Kinoull
There nature lay before me in its glory
Whether heather hillocks rise and fall unevenly
    my footsteps tread
And the rugged rocky peaks stood out before me

The trees wild scattered o'er the braes
Put there by natures haste
The green clad boughs sway softly
A solitude of wildest grace

The heather clumps grew in abundance
While the sweeping braes down to the lowlands fell
There nature grew in scattered beauty
Sheltered by the braes o' heather bell

So stalwart stood the scraggy peaks
Creative sculpture done by nature's power
Upon uneven lofty ledges
Grew clusters of the modest mountain flower

I wandered on to reach the end
Where heather brae and grassy bank divide
There green shrubbery in splendour grew
Where birds sang out their song at eventide

Indian Summer
William Davies, Jr.
Wispy fragrances of wild grapes,
crabgrass and elderberry
pass hurriedly in the truncated afternoon
like tramps through a railyard.
The sky is blue and quiet,
the geese have left early,
prodded from the meadow
by a September frost.
The trees have uncluttered their
limbs and revel like naked bathers
in the sun.

Hot And Cold
Micheal McParland
Your feelings for me were nearly strong, though never really deep
Your heart wanted mine just for a while, though certainly not to keep
Your kiss was not indifferent but yet not enthusiastic
Your tender words were very few, and much less than those sarcastic.

You wanted me on Monday but on Tuesday not at all
You phoned me all day Wednesday but on Thursday failed to call
You thought me a prince on Friday but by Saturday I'd become a rogue
You called me handsome most of Sunday, then my looks went out of vogue.

We could talk all night when on our own, when no one else was near
We would go out drinking, crowded pub, then somehow I'd disappear
We drank the beers and shed the tears and you blamed it all on me
We walked homeward bound on separate roads after just one apology.

I was hot when you were cold; and you were cold at will
I was summer in full bloom while you were winter still
I was the man in love with life, and life meant none but you
I was the man who felt the knife with each thoughtless thing you'd do.

My tears they now have ended and I am no longer weak
My heart no longer flutters when of you they casually speak
My dream is still of loving bliss, before my heart grows old
My prayer, beware, is that we meet when you're the hot and I the cold.

Brief Interlude
Roberta Anselmi
How I wish to be alone,
No futile conversations,
With all my minor worries gone,
Alone with meditations.

No people to demand my time,
Questions wanting answers.
No problems flitting 'round my mind
Like whirling dervish dancers.

Oh solitude, I need your peace,
Tranquility and calm.
Companionship has lost appeal,
Society its charm.

This is just a passing phase.
It will not last forever
So then I will need company,
And go where people gather.

But just for now, a little quiet,
A little time to be.
A time to be just by myself,
With no one here but me.

Be An Are!
Jason M. Mass

You'd rather be a could be
If you couldn't be an are.
"Cause a could be is a maybe
With a thought of flying far!

But you'd rather be a has been
than a might have been by far.
"Cause a might have been
Never has been
But a has been
Was an are!

Sunday Morning
Laurie A. Nicholson

When I bent over to ease on my slippers,
I felt the ache in my back, although I was very young.
And the face in the early mirror had dark pools
and crags and scars, like the shore.

I crept down the carpeted stairs,
my dancer's feet sending tiny creaks before me
mingling in the winter air with the smell of weak coffee,
and the absent smell of pancakes and daddy.

The TV was silent, and only one newspaper rustled.
There were two place settings,
and the napkins were rather clumsily placed.
And I glanced in at the empty armchair, right next to the full one,
and her calloused toes seemed to gasp for breaths in
her tiny, pink slippers.

I stood, and I stared— she didn't even notice I was there.
So I pretended, trembling, that I could hear his sniffles.

But the way her robe no longer fit snugly told me that
daddy was gone.
He had taken all his Neil Diamond records,
and left us with these Sunday mornings.

Springtime
Kenneth Scarff

Spring has arrived after a winter cold and long.
The birds fill the air with their melodious song.
From the top of an oak tree tall and proud.
Comes the call of a blackbird clear and loud.

The call resounds out over valley and hills.
And is soon taken up by a thousand bills.
It's the dawn chorus ringing out over the dale.
Proclaiming the wonders that nature is about to unveil.

The sun has risen up on a most wondrous sight.
Everything has changed almost overnight.
Cascading down the hillside like a mantle of gold.
Thousands of daffodils their petals unfold.

While down in the woods 'neath the shade of the trees.
Carpets of bluebells dance in the soft spring breeze.
Swallows glide swiftly through a clear blue sky.
Their beauty and grace a delight to the eye.

If only we humans would take time to rest.
And see the wonders of nature at her very best.
Revealed in all its glory by the rising sun.
The winter snow has gone, spring has begun.

Cool Nights In Town
David Riemenschneider

I wrote a love–song,
yesterday and tomorrow,
with a chorus of porch swings
and county fairs
movements, cozy sofas,
lollipops
But, for today,
I hum someone
else's melody,
while looking only for the
fire escape.

Visions Of Greece
Christina L. Yard

Pine–fragranced breeze. Turquoise seas.
Mountains that stretch forever.
Secluded bays. Hot sunny days.
Street markets selling leather.

Balmy nights. Ancient sights.
Old women dressed all in black.
Old men drinking. Sitting, thinking.
A donkey or two out the back.

Orchids growing. Fireflies glowing.
Crickets that chirp all night long.
Stray dogs and cats. Priests in tall hats.
A tavern with dance and song.

Sunsets to please. Lemon trees.
Olive groves, dark and cool.
Midday siesta. Plate smash fiesta.
And churches with bell towers tall.

Windows shuttered. Beaches uncluttered.
Tablecloths made from lace.
Walls painted pink. Ouzo to drink.
Oh! Greece is a wonderful place!

Iron Horses
G. Shankly

Faith, Hope and Charity, lie in state
Scrapyards wait, to decide their fate
Out of darkness, and into the sun
The colliery's closed the work is done

Three locomotives, souls of the pit
Hauling manriders, timber and grit
Iron horses, pulling loads to the face
Around the clock, no slack in the pace

Hope is the tortoise, who is slow but sure
No load is too heavy, her engine is pure
Charity is a flyer, a Peter Pan dream
She speeds through the tunnel, of the coal seam

Faith is the Bulldog, steadfast and true
She sets off in one pace, and always comes through
Three locomotives, each had different ways
I was their driver, in coal mining days.

Our careers are now ended, we begin anew
farewell, iron horses, adieu adieu.
I leave the scrapyard, close to tears
we were a good team, for all these years

Eden
Jonathan Rew–Dixon
In Eden's garden I have walked
And smelled each bloom within
But no aroma can erase
The perfume of your skin.

A thousand countries I have known
Swum seas, scaled mountains high.
Yet no pure beauty has outshone
The starlight in your eyes.

A wealth of statues I have touched
Of maidens tall and fair
But none have made my senses reel
Like the satin of your hair

In woodlands I have listened long
Heard nightingales rejoice
And yet no sound has held me bound
Like the softness of your voice.

So though we sleep alone tonight
For fate keeps us apart
I hold you close to me in thought
And still closer in my heart.

Alternative Modes
E. S. Gould
When I call, I sometimes reach you
More often, your answering machine.
Direct contact is better
But I hesitate and stammer
(Why should that be?)
With the machine, talk is easier
I can organize my thoughts
Be logical and concise
Or tender and solicitous
And perhaps add a touch of elegance
It is almost another art form

Grandma's Spring
G. Thom Edwards
A young girl romped across field
and marveled at her power,
she felt the sun, she felt the breeze
and stopped to smell a flower.

She watched a little mother squirrel
hide acorns for the winter.
She flew with eagles and she felt
the pulse of life within her.

As Grandma looked across the flowers,
her prince came into view,
the young girl grew into a bride
and began her life anew.

I watched her as she thought of life,
the triumphs and the tears.
I thought of all the pleasures that
she'd given us all these years.

A smile was upon her face
as she dreamed of things she'd tried.
Then, I softly laid my hand in hers,
and wept, as Grandma died.

Father Time
Michelle Hoffman
Time holds my judgment in the pocket of his tattered coat.
He carefully placed it there the day he found me weeping on my knees.
He stood beside me and placed his aged fingers on my face.
A promise of truth whispered in his old touch,
and a light glimmered in his knowing eyes.
As he helped me to my feet, I was suddenly alone in my journey.
Twenty paces ahead, I saw Time staggering away from my glance.
He stands now out of sight.
From time to time, he clutches his coat pocket,
to be sure he has not misplaced my destiny.
I chase him often, but I have never caught him yet.
I suppose on with such wisdom only trusts himself.

Is It Really Failure?
Debra Lynn Robinson
With a heart filled with hope, he came into her life,
With promises of love,
He took her as his wife.

The dreams of love and happiness,
Babies and white fences,
Soon would be replaced with pain,
Resentment and cold defenses.

The promise she had made to God,
She did not want to break,
She held on for as long as she could,
But it was more than she could take.

Her body was still living,
Her soul began to die,
She did all that she could do,
But she couldn't live this lie.

So was the promise broken?
Will God forgive this sin?
Physically she did not die,
The death was from within.

The Magic Of Life
C. Rushton
The smile of recognition of a musical note,
The significance of a tune on which lovers dote,
That old oak tree where we used to meet,
Magical moments from times so sweet.

Hoarfrost silhouettes with dramatic precision,
A white wonder world, a true Christmas card vision.
The kaleidoscope of greens on a summer's day,
Painted in the Lord's own inimitable way.

The eyes of a child on Christmas morn
Give memories revived, hopes reborn.
Emotional pride in a parent's face,
Seeing offspring begin life's steeplechase.

Watching kids struggle through the ups and downs,
Indulging and scrimping midst smiles and frowns.
Blessed with our grandchildren, their greatest thrill,
With fun, laughter and tears two lives fulfil.

Generations pay homage on Remembrance day,
To those who fell in battle so that we all may
Drink in the joys of life and pleasures untold,
A legacy from those who'll never grow old.

Last Rite
Erika Zettl
The early morning rain
left the dead peach tree
with a diamond–studded shroud.
A fragile fabric
strings of tiny globes
clinging and trembling in the sun
with brilliant magic.

A lively wren swoops down
and through its gentle touch
the diamonds drop like tears
in solemn silence—
all but one.

Untitled
Julia Brown
Winter is more a feeling than
a season.
I look out at the sun,
brightest now in June,
long days of waiting silent,
watching for the snowfall to return.
My toes pink stiffly wiggle, hardwood
floors freeze them
together
even in the summer heat;
I shiver.
Spider crawling
on the window pane stops
to watch me.

I hate him.

Winter is no more a season
than laughter.
It seeps cold, bruising my pink
tender flesh with biting snowflakes
of frozen tears.

Maritime September
Marion R. McManamy
Lovely September, I long for you to stay,
And lull my senses dreaming with your sounds.
Through crackle of your painted leaves I stray
And sense the winter's "baying of the hounds".

Your falling leaves like bright and playful children,
Frolic on lawns and tumble down the street,
Caught by the gusting winds of early autumn,
A carnival of colour at our feet.

Now here are wisps of gold and wisps of flame,
All intertwining in your glorious reign,
Like jewels shaken from a royal crown,
In glassy tumble, tap and rattle down.

Now think I on the Artist of the sky,
Inviting man to see how all things die,
How in their dying beauty they fulfill
A greater purpose of His loving will.

So when the flush of spring comes once again,
Renewing all with wash of sun and rain,
Reconciling land and blooms again.
A joyous world notes end of winter's reign.

Snow
Cassie Chester
Wet, cold snow
Tumbles from an emotionless,
gray sky
The mysterious crystals
cling together
Until they hit the soft, white,
blanketed earth
There will be more to fall from
the great canopy above
They will not stay for long
For spring is soon to come
and warm the crystals
To wet nothingness

Little Girl Dancing
Sara Roegge
Little girl dancing in your long white gown
With violet ribbons in your hair.
Rain streaming down your face
Mingling with the tears that stain your dress.
You open wide your arms
And gently smile at the heavens.
Welcoming God and the angels
To sing your silent lullaby.

Once I was you little girl;
Violet ribbons in my hair.
Hearing their silent song
Deep within my heart.
Beautiful melodies that connect
The soul with the mind...

Once I was you little one;
As you raise your arms to the heavens.
Innocently praying for peace within.
Innocently praying for love through–out.
I watch tears stain your dress little girl;
For you, I wish God took requests.

Majestic Madness
Andrea Marie Chenoweth
As still as the sphinx,
the dusty desert of anguish.
Then full of hijinx,
to the isles of outlandish.

Back and forth,
up, down, about and around.
South to north,
capriciousness abound.

Not to mope and grope,
or fear the dismal and doom.
To approach cope and hope,
time to bloom!

Banished, battered, and scattered,
the strife in life will cease.
Love is gathered,
the welcomed aura of peace.

Agony to zest,
dark to light.
A newfound best,
and so, a glorious fight.

The Hudson River
Emilia DeLisa

Cradled in the glory of mountains;
In the falling and rising of day and night.
Tucked with blankets and quilts in winter,
Pillowed in heaps of wrinkles and puffs,
It rocks in the wind with rhythmic motion...
Rocks the cradle of the Hudson River.

In genial weather, the satiny covers
Sparkle with rhinestones in the glint of sun.
Sprinkled with silver in moon glow and star glow,
The cradle rolls to the cadence of wind.
While birds fly over and sing in chorus...
Sing and flute a lullaby.

The Sea Sprite
Jean Jones

A haze hung over the ocean,
Its blue reflected the sky.
The gentle ripples washed the sand
And left the pebbles dry.
A sea sprite danced through the water,
Which rose in a shimmering spray,
A shower of glistening, sparkling drops
Caressing the sun–lit bay.

Black clouds obscure the horizon;
Their fury beats on the moor.
The breakers thunder on the rocks
And surge far up the shore.
A father stands on the shingle,
His arms reach out in despair,
The scything raindrops lash his face,
The wild wind buffets his hair.

The angry sea calms its raging,
The restless waves cease to churn.
The sun illumines the lonely watch;
His daughter will never return.

The Master's Touch
Chau Mai

I stood upon a windswept hill
and looked out toward the sea
The quiet thrill of solitude
came faintly to surround me

I saw the shadows shift and glide
across the silver sand
And race to meet the coming tide
that sweeps across the land

I watched the whitecaps of the waves
push high into the air
As if a mighty hand reached down
and flung them here and there

I feel alone and yet with joy
what I see in nature's plan
The things that heal each wounded soul
that's in the heart of man

Look to the east and to the west
wherever man has trod
And see in every countryside
the handiwork of God!

Christina
Ramona Seitzinger

The soft sound of a little girl asleep,
Slumbering, dreaming, alone in the deep,
deep sea of the nightly song,
of long ago journeys, and the merry throng
where children play and grow, and sing.
With hair so damp upon her cheek,
what does she dream? I ponder and think,
For to look at her, when sound asleep,
such an angel to behold, all the future lay at her feet.
with such thoughts, held closely dear.
I wish for you to grow, strong and sweet.
And go on dreaming your dreams for tomorrow you see,
is just the beginning, for you and me.

Alone
Emily Ferrill

An old man wakes up to stare out a frosty window,
Too cold to move, too lonely to care
The pain of his loneliness devours his insides–slowly.

The new kid at school sits alone at lunch,
No one speaks to her, only about her.
She slowly eats her sandwich as a glob of grape
jelly slides down her shirt
As slowly as a sloth, a single tear runs down her cheek

A middle–aged man in a well pressed suit comes
home to his money,
Eats his supper and slides into bed, alone
Money can't buy him happiness or love

An old woman wakes up to her empty room,
no flowers, no visitors, no love
The smell of the nursing home burns her old
Wrinkled nose.
And she sits alone.

They all sit alone.

I Ran
Epi Juarez

My mind was full of questions,
so I ran so far away,
with hopes to find the answers
and hopes to find the way.

I saw majestic mountains
and fields of lustrous green.
I saw the beauty of this great earth
as God's beauty was displayed to me.

But my questions were left unanswered,
and I still could not find my way –
then I realized what I had been missing,
for I'd forgotten to kneel and pray.

So I raised my head to the Lord
and shared my hopes and fears.
I prayed for the peace that only He brings
and asked him to stop the tears.

And when the Lord heard my cry,
He looked down and smiled at me.
With open arms He turned and said,
"My child, you need only run to me."

My Mother's Hands
Edith McGrail

My mother's hands are wrinkled now.
They're old and feeble too.
And yet there's nothing in the world,
for me they would not do.

They've helped me through a thousand times,
when things were good or bad.
They've often turned a gloomy day
into a day so glad.

They're always busy doing things,
to make my life worth while.
So tenderly, I touch them now
and see my mother smile.

The Mermaid Queen
John Leighton

By fountains clear, in spangled starlight sheen,
Quench'd in the chaste beams of the watery moon,
Of all the radiancy of the mermaid queen,
When she wakest, the sea birds croon,
Waxen in her mirth, with pious care,
She'll dance her ringlets in the flowing flood
A merrier hour was never wasted there,
With adorous chaplets for a crown,
Certain stars shot madly from their spheres
To here the mermaid's song in tears.

Oh mermaid, take my heart in yours to knit,
I'll give you sea–fairies to attend on thee
And they shall fetch thee jewels from the sea,
Your eyes are as blue as the sky at night,
Your bosom and neck are soft and bare,
No garment you wear save a kirtle bright
And your own long raven hair,
Hear on the edge of silence, in to the night,
I hear the waves and the sea gulls mocking cry,
And there was only night, the sea, and I.

Mom And Dad Are Aliens
Jared Terwilliger

My mom and my dad are not what they seem.
Their dull appearance is part of their scheme.
I know of their plans, I know their techniques.
My parents are outer space alien freaks!!!

They landed on Earth in space ships humongous.
Posing as grown ups, they now walk among us.
My parents deny this, but I know the truth.
They're here to enslave me and spoil my youth.

Early each morning, as the sun rises,
Mom and Dad put on their earthling disguises.
I knew right away their masks weren't legit.
Their faces are lined, they sag and don't fit.

They live by the clock, they're slaves to routines.
They work the year 'round, they're almost machines.
They deny that TV and fried food have much worth.
They cannot be human, they're not of this earth.

I cannot escape their alien gaze.
They're warping my mind with their alien ways.
For sinister plots, this one is a gem.
They're bringing me up to turn into them.

The Bridge
Wes Hyde

In the cold, swirling winter
I languish above this bridge's dark shadow
Gilt by the moon's sylvan glow.
I now disremember
From whence I did enter
Uncertain of which way to go.
As I stand here above I look down below
At my own silhouetted form at the center
Of the shadow as the waters rush on.
And its ripples catch moon beams
As it races along its dark way.
The river lies there below, but those waters are gone
Like when you awake from your dreams
And rise at the first light of day.

Frank's Rainbow
Amy B. Kehrli–DeDeaux

He loves the reflection of purple, pink and orange in the
blue ocean from the romantic sunsetting skies.
He loves the brown, the gold, the green and the
blue sparkles in his beautiful grandkids eyes.

He loves chips and salsa, margaritas, chimichangas and sliced
red tomatoes with spicy chili rellenoes.
He loves celebrations, 1931 Plymouths, windy
red hot balloon rides and the warm sand between his toes.

He loves peppermint candy, merry–go–rounds, friendly
yellow daises and lots and lots of treasures at his place.
He loves Lifesavers, Pecan Sandies and the bright
yellow sun (as long as there is a hat nearby) on his face.

He loves mocha–amaretto–hazelnut coffee, cheese made in the tall, lush
green mountains of Switzerland and the Giants in spring.
He loves to visit Santa in the city with its bright lights and decorated
green Christmas trees and the warmth his family brings.

For now He is in heaven above,
because of Him these are the things I love.

Untitled
David Atkinson

Alone in a place where chaos rules and blind planets collide
a ragged thief plays skeleton keys
confused as to his purpose.

Done with yesterday, his body and spirit are now
beyond the reach of tomorrow.
He can see the story in your eyes
a ragged thief to steal your sorrow.

Awkwardly confident as he walks from the shadows
He's not nervous, he's thoughtful; weary but sincere
stepping from truth to truth, with feelings not reasons.

And when your past is close behind
he'll be there to ease your mind
as brand new heart–shaped seas
fill you up with loving dreams
and hope swims in your eyes
at the unfixed edge of time
perfection sparkling the sky
on magic carpets as you fly
and all that's dark and deep and blue
will be shining at the sight of you.

The Wind
Susan Ann Fleckney

Sometimes it caresses her body like a warm blanket,
Folding its strong arms around her
And making her feel that she is cared for.
Bringing back memories of those who once cared
And of lost loves that she thought she had forgotten

But then its mood changes and it becomes angry with her,
Making her feel cold
And driving fear deep into her soul.
Pushing her back with force
And tossing her about like a rag doll.
Whipping up into a frenzy
And throwing aside whatever gets in its way.
With no regard for life

Just as quickly its anger dies
and it becomes peaceful again.
Lightly brushing the grass
And playing with the flowers.
Gently it runs through her hair like fingers,
Enveloping her face like strong masculine hands
And making her feel safe again

Disillusion
K. Spinks

Speak not to me of constancy or love,
For by such sweet deceits are we beguiled.
False words and promises, oft hand in glove,
Have countless times the purest hearts defiled.
When first, the petals of loves flower unfold
Their fragrance acts as opiate to the mind.
All actions be but by the heart controlled,
No faults within themselves can lovers find.
But all too soon this beauteous blossom fades,
Once heady perfume, turns to cloying musk.
Each lover now, the bitter truth evades,
Love's withered seed becomes an empty husk.
'Tis death to love, to passion, and to trust,
Thus, Cupid's dart becomes a rapier's thrust.

Last Mile
T. Pratt

Do you miss me when it rains, when dark clouds fill the sky
Memories come rushing back, a tear forms in my eye

We met on a stormy night, it was fate, our destiny
So quickly did we fall in love, an empty place you filled in me

Some things are hard to understand, life is filled with irony
The rain brought us together, then it took you away from me

Blacktop glistening in the night, thought we could make it almost there
Mountain curve, blinding light, sometimes life is so unfair

You would still be by my side, if we had made it one more mile
I still feel your hand in mine, I still see your playful smile

On nights like these you feel so close, my heart it aches inside
Are your tears mixed with the rain, until together, forever we ride

I think often of your loving eyes, I dream each night of our ride
When I will be whole again, without this emptiness inside

Natures tears bring happy memories, they help wash away the pain
Are you somewhere close out there, do you miss me when it rains

The Dropped Bottom Brigade
Marguerite Pratt

(Senior Citizens Keep Fit)
Under the leotards the flabby thighs
Bulge softly out. Strange hosiery wraps
The curving legs that are put proudly forth,
Patterned with veins like Royal Ordnance Maps;
And all are members, fully paid,
Of the Dropped Bottom Brigade.

Now Venus, in a shimmering leotard,
Controls the action while the music plays.
The ladies start to move, not quite in sync,
Directed by the goddess on the dais;
And all are members, fully paid,
Of the Dropped Bottom Brigade.

Ladies, lift up your hearts and undulant chins,
Beat off Time's fingers with your waving arms;
Enter a world of dreams and yesterdays,
Where you are ageless, with unfading charms,
And not all members, fully paid,
Of the Dropped Bottom Brigade.

Autumn Sonnet To A Sugar Maple
Jim Ploss

A sugar maple, caped in scarlet flames
That yesterday were leaves of many greens,
Provides a park where squirrels play Catch Me games!
Their busy chatter shattering to smithereens
The brittle autumn blueness of the afternoon,
That bright blue lightness past the mid of day,
'Til wooed to nest by rise of harvest moon,
By scent of burning leaves, of sun–dried hay.
When morning comes the tree is starkly bare,
As if with one tremendous shrug
The maple doffed its cape with careless air,
To spread it on the ground, a welcome rug.
And thus forewarned, the snowflakes fall all night
To drape the maple in a cape of virgin white.

Morning Coffee
Karen Hatcher

Lady in a hat and gloves,
blue–eyed fire
Painted nails of stone.

Strong, working German hands
A tight, loving grip

Jeweled heart in the lipstick drawer
combs and brushes in a line of laughter.

A cookie after dinner,
story books and an afternoon nap
a walk home from school.

Some days pass with little notice,
but memories never shall.

Jesse James took the West.
You captured life.

There is always time for a smile
With or without our cup of morning coffee.

Daydreams
John Tierney
If the world were a cartoon,
I'd be a superhero, I'd fly to the moon.
I'd float far away in a giant balloon.
I'd swing in a tree with a jungle baboon,
If the world were a cartoon.

If I lived in a storybook,
I'd sail the seas like Captain Hook.
I'd be a policeman and catch a crook.
I'd climb the tallest mountain and take a look,
If I lived in a storybook.

If I could be in a fairy tale,
I'd ride through the ocean on top of a whale.
I'd have magic powers that never would fail.
No matter what happened I'd always prevail,
If I could be in a fairy tale.

But daydreams are no fun when they always come true,
I'd miss my family if I left too.
So I'll just stay here and daydream with you.

Summer Night
Robin Leigh Portune
Cool and crisp, the air faintly humming,
The sunset gone, the stars soon coming.

The pond aglow with amethyst light,
Shimmering brightly in the night.

Fireflies slowly flutter by,
Pale gold against sapphire sky.

The moon's pale face, gazing at diamond stars,
Enveloped in a cool mist blown from afar.

Lavender butterflies, silent in flight,
A pale circle in the dark summer night.

The Transfiguration
Ted L. Barnes
In a small room furnished with just a bed and chair:
The sun filters through the window shade with a
yellowish cast on the old man sitting there:
His hands that once worked with careful skill, lay in his lap
His head tilted, cheek against shoulder as he pretends to nap
He hears the sounds as others busy around the house and
sees their shadow as they pause to glance at him
through the partial open door.
No words are shared as there's no interest in his repore.
"He's just a crazy old man", words he's heard them say
and, "who needs him anyway"?
He knows he's just a burden and yet sits helpless
through out each long day.
But now and then the door bursts open and a small figure appears
A little boy comes in climbs up in his lap, lays his small
hand on his and compares the size and prompts for a story.
The old man forgets his despair as he shares past
moments of glory
Then the child filled with wonderment goes on to play
Instilled with hopes of growing up to be just
like Grandpa some day.

What's Next?
Zoe Murphy Rudolph
Here among the scattered cardboard
I sit on the kitchen floor
By the sink folding and stacking dish
After dish in newspaper, hands stained
With ink.

I feel sad to leave this solitude
Behind to go into the new void of uncertainty.
Surely a new challenge awaits,
'Will it be kind?'
Rows and rows of boxes line the wall
Marked and taped
"Shall I put them in storage or bring them
Along. But please God don't let them fall."
They look like chess pieces waiting to be moved.

Sappho's Fire
Elizabeth Lyulkin
They move to the music
Of their own making
Forsaking proper forms
For the sheer fury of the dance
Hands flying, legs akimbo
Fingers gently, probing, searching
Eyes wide open
To the dangers before them
With people closing
Their minds and hearts
Turning their heads away
Unable to watch
Hidden by the balcony railing
I watch those same moves
And my heart stirs
Caught in flamenco's frenzied beat
Barefoot, I run
Taking two steps at a time
To join in their dance
Danced to the sacred music of our hearts

Parental Rights
Bobbi McLendon
There are those that use a
chisel on a bare heart
there are those that
use only the finest of carving
tools to engrave indulgent
irreverent messages
there are those that
utter their last
prescriptive breath into the
culmination of their
own existence
there are those that
hold tight to the magic of
small sure hands and
tender nose kisses
there are those that
cradle their
dead child
every night
before falling asleep.

A Midnight Rose
Matthew Dodge Gewirtz
A magnificent sight;
Shining in the night's lone moonbeam,
The evenings dew glistening on its petals;
Like a thin sheet of perspiration on skin.
Its stunning beauty takes your breath away;
As you stand in awe at its will to survive.
You approach this work of art,
As it sparkles like diamonds in a pool of crimson.
You reach forward to take the creation into your grasp,
But it is not a rose that you touch...

It is the hand of your love;
Gazing into the depths of your eyes,
Forever saying,

I Love You.

Kisses From God
Angelia O. Bell
These things are kisses from God:
the warm sun shining brightly on the tips of my eyelids
the fragrant smells of budding flowers
winds that softly brush against my skin
white cotton—candy clouds set against a powder blue sky
the sounds of distant barking and ongoing traffic
children laughing and playing their games
sheets hanging on the line
my toes threaded through crisp blades of fresh—cut grass—
me breathing slow and deep.
These things too are kisses from God:
the smell of fresh rain
droplets tickling my face and arms
puddles of water going pitter—pat, pitter—pat
little babies sticking their tongues out for a taste
the feel of cool, gusty winds that whip through my hair
brooding, dusky storm clouds
the street lights that suddenly click on as the sky darkens
thunder rolling beneath my feet as I stand witness—
me breathing slow and sleep.

More To Say
Robert Dye
We used to sing the colors of our dreams
for one another often in those days.
Can you remember passing summer evenings
in friendship's effortless communion,
when we danced across the waters with Cortez
until the hurricane swept loneliness away?

Later on, we sometimes talked long distance.
Time, at least, was something we could share,
although our journeys had diverged
and our commonalties had weakened...
you were growing...and seemed fewer every call.
"How are you?" still truly meant "Speak your soul to me."

Now, we prattle like strangers on a plane
or two bored old men in a barbershop
when we see each other once or twice a year.
But mostly, we just sit gazing vacantly
into the void between us, wondering why,
and maybe wishing we had something more to say.

Village Stores
Rosina Brown
Where has it gone? The village store
It sold so many things
Bacon, ham and pots of jam
And sausages on strings.
A wire cutter that sliced through cheese
Honeycombs from local bees
Those rolled up sticky papers that caught unsuspecting flies
Disinfectant, moth balls and soaps that stung the eyes
A tabby cat, curled up sleep immersed in feline dreams
Twixt the glass topped biscuit tins which held the custard creams.
Pungent odors lingered there, paraffin, coffee, spice.
Stiff paper bags of every hue and traps for catching mice.
There in rows of screw—topped jars, stripy humbugs, barley sugars
And twisted candy bars.
It was not so hygienic, the service not so fast.
But it was, oh! so friendly, this memory from the past.

Girl In The Chip Shop
Philip Stickley
The girl in the chip shop
Has caught my glad eye,
A white coat clad princess
She'll wrap and she'll fry,
With her oil blistered hands
And her red shiny face,
She can deep fry my haddock
Or batter my place,
As I order my food
I go weak at the knees,
As she sprinkles on salt
And spoons out the peas,
Five nights a week
I go in at eight,
I'm losing my money
And putting on weight,
My courage it fails me
All I can say,
Is a pound's worth of chips
And fish on a tray.

Lilacs After Rain
Bernice Wenzel
Lilacs after rain—
Harmony
Resounding again—
Young love!
New —
Purple with the strain of a melody
Bursting from an o'er—filled heart
That pounds like waves on
A clouded sea beach!
Pounds—
Releasing joy that stifles
Breath —
Making sighs caress
Lips
Full and tender!
Lips
Warmed by deep rich contact—

Lavender twilight—
Lilacs after rain!

Mama's Rocking Chair
George H. Randall

When the pressures from life's problems
Seem more than I can bear,
I wish that I could go back again
To mama's rocking chair.
My troubles always vanished
When I ascended there
And snuggled up for comfort
In mama's rocking chair.
There was magic in those moments
For I lost every earthly care.
In the loving arms that held me
In mama's rocking chair.
And though the years have slipped away
And mama is no longer there
Blessed memories of my youth return
To mama's rocking chair.

Fate
Elwyn Williams

I've watched the blossoms forming on the trees,
And flutter downwards with the breeze;
Have seen the bluebells bloom,
And fade away so soon;
Nature gives, then takes away,
Regardless what we do or say.

Have noticed people praying on their knees,
Yet suffer awful tyrannies,
Seen children laugh and cry,
Suffer, shrivel and die;
Nature gives and takes away,
No matter what we think or say.

Most people search and strive for precious peace,
Others are restless with unease,
Wild wars proliferate,
Sending souls through Hell's gate;
Man can give or take away,
Regardless, oft, of what we say.

Bedtime
Elise and Ryan Alcorn

Lay still, still, still,
It's time to go to sleep.
Be quiet, be quiet.
Do not make a peep.
Heavens to Betsy,
It's time to turn in.
On your mark, get set, go!
Let the sleeping begin.
You may not feel sleepy,
Not sleepy at all.
But somehow you'll get by that non-sleepy wall.
Quickly, quickly jump into bed.
But you better watch out, or you'll bump your head.
It's the time of the day,
You slowly wind down.
It's the time of the day,
After get back from town.
I'm so, so, so sorry,
I've run out of time.
I cannot continue this sleepytime rhyme.

Count Your Blessings
Karen Davies

I've got a third class ticket through life,
but I'm traveling in a rich man's seat,
and although it may rain upon my head,
I see sunshine across the street,
and when I walk in darkness,
the stars they shine so bright,
I also know the light of day,
will surely follow night.
Although I have a poor man's pocket,
I have a rich mans dreams,
and when my burdens feel too heavy I know,
it's just the way it seems.
When I think about my family and friends,
and the people I've yet to meet,
I may have a third class ticket through life,
but I'm traveling in a rich man's seat.

Melody
Cynthia D'Adamo

Sad and low, sad and low—
The echo of her constant song.
Eventually, he tired of its familiar melody
And abandoned her music for a time—
For other rhythms, other songs.
Until there came a day when he longed, once more
For her familiar melody—
Sad and low, sad and low.
Whispered summer lyrics, reminders of a time he lost—
Sad and low.
Reminders of a part of himself,
Reminders of a constancy, since abandoned—
Sad and low.
He played her song, once more
But with a realization—
Never again would her music be
Fresh, new, and undiscovered.
Never again would its echo—
Sad and low,
Touch him in her same summer way.

Don't Cry For Me
Deborah Fowles

Think of me when you see sunlight on the sea,
or hear a wintry wind moan through the trees.
When morning mists rise off the lake like steam,
or you hear the gurgling waters of a stream.
Think of me when snow cloaks branch and stick,
or when new buds pop out, so green and thick.
When you hear spring breezes dancing through the leaves,
or see the scarlet autumn clothes of trees.
Think of me when owls hoot in the night,
or when the stars above are diamond bright.
When you hear the haunting laughter of a loon,
or watch clouds scoot across the moon.
Think of me when wintry blizzards blow,
or when you hear a river's waters flow.
When you feel the ocean's spray upon your face,
or watch a dozen schooners in a race.
Think of me when waves crash on the rocks,
or you watch the lazy, soaring flight of hawks.
I am in these things and they're in me,
and I am with you and will always be.

Santa Didn't Come
P. J. Selby
It wasn't the same this Christmas Day,
Now the kids are grown and gone,
No shouts of joy to wake us up, an hour
Before the dawn,
No happy laughter filled the air, no toys
or games at play,
No wrapping paper rustling, four a.m. on
Christmas Day.
No Santa's sacks hung on their beds,
No junk cluttered up the floor,
Just empty beds, in a empty room, when I
Peeped in, round the door.
The lights on the tree, didn't seem so bright,
And we didn't trim up much, this year,
Cos, it wasn't the same, this Christmas Day,
Now the kids are no longer here.
So all of you, with children, should treasure
The gifts that are yours.
For with misty eyes, you will realize,
With no kids, there's no Santa Claus.

What You Took Away
Laurie Woods Sanders
For all that you could have given to me
you took many more things away.

You took a lonely heart
and gave it new life.

You took forgotten dreams
and gave them renewed hope.

You took a lost soul
and brought it home.

What you have taken from my life
will never be missed,
For all that you could have given
you took away, and helped me live again.

Single
Kathleen Linhardt
Faucet in the void of night
drop by drop

abandoned and forgotten—
in need of change.

Dawn after restless dreams.
The hot, humid air of summer

wraps around you like
a woolen shawl and smells

of thick greenery and steaming concrete.
On the bistro table

a cup of Java
stands single, by which

a ring is lying—ahead, the
shoreless ocean of the day.

Awakening
Elizabeth Gibson
Early morning...
Silvery mists rise dreamlike
from the surface of the lake.

Ghostly silhouette...
A lone goose creases the smoothness
of the water,
Regal, silent and proud.

Shards of sunlight pierce the veil
As shadows lift and disappear
into the coolness of the morning.

A lone melodious whistle echoes...
Gathers a swelling chorus,
as dawn gives birth
to the fullness of the day.

My Room
Sandy Mudger
A newfound treasure that lets me be me
Was right here among...my home and debris.
My life took a change from the "mothering" touch,
When my last son took flight, I'd lost my last crutch.

I floundered, I faltered, I had no direction.
Which way to go next? I may fade without mention.
A new beginning which will help me be a part
Of a life once again, I began to take heart.

An old family loveseat, a chest for a table,
Old lamps and new pillows, a room I can label.
Some books and some pictures, a pen and a plan,
To write down my thoughts of my "life" if I can.

This place I have made is mine for a while.
It lets me find me, who I am, no denial.
This "place" I have made is sweet as perfume,
My refuge, my strength, my comfort,..."My Room".

Lost Sheep
Keith J. Coleman
What's wrong with that child sitting on the sidewalk?
No shoes on her feet and God only knows
the last time she had something to eat
Can't help to think when she had a good nights sleep?
Truly this is one of God's lost sheep
You have passed her by on many occasions
On your way to the bank, late for work, on the run
going to the park to watch your children have fun
Not once did you stop to listen to her plead
Deaf ear to her cries not willing to take heed to her need
Yet you eat food in her face out of greed
One day on your way to the market
you over heard someone say "She was an easy target"
You get chills and stop in your tracks
Whispers catch your attention
Suddenly you see what they have mentioned
That same little girl lies on her back
As the crowd grows so does your conscience
In your mind there's the sight of a dove
reaching out for your love!

Atmospherics
Megan Guest
Leaden skies weighed down with rain,
the eerie air so hushed and still,
waiting for the storm to break.
Crouching clouds are haloed black;
from far away the thunder moves,
primeval, stirring from its lair;
unseen, the giant stalks its prey
and earth lies passive in its way.

Soon the rain comes pelting down,
hard on waiting paths and roofs.
Water streams along the gutters,
flushing out the dusty drains.
White forks of light impale the sky,
With static cracking space apart.
As thunder booms and flashes blind
such mighty grandeur splits the mind.

Climbing The Wind
Ivan Wampler
Climbing the wind – like thistledown
riding the first breath of morning...
the inner joy – and outer wonder,
by one who dares to dream...
or dreams to dare.
A shout above the earthbound,
spider trap of strife and toil...
reaching ever upward,
ethereal and free,
like a ballerina spinning
on waves of applause.
No longer indentured, the spirit soars:
wind shaken, and cobalt scoured.

But climbing the wind
is a hallowed dream,
born of thistledown and hope
in a secret corner of the mind –
at first light of morning.

My Dream
S. John Arber
Give me an isle 'neath a tropical sky
With a beach by a shallow lagoon;
Give me a bed 'neath a thousand lit stars
And the light from a rising moon.

Give me the song of a tropical bird
As he sings to his love in a glade;
Give me the flash of a cascading stream
Or the whisper of leaves in the shade.

Give me a glimpse of a tropical dawn
When the blossoms are tinged by the sun;
Give me the blush of an orchid in bloom,
Or the scent when the warm day is done.

Give me the years that I spent as a youth
And the hand of my love I could hold;
Give me my dream and I will give you
My riches, my wealth, and my gold.

Rocky Road Cake
Donna Pilch
He smoked way too much
for over thirty years,
and never understood
that's what caused my tears.

Now I picture him in heaven
asking God for a light,
wondering if he knows
that his family's in a fight.

He came back at least once,
of that I became sure
the night his coffee mug
inexplicably crashed on the floor.

Now I'm sitting at his table,
thinking of vacations he didn't take,
and then I take my fork
and stab Entenmann's new cake.

Final Pages
Joan Slatalla
Black on white,
A rambling page of grief,
Old age, dementia, isolation.
A paragraph of short reprieve,
time returned, pain relieved
before the final desolation.
What follows this unfinished
script; this story without end?
It's a guessing game
for all who came and,
stooped or still unbending,
have made their way
from the title page
with the help of God
to the epilogue, and now
bequeath their memories
to the critics.

Untitled
L. E. Brouse
For so long the little bird sat
That I thought he must be dead.
But on my approach he fled
With fluttering, varied mishap.

And looking at the spot where he had been
Found still mingling there, mites.
It was they had robbed him his flight,
Sapping the life's strength from him.

Had he only remained in his place,
I would have kindly offered relief
From the objects of his hurtful grief,
But could not follow his fearful haste.

How like the little bird we often are,
And in ignorant, frantic course
Flee the very benevolent source
That would rid our blightful mar.

The Forgotten
Michael J. Murray

Leave them be
for the truly unremembered
have earned their anonymity,
inhabiting as they do,
a sphere in time
so infinitely mysterious
that the jaundiced eyes of age
are eliminated.
Let them touch hearts
made weary by cynicism
with the thought
of their own reflecting images
trembling
on the brink of eternity,
and if they do,
then we few
existing at the edge,
will forever envy
their anonymous immortality.

The Doorway
Judi Westgate

I am standing in a doorway
But I cannot remain.
Soon I must make a choice
To move forward to adventure
Or move back where I am safe.
And if I should move forward
Would I find not great adventure
But despair and disappointment
And regret what I have lost.
But, if I should move backward
Would I find not a safe refuge,
But a prison, dull and lonely,
And despise my self–made chains.
I am standing in a doorway.
I know I cannot remain here.
Soon I must take a step
In one direction.

Three Wishes
Lora Sutterfield

I wish I Had a Telescope
To scan the starry skies
But, since I have no telescope,
I'm glad I have two eyes.

I wish I had a kitchen run
By push–button commands
But, while that kitchens still a dream
I'm glad I have two hands.

I wish I had a super car
To give my friends a treat
But, till that new car comes along,
I'm glad I have two feet.

"Two eyes to look to God above"
"Two hands to clasp in prayer"
"Two feet to carry me to church"
"Why, I'm a millionaire!"

Untitled
Christopher Billing

Build me a boat
inside a dream
arms crossed in peace
cut off from life

Cut off from life
between two shores
adrift in sleep
my dark eyes see

My dark eyes see
for once behold
through mists of doubts
a light ahead

A light ahead
a ray of hope
build me a boat
inside a dream.

Unrequited
Christi A. Hart

A breath, unlike one ever breathed,
So sweet, a cleansing sigh stays the swirling depths.
The sun bursts into countless fireflies,
all around, consuming me.
A spell, whose mystical fingers clutch me through the mist,
pulling me ever so tightly against its yielding breasts.
A star, twinkling brightly in the distance,
far away, begging not to be one of the forgotten among the masses.
A wave crashing over me,
a momentary plunge into oblivion.
A desert, feigning death,
all the while giving birth to unimaginable life.
The moon, serenely basking me in its glow.
A pond, its glassy smooth surface reflecting what only I can see.
A soul, yearning to finally touch
that, which it has been reaching for.
Alone, trapped by circumstance.

Life's Journey
Kevin Dittrich

Conceived in passion, born through pain,
The miracle of life begins again.
The first spoken words or steps taken,
Consciousness to become awaken.

Confusion and conflict, until your late teens,
Studying hard to fulfill your dreams.
The first kiss, the first touch,
Tender memories you will treasure so much.

Married, divorced, children moved out,
Mid–life crisis, surrounded by doubt.
Searching for reason, a purpose in life,
Longing to end this endless strife.

Old age descends, enveloping all,
There is no escaping the Grim Reaper's call.
Now death is at hand, it all becomes clear,
You make the rules, and the game ends here.

Shyness
Christopher Chivers
Shyness holds my thoughts for you
Encased as silent dreams.
Visions fueled by fantasy
Are held in high esteem.

A smile displays my like for you
When words are sure to fail.
Despair when lack of confidence
Is disguised to no avail.

Poems became my messenger
A voice to show I feel.
A visual piece of imagery
That caring can reveal.

So shyness is my mental lock
That holds my frightened voice,
And poetry is my written key
That lets my heart rejoice.

Outside The Window
Lorraine Horry
I look out the window and what do I see
A thousand spring flowers all laughing at me
They bounce up and down in the wind and the rain
They look towards me and start laughing again

I turn to my right and see children at play
I smile to myself and I'm aching to say,
'Hey kids don't you know that you're gonna get wet'
But they carry on playing, not seeing me yet

On my left there are houses, all standing up tall
I don't think I see any life there at all
Oh wait there's old Henry he's out for his walk
I'd better turn round or he'll want me to talk.

Back in my seat I sit down and sigh
A lonely old man sees the world going by.

Mama's Walk
Mary Christina Meadows
When Mama prays, God listens; her faith is strong and sure.
She has asked and will receive; in HIS love she's secure.
HIS word is true; she's learned it well, on HIM she can rely.
So, she stands on HIS promises; it's faith money cannot buy.

Mama's walk is constant; she's in the Word each day
Communicating with her Heavenly Father. Her focus undeterred.
Cards and letters that she sends all have verses written there
For us to read, apply and know she sent them with a prayer.

Her steps have slowed and she laments that she cannot always get
Tasks done she wants, or visits made, but I tell her not to fret.
She still can read the Word and pray and sing of HIS great love;
The blessings that she brings to others is manna from above.

So, Mama, know that as you've walked and obediently prayed,
A brow was cooled, a burden lifted, an important decision made —
Your prayers were answered and I know of many that will say,
"Thank you, Jesus, we are here, 'cause Grace took time to pray."

So Many Songs
L. A. Churchill
So many women
through the ages; so many tapestries
stitched, chambers paced, fingers
locked and laced, windows watched.

So many women
enduring pain; so many disappointed
smiles, disowned thought, lovers
shunned and sought, desires dreamt.

So many lives
wasted by time; so much despairing
grief, silent cries, bitter—
spoken lies, heartlost hours.

So many women
singing through life; those unrecognised
tunes, borrowed words, chorus
lost unheard, again, again.

Foreign Boy
Adelle Manning
Why won't you look at me, beautiful foreign boy?
Is your bitter coffee that absorbing?
Are these smells and sounds new to you,
and lonely women a constant?
Do you wear sunglasses just to keep me wondering?

Maybe I love you already,
maybe I don't know what love is,
maybe the sound of your breathing
is some huge part of heaven,
maybe I'm making too much out of this.

I see you walking daybreak streets,
eyes scratching the surface of my Monday paranoia.
Beautiful foreign boy,
with beautiful foreign hair and lips and tongue,
head tilting in every direction
except that half inch left to face me.

The One Within
Jo Wightman
I hate the thief who steals my time
Who lives my life and takes what's mine;
The one who defines every thought
And whisks it away before it's caught.
She is the temptress, the one who imprisons me
She shows me glimpses of the view I cannot see.
Through the bars she lends me flirtatious glances, offers me tendrils of
    music and
wisps of mysterious dances.
When I blink the curtain is raised
I see a land of possibility, a world to be praised
For one moment then the stage is bare,
The theatre dark and yawning no matter which way I stare.
The silence is loud — the pulse the drumbeat to which we dance
Living like robots rarely taking a chance.
The steps are mapped, the route is charted for fools
Yet still I feel lost, bewildered, not knowing the rules.
I am swept up, taken along for the ride
And the only one in whom I can confide is me — The Child Inside.

A Day In May
Elizabeth Morris–Pierce

He knelt and laid a fragrant flower
upon her grave to say "goodbye."
His broken heart could not bear the pain;
from his throat came a pathetic cry
as his hand reached toward the sealed urn
of the one laid in reliquiae.
He thought she'd be with him forever;
forever he would see her dear face,
forever share coffee together
in the small kitchen of their own place.
Ah! If only he once more could give her
a touch, a kiss, a parting embrace!
But he knew not how death's claim to stave
when at last it came to their gateway.
Gently they helped him up from her grave
and with loving arms led him away;
they dared not ask their dad to be brave
bereft of his wife that day in May.

The Blessing
Susan Allen

We hold this infant in our arms
And whisper in her ear
We look into her sparkling eyes
And wipe away her tear
We softly kiss rosy cheek
And count each finger dear
We smooth the worry from her brow
And ease her every fear
We'll watch this infant change and grow
Each accomplishment we'll cheer
This child was born within our hearts
Before 'twas ever here
We hold this infant in our arms
And feel the angels near

CHAPTER TWO

Noteworthy Works

Ben Johnson once said, "A good poet's made as well as born." These are words of encouragement to all of us who aspire to the craft. The following collection of poems is wonderfully varied and draws from the talents of numerous individuals. Although the poems featured in this chapter did not receive any awards, they should nevertheless serve as an inspiration. This chapter is devoted to those poets whose work shows true promise.

A May Day
Natalie Rock
I love a clear blue sky on a May day
When the sun is shining brightly —
At least no one can say
I don't have anything
For I have this day
So clear and blue
I could put all my energies into this day
And make it mine – –
All mine.

A Father's Plea
Nina Toste
Summer of 96
She was born
Torn away from her father
Both left to mom

Eyes of blue
Hair of gold
White as a dove
Will her story even be told

Never to see her father again
He is lost without her
They are two souls from a part
Together they never were

Trying to win custody
The fight will never end
If only her mother would understand
And try to be his friend

I want to help him out
But there's nothing I can do
It's not like I could make a wish
And all his dreams come true

I don't know Kiana
But I know enough to love her
Just enough
For me to be her stepmother

I love them both
And it hurts me deep down inside
Seeing both of them suffer
In whom could he confide

I can't handle all the suspense
All I can do is sit here and pray
For Kiana and Ryan
To see each other one sweet day

It's May 21 of '97
Ryan gets to see his little girl
What happiness it brings
To see him in such a whirl

She says "dada"
For the first time
How he falls a part
To him these words are soothing
as a chime

Every Saturday
Once a week
This is Ryan's time for love and joy
That they no longer have to seek

Mirage
Jay Andersen
Don't know where the pavement ends and life begins.
Driving, driving. Chasing water on the road.
Is it my imagination, where I hide myself?

Just going faster and faster...to catch some illusion
That isn't there, but is. Confused life on a lonely drive,
wish I had someone to stop me.

They say a death in sleep has no pain, but how would anyone know?
My eyes are open, but not seeing. What do they see that I don't?
How do they feel, and why?

What is it like to be dead?
I think it's finally overtaking
the water on the road...

I Never Shed A Tear For You
Nancy A. Huebler
In those years of old, those rose gardens, there was a
story beginning to unfold.
Missing too late, the one I truly always loved, I was
confused, lonely, and now unhappily expectant.
My mistake was made, and the little heartbeat inside,
shouldn't be ignored or denied.
I didn't follow through my original intentions, for a
different start in life.
And I gave in to other people's intent.
A soul full of misgivings, and a heart full all the while.
The whole new picture was rightfully due my innocent yet
unborn infant.
So I marched with his father, my groom, down the aisle.
The day had its good moments, the family, the friends, had a day
happily and hopefully spent.
I showed the world a smile.
They say I made an exceptionally beautiful bride.
Only I knew I was swelling with the pride.
I went through it all and prepared for the only real hour of joy.
Nine months later, a beautiful, healthy, baby boy.

Time has passed, he is handsome, and he has his
accomplishments, and he is, truly my pride.
I have a few but haunting regrets, those vacant rooms left
in my heart to rent.
It's time to pour out, what's been hidden deep inside my breast.
I had intended to mail my heart's desire, an invitation, but
not even a word, would I permit that day, to be sent.
The one I had prayed to belong to, I thought surely God had
made us to be meant.
In my silence, he never knew, the wishes, the prayers, I had
wished to come true.
But dreams, prayers, and wishes, are not enough, actions were
needed to be followed thru.
So because I lacked the courage, my secret love, I had only,
my shyness to communicate to.
Even though he was my special friend, since our childhood, I
never wanted to become a memorable vision, a martyr, a saint,
or a sinner, after all I had my pride.
I couldn't speak, so perhaps, I don't have the prettier picture,
in my album of memories, to paint.
And today, I look from my misty, but not unhappy eyes, and see
that young girl, all but a few years ago.
Now, and only now, can I understand, better her heart.
So long to the dreams, the prayers, the wishes, they seem but
little fishes, swimming back out to sea.
I say to myself, those tears, I should have shed for me – maybe.
The story is not finished, we'll have to wait and see, after
all what will be, will be.

The Eagle And The Rose
Linda Knowlton
The serenity of rivers and streams as they flow
The strength of the powerful bird
The heartiness of the flower that comes from the earth
The emerald waters so full of His awesome creatures
Can only make us spiritual believers
The Eagle and the Rose
What wonderful gifts for us He has chose
The beauty of life and the variety of things in our sight
Makes everything seem wonderful and spiritually right
The Eagle and the Rose
creations of God as we all know
So different yet so alike
They struggle lack day just to have life
We too as God's creatures struggle as a day
Comes and goes
Not unlike the Eagle and the Rose

A Smoker's Fix
Albert Marcus
Smoke, smoke, smoke
Just in case you don't know it
I do indeed smoke

Not for style
Not for reason
Vaingloriously pleasing

I just smoke

To my wife in the morning
I smoke

Arriving at work
I smoke

Kiss my daughter in the evening
I smoke

Sometimes just thinking
I smoke

Party happens
I smoke

Feeling just beginning
I smoke

This coughs bothers me
I smoke

God I'm confessing
I smoke

Pain in my chest
I still smoke

Guess I got a problem
I smoke

Friends are complaining
I smoke

At least it's not dope
I just smoke

Got to die from something
I'll smoke

In Memory Of My Mom
Luella M. Boer
'Twas on March first of ninety—one
Mother's days on earth were done.
Beside her bed in CCU I stood,
I'm sure my love she understood.
I held her hand till breath was gone.

It was so hard to part with one so dear,
But I was glad I was so near.
She was my mother and special friend,
I trusted God my broken heart to mend,
And knew the comfort He could send.

I gave her one last kiss good—bye
With tear filled eyes, I had to cry.
Three years have passed since you have gone,
But my love and memories go on and on.

Imagine
Jimmy P. Vereen
Imagine being as sweet as a pumpkin pie
Imagine finally living past that lie
Imagine being loved endlessly,
Imagine being blind but still can see

Imagine, Imagine, Imagine...

Imagine being totally free
Imagine whatever you want to be
Imagine releasing all of your fear
Imagine crying your last tear

Imagine, Imagine, Imagine...

Imagine your life being full of just light
Imagine being blind and finding sight
Imagine being in the tenderness of care
Imagine having all the love you can bear

Imagine, Imagine, Imagine...

Imagine reaching your whole life's desire
Imagine being upheld and always admired
Imagine being a flower that blooms every year
Imaging being plucked by someone who really cares

Imagine, Imagine, Imagine...

Imagine being on the beach playing in the sand
Imagine having everything at your command
Imaging being able to play such a game
Imagine waking up and everything is not the same

Imagine, Imagine, Imagine...

Imagine living without any pain
Imagine not having anything to gain
Imagine having all of your problems solved
Imagine being isolated and never involved

Imagine, Imagine, Imagine...

Imagine being a king for just one day
Imagine having everything going your way
Imagine having your palace full of knights
Imagine being protected all day and all night

Imagine, Imagine, Imagine...

Lilac Memories

Jeri Wilkinson

Soft breezes of springtime carry the scent
of seasons long past,
a childhood since spent;
When time held the promise of dreams
to come true,
and days were watercolored a lavender hue;

My youth like a symphony
played out in your presence,
each movement and nuance
underscored with your fragrance;

And when your time had passed,
your poignant beauty faded,
captured within my heart
was the magic you created,
of lilac memories.

Twinkle, Twinkle You And Me

Patricia A. Fehervari

Blissfully holding my little girl tight, on a summer's cool
Clear starry night

In our rocking chair by the window I said "let's count the stars
Before you go to bed".

My daughter sat up and said "how is this done?

And I told her "dear, you start with one".

"But which one mom, they're all so shiny, there's big and
There's small, there's huge and there's tiny!"

"Do I start from the left and go to the right, or go from the
Bottom to top?"

And I said "sweetheart it matters not, as long as you count till
You stop".

"Mom, do you think I can count all the stars that twinkle so
Bright in the sky?"

As I gave her a hug and kissed, I simply whispered "honey, just try".

So she started with one and continued to count till she got to
The number twenty

Then I heard her take a deep breath and sigh, "gee mom, I think
That is plenty".

"The next day can I count some more, how long will it take till
I'm through?"

And I said "Darlin', at twenty a day, you'll be about one
Hundred and two!"

We'll count more tomorrow and I'll tell you a tale I heard
When I was eleven, of angels with lanterns that light up the
Stars to help you see clear up to heaven."

Then I gazed at the sky and smiled to myself and suddenly
Heard not a peep.

And when I looked down on my dear daughter's face, the
moon's glow showed her fast asleep...

Dedication: My daughter Samantha, with love

Hills Of Dream

Bev Taubenfeld

Far away; yet not,
on a hillside of ceaseless fantasy
is a home for my wandering thoughts
where dreams come true
if I say it be
and reality stays as sought
I would, to live a very short while
with the honey–sweet folk
on the hills of dream.
To sing with a lute of self–made style
and set, with my emotions,
the ever–changing scene.
Then, would I leap
from my highest scheme
to safely, in the arms of reality, land.
I'd gaze at the beautiful
hills of dream and touch them,
once more, with the tip of my hand.

Dedicated To Jacob, Dan And Sharon

Laverne E. Burns

Daughter Dear, your precious child senses the American Dream you must achieve

As a nurse, you earn your way, skillfully, comforting parents when they grieve

The depth of our love is unexplainable, different and difficult for others to perceive

God and His Angels watch over us from above, giving us strength, I believe!

Restless babe, locked indoors, I'm touched by the warm little arms of my Grandson

Cold, delicate, little arms can give no hugs, only wonderful smiles from my own son

One is active, loves to tease, watches TV, bounces, jumps, up and down, just for fun

Briefly and cautiously my special child here is ever so gently rolled out under the sun

Hesitate, contemplate, is it fair that unbeknown our loving boys are intertwined.

Uncle in a wheelchair and three year old are a pair; one can see and one is blind

Together, childlike, tender, thoughtful, unassuming patience; a blessing, in our mind

Equally their spiritual, fortitude reminds us to pay attention, be considerate and kind

Disabled and normal children do relate, evaluate this normalcy if you dare!

Like a rainbow of gold and drops of heaven's rain, heartfelt love is what I share

Remembering our worthiness in the valuable gift of earthly, life; let's be well aware

That all God's creatures are individuals, still the same, needing devotion and care

Now, silently, the sun sets, behind our hills, my heart is singing, as I hear it say

Compassion for others is my gift today, there's always time for work time for play

The unknown future can often be contrite, God give us health, fervently, we pray

The Vision of Light is in my soul, joyfully together again, Bless this day!

Dedication: Heaven's special child, Daniel Foresta

Troubles
Beverly Trujillo
Troubles on my mind,
Troubles all the time,

Is there one who can say,
I never have to worry.

I'd trade places with that person,
Brother in a hurry.

These troubles that I have really get me down.
Especially when they keep going round and round.

You can smile today and think, my troubles are all through,
But don't you turn around because they'll creep on you.

There'll be a time when you can smile and you won't have to worry.
That time might be a long way off.

So until that day, don't worry.

How I Wish Upon My Dad
Debbie Poe
How I wish my dad were here, he would be so proud if he were near.

How I wish my dad could see, the woman and mother I've come to be.

How I wish my dad could hear, me tell him that I love him so very dear.

How I wish my dad could smell, the beautiful flowers he taught me to grow
so well.

How I wish my dad could taste, his birthday cake that I would love to
bake.

How I wish my dad could know, how I really didn't want him to go.

How I wish I could hug him again, and thank him for my life he began.

How I wish my dad were here, No one can take his place, he needn't fear.

How I wish he could again sing along, with and our family, his favorite
song.

How I wish my dad were here, I miss him as much today as I did when he
passed away.

How I wish my dad were here, he's in my dreams and my thoughts, I cherish
so dear.

How I wish my dad could see, how his grandsons have grown to appreciate
me.

How I wish I had my dad, it's too late now, inside I feel so sad.

How I wish everyone could know, how important it is and to let it show,
how much a daughter needs her dad, and he can make her whole life glow.

How I wish he could have lived longer, he could have made me so much
stronger.
Not only this time of year, but all year long, I long to have my dad sing
me his favorite song.

I know we'll meet again some day, I'll see you smile again in your special
way.
How I wish I could tell you today, I love you, dad, Happy Birthday!
Dedication: My dad, Harrison Edward Abbott

Alone
Tammi Kathleen Smith–Santoro
The wind blows fiercely down a cold city block.
A homeless man sits huddled in the corner of his box.
The skies darken overhead, and threaten to pour rain.
The man shivers, trying to keep warm is all in vain.
A woman rushes by, her eyes catch a glimpse sideways.
A businessman grimaces, tossing him a dime, wondering
What this world's coming to these days.
Nobody stops, nobody cares.
Stopping would mean they'd confront their own fears.
That they too could be the one in that box,
Shivering and alone on a cold city block.
The man huddles further into his retreat,
Knowing that him and death would eventually meet.
He closes his eyes for the very last time.
His pockets are empty except for a dime.
In the morning they'll find him, stiff in his box,
Not caring that he died alone on a cold, city block.
Dedication: For Nicholas, my soulmate

Changing Skies
Olivia Hall
Blue is the sky, clear and cloudless as the ocean waves

Time escapes, so fleeting its steps, it passes unnoticed

Suddenly, the sky becomes grey, then completely white

The wind swirls fresh snow about, laughing and flirting as
it gently falls

Dancing, going round and round until the winter blanket
covers all

Harmless merriment changes faces and soft whiteness becomes
a tempest

Force and fury rise to the taunts of the wind, hurling cold,
icy contempt

Answering back with a blinding chill, the blizzard rages on

As dusk approaches, the fading winter light takes with it
the last shred of hope

Enveloped by darkness, snow keeps falling, oblivious to the
fear of death

Huddled on the snowy ground, afraid to live, afraid to die,
nothing to be done but wait for the light

So fragile the spirit, it cannot remain, a tortured mind
keeps vigil with the frozen form

Sinking deeper and deeper, the mind desperate to hang on,
hallucinations form reality

Struggling to survive, the cold relentless, the night slips
into eternity

White, then grey, now blue sky appears under the fading moon

Dawn breaks with sunlight so brilliant, the nightmare loses
its hold

Calmness hushes the turmoil, the night has ended, and the
journey just begun.

Forty–Nine Forever
Ida Corradino

Birthdays seem to make us shiver
as the years go rolling by;
But a birthday that marks your 50th year
can even make grown men cry.

Although we know that with age you grow wiser
it's a frightening thing to behold;
There are trees and buildings and even a President
that are younger than fifty years old.

Fifty can mean a half of a century
or the point just "over the hill";
But you can still do the things you did years ago
as long as you take your "Geritol" pill.

No matter how old others think you may be
and no matter the jokes you may hear;
Fifty is the beginning of the rest of your life
and also the start of your 51st year.

Dedication: Everyone who believed in me.

Six Wishes
Lee Murphy

Six wishes I made
On the
Roses
You
Sent,

One each for
Health and
Happiness
And
Money
For rent.

Two more I
Used
For Money
And
Love,

And the last
I saved
For
A
Message from
Above.

If we let
Ourselves
Hold
Hands
And
Hearts,

Perhaps there
Will
Be
No
Ending,

But
Only
A
Start.

Winter Of My Soul
Susan Long

There are places
where there is more gray than blue,
closed down skies,
no sun can penetrate.
There is cold that strikes the body with despair and pain.

Earth quiet and unyielding,
winter of the soul,
the land, the firmament...

Yet underneath it all
the pulse of ever–changing life
brings forth the sun;
calls out the tender shoot
beneath the soil;
sets man's heart to beat
a new rhythm of hope,
a fresh desire to throw off the cold,
the fear, the despair.

The soul comes alive again
and learns not to look back

Visually Impaired
Tim Beck

Many times in the world of ours we get caught up into things, situations, and circumstances that
cause us to lose site of what's really important. Society looks upon the ones who may be
different from the norm — and they become outcast.

God leads our lives, and we are led down paths, that regardless of our Self–developed social
norms may not necessarily be accepted. Always look to what is really the true meaning for
our lives, not tailored for social gratification — but rather the fulfillment Life has to bring.

In our ever changing, Political, Ethical, Man–made micro–cosm; We do in fact become fooled
into thinking — Black or White. No longer is gray a shade that may be accepted. But others
blinded by the darkness of so–called worldly values — (In a desperate attempt to chain us to
normalcy) try and color us a shade darker or lighter so not to cause a disturbance.

A disturbance that creates turmoil within the conceived structured methodology of Men.
Men created by God, for God — Who have exploited their perceived impulses to be that of
an infinite power pertaining to all humankind.

Let us never lose sight or focus — of the visions that empower us. No matter what deep
sense of ambiguity that may be attached. Follow your heart — Always in a matter that's just —
Justice the way it was meant — Universally, not Restrictively.

There is a meaning to Life. Once you find it — Continue in your pursuit — for it is Never–
ending — and may bring about a joy that few find, and others believe is at best —
Incomprehensible. Follow — Or should I say, "Lead" — Yourself and others — through this
collage of color — while never fearing to embrace what is considered outside the lines.

Simple Things
Ellen Marie Cody
It's simple things that bring me joy
Things others may not see

You have to watch and listen
For them very carefully

It could be a child's first words
Or lovers walking hand in hand

Birds making nests, or Father and Son
Building castles in the sand.

The smell of a new doll at Christmas
Or the feel of a hard back book

The sound of our National Anthem
Catalogs, and time to look

The cry of a newborn baby
A wildflower in a vase

Simple things are often the best
Certainly too good to waste.

Reflections
Judy Magie–McKenzie
Between me and you I'm finally two.
Really sorry you missed my party.

Balloons and candles tuna and such,
Oh my goodness Mommy made such a fuss.

I'm all dressed up in my black and white,
Ready for a party but no more fights.

A lot has happened in this past year,
But I'm older and wiser than I appear.

The loss of my sister the trauma of a fight,
Has made me realize the delight of life.

But come next year when I'll be three,
I hope you will come just to visit me.

I have a secret and it's not a curse,
My Mommy's left arm is where I nurse.

Even though I like to nurse I'm not a little baby,
I keep myself so nice and clean I'm quite a pretty lady.

I love to have my belly rubbed day in and day out,
And when I play with all my toys I wish that I could shout.

My favorite food is Kitty Stew with all those vegetables,
And with my egg or tuna fish I really get quite full.

I am not spoiled oh no not much but you must understand,
My Mommy loves me very much and isn't that just grand.

I try to help my Mommy when she's doing her yard work,
But I prefer the cool, cool shade and not that dirty dirt.

Mommy says I'm good as good as I can be,
But Mommy spoils me rotten so how else could I be.

I am so glad that I love Mommy and that Mommy loves me,
It must be plain for all to see we are a loving family.

Left To Keep
Sandra Fowler
I watch the shadow take you as you sleep.
A bird sings from the clothesline deep too deep.
That moon is but a sliver left to keep.

Trees shiver in the spring wind on the hill,
And I can only hold by force of will,
The yellow gladness of a daffodil.

The planting of this flower made you so proud.
You said you saw your picture in a cloud.
One day in the year such dreams are allowed.

There was something so safe about your face.
Its planes and hollows were my true homeplace.
Such shelter weather boards cannot replace.

Go, little whippoorwill, now let me be,
Just what I was before you sang to me,
A woman married to a memory.

When morning rises over yonder hill,
As fine and golden as this daffodil,
His shadow will be gardening with me still.

Her Secret World
R. M. Hall
Her face always made up like a china dolls,
painted with rouge, concealer and bright red lips

She's a vision of natural beauty, a woman portraying
an outer image of a content, confident woman
thriving on perfection.

The reality is she's oblivious to her splendor, and
stares continuously into her hand mirror
finding imaginary flaws in her reflection

Her outer persona is just an illusion conjured up by
the alcoholic cider for confidence, she regular sips

For you don't see her nervously shaking as she does
but stand in her open doorway puffing on her
nicotine addiction so petrified

You don't wipe away her perspiration, the hot sweat
of fear that exudes soaking her wan skin

You can't feel her intense inner pain, that twists turns
tightly in her aching chest the sickness feeling within

You don't have to sit for days at a time staring at the
same four wall yearning for the courage to venture outside

To take that first initial step out into the world she fears
makes her heart beat rapidly race her strides quicker and
quicker for she feels scared and insecure

She can feel a million eyes glaring in her direction too much
hustle and bustle in the streets below
so she climbs up a desolate hill

For here she feels safe an escape a private paradise for in
her mind she obliterated the murky river and cold winter's chill

For alone she does but sit with no people or words to utter
she feels safe and happy in her secret world a second home
beyond her front locked door

We Wish You Love
Starr Vincnet
We wish you love forever
For eternity
Love forever
Then all things can be
When you join two hearts
And never set them free
You'll have love

With caring and two sharing
The world is open to you
There's no force in this world
That can stop you from what
You want to do

We wish you love forever
To strengthen fates you're bound
Love forever
The strongest ever found
When you join two hearts
And never set them free
You'll have love

Dedication: Karin and Travis for their wedding

The Great Bear Spirit
Stephanie Tyler
Oh Great Bear Spirit of the forest
touch me as I seek my soul.
Guide me over hill and knoll
to my Grandmother's place of rest.
Chained as I am for things not done
but guilty of a vision dimmed,
I pray to all the native spirits to lift me
from this life of sin.
Show me how to change those things
and lead me home on the eagle's wings.

Thank you spirits of the forest
for bringing me this earthly sign.
This gift of Sunlight quite divine.
I must protect this little warrior
But panic and dread lead me nowhere.
Only my ancestors of the past – my only
hope of getting there!
An answer to my frantic prayers,
Perhaps the Eagle, Sun, or Bear?

Oh Great Bear Spirit of the forest
you've come, at last, to claim your prey.
Oh no, you cannot take the Sun –
she's gift from the Milky Way.
Be brave, Oh Great One, this son must
slay thee.
So if you will, come dwell in me.

With graceful movement, the Great Bear
falls – the darkness now surrounds me.
Bound anew, I soon will be.
But at last, I see the sunlight and
joined with all, I see the light.
Courage yet to face the night
against the world I stand contrite.

Oh, Great Bear Spirit of the forest!
as you dwell within me now,
Indeed I am a soul that's free
to right the wrongs – Thanks to thee!

Tribute
Denise Kolojejchick
A woman known in darkness
who seldom sees the light
She does for everyone else before herself
in my book, she's all right.
She's there in my sadness
when tears fill my eyes
And she also shares my joy
when I'm filled with pride.
She's there to help me
when I need a hand
But she lets me go on my own
and she always understands.
When I make a mistake
to her I always turn
She helps me through it and lets me know
it's the best way to learn.
As I grow older
she'll always be there
To hold me and protect me
I know she'll always care.
When I'm finally grown up
by myself, but not alone
Hopefully I'll be like her
a woman and mother with children of my own.

Untitled
Sherrill Madore
Your family and friends all praise you
That's nothing to be denied
And when we tell you how much we love you
You know we've never lied

Only once in your life you will turn 50
That's 1/2 a century old
Nothing to be concerned about
Your path is paved with gold

Now 50 is just a number
It doesn't mean a thing
When you're as young and happy as you are
You can fly with just one wing

Now that you've hit the big one
You can say and do what you want
You can blame it all on menopause
While you kick up your heals and flaunt

50 used to be a time
When you sat in a rocking chair
You did a lot of knitting
And the gray showed in your hair
Your skin began to wrinkle
Your hands and legs did shake
And that was all before
You had your birthday cake

But times have changed and we all know
That after 50, you still have a long way to go
So lift that head and dye it brown
Wear a mini and hit the town

For Linda Pinkerton we all know
Will laugh and smile and let herself go
And we will all be around
When the year comes to a end
Just watching Linda
Turn 50 again

I Want To Live
Teresa Brereton

I want to live where a person's race, religion, or looks doesn't count.
Where children are happy and all prejudices are left out.
I want to live where crimes are punished,
Where good deeds prevail when all is said and finished.
I want to live where everyone has food in their stomachs and roofs over
    their head,
Where children feel safe when they're snuggled in bed.
I want to live where generations to come have bright futures,
Where they know we're done our best when they reminisce with old family
    pictures.
I want to live where you go to the beach and play in the sand,
Where you won't find dead fish or toxic trash in your hands.
I want to live where everyone recycles and is environmentally aware,
Where when our grandchildren look back they will know that we cared.
I want to live where adults and children are not victims of abuse,
Where they're not afraid to break the vicious cycle and put their
    experiences to good use.
I want to live where children aren't afraid to go to school,
Where drug and violence aren't said to be "cool."
There are many subjects yet to be touched upon,
But if I did this, this poem would be a mile long.
So in closing I will just say this,
"I want to live. Yes, I want to live!"

Dedication: My hope...Justin, Christina, and Brandon

May Tempest At The Shore
Ray Burns

Hazy sun gives way to gathering graying clouds. They darken as they swirl
    and move with haste
from West to East. A palpable pall blankets the shore and the day has
    become desolate and dim
hovering on the brink of a torrent. Gray to ebony gray skies to the West
    approach with a
vengeance and flashes like flickering fluorescence span the blackness from
    North to South. The
roll of distant thunder moves across a poised, anticipating Bay; it
    reverberates and rumbles
unobstructed to the Ocean.

To the West a silent flash leaps between the clouds and land and, as if by
    signal, a wind from
nowhere wails across the Barrier Island sweeping sand, like vapor, to the
    sea. The Crack,
Crackle, Crashing Crack of tumultuous bolts of blue white lightening shoot
    between the heavens
and the beach. The Gigundo Boom, Barooooom, of the accompanying spasmodic
    thunder
pounds into your chest and rolls through your bones. And again, Barooom,
    and again, and again
frightening and exciting in its relentless exhilarating fury.

The rain, torrential, cascades from turgid clouds in deluge but then with
    decreasing intensity
becomes a sprinkling spray. The booming becomes a rumbling as the storm
    with its turbulence
reluctantly drifts out to sea and oblivion. And there it is. The glorious
    "Oz" like rainbow arched in
splendor and mesmerizing resplendence evoking awe.

The air is different now, It's washed clean and it is calm as a soft
    breeze sighs across the Island.
Misty vapors rise from the boardwalk and crystal like droplets hang on the
    dune grass. There's a
magic in the air, a feeling of bestowed serenity.

Be here now. Smell the salt and witness the beauty of a storm at the Shore

How Do You Forget
Steven Sippel

the smile has all but vanished, the happiness has disappeared
a heart once filled with love, has become cold and barren
a soul once filled with the joy of life, has since become an empty void
a spirit once a tower of strength, has now become brittle and frail
a desire for life and a will matched by none, have all since crumbled to
    dust
all this pain, all this unhappiness, all this sorrow
and for what? all for the name of LOVE.
oh what powers you have to control a mans inner self so tightly
to dictate all he feels so that he has no control of how he feels
to build him up to a high unequaled by any drug and then
to push him off without a care as to where he may fall
from a high so wonderful, and so satisfying, to a low so painful that the
    heart is mortally wounded
and then they say to forget, move on with your life
someone more deserving of what you have to offer will come
but now can you forget the feelings that have embodied every part of your
    soul for so long and
yet so short a time. how do you forget, oh GOD, how do you forget and move
    on...

time is the wondrous healer, for in the future all pain subsides the
    present becomes the past and in
the past there is nothing but faint memories of what was.
maybe this is how one forgets!

On Healing
Patricia B. Toler

Self–doubt is a deep, dark pit
Filled with my tears of inadequacy.
Why should I stick my neck out
Only to have it chopped off?
It's better to keep my neck
Tucked under the wings of safety and security.

Depression slithers all around
The fathomless recesses of my mind.
Why can't I concentrate?
Why can't I carry a task all the way through?
It's better just not to start
Than be called a quitter.

Low self esteem is my own personal devil
Relentlessly poking and stabbing me along.
You can't do this.
You can't do that.
You're not as good.
Stay inside and keep to yourself.
One is the perfect number.

Thunder, lightning, heavy rains, and hail
Will eventually surrender to the calm.
A ray of light will peek above
the wind–battered tree–tops
Warming the clutter left by the storm,
Drying out the trash in the gutters.
Do I believe?

Time is the great healer, but it goes by so slow.
How can I shove those hands on the clock?
Pray for patience and wait.
Pray for guidance and strength.
Open my heart's door and let God in.
He is my friend.
He is my refuge.

This is my belief.

Tabitha Our Granddaughter
Myrna Sholly

Tabitha Lynn is her name, a bundle of joy from heaven came.
Sparkling eyes and a lovable smile helped make her a wonderful gal.
Nicknamed Tabby, not a day in her life did she look shabby.
She always is so proper and prim, like a beauty contest she's about to
    win.

As Tabby was growing up, there was a lot of laughter and a lot of tears.
She kept everyone on their toes, because of the friends and life she chose.
We never knew what Tabby would do next, we would always try hard to guess.
A lot of joy and laughter she gave us, without too much bother or fuss.

Then, as the years went by, a bond with us she did tie.
This bond would never break. A wonderful granddaughter she did make.
She has a great burden to bear, an illness she has, which isn't fair.
She has taught us so very much, and a lot of lives she did touch.

Courage has become her strong point in life.
She has handled her illness without too much strife.
God only knows the time we have left,
So we cherish every moment and will try to make it the best.

Granddaughters are a gift from above,
And we sure have the best one to love.
We thank God and her for all times shared.
With all that nothing can be compared.

Heaven
Pedro Tejeda

Heaven is one breath away, heaven is two steps away,
Heaven is a place where all poetic justice is prevails,
Where all citizens weak and strong, thrive to hear where all
    power belongs,
It is a place where ancient history can be told by footprints of
    heroes long, long ago,

Where blue jays fly, round, round with glee, and angels sing
    quite joyfully,

It is a place where you can assure, all your problems can be
    cured,
Where visions of old and new can come to past,
It is a place where the holy ground is paved with priceless
    gems and stone,

While you stand there in constant ah and observe,
a cool wind breeze blows the scent of lilacs in through your
    nose,
traveling down through your body, down, down to the very
    end of your toes,
leaving you with a wonderful tingly sensation spreading
    throughout your body,
leaving you dazed and breathless,

As you stretch your arms up higher and higher,
you suddenly fall back onto a cloud just happening to float
    right by you,
Then slowly, slowly your eyes begin to close inch by inch
    little by little,
then suddenly you remember that your time has not yet come,

You in an instant leap to your feet not willingly wanting to
    leave, but as
you turn to take one last look you suddenly see fire and
    brimstone leaping at your feet,
Then suddenly, suddenly you awake not quite sure what
    just took place—

The Master Builder
Marian S. DeLoatch

Ye are the temple, a house built not by hand brought to life,
fashion by the Master my friend.

A Master of the trade knows his work even before its time.
Professional designer, creator of all designs.

First class genius beyond all ages before the world was created
he knew its stages.

No blue print only his image, making vessels big and small,
molding and shaping; a potter he is called.

He knows the frame work using clay and dirt peculiar, no
hammer, no nail creating images from head to tail.

Upon his wheel he chips away putting every detail in its place.

His furnace is heated fiery hot testing holes, cracks and spots.

Beautifully created the things he made an artist giving it radiant
colors that won't fade.

Artistic, goes beyond the limit, no other before his time.
The Master Builder, the Great Architect, the True Creator
putting silence inquiring minds.

The Soldier Beats His Drum
Elizabeth A. Harse

The beating of the drum resides inside a shallow vessel, unleashed power a
    prelude
to its life, controlled spasm caressing warm palms across unbroken
    barriers. The
soldier's arms encircle the object of his pleasure.

The boom of the drum...membrane now greatly empowered, an awakened
    excitement
releasing hypnotic perfumes...Soothing waves sending shivers of
    expectation along
ridgeways of imagination.

How strong the beat of the drum...vibrant movement projecting its own
    purpose...
an airborne missile seeking out its beacon.

How loud the beat of the drum as it searches hidden corners of a secret
    world,
shrouded in darkness a fertile land allows the conqueror freedom to invade
    its
surrendering territory.

Clocks ticking...ears pounding...earth's vibrations on the move
    showering the
senses with immeasurable sensation, reaching...climbing...striving
    for
the exaltation on fine threads of heightened intensity...

As the final roll of the drum sheds its river of life throughout the
    steeped mountain
valley claiming victory...its echo falls to earth in the dying embers of
    lust...
the drum rests from its labour as it lies in total silence upon subdued
    ground in
the stillness of spent life.

For the soldier the battle begins at dawn...discern your final sunrise
    drummer
boy...for in your empire you ruled as sovereign only for a night!!!

New Beginnings
Candy D. Riley
I opened my heart, and let you in,
To share my life, and be my friend.

I fell in love, it seemed for life,
Praying, one day, we would be husband and wife.

My dreams were shattered, by the mistakes we made,
And now I rest, in the bed we laid.

Not a day goes by, you don't cross my mind,
I thank God, we were not blind.

But now I want, what we once had,
When life was good, and I wasn't sad.

Will you return with me,
To our life, with our own little sea.

Where we will share, our dreams and hopes,
And restart our lives, by climbing the ropes.

That leads to our heaven, not in the sky,
But here on earth, where we reside.

In my heart, my love beats true,
For the man I love, the one and only you.

Soul Of A Child
Joan A. Hopkins
He awakens in the morning filled with love and hope
Yet he knows this not for he knows no other way
Still he feels and fears another side of life
And thinks it lies in darkness
Is that from where he comes?
Couldn't we quicken our own soul?
And find peace the same.
For the mind misleads and tricks us up and causes so much pain

I think it was that way before in the golden age
When beauty was the ruling force
Which is only truth again
Another tried to tell us this
A great religion came, be as children he had said,
is this not the same?
For here we are years later caught in mans knowledge knot.
For all our know how will not show how.
Or all our knowledge save us
for look at what it's brought
A race to live from sphere to sphere at each others cost.

Curious minds asking how and why and if
Taking life all apart for life's simple pleasures.
They're not content to know their minds are meant for finer things
more challenging that show

Is it these men of learning or the monitory gain
that causes all the hell on earth of horror and of shame
One fixed in the others, what a deadly pair!

Oh can't you see—Oh can't you see that all there is really there
It is your birthright from the start until we are told prepare.
Prepare from what I ask you?
Must it be this way. A great long struggle to gather and achieve
Only to lie back and sigh and die and be relieved
The end is near, it's closer now which way will we all go.
Shall we execute the genius of our finest, make it our last show.
Or will we one more time with a guilty finger point?

Little Boy Of Mine
Trisa I. Johnsen
I look into your eyes, and I see a piece of me.
I look upon your face, and dream of things that are to be.

And I think about how blessed I am, that God has chosen me,
to raise this precious child of His, to mold his destiny.

I never could have dreamed that I'd ever feel this way
as I hold you in my arms, or watch your tiny hands at play.

But not a moment passes, that I don't want to capture for all time,
for time passes so quickly, Oh little boy of mine.

I love that sparkle in your bright blue eyes, as you discover great new
    things
Or the way you finally close those eyes, at night as mommy sings.

And then you sleep so sweetly, your tiny lashes curled,
over eyes that are so tired, from exploring this big world.

But here you are all safe and sound, in this home that we have made,
to raise this precious child of ours, as he grows from day to day.

And I hold these moments so dear in my heart, to reflect on for all time,
and think about how blessed I am, that this little boy is mine.
Dedication: In memory of "Papa"

Dear Sweet Mother
Deborah Dietrich
Oh what a friend I have in you,
especially when I'm feeling blue

A mother's love is like no other,
whether you're right or wrong it's
always strong

This bond comes from inside out
every mother knows without a
doubt

All too soon your baby's gone like
the winter snow, and this is
hard I know.

As life moves on we've had many
mountains and hills, as you know
this is God's will.

When I look back I thank you
for keeping me on track

We talk and reminisce about all
the times we miss as I greet you
with a hug and kiss

You will always be special to me
with every prayer on my knee.

I've been told I'm just like my
mother, but mom I'd rather be
like no other.

Thanks always to my mother as
I lay me down and
pull up my bed covers.
Dedication: Mom, children and husband, love always

Lost Prayer
Dundi J. Corbin

A lost prayer is all she sees, flying away in the far distance.
Where does it lead?

Her empty promises. Faith she was reluctant to show.
Only whispered threats, that were hers, secretly unknown.

She gazes through an opened window, what does it show?
Only her selfish prayer, to which know one knows.

Waiting alone, she lifts her hands.
The rain hits hard, she is bleeding drops of dry sand.

Her foolish sin has left her blind.
Only leading her lost prayer hidden in time.

She yearns to feel love. To find peace of mind.
Her stubbornness has killed her, she is denied.

Darkness covers her. Night demons arrive.
They take her body...her black soul, not kind.

Then her lost prayer flies, oh so high,
Never returning...

It was her choice.
God has left her behind.

Leisure Days
Charlotte Horn

Languishing lazily in a foreign
land.
By the blue, green, sea, on the
silver sand.
The white hot sun, in the
sky so blue
Can't be reached, by me, nor
you.
Its rays pour down upon
my skin.
To make me feel warm, and
good within.
The sea makes music, I
have found
When the tide softly
tumbles, with a swishing
sound.
A symphonic crescendo rises high
As white crested waves,
come crashing by.
When the rays of the sun
are too much to bear

I call my friend The wind
he's always there
Wafting, gently round my
heated frame,
Or tossing about – as if
playing a game
All we need is all at hand
The sun, the sea, the breeze
the land.
Let's not poison and
rape, our Mother Earth
But care and tend her
for all she's worth.

Dedication: My grandchildren, whom I adore

Look At Me!
Sherrye Gothard

Look at me, what do you see?
A little girl's mommy who wipes away tears?
Turns them to laughter, calms all her fears.
Another's loving wife?
Faithful and true in the midst of all strife.
Do you see me as a Woman?
Not mommy, Not wife.

Look at me and tell me true,
Do you feel anything when I reach out to touch you?
Do you feel desire? Does your heart start to flutter? Can you feel I'm
a Woman?
Not merely wife or just mother.

Look at me and dare to believe,
That a Woman is what I want you to see!

Reach out! Touch me! Look in my eyes!
Know that I'm just as mesmerized!

I ache for your touch. I dream of your kiss.
For you I feel too much. I've never felt like this!

If you look at me, I'm all aflutter,
In your presence, I'm only a Woman!
Nobody's wife. Nobody's mother.

To My Granny
Robert J. Thompson

To my Granny I love so well
Her great strength that's taught me move
forward, on the past do not dwell
I recall running in her orange grace,
so wild and free
I'd climb for the biggest orange,
in her navel orange tree
There was a swing, that there I
loved to swing
A tub in the entrance way, there
I remember bathing
She cooked our meals, made us the
best divinity
She curled my hair
I remember even being spanked,
Put on the right track by my granny
Her strength I so admire
Her love for the one that
there is no higher
She has a garden every year
which I'm sure beautifully does bloom
My Granny

I remember sitting with, in
her big white house, looking at
books in her living room
She told me at an age of young
While sitting on a bed I
was a chosen one
I'd not the knowledge then to
understand
Yet I know now it was for
God's great plan
for my Granny I pray that
She get better each new day
I just wanted to say
I love ya Granny, in a very
special way

Gone Are The Days
Kimberly Elmore

Gone are the days when I was young,
the things I've seen, the things I've done

The people who have shared with me
all of my hopes, and all of my dreams.

The days of cutting school, are finished
Oh those tears I shed over a facial blemish

Smokin' in the girls room, such a sneaky deed
Cussing out the teachers, that disagreed with me.

Fightin' in the parking lot, waiting for the bus
What did those grown ups ever think
That they could do with us.

Now I'm grown up and can't believe
the things I used to do
things I deemed so greatly loved, I eventually out grew

Well things have changed, and so have I
the days of childhood gone
there's only time to rearrange
these things that I have done

Dedication: Remembering "Granny", Irma S. Walters

Growing Up
Laurie Cianciotta

Growing up with a dad like you has made every little girl's
dream come true.
You granted every wish you knew even ones mom wished
you never to do.
You turned the radio off when it made me sick, as crazy as
it sounded you knew the trick.
We spent Saturdays watching a slap of a puck and made sure
to tell me when to duck.
We awoke on Sundays mornings and fled for the news, buns,
pasta, and bread.
You sat patiently as I played beauty shop let me do your nails
and comb your mop.
You taught a frightened girl how to ride a bike and knew when
to let go which she didn't like.
You knew when to make her smile and joked all day and laughed
a mile.
Crabs and pasta were our favorite meal, we picked at them until
we couldn't feel.
Many a day we sat outside and watched people walk or go for
a ride.
You did favors for me on a drop of a hat and welcomed all my
friends to our door mat.
We sat on edge and watched the Rangers and sweated it out
when they were in danger.
They defeated those Devils by a thin line, which to us was more
than fine.
They rose that Stanley Cup so high, our ultimate dream reached
the sky.
Messier promised us they would win and brought you and me
the biggest grin.
A memory that little girl will remember forever, the memories
of you and the time together.
The love shared throughout the times we had, no one can take
away which makes me glad.
I miss you more every day that goes by, and try really hard
not to cry.
I wrote this in memory of you, and hope you knew I loved you
too.

The Search
Mary Lena Govar

I climbed the highest mountain
Where man's feet had never trod,
And on that lofty, majestic summit,
I caught a glimpse of God.

I gazed upon a new born babe
As peacefully it did nod,
And in the tiny angelic face,
I caught a glimpse of God.

I walked through low green valleys
With flowers, trees, and streams.
I listened to the whippoorwill,
As he called his mate, from dreams.

I saw the sheep and cattle
As homeward they did plod.
There in the peaceful evening
I caught a glimpse of God.

I stood beside the roaring sea
And watched the rolling tide,
As the waves beat on the shore
And tore away the sod.

I knelt there on the sand and prayed,
And I knew, I had found my God.

A Mystical, Mysterious Journey
Denise McCroskey

Will my soul never cease to be moved to its very depths – its farthest
reaches, when I encounter you on my journey? Will I
never cease to feel as if I meet my cosmic twin, traveling parallel yet
separate paths? And each time it stirs a faint yet very
distant memory of another time, another place that I do dream about.
Somewhere that reaches far beyond the short time I
have known you here on earth.
Ah, my soul reaches back to ancient, heavenly times. I catch a glimpse,
for a moment...for a while...and then it is gone
once again. Fleeting and floating like the mist. Even my dreams speak to
me of it...when you and He appear in my sleep and
speak to my soul.

Something that saints and mystics and those of varied religions attempt
to describe and yet cannot fully explain. It reaches
beyond time and space and into the depths of the universe. No, it is not
the sometimes silly, frequently maudlin lyrics from
a love song or the wild imaginings of the feminine or a fleeting
sensuality.

I have existed with you forever it feels. Two very old souls, it seems.
My mind strains to remember after these encounters.
Like a person with amnesia, small pieces of memories appear. I know not
even what I write other than it is real, though
abstract. I almost have recollection of a time in the presence of our
Creator – together we were with Him. And we said, yes
it is time you send us to earth to complete our mission. And we begged
that he allow us to exist at the same time in the history
of the universe. Even though we knew the time to be brief, it would be
too difficult to bear if we didn't encounter each other
at all. He did so because it was a part of His plan.

Beyond traditional religious lines, it goes back to the Creator of the
cosmos. That which is beyond words and meaning. That
which is ethereal, yet so tangible.

It is mystical and mysterious. Do you know that of which I speak?

Butterfly Love
Robert A. Palmer

Spread your wings and fly
little butterfly fly
Fly to your new found flower
and then away from me.
No one can catch you
I know you want to be free
You've got to do what you've
always done
Fly from flower to flower
In the morning sun
You say you don't see your
life belonging to me.
Go do your thing, what ever that
will be. Fly away up in the
highest tree.
Spread your wings
Fly away, Fly away Free.
You'll never find a place to stay
Nothing new for you to see
Nothing left for you to do
No one will ever belong to you
Honesty and Devotion is not
your name —
You only want to play the
run away game

Dedication: Letha M. Shores of Selma, Ca

The Flag Flies High
Paula M. Pimentel

A midst of many stars, I saw the crimson stripes,
And couldn't help but feel proud,
As they represented all the blood shed to preserve my rights,

The bold white stripes that ran parallel to the red,
Reminded me of the peace,
The peace that rests with all those now dead,

And the stars, stood for the quiet sky,
That I sleep under,
Every night,

It rose above the earth with pride,
A tear fell,
But I felt safe inside,

Because for us, they fought and gave their souls,
So their children could live peacefully,
So our children could grow,

oppression, only a distant memory,
The names of many brave soldiers,
The only piece of war they would see,

Young men believing in themselves and the good to come,
Some died to save many,
And many live free, because of the wars won,

In war, overall glory is rarely a sight,
But someday,
We'll suffer through our last fight,

Then for once, maybe peace will unite mankind under a silent sky,
When it's no longer the American flag, but the world flag,
And we'll watch together, as the flag flies high...

Dedication: My father, Daniel Pimentel

Let Go
Richard Paul Salvaggio

To "let go" does not mean to stop caring. It means I can't do it for
    someone else,
To "let go" is not to cut myself off. It's the realization I can't control
    another.
To "let go" is not to enable, but to allow learning from natural
    consequences.
To "let go" is to admit powerlessness which means the outcome is not in my
    hands.
To "let go" is not to try to change of blame another. It is to make the
    most of myself.
To "let go" is not to care for, but to care about.
To "let go" is not to fix, but to be supportive.
To "let go" is not to judge, but to allow another to be a human being.
To "let go" is not to be in the middle arranging all the outcomes,
but to allow others to affect their destinies.
To "let go" is not to be protective. It is to permit another to face
    reality.
To "let go" is not to deny, but to accept.
To "let go" is not to nag, scold or argue,
but instead to search out my own shortcomings and correct them.
To "let go" is not to adjust everything to my desires,
but to take each day as it comes cherish myself in it.
To "let go" is not to criticize and regulate anybody,
but to try to become what I dream I can be.
To "let go" is not to regret the past, but to grow and live for the
    future.
To "let go" is to fear less, and love more.

An Expression Of Our Love
Michele A. Bayer

To My Sweet Heart, Thomas
Our friendship blossomed into pure magic over night.
In my heart, mind, and soul it felt so incredibly right.
When it rains, you are the sun in my sky.
You have paved the way and given me the wings to fly.
You have lifted me up into a world that I have never known before.
As long as we are together our love will continue to mature.

You are my galaxy of pure white stars.
You are the center of my universe just the way you are.
When you hold me close by your side,
You take my breath away each time our lips collide.
You are the river of dreams at the beginning and end of my rainbow.
I'll take you with me wherever I go.

We will walk through a path of truth that will guide us together.
On a journey that will last always and forever.
In the reality we have created we could never lose touch.
Because we love each other far too much.
No matter the difficult obstacles we may face,
Our passion and romance could never be replaced.

When we roam with the shadows of the night.
We will never get lost as long as we follow the light.
If we come to fog in the crossroad, I will choose to stand by you.
Without hesitation our love will pierce through.
We have a physical attraction that is meant to be.
In the ocean we swim babe, it's just you and me.

When you look deep into my eyes, I feel the warmth in your heart.
My heart sings a song of sadness when we are apart,
But the tears of happiness rekindle when your hand touches mine.
Every moment we share will be cherished until the end of time.
Honey, you are a precious gift from up above,
You are my very best friend and the man that I love.

Dedication: My best friend, Thomas J. Muccio

Unseen But Not Unknown
Ronald L. Overfield

Even in the darkness of night, there was Light.
She was her Lord's faithful and unfailing servant.
Each morning as the sun rays shone through the hospital window
One could not help being drawn to her beautiful sky–blue eyes.
Through those eyes a glimpse of heaven could be seen.

"I love you", I would say as a child, "Do you love me?"
"I sure do!" was her unfailing response.
Now as she slips closer to her reward of paradise, I asked again
"I love you. Do you love me?"
Belabored, she whispered her familiar, "I sure do!"

Lying motionless as a result of a stroke, she could barely talk.
But she continued to speak with her eyes – those incredible eyes.
What a great enduring gift God gave me when He blessed me with this
   mother.
This would not be goodbye, for I was confident I would see her again,
But next time it would be for eternity.

As her body grew weaker, her eyes were drawn upward.
They seemed to affirm her lifelong faith.
Quietly, but distinguishably, her last words were "I sure do!"
But this time I had not asked, "Do you love me?"
There was no doubt to Whom her response was directed – The Unseen
   Questioner!

Dedication: Mom– my everlasting thanks

Infinite
Annette Cooper

A tiny seed,
planted deep below the ground
soaking warmth supplied by sun
drinking waters of the sky
emerging life,

begins to grow,
reaching high towards the clouds
bending with the breath of trees
withstanding all the weathered days
enduring life.

As seasons change,
Its petals fall towards the earth.
The days are cold. The trees are bare,
Yet, soon there's sweetness in the air,
It starts again.

A little child,
one day born into this world
soaking warmth supplied by love
unaware what lies ahead
emerging life,

Begins to grow,
setting goals up in the clouds
seeking knowledge through his wonder
trudging over rocky roads.
enduring life.

As years pass by,
through his journey on this earth
with the changes, he adjusts
and now a man, he leaves his son
to start again.

And life remains...

Metanoia
Robert Calco

I have seen the red sun set
Beyond the midnight hour
And breathed the salted breeze
That shuffles the leaves
On a robust Siberian
summer's eve
And felt the rolling thunder
Make rage against the night

And I have been blinded by the Light
Of He Who Built the World
And set it all ablaze for a Word
That men might weep

And I've awakened from the deepest sleep
Only to find myself still dreaming
And to hear the Silence screaming
Its true meaning
Only to fall on deaf ears

And I have faced my deepest fears
And read them all to death
Between the lines of lost pages
Forged from the Book of Life

Fool that I am!

Dedication: Olga; my wife, my friend

Those Depression Days
Jennie Williams

I grew up in those depression days
when times were really bad
Kerosene lamps
and old wood stoves
worn–out shoes
and hand–me down clothes.

I walked to school
in snow to my knees
with burlap bags
tied around my feet.

I carried the water
from a pump down back
and the only bathroom
was that little old shack.

No washing machine
and no big TV's
just an old scrub board
to keep me clean.

Many a night before
going to bed
my evening meal
was peanut butter and bread.

The stove would burn out
in the middle of the night
and I'd shiver and shake
till the morning light.

Now as I look back
on those rough days
I wonder how I made it
to this ripe old age.

BAR – My Life Saver
Joseph Bertalan

I had a dream the other night I had never had before.
I was back in Luxembourg with my outfit during the Second World War
Since my rifle was not much help against the Germans, I did not feel secure

So I asked my sergeant for a BAR and he smiled and said, "Ok, sure
"Where do I get it?" I asked him, while looking all around.
"Oh, tomorrow you'll find one somewhere on the ground."
"On the ground?" I asked him, "Isn't that a funny place?"
"The guy who had it is dead out there," he said, with a serious face.
This shook me up quite a bit; my unit had just arrived.
We hadn't done any fighting yet and soldiers here had already died

The Germans lobbed mortars all night long, so nobody got any sleep
By dawn we were ready to go and fight and destroy those creeps
The sergeant was right, I found two BARS half hidden in the snow
Under tank exhaust they wouldn't thaw out, so I put them by a tree
After dark we returned and my BARS were waiting for me.

I cleaned them up and made them work, kept them by my side
The next day I was in front of our men, running from tree to tree
The BAR made all the difference – it really took care of me.
I never enjoyed killing, but since it was "them or us," I was willing.
For fifty years my constant prayer has been "Let there never be another war
BAR – Browning Automatic Rifle

Dedication: Joyce, my wife

My Mountain...My Friend
Rachel R. Diaz

Come by my mountain my friend, I want to show you my place of secret
    wonders
built through the years, that You my friend have been a part of. Where I
    laughed
with you, cried with you. I want to show you the top and point up to the
    sky and
show you who really loves you.

Come by my mountain my friend and see the millions of greeting cards I've
    piled up
through the years, some with meaning some without...they've been part of
    the
background music, my sense of purpose.

Come by my mountain my friend and share the earth, where if I'd have no
    sight...I'd
have no fears. My faith never shaken, on this rock all faces appear.

I really wish you visit my mountain my friend, for there is real spring
    here, where
old limbs mend with deep–welled beliefs that years fade like roses and
    laughter is
captured in the leafs. Lark the soul my friend, sing the songs, write the
    prose and
paint the wind...touch the sunshine...absorb the rain!

You see I reach the top much quicker now my friend. I now take steps that
guidance gives me. I have no maps, no roads are drawn, no signs are up but
    those
in my heart. I now stand where I used to stumble. I silhouette my face
    against the
sun, one side burns more than the other. C'mon let's go my friend, I want
    to bring
you to the top and point up to the sky and show Him my true brother.

Dedication: All creation, Ysalys and Johan

Behold This Day...
Sally Ploski

Behold this day you graduate...for you must be very proud.
Enjoy the time you celebrate...and thank the Lord aloud.

Take forth the things that you have learned...and apply them to your life.
For this diploma you have earned...with studies and tests a rife.

Your life will surely have many trials...and tribulations.
Look upon your future with many smiles...and great anticipation.

Think fondly of the days when you were small...and life was so carefree.
Now that you are big and tall...go forth with pride and glee.

In your realm you can meditate...and reflect without a sound.
Remember those who hesitate...are not outward bound.

Your family is very proud of you...and wants you to succeed.
So if you cry do not be blue...you've done yourself a good deed.

Do what you can to be creative...and stimulate your mind.
Apply with great incentive...and leave your mark for all mankind.

Take the time to speculate...in what you say and do.
And always try to reciprocate...those so nice to you.

Congratulations to you...on your high school graduation.
We all shall salute you...with love and admiration.

Dedication: Michelle and Rachelle Tabbutt, Thomaston, Maine

A New Beginning
Patricia A. Creem

A new season is upon us in all its
                                    splendor
As winter is a memory giving way to
                                    surrender.

Early blossoms of pastel on each
                                    flowering petal
A welcomed sight of spring is here
                                    to settle.

Rivers and streams now filled to their
                                    brim
As schools of tiny trout learn how to
                                    swim.

Days become longer with sunshine
                                    so warm
Sweet nectar enjoyed by bumble bees
                                    that swarm.

Robins earnestly search with their beaks for
                                    that worm
Bringing to their nests ones that wiggle
                                    and squirm.

For every season there is a time
                                    for change
A time to reflect and a time to
                                    rearrange.

How fortunate are we to be such a
                                    vital part
How thankful are we to embrace a
                                    new start.

Dedication: Aunt Anna, a great source of strength

Rodeo Tears
Betty Loechel
Talents are few for this young man you see,
He's tried many sports from
skateboards to skis.
He's become somewhat hooked on a sport
Dangerous and wild,
Yet, he only wanted to
Be recognized just like any other Mother's Child.

He looked in the crowd often with
Anticipation and fear.
Hoping he would see her and not
Have to shed tears.

He's not what you'd call a "regular" Child—
He's been up and down and often
Times wild.

Yet, on this day, he just wanted to shine—
Telling all of his friends—
"You'll soon meet that Mom of mine."

Well, the Rodeo came and the Rodeo went
He rode the bull with his head bowed and bent.
He looked in the crowd, and all he could see was
The seat that was EMPTY—
The one was to be, the one
That was waiting for his Mom,
Linda Lee.

My Dad
Wendy A. Garman
I know this man
Who is dear to my heart
Suddenly one day
It was torn all apart.

This man taught me everything
That I needed to know
But I never really listened
Until he had to go.

He gave me Love
And touched my life
It's all over now
He no longer had to fight...

He tried to teach me
Right from wrong
The day he left
I wasn't that strong.

He is gone now
It is hard to believe
This man is MY DAD
Who I will never see.

But, I will see him again
This I know
The day will come
When it's time for me to go.

So, I'll hold him dear
And close in my heart
'Cause the day that we meet
I know we'll never be torn apart!

Dedication: "My dad", James H. Garman Sr. 4–12–97

Why
Stephanie Pociasek
Why do your eyes radiate such torturously
unbearable kindness?

Why does your smile make my insides bubble
over with the sweet pain of longing?

Why do your words make my body ache with
the incredibly lonely wanting of your love?

Why does the brilliance of your glowing soul
show through you making you irresistible?

Why does your touch bring emptiness and a
craving for you to embrace me always?

Why does the thought of you equal the soft sting
of a knife piercing through my love–sick heart

Why do you hypnotize me into needing the
passion you hold?

Why do I fear our time together is limited and I
may lose you to the bitter hatred of things that never were?

Why can't I find the answers to the problems
that wretched me from the happiness I once knew?

Why?

A Rose
Jack L. Harden
In the beginning
As everyone knows
God the Creator
Also made the rose
He made this lovely flower
For he knew that someday
It would be needed to express
What words cannot say
The rose has a language
Everyone understands
Throughout this country
And in all foreign lands
It says Congratulations
For a job well done
It says I love you
To a special someone
It will say farewell
When you've lost a friend
It cries with you softly
To help your heart mend
When a loved one dies
And flowers are sent
It carries the message
Of the feeling that is meant
It will cheer you up
When you're feeling blue
It will say I am sorry
If I have hurt you
Whatever the message
That you want to be heard
The rose will say it
Without speaking a word
God is Love
And through this flower it shows
For the Love of his people
He created the Rose.

So Noble, So Fair
Diane D. McCormick

Am I making a fool of myself
To believe you could possibly care?
What makes me think I could attract you,
You, the one so noble, so fair.

Am I making a fool of myself
To tell you what's hidden inside
The tenderest part of my beat up old heart
Where the love for you constantly hides.

Am I making a fool of myself
To believe in forever with you,
To believe there is one that might love me
And to believe that just maybe its you?

Am I making a fool of myself
Can you see it all over my face
The unbridled joy and the unfettered love
That I feel when you enter my space.

Am I making a fool of myself
To cry endless hours all alone
To accept with such grace the goodbyes every day
And to watch you just drive away home.

Am I making a fool myself
To believe you could possibly care?
What makes me think I could attract you,
You, the one so noble, so fair.

Love and Life Am I
Bryan Keith McGlasson

Love is within Me And me
within Love

I flow within the streams of
Meadows

I Am the wind that whispers
through the Air

I Am the precious seed

that germinates into a beautiful
sycamore

I endure the seasons and
generations

I rise within the peaks of
snowcapped mountains

I live within the clouds in the
sky

I Am the light from the stars
in Heaven

I Live within you and you
within Me

I Am The Love,
Light and Life of the
world

I Am Jehovah the
Almighty God

Warm Rain And Sunshine
Anita Spreacker

There are tragedies in life I'll never understand,
Why you left when you did I can't comprehend.

Your demise was so sudden — you didn't say goodbye,
I pray you are happy, yet I still wonder why.

We shared good times and bad times over the years,
All that's left are the memories and heart rending tears.

Mom, I know you can hear what I have to say,
The love that I feel remains to this day.

I can see you in your kitchen with a apron 'round your waist,
Cooking Sunday dinner, just season to taste.

Warm rain and sunshine remind me of you,
I can feel you beside me, do you feel it too?

The purple flowers in your garden were always your favorite,
With loving hands they were planted, and blooming there yet.

The German stubbornness I inherited from dad and from you,
I thank God every day that I told you I loved you.

I can't say goodbye, because to me you're still here,
Warm rain and sunshine and I know you are near.

God keep and protect you from sorrow and pain,
For I know in my heart that I will see you again.

Quilting Life
Margaret A. Westall

I remember walking down the rock–encrusted road to the house below with my
Mother...
Holding her hand and kicking rocks as we went, the sun was bright and I
was happy to be
on an outing. Stepping upon the weathered grey wooden porch we knocked at
the door
and were welcomed inside. Within flowers adorned wallpapered walls. The
bare wooden
floors echoed as we stepped. The smell of wood smoke scented the rooms as
sunshine
invaded the cracks between the homemade window curtains and brightened the
cozy cool
darkness within...Freshly baked cookies were offered the smaller members
of this
exclusive group. As did the others, I quickly filled both hands, each with
a big cookie.
Forward I marched, to and fro beneath the magic canopy that was lowered
from its
resting place at the ceiling. Alone there beneath the quilt I watched as
chairs were placed
and shoes black and brown filled with legs that stood erect beneath my
kaleidoscope sky
surrounded me. The hum of female voices blended as needles, thimbles and
thread
appeared from bags and pockets. Multi–colored squares fell to their
predetermined spot as
identical methodical stitches appeared struck and left with hushed
obedience, one after
another, time upon time in rhythmic cadence to some syncopated rhythm that
grew and
ebbed. Warmed by cookies, by the canopy, by the quilting and by hum of
life, I rested
and slept and dreamt of magical places with humming trees, with sweet
oatmeal cookie
bumblebees floating above beds of tri–colored dandelions.

Today, Tomorrow and Yesterday
Anna G. Marzano–Sajna

Each day that we live we seem to ponder on each day
that has past.

Wondering whether we should have changed a few things or
simply try to forget fast.

But, forgetting may be difficult when your heart is
filled with sorrow.

Just knowing you can't go back to change "Yesterday",
but have to face "Tomorrow".

We need not waste so much time living in
"Yesterday's" steps.

For with the power of God we can learn to
"Forgive and Forget".

So, onward we go and backward
no more.

Our God is leading the way and our
sights are set before.

So let us focus on God and do what is right for
"Today".

For then there will be no regrets for your
"Tomorrows, Yesterday".

Bubba, Ten Years Without You!!
Sandy A. Snell

When I stop and close my eyes Bubba, do you know what I see? A
   happy–go–lucky guy who loved to
pick and tease.
We miss that crooked smile of yours and that sparkle in your eyes.
   Yes we miss you very badly, it's like
a part of us has died.
Your unborn child never got the chance to know his father's love,
   but he sure knows he has one terrific
dad above.
Yes, you have a son Bubba, he has your looks as you can see. He is
   Granny and Paw Paw's pride and
joy. The apple never falls far from the tree.
Your baby brother at the time who was not quite yet two, he thought
   the sun rose and set in you. When
he heard your maroon truck coming up the road to the window he flew.
Your Mom and Dad, what pain and hurt, the tears they wept for you. I
   could only hang my head, for
my heart was breaking too.
The guy who cruelly took your life, just ten short years ago. I wish he
   only knew the pain and hurt he
put your friends and family through.
What's so sad about it all? You know your car he stole, he has no use
   for it now, for he still sits on death row.
So much has changed since you left, divorces, marriages, births, and
   deaths. But we still take life day
by day. Bubba, please ask God to hear us pray!
Watch over the ones who have joined you there. Like Granny Allen, with her
   silver hair. Tell her we
love and miss her too and we're sure glad she's in heaven with you.
So many times we have asked God Why? Why did this happen to such a great
   guy? The answer to that
we may never know. We still love and miss you so.
As I wipe the tears from my eyes, I would like to say again, we love and
   miss you Bubba!! Our dear
Brother, Father, Son, Grandson, and Friend.

Untitled
Vickie Townsend

I set my concerns aside for awhile
to marvel at your sweet delight
my heart can do nothing but be lifted up
when you eyes fascinated alight!

I wonder beholding the joy on your face
first time partaker the samplings of life
its pleasantries and curiosities

A moment I sit on the sidewalk
beside you we stare at a snail plodding on
your unintelligibly query of me
I answer "he's is trying to outrun the fast–rising sun"

Moment overshadowed overtaken right there
by a vast roar growing and growing more
I am afraid that you will be so I pick you up before
Behemoth garbage truck filling our view
I look at it with your open eyes unjaded unshaded eyes
It appears as, again, something new

We stand there we watch it my baby and I
this truck–thing until it is through

Time to return to all I have to do I must let you down
But first I gaze at you amazed, and I weep without sound
At the love I have for you, so precious and profound

Dedication: My five beautiful little girls

Reflections: A Tribute To An American Farm
Patricia D. Senter

My reflections of rowing up on a farm in the Midwest include:
The sight of the morning dew sparkling on the grass as the sun rises
Looking upward at puffy, white cumulus clouds in a sea of blue sky while
   laying in the grass
on a hot, summer day
Seeing bright–colored yellow, orange, and brown autumn leaves as they sway
   in the breeze
while walking in the woods
The glistening of small, crystal clear ice particles on the bare trees and
   the telephone wires
on a bright, cold winter day
The smell of the wild flowers and the leaves of the trees after a spring
   rain
Smelling freshly mown hay located in vast fields of green
The scents of chicken being barbecued in the backyard on a Sunday
   afternoon
Sounds of a babbling brook with birds singing and the chattering of
   squirrels serenading
in the background
The sound of the fish jumping in a clear blue lake on a hot, still summer
   evening.
Hearing a frightened baby kitten purring in your lap for the first time
The sound of deer bristling in the bushes at dusk as they come out of the
   shadows to feed
Tasting the first fresh watermelon of the summer that you've picked — out
   of a neighbor's yard
The taste of homemade ice cream and fresh cherry pie at the annual 4th of
   July picnic after the parade
The taste of freshly caught fish on an open campfire while sitting beside
   the creek with friends
Eating marshmallows that you've cooked over a crackling fire — even
   though they're a little
over done
There are my reflections that shall always be treasured and never
   forgotten.

Untitled

Di Maries E. Serrano–Gonzalez

when God comes, does he really come?
or is he just a figment of the imagination.
do people really believe entirely in the
Almighty, the only son of God. do people
really follow all of the teachings or do they
believe in what is convenient for them at that
particular moment.
now for the five percent of the complete
population of the Earth, who know who the
true and living God is, my? for you is: are
men really gods and women the Earth, or
is that speculation from someone who
again, thinks that he knows.
in this gloom world that humans call theirs is
everyone consumed by the intelligence of just
one man's saying, or are they really researching
the actual facts of their beliefs, of "their" so called
intelligence.
don't perceive me to be the person that knows all
the answers or that I am saying that your beliefs are
wrong, because fornication alone makes me a sinner,
possibly even a believer of circumstance, but are you
as aware of your sins as I am.
or are you hiding behind your beliefs of circumstance, so
that you won't have to be responsible for your actions and
look at yourself in the mirror of YOUR CREATOR and
deal with the possibility of being persecuted for YOUR TRUE SELF.

is HE real

It

Nancy S. Gregory

Oh feeble moth, your drab, grey being goes unnoticed and unseen by the
keen eye of the expert connoisseur of beauty in his quest for the sight of
the most exquisite butterfly.

But unlovely as you seem, you may delight the eye that has never known
the sight of a lovely butterfly, or gladden the heart that is blind to
the marks carved by man on a yardstick to measure beauty, love and
     perfection.

Your divined assets did not include the ominous whine of the mosquito to
make your presence known/nor the sting of the wasp to command respect
for your allotted space in the infinite scheme of creation.

You do not possess the exotic beauty of the butterfly that satisfies the
thirst of sight, nor do you make honey like the bee to appease the crave
of sweets, and when gratified ceases to cry out and peacefully goes to
sleep.

But, feeble moth, what have you done? In your quiet and almost unnoticed
retreat from the glare, the glamour and the clamour of life, you have
caused a quake that rocks the emotions of the world — you have peaked the
curiosity of man and sent him on a long journey through life in search
of the evasive truth.

Your drab life and humble silence caused the world to rise and cry —
it evoked the eternal questions of mortal man, the question of How and
Why.

Your only physical acts of life to be seen by those concerned were your
many flights into the flame and without the faith that made you fly,
you would surely have burned — you see to seek the facts of life as you,
flutter toward the glare — this act is similar to that of man as he
asks for light in prayer.

Dedication: My late husband, Ernest Gregroy

To Hurt And Heal

Gregory R. Schoenbaum

The familiar touch of a passionate lover is now just a
Memory to me,

The joy that once made my heart leap and sing is now
simply quiet misery.

The hurt and frustration now that ensue make nothing
Important it seems,

For what once was so real, the sense and the feel, can
Now only be found in my dreams.

To want so much to talk and to touch, with the one who
felt right at my side,

Only conflicts with what my mind predicts, that again my
Poor heart has lied.

Tired of trying to win someone's love, by the rules of this
Ancient game,

Discouraged to think after playing so long, the results
Will be always the same.

Yet despite tries in vain, and despite all the pain, my heart
is beginning to mend.

And it won't be too long 'til my mind was all wrong, and
I'll be playing that old game again.

My Dear Sister

Kingsleigh James Hammond

Is this a dream or reality
Your life so close to fatality

I held your hand thinking you not to die
You just smiled, I see a sparkle in your eye

I could not help but shed my tears
All these thoughts and so many fears

I can't believe how you were so strong and so brave
My dear sister I prayed God was to save

Seeing you in such pain and distress
My feelings inside I cannot express

You were in agony, there was nothing I could do
I just thought of how much I LOVE YOU

I know now it's going to be alright
As you are strong and you can fight

I watched your baby sleeping so quiet and peaceful
My heart beating fast as she is so beautiful

So small and wonderful a baby you made
These special memories will never fade

A baby girl which you have named Chanice
She is someone special, she is my niece

My prayers were answered, you're here today
There's just one thing I wish to say
I LOVE YOU BOTH.

Dedication: To my dear sister, Sarita

Holes
Henrietta Correll

What a hole it has made,
Your passing!

A hole in the space you
Occupied on earth,
Pretty Big!

A hole in our hearts,
Even Bigger!

A hole in my mind!
Now all my thoughts slide
Right through!

What are we to do?

Whoever tries to step in
That space will fall right
Through.

If I move the blood
will flow out.

The time of my thoughts
In my mind is too brief.

I have become immobilized by grief.

Dedication: In memory of Archie Dewey

For Whatever A Love
Eugenia Murry

To the love of my life who I've promised each day to honor and cherish your
    being always,
You are the wind in my song that lullabies my troubled days, the right in
    my wrong when my world seems so crazed.
Each day that passes it's still hard to perceive, that a love like yours
    could ever nest upon me.
Do you remember the moment when I first laid eyes upon your face? It was
    the day when all my loneliness would soon be erased.
From that day forward you have penetrated my world with intense emotions
    and a desire to love you more.
My life is now perfect and in a wonderful place to be, forever we shall
    linger in the light of pure ecstasy.
Never should you wonder, you may forever rest your worries aside, for the
    love I carry for you—no one else could ever provide.
For whatever you want or whatever you may need, I want you to rely on the
    trusted faith I have within me.
With all my heart I give you all that I can be and pray that you will
    forever a lifetime—be in love with me...

...To the love of my life who vanished without a trace, I cannot question
    the reasons why you up and walked away.
Our life had been a perfect place and together we would always be, but our
    fairy tales of love ended all so suddenly.
Yesterday was a blessed day because I was wrapped within your warmth and
    sheltered in your love, all I felt was comfort.
Today my heart was broken and I began to cry. My life which seemed
    immaculate to me, laid down its fight to die.
I wanted to give up my troubles and bleed them all away, and deep within my
    soul I felt I'd never see better days.
Tomorrow the pain will still linger, holding on to dear life, without my
    ever questioning: "How did this happen and why?"
So to the love of my life who I promised always, to honor and cherish your
    being always.
'There's no right in my wrong for you to fulfill, only a broken heart to
    mend—time shall one day slowly heal.'

Philharmonic
Charles Douglas Ricks

The maestro's head is bowed. He prays that we do him proud. All of our
instruments are held still. They wait to serve the master's will. In the
    air hangs a chill.
No mistakes are allowed.

We are all rehearsed and carefully tuned. It's our first concert. Nothing
    has been
assumed. At once our beloved maestro lifts his head and wand. His face is
    aglow and
fond. Our minuet begins softly and then is mushroomed.

Each musician has his own part to play. Our instruments each have special
    things
to say. The instrument and its player are one and the same. They make a
    unit in the heart
of the orchestral frame.

The maestro's music can sing to a troubled heart. The sonata will give a
    mind its
new start, his music carries our souls to the heavenly day. Our worries
    are seen as
meaningless and gone along the way.

This symphony is the maestro's master piece. It's written for our lives
    to give us
the new lease. Let the soft melody come inside. Let it open our ears and
    minds wide. Let
the master's symphony make the love to increase.

The maestro's head is bowed. He prays that we do him proud.

There Is No Beginning Without An End
Derrick Horner

Videocassettes of home movies
Show happier times of you and me
Here's a scene on our wedding day
With our faces smeared with the cake's icing

There we are moving in our first place
When you were pregnant with our son
We were just beginning a life together
Not knowing an end would come

There is no beginning without an end
You were my sunshine but sunset had to eventually set in
Each chapter that starts in one's life has a conclusion
There is no beginning without an end

Next you're seen on our last Christmas eve
Flirting under the mistletoe
As I watch I remember the nights we spent
By the fireplace while the fire glowed

Here is a close up of you
And I touch the screen as if it were your skin
I wish time could be like these tapes
That can rewind back and begin again

There is no beginning without an end
You were my sunshine but sunset had to eventually set in
Each chapter that starts in one's life has a conclusion
There is no beginning without an end

The clock on the VCR catches my eyes
As the last home movie ends
It's time for me to go and get to your funeral
Before it begins

I Am Only A Shadow
Catherine Thomson

I am only a shadow, whose existence depends upon light.
I cannot be defined when darkness blankets the night.

Moving like a mirror, I mimic a child at play;
In careless abandon I follow, but only in daylight I stay.

The child is beckoned indoors, when the day is at its end;
Just one more game of hide–and–seek before I vanish from my friend.

Tomorrow finds me, when daylight again is new:
I am the shadow of the flowers drinking drops of morning dew.

My petals are not as vibrant as the rose that I portray,
But its beauty is cast upon me, and I will stay the day.

Another dawning at hand, another night has ceased,
How refreshing to find my way wherever sunlight is released.

When it placed me by the side the heart of a lonely man,
He offered me my confidence, I found trust without demand.

When he reaches for my hand, I am reaching for his—
And for these gracious moments, I share the life he lives.

When daylight fades to black, and the weather decides to cloud,
This shadow will remember the love the sun allowed.

I am only a shadow, whose existence depends upon light.
Wishing the sun would somehow still shine, when the day becomes the
    night.

Hey Boy...Hey Girl
Rose A. Bennett

Let me introduce...myself to you
Most people call me "crack"...but I'm "Jum" to you
If I don't get you that first time...second or third
I'll certainly get you that fourth time...mark my word

Hey boy, come on...and feel my blast
Hey girl, watch out...I may be your last
Some say I only last...a minute or two
And you know what...that's probably true

I'll make you feel good...'cause I'm so bad
I'll make you give up everything...you ever had
Your whole pay check...will come to me
And I'll give you a blast...for a day or three

When that blasts all over...and gone you see
You'll bring your watch...and stereo to me
Next you'll bring your TV...and then your VCR
And soon enough...I'll have your car

Hey boy, hey girl...why don't you wake up
For I'm not even worth...your every buck
I tried to make you feel...like I'm your friend
But look what I do to you...in the end

I'll strip you of everything...including your pride
I'll make you feel...as if you just died
Let me tell you something...that's very, very true
You don't do me...I do you

If you still doubt...which way to go
When you see me...just say no
Hey boy, hey girl...don't come my way
'Cause I'm not a toy...and I don't play

Beyond The Veil
Tracy Armstrong

Cocooned by the night, this angel dreams
of boundless worlds, on fearless wings

With graceful flutter, they carry her through
fairy dust storms, and skies of blue

To a land called Freedom, where her heart is whole
and the miracles of life, nurture her soul

Poppies and pansies, bursting with color, sway in a fragrant meadow
of lilac and lavender, she dances with bees, beneath a hummingbird's
    shadow

Amber and gold, streak the sky, the sun waves as the day closes
her heart is full, as she lay to rest, on a bed of purple roses

Morning is cruel, and brings the veil, that separates her from life
it dampens the fragrance
dulls the colors
and filters out the light

Anchored by anger, afraid to fly, she grounds herself in the mud
and dreams of the magic, beyond the veil, to flower this perpetual bud

The fabric was woven, by the angel herself, its threads are fear and pride
now she waits, for her wings in the night, to glimpse the other side

A leap of faith, is all that is needed, to bathe in a warm summer's rain
step out from behind the veil that shields you, feel the laughter, the
    love, and the pain

My Mother's Hands
Norm Klingler

Her hands are creased with many sorrows.

They have traveled through a divorce, trying to get her life
back in order.

At the same time they were telling her two very young boys not
to worry, everything will be okay.

Her hands have wiped away many tears that have fallen from her
eyes.

Her hands were there for my younger brother and I throughout
the divorce.

They were there to comfort us when the world seemed hateful.

Her hands kept us together as a family when times were tough
and confusing.

Throughout all of this, her hands still took on many other tasks.

The worked all day and then came home to do the household chores
that awaited her.

They cooked, cleaned, and washed my dirty laundry.

They sewed my torn clothes.

Even though they did all this, they still found time to make
me cookies.

Even though a lot of time has passed since then, her hands are
still the same comforting hands that have always been there
and done things for me.

The Real World
Kendra St. Peter

Liars often dream, dreamers often lie.
The world is a horrible place and I long to die.

Death's pale flag is a fool's paradise,
We are all so quiet just like mice.

I live to look and look to like,
Love is nothing but a sharp, terrible spike.

We are all destined for great things,
Sometimes all that we need is a pair of wings.

The world has many views,
But sometimes it makes us choose.

We all have to do more, we all have to be more,
If we want to win this lifetime war.

Only in our dreams can we truly be free,
Even if we're way at the top of the tree.

This world we're living in is a field of dreams,
Sometimes I just want to scream.

Even if it kills you we still have to try,
But the question is why.

Liars often dream, dreamers often lie,

If you love thee, what must be shall be.

Homeless Woman
Lela M. Puckett

She walked along the beach picking up seashells
And placed them tenderly in her little basket

Then she went to the mission for a meal and a bath
And a prayer for the salvation of her soul.

She seemed happy contented with her lot never wondering
Why those who weeped for her soul had no mercy for her in
this world.

I am like one of the greats she said— those who were spiritual
and enlightened. They had no home on this earth.

What an honor to be unencumbered for I may go anywhere
And be anyone and I like who I am. I have harmed no one.

I have the blue of the ocean, the sun kissing my face to wake
Me from my bed upon the sand. I am rich among women.

Most of all I know that it is not big homes or expensive cars
or even prominent positions that bring success.

It is how much love you give while you are here. I will gladly
share what I have gladly and what I have to give is much
much more than what this world calls success.

Homeless, well perhaps. How many have a home they do not
appreciate? How many have fine cars they take for granted?
How many have positions they use to hurt others.

I sleep very well on the wet sand. I build sand castles, paint
pictures and write my poetry to touch the heart even of those
who have hurt me for I would use what I do have or help them
in their time of need.

Blind Promises
Chad Johnson

Tragedy strikes as an arrow flies
Magical love stares me in the eyes

I cannot hold her, she's too far away
This pain does haunt me, day by day

Love so few and far between
I hold my love for one not seen

She's in my future and there she stands
And I am holding her with by future hand

Her name for now is hidden from me
I wait patiently...patiently to see

By the dark of night and the light of day
I wait for her as I make my way

I can't describe her though she's a beautiful sight
I hold her close and with all my might

She'll never forget my love is strong
And never will I do her wrong

Always faithful and forever there
I'm with her always though I know not where

These vows for her I do take
these blind promises I do make

Dedication: Dany – Love of a lifetime

Find Your Child
Katrina Paananen

The spirit of a child is free and whole; Unaware of the inevitable.
The world tries to destroy the beauty of individuality with its
claws of hatred—
Tearing, ripping, and pulling away viciously at the soul of the
child.
Shaping it to become its own desire; The image of itself.
The child's soul cries out in pain and confusion settles into the
hurting heart.
And it spreads to a point where the child no longer knows her
identity—
She doesn't even recognize her own heart anymore. No longer
a child.
She struggles against everything they've taught her to find her
dying soul.
And they don't understand the child's frustration because they
have forgotten.
Or perhaps they lost the battle between trying to be your own
person
While others try to make you become the person they were
made to become.
But she must remain strong if she's to grow into herself.
Take hold of the world's claws and release their grip from your
soul.
Remove the lies that were placed on your heart. Find your child.
Let your spirit free to be carried with the wind
And fly among the angels high above the earth, as it was meant
to be.
Do not live your life with a withering soul but add to the spirit of
others.
Find your child.
For the spirit can live without the body—but the body cannot live
without the spirit.
Find your child.

My Mother
Bernadette Melrath

My mother was very giving,
when she was living.

I was the youngest of three.
I thought she would always be.

Elvis Presley movies, we used to share.
It's really not fair.

Why did God take her from me?
This blinds me and I cannot see.

Does she hear me, when I call her name.
Things will never be the same.

Louie Armstrong was the singer she liked.
I remember the first time, I rode my bike.

My mother lost her father at five or nine.
There was never any sign.

She would always ease my pain.
A lot of times she took the blame.

My friend! My Mother!
To this day there is no other.

She will always be in my heart.
I feel with that, we will never be apart.

Dedication: My mother, my inspiration

The Essential One
Matthew R. Jubak

The burning sun descends, like she always must, when the sky screams to
    dream;
leaving the moonlight shine as the only road to a love so true. An aching
    sea lusts for
the next gentle touch, from her smooth, delicate tongue; to soar over his
    bare blue
water, with that unforgettable west wind. A madman with a sad cry was
    heard, as his
spirit began to lose its sound; feeling heartache and pain, as he falls
    deeper into the
ground. And it is with yet one last glimpse, as their eyes meet across
    this land so free;
that you feel his pain and can truly see why their love will never be.
    Jealously
watching, as the dawn boosts this vision into the wide open skies; always
    wishing that
he was the one, as tears fell from his eyes. Her extravagant color
    increased, with a
beautiful array of heat and passion; higher and higher she arose, in her
    usual,
seductive fashion. Time and time again, he would attempt to make it known
    she is the
one; but never could she hear him, for she is the sun. As quickly as day
    turns to night,
he would arise to watch her sleep; and with the help of the stars, he'd
    pronounce his
love so deep. Sometimes around midnight, when destiny provides him buoyant
    and whole; he will testify his love with romance,
in a full moon's ode...
It's easy to see why the entire world awaits for the sun; for I am in
    love, with the essential one.

Dedication: The true essential one

The Harp
Tadeusz T. Kosnikowski

Magical fingers tickle the chords,
Delicate tunes caress our ears —
Sometimes are heard menacing words,
When Chopin's Etude vents anger and fears.

O, harp, thou are, as this world old!
The artist feelings, thou renders best —
The warmth of dreams and the war's cold,
when sounds of despair your chords express.

Murmur of streamlet, running amid fields,
hard rhythm of sea waves, striking the shores —
All subtle sounds, harp clearly yields,
distributes them, in air, outdoors.

Artist masterly governs her harp,
Listeners forget all other things,
Divine melody, once sweet, once sharp,
well known to many, to all of us is akin.

Oh artist, touch sensitive chords,
Shower on us the charming way
and add a sunshine to yearning souls,
change into a dream, a common, drab day.

For that caress of our ears
through a music charm bestowed upon us,
let me pay homage to you an Artist, so dear,
in simple words uttered over here.

Dedication: Mrs. Liliana Osses Adams

Untitled
Kim De Simone

I hold the image of your face so closely to my heart
I know being without you would tear it apart

How could I ever manage being all alone
Locked up inside a heart filled of stone

To me you are the world, the colors that I see
You have given me memories to cherish, you have shown me what
Life is to be

You mean to me a world of love never sorrow
And living for today never yesterday or tomorrow

The happiness we share is one of a kind
If looked for again we will never find

Now I realize what I am trying to say
I could never be without you and I need you to stay

These are not childish gestures I know how I feel
Everything inside me tells me this love is for real

You cannot ever say goodbye
Because then part of both of us will die

There is a strong bond between me and you
No one can break it, it is too strong to

Only we have the power to break it apart
Causing much damage to our heart

Babe we have got it all
Let's just keep it going, let's not let it fall

Remember When...
Carol Colburn

It doesn't seem so long ago, when we were rocking to and fro.

Wondering how your life would be, and hoping good things for you and me.

As you grew older I could see, the times ahead would be hard to foresee.

Despite some hard times which life had brought, we searched our problems to be sought. Not always such an easy road, but together we could carry the load. With you by my side I knew we would complete life's ride.

You weren't the perfect child you know? And sometime you would let it show! Though not the perfect one you see, the perfect one you were to me.

I am so proud to call you mine, for now and always and all the time. You've grown to be a son well taught, a son I am glad that God had brought.

I hope your future will be complete, for you have earned a life so sweet.

If you still need me by your side, I am always waiting to abide.

I'll love you forever as you will see, please know how much you mean to me.

Dedication: To Douglas, whom I love

Vision Of A Friend
Sandra Hernandez

I found myself
in a state of
depression and sorrow
Walking the corridors of
loneliness and remorse

Ahead of me
the shadow of a man

I feared
impulsively I looked on!

His forehead scarred
long wild hair
He quickened towards me
His hands extended

In a fast/slow motion way
He embraced me

Without speaking
He questioned
Is it a friend you need
Will I do

In the midst of this vision
I heard myself say:
Lord a friend

With a gesture
Our spirits were sealed

Dedication: To God, be the glory

Untitled
Darrelyn Phillips

The last days of childhood are soon drawing nigh.
My early remembrances now pass me by.

The hands on a clock are no longer my friend,
the days of my play time have come to an end.

I'm all grown up now, time to be on my own—
to face the cruel world but fears have not flown.

I'm still a scared child knowing now where to turn,
which bridges to cross or which bridges to burn.

Many heartaches and sorrows will soon by mine
like a strenuous chain, myself will they bind.

Some mistakes lie ahead, with trouble in store.
The barren roads I must take lead to new shores.

With sweat on my brow and some shadows of doubt
Burdened and weighted, can I find my way out?

A strength I must gain with my fears laid aside
to come out the victor what ere be the tide.

A fresh place lies waiting for my mark in life,
to take a firm stand and overcome all strife.

Now a worn book on a shelf, my childhood rests,
I open another, to conquer life's quests.

Dedication: To mother, my continuous love

Love's Life Travels
Gage M. Gardner

My heart once full of jubilant joy has now tasted the pangs of love's
    winter garden.

Bitter reminders of lovelife's relationships held in place, written in
    time and space.

My arteries stiffen now as I remember the past.

Temperature so slow, love's fire and the eternal flame of hope
sit as captured prisoners waiting to be stoked.

Once I remember love running free, but now it's only life's rigor mortis
    setting
deep inside of me.

It's almost complete now, run its course as some would say.

My heart has turned to stone.

I now stand statuesque as life's attestment to love's winter garden.

As the frigid wind blows through this garden I can only feel cold.

Inside there is that ember covered with ash, patiently waiting to glow.

In impassioned hopes that there is a Spring, in order for this heart to
    blossom...

Love is an experience, one of the unknown.

An experience we all should foster, protect, and cherish in order to grow.

Love's life travels...something we all know...

Creativity: A Multitalented Person
Monica Regina Alston

From my mind I can transform many things,
Into bright and vivid features with the talent that it brings.
With a pencil on paper, I restore animation,
And drawings breathe, true to manifestation.

I sometimes sit and wonder in amazement of the anatomy of
various organisms.
This time is executed some what wasted, yet well spent.

I love to listen to music, because it has a certain type ring,
That leads me to thinking: I could do the same thing.

With this precise notion, I conjure a beat,
With base that enlightens, and renders it complete.

To fit the pattern, I then produce a verse
To which I give a style that reimburse.

I am most for playing a role which involves real—life situations
Yes, acting and having a dramatic variety of relations.

I am good at drawing, and excellent when singing,
Great at acting: Me, a creative human being.

I design my own drawings and write my own songs and create my own
music.
I can also act in exhibition a character's role very elucid.

With all of these type talents, creativity is the version
Of my being one of millions, A Multitalented Person.

Dedication: To all those talented

Love
Nancy Bursik

Is waking up to someone who greets you
With a smile and a kiss

Is knowing that each day you spend together
Will be a special memory

Is wanting to make each other laugh
No matter how rough it is

Is that peaceful feeling you get
When you're in each others arms

Is not taking for granted
All that you do for each other

Is tough and only those who
Respect the hardships last through it

Is willing to spend the rest of your life
With the one who means the most

Is always keeping in mind
The feelings of the one who means the most

Is telling all your secret desires
To the only one who can make them come true

Is the most
Wonderful feeling in the world

Dedication: My ever—loving husband, Matthew

Tides
T. H. Wilcox

I went to the ocean last night
Motionless, I sat alone
As the tide was coming in
I listened to its endless drone
The water was slowly
Covering the rocky beach
Ever so carefully,
It was coming within my reach
It made me think of you
Or, rather, you and me
Of how things were, are,
And how they are to be
Do you remember the height
We once soared
It seemed our bond
Was an unbreakable cord
But now I look through that window
And I see shattered glass
A testimony of stones
You've thrown in the past
I keep replacing that window
Because I want to see
Walking down the path
Of life you and me
Just like the tide
You come and you go
My time here alone
Has helped me to know
The water is quickly
Uncovering the rocky beach
And I can see you
Falling from my reach

I'll Never Stop Loving You
Lisa Edwards

When the answers are never
found.
When the truth is hard to
find,
When there are tears without
a sound, you'll never leave
my mind.

When the daylight never comes,
and my heart is full of
Sorrow, I'll realize that you
are gone, and there will
be no tomorrow.

When the world seems un—
bearable, and the hurt gets
too much, I'll miss your
tender kisses, and the way
we used to touch.

When my eyes have no
more tears, and my heart
is empty inside, I'll know
the end is here, and I'll
have no where to hide.

The end is here at last,
and all my dreams untrue, but
as long as my heart beats, I'll
never stop loving you.

Dedication: Kenneth Edwards, my soulmate for 17 years

Is Anyone Listening?
Sharron Spain

Why should we have to prove
in everyday life
Why should we have to prove
the constant 24hr strife.

Why should we have to prove
whilst trying to be realistic
Why should we have to prove
the confines of being Autistic.

Why should we have to prove
to the powers that hold the reins
Why should we have to prove
that these children have functioning brains.

Why should we have to prove
to establishment, so unfeeling
Why should we have to prove
that their responses send us reeling.

Why should we have to prove
that our family is close to breaking
Why should we have to prove
that, my friend, we are not faking.

Why should we have to prove
that our children's need is real
Why should we have to prove
that you have to live the life to really feel...

the needs, the wants, the frustration, the hell
this, my friend, is facing Autism, not hiding in your shell.

GOA
Ann–Marie Meagan

Peaceful sights, peaceful sounds, await the tourist upon the grounds that
    border
beaches flickered with sunlight where palm trees stretch lazily over the
    shore and the rush of the waves whisper once more.

The people smile constantly, no surprise, when life in Goa is full of new
    wonders
on each path you take. What's that? a Kingfisher, dazzling blue, sleeps in
    the shade of the morning dew.

Where will his day take him? Over the river to bask again in a Crocodile's
    lair
or meet with the Eagles so strong in the air gliding the breeze against
    pure blue
sheets of sky protecting his mate where she and babes lie.

The fishermen arrive on the shore trailing nets of King Prawns and fish for
    my
supper. Look, there he is served up with incredible flavour that fresh,
    sweet,
delicious Snapper. Stunning aromas from the kitchen at night enhanced by
excitement from the fireworks light.

The service smiles are contagious and you will soon find that you smile
    along with
them, so genuine, so kind. A race of people so eager to please, so
    friendly, so caring your stresses they ease.

My mind and my soul so peaceful Goa made and a part of my heart in Goa,
    it stayed.

Dedication: All held in my heart

Grandpa Did You Ever Say "I Love You?"
Matthew Anderson

I know I never heard it, I always wondered why
but every time I left the house you always said goodbye

Never "I love you" did I hear you say not to Mom, Mamaw or Me
Never did I expect it, I got used to it you see

We often said it to you, every day I think
Sometimes I waited for a reply, but I settled for a wink

You never said a lot, you were quiet as mute birds
But when you did speak up, I never heard those three words

Why did you never say it, did you have it on your mind?
Were you mad at me or nervous, or did you just pass on that time?

Now that you are gone, I cannot expect to know
Why you never said those words that I always cherished so

As these three days have passed the answer has come to me
You had given me the answer I was too blind to see

Your love was not in words it was in your special ways
You never had to say it you showed it all the days

As I grow old and grow into a man I'll never wonder why
My grandpa never said "I love you" I saw it in his eye

So if you ever wonder if and really stop to think
Did he reply, "I love you?" No, he probably gave a wink

Dedication: My papaw Ed

The Dark Screams
Ronnisha Davis

I hear the children's screams.
I see them only in my dreams
I reach out to them, they're not
there. The little boy disappeared
into thin air.

They have problems I can't solve
They cry for me but the pain
doesn't dissolve.
I can't believe they've been
through so much.
All the words, the beating, and such.

Why do they have to suffer so?
They try to run, but there is
no open door. I wish they could
get out, but they can't escape
without a doubt.

If I could help them, I really would,
I would comfort them and let
them know it would be all good.

All they would need is shelter
from the rain.
To take away the despair.
To ease their pain.

The dark screams are haunting
When there is nothing you can do.
You never realize how serious
it is until it happens to you.

On Your Own
Kathy Ortiz

As you head out to start life on your own
Know that even by yourself, you're never alone

Although you're far away, in our hearts you're very near
With God and us close by, there's no need to fear

So as you prepare to leave the comforts of home
No longer a child but a man making roots of his own

It's your life's story make it unique and rare
Do it with patience Do it with care

And when you take chances as we often do
Be careful and cautious Do it for you

Always remember that life is borrowed time
Make each day your best, Then you will find

That determination can make dreams come true
So give it your all in whatever you choose to do

With your strengths of honesty and your love of living
Hard times will pass and a new day you'll be receiving

So with this we set you free, and out on your own
To do what must be To set your milestone

Always know that you're welcomed home
Even with making life on your own.

Dedication: My children

Love
Jon Portelli

Have you ever loved someone,
And you know that they didn't love you?

Did you ever feel like crying,
But then what good would it do?

Did you ever look into their eyes,
And say a little prayer?

Did you ever look into their heart,
And wish that you were there?

Did you ever see them thinking,
When the lights were way down low?

Did you ever say, "I love you,"
But didn't let them know?

Please don't fall in love my friend,
You'll find it doesn't pay.

You may end up with a broken heart,
It happens every day.

So now you see you're losing them,
You'll find the price is high.

If I could choose between love and death,
I think I'd rather die.

Dedication: My best friend, J.S.C.

My Mother
Nikki Seymour

My mother had an adorable chin and
smooth, soft skin. Her blond hair glittered
like the ocean water in the sun. She had a
toothless smile and her eyes wandered
around the room like an owl in the night,
when she was a baby.

My mother wore a summer dress with bows
and buttons, ribbon and lace. On her lap sat
a play telephone waiting to ring, when she was a baby.

If the picture could talk my mother would say, "Hi Mommy" into the
phone, when she was a baby.

My mother looks shy in the picture, and curious about what is going
on. A big light flashes before her eyes, when she was a baby.

In front of my mother stood a man holding a rubber duck, and a
teddy bear trying to get her to laugh, when she was a baby.

"Look," my mom would say. There are many other children dressed in
dresses and suits. She probably
wondered what they were doing, when she was a baby.

My mother's life was so simple and great. People would give her hugs
and kisses. Relatives would take her places, give her things and spoil
her rotten, when she was a baby.

My mom is so special to me. I think she looks like me in every way:
her glittering eyes, her silky blond hair, her beautiful smile, and her
button nose. She is my mom.

Untitled
Basil Hemstock

My Love Is My Wife The Season Spring
But Oh What Joy A Girl Would Bring

I Have Two Sons So Precious And Bright
Would I Deny Them To Change My Life

To Our Surprise My Wife Was Caught
In The Biggest Battle That We've Ever Fought

Could This Be The Girl And Does It Seem
That my wife would fill my wildest dream

The Battle Fought The Battle Lost
Which Left Us Both To Count The Cost

To Me It Made Me Realize
My Wife Was With Me And Still Alive

I Haven't A Girl But I Thank God Above
I still Have Two Sons And A Wife That I Love

To Continue The Story Of My Life
Today I Am A Grandad By My Son And His Wife

Now They Have Filled My Wildest Dream
They Have Given Me A Girl A Real Beauty Queen

All These Events Happened On The Eve Of Spring
Now I Know What It Feels Like The Joy A Girl Can Bring

Dedication: To Chloe, a beautiful granddaughter

Daddy's Vision
Dessie Tanksley

My father was a farmer man by hand...who took great pride in harvesting
 his land...but above
all...he was a family man...To this Day, I proudly wear his Name...my
 3 siblings – they feel
the same...

Now, listen to why we honor this man! Years ago as this story unfolds...
 Daddy had a Vision
he would never grow old...or live to be age 30...Since he did not take
 this fate for granted...
he worked real hard from dawn to dusk: tilling soil and hauling logs...as
 well as working other
odd jobs to pay the mortgage on our farm...

He taught my ma the pros and cons to prepare her for a tough widow's
 life...She thought
this was foolishness...but Dad knew it was his Destiny...so he ignored
 her pleas and
persevered...to earn stability for his kids...According to him: When he
 lay cold...we
would not have to go from pillar to post...or even live with our
 relatives...for we would have a
home to call our own...

In January of 51...when I was almost 6 months old...and my baby brother
 was not yet born...
Pa's premonition took its toll: while crossing a bridge in the State of
 Georgia...he was killed at
the wheel of an automobile...Ironically, he was 29!...

Believe it or not: Daddy's Vision is not fictitious...

Oh To Sleep
James Atkinson

Fleeting shadows fly by me, a clock
Ticks each and every hour.

Morning comes, we all arise, as do the
Smallest of flower – Oh to sleep.

Unconscious the mind drifts, dreams that
Night is light, the day is dark.

Even children playing, swinging, in a far
Distant park – Oh to sleep.

Doctor assure you, with how many pills
Sleep you cannot get, can he cure all that ills.

Some that cannot sleep, will try their best,
Not to stay awake. –

Prisms of blue all shades, of colours a
Kaleidoscope makes. – Oh to sleep.

Nervous no sleep, that be as may.
Dark in the mind, clouds took the moon away.

Cannot sleep? Twists and turns, that's
Just like me.

The sleepless are going through, A
thousand hours of misery! – Oh to sleep.

Dedication: To Mam, Margret, Kelly, love always

I Am A Mountain
Susan T. Howard

I am a mountain solid at the core. The trees sway in the wind.
 The birds sing as they
nest in my trees. The wildlife surrounds and protects my inner
 core. Only natural
erosion will expose me to the continuous beginning of my life.

But man blew a section of my mountain and tore out all my
 protection to expose a part
of my nakedness that cannot survive alone.

The earthen wind had forgotten the mountain, so the mountain
 had thought.
And when the wind blew her seeds of life, the mountain was at
 loss, for despair lived within the core of herself.

Then the wind changed and sang a sweet song that reminded
 the mountain of a time when she loved life.
The winds blew the earthen soils toward the mountain.

The mountain clung on to the soil and coated her exposed inner
 core. Then the winds blew
seeds, the mountain reached and snatched the seeds in hopes
 of germination and full life would once be restored.

Now the soil is becoming enriched with nutrients and the trees
 are reaching for the sky.
The birds will begin to nest and wildlife will surround and
 protect the mountain again.

Only natural erosion will occur again, to show life is a
 continuous beginning.

An American Dream
Cheryl Ritch

White picket fences on a suburban street
Smiles on the faces of neighbors we meet
Children laughing and playing not fighting at all
Drugs are no longer the cause of their fall

An American Dream, An American Dream
I know I am living, An American Dream

Down on the corner there stands a church steeple
Gathered outside are all of its people
Laughing and joking of the work week gone by
Proudly pulling together, No tears in their eyes

An American Dream, An American Dream
I know I am living, An American Dream

Grandmas and Grandpas in their old rocking chairs
Holding the children of the offspring they bear
There's no old folks homes to take them away
It's all in the family they're welcome to stay

An American Dream, An American Dream
I know I am living, An American Dream

As I walk down the street to the old city park
There's no homeless people no fear in the dark
And as I looked above me on the flag poll I say
The Red, White, and Blue representing us all

An American Dream, An American Dream
I know that I'm living, An American Dream

The Tamarack
Geoffrey Newton
As I awoke at the end of day
I saw two paths stretch far and away.
One lead back past a tamarack,
To the setting sun and a place I could run.

The other extended far to the east;
To a distant horizon I seemed to know least.
Beyond the furthest reaches beyond the farthest sea,
To a faint and distant mountain I could but see.

Sitting down to ponder which way to wander,
There came into view a flock of cockatoos.
Chattering and squawking as they sailed through the sky,
Floating on winds they flew higher than high.

Off to the east I could see they would reach,
To the rising sun and a place full of fun,
Sailing on clouds which bore them swiftly afar,
They seemed to know it was time to go
Leaving behind all that was fine.

I got up in a instant,
Following sounds in the distance,
It was strange to think I was on the brink,
So I turned to the west and said fare—ye—well,
My home is not back past the tamarack.

For I thought to myself as I travel the roe,
Why should I fear which way to go?
When I knew all along that the mountain of Hope,
Always resides in the valley of fear.

Untitled
Nancy E. Brady
When I was an infant
THEY cradled me;

Learning to stand and walk
THEY supported me;

When the family played
THEY hugged me close;

Watching him work
THEY seemed massive;

Learning to drive
THEY patiently guided me;

When I left the nest
THEY reluctantly let me go;

Through uncertainty and growing
THEY held mine tight;

As I struggle with life's challenges
THEY surround my shoulders;

THEY are LOVE

THEY are my Father's Hands;

When they are no longer with me
THEIR memory will be cherished
as the Man has always been.

Untitled
Stacie Salipek
I don't know why I'm feeling fear instead of relief.
I'm afraid your love will stray, leaving me in grief.

I wasn't the only one broken, this I understand,
But why am I sad when you're away, and insecure without the touch of
your hand?

I can't explain why I'm empty, why the hurt is still inside.
Why the broken pieces are not yet together,
Why I can still trace the tears I've cried.

Why can't I raise my head to the sunshine and forget the pouring rain?
Once again hold onto your love and say good—bye to the pain.

I want to welcome the feeling of warmth back to my heart.
Please take away the cold darkness, don't let me fall a part.

Please be my shelter when a storm is on the rise.
Try to keep the rain clouds from shadowing my eyes.

Make the rolling thunder halt, rid its noise from my ears.
I want to hear your voice gently calming my fears.

Don't let the lightening strike me. Keep me safe from harm.
Protect me from the dangers that sound my heart's alarm.

Make me warm inside, I want to feel the sun's rays.
Make life's forecast brilliant, shield me from the blackening haze.

Please tell me that you love me, that you mean it from deep within.
I want love to rekindle and set my soul aflame again.

Dreams Of A Rising Sun
Joshua Shipp
Dear Rising Sun,
As the sun sets, my hopes and dreams are put off for another day. As the
last
flaming bursts of energy goes down across the horizon, my thoughts of you
disappear into the night time sky. Losing the love of a lifetime is like
the setting
sun...it becomes cold and lonely. You are just wishing for that certain
someone to
grasp you, the earth, in their loving embrace to keep you warm.
The rising sun is here and comforting...the ideas are still alive...alive
with the hopes
and dreams that someday soon your focus will soon again be on us. Together
as
two souls that make the days cheerful and the nights full of passion and'
romance.
The love that we share can compare to no other.
We have made history in the eyes of the rising sun. That rising sun is the
new hopes
and dreams of an even brighter future. One that is filled with romance,
dreams, happiness and love. A love that is so true and desirable that no
multiple of
stormy, cloud covered mornings can bring dismay. Loneliness and feelings of
separation are no longer a factor. As the sun rises, new hopes and dreams
find
their way into the hearts of best friends, lovers, soul mates through out
eternity.
Come back sweet girl, for I am cold and need the love of a lifetime.
Love,
the Earth

Dedication: The woman of my dreams, the love of my life

Why I Am Thankful
Latifa Jones

I pray to you each day
I pray to you with all my heart
in every way
I know I've made mistakes before
But you Lord, has given me a second
chance once more.
I pray to you each day
I pray to you will all my heart
in every way.

You have blessed me, and the ones
I love.
You have given them strength,
and many things to dream of.
Why I am thankful,
Is one thing everyone should understand.
For a life without you has no plan.
I pray to you each day
I pray to you will all my heart
in every way.

Why I am thankful, is for all
you've done.
For you have given me all I
need to see the morning sun.
I pray to you each day
I pray to you will all my heart
in every way.
Thank you Lord
Amen!

Treasures From The Sea
Mary B. Conyers

The ocean rises and falls depositing its treasures on the shore. The sun
    is setting with an incredible
display of color painted on the western sky by its artist. Fishermen not
    seeing the treasures, step on
them. Women walking fast in the brisk fall dusk, not noticing them. Four
    wheel drive vehicles make
deep tracks in the sand, crushing them.
Why don't they see these treasures lying at their feet? Is it because they
    cannot be seen by the
naked eye?
A fishing vessel passes just off shore dragging its heavy nets, followed
    by a black cloud of gulls and
sea birds. They, too, don't know about the treasures—these jewels of the
    sea.
To see these precious gems you must look with your heart. At first glance,
    they appear to be only
broken, worthless pieces of shell. But, if you look from your heart you
    see beautiful shells, battered
with time—broken but smooth from perhaps years of wear from the sea. From
    stress, from time, being
tossed about from one direction to another, flowing with the tide. But age
    and time have given them
something the others don't have. Beautiful, smooth lines, no rough edges.
    They have existed through
storms, through calm, through dark and light to be seen by the eye of our
    hearts as a treasure from the
sea—hand–crafted by God in His workshop, the ocean. The wear has only
    added to their beauty.

Dedication: My father, Jack H. Byrum

The Days Of Life
Kristina S. McCreary

Like the night,
I am dark
As an animal,
I hunt
Without fear,
I live
Beneath the stars,
I sleep
On the ground,
I lay
Like the night,
I grow old
As an animal,
I hurt
Without fear,
I wither away
Beneath the stars
I run
On the ground,
I fight
Like the night,
I have seen
As an animal,
I am hunted
Without fear,
I am taken,
Beneath the stars,
I am!

Dedication: Billy Alton McCreary, Jr.

Please Rescue Me
Donna M. Erickson

Holding my plane at the gate,
Lost in traffic, I'm really late.

When I arrive, friendly faces I do not meet,
Then, I'm rudely rushed and shone my seat.

Oh so high in the vast sky,
I smell smoke, I don't know why.

The pilot says, we're going down,
I hear screams all around.

I brace myself and pray I don't feel,
As I talk to God, I make a deal.

The impact of the crash, is awfully great,
Confused and still alive, that's my fate.

Please Rescue Me!

If you don't, I will drown at the bottom of the sea,
Did error of the pilot, do this to me?

Swimming with horror on my mind,
Clobbering of waves, bring chills to my spine.

Thinking of my life, as I saw it all planned,
Everything's a dream, until I'm rescued with a stranger's gentle hand.

Dedication: Joey and Randi, love you!

A Woman
Doris Thomas Ariyibi

Look beyond what I am today, Because it's not
what I want to be anyway.

Potential, I'm sure we've all got some, But most of
us can't tell if we're to go or come.

Why can't I be what I want to be, Someone's always
trying to pull strings on me.

They feel this way and they feel that, And truly
believe that they are where it's at.

I can't feed your desires before quenching my thirst,
Before I'm a woman I'm a human first.

I've got a thirst for knowledge, things I really
need to know, I've got a need to explore the places
I know I can go.

I've loved and lost times too many, Yet I have love
to share if someone special needs any.

I'm not bitter about the things in the past, I
feel in my heart that I'm free at last.

So if you're thinking of holding me back or keeping
me down, Just remember one thing I started
from the ground.

Dedication: My children, Twila and Sterling Evans

The Problem
Ilse–Dore Pulliam

"Don't we have any milk, any cheese, or at least meat?"
complains husband Joe, finding nothing to eat.

"Sorry, 'ran out of time," was Pam's reply.
"You'll have it tomorrow. Trust me, I don't lie."

In managing money, Pam's not the greatest.
She is looking for coupons, the very latest.

Now she can go shopping, a little while later,
to fill and restock the refrigerator.

The phone is ringing, her friend makes a call,
"Plan nothing," she says, "if you did, drop it all!"

"Bring plenty of money, hurry up and let's go!
It's our last chance for the Flea Market Show."

In the evening Pam noticed the mistake she has made,
going Flea Market shopping with her best friend, Kate.

Milk, cheese and meat, she had promised her honey.
She simply can't get it. She is plum out of money.

What should she now do? What can she now say?
The solution appears in the "Womans Day".

Page twenty–nine reads: "Your Poem Could Win"
Her problem seems solved, if she just sends it in.

Lies
Rose Mary Arocho–Fullam

If you begin life with a lie;
You'll end up lonely deep inside.

A simple lie distorts the fact;
Don't reach a point of no turning back.

Pain and sorrow, a lie can cause;
The meaning of truth shall be your loss.

These state of minds forever collide;
Which is stronger? One must decide.

Please judge this carefully, for in time;
You may not like what shall unwind.

Think back to a moment in time;
When honesty wasn't your frame of mind.

A lie is the catalyst of your present pain;
On a foundation of lies, truth can't sustain.

Honesty can fill that empty space;
Bring light forth to that dark place.

Like most things in life, once truth is dead;
It can never voice what needs to be said.

We all must face "JUDGEMENT DAY";
Please, try not to lose your way...,

Escape From Reality
E. Murphy

I welcome the shadows of the night in the
heavens the bright stars shine. In the peace
quiet and tranquility I can escape from
reality

To rest sleep and dream of a happy yesteryear
No tears or sorrow in my dreams, only happiness
and joy. For in my escape from reality I can
fulfill the aspirations I had when just
a boy.

In my dreams I return in time to find
where I went wrong. To remember relations
and friends lost over the passing years,
and remember the words of a nursery rhyme
the lyrics of a long forgotten song.

Sweet aromas of the past and the taste
of good mint toffee. But the special thing
most pleasant to me was the smell of
fresh ground coffee.

So sweet slumber I say farewell to you
and awake to the stresses of the day.
For with you, I've been able to relax and
make my mind afresh, for any obstacles
in my way. For you and only you are my
escape from reality.

Dedication: Susie Q, my friend

Adagio For Fallen Spark
Robert Abbate
The phone rang amidst the pre–dawn chatter of robins.
The gray mocking birds with white–tipped wings
were nesting in the eaves of the house,
announcing the incubation of the seasonal clutch,
anticipating the hatchlings arrival;
while outside, the daffodils bloomed early.
But the morning message brought wintered grief
to stall spring's premature appearance.

Spartacus Carpenter, his name with the resonance
of a Roman gladiator, lost his mount on snow chariot
while crossing Lake Winnipesaukee's frozen circus.

How then can a walk to Emmaus not be without tears?
Were not our hearts tearing and rending at the news?
Did we not yearn for that glorious day beside the family pond,
a relapse in time to a wedding on a cool June day,
Spark wearing the linen suit with collarless shirt,
his brother's best man?

Somehow heaven is likened to just such a feast,
where the breaking of bread and reclining at table
with family and friends supplants the desolation of aftermath.

Spark, alone now, paddles a canoe with imperishable hull
across resplendent waters to the far shore, disappearing
from sight; as we recognized the Lord in his brokenness:

Dedication: To the Carpenter family

Who Am I
Lynda Taylor
The Suffering Of Alzheimer's
I wander and wander, up and down,
A long, long corridor, with doors all brown,
My legs are aching, and my feet are sore,
What am I doing? It's such a bore.

I feel confused, I want to cry,
I want to remember, really I try,
My words are messed up, and all of a jumble,
And when I do talk, it comes out a mumble.

I know my name, I'll never forget,
But I now live with people, that I've never met,
I'm lost and scared, and I try not to moan,
Just show me the door, and I'll find my way home.

I can't find my handbag, where can it be?
My glasses, my book and my door key,
I've moved all the cushions, looked under the chair,
What am I doing? I don't really care.

Two ladies are shouting, I don't know why,
I won't interfere, just walk on by,
I've eaten my dinner, I wanted some more,
So why have I just thrown it, all over the floor.

Back down the corridor, I'm feeling unsteady,
I'll sit in a chair and wait till I'm ready,
I'm in a strange room, someone's put me to bed,
Is this my life now?...Surely I'm dead.

Nana Blue
Nathalie Belkin
I sat beside you and held your hand, so cold and stiff, blue and gnarled.
I started to talk to you, I wanted to tell you everything, I wanted to
        tell you anything,
The words seemed to stick in my throat as the tears filled up and
        swallowed me.
The pain I experienced watching you, the love I felt for you
        overwhelming me.
Unable to give you up, unable to let you go,
I prayed for you to return, open your eyes with recognition,
but this time it wasn't meant to be

They told us the time was close,
you couldn't keep fighting, your body needed rest, but nothing could
        prepare me
seeing all those doctors running towards you,
my pain exploded like a fireball, ripped through me at the speed of light.
I knew I had to say goodbye, yet denial hung in the shadows.

You looked so small and peaceful, the forced breathing stopped and the
        bruises covered,
I sat once again beside you,
I kissed your cheek, now cold, remembering once its warmth.
I told you how much I loved you, how you will always be in my heart, how I
        will try not to be so upset,
but Nana I miss you so much and I can't make it stop
I hope you are in peace now and the pain has ceased
I hope you are looking over me as I look up at you.

Throw Away Child
Ethyl Lyons
–ignored, unnoticed, never visited
basic amenities only

Spring
Amy Dorsey
The flowers start to bloom,
The grass grows greener.
That's when you know,
Spring is here.
Mom and Dad call you in,
from your games.
It's dinner on the grill.
The sun is so bright,
Yet the wind keeps you cool.

The flowers attract the honeybees,
while brother swats at them.
The cool air whispers,
Spring is here.
Baseball season is just beginning,
the President throws the
first pitch.
We all cheer,
because Spring is finally here.

The garden starts sprouting,
yummy vegetables.
Lightly it starts to rain,
the sun starts running away.
Time to come in,
and play inside.
Spring is here,
in rain and sun.
The trees are budding,
for the next season's sun.

Velvet Blue
Wanda Hancock Rohman
Like a ribbon that's floating
In the wind
This love of ours, stirring memories
Of what might have been
As I search for the sky of
Velvet blue
Velvet blue for me and
For you

Crimson flashes of birds on the
Wing
Wishing that I, like the bird
Could spread it's wings
I watch the lightning rip apart
The love we knew
But I'll keep looking for our
Sky of velvet blue
Velvet blue for me and
For you

The wind whispers sweet words from
Days gone by
And silver spikes of rain, fall on a
Lonely night
But still I long for sky of
Velvet blue
Velvet blue for me and
For you

Untitled
Jean Lehr
Goodness reaps freedom
While evil entraps oneself.

Free
Gloria Turner
One morning as I sit in my breakfast nook
Out the window I turned to take a look

A small bluebird was flitting from tree to tree
I thought how wonderful to be so free

Then suddenly it hit the window with a thump
Oh there it laid in a small lump

Out the door I went as fast as could be
For this little bluebird I had to see

I picked it up with loving care
Sure was glad no cat was there

Its heart was pounding one two three
I know it was afraid of me

I sit it on the birdbath to revive
Bet it was glad to be alive

It soon recovered and flew away
I will never forget that day

In my hand a bluebird I did hold
It felt better than a pot of gold

I feel special so you see
To have held something that is so free

Sunset At Milton
Lolita Arreola Mendoza
When the sun goes down,
At five o'clock in the afternoon.
I try to sit by the window, rest and think,
All of a sudden it came to my mind
I know it's time for recollection.

I think of the present and of the past,
My children, grandchildren, and my nipa hut.
The garden I'd love to see
With the flowers blooming around,
All of these made me lonely at last.

Yes, I was daydreaming,
For I thought I was in my own hometown.
But when I pondered around
It's not what I daydreamed about,
It was a sun setting at the horizon.

A second thought came to my mind,
About a love one I once had,
Oh, I miss him a lot at present,
and all the days that have passed.
Then I said to myself alone,
"What a wonderful life to think
when it's sunset at Milton."
Dedication: To my loving children and grandchildren

Spam
Scott J. Hammond
Spam is taste acquired
pink secret on a shingle
My stomach demurs.

I'm Only A Child
Marjorie A. Marks
Don't you hear my cries?
Dry your tears, it's only a nightmare...

Why are you so mad?
What have I done?

Can't tell mom, it would break her heart.
Should have done something, from the start.

This is Daddy, he's supposed to love and care
This is not love...
It's not a nightmare...

This is real, it's happening to me!
Hear my cries, hear my plea!

Can't face anyone, I'm numb...
this is dumb, got to tell someone...

Mom and me, we're all alone, what have I done
It's not a home anymore, what else was there to do

Daddy's gone, was it my fault?
In my heart, it was for the best.
Finally, it's time to rest!

Listen, listen, to me, hear my cries hear my plea

"I'm only a child"...

The Healing Hand
Laura Anderson
None other than the touch of a friend
can heal the mind and body by a touch to mend,
always to be there, always to tend...
everything is perfect with the touch of a friend.

Heart And Hand
Regina Anne Cosenza
Be blessed, be loved, my dearest one,
It seems to be so long a time,
That I have seen your shining eyes,
And held your heart and hand in mine.

Be it seconds, be it years. They seem both quite the same.
When you're away and we're apart, forever is my pain.

My soul it aches, my mind it longs, to be your only star.
Never changing, ever lasting, guiding you both near and far.

I'd be the brightest light for you, travel where you may.
If decades prove you need me not, just blow your star away.

I will leave you quietly, without a single tear.
I will know I've loved you well, through every passing year.

God gave the world I knew before, your spirit polished fine.
He let me learn, He let me grow, however short the time.

You will remain my dearest one.
Always on my mind.
Although I'll not see you again
Or hold your heart and hand in mine.
Dedication: All lovers separated in time

Kathleen
Rex Hodges
More than the twinkling of a thousand fireflies
lighting up a soft summer eve

More than the outstretched fingers of a solitary oak
after the wind has stolen away its leaves

More than the dancing spray flung skyward
in a storm–tossed sea

More than the frenzied wing beats of a hatching chick
as it struggles to be free

More than the wildflowers that paint the hills
by a lonely country lane

More than the pools of silver that dot the meadows
after an early spring rain

More than the stars that return each night
to light up the heavens above

More than the wondrous warmth and care
of a new mother's love

More Kathleen, much, much more are the ways
you make my whole being soar

You are my love, you are my life —
with each passing day I only love you more.

Untitled
Gladys E. Lytle
Today I baked two pumpkin pies, so big and round and creamy.
and who could know two little eyes were anything but dreamy.
Tonight I found my angel cake angelic still but shifted,
Those pumpkin pies I found too late...they'd had their faces lifted.

Dreams
Melanie K. Graves
What do you dream of?
With your eyes shut tight.

What do you dream of?
In the dark, silent night

Do you take flight with your dreams and discover new lands?
Do you become a "baseball man"?

Are you playing in the mud and grass?
Are you running very fast?

Have you made the game–winning play?
Have you pitched a winning save?

Do you see your Mom and Dad?
Cheering you on, from the stands.

Whatever you dream, large or small,
Remember you can be anything at all.

No limits, no boundaries should exist in your dreams,
What is important, is that you believe.

Believe with your heart, believe with your soul,
Believe, Believe, that is your goal!

Almost Perfect
Candee Garo
The "almost" perfect things you'd say
The "almost" things you'd do,
"almost" had me believing
Our love was "almost" true.

I "almost" want to thank you
For "almost" being there,
For "almost" always showing
How much you "almost" care.

We "almost" had everything
It "almost" was enough,
We "almost" had each other
We "almost" fell in love.

We "almost" has some good times
To "almost" build upon,
We "almost" came together
We "almost" were as one.

When you were "almost" honest
You "almost" seemed sincere,
We "almost" saw forever
"almost" perfectly clear.

We were "almost" over
"almost" when we begun,
I'll "almost" always love you,
You "almost" were the one.

Untitled
Morgan Bedard
On crying at her first Easter Passion Play.
"My chin just wrinkled up
and pushed the tears out
of my eyes."

To Dad
Diane Easter
To look back when I was little
Around 5 I must have been
Yelling to the kids in the neighborhood
"My daddy's home again!"

Every Summer you went fishing
for Salmon in the Alaska bay
To Supplement the other job
Driving truck, until late May

You taught me that I'm special
And you taught me to pray
You held me when I cried
And you Knew just what to say.

The years they go so quickly
Somehow you need to know
The place in my heart you dominate
Is more than I can show

As the laughter and the wisdom
You continue to share with me
Now that I'm a grown woman
Means the world to me;

...like you always have

A Wonderful World!
Angele Bassole—Ouedraogo
They told me
Before I entered their world
What a Wonderful World!

Reminding me of Armstrong's unbeatable Poetry
Now that I'm deeply involved in it
I've been yet looking for his wonder

A wonderful World! They told me
What I'm seeing is just Injustice, Lies, Rape.

Inside my body there is a huge fire
Burning and burning again

The fire of Betrayal
The fire of Violence
The fire of Misery!

What a Wonderful World!

My Memories are warm and sad
The sadness of Betrayal
The sadness of Violence
The sadness of Misery

Wonderful! They told me it was Wonderful!
Shame!

Dedication: My beloved son, Eddy—Lionel Bassole

I Will Wed
Cynthia Ghee—Massey
Please don't anguish,
the one who born me.
I love you,
she is my life.

Ivory Keys
H. E. Wilmore, Jr.
Ivory keys that fascinate you
Bring a happiness with a smile
Songs are played and kept in tune
From the piano you play with style

Play the songs that mean so much
Songs that come from your heart
Songs that say you're so in love
Never to grow apart

Beside you I shall sit
To listen to your heart
Will you tell me you love me
Forever from the start

Fingers touching the ivory keys
Gazing eyes that intertwine
Whispers in a soft sweet voice
Love shall last for all time

Play your favorite love song
One that says it's true
The one you hold deep in your heart
A song of love renewed

The Ivory Keys have spoken

The Rose
Cynthia R. Lewis
It seems we always end up this way:
we quarrel, then avoid each other for days—
and then you pay a visit with a rose.
We forgive each other, and are again the best of friends.

I can't count the vases I've filled; afterwards, it seems so trivial.

But then, the fight to top all battles—how we argued!!!
I stormed into my house, and wouldn't come out,
fiendishly stubborn, alone and without.

After a few days came your tap at the door—I didn't answer.
I let days pass in this manner.

I sat, tightly wrapped, in my iron resistance, yet—
daunted by the phone's persistence—in forgetting who was "wrong",
I snatched up the receiver to find out you were gone:

an accident, they said; in only seconds, you were dead.

It happened so fast...and all the time I'd been too stubborn
to apologize for what had passed.

I gave in to my grief and wept, and, in between the tears, I slept.
It was weeks before I went outside. Was it a month? Or maybe more...

yet, it was there I tripped and stumbled—my guilt was honed, my nature
  humble
on a pile of wilted roses that were lying by the door.

Untitled
J. MacGregor
Here I lie in my hospital bed
Dreaming that I am dead.
I wake up
And I am.

The Eagle And The Wind (Master On The Wing)
Aleata Carpenter
He stands on top of the cliff edge
An eagle majestic and strong
He listens to the forest
The heavens, the earth, and their song

Then the wind like a phantom whose risen
With gossamer hair and wings
Charms and delights the eagle
As she passionately dances in rings

Transparent she rises beneath him
His wings beating in time like a drum
Soaring high to the heavens
Till they meet and then become one

With grace they continue the ballad
Serenading the valley with dance
Falling and rising in rhythm
Like composers inciting romance

He floats gently home to his kingdom
The wind becomes still for the night
The world stands in awe of this union
The eagle, the wind, and their flight
Dedication: My sister, Brenda Piatka

True Love
Allen Ladner
A boy who thinks he's become a man
Puts his life in God's mighty hand
He would fight for her as a bard or king
She gently caresses his last heart string

She is a princess in a dragon's world
Oh how he loves this precious girl
About this girl is all he can think
And within her beauty he takes a drink

A shining knight riding the wind
Does his love constitute a sin
To die in her arms or by her side
With her he would forever ride

She blows him a kiss on a cool summer night
As he rides with a king to do what's right
As he lay dying on a lonely plain
He sees her dance in the cool summer rain

She holds his hand as his eyes do close
And upon his breast she places a rose
At deaths door she begins to cry
Knight and Lady rise up into the sky

Hand in hand they ride the wind
Until their time to live again
Dedication: Mandy Sanders

Jack–In–The–Box
Samantha Hemmings
Turn the handle,
Turn it quick,
Out jumps jack,
And does a little trick.

Hope
Luis Marquez
Generation and revelations
time appears away
sunlight by night
moonlight by day

Velvet circus known as life
formed anorexia called planet
genocide by homicide
suicide of mankind

Melted soils and fossils
painful source of mental failure
cold bloody eyes in angry shadows
as the swastika stamps on your forehead...

Abhorred by silent sadness
lunatic creatures run through my life
while endless waves of deepest wisdom
surround the shores of my mind

As I secure my peaceful destiny
by overcoming guilty thoughts
I laugh at your confused ministry
and cover this world with holy dust

I'LL MEET YOU AT THE GALLOWS

Love
Adam Huening
the smile on my face
the tears in my soul

the tickle of warm waves
the shivering in my spine

the air beneath my feet
the gravity holding me to the ground

the whistle in my work
the giggle in my asylum

the roses in my garden
the temptress in my Eden

the buds of my spring
the wilting of my petals

the caress of silk
the burning of my ashes

the sunrise on my arctic nights
the sound of vast mountain silence

the chromosomes in my sperm
the bullet in my gun

the pillow for my head
the closing of my casket

Untitled
Dawn Sams
I'm madder then sad,
I'm sadder then mad,
Let's sneak out the door
and go to the store

An Island Lad
Spence McIntosh
A young lad, a smiling face
Oh to love a youth.
The need to care comes a pace
One's love becomes the truth.

Years pass, the longing fall
And then one fateful time
The Gods conspire against the all
We're thrust together for another "lim..."!

The heart throbs, the breath is short
The stomach churns
The mind tries to abort
But nothing stops the yearn.

Oh young man, love me
Do not judge or be of fright
For all I want of thee
Is your hand so tight.

Don't let me go into darkness
Leaving the world guessing
Come to me in your nakedness
And change what is missing.

Dedication: To my dear friend, Deen

Children In Need
Deborah Waite
Without protection, the tender sapling
Will never be a tree.
Without the care of the pride
The lion couldn't be.

Throughout the world, in every species,
The unwritten rule remains
Protect the young, and let them grow
To find their own domain.

So why are we the only ones
Who seem to have forgotten
Our children are our future,
Without them, we'd be nothing.

But every day these young ones suffer,
At the hands of their own kind,
Abuse and violence, or pure neglect,
Of body soul and mind.

Eyes so young should never see
The horrors that they see,
Innocent minds should not be filled
with pain and agony.

When will we learn, our children are,
our one and only treasure,
And by the way we treat them
Is how God will take our measure.

Torn Brotherhood
Nicholas J. Leistra
The beautiful valley is so peaceful;
to the north the blue sky is sweet,
but to the south the gray clouds are swirling.
when they collide the nation shall weep.

The Tree
Mary Jeanne Carlin
In case you may wonder about me
I am the roots that hold up the tree.
Every branch is a part of me.
Although the fruits I bare, I share with thee.

I strengthen my roots beneath the earth
Scatter seedlings giving children birth
I grow stronger, wiser each new day
And with the wind I gently sway

I spread my arms the earth I shade
Where all God's creatures heads are laid
I nurture my limbs with all I can know
For I am the foundation of which I grow

And if you were to cut me down
Or pull me out of the earthen ground
I'd just grow back In Spring you'd see
As a wiser stronger rooted tree.

I'd bare my fruits to you once more
Scatter more seedlings on the earthen floor
For I am the roots that hold up the tree
In case you may wonder about me.

Dedication: Michael, Marcus, and James, my angel babies

Not Yet!
Lawrence Ferris
Do you know the answer?
No, not yet!
Do you know the finish?
No, not yet!

Do you hear the music?
No, not yet!
Do you know the rhythm?
No, not yet!

Do you know the meaning?
No, not yet!
Have you got the measure?
No, not yet!

Do you know the plot?
No, not yet!
Do you know the theme?
No, not yet!

Have you got the map?
No, not yet!
Do you know the way?
No, not yet!

Do you know the question?
No, not yet!
Have you seen the script?
No, not yet!

Living
Sharon Smith
Always dream about tomorrows,
Keep yesterday's memories in a box,
Live for today as you would hope for the best,
And your tomorrows will be today and full of success.

An Autumn Walk
Faye B. Wright
I walked today on a woodland trail
The wind blew leaves in a gusty gale
They showered my face with red and gold
And tangled my hair with fingers bold

The great trees swayed and sighed above me
Rustled and whispered endlessly
And told a story, old as time
Of God's creation so sublime

Tall green ferns grew at my feet
The woodland smell was damp and sweet
A noisy squirrel scolded high in a tree
As he looked suspiciously down at me

I crossed a tiny rushing stream
Lit by the sunlight's golden beams
It murmured and hurried on by me
In its restless journey toward the sea

It turned and twisted then stood quietly still
Then rushed on again, as it always will
I marveled at this as I stood on the banks
My heart filled, and I gave thanks

Dedication: My granddaughter – Stephanie

Jamaican Market
Nicki Lodge–Mclachlan
Market day vendors,
In colourful dresses,
Headwraps and aprons
With very large pockets,
Create a kaleidoscope
Of blazing colour.

Baskets piled high with golden, ruby
And emerald fruit,
Atop erect vendor's heads,
"Star apples, tangerines, mangoes
And naseberries too!" they croon,
This is all part,
Of the splendour of market day.

Feeling and weighing of ripened goods,
A joke shared, a bargain struck,
As lively anecdotes flow to and fro,
Between Miss Matty and pastor Jones.

And on large green cloths,
Lining wooden stalls,
Lay circles of red and white candy
And paradise plums,
Causing small faces to shine with glee,
At the glorious display of sticky treats,
To be found in mother's basket – On market day.

Dedication: Jimmy, Tammy, Tano, with love

Fatalism
JoAnita M. Booth
My sisters are now my brothers
My brothers are now my sisters
My mother is my father, and her
children are mine.

My thoughts are not my own,
emotions I know nothing of.
Often I am forgotten as a tree
is in winter,
until something is needed of me.

In my search for divine truth
I have become increasingly aware of
the clever lie.

In my quest for the rights to immortality
I have become fearful of our everyday
existence.

In a time where innocence is no longer
a virtue, honesty is a disease, and
peace cannot be found even in one's sleep

I fall upon my knees.

Dedication: Asia Christian Sims, "my joy"

Daffodil
Kathy Pool
I saw a yellow Daffodil,
Sitting on a window sill,
Sitting still...
I saw a yellow Daffodil.

Awakening
Eileen Wilder
The wind did whistle a merry tune
foretelling rain would come real soon.

Home a doorway for the night,
a mystery how I befell this plight,

Questions unanswered race in my head,
legs so cold they feel like lead.

Cardboard mattress to repel the damp,
ungiving tho' for painful cramp.

Yesterday's news has great worth,
shoes to insulate from chilled earth.

No tears left, I cannot cry,
from parched lips escapes a sigh.

Nose does twitch with great glee,
bacon frying, it cannot be!

Wake–up, wake–up, a known voice says,
on a lovely breakfast my eyes gaze.

Reality dawns with sharp clarity,
I am safe with a roof o'er me.

Another's fate, would it leave its mark,
beyond belief a life so stark.

Unknown 1 (A Tanka)
Susan C. Lesko
Look in the mirrors
One place, reflections abound
I become many.
Few have peered through and saw what
They have forgotten by choice.

Man's Tribute To Woman
Gerald Chokas
One minute with you fills my emptiness for days
You have no idea of the effect you have
You have taken away my pain and restored me
The beauty, Oh Lord, the beauty is incomparable
Please don't misunderstand

You are my addiction, my weakness, my strength
If only I could tell you; but no; no never
I must bear this pain, this sorrow, this loneliness
For to touch you even is unacceptable, unforgivable
Please don't misunderstand

Although we remain apart, I am always there
Go, seek, find, Live as you must; I still remain
without a revelation, nothing can be revealed
In time dear lady, only in time; time is a season
Please don't misunderstand

As a child grows in flesh, we must also in spirit
Only God is Love; Yet through the spirit we experience
You are my experience: Your time, my reward
Until the darkness is overtaken by the dawn; this is all.
Please understand

Dedication: The Variable of X

What Shouldn't Be...
Karen Bilodeau
The sky is shining
Our eyes are falling

The rain is crying
Our fears are shedding

The clouds are leaving
The sun is coming

The earth is stopping
The birds are speaking

The snow is melting
The rivers are escaping

The brooks are breaking
The fish are drowning

People are smiling
Children are playing

Criminals are judging
Lawyers are praying

In the END

GOD

is SIGHING ...

Wisdom
Jeff Rushton
Knowledge is nothing unless
Knowledge is followed by action.
To know and to do is great.
To know and do contrary or askew is
The testimony of him that never knew.

Love
Marquetta Bryant
Time has a way of
slipping by
Almost in the wink
of an eye.

If we could see
what life would be,
I'd choose the love
between you and me.

The looks that pass
between say so much,
I feel life in your
loving touch.

Life is worth living
when you have someone
so loving and so giving.

I thank God he sent
you to me.
You are the joy I
knew life could be.

Dedication: With love to Dwight

Angels
Christina Montenegrino
Do you believe in angels?
I think I just might.
They're always watching,
Although not in sight.

Angels of God,
High up above.
Always helping,
Sending love.

A presence of beauty.
So pretty in white.
Do they come in the day,
Or show up at night?

Mysterious they seem,
With halos that gleam.
A voice that sings,
And big, fluffy wings.

Rosy cheeks,
And curly hair,
You feel their presence,
But no one's there.

Do you believe in angels?
I know I do.
A guardian angel,
Guarding me and you.

Not Alone
John Burke
He stares, empty eyes beckon a warming hand.
The drop of money, faintly fills his cap.
Droplets of rain blur his vision, kind footsteps diminish into
a bustling crowd.
Weakly, his lips barely parted, his heart thanks the stranger.

Child Of Light
Richard A. Knutson
As winter lies upon the land
Trees bow low before the storm
And tiny fires reflect their glow
Upon the grains of winter's sand

Fog grows thick in the fading day
Smothering light that might have been
Freezes slick upon the road
Trod by many along life's way

Dangerous pitfalls mar the trail
Hoarfrost, ice and covered pond
Snaring all along the way
The rising wind to screen the wail

Scars like livid maps of fate
Crisscross the hills of nature's mind
Rivers running, swiftly crest
Submerging all with soulless hate

In black of night the tale is told
Bereaved, the widow stand and mourns
Mother Nature's child of light
Within his mother's breast she folds

Sailing On A Moonbeam
Martin J. Dahlgren
The yellow crescent moon hung in the darkness
catching the night in the western sky
greeting the Unicorn in Winter...
Today the singer said goodbye
his song sings to the echo of memory, deep in the heart of the Earth
now on the banks of Lethe, going to the afterworld...

Sailing on a Moonbeam, above the astral plane
like the snowflakes make a sound
a chord, as they fall silently to the good white earth, tasting stone...

Still, the cat catches the moonbeam by the fireplace and holds it in his
eyes...

Blown there by a windbeam...

sailing on a moonbeam
the dream came true, if only for awhile
to touch the tide in the waves of wishing...

Still, now, the desire is at peace
the crumpled brown flowers catch and are covered by tufts of snow...

the little blue flowers on the windowsill
catch the icy moon white in the day and night sky

and so we will remember

The cat sits in the shadows of the window–shade, sailing on a moonbeam...

Life
Diane Johannessen
Confused and amused
To waken and know
We would do it all
Again but, with love
One survives.

The Chair
Peggy Marasco
Her boundaries are limited but she does not care;
normalcy must continue despite this new chair.
High counter–tops and street curbs are challenges, at best;
aware that her future activities depend on passing these tests.

Years ago life was carefree, fresh with youth and full of fun;
few things got the best of her for life's obstacles were ultimately won.
But for now, many things are different, what was once taken for granted is
nevermore;
she's on a road that's less traveled; her heart quickens as she encounters
a door.

What lies beyond this barrier is freedom to move about as others do.
but she's scared that she won't make it, the "handicapped–door" law is
apparently too new.
Frustrated, she retreats to find an answer as to how she can pass through
that door,
knowing her chair was too large and the entrance was smaller, she was sure.
To her delight, did she then notice ramp to the left that was obviously
new;
excited, for at this short summit, was now a door her chair could pass
through!

Too often we fail to realize what chaired people must endure to survive;
their main need is simply to function like us—be productive to feel alive.

Lost Love And Heartache
Rosemary Lynch
I'm feeling very lonely now
I don't know how much I can take
ever since you left me
my heart began to break.

If only you could understand
the feelings I'm feeling inside
The feelings that I have for you
So strong I cannot hide

Please come back to me
and stay with me forever
Please come home to me
and say you'll leave me never

I cannot be without you now
It's tearing me apart
and I will always love you
with all of my heart

If you won't come back to me
and your love I cannot keep
I'll just lay my head on
my pillow and permanently sleep

And then when they bury me
and you begin to cry
Remember here lies a broken
heart broken by her guy.

Poem
Julie M. Ulreich

There once was hog the dog
that liked to jog,
and one day,
he tripped on a log,
because of a frog

Sisters
Janice Wilkins

Sisters we were born
Sisters we will always be
We couldn't get any closer
If we were black–eyed peas

You've been my best friend
My councilor and adviser
You listen to my problems
Sometimes you help me solve them

I think the good Lord knew
That we would need each other
That's why he made us sisters
Instead of brothers

We could have been twins
Don't you think
But just between us
There couldn't have been a stronger link
Through thick and thin
Till the very end
I've never had a better sister
Or a better friend

Dedication: To Mary, with love

A War Of Faces
Brenda Greyeyes

One
A single person
With no one by their side
Lonely
Just another body
Another blank face
Empty
One of many faces in the crowd
Expressionless
Showing no emotion
Physically dead
Everyone is for themselves
Unconcerned
Minding their own business
Self–Centered
With no desire to communicate
One of the lonely faces in the crowd
Complete strangers
Living side by side
Unfriendly
Faces that think they know everything
Ignorant
Stupid and hostile
Unwilling to learn
A war of faces against each other
This is war, this is life
Feelings don't count
Just One of the many Lonely
Faces in the crowd.

Limerick
Tara Osborne

There once was a dog named Sam
Who liked to eat Spam,
and liked to clog,
he ate logs,
and then went out for clams!

The Special Place
Sandra Dolezal

You bring me to a special place;
a place of rest
A place where I can just relax and be myself
A place where I don't have to play games
or prove anything.

You bring me to a special place;
a place of truth.
A place where my secrets are revealed
and sorted through, and understood;
a place where I can release the tigers within
because they don't scare me anymore.

You bring me to a place of peace
where love is felt, although unspoken.
where time stands still
and nothing else is known, nothing else matters...
except that moment.

Everything else disappears
as though a vapor; without substance.
And I become lost in the dream...
never wanting to return to the world.

Dedication: Dan, my hero, my friend

Tomorrow, Today, and Yesterday...
Aljokhina Valentina

We are turned to the future "TOMORROWS",
Full of mysteries, always appealing,
And in "TODAY" we're leaving all sorrows,
All with what we were fighting and dealing.

In "TODAY" we are staying in present,
Rather common, routine, and sad,
Not an easy, or kind, or gracious,
Very simple as water and bread.

Only seldom it comes to be bright,
Full of colours, like blossoming heaven,
And we love it with all our might,
And we pray to keep it forever.

But "TOMORROW'S" already waiting,
Urging on the run of the clock,
All the present events are melting,
Carrying streams to the memory stock.

And again will be new "TOMORROW"
Making "YESTERDAY'S" irreversible traces...
From this stock we can only borrow
Precious moments, people's faces...

Weightless load of memories stays
In our souls and hearts forever
Making life which is fragmented of days
Bringing happiness, so anxious, hard and clever...

Another Christmas
Jean Janke
I try each day to do my best,
with heavy burden and unrest,
My mind is busy, but, my
soul's at ease,
And every one I try to please.
At Christmas time you scurry
around, toys and presents
can't be found.
There's decorating and
baking too, and all the
things you need to do.
There's friends and family
from out of town, you
must smile and show
them around.
There's cookies candy and
apple cider, all these
treats make you wider
and wider.
Christmas comes but once
a year,
Hold on, because, you'll make
it my dear...
Dedication: My sons, John and Brent

Untitled
M. E. Ragsdale
The awakening dawn spreads
Its light on my lawn,
Making crystalline dew from
The earth's sweet air, and
Beckons her sleeping flowers.

Forbidden Lust
Gareth M. Hogg
It caused weeks of tears and sadness
Arguments, jealousy and mistrust
It caused heartbreak, cursing and bitterness
That one hour of forbidden lust.

For lust it was, she said, not love
And vowed she loved me true
But I cannot help but wonder
Is he the first of an endless queue.

Every time we kiss, every time we touch
The thrill for me has gone
Instead I think, his lips, his hands,
His body has sung my song.

She cries and tell me, it was nothing
That I'm bigger and better than him
But how to I know, that she didn't also
Whisper the same encouragement to him.

I wish I could go back in time
And omit that night in September
When she gave herself to another man
And gave me tears and heartaches to remember

They say, time is a wonderful healer
And I must learn to forgive and trust
But in my heart I know, I shall take to my grave
That one hour of forbidden lust.

Tomorrow Counts
Nancy Schettig
Today we must realize—this is the first day of our life

We spend so much time dealings with problems and strife

Life is uncertain as we pass through each day

We try to find answers—but we forget to pray

We promise ourselves—when our problems get solved

We'll get into living and again get involved

But tomorrow arrives and what do we do?

Fall back in our rut—feeling unhappy and blue

Remembering we are not promised a tomorrow

No guarantee of all happiness no sorrows

What we do with each day is strictly up to us

Lets look for the positives and then we'll enjoy all the pluses.
Dedication: My children (Rick, Tim and Doug)

Star Gazing
Rhonda A. Henry
Lonely stars thought earthly bars we watch and never touch,
and love them thought they never know really just how much.
A comet's light that burns so bright in our lonely heart,
never to be seen again in this life's time,
like the fallen meteor, into the sublime.

Reflections From A Cruise
Lee E. Ecke
The water is blue, the sky is too, let's sail the ocean we never knew.
Come along and sail the blue, food is great and so much to do.

When aboard it may cross your mind, the world I knew I left behind.
Sailing smooth, weather fine, a breeze later we should not mind.

All the crew, waiters too, can make this trip too good to be true.
Among things to do, visit the bridge is something new.

To take a cruise and have some fun, get on deck and see the sun.
Should you have the urge to run, outside deck is a lot of fun.

If fun you want, just take a glance, match numbers, take a chance,
Or to the movies, have a glance, or get up and have a dance.

Even though you may not care that Christmas is a time to share,
Since Santa travels through the air, he is to find you anywhere.

To cruise the sea is really great, to enjoy in full, participate.
A Christmas cruise is so great; especially with a New Years date.

Begin the year on a cruise at sea, is the dream of things to be.
Even though you are at sea, you can go a shopping spree.

New Years Eve can be so neat, sailing the blue is hard to beat.
For sure it is to be a treat, the day the Captain you will meet.

Comes the day we bemoan, we see the port the ship calls home,
We take memories we own, back to the world we call "our" home.

Memories
Barbara B. Benz
The Circles echo when a leaf descends
To drift upon a stream; thus in my mind,
The echoed circles of evasive thought
Return to me the wisps of memory,
Regressed, forgotten, 'til encircled now
By echoes of the past. I find no end.

The Day Of His Triumph
Joshua G. Weese
At first, the devil will unleash his pawn;
He will mesmerize the world with his strength and brawn.
He will march with all his army west;
and put the great country Israel to the ultimate test.

In a flash, the greatest country, America, will be on its knees;
Its people forced from their homes to take shelter under the trees.
Immediately afterward, Israel is pushed towards the sea;
Cornered by a madman who only evil can see.

No one can come to help, some won't even consider the chance;
Not America, Great Britain, Canada or France.
After a few months, it appears as if the madman has won;
Then, He comes from the clouds and challenges the mighty one.

Then the magnificent one and the new one;
gather their great armies and prepare for the Battle of Armageddon.
In the end, only one stands alone;
amidst a hundred square miles of fire and brimstone.

And now you can finish the remainder of this;
Who do you think it is standing amidst with a clasped fist?
Who could have won with a single "wumph"?
Jesus Christ Himself, during the day of His triumph!

Final Desecration
Sharon Thayer Kostenbauder
The beautiful waving colors that are seen waving high
Blood, Purity and Honor reflections to signify

The flag I salute is distributed to many!
The flag's vast presence is overwhelmingly uncanny!

The only running color was crimson from the dying
While survivors in shock, just helplessly sat crying

Valor, Good and Respect are the images projected
Even the right to desecrate ironically, is protected!

A target of reproach, this emblem has become
While it is denounced by a few, it is tattered by some

Each time one flag is tattered or destroyed to the core
It is merely a small battle lost, not the entire war!

Citizens of malice miscalculate their aim!
Negligence of empathy are present in the same

A cloth alone does not empower those who are despaired!
United actions against evil forces demand to be declared!

A sudden seizure of the flag foiled plans of desecration!
Screams of rights to do so, were silenced in devastation!

Realization tolled, those rights were finally gone!
For America's freedom vanished, leaving the perpetrator alone!

My Friend Po
Katie S. Davidson
Po's my friend my very best friend,
She's so caring and will always lend,
Me money, support and friendship too,
She is fun and helps me through,
The great times and the bad
She's the greatest friend I've ever had.

Memories
Julia Weatherbee
Memories that walk into our lives
Childhood memories that we recall
Young and barefoot and oh so tan
Memories

Walking on dusty country roads
Laughing faces as we stroll
Trips to the farms nearby
Memories

Large straw hats touched by the sun
Floating butterflies of orange and blue
That brushed our faces as we go by
Memories

Wild strawberries, growing along the way
Sweet blueberries on bushes
With their silvery glow
Memories

Pausing long enough now to recall
Joys of our youth, So long gone by
Suddenly fall is now ever so near
Memories.

The "A" Disease
Ada Marie Poindexter
The "A" disease strikes millions
across the country, yet goes
unrecognized. It begins as sort
of a trance. A blank stare! Then
it slowly attacks the heart and
fills it with emptiness.
The pain! Ahh! Ahh!
It is agony beyond belief, but
do not fear! For this disease has
been diagnosed and is treatable and
possibly curable with extensive
and excessive care.
Wait! Wait! Wait!
Wipe the sweat from your brow.
Relax! Put the check book up.
This "A" disease. This problem is
loneliness. This treatment, this
care is so simple. So economical,
yet feels so good. It's love,
attention and affection daily from
the opposite sex.
Wait! Wait! Wait!
Loneliness is no laughing
matter. It's not to be taken
lightly. It's more widespread
than any disease. Yet goes
unrecognized as a problem;
a very serious, a very real,
a very lonely problem.

Earth
Jonathan Fasulo
Old beautiful
Astounding, spring, relaxing
Trees, habitats, wild life, nature
Amazing, shimmering, glistening
Round, green
Planet

Beyond Eon
J. Gordon Alderman
They have watched worlds collide
across the heavens far and wide

Held the fate within their sand
of countless stars however grand

They awakened fire in an ancient sea
where some said land could never be

Saw the mountains smoke and grow
then watched them covered beneath the snow

Many times they saw the fall
of nature's creatures large and small

They road with travelers from many worlds
as they launched their ships upon the perils

Who brings to bear God's heavenly light
to brighten his own eternal night

Let us join them in their home they set a table prime
step inside the hourglass and meet the sands of time

Dedication: My wife, Betty, and our time

My Precious, Special Miracle
Theresa Morales
When things didn't seem to be right,
from the start, I had this pain in my heart.
When I gave birth to you, I had this dream.
Until the diagnosis, my life was serene.
As I look into your beautiful eyes, you have a blank stare.
Do you love me? Do you care?
I hope you believe this to be true, that I will never give up
on you.
You are my precious, special miracle – the one love of my life.
This whole thing just cuts me like a knife.
Come into my world, come within my reach. Don't be afraid,
just let me teach.
I know you have no choice, but please, sweetheart, let me hear
your voice.
How can I make people understand that this child is such a
demand.
When I hear the laughter of the children outside,
it is my "true" feelings that I must hide.
Why can't it be you out there? It just doesn't seem to be fair!
My sweet baby, I am so proud of you. You've come a long way.
We have a long road ahead of us, but it will be worth it. You'll
see, someday
Won't you please come out of your shell? This hurts so much,
like hell.
Maybe one day, you'll read and understand this poem.
That's when I'll know you will truly "be home."

Dedication: My beautiful daughter, Christina

God's Garden
Cynthia D. Williams
In God's garden little children grow.
God chooses the hands that tend His precious flowers.
May all we do be done in love, as we nurture, and water
these precious little ones.
As we do we will fulfill this ministry He's given,
to care for these His precious little children.

Your Cabin
Louise Evans
In the silence of the East Texas pines,
Time becomes insignificant, as you enjoy life around you.
The trees sway in the gentle breeze, as if praising God.
The woodland creatures silently observe, as you begin to fall trees.

You smile, envisioning the cabin you are about to assemble.
Your dream is about to unfold before you.
A tremendous amount of labor is ahead of you, but it becomes a labor of
love.
Your inner–most being longs for communion with nature.

The logs go up, one by one. Soon the walls are established.
You feel proud, surveying your accomplishments.
As the roof is completed, you consume the excitement that is within you.
Your cabin. Your dream. Life is wonderful!

Circumstances change as life continues. Sometimes unbearable.
It becomes difficult to make rational decisions.
There is a yearning for inner peace.
The decision is determined.

Now, you walk along the shore of the crystal sea.
There's a smile on your face, as you enjoy the beauty that surrounds you.
You relax in your cabin, that is nestled within the celestial forest.
It's more magnificent than you ever dreamed. Your cabin!

Invisibility
Sandra Vincent
In the morning,
We don't always see the sunrise –
But – it's there.

In the evening,
We don't always see the stars shine –
But – they're there.

We don't see the trees filtering the air that we breathe,
Nor the wetlands purifying our water –
But they are.

We don't always see where the birds fly –
Nor the animals and others living in the wild,
But they're there – At least for now –

And sometimes we get all confused, hurt and bewildered –
Looking for something, someone, somewhere –

Calm your thoughts –
Breathe – Relax –

Enjoy the sunset!
Look inside –
You will find yourself –
You are there.

Dedication: Carol, David, Renee, Karen–Kim

The Journey
Pamela Pugliese
Perhaps she is the only one aware of this journey
She whispers welcome to the summer breeze
They huddled together blinded by secrets
Casting glances at those all alone
But she has touched the moon
And her soul is free

Teenagers
Jane McKnight
Teenager are people
Just like you and me
They are thoughtful and happy
Well, maybe a little more carefree
They like to have fun
Like all of the rest
But really and truly they do their best
They love their mother and daddy
And to their friends they're always true
As for me I'm a teacher
To teach one and all
I'm here to help you
So you will not fall
So please be careful and keep the hope
And always say no to this thing called dope
Then when you're out into the world
You will be a respected boy or girl
You will have a very wonderful life
When you decide to become a husband or wife
So learn all you can while you're in school
Then you will grow up to be nobody's fool
You can go through life without a worry
Because as you know life passes in a hurry
Remember you're the one who has to choose
Whether you win or whether you loose

Three Little Brown Eyed Girls
Inna J. Martin
I have three little brown eyed girls, different
in every way.
One says yes, one says no, and one says maybe so?
Three little brown eyed girls, different in every way.
One says I want to be like mom, one says I am
like mom, and one says maybe, someday?
Three little brown eyed girls, different in every way.
One is tall, she's quite jazzy, she's a genius, and
somewhat sassy.
One is short, she's a songbird, she's petite, and
quite unique.
One is an angel, she's yet small, a bundle of
fluff, and a barrel of fuss.
Three little brown eyed girls, I love them each
so much.
When one sighs, another cries, and the other one
just bellows out!
Three little brown eyed girls, different in every way.
But, wait a minute, make no mistake, there are
three common traits:
Their beautiful brown eyes.
Their lovely black hair.
Their love for their father.
And that love is majestic and rare.
Three little brown eyed girls, different, yet,
the same.

Dedication: My husband and children, lovingly

Mom, I Miss You
Nancy C. Rashid
Mom, you have been gone too many years.
Perhaps you have only been gone for three –
But I remember you every day –
And I hope you remember me.
Every day I ask the Lord to take care of
And I hope you ask him to take care of me.

Grandma's Little Girl
Mavis J. Cope
My granddaughter called her Mom today,
Since there wasn't much else to do,
And said, "Well, Mom, why don't you come over
So I can spend some time with you."

But Mom just couldn't make it.
She said she had things to do.
When you're only six years old,
That leaves you feeling blue.

Her Daddy's girlfriend just had a baby,
And last night they were here.
She said, "Daddy, holding that baby is all you want to do."
When you're only six years old,
That leaves you feeling blue.

I don't know if her parents care
About what they're doing to the world.
But for now, forever and always,
She'll be Grandma's Little Girl.

She's not at fault for wanting their attention
That she's missed out on for so long.
The fault lies with the parents
For not seeing where love belongs.

Friends
Andrew Stallworth
Friends are God's creation to fill voids, they are
Precious commodities you seek when in doubt,

Someone seeming you can't live without.

Friends share you anxieties, your love, your fears,

But remain steadfast throughout the years.

To find a friend is finding a four–leaf clover, which
Is something rare,

Someone whom special feelings and secrets you share.

A friend has answers when questions seems too difficult
To ask

A friend hears your needs tho you have not spoken and
Accepts the arduous task.

The law of gravity does not apply in friendship, for
the high esteem we have for each other never falls.

A friend is a diamond of life who's value appreciates
And last forever.

A good friend should be cherished and forgotten
...NEVER!

Nature
Emily Jayne Piper
N is for the nightingale and his sweet song.
A is for the alligator that snaps hard and long.
T is for the turtle in the backyard.
U is for the umbrella tree whose bark is hard
R is for the reindeer with his big horns.
E is for the elephant with her new–born.

A Mother's Poem
Michele H. Wilkinson
My little newborn so tiny and sweet
I can sit here all night and rock you to sleep.
I whisper to you and say with a smile,
Please slow down, stop growing for awhile!
I love to count your piggy toes, and hold your
Little hands, and now I watch you run and play
With your friends in the sand. I say to you
With a laughing smile, please slow down,
Stop growing for awhile.
Before we know it you'll be in school
Learning to read and write. And soon you'll be
driving Daddy's car instead of flying your kite.
I yell to you with a joking smile,
Please slow down! Stop growing for awhile.
I know soon the day will come, that you
Will be all grown up. As we hug and say
Good–bye, I say to you please slow down...
you turn and smile...I know mom, stop growing
For awhile.
I know someday you'll understand, when you
Hold your child's little hand. You'll look at him
And say, with a proud smile, please slow down
Stop growing for awhile.

Dedication: My sons, Corbin and Tyler

Where Is God
M. Brown
So often have I heard these words said, if there
is a God, why is she dead?
She was so young, it is so unfair, she was his
Life, such a sweet devoted pair.

Many times have I heard people say, God watches
People doing wrong every single day,
Children being abused, and elderly mugged and
just left there to die,
Why does He not do something? Surely He hears them cry.
Why does God watch whole families being starved
With rich countries' food glut, deaths could be halved,
So much suffering in third world countries,
Why? When so many rich people could help with their monies.
When no one can help with our everyday tasks
We look to the heavens, and in prayer to Him ask,
"God up above I beg you please help me
My life seems so pointless, no end to the misery."

God gave us life to help and love one another
Not to quarrel and fight and kill each other
He gave us Ten Commandments we should all obey
If we did, we would never go astray.

We ought to live side by side, without any bother
Not kill and maim, just to prove some point or other
We should look at a man as a son, Father or brother
To a woman who is his sister daughter or Mother

Sunset Afternoon
Anna Galt
Everyone needs a time to think,
Everyone needs a place,
Everyone needs the sunset to place us
into dreams,
Everyone needs the sunset to dream in,
Do you need the sunset to so often dream in?

The Weight Of A Feather
Joan McLemore
One's life begins;
as a drifting,
weightless,
feather.

Blowing aimlessly along.

Seemingly care–free;
until the awareness of the concerns of life,
creep upon us, ever so slowly.

Accumulating feathers;
heavy,
dense,
smothering burdens.

Now with certain aim;
falling,
crashing,
lying unmovable.

THE WEIGHT OF A FEATHER IS THE SUM OF THE WHOLE.

Until a fresh wind blows,
lightening the soul.

The Qualm Within
Jodie Carter
Framed in your soul fear sealed with
numbness of inability

Why do you clothe the inner fear?

It has stolen the sun replace it
soon black hole within shallow, empty

Should you continue being helpless
and wondering choking on the mist
of pain?

Remaining light turned dark
Why!
Fear can you see its not real

Perched upon you fear weighing
You down to be free

Why Not!

This fear is only the foe of the
hearts agonies

But –
Its secretly taking over till no
longer
YOU ARE THE FEAR

Dreams Alive
Raymond Damont
Hollow how's I feel
Sorrow's all a lie
Life's a living cycle
Eyes are down
But I still dream of
Paradise

An Eternal Music
Vishnu P. Joshi
Like a flutist and his flute, or
Like a writer and his pen
The mind and the body
Play the music—Life;

The music of today
It comes from the melody
They composed yesterday;

The music of tomorrow
Will come from the melody
They will write today;

One day they will compose
The music
That Christ heard on the Cross;

An eternal music –
That Angels sing in heaven,
A music of souls in the God's kingdom,

A melody –
End of Pleasure and Pain,
That Buddha heard
Under the Bo–Tree.

A Friend In Need
Melissa Gail Bouldin
The day you were born onto this earth, your future was all planned.
God sent an angel to watch over you and lend a helping hand.

This angel taught you patience and gave you strength and love; as the
Lord watched, smiling down on you from the heavens above.

Sometimes your days seemed long and hard, and not too often bright,
but the angel was there watching over you to help you win the fight.

As you grew older, the angel had taught you so much, so she left this
world peacefully, with just a gentle touch.

She has taught you selflessness and let you take the lead; She taught
you how to love someone and not give in to greed.

She taught you how to have patience with those who had lost their
way, and taught you how to live your life as if it were your last day.

She taught you how to give to those who had nothing left to give,
and with the special things she taught you, you learned how to truly
live.

You learned to be a seed, to flourish around the lost, and so you did
what you had learned, no matter what the cost.

You have taught these lost ones what you have learned and let them
take the lead...and then you went off searching for another...
Friend in need!!!!

Untitled
U. H. Berner
Pictures and Poems
Both a Thought removed
Frozen in their moment
Enlarged
by Frame or Verse
to be kept forever.

Nelon Park
Barbara Wirthlin
My house sits on a corner lot;
One small tree shading me,
The backyard small, a tiny plot.

Spongy lawns and leafless trees
Adjacent to my house and fence
Spread far beyond its boundaries.

I feel the air so chill and hence
I cannot stroll next door today.
A peek outside past grass so dense

Shows swings hung still to my dismay;
No squealing children's reddened faces
Breathless from their joyous play.

The baseball diamond's empty bases
Meet bleachers lonely for a crowd.
The drab dugout's vacant spaces

Shadowed by a darkening cloud.
But restful fires warm my hearth
Against the stillness—oh, so loud.
Dedication: For Dad, who inspires me

Who You Are
Michael Chalmers
I know who you are.

I love to laugh
so why do I cry?

Why must I smile
through the tears;

too many years.

I know where you are,
you don't care,
to you I am no longer there.

Wilted dreams and
muted screams,

illusionary love.

I cannot remain above,
the depths they beckon,

pain,
deceit,
despair.

Did you ever know
I was there?

Let It Flow
Julie Buckman
Your love is like a river over flowing into my stream
We are drifting together soon we will be one naturally
If their ever a rapid current try to slow it down please
Cause a love drifting together should be slow naturally
For a love is like water use it cautiously
And you can have it forever naturally

The Future
Norma Jean McCann
A subtle sadness steals across her empty heart.
But is the emptiness for real?
Or merely a thin veil,
a meager attempt to hide,
the rage and passion,
and bitter loneliness hidden deep inside.

But what of death?
Is it truly a comforting blanket of nothingness,
or a door to another world?
One key swinging open the door to paradise,
the other opening the door to hell.

Perhaps it is enough to float among the muck
of one's self pity.
To pretend to own no fault,
to have no say about the story's ending.

Is it too much trouble to choose,
or is it just too easy to let other's lead you along
and take the blame.
It's easier to hide in the darkness than to chance,
to hope to see the Future.

Dedication: Michael Shane Grove, U.S. Navy

MacKenzie Grace Parry – Jayme's Baby Sister
Nixeon Civille Handy
Loved
Into
Being

Father Ted
Mother Gwen

Born precious
Angels attending

23rd Holy day
2nd month
6:15 am
1997

9 pounds 13 ounces
Northwest Hospital
Seattle, Washington

Extended family
welcomes her
with a birthday cake
(one lighted candle)

MacKenzie
Our
Beloved
Darling

Leaves
Mary Wagener
sweet sour small
lemon lime
yellow and tall
bright dull
it's time for fall
now we see none at all

The First Day Of Fall
Barbara L. Celello
This
I breathe
the first day of Fall
an autumnal haven
called Indian Summer

Pondering
I cry
looking back to Spring
remembering green leaves
and how they changed

Sweet
but sad
to see the pinks and blues
of Season's birth
turn to gold and brown

Wondering
I try
to understand how
the plan began
in the womb of Life.

Dedication: All "angels" in my life

New Car Old Feet
C. A. Wardell
Buying a car
can be really good fun
if you think about
walking or having to run
for a train or a bus
that's running on time
or queuing for taxis
and standing in line.

A shiny new car
with chrome and good tyres
and a bang in its exhaust
when the engine backfires
a Ford or a Renault
or a Honda Accord
the choice is yours
but can you afford

The road tax, insurance
not forgetting MOT
a weekly car wash
on Sunday before tea
Petrol, Oil and Lubricants
a service when its due
my feet will last forever
I'll leave the car to you.

Dedication: My mate Tim, your choice

My Child Too
Regina Rena West
We haven't met yet but to my heart I know that you will bring joy.
For now through the love your father and I share I have a little boy.
I am not your real mother, this is true.
But it doesn't mean that I can't love you too.
I hope that the same feelings for me you will share.
Because the way you feel for me you will never know how much I care.

My Dream
Sheryl Smith
I dream of owning a house some day
Where my daughter can run and play.

I guarantee all the walls would not be white.
There'd be colors so our hearts squeal with delight!

In spring we'd plant flowers, that later would bloom.
And we would pick them to brighten up our rooms!

It would have a large porch for long summer nights,
of dreaming and wishing on stars so bright.

In fall we would rake the leaves so high
And jump in the piles to watch them fly.

We would bake cookies on snowy days.
To help chase the winter blues away.

This house is just a wish right now
But I will find a way somehow

To make this dream come true
Within a year, maybe two!
Dedication: My daughter, Emily

Darlene And Noel
Noel Patterson
Darlene when our eyes first met, I knew
our love was meant to be.

Me for you! and You for me!

"Darlene and Noel", we are as one.

Together we will do what must be done,
There is nothing we can't do, as long as
you have me and I have you,

"Darlene and Noel"

We are a special pair as long as we have
each other, we haven't a single care.

"Darlene and Noel"

Our love is a special kind, we have found
what others my never find.

"Darlene and Noel"

We've had bad times, more than our share.
But here we stand a beautiful pair,
"Darlene and Noel"

Together till the end, husband and wife, lover and friends.

Only
B. J. Naeem
The wind blows and thoughts of you are in my mind.
Night falls and you are in my heart.
The dawn draws nigh and you are in my soul.
Only thoughts of you fill the hours of the day.
Memories of long awaited hours alone,
and only moments together.
Hoping and praying to be with you once again;
only knowing it will never be because your love
for me will never exist.
Depression has filled my mind.
Only sadness is in my heat and loneliness
fills my soul.
Tears now cloud my vision; no longer do I see
the rainbow.
Only darkness fills my sky.
No longer shall I hear the bird's sweet song.
Only the droning sound of clocks passing
time is heard.
Precious touches my body shall no longer feel.
Only pain and longing will fill me up.
Shall I never taste the dew of morning's sweet light
only bitters shall I eat.
The scent of flowers is no longer.
Only the stench of burning memories of you
remains.

Untitled
Mary F. Schwartz
I needed love. God sent me you.
I needed strength and courage, too.
I lacked the rhyme; the "why" of living,
God gave me you, and in the giving,
I found new eyes with which to see.
God gave me the world when He sent you to me.

H2O4U
Jaime Britt
Who will take me in and who will love me so?
I don't think I'm that bad, if people could only know...

What I do for them and how they need me.
I am only a commodity of liquid, or at least that's what most see.

But flowers and plants, Oh sweet flowers and plants, they appreciate me so!
And they also realize their existence relies on me alone.

As they drink me in, to nourish their fragile souls...
They thank me by showing the colors they stole.

From the Mighty Creator, who actually graciously gave it.
But people still don't recognize His importance and choose to go on by
   their own wit.

But I say, they would not last if it weren't for me.
And they should know that I am almost everywhere they see.

They even pollute me as if I were something not needed.
But if they continue to mistreat me, it will produce a consequence not
   heeded.

For I am what they drink and even survive on.
Because without water in their body, they have nothing to thrive on.

So here is some advice, for more than just a few...
Take good care of me, and I'll take care of you.

Untitled
Jessyca Rodriguez
to get, you must give
to die, you must live
to love, you must hate
to learn, you must make mistakes

Dedication: Matthew and Henry, with love

Life In My Heart
Alene Sibley
The field lays down for him, calling. The dewy grass is in love.
It's the whispering hairs upon my outstretched arms, loudened by a grabbing
   sunlight.

From uncloseable window—eyes he regards
hazy and misted teal air beauty,
that is my romance. My kiss at midnight from a fab date.
He was gorgeous.

So sympathetic, the atmosphere shivers in sigh,
a complete galaxy focused.
It is my memory frisking the universe for one more moment.
One teensy word able to alter tall sacrifices.

Who knew a burial would uncover to him my beauty
that even I do not see?
My searching stars cannot find him,

yet

tonight he cups water from Heaven's stream,
where the pounding of my heart shakes startled liquid from his fingertips
to be tears of his caress massaging through my veins.

and no less will be my ache,
yet.

Untitled
Mitchell D. McCommon
From darkness
to kindergarten
Another moment's passed
I'll never get back,

First grade to graduation
Another moment's passed
I'll never get back

My first kiss
to going down the aisle
Another moment's passed
I'll never get back

From cutting the cord
to changing her diapers
Another moment's passed
I'll never get back

Holding her hand to steady her first steps
to giving her hand in marriage
Another moment's passed
I'll never get back

So treasure all moments in life, cause you can't get them back.

Dedication: Reba Lipscomb and Ashley N. McCommons

High School Graduation
Mary Jane Morrison
Your graduation from high school was a
celebration we all joyfully shared with you.
We were all there – your Mom and Dad, sister,
grandparents, aunts, uncles, and nephews too.

I was also there the day you were born –
your parents were ecstatic and filled with much joy.
They beamed with happiness at the sight
of their new baby boy.

The day that I held my first grandchild
was indeed a precious moment for me.
What a pleasure to watch you grow into
the fine young man you've turned out to be.

Set your goals high as you go off to
college now, all on your own.
You'll be covered by my prayers and
may you never feel alone.

Grandpa and I wish you the very best
for each and every day.
Graduation from high school is a
real milestone along life's way.

Dedication: Our daughter Julie...Chase's mother

Untitled
Tom Morgan
The simple plans
of a feeble man
rock the boat momentarily
evil plans
of the challenged man
shake the world eternally

The Mountain
Flo Carjile
High up on the mountain where trees grow tall and straight
I had an urge to climb it I couldn't hardly wait
up there I had a vision how great our life would be
I'd take my honey with me just her just me

So we got our gear in order and began to climb
Each day took us higher with no danger on our mind
We finally reached the very top there was beauty all around
But the wind that blew through the long tall tree
Made a sickening moaning sound

The ice and snow began to fall the rain began to pour
The mountain took her from me I won't be seeing her any more
She was my golden angel, she was my love my life
She was all I had to live for my darling and my wife

The gold won't ever take her and that love is next in line
I can see my love beside me oh what an awful climb
We made the top we've done it all we've done what we had to do
Her love for me was sacred my love was sacred too

So I'll get my gear in order now
Leaving hers behind
I'll think of her and see her there as down the hill I climb
We made our vows together that we would never part
I'll leave her here and disappear
With a sad and broken heart

Take The Memories
Sandy Meloche

I'll take the memories
To remember days gone by,
And treasure all the happiness
How we used to laugh and cry.

I'll take the memories
How we shared a joke or two
We talked about the good times
In the lives of me and you.

I'll take the memories
How we sat and didn't speak
We knew each other's feelings
Our strength would not grow weak.

I'll take the memories
How you always seemed to care
When mixed emotions stood me up
Your Faith was always there.

I'll take the memories
How you taught me how to pray
Not for miracles but for guidance
How to live from day to day

Dedication: To Donald, a special friend

Life
Diane Jaquis

Life is here and now
what will happen tomorrow
or in the future.
Remember now
that's all we have for now
'til we get to the future.

She Is Here
Renee Lenerville Leach

When I look into your face,
When I hear you laugh...
I know she is here.

Her memory enfolds me,
Like a warm breeze on a sunny day
And I know, she is here.

I see you gesture,
or look at me that way
And I know, she is here.

I feel you reach out,
Each time I take a fall
And I know, She is here.

I see you cheer,
for each goal I reach
And I know, she is here.

I have not lost her,
Though I cannot see her face.
She has gone, and left you in her place.
I have you and I know,
She is here.

Dedication: Mom, we miss you

No One...I Think Not
Kim M. Sell

Does anyone have the right to judge or criticize you?
Is he/she better than you, for if they do?

Who must condescend to make oneself feel better?
Is it necessary to make others feel lesser?

What kind of friend has no respect for you?
Will this type of person do?

What type of companion thinks only of his/her own desires?
Will he/she be around when you have flat tires?

Does a friend offer of him/herself less than you have to offer?
Is it right or fair to make another suffer?

Should a friend physically or mentally abuse you?
Can he/she make you do or say anything you don't want to?

Do you want to be with a person that doesn't know how to have fun?
Is it someone you want to spend time with over and over again?

What type of person does not trust or support you?
Will this someone be loyal because you need him too?

Is there a future with any kind of person such as these?
No one, I think not...So we'll move on as we please.

Aids
Amir Elzeni

If flowers spoke
would they speak
fondly of the rain?

Is love the enemy
of every rose in pain?

Life Real, Freedom A Dream
Tom Szymecko

Maybe it has to be this way...(Dr. King would know what
I'm talking about.)
Saturday night, the busses stopped.
The cold, slow walk from work, silent scrape of heavy—
frictioned feet,
hungry, bladder aching, as cars speed and hiss and mock
me going by,
makes me think of comfort of course, independence,
the absolute freedom of my own business(!)
until I get to the pizza joint.

One table full, pizza man owner doing everything, alone.
I order, we talk 'til 2 (my cold bag of food ignored),
we talk of his business, growth, profits, quality, quality,
(as I think of "quality of life").
But we know the real world demands quantity, quantity,
quantity hard enough to squeeze and burden our dreams
(especially as the years go on), but not kill them.

We hope of lowered rents. I easy work, a car;
he easy franchise, vacations,
and of course we both the non—materials, peace of mind.
Ah yes,! Our freedom perfect dreams!
(Despite the real rough—stoned pavement and blood—soaked rent)
the more tangible, if unattainable, vividly stronger, dreams.

Dedication: My friend, Shah Jahan Kabir

A Cat Lover's Observations
Beverly J. Hardy
As a cat lover, I am compelled to say
Cats are better than us in so many a way.

Their intelligence is a tangible thing
Worthy of the respect that should bring.

Questing for knowledge they never tire
Plowing ahead, spurred on by a secret fire.

Cats are relentless in every pursuit
Their labor almost always bearing fruit.

Cats accept other cats on merit alone
Never failing to make them feel at home.

Cats never hesitate to express their feelings,
Seldom resorting to subterfuge in their dealings.

And when it comes to you – the one they adore,
With this love, you couldn't want for more.

Cats sense when your world is torn in half
And possess the ability to make you laugh.

The one thing you can depend upon, too,
Is your cat loves you because you're you.

I Came And I Went
Penny Lawson
I awoke one morning to get on with my day
I listened to some words of wisdom a child had to say
The rest of the day, I loved and I toiled so a day well spent
And into another day, I came and I went

Dedication: To Danielle, with love

As The Wind Carries My Words Away
Marcy S. Deneweth
Catch my thoughts as they ride the wind
Drink my words as they escape my lips
I'm tempted by fascination
my eyes hold onto my imagination

See my words as they paint a picture
Taste the flavor from what I say
Feel the heat from deep inside, you listen
The night is gone, it's almost day

Flesh and bones hold my words together
As the wind carries my words away
stick with me and I'll lead the way
Trust me with all that is unknown
Because I am held together with flesh and bones

Time is a soldier that stands tall and proud
It's in front of you, but you can't catch it
It's running fast and running out
We're living on the edge of time

Catch my thoughts as they ride the wind
Lick the flavor from what I say
Flesh and bones hold my thoughts together
As the wind carries my words away

Dedication: Jesse, my only love

Epitaph To A Queen
Sarah E. Glavinic
Here lies the body of Cleopatra, born 69 BC
Spent her entire existence
As though it were in a boundless bank.
Unleashed from Life and rested for a brief moment
Beside her lover
Before continuing a journey began in the common Earth,
On the last day of August, 30 BC

Departure
Leslie–Ann Carabin
The road to his future is where he'll head
How often I'll see him has not yet been said

I will miss him, for he is my companion
I still will hold the memories inside

The joys we shared will never be forgotten
The few hardships we bore will fade away

I must be strong, I will not cry
He must go on with his life, but why, oh why...?

must he leave me behind to finish my life
without his brilliant mind...

to back me up when I am wrong?
Until our parting, it won't be long.

Our house will seem empty without his jokes
My eyes will gleam with the tears of sadness

My brother, my ally, will soon depart
And his leaving will leave a void in all our hearts.

Dedication: My great brother, George

Sunset
C. Edwards
Far beyond the distant hills, the sun is dipping
Low,
And everything is quiet, save the river's
Rippling flow.
The songsters all have gone to rest among
The leafy trees,
For is it not the sunset hour when, homeward,
Come the bees?

Look how the hills, a hazy blue, reflect the
Sun's last peep.
The shadows creep along the glens and up
The hillside steep.
You could not wish a fairer sight to charm
An artist's heart,
For there's no jarring colours there – yes,
Nature plays her part.
Now the sun has disappeared and night
Begins to fall,
The lonely beauties of the west are fading
One and all,
Both man and beast retire to rest, soon to
Be fast asleep,
Secure beneath the care of him who silent
Watch doth keep.

Dedication: George, my dear, late husband

My Pocket
Kaitlyn Culliton

In my pocket there are lots of things
There are buttons and beads
Oceans and seas
Waves and caves
Farms unharmed
Light beams and dreams
and a bed for my sleepy head.

It Makes Me A Jolly Good Fellow
Christina Strom

He stares into his half full glass,
Memories of his once full past,
Her face, entwined within his mind,
A little girl not far behind.

He wonders what he did so wrong?
To lose the laughter, love and song.
To lose his safe and sacred shrine
No more the master of his mind.

"Relief," he searches, from his pain,
But what he reaps, is guilt and shame
Respect, was lost inside a maze,
Of long lost nights, and "boys" gone crazed

His face, a novel of his life,
Show agonies of lows and strife
The path he's chosen, taken toll,
The "serpent" rapes another soul.

Regrets are many, answers nil,
The harvest is a bitter pill,
Three broken hearts — he wipes
a tear.
And orders up, another beer!

To My Wife
Mike D. Palmer

Deep in my heart
I know its true,
Is a very special spot
I've reserved for you!
way down deep,
Where love should be
Is a special love for you and me

Its always been there
I suppose its true
this thing called love
that's only for you!

As time goes on
this love gets strong
and never will it weaken,
cause by my side
you'll stay the bride
that through my life I was seeking

I'll always be true
In the things I do,
for I never want to let you go,

So this day is yours honey,

Because I love you so!

Know Me Right
Flora Dalton

Look at my heart, not my face
Listen to my voice, not your mind
Realize I'm breakable, not shatter–proof
Understand I'm real, I don't just exist
Know that I'm human, not a used old
rag doll to throw in a corner and
forget about.

Memories
Martha Beschi

We all have our memories
that we seem to re–call
Some maybe happy–others may be very sad
But we learn–through this life we pass
Some are good, others even bad.
Some memories come upon us
while others pass us by.
Yet we will have our memory
until the day we die.
So what ever we do with our lives
are carved upon a stone
In a short time we create a memory
In a moment, it can be gone.
Though it is not forgotten,
But stored in the mind,
And return without warning
any place – any time.
So a stranger may knock upon our
door
Strange faces may appear
It is not who is standing
there
But – our memory – that we fear.

Dedication: Mary Smith– special cousin

Voices In The Sand
Gillian Sterling

Voices on the sand,
look around a hundred and one
Voices on the sand,
people, places, time and sun,
to them unknown you speak to me
a voice unheard by a hundred but one.

Voices on the sand,
many come many go
Voices on the sand,
look around me, look I about
where are you now that they go
do you dare to utter a word.

Voices on the sand,
speak softly, speak loudly
Voices on the sand,
do I perceive you try to say
oh! I heard you then, OK!
I listen then, I listen now.

Voices on the sand,
homeward goes a hundred but one
Voices on the sand,
I listen like the fool I am
yes! I go, but you won't tell
why you hide deep in your shell.

Love
Gladys Caraballo
Love is like a blooming flower
In an open field
A flower that will make you feel good
When you're so, so sad.
Love is one's eternal hope in life to find.
Love is a
Miracle . . .

My Guardian Whispers
Paula Hawkins
You whisper in my ear, that you are still around
Although you cannot speak, your love makes this sound
A breeze through a door that is tightly locked
A photo falls that wasn't touched or knocked
A faint light shining in a room pitch black
Somebody following me, back to back
This presence I can feel deep down in my heart
You have been at my side, ever since you did depart
Speaking to me, talking to me although I cannot hear
Saying not to worry, that you'll always be near
I cannot see you, or hear you, or feel your touch
All of these things I miss very much
You are the breeze in the room, when all is calm
You are the person who is softly touching my arm
You are the rain, when all around is dry
You sit and comfort me when I break down and cry
The person who whispers the kind words is you
You have been my guardian, my whole life through
You are the stars, the moon and the sun
You are the greatest, the only one
You are in everything the light does show
And when night time comes you do not go
You shine brightly like a new born star
Sparkling clear, like the star that you are
My Guardian, My Brother

Untitled
Kelly–Ann Waugh
Our hearts are
together
Forever you and I.
Bounded by
love,
As darkness
to a cold winter's
night.
We have reached
the heights of heaven,
Moonbeams
glare
forever
from within our
eyes,
Fire burns a
fuel of passion.
The amount,
our hearts
decide.
When ghosts
of last,
our passions,
go flying
in the sky
singing free,
"Our love will never die."

Spring
Elizabeth Hackworth
I saw them two days ago
Heading upwards towards the sky
Soft, white snowdrops.
I saw the sun too
And not just for a fleeting moment
A whole morning of warmth
I went out without my coat

Old Flame Of Mine
Karen L. Morgan
Old flame of mine, you still burn bright
I wonder where you are
I wonder if you're alright
Can you be far?

I think of you even now
Though many years have gone by
Could it have turned out for us, I wonder how
I listened to logic instead of my heart, but why?

If fate was to grant us one more chance
Would we be smart enough to grab it?
Sometimes we only get but one chance
Oh, if love only came in a kit

Yes, "we" were a long time ago
But we were together for a while
I long for you so, I miss your smile

Old flame of mine, I hope you'll always burn bright
My memories of you always comfort me
When things seem darkest, your flame shines bright
For memories are all I have of you, don't you see

Old flame of mine, you're so dear to me

Look And You Shall Seek
Coreen Keech
Life can be such a funny game, always taking
and giving back pain. Never stopping to realize if
someone is really hurt or cares if they die.

Years have passed and the days roll by, with nothing
to show but a tear in my eye. So down on my
knees I called out his name "Oh Lord have you
forgotten me? Is my life all in vain?"

He came to me in a vision so calm and gently
And showed me, myself in a moment of grief.
There right beside me in all his glory he stood.
Wanting to comfort and dry up my tears, he knew
All my sorrows, he knew all my fears.

My spirit was renewed with a new found peace.
Nothing in this life can turn me from this
glorious belief. "Jesus" he was the Savior who
appeared to me. He was here all along, I simply
was just to blind to see.

Life is now a game no more, my heart is filled
with hope for what he has in store. Eternal life
of love, peace and joy has been promised to me
My debt he paid on Calvary.

Amen

Winter Morning
Malachy Gribbin

Before I am fully awake I sense your presence
There is a stronger silence on these mornings
A calmness
And even in adulthood I still rush from bed to greet you
Your whiteness strains my eyes more than other mornings
"It Snowed" I say in a voice for each to hear
And smile as childhood memories flutter in my head

Nicola
R. Simpson

You're the oldest, I love you so,
You're the one who's special and this you know
When you were a kid, I was always there,
Now being without you is so hard to bare.

There's a million things I'd like to say,
But it's hard for me whilst I'm away.
When I come home, I'll show to you.
All the love from the dad, that you once knew,

But for now Nicola you stay strong,
Just let the months roll on and on,
And one day soon I will be home,
Then never again will we be alone,

From when you were small, we used to talk,
I'd tell you anything we'd laugh and we'd joke,
You were always there, what–ever I'd done,
I love you Nicola, like I love your Mum,

I wanted so much, good things for you all,
I was never a man to sit on the dole,
I made mistakes, but all men do,
But I always loved you and you know
that's true xxx.

A Diamond Is Forever
Mary Dinsdale

I would like the people of the world to
know that a diamond can be forever.

A Diamond for me. A Diamond for you
When we first meet. I knew it was for true.
When we fell in love. I knew that we
were meant to be together from the Heavens above

We went for a walk down Lovers Lane. We stopped
and stared at each other. But suddenly it
started to rain. The rain stopped not long
after. Soon we were fitted with great joy and laughter.
Then the sun begin to shine down upon
the beautiful flowers trees and everything. It
was then when he presented with a diamond ring.

As we walked past Robin's Bay – I said
to him. Thank you for the Beautiful day.

He turned and looked at me with a big grin
He said that he got a job. The very next day
digging for gold. But instead he got a very nasty cold.
When he come home. He started to shiver. I
said to him. Why don't you join me in this
candle–lit–dinner. Then he give me a little
box all rapped up in silver. When I looked
inside. It was a diamond forever.

Teenager Un–Loved?
Neil Scott

I dream of love through my teenage years,
The kind of love I fear I will never find,
I long for love, when I am only young,
Am I longing for the stories to tell,
Am I searching for love out of jealousy?

Friends tell of their tales,
Whether I believe them or not,
I still wish for my turn in the game of love,
My love would not be a game,
My love is real.

Am I critical?
Am I naive?
Or being unfair,
All I wish for is my teenage love,
To complete my teenage wishes.

I write these poems,
To anyone who will read without judgement,
Of style or personal character,
I have these feelings through no fault of my own,
Sat for evenings on end recording my thoughts,
For whom?
Me.

Windstorm
Jeannette Cronin

Power and excitement embraced with fear
In one swift moment strong trees fall
Lie prostrate on the very grass they shaded.
The wind with ferocious and blatant glee
Destroys the tribute of the sun and soil.
Is it the laughter of an unconquered king
Or Mother Nature in an angry mood?

I Have Seen Dragons And Other Wonderful Things
Denis K. Hirayama

When I was a young person I used to lie on my back and look at the clouds.

A young person's imaginations is pure and unspoiled. There is neither black nor white.

You will never see black or white in a rainbow.
Black or white, yes or no, these are not the thoughts of a young person.

When I was young, I saw dragons and other wonderful things in the clouds.
No limitations, just my vivid imagination.

Answer like, "I'm not sure", "I don't know," or "just maybe", were more common for me and my friends. I guess we all saw dragons at one time or another...I think that was nice.

Now that I am a adult, I still see clouds. They are usually black or white. When I ask if it's going to rain. The answer is usually yes or no. I asked
  a
friend recently if he believed in dragons. He said, "no." I was kind of hoping
he would have said, "I'm not sure", "I don't know" or "just maybe." "yes, I have." "I have seen them with my own two eyes".

Now that I am a grandfather, my grandson ask me if there are dragons out there. I look into his young eyes and say, "of course there are, and there are also knights in shining armor to protect us and our castles." My grandson grabs my hand and smiles...

Heavenly Intervention
Jane Ulrich
The angels must have listened
Though I didn't say a word,
My aching was a silent ache
But the angels always heard.

One day they must have gathered
And in thought became as one,
Then the angels did in heaven
What on earth could not be done:

They looked at me through angel eyes
They looked inside my soul,
They looked – but only found a half
And a longing to be whole.

They looked and soon discovered
What no one else could know,
And they said, "We must give back to her
What she lost so long ago."

So they, in all their wisdom
Knew exactly what to do,
The angels gave me back my heart...
The angels gave me you.

Dedication: To my Todd...

Mid Summers Eve
Susan Kay Spohn
Oh! How wonderful it is to sit upon the porch on a hot summers eve
Waiting patiently for a cool night breeze
As I sip ice tea from my glass I watch fire flies rise from the grass
While moonbeams flow to the ground I listen to the frogs croaking
All around oh! How wonderful it is a mid summers eve.

Dedication: William, my husband, my friend

I Want You To Be My Daughter
Robin Schwarz
I married your Dad ten years ago,
Then your age was about ten or so.
You needed a Mom then, I didn't know,
I want you to be my daughter.

So much has happened, I don't know why,
Your wings were clipped before you could fly,
If I were your Mom I would have seen you cry,
I want you to be my daughter.

I will never understand why she went with him.
A daughter is such an important friend.
I promise I will be there to the very end,
I want you to be my daughter.

You are so strong, and I am so proud,
You're free to ride high on that cloud,
I want to yell and scream out loud,
I want you to be my daughter.

The past is over, not much I can do,
I can't change it, but I will help you through
The future ahead, we will have that's new,
Knowing you'll be my daughter.

Dedication: Jennifer, thanks for saying "yes"

Reflections
Margaret D. Burcham
Does everyone hold in the heart
A special spot reserved for that one young love?
It may have lasted a short while –
It may have lasted longer.
But, sometimes, the heart opens
And, for a moment, the memory returns –
Beautiful! Treasured!
Doesn't everyone?

Being Sick
Joyce P. Arnold
Being sick is not much fun.
You can't go play, you can't go run.
In the bed you have to stay, why won't this germ just go away?

Being sick is not much fun.
You can't go outside and get some sun.
In your room there are books and toys, but they don't bring you lots of
  joys.

Being sick is not much fun.
Your body feels like it weighs a ton.
A bowl of soup you must first eat and then your Mother brings you a treat.

Being sick is not much fun.
But you feel better when it's all done.
The medicine you had to take, the fever's gone that made you ache.

Being sick was not much fun.
But now I can jump and now I can run.
No more stuck up in my room, no more sadness, no more gloom.

Being well is really GREAT!!!
I'm going fishing, I just can't wait.
Going to ride my bike, play ball and skate.
Gee! Being well is really GREAT...

Memories
Robert Wilson, Jr.
On cobalt seas– of memories
I drift without a care,
and reminisce the tender kiss
that made my soul aware–

I cast my eyes– unto the skies
and there I see your face,
in softest hues of velvet blues
where clouds are not a trace–

The smile I see– reminding me
of all my childhood dreams,
to rise above and share a love
much sweeter than it seems–

your eyes touch mine– the sweetest wine
my soul could ever taste
I long to drink and dare not think
one drop should go to waste,

The light of grace– above your face
turns sunlight into stars
and there I see where I should be
asleep within your arms.

Dedication: My true love, Tommie Tears

Tears
Renee R. Ming
It falls from the source
And rolls down the cheek.
A salt–filled drop of life.

It carries the pain released from within.
A mortals plead for

Love.

A Stranger To War
Martha–Claire Denniff
Orange people, masked people, armed people, dead people,
Takes all kinds to make up a war,
Yet I can't comprehend, what the fighting is for.
Surely there's a way for the anger to stop?
A tear falls, a stranger watches it drop.

Wanting freedom to walk, sounds simple to innocent ears,
But it is so much more than it sounds,
It's the hatred, anger and violence that's bound.
I can only watch in disbelief and cry,
A smile fades, the stranger watches it die.

I want to have peace, like so many others in this world,
Yet my reasons so different to theirs,
Thoughts of him are with me night and day, always in my prayers.
A loved one so far from me, I am left only memories of you,
A heart breaks and the stranger watches it tear in two.

It maybe too late to pray for peace,
As the world is already crying.
Why does it cry? Innocence calls out.
But to this there was no answer as the world always cries.
The stranger turns his back and sighs.

Dedication: Scott – always on my mind

Lessons Well Learned
Edgar M. Greenwood
While growing up on a farm in southern Arkansas
Where the wilderness was a fascination to me
There was so much to learn about nature and it's surrounding
And there was so much there to see.

I learned from my parents, "nothing comes easy."
Hard work and responsibility will bring me respect
Honesty and fairness will make me a better person
And I will never become a reject.

I also learned the importance of a family
We learned to respect each other's rights
And there was someone ready to settle all arguments
Before they developed into a fight.

We learned lessons in reasoning and how to make peace
And to listen to others point of view
And when we lay down to rest after a long day's work
There was nothing left to do.

The farm was like a training center for all of us
For there were so many lessons to learn
But despite the fact I grew up and left home
My greatest desire was to return.

Dedication: My understanding wife, Erma

Untitled
Eleanor M. Vogel
Be happy you're living
That's my philosophy
Always loving and giving
That's the way to be
I'll make you happy
And others too
The world will be a better place
for you and you and you.

Butterflies Are Free
Karen Jarmon
Some days I feel like
I want to live the life
of a Butterfly

Starting out so secure
Wrapped up inside
the nice protective shell
of a Cocoon

Growing, maturing until
Nature decides
It is time
To Awaken
from hibernation

Spiritually Awaken
Spread my wings and
Take Flight...
BE FREE!!

Come ALIVE with Color
So BRIGHT AND BEAUTIFUL
Become one with Nature...

Fly Away and BE FREE!!

Love Of My Life
Carolene J. Lund
I love a sunny day,
the cheeriness it displays,
accompanied by warmth and brightness.

I also love a day,
when the sky is filled with
beautiful white, soft fluffy clouds.

I think of my husband when I see them.
Flying across the Atlantic Ocean they were so gorgeous,
it seemed he was just outside the window going with me.

I felt so close to him, hardly remembering he was cargo in a box.
The comfort of knowing God was in the clouds as well,
was very sustaining to me as I flew alone.

A little chorus kept going through my head,
at times I was even humming;
"In moments like this, I sing out a song,
I sing out a love song to you."

It was special to realize how much God loves me;
how thankful I was to have a love like my husband.

I cannot walk and see the clouds,
without a consuming realization of the "love of my life".

My Dream

Sarah A. Carmon

My Dream is this
Our last Kiss
The final embrace
I see your face
I look into your eyes
I am lost in our sighs
Of Joy, the thrill of our love
Sealed by heaven above.

Childhood Days

Marion Holt

Thinking back over days gone by
When the sun up in the sky
Shining down on birds in flight
Filled our hearts with delight

In the park where we went to play
You could be princess for a day
With daisy chains we made and wore
Who could ever ask for more

What a thrill it was to ride
On a tramcar by mother's side
Especially when we went upstairs
To ride out in the open air

Steam trains, that took us on our way
To the seaside to spend the day
With our rusty bucket and spade
The huge sand castles that we made

When the ice–cream man came to call
That was the best treat of all
Get a cornet and lick it all round
To stop any drops falling on the
ground.

When I Came To Your Door Today

Nancyann Laroche

When I came to your door today...
I heard a whisper say,
"Can I help you if I may?
Come on in...Have a seat...
Take all the time you need.

You'll talk and I'll listen,
When you're done I'll give
my opinion.

You are the seed, and I'm the sun.
When you came to the door,
that's when it really begun.

You showed me that you made
the right choice,
When you came to the door.
Because you wouldn't done that before.

You remember what I told you,
And I'll see you tomorrow.
Only if it's a word, or even a laugh.
But mind you, I'm not four miles.
But just a warm smile."

Dedication: Chesbrough and Richford Elementary Family

Rain

Kim Collings

Rain Rain patting at the windowpane
How very sad you seem
Dropping Drops filling pots and adding to the stream
Growing flowing ever bigger
Until you reach the mighty river
Then rushing down to meet the sea

Dedication: The memory of Charles S. Collings

Care About The Earth

Carrie Catterall

Why do so many of us not care?
Why can't we see all things on
Earth have meanings?
We were placed on earth to get
along,
But what do we do? DESTROY!

There were once beautiful rainforest.
Covering the earth,
Magnificent creatures creating new
birth,
The skies were so clear,
You could almost see your face,
But then all of a sudden,
There was a start to a new race.

The forests disappeared,
The creatures became extinct,
The skies became covered in muck,
So why should we care?
Forget we were there,
But don't look back and regret,
Soon the earth will be gone,
And it will be too late,
Don't wait take action NOW!

Shadows Of Memory

Glenda K. Phipps

The trim of an apron, the hue of her hair, the feel of her fingers, I was
there.
The sound of my shoes across the floor, the hint of breeze from her back
door.
With colors of pink upon the walls, in hazy mirrors, was me I saw.
Through tricks of light I played the day, I hear the laughter from far
away.
I smell the scent of fruit–filled draws, I know the place, I was there.
Her table is full with bowls of fluff and clouds of steam, I should not
touch.
Outside I see awaiting me, the basket I take when flowers were, free.
I gather the ones with pink and white, and take them to her with great
surprise.
My eyes awake, the sun a flare, the touch of her hand, I know, I was
there.
The days we shared belonged to me, her joy and heart others would see.
My time with her is wrapped in warmth, with rivers of color, gold and
true...
I see the picture I hold in my hands, I touch the face of grandmother
fair.
The image I see in shadows below, her hand in mine and smiles on both.
With walls of pink and draws around, I hear the voice, I hear the sounds.
When tears were wiped and love was needed, it was you I saw, you were
there.

Dedication: The Conley and Phipps families

Love
Sandra Minnie
Love is a four letter word
it covers lots of ground
it is a might powerful word
as it travels the world around
it shows many feelings
of peace and joy and hurt
for such a little word
it's filled with lots of worth

Clouds
Robert John Charlton
I'm lying in a field on a bright sunny morn, watching the clouds
And shapes that they form, some are white fluffy, others grey and
vast, making me feel small in contrast.

I could lay here forever in the bright warmth of the sun,
Watching the clouds as they drift along.

I notice in the distance the clouds turning black, bad weather
They promise there's no turning back.

They're rumbling towards me at a frightening pace, as though
The light and darkness are set in a race, the light is winning
But the darkness is strong, and gaining its grip as the day
Pushes on.

Soon the dark clouds like a blanket of night, will rob the sun
Of its wonderful light, and when the darkness is whole and
Complete, it will send down the rains for God's gardens to drink.

My day will be ended no more dreaming in the sun, but I am not
Sad, no cause there's more to come, soon there'll be a rainbow
And the rains they will end, then again in the sun I will lay in
The grass, and watch as the clouds drift slowly past.

Dedication: Thanks Dad, for your encouragement

Jesus Has A Tag A Long
Marie Williams
Jesus has a "Tag A Long" that walks
In and out with Him,
A shadow of the man
That's me.

He travels up and down
And all over the land.
When the sun shines brightly,
He says come..."Tag A Long" with me.

He knows every crook and cranny
Where sinners like to go.
He despises their sinful ways,
But has mercy for their soul.

Come to "Jesus" through the cross,
He shed his blood for thee,
So won't you come
And be a "Tag A Long" with Him?

There is no other place
I'd like to be
Then to be a "Tag A Long" for Jesus,
But I would like your company.

Dedication: My children, grandchildren and friends

A Winter Dream
Kate Lee
The frosty air feels so fine,
It sends a shiver down my spine.
The cold upon my cheeks and nose,
Sends a tingle to my toes.
As I wander in the snow—filled day,
I hope the snow is here to stay.
And all my dreams have been surpassed,
'Cuz winter has arrived...at last!

Boundaries
Liza Quinn
Be oh so careful with this heart
Its been strongly protected and now belongs to you
Its universe so sheltered from the depths of pain
Be oh so careful with this heart
It gives itself completely from the start

Be oh so careful with this love
It needs laughter and joy to mature and grow
It requires understanding, compassion and trust
Be oh so careful with this love
It needs to be held tightly with gentle gloves

Be oh so careful with this soul
It needs security, passion, and a soulmate so true
It will blossom with honesty and devotion
Be oh so careful with this soul
In your hands, its world you hold

Be oh so careful with all of me
My dreams and desires I will share with only you
Me emotional boundaries are written plainly above
Be oh so careful with all of me
Given the chance we can love for eternity

Dedication: H. B. ...Thanks

Happy Father's Day
Sandra Gaulke
On this Father's Day
May you never regret,
That your job with me
Is far from over yet.

Words like "I Love You"
May sometimes go unsaid,
But your guiding hand
Tells it all instead.

In the next year or so
As each day goes by,
Be patient with me
My wings I will try.

May our time together
Not be measured by length,
We'll be building memories
From which to gather strength.

I will always need you
Whether I'm young or old,
The blessing you've given me
Are too many to be told.

Dedication: Ernest Myers, never too late

Beautiful Tree
J. Skinner
You are so strong
Your branches free
Your leaves do flutter for all to see
The wind blows through you high and low
The sun shines through you all aglow
Then autumn comes then it's the snow
But I know you will still be free
Standing there for all to see

Streetlife: Is It Hard Or Okay
LaQuanda Riggins
The streets can be hard at times
When you have loved ones on your
Mind
Being hard all the time is not the way
Killing and stealing is how they get
through the day

Why is it so hard being on the streets
Because of the sick people you intend
to meet
Being hard will get you knocked out
Only because you opened your mouth

Being kind of nice is the way
Only if you intend to be okay
If you mind your business and get
to your place
You won't have to worry about people
In your face

Being okay is walking away from the
Crowd
Don't get in the situation or try to get loud
All you need to do is to go on your way
So the bullets that's shot will not be astray

I Have A Vision
Diane Case
Everyone is born with a God–given vision.
That vision brings fire to our souls.
You only will have one true vision or dream in a lifetime
Before that vision can come to life, we have to pray about

The prayer of your life's vision will always be there.
Go after it with all of your might.
Wait patiently, for He will anoint you,
to have your vision come true

Have a focused vision of what you want.
Be determined. God implants it, we decide it.
Announce it explain it with excitement.
Words carry power.

Develop a plan to succeed,
for a wise man looks ahead.
Have the skill and the right people around you.
Do not be negative or be around others who are.

Wise men don't walk with fools,
for they will only break you down.
Being around the right people
will enable you to accomplish your vision.
Dedication: My friend, the Holy Spirit

Lighthouse
Diane McCalmont
A lighthouse stands strong and proud,
Yet it stands alone.
It braves the storms to provide safety
To those who are lost.
Onlookers through time fall in love
With its steadfast power.
Yet still, in the dark of the night,
A lighthouse stands alone.

Lakeyia
Lonia M. Cook
I love you more than words can tell
Each and every day, I wish you well.
Always know how much I love you
Forever keep this in mind in everything you do.

Remember to put God first in your every day life
You will be surprised how much he can ease the strife.
God can make you a better person without and within
Just open up your heart and ask, He will forgive all your sins.

May you be successful in everything you do
With God's help, you will get through.
May your future be filled with joy and success
Give life the best you have to offer, God will do the rest.

There must be rain as well as sunshine
Mountains may often seem too high to climb.
Keep your hand in God's hand as you travel this road
Chin and head upward, He'll ease the load.

Treat everyone the way you want them to treat you
Because deep down within, you know this is the thing to do.
Ugliness is not a becoming trait
Prayer, love, kindness, faith and forgiveness will help you enter
the heavenly gate.

The Light
George A. Weston
There is a great love in me,
Deeper than the deepest sea.

To find someone which to give,
Is a hard life I must live.

It's been so long the hall is dark
The light is out the door is locked.

So follow me I'll light the way,
And unlock the door come what may.

I'd give my life for love so pure.
For without risk it's death for sure.

It's funny how just one word,
Can save or kill if it's heard.

Don't fall back we are almost there,
Yet I can see it in your stare.

You're not sure of what you want
So I continue my life long hunt.

I'll sit here and wait until when.
I light the way and start again.

Life Today
Amy Savage

Man's idea of life, was never meant
to be
The earth belongs to all of us, folk
like you and me.
We think it right to use the creature
to fill the rules we make
Who are all these people? who decision make
He really has no status, no better
than another
But always hiding in the clouds
The rough hand of big brother
But God created many rules of
which we cannot break
We shall live, and we shall die whatever
path we take
And when at last a life shall
end
No matter what we obtain in
life
No matter of our worth, God will
return us
To the soil and to the earth
To the people who are left, they too
will take the call
And it will be as if we had never lived at all.

Friends
Grace Ellen Kurth

True friends last forever,
losing touch they will never.
In their hearts they always share
feelings of trust, truth and fear.
Always remember, it won't be far,
just look up in the sky and wish on a star.

Dedication: Timothy Vincent Daleiden, my true friend

Homeward Bound Angels
Mary E. Lamie

Oh what a senseless thing!
People and loved ones in so much
pain
Loved ones gone in a flash!
They are "Homeward bound
angels at last."
Pray, don't lose faith, look to the
sky
Your love will go on forever,
you'll see!
Your angels, are in a truly better
place to be
God's littlest angels that were
in the day care there.
Oh they miss you so very much
but they are much happier now;
up in the heavens, but they still
care.
Homeward bound angels, at peace,
tears are no more, they all at rest.
Heroes on earth you are, you
have all done your best.
Your love remains and will not
fade away.

Dedication: The Oklahoma Bombing Victims

Infinity
Barbara Andrus

Infinity is timeless, as the ever—rolling sea.
The sands of time drift aimlessly, to find where they should be.
They stand as silent sentinels, protecting you and me.

And as they stand, so silent in their never—ending task,
They beckon through the ages
And call us from the stages of the world where we may pass.

The call...it is a song of life, a melody sublime,
Enriched by many harmonies
With ever—changing cadences of haunting, restless rhyme.

At times, the harmonies are harsh, and jarring to the soul.
Their rhythms racing helter—skelter, trying to find the goal.

But then...through all the noise, the stark cacophony, the maze...
There winds a tiny melody...a small intrusive courier
That speaks of better days.

This melody remembers when the earth was just begun,
The mystery, the moodiness, the rising of the sun.
It hears an infant's feeble cry...the ecstasy of love.
It strokes the soil with healing balm; It celebrates the poet's song;
It rights our worst—imagined wrong
And sets our path, directs, displays the time that's yet to come.

Firecrackers
Joanna Nightingale

Firecrackers are special because they
light up the sky with beautiful colors.
A firecracker can come in all shapes
and sizes. When it is lit it flies to the
sky and bursts into a rainbow of
colors. It soars up to the stars
then cracks with a bang. And
that is why firecrackers are so special.

My Dream
Velma Robertson Klinger

I had a dream before I woke,
arrived in Heaven to find I was broke.

I said to St. Peter, "Please may I come in?"
He open the gate with a great big grin.

He said "Come in sister and take a look,
your faith in God was all it took."

I went for a walk in the garden of love,
heard the coo of a sweet turtle dove.

As I walked up the street of gold,
Oh! Such beauty can never be told.

Then a soft whisper as he called my name
My heart stood still, I was filled with shame.

I think of the many, who are lost in sin,
and I could tell them how to get in!

I said "Lord, grant me this plea before I awake,
let me hasten quickly to correct this mistake."

I'll tell how He died to save us from sin.
When we return, may we all come in.

The Woman's In Love
Ron M. Polikoff
You can tell by the way she smiles at him.
The woman's in love.

Look at the way she holds him.
The woman's in love.

See how she strokes his chin?
Caresses his brow?
The woman's in love.

He looks up at her and smiles.
He can feel it too.
The woman's in love.

She clutches him closer to her breast,
adjusting his bottle.
He feeds until he sleeps.
Content.
Happy.
His appetite sated.

She stares at her infant son, wipes his mouth
and smiles.

Yes. The woman's in love.

Untitled
Glenda Whittemore
Thank you Lord for this
glorious day,
The love and the joy that
You send our way.
The peace and tranquility,
the blessings untold.
The wonderful comforting
feel of Your hold.

Happy Birthday
Maureen Sanchez
Happy Birthday, Honey,
To the little man that I love.

You're a blessing in disguise,
a gift from up above,

Sent to me from Heaven,
to nurture, and to love.

I dedicate my life to you,
It comes so easy to me.

I'll watch you grow up,
and then I'll set you free.

Letting you know all along,
that mommy's love is there.

You need not ever worry,
because I'll always care,
for you my love, please always
know,
In my heart, I will never let you
go!

Dedication: Lil Jimmy, my love, my life

Tame
Marlo Gierczynski
Golden sun, leaves of grey, mystical shadow on death's path
Lofty
If I look at you will you cringe
Only in fear for the unknown

I'm thinking of this bird singing on a branch
And you, I want to feel you
What happens if it goes

Will this warrior finally be tamed
Or will all of the inside cover you in wrath
Do you want that, or the quiet bird

I want the road that my shadow takes
It's free and has no boundaries, no cares

Is there nothing in the center of light and dark?
Or is it everything, all existence?
In that case, why not take what is needed?

It's a spirit that cannot be tame
Nothing there to tame it with
No body, no feeling, no soul
Maybe a thought
Perhaps a sword

The Last Day Of School Has Come
Mary Taylor
The students are yelling and jumping and waving
Saying goodbye and sayonara and all.

The hugs and good wishes and the tears are coming
The books are flying, the big rush for the doors

For freedom is out there with no assignments to do.
The last day of school has come.

Beside Still Waters
Anita D. Abbott
Come my child
Sit at my feet
And we will have fellowship
Oh so sweet

Listen to the voice
Deep inside
While you come away
We will abide

Shut out the world
And the noise around
And have fellowship
With this love you've found

Many have searched
Running here and there
Not really knowing
It's not out there

The happiness you've found
Comes from deep within
When nothing else matters
But your love for him

Dedication: All who can comprehend

White Silent Moments
Mary E. Kerby

Our red tongues looked funny as we caught flakes of white,
frozen lace.
As flake after flake drifted silently down, I pretended each
icy touch was a promise.
A promise of time. Time to taste and feel and see
the joys of Christmas once more.

We were invincible at fifteen.
We wore this magic white together and it was Christmas!
but even Christmas could not stop the whispers.

My friend knew each flake differently than I.
I think she imagined each icy touch
A promise of memories frozen in time.

Memories more precious than the crystal snow that
painted our uplifted faces with delicate and timeless jewels.
As each flakes touched our tongues, she'd recall funny memories
So in that silent world we became frosty clowns
joking with white breath.
I laughed so hard I thought I'd die.

And she did. After Christmas, in a white silent moment
she was gone. We were fifteen and dreamers in white.
She is gone and I don't catch frozen lace anymore.

Poppies
Emily Victoria Lamb

Poppies poppies everywhere
the red petal from
the blood that makes me shudder everywhere.
I wonder why there had to be a First World
War
and all the others.
But now the world is a better place.
I wonder how it happened in the first place.

Thank You Lord For Mom And Dad
Pauline Davis

Thank you Lord that I was born
Many years ago, on an Autumn morn
To parents whom I hold so dear,
When in their love I knew no tear.

You gave me sisters whom I adore
And we share our love more and more
The brother you gave us, the eldest of all
A giant to us, so big and tall!

We each grew up and went our ways,
But never will we forget all the days
Mom and dad working so hard
To feed and clothe us...Thank you Lord!!

When I was only twenty—three
You called my dad to live with thee
And just two short years ago
My mom joined him through your open door.

Oh, how we miss them not being here
But Lord you know we hold them dear
And even though my heart is broken and sad
Thank you Lord for a Loving mom and dad.

Dedication: Mom and dad, with love

To The Chaplain
Ida Rogers

From: A Volunteer
I walked down the long dark corridor
to the Chapel where candles glow.
And a man of God stands waiting
to welcome me at the door.

I have just started my morning.
He has just finished his watch.
For he is the Hospital Chaplain,
who watches through the long dark night.

And God watches with the chaplain,
the Sculptor he has called to repair.
To patch up the hurts and the scars
on the Souls of men with his Prayers.

He meets sin with a challenge,
to call me from their fate.
By patient creative effort,
a new life before it's too late.

And who is this Hospital Chaplain,
with talents so rich and rare?
Oh, he is only God's Servant,
serving humbly everywhere.

Untitled
Wanda Means

I wish you happiness now...
When the trees are green,
And the stairs aren't too steep
And everything seems easy.
But mostly I wish you happiness later...
When the trees turn brown,
And the stairs seem like mountain
And everything isn't too easy.

Ode To A Ford Service Manager
L. H. Bishop

My prior complaints have reached fruition
Something has to be done with my truck's transmission.

The mechanical parts are breaking down
On rural roads or often in town.

It slips and shudders as it goes thru gears
Acting much older than its actual years.

It tries so hard the right speed to find
But it just can't seem to make up its mind.

On the interstate highways so flat and level
It comes to cruise speed and runs like the devil.

The engine performs likes a year old pup
Too bad the transmission can't keep up.

It vibrates and chatters while rolling along
With occasional grabs to prove something's wrong.

So please Mister Servicemen, hear my plaintiff plea
And correct, while we're still under warrantee.

This poem now serves as your written commission
Whatever it takes—please fix the transmission

Little Bird
Pamela L. Drake

I set you free,
Little Bird.

From your nest,
lovingly I lifted you
and set you free.

No longer will your song
fill the emptiness.
No longer will you nestle
in the bosom of your home.

I set you free,
Little Bird.

You stopped
and questioned my actions
then understood the pain
of losing you.

I set you free,
Little Bird.

Because he asked me to,
I set you free.

Christmas Time Is Here
Connie Anderson

Christmas time is here
Things are bad all over
but we'll have lots of cheer
Christ was born that starry
night to give us hope and
love and this Christmas
season He'll be watching
from above.

Quantum Regression
Geraldine Springston

Today my heartstrings beckoned me back
To my nearly forgotten homestead.
I just had to see my youth home shack,
Though all former owners are long since dead.

Our dear old log cabin that Grandpa had built
Was only a fond memory of where it had stood,
But jonquils still bloomed near ashes and silt
And our old farm was covered by forest and wood.

I stood reminiscing as the tears started flowing
Knowing that my youth could not return to me,
And regretted the years of not knowing
How precious memories would come to be.

I mentally pictured my mother and dad
As they had sat on the porch where it once had stood,
Resting from hard labors when times were bad,
Giving thanks for all the things that were good.

Then I glanced to the west, and to my surprise
Our old lilac bush still bloomed faithfully,
While Mom's beloved weeping willow had tripled in size.
Now weeping not for loved ones gone on, but weeping for me.

Dedication: My children, Harvey, Jeff and Mona

A Child's Nightmare
Timothy M. Albertson

Shattered Shutters
Clutter
On the weather–warped house.
The bottle hits the lips.
The lightning
Flared.
The stairs
Creaked.
The shadow of the old maple
Lunged forward.
The door slammed open
The hideous Monster appeared
Tearing my clothes,
Fists flying,
Tears falling,
Bodies moving,
Screaming,
Pain.
When I awoke
Bruises on my face.
Sirens blared,
Handcuffs clicked.
My father was the Monster
It was not a nightmare
But it was now over

Fantasy
Heather Kinsey

If in dreams
we're heaven's light,
Smeared across
the frosty night,
I'd wake and wonder
where I've been,
To return to the moment,
living in sin.

Main Street U.S.A.
Mildred Birdsall

I'm fading away, don't let me go,
I need refurbishing to help me grow.

Rebuild my facings and polish my bricks,
Hang new lights, or clean the wicks.

You can see that I'm gathering dust,
Some run down buildings and some rust.

Repave my streets, and the side–walk,
Where people come together and talk.

Will you save me from rotting away,
And save me from the shambles of decay?

Make the repairs where they are needed,
Keep my grounds clean and neatly weeded?

By giving my front a new face lift,
You'll be giving yourself and me a gift.

Please! help my image for future years,
Bringing more laughter instead of tears.

Don't let me crumble and fade away,
Our heritage will be gone and missed someday.

Moonlight
Brian P. Timmons

The silvery moon casts shadows of beauty.
The full opened face show scenes of serenity.
The reflection of light pierces my eyes.
I look for the future of my wonderful life.
The warmth it gives is felt in my heart.
At times it grows only in parts.
Once a night gaze up to the sky,
To feel the warm love this great orb provides.

Big Enough
Wiley Martin

She wasn't a very big dog.
Nor was she even tough.
She was just a playful happy dog,
My little "Big enough".

She loved to play with tennis balls.
They were her favorite toy.
Of all the dogs we've ever had,
She was my pride and joy.

Maybe the driver didn't see her
As she was standing there.
He didn't honk or even stop.
I guess he didn't care.

My little dog is gone now
And I find it sort of rough
I'll miss my friend – my buddy,
My little "Big enough".

If dogs really go to heaven
I hope that there will be
A little dog called "Big enough",
Waiting there for me.

Sing Me A Song
Cherylann Foster

Oh sing me a song from the grassy green blade,
as I lay on the carpet that heaven has made,
sing me a song of the gold glimm'ring light,
that bathes me so warmly,
and colors me bright.

Sing of the songs that I write just for thee,
of the dances I do, that no others can see,
of the breath that surrounds me, the earth in the air,
of the notes from my pipe, as I play sitting there.

Oh sing me a song, for this day soon will pass,
remember I'm fickle, my enjoyment too fast!
I'm wrapped in this sweetness, of sunshine and honey,
Oh glory, Oh greatness, my God is upon me!

Sing me a song from the grassy green blade,
of the wonders I live for before they all fade,
in the dusk, as the sun falls, the world then to sleep,
reciting my mem'ries,
that all I may keep.

Sing, sing, and I'll love you forever,
sing songs of this glory, and please leave me never,
at dusk, as the sun sinks, a pink grand finale,
to wait, in the grass, hoping night never finds me.

Love's Perfect Light
Ruth A. Parks

From out of love's light
Comes a gentle hand
That takes mine
And leads me on
Through a grave land
As dark as night
Leading me on
Into love's perfect light

Witness
Philip Cohen

The graceful oak blankets its shadow over the grassy plain.
A bluebird flutters beyond the out–stretched limbs of the elderly tree.
A feather slips away from the creature's soft body and hovers above
the greens, reds, browns, and gold's of the autumn–painted leaves.

The lifeless yet graceful, cottony snip swirls round the fall breezes.
It spirals downward, plummeting towards the pollen–infested earth.
It suddenly halts to a slow cascade; inch by inch, bit by bit, drop by
    drop,
until it cushions itself upon the cool comfort of grass and moss.

The majestic sun begins her journey to a bed of mountains and hills,
    crystallizing the sky
in stains of purple, wine, rust, and tangerine.
The moon glows faintly through the heaving sky and the world prepares for
serene moments in the eager awaiting darkness.

A star breaks through dusk, forcing the day to slumber and the night to
    rise from its sacred sleep.
The moon's light of pale gentleness sprays over the oak's lofty silhouette
    as another day ends.

Again the cycle is completed; the winds have ceased.
The great tree proudly stands tall as a witness of time.

New Beginning
Joanne Dalziel

I remember September, when I began at A.C.E. I really didn't think I
    could learn and keep up the steady pace.

I was quiet, scared, and shy. I felt like a lost puppy with no place to
    hide.
But in my heart, I knew I could learn with the help of the teachers and
    their concern.

It took a little time, and they got to know me, and I got to know them.
All the teachers from the grad section were there for me, whenever
    I needed a friend.

They reassured me of my need to learn, and put it at the forefront of my
mind. The darkness that I lived with disappeared and I was glad to leave
    it behind.

A new beginning was happening, and I just wanted to shout everything I
learned out loud.
The struggling has stopped and I'm feeling extremely proud.

I can't express my feeling that are all bundled up inside. I had no idea
that learning could fill a person full of pride.

All my teachers, Ward, Don, James, and Deane deserve to be
commended. They played a big role in my life and I am sorry
this year has ended.

My Little Angel

Ruth Stavely

Today I was watching my lovely granddaughter.
One might think she was made–to–order.
Her lovely brown hair and beautiful smile
Along with those eyes make life worthwhile.
She's so innocent and playful at the age of four
One can't help wonder what her life has in store.
As she grows through the years to whatever age,
I wish lots of success and happiness to my darling Paige

Patched Pants

Diane R. Simon

Out of love, she bought him a pair of pants,
Soon his favorite, he wore them every chance.
Indoors, outdoors, everywhere he'd stroll,
With all that wearing, life took its toll.

She kept washing them to keep them clean,
Then right back on him is what she'd seen.
After awhile the knee wore through,
They wondered together what to do.

Should they or shouldn't they repair the hole?
They were concerned if it'd last life's role.
Remembering how nice they were when new,
Investing in them seemed the thing to do.

Deciding to repair topped throwing them out,
A patch was bought and worked round about.
Both took better care of that old pair of pants,
She laundered on gentle, he'd wear them by chance.

Now each adhered to their original oath,
And the pants are still being cared for by both.
They discovered a good patch upon the knee
Can last a pair of pants till eternity.

Have You

Sheila M. Smith

Have you ever heard the willow weep...
for all the lives buried at her feet?
or have you listened to the river cry...
for all the souls it holds inside?
or maybe you've watched a storm roll in
and shuddered at the anger in the lightning's din.

Have you ever sat, watching a friend and
felt the walls they've built within?
Have you ever heard a final breath
then wept gratefully that at last came death?
or may be you've watched the world go by
no one knowing you've died inside.

Have you ever listened to the lonely laughter
in a room full of people, meaningless chatter.
Or maybe you've wished you could sail away
to be born again, a different time or day
and have you ever wished you could ease the pain
wash it away, with a gentle rain.

Have you ever given a smile, a hug, or just a soft
word? Planted a seed of salvation, quiet as a bird
Have you, hmmm, have you?

Dedication: Angels on earth and Gramma B.

Light The Way

Daniel Cowle

I'm in a dark cave
Living in fear
Pain and sorrow
Peace
Please
Let me see
Light the way
Haven't seen the way out

I Dialed You In Heaven

Eileen Lawrence

My Daddy's gone and I know where.
He's up in Heaven, my Mommy said he's there.
I love you Daddy and miss you, too.
I'll call God long distance, just to talk to you.

I dialed you in Heaven and nobody was there.
I wonder what was wrong up there.
I know God is really busy, Mommy says, he's everywhere.
Please God, tell my Daddy I'm calling him up there.

I dialed you in Heaven, the phone didn't ring.
I told my Mommy it's the strangest thing.
I dialed real careful, just like Mommy said.
Nobody answered, maybe God is tired and everyone's in bed.
It's alright Daddy, Mommy explained it to me.

I can't call you, but you can call me.
If God wants me and you want to call.
Dial us direct, and Mommy will accept the call.
I can't call you again, Mommy says that's a no, no.
But I'll think of you always, wherever I go.

Me and Dolly will sleep real tight.
I LOVE YOU DADDY, and tell God good night.

A Special Gift From Heaven

Joyce Malaske

No words can describe the love of a mother
No matter what your baby looks like, there is no other
More beautiful than your darling newborn baby
What a joy and someday she will be a little lady.

This one and a half year younger sister of mine
How beautiful, how precious, and how mom's eyes did shine.
It didn't matter that she had a blank look and did not smile
Mom said "she is just a little different but she will catch on after a
      while".

Down's Syndrome was what several doctors said
To Mom, that did not matter, she loved baby Patty, who was asleep in her
      bed.
It took a very long time for Patty to learn how to walk
I am certain Mom wondered "would she ever learn to talk?"

When Patty started school, that was the only time Mom was overwrought
For her teachers kept saying "Patty just can never be taught".
Mom never did believe that to be true
"To never give in and never give up" that was our Mom's rule.

Now Mom is very frail and her age ninety four
Patty comes to the nursing home to visit weekly–sometimes more.
It is a joy to see them look at one another and just smile
I know that Mom still believes that "She will catch on after a while".

87

Prayer
Rachel Swanson
The sun slowly sets,
and I drift away.
I don't want to go,
yet I don't want to stay.
I know I am loved,
but they do not say.
I would like to go back,
so I sit here and pray.

Love
Cassie D. Wray
Love is such a beautiful thing
With nothing it can be compared

It is something everyone needs
and something which should be shared

Sometimes love can hurt and it
May break your heart in two

But love is also great cause
it helps you make it thru.

Without love the world would
be such a hateful place, we
couldn't bear to live.

That is why God gave us love,
to receive and also give

So for when the night comes
and you're wishing on the stars above.

Don't wish for fame or money
Wish for someone to love

The End
James Early
Picking up the pieces,
of a shattered heart,
I realize I was foolish,
to think we'd never be apart.
I stand and question myself,
but you've got the answers,
so I may never know why,
because the answers are yours.

Plucking out the petals,
of a wilted flower,
I always think of you,
every minute every hour.
A single row of footsteps,
as I let God carry me,
He knows what I should do,
I only hope you'll see.

Squeezing on the fingers,
of a confused girl,
I cry for a second,
remember how things were.
You shouldn't have let me go,
but it was up to you,
let God carry you too,
He knows what you should do.

The Search
Bobby Mullis
Grandfather said those are Irish bones in ye
So an American journeyed o'er the sea
To visit the place my ancestry would be
But research scripts revealed a surprise to me
It is English blood only that flows in thee!

Yet making new friends on the Isle emerald grand
I discovered 'tis my heart that's from Eire land

The Fear Of Loving
Linda Kemer
The fear of loving and being loved in return,
Can be such a sad feeling that it will make your
Heart burn.

The pain will fill your body right to the very core.
It's not like any other pain that you have known before.

It will cause you disbelief and doubts about those
You love.
It will also make you wonder about miracles that come
From above

It will stop you from reaching out and touching those
You need,
Because the fear of being hurt is such a dreadful pain
Indeed.

You cannot make decisions because you cannot move
Ahead.
It's hard to deal with the present because the past is
Not dead.

Yes, the fear of loving and being loved in return,
Can be such a sad feeling if we are not ready to learn.

4 Of A Kind
Damon E. Luke
Yeah, there are some similarities between us
but we rarely discuss.
Only, "In God We Trust".
When lacking, we fuss.

Yeah it must be wrong
for us to stay strong
when we didn't get along
because one didn't belong.

What about now,
on common ground,
not because we're brown
but for the love we drowned?

I remember you
and the other two.
When we used to "boo–hoo"
over the things we'd do.

Can't you see
it's supposed to be
one and three (four)
Luke Unity!!

Dedication: My loving siblings

88

Golden Yesterdays
Evelyn J. Daniels
Take your Golden Yesterdays
and, one by one —
string them up on a strand of crystal
to have them shine
in the Sun's bright light,
this, then — you hold in your heart
as a Sweet Melody
to help you remember.

Missing My Grandfather
Rossana E. McHugh
Purple sunsets in the summer sky,
Ice white color in the winter snow,
Jade green eyes that look upon me,
The dew wet droplets that fall upon
My face,
Looking beyond with a smile,
The orange leaves that twirl in
Circles,
Thinking of him,
Once upon a time once upon a place.
Together again with a heart full of
Joy...someday.

A lost rainbow waiting to be found,
Togetherness – a bonding of none,
Under an endless lit sky.
Breaking away.
Mending with a stitch.
A splash of memories,
Ancient, new, and everlasting –
Even when we reach the golden clouds
Of eternity. I miss you Nonno.

Dedication: My loving and devoted, Nonno

Time
Patricia L. Wilson
There is a time to go
There is a time to wait
A time to tune in, and another to tune out.

The biggest time of all is not to stop
Never stop giving up on someone,
No matter what.

Never wait for the best to arrive
Tune into your heart and feelings
Tune out those who only wait for trouble
But Never...Never
Stop helping and loving your fellow man
Give him a lift–a helping hand

The good feelings you'll get inside
is better than words could ever say
The little pleasures and comfort you give to someone else
Will give you greater pleasure, and comfort
from within
A debt will have been paid
Another,
Then another
Shall take the time to turn the tide.

Dedication: My best friend, my husband Richard

A Soldier's Anguish
Joan E. Hayes
As a soldier, part of me is forever at the foot of a hill
Memories surround my mind like a dark cave
Seeking lost comrades and friends, forever buried in their graves

Beyond control the past seems to continually haunt me
Although I want to run, I just can't escape
For was I lucky to return to the real world
Or where the others better off with their fate

Returning home I expected to be granted
A hero's welcome, a thank you second to none
But all that I was greeted with was silence, confusion and shame
For a war that society wished never happened
And fellow soldiers who felt empty and drained

As a soldier I have come to the conclusion
That war is various degrees of complexity for anyone
Who is not directly involved to understand

The fate of war reaches out beyond human boundaries
Touches those souls who actively participate
Leaves them forever mentally and physically changed
Stretches our focus and shakes our balance of the world
Leaving strands of character shaken and rearranged.

Seasons Of Life
Erica Sneeringer
I am like the leaves that die in Winter,
and are left behind.
To be alone, to disappear.
You are like the green buds that come in Spring,
to take the place of the dead.
They grow and grow and become new, alive leaves.
But they too must die and become what I am,
But I cannot come alive and become what you are.

A Child's Dream
Darlyn S. Murray
One night in the garden
I saw a strange sight
The fairies were dancing
In the pale moonlight

The flowers and the foliage
Seemed to sway in the breeze
As each tiny fairy
Danced around with ease

One little fellow sat
Upon a flower
He seemed to be staring
At a far–away star

I wanted to ask him
Why he wasn't merry
But was afraid if I spoke
No longer he'd tarry

And then, just when I'd begun
To believe what I saw
A curtain of darkness
Around me did fall!

Dedication: All who've shared my dreams

Rest
Bernice Pelles
O' Where is this place in Life
We travel up and down roads
Only we find heartache and strife
Money soon has no taste
Fame comes and leaves in a flash
The efforts become a waste
When we think we did our best
What will our marker read?
Will it be true or, the start of unrest?!

In My Mother's Kitchen
Martha J. Murphy
In my Mother's kitchen was a welcome mat
For any one to come for coffee or a chat
And in that room you could always find true
Food and love just waiting for me and you.

Her kitchen was filled with sounds of laughter
For you to take along with you thereafter
When you had gone away full and always sure
That no where else the smells so pure.

Her Kitchen not always so spic and span
For there usually was at least one stray pan
That sat along with the kettle on the range
Or you heard her put them away with a bang.

Her kitchen with all treasures was filled
Each Monday a letter to Grandma to write and seal
And at the table sometimes with a puzzle or book
Mother was in her Kitchen when you went for a look.

In My Mother's Kitchen was a table for only two
But there was always room for me and for you
She opened her heart just like her kitchen door
And all the ones she served she never kept score.

Under The Sea
Domitila R. Tablason
I like to be under the sea
Where school of fish can play with me,
I don't know if mermaids are true
I'll discover it so we'll know.

Colorful corals can be seen.
With sea urchins hiding between,
Green and brown sea weeds can be found
With sea anemones around.

We can hear friendly dolphins cry
As we watch them all passing by,
All of a sudden a big splash
By the whales like boat that is crash.

At the bottom as we go round
Are creatures dancing on the ground,
Octopus, squids and cuttle fish
With tentacles they can squeeze

How do you like to be with me
To spend our lives under the sea?
Tell me if you will not complain
We will be in a submarine.

Dedication: All my loved ones

Untitled
Bill Elden
What did I Know?
I was but 18, when
They told me of the
American dream
They failed to say.
Divorce – Downsizing
– Illness may get
in the way
What did I Know?

A Mother's Dream
Abigail Rodriques
Child born to be free
Free from problem
Free from needs
Born to enjoy life
Born to see what it's
Like to be free

Child born from friends
Friends that became lovers
Friends that gave themselves
To each other
Friends that swear to be
Together forever

A child grew up to be an adult
Adult that know responsibility
Adult that want to do right
Adult that want to help the world

But the child was naive
The child who was taught to be free
Free to think, free to choose
The adult realizes this isn't true
The child was born only to lose

Steel, Brass And Lead
Wilson P. Levron
A man once used a gun of steel, brass, and lead
He used it against other men who soon were dead

Those men used steel, brass, and lead
to try to take away life
And now they are dead
Life is worth more than steel, brass, and lead
Steel, brass, and lead are no use to a man that's dead

Steel, brass, and lead
Are immaterial things
They are nothing compared to the things
That life can bring

Happiness and love are two things
That life can bring
Happiness and love are worth more than steel, brass, and lead
Happiness and love are no use to a man that's dead

So when a gun does fit your palm
Use it with good judgement
Happiness and love are things that life can bring
And they, like steel, brass, and lead
Are no use to a man that's dead

Dedication: My wife, Diane Levron

Our Roots

Catherine Rose

No two people are ever the same,
When we were born we were given a name,
In our own home land or travelling afar,
It is so important to know who you are.

Your heritage be proud of and carry it on,
Don't be fooled in thinking you're wrong,
The way that you express the words you use,
They are "Our Roots", and no one should abuse.

Follow Your Heart

Alison Atwood

Don't tell me what you think I want to hear.
Don't tell me anything that's not straight from your heart.

I don't want to hear a line out of your pretty little lips.
I don't want to see the light of love in your eyes,
If it's only covering up for the thunder of your lies.

I want to feel the tenderness of your touch,
But not unless we're bounded by a truth that only you knew.

I want to give you all this love in my heart,
But I don't want to give it all up only to be left with a hollowness in my
heart.

Still don't tell me what I want to hear just so you don't have to face the
world alone.

We can face the world hand in hand if only I knew what you knew.

Don't ever stop these tears from falling down my face.
Don't try to wipe them away by a hand so swift.

But please just kiss my tear-stained cheeks once more,
And then do what you feel, in your heart, to be right.

The Lover's Plight

Marie Cormell

Alongside the babbling brook
my love and I were stood
Our vow to love and cherish forever,
We'd be as one always, together

I left for war against my will
and left her alone in the evening still
Her heart was broken her promise not
Those tearful eyes I have ne'er forgot.

Of the battle of bloodied men dying
Gun's rattle bombs shatter soldiers crying
My mind is racing my heart beats fast
Praying this war will soon be the past.

So far away from the babbling brook
from my love this was has took
With tears of sadness I say goodbye
Not from war, but pain would I die

And still the war goes on and on
I dream of my beloved one
the moonlight dancing in her hair
Not long now my love I will be there.

Dedication: Mom and Dad, with love

I Dream A World

Margaret Riley

I dream a world where man,
Knows how to take care of what little they have.
Where there was peace everywhere,
And there were no wars to tear a family apart.
I dream a world where everyone was created equal,
Where no one would think they were better than others,
And no one would kill someone for the fun of watching them die.
I dream a world of hopes, happiness, love, and peace.
Of such I dream our world!

Twins

Mark Dawson

While I think of you
And call softly your name
I know your thoughts are of me, too
And mine are just the same

We lay in tiny isolettes
Acrylic greenhouses they seem
In an ICU, separated
Where no one can hear you scream

Medically, politically, socially, legally
All decisions for us permeate
Each stare our way so blindly
While great costs we mitigate

But our thought processes ponder
Pulling you through as you did me
Never pausing to wonder
What twins we'll ever be

Several times you begged leave
But I gave all my strength to you
To fight, to struggle; until the final scene
When I chose to bow out, too.

The Uncompleted Tapestry

G. B. Browning

After a bereavement when the last word has been spoken
The tapestry is laid aside
The thread of life is broken

The growing pattern that evolved
Out of the worst and best
Can never be completed now unfinished it must rest

The hand that held the needle
Can no longer draw the strand
But somewhere on the other side a new design is planned

And you now left alone,
Must take the skeins of mingled hues
The crimsons and the violets
The scarlets and the blues

And start to work upon the tapestry
Not the same but different
And lovely it could be

With glowing tints of memory to give a brief relief
Like threads of fine embroidery
On the canvas of your grief.

Dedication: For Victor, now in heaven

The Chesapeake Bay
Dawn Doty
She is beautiful to the naked eye.
You can hear her come alive with her waters crashing
against the rocks.
You can see the life that lives in her and surrounds her.
But soon you will not be able to see the living things
or her beauty.
You won't be able to hear her come to life.
Because of abuse, we the people of this world are destroying
her beauty, life and sound. She is our Chesapeake Bay.

Autumn Song
Cheryl Walker
Autumn leaves are tumbling off trees
Swept upwards by a spirited breeze
Twirling madly in their flight—
To every observer, a dazzling sight!

Then MORE join the party in the sky
A rainbow of color meets the eye
Red, orange, yellow, a vivid gold
Some multicolored – extremely bold!

Now with a firm hold on the land
Painting the landscape with loving hand
And elegant strokes do beautify the trees
Autumn's portrait of perfection, nice as you please!

The heat of summer has faded away
Promising to return another day
Autumn's brilliance has burst upon us
Trumpeting its glory with plenty of fuss!

There is no lovelier sight than this –
The dance of colors with autumn's kiss
Take time to enjoy it while you're able
All too soon winter will be upon the table!

My Wife And Her Shoes
Richard Walter Burrell
She's got shoes in the attic and shoes in the shed
and two dozen pairs under our bed.
yet still she says "I need more shoes
perhaps you'll come and help me choose".

So I pick out a pair which are sturdy and fin
and notice the price—only nine–ninety–nine.

But says she. "They're not to my liking
they're no good for dancing, but are more for hiking."

I wait in the shop, it seems like a year,
while she tries on another pair.

I must give the sales lady her due
she's been back and forth with quite a few.
At last she finds a pair that will do;
they're no real tops and the toes poke through.

She takes them home but I knew in a week
she'll complain bitterly. "they hurt my feet."
For all the money she's wasted on shoes
could have easily taken us on a world cruise.

Women! What a peculiar breed.
I think I've married a centipede!

My Emotional Mayhem
Mark Smith
I have so many questions, I'd like to put to you.
I have so much confusion, Its ripping me in two.
I once had so much gladness, but now live only pain
I have this awful sadness that's driving me insane.

I can't foresee a future, with all this hurt I feel.
I can't imagine loving, the thought is just unreal!
I do not want another, For I can't forget you
My hopes, my thoughts, my everything, were all wrapped up in you.

The Ocean's Cry For Help
Stephanie A. Melley
The ocean remembers days gone past
When untouched beaches stretched for miles
Silken sands of primitive lands
heard long days of silence from a desolate isle

A synchronous aquarium
containing sea–life so exquisite
An unparalleled beauty
With diversity so vivid

Set on the ocean
far from civilized minds
Never knowing progress,
this destruction of mankind

For the broken reefs are crying out
and the ocean beds lie cluttered
This once thriving underworld environment
is left holding mostly damaged treasures

The choice is in the hands of all mankind
to protect the marine life and their home
for capturing renewed resplendence
deciding a future which is still unknown.

My Dearest Darling Mother
Monica Chambers
You doze beside the dying embers,
I watch you in their glow.
You look peaceful and contented...
But I wonder If that's so.

'Cause now and then you twist and turn,
On your cheek, are there some tears?
Is it a sad and heartfelt misery
That's been locked away for years?

Has a memory just unfolded,
Of a favourite song or rhyme?
Or perhaps a dear departed
Or a not so happy time.

If I could take the hurt away
And once more see your smiles
God knows that I'd do all I can...
Even walk a million miles.

So as I gaze upon your face.
I whisper "there's no other"
And I'll love you now and always...
"My Dearest Darling Mother"

Dedication: To Robert, "always and forever"

Untitled
Michelle Larsen
Looking down on you
Looking so cold
And there is nothing I can do
My heart torn apart
I don't know where to start
I know I will never fear
Cause you will always still be near
The things we had will
always be forever!

Future Reclaimed
Josephine Butler Young
The leaves came softly floating down,
Red, yellow, gold, and brown;
Mother nature, willing to set them free,
As if knowing what the future will be.

West wind helps persuade the leaves
To listen to the whisper of the breeze,
And show their colors of gold and red,
Spread as a blanket upon a bed.

West wind gives way to Old Man North,
As snow clouds break and send drifts forth;
It leaves the forest and all things quiet,
Things which were colorful are all now white.

The sun breaks forth, the storm has passed
Beneath the canopy, rest at last
Until the bright warm sun of spring
Brings new life, vitality and the rain.

A life passes, a new season at last
The sign of future and the past;
Again, revival, renewal, new dawn;
The miracle that the flow of life moves on.

The Drug Was Me
Barbara Wright
You made me love you with your seductive and venomous charm,
So why did I ever expect to escape, not damaged and unharmed.

A taste of your sweetness, with a flavor all its own,
Made it hard to partake and then leave you alone.
Enticing me cautiously; Tempting me slow;
Flirting subtly; Playing games with my soul.
Cunning and deceitful; Wanting more and more
In danger of an overdose; Losing control.

Gladly, I participated in this game you did play,
Giving you my permission to drain my life away.
My spirit now weakened, not much to say,
Just enough strength summoned, to talk with the Grim Reaper today.

Anything poisonous has the potential to be deadly,
But by grace, I escaped in the nick of time; Scared, trembling, and
    sweating.

It makes no sense for me to walk around blaming this all, on you, you see;
For we could not have had this dance of destruction,
Without my consenting totally.

So if anyone is to take the blame, and accept full responsibility,
I'd have to say addiction was the driving force.
But in all honesty THE DRUG WAS ME.

Rage
Sharon Rabideau Derr
Hostile, hammering hands,
pounding fists, pushing doors,
shaking walls, rattling window glass,
glazed features on frightened face as
nefarious neighbor raves relentlessly
seeking relief from restricted rage
held holy as childhood's
unchosen penance
for parental parsimony.

Poetry
Barbara A. Flynn
Poetry can bring to life
The color of a rose
Even words put down in Braille
Can make the blossom grow

It captivates the mind
With words of old and new
And brings about great memories
Of everything we do

Poetry doesn't always rhyme
But, then neither do our lives
It comes in shapes and sizes
Befitting our desires

But, if you can take a terrible day
And turn it into rhyme
Letters on a blank sheet of paper
Can have no better times

Love becomes much more intense
Humor more sublime
Even pain finds meaning
With poetry and wine

Her
Paula Denning
To be seen as the bad,
To be seen as the cheat,
To be seen as the wrong,
the dirt under their feet.

The one who's so stupid,
The one who tells lies,
The one who's not special,
Just the one who gets by.

The one to whom no respect is due,
The one nobody wants to know,
The one with no looks, brain, or soul,
The one whose indignities always on show.

Why not get to know her?
Why not see what's inside?
Why push her on over,
to the broken down ride?

If only they knew her,
her beauty, her youth,
If only they loved her,
then there would be truth.

Dedication: Those who love her

Prayer And Thank You
Margaret Gardner

The rainbow chases each drop of rain,
Sun sparkling on my window pane.
The hand of a friend is always near,
To help fill your life,
With love and good cheer.
May your hands be always—busy,
With many things to do,
Never let a day go by,
Without a prayer and thank you.

This Poem
Betty J. Keys

Nancy is a fine Christian lady and friend
Who knows I dabble in poetry every now and then
She saw your "call for entries" and clipped it out
Gave it to me and said, "now get your pen out",

Since I write by inspiration and not by whim
And it wasn't long before entries had to be in
I thought, what can I write about, oh inspiration come
In just a short while I had the words to this poem

I truly enjoy writing whenever I can
But I rarely get to unless something specials at hand
People, anniversaries and birthdays, to name a few
Are the kinds of poems that I mostly do.

This poem is special as well as unique
It's fresh off the press, so to speak
I created it solely for your competition
Would be nice to win at the contest's completion

Twenty lines or less your rules say
I'm always there, just two lines away
So, I'll close this poem with thanks to you
For allowing me to show what I can do.

Goodbye
Veronica Tett

Eighteen years since we first said 'Hi'
Just one year since we said 'Goodbye',
A long sad year of missing you
But yet my life must start anew.

I feel your presence every day,
You're in my heart still having your say,
I hear your purr and gentle miew
But yet my life must start anew.

I see your eyes that with one look,
Could always read me like a book,
You were my friend so faithful and true
But yet my life must start anew.

Inside me I feel this crushing pain,
Knowing I'll never touch you again,
My tears still flow when I think of you
But yet my life must start anew.

I know I have to let you go,
My very, very special Mo
And so for now, I'll say adieu
And yes, my life will start anew.

Dedication: Mo Mo, my Number One

Trapped
Sharon Viner

You have trapped me,
Entangled and twisted in your web,
There I'm left, waiting,
Waiting for you to feast upon me.

I live in hope of freedom,
Wishing I could escape this web,
But left dangling for your return,
Return, you never will.

Life, Then And Now
Evelyn M. Knouse

Oh, for the wonderful, happy, long ago days of childhood,
When life was simple, uncomplicated and carefree;
When you thought in terms of wonder and enjoyment,
And didn't suspect for a moment, it would not always be.

The learning years were so much fun,
Learning to count, saying the A B C'S, printing your name;
Each feat accomplished was no small gain,
Learning to live life was such a happy game.

The growing up years were so bewildering and exciting,
So many choices to make, so many things to do;
People, places and things now take over the day,
And the quiet, peaceful, unscheduled hours now are so few.

Each stage of life brings added and responsibilities,
Sometimes far outweighing all the happiness and good times;
The secret of living above a level of survival,
Is learning to adjust to changing modes and climes.

Life has been and always will be hectic and unpredictable,
But there's one unfailing truth you can be sure of;
God sent his Son into this cruel, sinful world,
To die for you and me to prove His abiding, unchanging love.

Ode To A Catalpa Tree
Deborah A. Runyan

Oh, catalpa tree!
You stand strong and steady through the years.
From season to season, the stories you could tell.

In the fall, dropping your leaves so gently to the ground,
My world started spinning, spinning 'round.
Raking your leaves would have been my joy . . .

But winter came.
Against the cold December days, we awaited word:
"BRAIN TUMOR" were the words I heard.
With the bustle of the season, I lie, awaiting my incision.

The knife came. So did deep, dark winter nights.

Then one March day the sun broke through . . .
You brandished leaves of green: greener and greenest.
I embraced a promise of hope: health, healthier and healthiest.

In your summer splendor orchid—like blossoms burst forth a beauty rare,
My life, restored, radiates love everywhere.

While time marches, marches on the seasons change; I change, too.
But for now, oh catalpa tree

We'll swing with new life . . . a life given back to me!

National Service – An Aspect
David Goar
Departing troopship gathering weigh,
Tearclouds hovering to waylay,
Bow dips deeper, wave on wave,
'Tween deck and harbour, wave and wave.

All seem to fade, we two are left,
On ship and shore, each one bereft,
In Winter gloom, receding, gone,
Letters later, — "Dear John".

Those Of The Wind
Vickie Fuller
I have known those who are like the wind, powerful and
destructive. They come into your life like the whirling wind of a
tornado, uprooting your life in a blink of an eye.

I have known those who are like the wind, soft and gentle. They
embrace the world around them, carrying the sweet smell of a
summer garden, cooling and soothing, such a wonderful delight.

I have known those who are like the wind, harsh and cruel. They
whip up the dust around them, stirring uneasiness or leaving you
frozen from their chill.

I have known those who are like the wind, playful and silly.
They dance thru the leaves or ruffle your hair, then lift a kite
higher into the sky.

I have known those who are like the wind, after they are gone,
all is musty, and the air hangs heavy. Your wish again for the
wind's arrival, not knowing how they come or what they will bring.

I have known those who are like the wind, you cannot control or
stop them. Unpredictable, they come and they go touching our
lives, sometimes changing it forever, and like the wind you can
feel them around you but can never really touch or hold them.

Mississippi — My Home
Janet L. Parr
I yearn to know Old Mississippi,
full of beautiful and enchanting sounds, sights, and scents.
I was born there,
greeted by the musical mist of her flowing shores.
She is like a sweet lady
who captures my imagination.
She is the Gulf of Mexico,
bathing her playful children in a salty embrace.

How I would love to sweep up her colorful shells
and bundle them in my dress.
Oh, to step into her cool waters, so gentle and calm,
while waving at the sea gulls hovering above.
I would delight to capture her great live oaks
as they extend their long moss covered arms to the ground.
She is the sweet smell of succulent magnolia,
delicate, creamy, and the size of my hand.

I would love to walk through her verdant forests in the evening,
when humidity drips crystal beads from leafy pitchers.
I hear the mockingbird cry out
in joyful serenade, a fond farewell.
He sends his cheerful song at evening.
thanking me for my homecoming.
"Come back again," says he,
and I keep it in my hope chest of memories.

From The Heart
Gladys M. Smith
I visited you when you were ill to assure you that I care.
I listen to the troubles on your mind the need we all should share
The task of cleaning was easy, as I hum a song or two.
I could hardly wait until I finished because I had a special gift for you.
The meal I prepared brought tears to your eyes but the smile was still
　　there too.
We prayed to the Lord for guidance because he knows what's best for you.
It is time to go now, tomorrow is another day.
May good health, love and blessings forever come your way.

Theater Of My Mind
Nicholas G. Shucet
No matter what God has in store for me
Perhaps, a sun that is hard to find,
I just know – I'll find a rainbow
In the theater of my mind.

When I think of friends and relations.
The thoughts are lovely and kind.
I place them in the role I like best,
In the theater of my mind.

Over the years many thespians
Came into my life to play a part
When a container was needed, to place the reel,
I let them use my heart.

Old age keeps stealing my memories,
Even the ones I kept confined.
Most come back in dreams that play
In the theater of my mind.

My long days of toil are over.
Its time for me to unwind.
Sit back, relax, and enjoy the memories
In the theater of my mind.

Rebirth
Chad Bradshaw
I have pain.
I have fear of having to live another year.

Time goes by
I refuse to die.

Because one day soon I will see the light.

Blind faith that's all I have
But one day that too will pass.

Another day
Another month
Another year
Another tear

All my fear shall go away, for tomorrow is a
Brand new day.

Life is new, void of fear

The hate is gone and no more tears.

Happiness and joy fills my heart

For I have been given a brand new start.

A Dream
Colleen Hansen
I awaken still caught in your warm embrace.
It is that time of uncertainty
When dreams and reality collide.
Was there a mention of fragrance?

You were closer than is ever physically possible.
Years have not dimmed any desire.
But reality does not allow such intimate time
Except in that collision of dreams and reality.

The Old Woman Of Carrigan County
Martina Farrah–Pugh
The stories told us she was a witch
And I wondered if it was true
She lived in a cabin in the hills
And in her pot was a witches brew

She cooked strange herbs and potions
Guaranteed to cure an ache or a pain
She could give you the strength of Samson
Or your energy she could drain

She wasn't ugly as a witch should be
Snow white hair flowed down her back
She wore lots of baubles and bangles
And some garlic in a brown cotton sack

She never frightened anyone
And wild animals loved her dear
When she sang the songs of the gospel
Her voice was angelic clear

This old woman of Carrigan county
Lived to be a hundred or more
And they talk of her still, as people will
Telling witches tales by the score

Our Wedding Prayer
Pat Hare
O Lord, on this our wedding day
Before the altar we do stand
Two hearts beating though as one
To face the future hand in hand

Amidst exchanging of sacred vows
Promises to honor and to love
Keep us ever mindful
That marriage is a gift from above

As side by side we journey life's pathway
Give us strength for all our tomorrows
Through sunshine, shadows, laughter, tears
Through our joys and through our sorrows

May our love grow stronger each passing day
As together we establish our home
We pray your blessings upon this union
For You are the cornerstone

We pledge our love and faithfulness
Throughout all eternity
Not to each other only
But always, Lord, to Thee.

Dedication: Brian and Christa Hare

Divorce
Michael Turner
The woman and man who once held hands
no longer see the light.
The thought of tearing themselves in half
just doesn't seem very right.
The reality of breaking up scares them
both to death.
Chilling their blood.
Stopping their hearts.
Taking their last breath.

Shades Of Blue
Betty Wood
As silent as a snowfall the darkness came,
and then the light
Crept slowly over mountains tall
and quietly shown throughout the night.

Like a path across the water, and on the
mountains tipped with snow;
Moonlight made the lake a mirror – reflecting
cold, blue, midnight glow.

And on a rocklike hill before him,
a tree disrobed of all her leaves
Stood ageless in blue moonlight dim
quiet and still despite the breeze:

That whistled through her barren branches
and rippled water in the moons glow;
And chilled the artist as he painted
cold blue mountains capped with snow.

And captured magic of the nighttime,
mountains, lake and barren tree
With shades of blue, and a work sublime,
he captured moonlight destiny.

Untitled
Ted Cahill
Please pierce me with
Those diamond eyes
Open this heart
You fill with sighs

Those cool blue gems
So sweetly gaze
And capture me
A thousand ways

Hold me again
Within your arms
So I might dwell
Amongst your charms

They are merely holes
In the vaulted ceiling
Of the evening sky
Glimmering with hope
For tomorrow's dawn

Blinking in their tiny dances
As the daylight trapped behind
Tries to pour back in
Through the tiny wounds
Of Cupid's errant arrows

Wishful Thinking
Marianna J. Arolin
My diets made me delirious,
I knew someday it would.
Everyone keeps telling me
It's for my own good.

The clouds I see up in the sky,
Are not clouds at all.
They're meringue topped lemon pies.
I wish that one would fall.

Clothes
Alvin Zaragoza
I have a hard time with my clothes
they are either too long or too short
they're big or they're small heaven knows
They are always of quite the wrong sort!

They are either too long or too short
they are hopeless as soon as they're home
they are always of quite the wrong sort
No matter how far I may roam

They are hopeless as soon as they are home
and no matter how much I complain
no matter how far I may roam
they continue to give me a pain

No matter how much I complain
there is no one to help me with them
they continue to give me a pain
and I wish I could continue without them

There is no one to help me with them
they're too big or they're too small—heaven knows
I wish I could get on without them
I have a hard time with my clothes

What You Need
David A. Crawford
Rich man, poor man, white–collar, blue —
If you wanna be happy, wanna have victory,
you need to know, know what to do.
You want God's love, salvation from above, family and friends — beloved.

You wanna feel the summer's warm rays — the rain of spring days,
the autumn blow, and the winter snow.
You wanna feel your lover's embrace; you wanna feel, this you know.

You wanna see the sunrise and the blue, blue skies,
white clouds sailing by, stars glittering on high.

You wanna hear God's gift of sound — wind blowing in your ear,
music so close, music so dear.

You wanna touch the love of your life — touch that life right,
touch your sweetheart's dreams.
You wanna touch the leaves of the trees —
touch the green grass of spring, touch cold icy things.

You wanna smell the saltwater; the scent of perfume,
flowers and weeds — pine trees.

You want your sense of taste —
Taste your lover's lips, taste the snowy bliss.
You wanna taste the victory, Jesus paid for you — lovingly.

Seduction
Anja M. Audersch
See me in your nightmares
I'm the one dressed in velvet red—
Carriage ride on fallen snow
Love is never dead.

See me in your dreams
I'm dressed in virgin white
Cool sea breeze on the ocean shore
Our love is so alive.

The Race
Tammy Frew
As I run this race
on the track of life,
I am faced with days of joy
and even some are filled with strife.

Many spectators come
to show their love and support.
Some of them even come
to see whose plans that they may thwart.

Though the length and course of this race
is sometimes a mystery,
I must press on to win the prize;
I must never grow weary.

What is this prize?
The reason the that I persevere?
Is it for all the glory?
That I may be revered?

I run this challenging race
that is set before me
So that others may know
of my Savior at Calvary.

Reality
Kathleen W. McConville
A baby's cry at 3 A.M.
Your child's room–a near pig pen!

This is the stuff that makes life real.
Isn't always the fairest deal...

Losing a job, breaking a bone
Being in love, living alone.

The little things that mean so much...
A grandpa's smile, a Mother's touch.

Jingle bells and birthday cakes
Guess we need to appreciate

The rollercoaster ups and downs
The sunny skies, the rain, the clouds.

A hardy laugh, a heart–felt sigh,
A new found friend, a sad good–bye.

Your sister's graduation day
Lilacs caressing the month of May.

Emotions are proof that we're alive.
Two steps backward, ahead one long stride!

Reminders
Leslie E. Whipple
The sweet smell of a rose
reminds me so much of you.
The gentle blowing wind
reminds me of your gentle touch.
The darkest of blue sky
reminds me of the feeling I had
when we were apart.
The singing of the birds
remind me of the love that was in our hearts.

The Cowboy
Phillip Merrell
The rider pulled up at the top of the hill.
He knew they were waiting, ready to kill.
He'd been thru this before, many a time.
He knew that his chances weren't worth a plug dime.
He tightened the girth to gain time to think,
Rinsed out his mouth and took a short drink.
His attention was drawn to a rabbit down there!
It was hopping along, then took off as if scared!
He knew this meant ambush and was gone at a trot.
A feller jumped up and he took his first shot.
The bad guy feel dead as the bullets went flyin'.
He was in a bad spot, there was no denyin'.
They had him pinned down and were gettin' his range.
His forty fours jammed and his horse had been slain!
But the outlaws were payin', for his rifle shot true.
Almost out of bullets when he was, he was through!
Then just in the nick of time, the cavalry appears.
From the kitchen rings out, Mom's voice loud and clear,
"Come in and wash up. Hurry now, you've been told."
He waves "Bye" to the outlaws, doesn't want his supper cold!
Silence breathes a shred of gold,
dawn speaks slowly now, comforting these ageless foes
who now in daylight,
bow.

An Ode To The Twins
Elaine G. Arneson
The good news was a thrilling surprise,
Bringing joy to my heart and tears to my eyes,
When your mother called and told me
That I was going to be "Gigi"!
And soon the happy excitement grew
When I learned there would be two!

Then on the date of February Seven
Arrived a special bundle from heaven,
With much love, happiness and joy –
A darling baby girl and a precious baby boy.

Juliana Claire, a beautiful name for a little star;
Befitting the princess that you are –
A loving tribute to your great granddaddy, Clair;
As from above I am sure he is aware.

Andrew Joseph, a saintly name for the other member of "the team".
Namesake of your grandfather, Joseph, whose eyes must glean
As he looks down from that special place
With a big smile on his face.

A happy childhood is this twin grandmother's dream for you,
With lots of fun, laughter and love too.
Then a lifetime of happiness for you I pray,
As you travel down life's way.

Thunderstorm
Nicole Newman
Lightning strikes as the sun goes down
Crackles of thunder fills the sky
Wind blows a whistling sound
Many people look around.

Trees swaying back and forth
Bottles blowing every way
The people are frightened
especially the people by the bay.

The Other Way
Edie Holdgrafer
Don't look up to see heaven,
You sure won't see it there!
Instead; look just the opposite,
Inside of yourself, somewhere.

Heaven's supposed to be comfort
To souls who have earned their place.
But; earning means charity and love;
For the whole of the human race.

Love for your fellow man,
Nature and the animals too!
Yes! That's what heaven is all about;
So; think of the good you can do!

When you die, you go to dust;
Having fought life's final inning,
So, it seems that all of life
Goes back to its beginning!

So! Heaven's so vast, you can't see it;
And it makes a lot of sense;
To look far deep inside yourself;
To heaven – what excellence!

Marynhor: The Child In Search Of Her Identity
Jesus J. Arambulo
You would not know for sure how the
fish that swam in the clouds and the
cock which soared up the sky had pieced you
together, as they were strangers to each others –

Yet burros, churros, tacos were either
compelling, or more so, persuading, "Come
to the Big Apple," where Washington and
Lincoln, sixteen spring times and four apart, not

Wanting to be ignored, for after all, each soul from
the four winds gathered one after the other,
clasping to unify themselves, are cooing: "color,
creed, language...why? This is the "land of the

Free..." the sun comes forth to the fish
in the East, and it sets down on the cock in
the West. Is there now any difference if you,
Marynhor, give your breath freely? American Indians

Will holler: "We are first!" The Blacks come forth,
yelling: "We owe you nothin'..." and the others
arguing: "Give us a bite..." and Marynhor crying
out, "Hey, I wanna bite! I wanna bite, too:

Dedication: Wife Sylvia, Bambi and Jonathan

The Glory Of Nursing
Mary Mosley

The glory of nursing is very real
When the need of the patient you can feel.
With such good deeds that you have done
The wonder of health has thus begun.

So with each thing that you can do
To lighten a burden and bring life anew,
With this each nurse that God does bless
The glory of Nursing is a success

The House
Margaret B. Compton

The empty house stands waiting
It looks with vacant eyes
Through windows stark and naked –
Bereft of human ties.

Many are the memories
That flit from room to room –
Brilliant colors woven through
The pattern of life's loom.

Sad it is to move a home
And leave behind a house –
A place without the laughter
Of children, man, and spouse.

If home were just a building,
A place to eat and sleep,
No sighs would sound in gables,
And willows would not weep.

But home is a condition –
A meeting place of hearts,
Where lives are shaped and shared,
And love oils all its parts.

A Prayer For A Free American Sunset
Doris Berg

American sunset so crimson lovely and free
Only you truly are home and heaven to me
Now lighting on a lonely far distant shore
Oh how my heart yearns to see you once more

In my mind's eye on the North Dakota plains
My brave beautiful Norsk Mama I see
Praying, pleading, for her five sons sent off to war

In her dear heart there is much fear
On her apron she wipes away a silent tear
As she faces war for yet another year or more

No disrespecting, disgusting flag burning
for my brothers and me
Because for freedom we fight wholeheartedly
To keep free our precious flag of red, white, and blue
To this sacred flag may we ever be true

I thank God that it is freely beautifully rippling
In our crisp crimson North Dakota sunset and breeze
A most glorious sight to see it tugs at the very heart of me

Now for my mama I to shed a silent tear
As I sigh and pray dear Lord please keep America forever free
for all God's Children don't you see?

Sister Love
Charlotte Ellis Maxwell

Mother love is most certain,
Father love completes the chain;
Brother love is a most precious gem
But sister love calls my name.

As sure as stars sparkle in heaven,
As sure as the moon rules from above;
As sure as night follows day,
I'm sure of my sister's love.

Sister love means commitment,
It means we speak without bitterness or shame;
Sister love is my salvation,
Because sister love calls my name.

Sister love is unchanging
traversed by life's highs and passion's lows;
Amid dusky dawns and hazy days,
Sister love will forever show.

Sister love is my redeemer
Tinged with friendship but never bane;
Sister love is the core of me
Because sister love calls my name.

Life's Lesson
Roberta J. Kennedy

The candles on the cake are quite a few
the lines on the face are many too.

Wise aged eyes look around and see
family and friends that mean so much,
as the years pass by and the numbers add up.

The importance of life we learn as we age
is not what we get but what we give away.

Old Age
Tamsin Winter

My washing ends up in everyone's
sink but my own.
My meals are cooked by everyone
but me.
My shopping is ready on the doorstep
when I get up.
They turn and are gone again
after a brief "Hello".
They don't talk to me. My
only friend is a paper.
Just another burden on a
hypocrite's life.
Walking down the street they
don't want to look me in the eye.
Only glanceful looks of sorrow
but never a word.
I am just another tree in a jungle,
but of no importance.
I know I won't score another
goal, or run another mile.
I won't ever get another
valentine card from a secret
sweetheart,
Once my door is closed they
will forget me, and will
carry on as usual.

In The Corner Of Her Heart!
Mary Grace Hudson
In the corner of her heart
There's twinkles of love that shine
In the corner of her heart
There's a smile of every kind.

In the corner of her heart
There's a song she softly sings
In the corner of her heart
There's joy for all the kindness she brings.

In the corner of her heart
There's something lovely that blossoms each day
In the corner of her heart
There's the fragrance of her love along life's way.

In the corner of her heart
There's memories of blessings each day of the year
In the corner of her heart
There's the hope of knowing that God is always near.

In the corner of her heart
There's love like a candle glowing bright
In the corner of her heart
There's just a touch of a fragrance of an angel of light.

Searching
K. M. Abraham
That dear pretty face,
Blazon with excitement and joy,
Appeared under the shadow
Of a speckled umbrella.

Swift was she on her feet
Gliding towards him, her "dear",
Under the burning noon day sun
Braved she the crowed, heat and sweat.

I'll Be There
Teresa Reno
Broken hearts; shattered dreams;
Thoughts of love and wedding rings!
A baby's breath; a puppy's smell;
A falling star; a wishing well!
Thoughtful kisses; loving sighs;
Stolen moments; sad goodbyes!

I see your face, I hear your voice;
I know, in my heart, you're my only choice!
I think of you while you're away;
And remember all the things you say!

With all the laughter; All the tears;
All the changes throughout the years!
Through all the good times and the bad;
You're the only friend I've ever had!

We've had our ups; we've had our downs;
We've faced each other in the final rounds!
We shared our hopes, we shared our dream;
We shared our love and everything!

I think of you while you're away;
And wonder if you'll come back someday!
I still love you; I do care;
If you should need me, "I'll Be There"!

Each Day This Prayer
Diane Groth
Dear Lord I come to you in prayer
To ask for guidance from above,
To live this day with praise to you,
To give to all I meet, your love.

Give me patience when annoyed
So good can come of those things too.
May I not fail to stop and see
How I've been blessed each day by you.

Please give me strength to carry on.
To do, what's right each day I live.
I know you'll ask not more of me
Then you will know that I can give.

If someone ever needs a friend
May they soon know my hand is there.
Then might all turn in prayer to you
Please help them know like you, I care.

If when I rest at end of day
I've put a smile on someone's face;
And if you choose to call me home
Please find this world a better place.—Amen

In Search Of Life
Naila Javed
Like a destitute I wandered through life
In search of destiny.
I found only mutiny.
A decrepit world of selfish gains,
Like assassins in shrouded manes.
Disguised as friends, but enemies at heart;
Most in the world of survival
Of material gains.
and sanctimonious vows!

The Mortician
Stella J. Follansbee
To be a mortician is wonderful, some people say
But it gets mighty tiresome, day after day

They think you get rich, with no work to do
But the way it really is, is the way I'll tell you.

You can't do as you please, your life's not your own
You always have to be close to that old telephone

You may be eating dinner, or just get in bed
When the telephone rings, and someone is dead

You start on a trip you have planned since last fall
As you get in the car, there's another call

You can't even go fishing down by the shack
You just put the line in and you're called to come back

Then you sit for days with nothing to do
Hoping if someone dies, they will call you

When you get one call, before long there are two
They you are so busy, you don't know what to do

But it's all in the job and a very fine life
If you have steady nerves and a very patient wife.

My Best Friend
Becky Lord
My friend has always been there,
My friend is always true,
My friend knows all my problems
And helps me see them through.

He listens when I'm speaking,
And even when I'm not,
He makes me feel so special,
Lets me know I'm not forgot.

His shoulder is there to cry on
If life gets a little too rough;
When it comes to saying 'thank you'
I never say it enough.

He works all day and through the night,
And his family is his life.
Never once is he heard to complain,
For he loves us so, his children and his wife.

He's not just any man, you see,
And he will be there to the end.
I hope he will say the same of me,
My husband, my lover, and my best friend.

Individuality
Carl J. Proia
I am
Who I am
For the reason that
My soul was created and
Placed into my body. My mind
Was formed to stimulate a spiritual union
Between God's image and my inner peace. My
Inner peace is; The constant pleasure of being
Myself, allowing nothing to destroy my individuality.

Paula
Philip Drayton
Your face appears within my head,
I cannot help but smile.
Now you are in a better place,
But with us all the while.

I feel a warmth here with your friends,
The ones you've left behind.
I know they hurt and miss you too,
You're such a special kind.

You are my sister, my dearest friend
A bond that does not die
Though you'll be with me all my life
For you these tears I'll cry.

Things may change but you're timeless
We'll watch your young ones grow.
We're all here to watch over them,
We know they'll make you proud.

You took a part of me with you,
When you closed your eyes,
You live on deep within my heart,
You're here deep in my life.

But I'll still miss you.

Make A Brand New Start
Stephen D. Hunt
I live a life of constant dreaming,
The things I see are still unclear.
The path of love seems far behind me,
We touched, we kissed, but you're not here.

Much time has passed before our eyes,
Your memory still remains.
Our love was full and needed then,
Much hopes, much cares, and gains.

You cannot see the tears I shed,
'Cause we're so far apart.
I need you back so desperately,
To make a brand new start.

I pray the day when you'll appear,
I miss your touch, your smile.
Your gleaming eyes, your graceful step,
And, your innocent style.

All through my ups and downs I'm sure,
My nights and days I see.
I'm always dreaming of our times,
Just dreaming of you and me.

True Love
Mary Ellen McCormack
Tenderness beyond compare,
Realizing that he'll always be there,
Understanding those living sighs,
Enduring, lasting, never dies.

Laughing at that one sad time,
Opening heart, and silencing mind,
Voicing joyous cries of hope,
Entwining you and I; One rope.

Listen
Dorothy Lee
Listen it's hard to do, listen let God talk to you.
Listen be amazed at what he has to say, listen let the Lord talk to you
    today.
Sit quietly in your chair, listen and feel God's presence there.
Now I wonder what I have to do, listen God will tell you.
Listen; can you hear me now, listen I'll talk to you somehow.
You have got to want me to, so listen and talk to you.
Listen; be amazed at what you hear, listen I'll take away your fear.
Listen I think a lot of you, so please listen, let God talk to you.
Don't be frightened I'm holding your palm, listen and try to stay calm.
You're one of my chosen few, listen I'll send messages from me to you.
I know you will send them on, think of it this way, you have won.
Listen; let God talk to you, In this way you'll know what to do.
Read up and down to get the rhyme.

Listen let God talk to you.

In this way you'll know what to do.

Sometimes you talk always.

To listen hear what I have to say.

Every time you want to chat.

Now stop doing that.

When I Met You
Donna M. Keene

I met you in October,
you swept me off my feet.
The talks we had, the kiss you gave,
made of something sweet.

Your eyes that gleamed when we touched,
the love we made that meant so much.

As time went on you made me see,
there was only one way it could be.
With you by my side, your love so deep,
I knew my life would be complete.

I've learned a lot and grown to love you
more and more each day.
For in my heart I know,
forever will I stay.

The love we share so passionate,
the love forever true.
A Lifetime Commitment from me to you.

You are my world to the end,
My husband, my lover, my friend.

Twilight
Lacy Yager

In the twilight, in the twilight,
as the day draws to a close,
the birds will sing their evening song,
the wording to their prose.

The orangish sky, the blowing breeze,
the "Golden Time" of day,
the time when all is nice and good,
and troubles stay at bay.

Wounded Soul
Mike Dollard

I know you've been hurt
That is plain to see.

Your heart is too big
And your trust too small.

You love undyingly
But what has it gotten you?

More pain and misery
Than you should have to endure.

Your spirit is pure,
But jagged and torn

From the tangle of lies
That are pulling at you.

You need a heart
To beat love into your soul.

You so desperately need
The love of rose.

But you end up with
The pain from the thorns.

Dove's Wings
Stormey Wingert

Free to be...
In the Golden Years...would it not be grand
not to worry about the fluttering wings
of the Doves, but only to know loves
free to be...
In the Golden Years...not to know tears or
to have fears. For tears and fears are for the
young. In the Golden Years, days should only
be filled with thoughts of love not the fluttering
wings of the Doves
free to be...
In the Golden Years...not to know pain
or to have sorrow. Know not to borrow
trouble for tomorrow, just to know that you
have gained from the pain and sorrow.
free to be...
In the Golden Years...peace comes when
the fluttering of the Dove's wings cease
for the stillness brings peace.
free to be...
In the Golden Years...at a place free
from tears, fears, pain and sorrow,
To know that the fluttering wings of
the Doves, has brought forth only love.

Love Is
Christina Wright

giving your heart to that special one
a tender kiss you give that one
making time for that special one
little things you do to make their day
always being honest
taking the time to listen
being patient even when it is hard
trying to be understanding
not always explainable

A Sunrise Spectacular
Timothy W. Strock

As the morning sun rose,
its rays did disclose.
Yesterday's forest so bare,
now a blown glass fair.

Everything in sight,
is dressed in ice.
The trees so fragile, and yet so strong,
their branches crack, and come crashing down.

In an instant, lifelines of electric and phone are cut,
roads and highways are shut.
Pines majestically bow to the Earth below,
dusting each vehicle that passes so slow.

The farmer's fence shimmers in the brilliant sun,
draped so elegantly with its string of ice diamonds.
The grass stands firm and tall,
at attention commanding all.

As the evening sun set,
its rays did forget.
Today's blown glass fair,
soon to be tomorrows forest bare.

The Color Of Love
James P. Kass
Roses are red and violets are blue,
it's an age–old saying, that is held to be true.
But what about love, in the darkness of the night,
does it also have a color in the absence of light?

When we look upon the darkness, it is plain to see,
without light, everything looks the same, as it was meant to be.
If we were alone in the dark, and we perceived by our touch,
would not being able to see, really matter so much?

There are many colors, that we can compare love to,
from the falling maple leaves, to the magnificent skies of blue.
What if we were all blind, and none of us could not see,
what color would we call it then, what could it possibly be?

If we were to make love, and together we became one,
would any color have a significance, in what we had done?
In our throes of passion, when we whisper each others name,
what would it even matter, if we see love's color, as the same?

Try to picture love, as our eyes might see,
close your eyes and imagine, what color it might be.
It could be many colors, pleasurable and appealing,
or maybe, it is just beyond our sight, and only what we are feeling.

If
Judith S. Berson
If you can allow me to be myself
If you can give me the freedom I need
If you won't feel threatened should
I become overbearing at times
If you can retain your respect for me
in spite of day to day annoyances
If you can love me as much as I love you,
I will make you
THE HAPPIEST PERSON IN THE WORLD

The Finger Of God
Barbara Olnick
I search my heart
for how I feel,
searching for truth
Was this experience real?

Last night as at the
altar I knelt.
Was it the finger of
God I felt?

My heart says yes,
I know it was real
I'm wondrously saved
I'm changed, Jesus heals.

Jesus, oh how can I
thank you my Lord?
Your forgiveness and love,
is like an unbroken chord

My soul gives you praise
that shall never end,
My Jesus who walks
on the wings of the wind.

What's Love and Hatred
Amber Gordy
No man can see through me
For I am just an invisible memory to others and myself,
If I was in hatred because of the mind and body
I would shed tears on the world.

Love is supposed to be about
Respect of others and their happiness
Towards others,
The soul enables us to fly free and do
What we think is right.

Finding Dreams
Kris Whitten
It seems like only yesterday,
I played my little girl games
I wished for fairies and angels and queens
And storybook endings, of course.

Then the fairies faded away
The angels, gone in the mist
I remember hoping they'd always stay
Still knowing I had to let them go

I lived without my dreams quite some time
I had to be grown up and strong
My life had no room for an angel's touch
Though there were times I could have used one

Yet in one moment, they all came back
When I met one who had hidden dreams too
And now again I can see angels smiling,
As I think of my future with him

He taught me to love, how to hope again
And together we dream of tomorrow
Where our children will slide down rainbows
Into a laughing angel's embrace

Sweet Lyrical Lies
Melissa Semana
The poetic harmony of the
words you speak
They sound so beautiful
and so often sweet

They sound like a melody
just like a song
Like nothing in our lives
is painfully wrong

My heart pounding in harmony
as your words come out
Tension in my body makes
me want to shout

The tempo of your voice
finding its way in
something so creative
should be a sin

Your masculine voice
Your deep caring eyes
Its amazing you came up
with those sweet lyrical lies

A Spectrum Colors Of A Rainbow
Alice Covarrubias
Red is for the beauty creation of a rose.
Orange is for the magnificent view of the sunset, after an horizon.
Yellow is for the shining of the Son.
Green is for the dew in the glittering of the grass.
Blue is for the silver lining in the sky so high above.
Violet is for the flowers lying on the ground, so peacefully.
Indigo is for the majestic mountains, after a rainy day.

"This is the creation of a rainbow, that
God has created, for all to see."

If There's A Path...
Gila Ashtor
Before you cried and pled for more
G–d knew your death, and birth,
Your days were counted long before –
You set foot on this earth.

And some, upon arrival wonder
Too fearful too fulfill,
While others stand outside in thunder,
And hope not to be killed.

And in their days some people lead
Or stand firm with defiance,
The rest can't hunt, nor kill a weed,
Their lives based on reliance.

Some in each day, find time to heal
While others are in need.
Some fail to see, life's path is real,
While in that path, others succeed.

Some see a path, but do not try
Too scared of unknown fate,
Now, life's seen them, and passed them by,
They'd go– but it's too late!!!!

A Talk With God
Floyd Cook
I walk this ground, and I'm so glad
That God gave me life, and all that I've had.
I think, to know pleasure, you have to know pain,
through my many years of sorrow, I have been so vain.

I never turned to Jesus, through each troubled time,
I always hurt by myself, it was a sinner's crime.
Why, oh why, did I turn away?
My heart has been heavy, for years, until today...

I want to know Jesus, I want him to fill me up,
It's taken so long, my life is so corrupt.
I believe in beginnings, and this is my start,
After most of my life, I now want Christ in my heart.

I know it won't be easy, after living life in sin,
God has waited on me, just to begin.
I will not let him down, when I get down on my knees,
I cannot, will not, because he holds the keys.

To Heaven and life eternal, and my soul will soar,
I will never go back, to where I've been before.
Thank you, Jesus, for what you did for me,
I ask for forgiveness, my final plea.

The Dandelion
Margaret P. Baum
Nobody likes the
dandelion
It's a plant that
no one needs.

Yet there is a beauty
in its golden blooms
and lacy green leaves–
What a pity, it has
to be weeds.

Mary And I
Beverly Dollarhite
The leader and me
Have more fun, don't you see,
Doing things that we couldn't
If we didn't be

A friend of our girls
Of the ages that do
All the things that we like
But just wouldn't do

So we stand up in front
In a size bigger than
All those little wee girls.
Now you see how we can

Get to do lots of things
That really are fun.
And the girls like it to.
That's why they begun

Brownie Scouts in our care
And I wish you could see
All the smiles on the faces
Of the Brownies and We.

When Friends Part
Veronicka J. Thompson
I once knew a girl named Katie
She was my best friend of all
Then she ended her life
Without so much as a call

I never knew it was coming
She always seemed just fine
If she was hurting at all
She must have kept it inside

Katie was very quiet
I thought she was just shy
And when her eyes twinkled
I never knew she wanted to cry

If she would have stayed around
God would've taken away the hurt
But when she killed herself
It only made matters worse

When two friends part
It's the worst feeling I know
I really miss you Katie
Even though you didn't have to go

Moon Light
Michael W. Thomas

The moon–drenched world is a dreamy wonderland. Walking through forest
paths lit by the gazing moon. The moon's mystery enchants us, speaking
    some riddle
within our hearts; it's a face that watches us all through the night.
    It dances
above three tops making merry the sky, a peek–a–boo pearl through the
    clouds
on high. The master of the sprinkled starlit sky, it's the mystery of
    moonlight
that assails the night.

Seven
Marilyn S. Matthews

I stand upon the windswept shore and watch;
And silent, inadvertently I number as I gaze,
Rememb'ring when I numbered last.
The winds were singing, gently urging,
But I heeded not their pleading
As the waves came racing, rolling, cresting, dashing hard against the
    sand.
Watched the fourth one tumble shoreward, watched the fifth, then sixth
    ones break.
Trance–like still, I saw the seventh crest and crash and foam away.

Then my hypnosis was broken, then I acted; then, too late;
For the first wave was upon me gently swelling to the shore,
And the foamy bubbles rolling, drifting, backward to the sea returning,
Told my soul that mighty Seven now had left me evermore.

Time has passed but memories never.
Still I gaze and dream and number.
Mighty Seven, will it answer?
Will it heed the prayer I breathe?

No one knows the whim of Seven. None can tell if it will hear.
But my soul has made its dwelling there upon that wind–swept shore.
Still I stand before the ocean, gazing, praying, numb'ring still.

Petals On The Wind
Kimberly Watkins

Three fragile flower petals dancing on the wind
To speak of their beauty where can one begin
The most blessed play of nature for us to behold
within these petals the pleasures of motherhood unfold
Three little girls so intricately perfect in design
so different, each of them gloriously one of a kind.
The little mother, the happy face clown, the needy baby
All three the most wonderful blessings to me be.
What will become of nature's babies, what is their destiny.
As our Father replenishes his glorious gardens here on earth.
He plants the seed of human life, little fragments of ourselves to be
    rebirthed
Into each flower we pour all our hopes and dreams, and pray fervently life
is not as cruel as it seems.
A mother, the most earthy part of nature she be, strives to provide her
young with the love and nurturance they need.
Just as the flowers need the gentle kiss of the rain.
God only knows through the love of a mother what each human petal gain
The tremendous bend stands the test of time without being broken. Three
simple words lavishly relayed, to them forever spoken.
Three petals floating on the wind. God grant them the ability to float into
    my ever waiting arms again.

Dedication: Falon, Hannah, & Kayla

The Man Of My Dreams
Martha Fender

Did you know that you are the man of my dreams?
You've always kept me safe and warm.
You are my knight in shining armor.
You are my brave Indian warrior.
You are my hero, my everything.
You are my strength, my life and my love.
Without you I would be nothing.
Just an empty shell with no sound.
There is no other who could ever take your place.
You will always be the man of my dreams.

Shanon
Rose P. Williamson

In a reflective moment, I contemplate the passing of the years,
Realizing now that time has, indeed, gone by in the "blink of an
Eye."

Still, you are who you've always been, daughter, sister, wife and
Mother, but most of all, you are a friend, laying up your stars
In heaven, by your unselfish deeds and selfless love.

Now, you've reached your 40th year of life, can it have been so
Long ago that your gift of life was given to us, your family?
But, what gift can we, Mother and I, give to you on this
Momentous occasion? Material things are too trite, we find, so
Instead, we give to you the very essence of our loving spirit.
Knowing in the not too distant future, you must travel your road
Alone, for surely we will have "gone the way of all flesh."

Never despair, however, the spirit of our love for you will
Continue to touch you always, in a memory, in a song, in a
Familiar word.

Happy Birthday, dear sister, may God grant you all the joy you
Give to others, now and always. We love you.

Dedication: My mother Duretta, my champion

In Memoriam: The Family Physician
Eva Anderson

Christ, the Healer, the Great Physician, bids all to come—
The lame, the blind, the deaf, the leper.
Through faith and love their ills He cured.

Christ, the Lord, commanded man to go forth and do His work.

To man, the physician, many come.
Man cures also by love, and by the grace of Christ.

The family physician truly works through Christ—
He delivers the mother, and places the newborn infant in her arms;
He watches over the infant and guides it through its life.
He sets the broken bones—
He bandages the wounds.
He is there when Christ calls one of the family home—
He consoles and supports those who remain behind.

Man, the physician, is truly blessed,
For he does Christ's work on earth.

Christ, the Lord and Healer, has called man, the physician, home.
His labors are through,
His tasks are done;
He has earned his rewards.

To Grandpa
Verna E. Day

'Twas always with a smile you greeted us,
When you were here on earth with us.
You helped to guide our childhood flight
At anytime, from morn till night.
A broken bike or toy you'd mend,
A helping hand, you'd always lend.
Now you've left us for the great beyond,
Grandpa, of you we were so fond.
Though out of sight – not out of mind,
Please Gramps – pray for us – the ones behind.

Alzheimer's
Donna Kijowski

I see his face, I see his smile
He knows me now—just for a while
We walk the halls
We go for ice cream
What ever happened to our dream?

A wonderful husband, father, grandfather and son
He had the time and love for us all, each and every one

Whoever knew what life would bring?
It hurts so much
You try to cling
To the one true love you ever knew
Who at this time does not know you

Our love runs deep, our hopes are shallow
We're losing such a wonderful fellow
All we can do is comfort him now
In every way that we know how

God bless you Mike
We love you so
It's painfully hard
To watch you go

When Grandma Was A Girl
Edwinnie C. Blackstock

When Grandma was a girl
Things were different, I'll allow.
She may have been a lady, once.
There a streak of hussy in her now.

She's lived her threescore years and ten,
Give or take a few
Grandma's a classy lady now
She doesn't need no one to tell her what to do.

She's still got that twinkle in her eyes—
But this is enough to make her balk
Mother Nature threw her a curve,
And took the wiggle right out of her walk

"Ole Arthur" visits Grandma now
And brings along his bag of pain.
So instead of her prissing down the street
Grandma has to use a cane!

But she doesn't need your pity yet,
So step aside for goodness sake,
Give the lady room to move,
Grandma's still got what it takes.

I Have Nothing
Kimberly Smith

My dear I love you, but I have nothing to offer.
I told them I'd holler,
but still, I have nothing.
Without you, I could not live.
If you married me, my heart, I'd give.
But still I have nothing.
I'd kiss the grass for you my dear,
I'd promise not to ever drink a beer.
I love you more than anything,
but still I have nothing.

Losing A Loved One
Linda F. Grace

Losing a loved one causes great pain and tears.
I sit alone and wonder why,
Why did you have to die?
My heart feels so empty now,
I must go on but I don't know how,
We shared our joys, our sorrows, our tears,
Things I thought we would share for years.

Then I remember like it was yesterday,
The way you would smile in your special way.
I remember special moments we shared,
All the little things you did to show you cared
I can remember when things got me down,
You would be there to wipe away the frown.
I remember and always will,
You loved me then and you love me still.

So dear, I want you to know,
My love for you continues to grow.
And when I'm feeling low and want to run and hide
I know I can look up and you'll be there saying,
"Honey I'm here, right by your side."

Dedication: Gwen, a special friend always

Chopping Wood
Julie Mahoney

Snow–covered maple trees and chipmunks squirreling for food
temperature dropping, winter chill in air
on my frost–covered window pane I make a small hole
watching children making angels in the snow
and from a distance echoes the sound of chopping wood.

Early Sunday morning air is brisk
passing pheasant hunters and horseback riders
my dog stopping dead in his tracks
to an old man chopping wood for fire
the only warmth he gets.

Straggly gray beard and sunken dark eyes
deep crevice wrinkles along his high cheekbones
his hands chapped and worn.

Feeling a blustery winter's bite down my back
I whistle my dog along
listening to the crisp sound of his paws hitting the freshly fallen snow
between the continuous rows of birch trees a few more miles we travel
and in the distance echoes the sound of chopping wood
the only warmth he gets.

Dedication: Donald MacDonald, my mentor

Tree
Robert Henderson
Sown and grown
Seeds awaken by the fire
Discussion revolution
I've seen sunshine I've seen rain
I was happy now I feel pain
Destruction construction
I am the air for earth
Without me you can't breathe
Don't cut me down
Please!

A Reflection Of You
Sarah Fausett
Mother I am a Reflection of You.
Your love, Your fear, and all you do.

The smile, the feel of that special look,
Seems like it comes from a fairy tale book.

From when I was young,
I now have begun,
To quite understand your job.

The worry, the pain,
Of a childish gain,
As I grab forbidden door knob.

And I'll walk through life so unaware,
That once again I'll give you a scare.

But when a single tear, trickles down your cheek,
I'll come back to you so sorry, so meek.

So I've learned a lesson from a mother so true,
And I really am A reflection of You!

Dedication: To my mother

Poetry
Elizabeth Gorman
What is poetry? – We all ask,
To describe it we have a task
It is the opening and closing of a door,
Another world to explore.

It is a beautiful way to express
Either sadness or happiness.
And also it seems,
A description of our dreams.

Poetry can cause us to see light,
After a dark and dreadful night.
Like the finding of May flowers
After the lengthy April showers.

With poetry express in part
The feelings within our heart.
Poetry is God's gift
That gives us quite a lift.

I thank God each day,
As I kneel down to pray,
For the poetry He has given me,
Makes me feel alive and free.

Cosmic Tidbit Of Information
Eric Robertson
Twisting world on shallow time—
This earth we exist upon is not mine...
It is energy and mass combined as one—
Emotions pressed to our very core—
There is no reason to ever just sit and bore.
We are existing simultaneously in space—
Magnetic and totally full of grace...
Why must the devil constantly be in our face?
Questions have answers, but none of mine.
We exist only once, as the human kind...

The Haunted House Of Applegate
Joseph Dragan
Down the road not too far
And on the other side,
There is an old deserted farmhouse
In which a ghost does there abide.

Some windows are broken and some boards are off,
And the house is bare of paint
And everything in and around the house
Has an old and weathered taint.

In the kitchen, there is still
The table and the stove.
And through the window, one can see
The tractors that he drove.

They lay out back where the yard once was
In a thicket of thistle and weed.
There are no elaborate furnishings
As he was not a man of greed

When the moon is high, and the wind is howling
If you hide somewhere and wait,
Sooner or later you will see
The ghost of Applegate.

Through The Windows Of Heaven
Sherri Warner
We'll never forget all your smiles and your hugs
The comfort you gave with all of your love.
You devoted your life to your family and friends
So now we'll remember your love never ends.

The days seem so empty where they were once full
With your helping hand to complete each days goal.
We know from the footprints of which there are two
That you are well cared for by the one who is true.

You touched our lives in so many ways
As a wife, grandmother you helped fill our days.
We miss you so much and wish you were here
But the windows of Heaven will help draw us near.

Through the windows of Heaven
You see our lives
We feel your presence
When we look to the skies.

Our lives are a circle
And Yours is complete
With the Father above
Who we all will once meet.

Life

Jigme Dojee

Life is not a long story
and not a short poem
Life is full of difficulties
until it carries you to the gate of death
You cannot make it shorter
when the sorrow comes
and you cannot make it longer
when the happiness comes!

Dedication: Akong Rinpoche, Founder Rokpa International

Sweet Child Of Mine

Cindy Embury–Parker

As I closed my eyes I heard a man's voice,
He whispered in my ear, sweet child make a choice
Reach out your hand cause times passing by,
Those words I heard allowed me to cry,

With tears of anger, fear and despair,
I never knew that someone would care,
I fell to my knees and reached out my hand,
He said sweet child I understand,

I held his hand I didn't let go,
He said sweet child I'll help you grow,
It's up to you if you want to live,
But your will and life you must give,

So I turned it over and again I cried,
Without His voice I could have died,
Serenity and courage you shall find,
He said sweet child, you're a child of mine,

Walk with me I'll show you the way,
Sweet child of mine it's a beautiful day,
Get up from your knees it's time to stand
Sweet child of mine, I'm holding your hand.

Our Wedding Day

Sharon Vega

As I start to walk down the aisle,
You turn to look at me with that wonderful smile.
As I take them steps to you,
All my worries now seem so few.

As my father now gives you my hand,
I step up beside you and now proudly stand.
As we begin to recite our vows,
It's you and I forever now.

As the Reverend says you may kiss your bride
I now look into your eyes and see your pride
He now says you are man and wife,
We now become as one for life.

As we now turn to our family and friends,
I realize never a lonely night shall I ever spend.
As we begin our walk to the doors,
You turn to me and you shall hurt no more.

Now years have passed and we are old and gray,
I now look back to our wedding day.
Remembering the smile upon your face,
I now close my eyes and come to my final resting place.

Love

Gloria L. Richardson

There once was a man
so bright and charming
Everyone knew he'd be true blue,
soon the girl found he
was in farming
Happy and loving all day through
We shall find the happiness
in everything they do,
Because they both stayed
true blue

Days Gone By

Kerri L. Kennedy

She sits alone in darkness
A single tear runs down her face,
She wonders where she's headed
She searches for a better place

In the distant shadows
The past comes rushing back so clear
Another tear falls silently,
The pain is getting near

The pain inside her heart
It goes so very deep
The memories of years gone by,
In her heart she'll always keep

All the broken promises
They haunt her thoughts all day
They fill her dreams at night
But they just won't go away

Each day that goes by
She'll always wonder why
The life she used to know
Just seem to pass her by

When Day Is Done

Philip L. Smith

After tomorrow
When day is done
We'll be with Jesus
For He said come

We'll see his glory
We'll see his crown
When we see Jesus
When day is done

When day is over
We're in his care
A day of loving
We'll all be there

When we see Jesus
Upon His throne
We'll praise Him ever
For He's our own

He is our Savior
And He's our friend
We'll be with Him ever
Where there's no end.

Summer
Megan Simonson
Snowcones dripping down my wrist
Everyone adding to the grocery list.
Flipflops tripping feet
Grilling barbecue meat.
Bathing suits drying on the porch
Night time lit by the burning torch.
Laughing and excited
TV Commercials recited.
Mom going out of her mind
It's SUMMER!

Dusk
Diane Kennedy
The tide rolls on across the beach
while gulls indent the sand.
The sun dips deep into the waves.
There is no sign of man.

The froth turns orange, then disappears
into the melting beach;
while crabs emerge to scurry 'round
their homes yet within reach.

The rocks, arranged like broken teeth,
bite through the beating surf.
As gulls and pipers gather near
the sparse and dead brown turf.

The jutting rocks all seem to writhe
with life all of their own.
The orange descends into the sea.
Now enters silver moon.

The waves roll slowly to the shore
like liquid mercury.
The breeze rolls in. A chill arrives,
preceding the cold sea.

I Thought It Would Be Different
Dolly K. Robinson
I thought it would be different
As I reached those golden years
With children grown and time to spare
He'd have more listening ears

I thought it would be different
As I advanced in life
With memories and wisdom
That I'd still be his wife

I thought it would be different
Because we had shared so much
But many things had happened
To hold back his loving touch

I thought it would be different
They say love never fails
But love is like a roadway
And there are many trails

So I'll go down another
And try to understand
Although it cannot be the same
It once was very grand

Mustang
Catherine A. Strong
She is strong and powerful
as wild as they come.
She moves so swiftly
along the side of the other.
They stop and stare,
They know she is mean
so they do not cause trouble
and they let her go by.

My Little Blue Mustang Car.

A Joyous Memory
Amy Marble
The season of red and green,
neatly packaged in bows and string.
Children's anticipation of old jolly,
and lovers kissing under the holly.
Pies and cakes so sweet to taste,
puts a glow on many a happy face.
The tree is covered with thousands of lights,
that twinkle brightly with each glancing sight.
Ornaments are placed with the tenderest of care,
as grandpa sleeps in his cozy chair.
The air is filled with laughter and cheer,
as the time to open gifts draws near.
The wind is chilling and the moon is bright,
as the stars shine their heavenly light.
Bells can be heard as the restful town sleeps,
as Santa and the deer make no peeps.
As little heads begin to nod,
the reindeer's hooves begin to trod.
The sun greets the white with radiant beams,
as the children awake with delightful screams.
Santa has come and briskly gone,
but he has left enjoyment to last all year long.
Dedication: My best friend, my mother

A Summer's Day
Janet M. Van Kirk
The clear cool dancing waters,
Flows over smooth white rocks below;
It sings and beckons to me,
So a–wading I will go.

It whispers, "Come go with me
To the yonder bend beyond,"
"Come wander along with me
And sing my happy song".

As I stepped into the water,
As its coolness touched my skin,
I knew I'd go on with it
For I felt such peace within.

I wandered till I came upon
A mini– waterfall,
It was my secret place I'd found there,
And I named it, Fairy Falls.

Oh, how I love to go a–wading,
In the waters clear and warm;
That flows on and on forever,
In the creek on my Dad's farm.

Ocean View
Sandy Thew
The tide is humming and waves are singing
for the joy of the day is rising in the east.
Sea gulls start flying and squirrels start feeding
for there's much to be done before the end of the feast.
The sun smiles down on the busy lot
and remembers the evolution it almost forgot.
For the creatures of the world Earth have advanced
and how it enjoys their every day dance.
They twirl and swirl till they're dizzy with jest
and the sun bids farewell and sleeps in the west.

Lonely Person Happy Moths
Stephen L. Jones
In a dimly lighted room
A single light bulb glistens.
As if it was a speaker
The moths gather 'round to listen.

They'll die someday,
But they don't know it.
They're not butterflies,
But they don't show it.

And they bounce up and down,
From the worn ceiling tile.
It could bring the loneliest person,
To stop and smile.

Speaking of which,
A screen door slams.
The moths pay no attention
As in comes a man.

And his sad countenance,
Contradicts his company.
Flying around the light
With no worry or empathy.

Out On A Limb
Christina Hurst
Since Adam and Eve in the Garden of Eden,
Were tempted by Satan to eat fruit forbidden,
Man has been tempted to this very day
To deny his God, and go his own way.

True, God is merciful, but He also is just,
And for all our sins, His law condemns us.
But His love for each soul is enormously great,
So He provided a way through the Pearly Gate.

He had a Son, whom He loved very dearly,
But He realized, and ever so clearly,
That through the death of His only Son,
Mankind to Him, would then be won.

They cut down the limb and carved out a cross,
When they nailed Him to it, they thought sure He'd lost.
Little did they know that it was all in God's plan
To save the soul and spirit of every living man.

And that brings a question to my little ol' mind,
A question I've had for quite some time.
If for your life, He went out on a limb,
What then, are you willing to do for Him?

Soldier
Vessela Vassileva
Lies the soldier with a wound so fresh.
Bleeding to death, but yet he is not sad,
nor is he crying for help,
because he feels not the pain,
but the joy, the truth and the freedom.
Lies the young hero, covered in blood,
and embraces death with all his heart.
He knows that now he can sleep in peace,
that his country is forever the happy mother
for which he gave his own life.

The Wish
Christina Baker
Solitude I wished for, isolation I did receive
Their oddly gawking faces say that strange indeed they see me
But strange have they always looked upon this human child
trying hard to apprehend, but not, thus call me wild

Oh Solitude so wished for, makes one a beast or god
Far from divinity I know I am, thus cast me with the dogs
So strange Solitude to wish for, though reasons do not overlook
Alone a friend I know too well, the only that has never forsook

my dwelling, even with others present. Call me mad but no beast
What is not understood is deemed insane, cast aside, forgot, deceased
I am ignorant to affection, for never have they witnessed me
though I stand at their feet, waiting, hoping to meet their decree

But This they cannot know, it is impossible for them to understand
thus alone becomes my only companion, even with guests at hand
I would rather have Solitude, actually be in the condition of Alone
than be with all acquaintance, presenting someone they've not known

Puzzled eyes and shaking heads when I scream, Here I am, know This
So to my lonely chamber I fly, comforted at last by silence
Granted wish of Solitude, escape from that lonely land
With no one even trying, thus no one failing to understand

Childhood Friendships
Ruth Durnford
Friendships of our childhood years,
Leave memories to enjoy.
Adventures, quiet times and arguments,
Activities of each girl and boy.

Then comes the time there's a parting of ways,
As each his interest pursues,
Many times these memories are all that remain,
Of those friendships replaced with new.

Oh! what a blessing, as down thru the years,
An old friendship can be renewed,
To find the dreams that you both have shared,
Did, actually come true.

Again you share the struggles and joys,
Sad times, accomplishments galore.
Thru laughter and tears you cover the years,
Catching up on the times gone before.

How nice it would be if each could but meet,
A friend of long ago.
And find that life has blessed you both,
Better than either could know.

Untitled
Rafael W. Rocha

The quietness of the night surrounds me
Tears fall in silence
Like the rain and the quietness of the night
My questions fall in the silence of the night
Then a gentle voice speaks,
One more day, please just one more day.
The day comes and goes like every other day.
So quietly, like all the other days.
That inner voice comforts me.
A silent friend looking over me.

A Judge
Paul Zellermaier

A laughing scornful deluded man
A judge perhaps at gates of death
Does doom to crush the life of man
With humor in his laughing heart

Behead that fool! He does command
Dim that flame! That glowing life
Plunge and roll that savage beast!
To the clutches Satan's hand

Flung at once that heap of scrap
Down towards the gates of hell
Leaving clutching life itself
Behind in tears of frightened men

With that vain command, he does induce
Bursting tears in disbelief
Broken cries and sobs of hate
Too much whispers, screaming death

So the judged becomes with fear
Screaming, kicking in disdain
Promising with poisoned pride
Vengeance on a starlet night

Tomorrow's Door
Cynthia Ruth Flynn

It seems forever mine eyes hit the sun
perceiving ever changing gleams of singular puns
but now and again the message shines clear
its just my own dreams, there's nothing to fear

Just my own dreams
they're far yet so near
surrounded by chatter
such patience to rear

Darkened skies beyond the sunlit horizon
Beckoning with whispers sheer
Blowing cloths of dresses seared
But who in the world would think to hear

Do others turn as vibrations churn
Throughout the crowded streets we yearn
Or do they learn as fire burns
Across their souls when failure spurns

Now is the chance for all hope to survive
whomever says never, that's just a lie
Spread your wings, it's time to soar
Today is what opens tomorrow's door.

Wandering Mind Of Mine
Patricia G. Pond

Sitting in a bubble bath by candlelight
Lying on a rug by the fire so bright
I know everything will be all right
Listening and watching your silent gait
my mind wanders and happily waits
Caress my face and draw me near
Plant one of those kisses right here
The day is unwinding and the night is inviting
I long for tomorrow and wish away the week to come
When once again the cycle is begun.

The Bus Stop
Sandra Santana

Violence doesn't have a color or hold race,
Prejudice! does it hold justice?
While some parents choose to let their
Children fight, Others refuse!
Violence is not the way,
While trying to let them know and
refusing to let their child fight,
Others say let them fight!
Still refusing,
Violence is not the way!
not liked by others, refusing,
standing alone,
Violence is not the way!
While the problem is settled
in school, Parents still in an uproar,
shouting profanities, Where is their
example to their children? Now, While
the tables are turned they are still
shouting fight! I still stand alone
and will continue to stand in what
I believe.
Violence is not the way!

Dedication: The breath that fills my soul

Wanting
Sharon A. Brown

I've never wanted much because I've always had what I needed.
Was I loved? Am I loved?
Yes, but loved like I need to be loved —
I don't know.

I wanted him because I thought I needed him
But, like a bee, he flew from flower to flower
Drinking their forbidden nectar
While my flower stayed rooted, wilting and wanting.

I wanted them because they would need me as much as I needed them.
Never changing, never ending,
Reciprocating love, loving unconditionally,
Simple, the way it should be.

I still wanted, but what did I want? Who did I want?
He found me and we formed a most perfect, yet imperfect union —
Loving, not loving, trusting, not trusting, hopeful, hopeless,
Clarity, utter confusion, a void filled, a vacuum created.

Happy? Not completely. I'm still wanting, needing.
Will I ever find It?
I decided to go to that secret room where the answer was all along.
I opened the door and there he was — Smiling.

The Elk
Carole Klock

I wish I were a poet,
For then I could tell you in noble words
about the elk.
He hovers on the side of the road at night,
Like a mere shadow, an apparition.
Then, when he crosses over,
He goes with proud head held high.
His hooves seem barely to touch the ground.
When God made this glorious creature,
He endowed it with a little of His very own beauty and grace.

To Know My Father By Number
Debra H. Bader

To know a man by his face,
the curve of his lips when he smiles,
the pattern of his lines time engraved around his eyes,
and the eyes themselves, speak a language truer than words,
they have seen what no man was meant to see and cannot look away,
the sight is imprinted on the air.

To know a man by his voice as the harsh laugh softens with years,
to know him by words and deed, by touch and kiss and embrace,
by his old plaid windbreaker and favorite lopsided hat,
by his silence,
to know him by the fringe of his tallis
I have counted and recounted beside him in Schul.

But to know a man by number 133527,
this defies knowledge,
the imprint of indelible past, indelible pain, indelible loss,
and yet,
as a very little girl, across from my father at the breakfast table,
he in his T–shirt eating a grapefruit,
I smiled, and he smiled back, and I knew
he was numbered among G–d's chosen.

Dedication: To my father, who inspired this poem

Thanks To My Friend
Thelma Meaney

Life seemed so dark,
With no direction,
When things were going wrong,
God sent me a friend!

It seemed like ages,
But it was only days,
Of darkness and despair,
God sent you to me!

The feeling of being alone,
Of no place to turn,
Where had I erred?
What decision was wrong?

The inner struggle, feeling of falling,
The fear became overwhelming,
But God cared,
He sent me a friend!

Your encouragement,
The support for me to rebuild,
My foundation within,
Thanks, God sent me a friend!

Subtle, Simple, Imp.
Billy Philipp

Go back to the blackness
that stole from me my twin,
oh deceitful devil of evil and sin.
My life, though unsteady, is mine once again.
Art thou not a liar, an imp of the dark,
who scribbles and scrabbles on sill like a lark?
Thy promises hollow, thy favors with strings.
The path of dark doings inevitably stings
those who would follow a voice in the night.
Heed not the voices, walk to the night!

Cavalier
Cody A. Jennings

Behind the shield is a heart of gold, being the eyes is a mind of a poet
Gauntlets protect the healing hands, while the sword protects the One,
    Loved.
Helmut, seals a destiny already written.

Behind the shield is a heart of gold, strong in struggle of life yet
    fragile in the hands of love
A shield that offers protection in times of war for what heart can survive
    every arrow
A shield and nothing more for wall's shelter without allowing God's wish to
    enter
Behind my shield I am shy yet kind for only the strongest of hearts can be
    open to all pain
No matter how strong I become no shield can stop the soft touch of love

The sword protects the one loved, but war has not ended without claiming
    one more life
Wounded, broken, dying, the hero needs the healer
Strength has left his body as his blood flows thin
As he fades away he feels a soft touch unlike any other
He knows it is she and thanks God for this lost moment together
Soaked with sorrow she holds him close..."...no" she says softly
Within her arms he feels her love flow through him and begins to live
    again

Fathers, Daddys And Men
Arieona R. McKune

God bless those Daddys,
who are not just Men.
They are the true Fathers who make time,
to be Fathers, Daddys and Men.

God bless those Men who are real Men,
who do not stray.
Those Daddys who are truly kind,
and who are forever there.

These Fathers, Daddys, and Men
are not just the average.
For these Men go way beyond,
the call of duty for their children.

I bless every Man who has stood by,
and not been a coward to their family.
Who have cared for and loved their family,
like no others have.

I would like to honor these Fathers, Daddys and Men,
for they have done far more than any others would.
These Men deserve to be called Fathers, Daddys, and Men,
they are the true Heroes in my eyes.

Silence Encompasses The Night
Richard Hale
Silence encompasses the night.
The pale forest grips us,
Taking with it our tired souls.
Forgetting what will make us laugh
Is worse than the events of our past.
The dense trees hide our sodden tears
And will bring us closer to the edge.
Only light will lead us through,
Because love exists beyond what is real,
Beyond what is natural.

Grandma's Shoes
Rona Leach
Grandma's Shoes all turned over, dirty, old, ragged and stained
Grandma's Shoes walked the fields,
the dirt roads, paths, through mud and sand
Yes, Grandma's Shoes.

Grandma's Shoes went to church, visited the sick and plowed the fields.
Grandma's Shoes even ran me down,
just so I might experience the taste of castor oil upon my tongue
Yes, Grandma's Shoes.

Grandma's Shoes saw lots of pain in her day...suffering, hunger,
loneliness and death.
They stomped to the rhythm of old gospel hymns, and danced because of
joy deep down in her soul.
Yes, Grandma's Shoes.

But Grandma's Shoes now set still beneath the table,
Grandma's Shoes will no longer pace the floor,
Grandma's Shoes stand still—less for the moment,
for her mildewed shoes will be no more.

Yes, Grandma's Shoes now heavenly slippers,
As she enters the Kingdom's Door,
Yes, that's my Grandma's Shoes!

An Angel
Annie Mayhew
Angels are sent from heaven;
They are very rare and few.
Angels are precious gifts from God;
They spread joy that is true.

I saw an angel with the warmest smile;
His eyes were comforting when life was cruel and cold.
I met him and he touched my heart;
He reached into my soul.

When he talks to me so sweet,
I can tell how much he cares;
But when doubt takes over,
I question how long he'll really be there.

I can call him my angel,
I can say he's my destiny;
But what he is in reality
May be different that what he is to me.

When I see an indescribable beauty,
I think of the angel's face.
Will this angel be around to guard me,
Or will he disappear without a trace?

Alone And Lost
Angela R. Mason
Alone is the way I feel
Lost is where I am
There's no one here to soothe my pain
I am not in reality nor am I in fantasy
I've looked for so long for someone to listen to me
My body is here but my mind is somewhere else somewhere dark and cold
I'm longing for someone or something to get my mind out of that cold, dark
   place
Alone is the way I feel
Lost is where I am

The Grandchild
Debbie Schneider
I love the feel of your little hand,
Always so trusting and warm,
And when I am upset or sad
Your little eyes seem to understand.

One look at that precious, innocent face
Proves you were placed by the angels above,
Maybe to remind us how special life is,
For everyone you touch, is filled with love.

Now I yearn to live forever
And watch you grow year after year,
It hurts to even miss a day with you,
For you have become so dear.

Alas, one day I will have to leave
To a new home nice and snug,
Where I'll treasure our times together
Like your smell and the feel of a hug.

And when I hear my Father say,
"I'll walk with you this last mile"
I'll keep in my heart the memory
Of that little Shala smile.

Impossible To Shatter The Glass
Erin Attfield
Hit my dream with my wonder
will I ever become...?
Sickness pouring like rain
drops leaving remain
beneath the moist soil I see the clear day.

Do you hear my echo
cracking the devil's mouth
splitting the lips of my phantom friend
still to dry to make a spark.

Do the lines on my palm say some truth
how do the rivers flow
curve to and fro
who will ever know?

Look back at the trail of the past
how baby-faced you looked,
still no shame for the game.

What shall I do next
to become the pathetic source
a criminal within heart
a dark night within mind.

The Price Of War
Joseph Ayton
The pilot who is flying overhead,
Unaware civilians will soon be dead.
Is this the price of war?
The machine gun fire overhead,
The soldier dying on a makeshift bed.
Is this the price of war?
Fire and smoke raging everywhere,
Children helpless in need of care.
Is this the price of war?
The innocent pay the price.

Thoughts Of An Orphan In Rwanda
Joan M. Hallett
God, what is peace?
I do not understand
I know of guns and bombs and death
It covers all our land.

God, what is food?
Will it stop me being hungry?
Please ask someone to send some help
So that we can live humanely.

God, what is love?
I do not know the feeling
An orphan is a sorry sight
And life, it has no meaning.

The Red Cross heard this tale of woe
And came to some decisions
To help in any way they could
With milk, toys and provisions.

God, please thank all these people
I now know someone cares
For their love and understanding
But most of all their prayers.

Modern Man
Darren Cross
Kicking and screaming, awoke from a sleep,
A child is born, still frail and weak,
His life will change as his young mind ages,
Progressing through modern man's seven stages,
The smiling infant, giggling and staring,
His doting mother, so loving and caring,
And on to the schoolboy with personal computer,
Storing information, divulged by his tutor,
Then into his teens, dancing and drinking,
Of the opposite sex, he has started thinking,
So now the young man with qualifications,
Progressing neatly through higher education,
He's leaving home shortly, away from his mother,
Renting a flat with his besotted lover,
Studying philosophy at a state funded college,
Trying so hard to add to his knowledge,
In just a few years he has a wife and a daughter,
She'll grow up well using things he has taught her,
He has a big mortgage, there are bills everywhere,
He is behind with his payments, the bank does not care,
He's down and depressed but his life soon changes,
A win on the lottery, he's been trying for ages,
A rich grandfather now with millions to spend,
No more worries: Fun to the end.

Mirror Mirror
Freda Wilshaw
I look in the mirror and what do I see
Some sad stranger looking back at me
I say who are you? Please give me a clue
Why oh why do you look so blue!
You have all that God has to give
So get a life and start to live
Wipe that tear from your face, and please don't cry
I know with God's help you will get by
I look again and what do I see
HELP! That's no stranger that is me.

Memories
Joyce Costello
The old man sat there dreaming
of happy days gone by,
They're now all buried in the past,
and in his own mind's eye,

He thought of days when he was young,
a soldier tall and strong,
Fighting on the front lire
amidst the mighty throng.

The happiest day, he always said,
was when he met his wife,
And how he took her by the hand
to vow his love for life,

His life is nearly over,
he doesn't really care,
For what is life upon this earth
without his wife to share,

For she's been gone a long time now,
and he has been alone,
Waiting for the Lord to see his pain
and call him home.

Red Bird
Christina M. Smith
Red Bird, Red Bird,
sing me your song.
Every note so perfect,
neither a right or a wrong.

Your notes float so free,
like the breeze on the air.
Drifting through the clouds,
with never a care

Red Bird, Red Bird,
high above the loft.
Sing me your song.
Ever so soft.

Even through the rain,
I can hear your song.
The perfect rhythm,
we all long.

Red Bird, Red Bird,
come again one day.
Sing me your song,
and then fly away.

Love's Death Knell
John Rose
Please be seated in wooden rows
My love lies in state, drag the lid closed
In silent reflection hear my prayer
I'm brought to my knees; this heart is bare
As the anointed baby my face is damp
Extinguish the candles, shine not your lamp
Infancy to obsolescence; idyllic for a while
Here comes the bride in some fantasy aisle
Solitary, cheated and deprived at best
Lower the box, lay my feelings to rest.

Untitled
Mary L. Stiles
If today was over
never to happen again,
and tomorrow was a day
I would never see,
could I look to the heavens and openly share...

"My last day was incredible"
all full of laughter and joy,
all happy and positive,
in all that was endured.
Kind thoughts and words for strangers
Sincere words and thoughts for my friends.

"My last day was what I made it"
For that I am fulfilled
Today can never be again
Things that happened today cannot be redone.

"Today was as it should be"
and if tomorrow never comes,

"My last day was incredibie"
because I made it that way.
I am proud.

The Sorrowful Dream
James Gribben
As I sat and watched the firelight fade,
With its dying flickering flame.
My body shuddered as those dancing shadows,
Reached out as if to maim.

The probing thrust of that darkened lance,
Struck home and caused me sleep.
And now I watch the rising sun,
With red—rimmed eyes that weep.

As Morpheus held me in his arms,
He made that I should dream.
To see a youth brimful of charm,
And a life that might have been.

I saw his carefree zest for life,
Yet tempered with loving care.
Fruits of life that he had earned,
With others he did share.

Now I with envy for his blessings,
In sorrow count the cost.
Bitter loneliness my sole companion,
For wasted years now lost.

Love Me Tender
Phillip M. Garcia
Please help me climb that mountain
To my cabin in the sky
I need your love and your devotion
Or I know that I would cry
I pray to God and Jesus
As my days go passing by
And when it comes my time to die
I'll find my place in heaven
With my guardian angel waiting
In my cabin in the sky

The Dancer
Edward Jay
She dances alone to a silent tune
Perfect symmetry in a crowded room
Feeling nothing, seeing only instead
Dark painful pictures inside her head

Grief has laid tracks across her face
Once auburn hair now grey in place
She dances alone forever lost to us all
Screaming silently within unable to call

Who stole the love that surrounded her life
From whence came his turmoil heartache and strife
Where are the arms that held her so tight
Where gone the body that warmed her at night

She moves in sorrow with head held high
No matter the cost she will not cry
Around broken furniture and scattered books
And torn lover's photographs with reproachful looks

She dances alone but still her arms entwine
The memory of a love she believed divine
Each step now taken with agonized breath
Accepting the pain yet denying the death

Untitled
Margaret Pash
Up there in a cosmic zone, the adventurous ones fly
so far from home.
They see the world from a different view,
Surrounded by clouds with a bluish hue.

Floating through their daily tasks, if things go
Wrong they have to mask,
The anguish they must feel inside,
For there is no place to run and hide.

Personal items they are but few, toothbrush, toothpaste,
—Photographs one or two.
Simple things you may not treasure,
But to lose them up there — we could not measure.

So when you look up towards the stars, either facing
Jupiter or maybe Mars.
Just stop for a moment and begin to wonder,
What courage it took to go out yonder.

So what's in the future, where will it all end,
Where next will they decide to send,
And — no matter how low they may proceed,
Man — will eventually succeed.

Why?
Mathew McNeil

Why is the sky blue, miss?
Why are the trees green?
Why are there waves in the sea, miss?
Why is the wind never seen?

Why do we live on Earth, miss?
Why is the planet round?
Why can't we float in the air, miss?
But have to stay on the ground?

Why is the sun hot, miss?
Why is snow cold?
Why can't we stay young, miss?
But have to grow old?

Why do dogs have four legs, miss?
Why have humans got two?
Why do sheep go BAA, miss?
Why do cows go MOO?

Why have you got that gun, miss?
Why is it next to your head?
I haven't finished my questions, miss,
And I can't ask you if you're dead!

Caught
Francesca Wrigley

Fluttering away,
Unable to play,
Tears drip like rain,
Truth tells the pain.
Enter we try,
To reach to the sky,
Wriggling, flapping wings,
Leaping to their feet.
No time to sing,
Capture is complete.

Ode To A Tree
Carol Fisher

A tree died tonight

They just tied a rope around its capacious ochre trunk and using
a tractor tore it by its roots from its loamy terrestrial bed

I heard it scream

A translucent heart rending scream echoing through time, the
vibrations breaking natures autumn tranquillity with tones of
slow torturous death

I heard its last breath

whispering painful pleas, a death melos of melancholy memories of two
hundred years from sparkling sapling to majestic earthbound living
landmark

I heard it die

an exhalation of spring sweet breezes, like the fragrance of new mown
grass blending ethereal in the all consuming atmosphere, then the lament
lost in time forever

I cried for that tree

The Good Shepherd
Dallas Jacobs

The Lord is my Shepherd my needs He'll supply
In pastures so green He maketh me lie
Beside the still waters I find peace and rest
I'll give Him my life for He knoweth what's best.

Through the valley of death, surrounded by fear
In Him I find comfort, He always is near
He will not allow any harm to befall
If I will but follow, and answer His call.

He leadeth me not, to a dry barren land
But bringeth me back with His own gentle hand
His Spirit will guide me, His love He'll disclose
With His wonderful blessings, my cup overflows.

He is the Good Shepherd, He cares for His own
He hung on the cross for my sins to atone
His goodness and mercy will show me the way
With His love He restoreth my soul every day.

With His rod and His staff, my protector He'll be
What a wonderful Saviour, and Shepherd is He
And when life is over in this troublesome land
I'll be with Him yonder in Heaven so grand.

Farewell
Cherry Mason

It seems I've only known you
For just a little white
Your surroundings will be missed
Your laughter and your smile
Even though you've gone away
We won't be far apart
For I'll hold a secret place for
you here with in my heart
So I won't say, good—bye for
Now I'll only say, farewell.

Faith
Sylvia J. Kaye

If you have Faith, you have it all
The sweet seas though far away
Seem closer, stronger, nearer, tall
Even though there may be some weeds gray.

They're not for you, all that is true
Are skies azure without the tears
Close by singing to you that bird so blue
Winged with Faith the waiting years.

If you have Faith you have it all
God's eyes and heart are always yours
No bleak winds or pitfalls near
Where Faith abides and soars.

Unending – ageless in this boon
The blessed sight of Faith
Creates the stars and golden moon
Though ecstasy may have to wait.

With Faith we gather flowers
And heed not the stones beneath
Only o'erhead we live the hour
For into Faith a life is complete.

Saved To Serve
Samuel Dartey–Baah
See men daily dying
Knowing not Christ as Lord and King
Damnation they enter with loads of guilt and sin
While children of God sing and rejoice in God their King
Devoid of compassion, watching them daily dying

You have been saved to serve
Not just to stand and stare at a world lost in despair
You have been called to declare
The gospel of Christ so clear
That he came to save and bear
All our sin trouble and care
And free us from every snare

Child of God arise and tell
Every man, woman, boy and girl
That Satan aims just to swell
The number of souls bound for hell
Let them buy the truth we sell
It is such a precious pearl
And each shall be your jewel
When Heaven come for us to dwell.

Dedication: Wife, Sandra and our families

The City Awakes
Betsey Adkins
Birds sing at morning light,
Waking from their restful night.
Flowers bloom along the way,
Reaching for the sun's first ray.
Street sweepers join the morning song,
As traffic slowly moves along.
A squirrel does his high wire dance.
On nimble feet we see him prance.
The peaceful night slips slow away.
The city greets another day.

Shangri–La
Rose Wilson
I dream of an island bathed in sun
Completely unknown to any one
Where I can be each precious day
At one with God as I kneel and pray

This paradise is a haven of rest
For this troubled and weary mortal
I can lie here in a sweet content
Without window, walls, or portal

The sky so blue above my head
There is no roof to steal my view
The colour so perfect, no artist could paint
Such a breathtaking and beautiful hue

The sea so clear, a shimmering jewel
Lapping at the sands so warm and white
This beauty makes me catch my breath
I gaze overawed with wonder and delight

Time stands still in this "Shangri–La"
The rat race left far behind
How I wish this could be a reality
For this poor solitary member of mankind.

To Daphne
Daphne Boket
I will always remember with pleasure
The day that our little one came.
To bless us with joy overflowing.
And how she required her first name.

We gave her the fair name of "Daphne".
Because as she lay in my arms.
I thought of the bright yellow daffies.
Those flowers of such golden charms.

They are flowers I love oh so dearly.
that on being given the chance.
I would fill every vase in the household.
And feast my soul on their fragrance

And I would that our little one blossomed.
And grew with a nature as fair.
And as golden as those pretty flowers.
By carrying joy everywhere.

Growing from childhood to wisdom.
And building a character fine.
Showing a bright happy future.
Like those yellow favourites of mine.

Romantic Chantings
Gregory L. Kelly
Romantic chantings, going through my head, and every thought
I think about you, is something to be said.
Every whisper that I hear, is saying to me, that, I wish
you were near.
Believing one thing about all else, that my love for you, is
greater than wealth.
This love that we have is one of a kind, because, there is
no love, better than yours and mine.

Dedication: My wife, Leona Kelly

The Highlands Of Scotland
J. H. Lightbody
Lochs, mountains and valleys,
Purple heather, eagles, wildlife in the glens and alleys.
Roads, rivers and rail,
A picture that cannot fail.

Highland cattle roam in the fields,
Motorists stopping with camera reels.
Rivers flow into the lochs with a song,
Passers–by, pause; then pass along.

History surrounds to tell the tale;
The commando–monument, museums and other regale.
From Fort William to Fort Augustus and beyond,
The magnetism draws people to respond.

Admire Glenfinnan's Pass,
And the forests flourishing in mass.
Fishermen on the rivers making a cast,
For rainbow trout, salmon or even bass.

Views of beauty await inspection,
Caught by the traveller from every direction.
The awe–inspiring scenes – an album collection,
The friendliness of Highland people a vital connection.

Heaven
Stan Gresswell

I have confidence in Heaven
that you'll forget me not,
although you're far away dear
You're in the sacred spot.

Heaven's door will open
and let my love flow through,
and all the years that follows dear
I'll be true to you.

Although you're far away dear
you're always by my side,
Good or bad I'll not be sad
My time I'll just abide.

Heaven's door has opened
And all my love's flown through,
for all the years that follow dear
I'll be true to you.

Although you're far away dear
you're always by my side,
Good or bad I'll not be sad
My time I'll just abide.

Untitled
Dawn Marie Santiago

As the bright sun is falling
My darknight is calling for you
Its a very lonely time
Even though your heart is in mine
I still can't help the feelings I have
Sometimes depressed and even stressed
I long for the day to come
for us to be all alone
I love you and I'll wait
You see, we are together because of fate

Red Ribbons
Gail Dyson

Red ribbons were always in my childhood
Matching my home—made dresses
With their tulips and poppies
Red ribbons decorated my hair and
Spoke of summer days and picnics

Red ribbons came with me to gymkhanas
A warning that a horse might kick
They accompanied Christmas presents
Easter eggs, birthday treats
Giving vibrant energy to all they touched

Red ribbons now bring awareness of a totally different scene
A warning of a virus as unpredictable as
The horse at the gymkhana
With energy as vibrant as Christmas

Red ribbons symbolise lifeblood for me now,
Infected, immune deficient, immoral
Red, reckless ribbons
Remembering those lost – in scarlet style
Red for blood – red for dead...

Dedication: For my friend, Darren

Love
Carla Tarpey

They say love
Grows stronger, day by day.
In a sense I suppose its true.
But if our love is growing stronger
Then why do I feel I'm losing you.

As I love you more
The hurt just seems to grow.
Simple things, change to something big
Making so many problems
And causing so much aggro.

What are we supposed to do.
Take the difficult option
And try to sort things out,
Or take the simple option
Split up and forget.

Things just seem to get harder
Causing so much pain.
How can love,
Which is supposed to be a good thing,
Cause so much sadness.

Wintertime
Wendy L. Shryock

Outside the freezing wind chills to the bone
Covering the ground a patch of fluffy white snow.
Icicles hanging from the top of the house
everything here as quiet as a mouse.
It is time for hot cocoa and gathering around the fire
and telling stories for hours and hours.
There is nothing to do this time of year for summer
is gone and wintertime is here.

Dedication: My husband, Duane

A Look At Life
Christian Clarke

As I look at life I really do begin to wonder
Surely to have been born at all was not just a tragic
Blunder
Born not by accident but by some far greater design
Another unique specimen of God's homo sapien line
Involuntarily ejected in a steaming watery slide
Then the last maternal attachment is torn aside
A slap a cry followed by faint beating heart
Yes this is it life just the first painful start
Suckling and sighing never ever seeming at rest
But almost permanently attached to mother's ample breast
This tiny piece of humanity be it girl or boy
'Tis its mother's delight, its father's pride and joy
Noisily gurgling and bumbling even beginning to talk
Crawling, standing, falling and starting to walk
Growing so fast with fierce longing and yearning
Accompanied by an insatiable desire for learning
Questions, questions, my oh my when? Where? and why why
why?
why do I laugh why do I cry – If I was born why must I
Die?
Now a teenager – puberty reigns creating great emotion
strains.
A totally confused juvenile with no ambitions or aims

118

Believing
Martha A. Whiting

You always said we'd be together
and I believe we'll be,
as long as there are waves
tossing around upon the sea;

I believe that every word
you utter to be true
as long as there are fluffy clouds
drifting around in skies of blue;

As long as there are mountains
whose heights you can't attain,
and flowers are still being kissed
by springtime's gentle rain;

As long as there is sunshine
to brighten up the day,
and the moon and twinkling stars at night
to lead us on our way;

To think that all these things will end
would just be too absurd
and so, my dear, until they do
I'll go on believing every word.

Dead Grass
Mandy Rasler

The dead grass
like mean people
Their blades
rip my feet
Crack underneath
each step
They come to
attack me
Where to run
Where to hide

Lancaster's Lady
Jill Galloso

A Lancaster flew over like a beautiful bird.
The emotion I felt seemed very absurd.
A flashback to a time, I do not know when.
I don't understand now, and didn't do then.

The Merlin engines, deep and low.
Faces surround me from a long time ago.
Huddled together as we flew darkened skies.
Watching for fighter planes with terrified eyes.

Corkscrewing down to get out of the way.
Hoping to live for just one more day.
How can I know just how these men felt.
Or question my hand that God must have dealt.

I cannot explain my love of this plane.
Nor cannot shed light – was I going insane
To believe I could, in another time,
Have flown in a Lanc. for this country of mine.

Was I a part of that terrible war?
Are the memories I have from sights that I saw?
They say "Ours is not to reason why",
So I'll live with these questions 'til the day that I die.

Sweet Sixteen
Joan Matthews

At sweet sixteen and bonny,
The world is at her feet.
She has that certain SOMETHING,
Charms everyone she meets.

Our young lady has her moments,
But is sunny as a rule.
Sums up situations quickly,
To prove she is nobody's fool.

Always studious in the classroom,
Pays attention and works with zest.
Feet firmly planted on the ladder,
Intends to climb overtaking the rest.

When in school tie ever decorous,
This young miss also knows how to play.
At the disco with earrings twirling,
She lets the music carry her away.

What did we do to deserve this Jewel,
Adorning our family tree?
Don't know, but I'm really grateful,
That sweet sixteen is related to me.

Climb
Judy K. Glasscock

It often seems
That too many dream
Of climbing
To the top
Of the ladder
And if the dream
Becomes reality
It often seems
That too many scream
"What does it matter?"

Beta Sigma Phi
A. Mae Reinholdt

Life is the span of time between two eternities,
The way uncharted; and ours is the will,
If we so choose, to make of it a temple
Set high upon a hill.

Learning is the golden stairway
Leading upward toward the stars,
Which we mount to realms of wisdom
And thereby enrich this life of ours.

Our friends are the yellow roses
Which we pick along life's way;
And through the years the fragrance lingers
Although we stumble and the skies are gray.

Life, learning and friendship,
And true friendship is by far the best,
For there we find a blessed haven
In which our weary hearts may rest.

'Tis there we learn life's true meaning:
To love, and be loved, and then to find
The promise of eternal life,
The great golden dream of mankind.

I Am Not Alone
Lois B. Weber

I am not alone His hand
is in mine,
As I walk thru life
one day at a time.

I am not alone when I
face life's woes,
The Lord alone His
mercy shows.

I am not alone when
everything is great,
My God is there to help
me celebrate.

I am not alone when I
kneel in prayer,
The Lord has promised
"I'll be there."

I am not alone with all
my fears,
For God holds my hand
and wipes my tears.

Jake
Melissa Long

Who is Jake?
Jake has pretty skin,
but is not thin.
Jake slithers,
but does not wither.
Jake is real long,
but cannot sing a song.
Do you know who Jake is now?
Jake is my pet Python,
that ran in the Marathon.

Missing You
Jeannie Zarrella–Schneider

It seems like decades since our last embrace,
Centuries since I last saw your face.
Every conscious moment I see you in all that I do.
My Dear, I'm missing you.

When was the last time we kissed?
The time in between and all we missed?
The last time it was only me and you?
Honey, I'm missing you.

Every time you looked into my eyes
Your smile wiped away my cries.
You understood without my having to tell you.
Darling, I'm missing you.

You were the calm during my storm,
The thread to sew my heart that was torn.
I remember everything that you would say or do.
Sweetheart, I'm missing you.

You could find the answer to every problem but one,
And now our earthly time together is done.
But at some future time I will again find you.
My Love, I'm missing you.

Rolling Waves
Pamela Waller

Rolling waves come up to me.
Granules of sand surround my feet.
A sea gull flies high above I see,
Watching, waiting and ready to seek.

In a distance a boat goes forth.
The sun beams down upon its sails.
A firm but steady course of north.
Ropes tied tight on its rails.

To my left a child does play,
Pail and shovel held in hands.
Builds a castle that must stay,
Waves take as it lands.

To my right two lovers lay,
Wanting a mere golden tan.
On this bright and sunny day,
A breeze hits like a fan.

Rolling waves come up to me.
A smile does paint my lips a glow.
I feel alive and so free,
As I turn and walk steady, but slow.

The Transformation
John Burch

The change is electric, electric and fast
the transformation to mother, to mother from lass.
The natural process from one into two
an unbreakable tie between the new.
The pace of the race forever slowed
a new direction accepted, an unknown road.
To be a mother, how wonderful it must be
to know this new life was conceived within thee.
Forever connected by spirit and soul
the transformation of woman from half into whole.

The Date
Kenneth E. Webb

I had been with her before
Way back in o—when,
So I called on the telephone
Said, I'd like to see her again.

She was something special to me
And a lady I would say,
So a date was set up
Would be the 6th of May.

I wasn't stepping out on my wife
And I wasn't being untrue,
I just had to see her again
This is something I wanted to do.

When I went into her room
She said you can sit over there,
So I got real comfortable
In that big old chair.

My heart skipped a beat
When she walked to me that day,
She said open your mouth
I'll start cleaning teeth right—a—way.

Where Have All The Elders Gone?
Lois A. McCartney
Are you a grandparent, and if you are
Do you feel left out, wonder what goes on?
Within your family; sometimes, so far
Away from the love of grand— daughter or son.

There is nothing so precious, don't you agree?
As a hug or a question from a little one
To look out your window and there to see
A grandchild who's come to visit — your day's begun.

There must be a void when a child doesn't experience
A relationship with an elder; nothing can replace
A walk with grandfather; he explains the difference
Between what's on the inside and on one's face.

All questions answered; a cup of cocoa
Food tastes best at Grandmothers, there's no doubt
The hugs are great, but it's time to go
"I want to stay here", you'd like to shout.

Cherish the moments, time goes so fast
No matter who you are, when all's said and done
The clock stops for no one, but memories last
Where have all the Elders gone?

Tenderly Attached
Linda Ferraro
Every time you touch my face,
No one could ever take your place.
Kiss me softly on my cheek,
Hold me tightly, make me weak.
Could love like this last forever,
Help me, we'll make the wish together.
Love me, please never let me go.
And I'll hold you close to let you know,
That every time you touch my face,
No one could ever take your place.

Lake Michigan
Ruth Webb Murphy
There is a fog out over Lake Michigan to night,
I can hear the fog horns blow.
The water is still and the wind is light,
There is little movement to and fro.

I like to walk along the lake
And observe the mood she's in,
If the waves are calm and do not break,
Then I know there is peace within.

Sometimes the lake begins to roar
The waves seem full of anger and ire—
They splash and pound against the shore
Tearing buildings into rubble and to mire.

Gradually, the waves become weary and worn out,
For their wrath is almost spent.
Then peace descends upon all about
And the lake again, is content.

How like the lake is our very life,
Sometimes we are happy and gay.
Again we are filled with sadness and strife
Then peace comes at the close of day.

I Won't Quit
Debbie Carpenter–Harnish
When the sky is turning the darkest of grey,
When the brightest of light is fading away,
When the azure morning is changing to haze,
I won't quit.

When the river becomes wider, and too fast to swim,
When the bright sunlit shore is beginning to dim,
When the last boat has left, and I'm out on limb,
I won't quit.

When the mountain is becoming too hard to climb,
When the rocks are slipping from underfoot I find,
When the peak is hidden far beyond reason and rhyme,
I won't quit.

My life is not ending, it has only begun,
The race is not over until it is won,
And I have but one chance to reach for the sun,
I won't quit.

Grant me strength to help others, family or friend,
When their perseverance has come to an end,
When our lives have just started around the last bend,
I won't quit.

Peace
Kelly A. McCaulla
There is something that is needed
in this world today,
That will solve many problems of
mankind and the things we say!
Instead we are striving and fighting
for our lives, we need to know where
we stand and know our every rights.
Just imagine how it would be if we
could see that this world is in need
of...Perfect Peace!

Untitled
Rachel Williams
I want to create
A memory for you
One that will last forever
And a lifetime or two.

A quick little experience
That will seem like nothing
And then one day
Will return a lasting recollection.

Maybe a tear
Maybe some laughter
Maybe a sight or sound
Will bring it gushing forth.

A memory to recall
When you're feeling blue
When no one is there
To lend a shoulder.

Memories
A lifetime of remembrances
Please let me
Make a memory for you.

The Ballad About Cape Cod
Vera Neyman

It was my dearest dream if allows the G–d
to travel one day to a mysterious place named simply Cape Cod.

And the day has come – it was a beautiful dawn
when we took a flight that brought us to Boston.
All historical names familiar from textbooks–
Providence Town, Nutcracker, Plymouth.
But the biggest surprise was when we got to the shore
We saw the un–human beauty we would like to explore.
And the sun was all shining and the breeze was so nice
The trip gave us a pleasure that adds life a spice.

And walking the destinations it seemed you can never reach,
I will always keep in my memory the taste of the salty breeze,
as the days filled with sunshine and the nights that were full of love...
That was the time you can only strive for, for the rest of your whole life.

And as a precious jewel in a crown, as the most wonderful gift
I recall our visit to "Mayflower" – the temptation I couldn't resist.
And the conversation to "real" Pilgrims – what a life those people lived
I am proud to be an American, I am proud of what they once did!

And I will ALWAYS remember the place you are close to G–d,
the place no longer mysterious with a romantic name Cape Cod.

Red Moon
Debra Anne Chapman

Red moon glowing symbol of rarity
unseen often illuminating Earth's Ozark heart.
Clouds float with caring comfort
shielding fragments of moon shared rays.
Watching from Earth's yard
the one that I temporarily will occupy,
I am honored to share in this colorful pageant
presented by the moon and clouds,
thankful to view the grandeur
by the red moon artist of Earth's sky.

Untitled
Daniel Bishop

It wasn't the roll of the dice.
It was love and sacrifice
That brought to be
The children you see.

We are so very glad
You are our mom and dad.
You brought us up in the way we should go
And our thankfulness we want you to know.

We are so very glad
'Cause you're the kind of parents
Every child wishes they had.
We love you Mom and Dad.

We thank you for your example,
The Godly example parents should give
And that example, Mom and Dad,
Has shown us how to live.

We love you, Mom and Dad.
You're the best.
We're glad we can say we love you
As our love does attest.

Perceptions
Frances L. Smith

Perceive, if you will
a golden hill
a lily pond
a daffodil

But you will say
a mound of clay
a muddy lake
flowers forsake

How do we see so differently?
Perceptions are not of the eye
but, of the mind
and heart rely

So, perceive if you will
my golden hill
my lily pond
a daffodil

And, I shall see
you've made a start
seeing not with your eyes
but with your heart!

Holy Matrimony
Georgia Gnann

On adventure, the two of us,
with one another's hand to hold,
for the road is tortuous,
slosh through mud
and rock–strewn floods, scale hills,
scorched by sun, then, bent by gales,
slip, almost, into the cracks,
crawl into caves,
but save our grip, coming through,
coming out, together, as One.

The Eternal Plan Of Salvation
Esther Din Brooks

Once there was a time in the presence of God:
Where each of us here was his spirit child,
We talked and walked beside Him, we beheld His face,
Oh, what a wondrous time we spent in that place!

God presented a plan and we all have agreed,
He was very pleased with our choice indeed,
That He gave us bodies in our spiritself;
We all came down and live on the face of the earth.

And when the time is come that life on earth is through,
God will lay our bodies in the ground below;
Our spirits will rise and will go back to Him,
Did we obey the Lord and endure to the end?

Our spirit will wait in the spirit world,
They'll rest in paradise if they've obeyed God's word;
Waiting for the resurrection and God's kingdom to come,
While those of the wicked shall still be in the ground.

The Lord will judge us and will give us glory,
According to our thoughts, to our actions, and the words we say;
Telestial and Terrestrial are the kingdoms for the wicked to stay,
And the righteous will be with God in the celestial glory.

G–R–A–N–D–M–A
Leeann Hogg
Grandma – is: Great – G
Grandma – is: Really cool – R
Grandma – is: Awesome – A
Grandma – is: Nice – N
Grandma – is: Downright – D
    Loved
Grandma – is: Marvelous – M
Grandma – is: Adorable – A

But most of all Grandma
is (Irreplaceable).

Sweet Sixteen
Susan Baldwin
These sixteen roses are a symbol of love
A love that grows each day
One for each year of happiness
Your life has brought my way

From baby tears to teenage tears
We've worked each problem through
For no one in this world of ours
Means more to me than you

I've watched you grow and learn and love
And cherished every step
We've laughed and played and argued
Sometimes we've even wept

Wherever your life may take you
Wherever your heart will go
Don't forget I'll always love you
More than you'll ever know

I will not be around forever
To help you along the way
Just remember all I've taught you
And you will make it through okay.

Victory
Belinda Jean Proietti
I felt a gentle breeze this morning,
blowing deep within my heart.
Assuring me of much better things,
now being so very broken apart.

This was indeed a need fulfilled,
restoring again a confidence of hope,
Releasing me of this world's strife,
enabling me to further cope.

Having come from my Lord above,
I welcomed such good news.
For the storm of days now past,
had left me battered and bruised.

But my God, He is always faithful,
when life presents itself unfair.
Sending his comforting Holy Spirit,
when there's pain too great to bear

I praise Him for His deliverance,
from my many enemies at hand.
For it is only in His loving care,
that I am able to firmly stand.

For My Love
Jennifer M. Vogel
All the love I have is for you.
You brighten up my day,
When nothing else goes right.
I can count on you to cheer me up,
You don't even have to say a word,
Just seeing you there next to me makes me smile.
I think of all the wonderful times we have together
and pray they shall never end.
But if we should ever part,
I want you to know that I will always love you
Love you till the end of time.

An Old Woman's Eyes
Ann Hunot Mendenhall
"Grandma, could you come to our recital at the School?"
"The ballet is so exciting, and the music oh! so cool!"
"The dancers keep a tapping to every note and beat;
The rhythm is so fast, you'll never see their feet".

"The costumes are so pretty; they sparkle in the light."
"The many different colors are beautiful and bright."
"My hairdo will be piled up high, on top of my head;
My slippers are of satin; my tutu all in red."

"For many months I've practiced to get my twirls just right."
"My curtsy is so graceful and my leaps are out of sight."
"If you do come, Grandma, please sit way up in front,
So you won't have to stretch your neck and weary from the hunt."

"I'll be looking for you Grandma, I'm the smallest of the bunch."
"I know you will enjoy it, I have a certain hunch."
I went to the recital, all dressed in Sunday best,
To watch my Emily pirouette and put her to the test.

My tired eyes focussed on a tiny figure fair,
Who danced and pranced with the flowers in her hair.
She looked like an angel with tutu all aflutter.
I'm sure the stage was crowded but to me, there was no other.

When God Made Friends...
Cheri A. Fortmeyer
The Angels came to God, and said,
'Dear Lord? if we may ask?
exactly, how, you did create,
What must of seemed, a task.

He said, so softly, unto them,
'Come sit here, close to me
I'll now explain, what I believe
A friend, should truly be...

'First of all, it matters, not,
What size or shape, or form
I'd rather, shape, their souls, to be,
So gentle, yet, so warm...

'It's true that I am everywhere,
Yet, felt the need, to send,
That, someone who, on which, to learn,
What I define, A friend...

That's the way it all went down
Forever, it shall be
And, all because, "When God Made Friends"
He made, you just for me!

Existence
Natalie Perez
What is the meaning to life?
I need it so.
Why do we have night?
Is it to be filled with emptiness –
Dreams of unreality – peace.
Wakeful hours filled to explosion
With unfulfilledness!
Is the destiny to be desolate solitude?
I wake at night to wake in day
Only to Die – Change – Fall – Die – Nothing.
An ever lasting carbon monoxide flower.

The Legacy
Ragini Macaden
Your tiny hands clutch my finger
I gaze into your eyes and wonder...
When the years roll by and your path you find...
Come, take your place, my little one.

Concrete towers offer to you only a glimpse of blue.
I remember the great blue dome and leaves with dew
Do you smell the flowers, my little one?

The magical tales spun around the fire place
Have given in to the marvels of cyber space.
Then, the family gathered around warm soup and bread,
Now, the cold "take–away" with every info provided!
Are you hungry, my little one?

The feel of the stony path, the gushing cold steam,
And sand in my toes are familiar to me.
Designed shoes, now befit every activity.
Are you safe, my little one?

The world spreads its choices before you...
Fame, Fortune, Glitz, Glamour and Happiness too.
May the legacy of Love and Truth guide your way through.
God be with you, my little one.

The Alcoholic
Pierre J. Lafrance
A quiet, unpeaceful tenseness
Surrounds my very soul
MY family sits far–in closeness
But I'm trapped deep in this hole

This poisoned bottle keeps me sane
From what – I just don't know
My life, a hell it shall remain
For the Bible tells me so

I understand, deep down inside
I feel, I love, I care
But all these things I tend to hide
Underneath this mask I wear

I want so much to share my hurt
Yet I fear the world's attack
So when I'm down, low in the dirt
I tend to hold it all back

Tormented by this evil drink
That lives to make me sick
The blaming makes me stop and think
That I'm the alcoholic.

Cold Compassion
Brian Owens
Romantic love
Knock not at my door,
Ply not thy wares
Without these walls.
Allow this winter to take hold,
Run its course—
Regardless of extended seasons length.
Why does sun bother to shine its shining head,
Tantalizing with rays of hope and warmth?
Turn away and let winter's chill
Encapsulate with cold compassion.

Call Of The Quitter
M. E. Johnson
Red tip on a cig
puff puff
Nicotine sure is keen
puff puff

Grey smoke from a cig
puff puff
Clean air, do I care?
puff puff

White ash on a cig
puff puff
Makes me stink, do you think?
puff puff

Yellow tar from a cig
puff puff
In my lung, I'm too young!
puff puff

Brown butt of a cig
puff puff
Nicotine, how obscene!
quit quit

Little Boy
Beryl T. Conto
Little boy upon the hay,
The grown–up folks all say,
You suffered and died for me
On a hill called Calvary.

They say men spit at You
And knocked You down,
Then put a crown
Of thorns upon Your head.

Little boy upon the hay,
I'm sorry You suffered
In such a way
For me.

I will be real good,
And do everything I should.
Till I get to be a man —
Could I just hold Your hand?

Little boy upon the hay,
Please guide me on the way,
Until in Heaven someday I'll be
With You through all eternity.

I Don't Ask For Much Out Of Life
C. Rodgers
I watch the grass the flowers and trees grow, I see the puppies grow into dogs, the kittens grow into cats, All around there is war and fighting. "Why oh Why can't the world live in peace?" "I'll never understand" does everyone and everything in the world have to die before there is peace. Babies in their mother's arms don't understand what they are being brought up to be just a few more deaths on somebody's hands no–doubt why does the world behave like this "won't somebody tell me why" if there is a God then why can't He wave His Almighty hand and make the world a safe and happy land,
so all brothers and sisters can walk hand in hand and all God's creatures can live in harmony as one.

Corey
Kathleen R. Polasek
Precious memories live in this house,
loving thoughts fill every room.
It seems as though you just stepped out,
and will be returning soon.

Everything is just the same,
as when you went away.
But now my life is touched with sadness,
as I pass through life each day.

Sometimes I hear your footsteps,
in the hall outside my room.
And there are times I see your loving face,
as I go from room to room.

I know you're watching over me,
at times you feel so near.
My heart then fills with sadness,
my eyes will fill with tears.

Yes, this house is full of memories,
each one I hold so dear.
The memory most beloved
is knowing you lived here.

Confusion Of The Mind
Sue H. Horn
Through the twists and turns of my consciousness
Memories, thoughts, dreams of things to come
Racing along their pathways
Each in turn wanting to be recognized

I search back through the jumble
What was it I was looking for
I know it's there
Why can't I find it

Looking outward through these eyes
What I see may be calm and serene
Looking inward the picture is quite different
We fool ourselves and others

Would that I could clean them out like a drawer or closet
To throw away all the old stuff
The useless bits of junk we store
All the pain and sorrow

I think I'll do an early spring cleaning
Get in there and sweep all the negative thoughts away
Dust out all those corners full of worry and self–doubt
Open the windows of my mind to the sunshine of all my tomorrows

Love
Erin K. Pielin
A Love once there
Slowly fades away
Once blossoming with
laughter, you thought
was there to stay
Full of loving eyes
and joyful smiles
and
Love that with hope
would last
For miles and miles and miles.

Taking Things For Granted
Gay Turner
We often take things for granted
As we live here day by day
We don't miss our eyesight, hearing or voice
Until they are taken away.

We often take for granted
The sunshine and the rain
And we don't miss our good health
Until, all we have is pain

When we wish to do all the things
That we did once before
That's when we wish that we had
Our good health back once more

We make resolutions
At the first of the year
But how many of us start
Our day off with prayer

Many things we take for granted
Like our families and our jobs
And once we reach our destination
We don't take time to even thank God.

Grandma Is Coming
Florence E. Estes
Grandma is coming
To our house to stay
For a most lovely Christmas,
And a gay Holiday.

The tree has been trimmed
The gifts boxed and bowed
The corner with presents
Has just overflowed.

The hustle and bustle,
The paper and string
Are now looking like
Quite a nice thing.

The surprises and secrets,
The smiles and the grins
Show that this big occasion
Is more than a whim.

For a visit from Grandma
Is for this family,
Just the very best gift
There ever could be.

Fall
Bonnie L. Slagle

As the breeze blows
And the leaves tumble to the ground
The sun slips in and out
From behind white clouds
I know that fall is here.

The trees becoming slowly bare
The green grass is
Surely turning to brown.
The next season can come in
And decorate with white.

Fatal Act
Sherry L. Lisby

I watch as the blue smoke
Drifts lazily into the still air
Taking seconds or minutes of life
Without the slightest of care

It invites a host of diseases
Some fatal and all life–altering
Into my body oh so quietly
I can feel it's already changing

I've developed a smoker's cough
It's embarrassing, hard to control
Yet I'm hooked in Nicotine's play
I cannot quit my hated role

I never intended to audition
I loathed this play all my life
Then it happened quite suddenly
In a period of stress and strife

I want so much to stop
Yet I can't—I feel confusion
I don't want to act out this role
To its obvious and fatal conclusion

Love Beyond All Bounds
Ruth Dixon

Oh, how I long for an enduring love
That time could not destroy
With one beside, I would soar above
And yet you think I'm coy

I've won you and your heart too
I really don't know why
Though affections have been shown to you
Your thoughts are just a lie

The reason that I have not shared, sir
The feelings deep within,
Is not shyness to which you refer
Further silence, a sin

Unlike you, my heads not with a book,
Always with poetry
Now if you would take a closer look
Our love you would not see

Time goes fast and thus it makes me fear
True love I'll never find
To love for the sake of loving, dear,
Gives no one peace of mind

Loneliness
Tiffany Epley

I see the freedom right down the street
Yet I stick around to find out if you still love me
My family out of touch to what's happening to me
It all seems the same as the last one did
But you still haunt me
The rain falls all around me like demons are striking me dead
I try to change my thought of life but something tells me to stop
My open wounds from bleeding
I'm so frail to the world as if one bite of the neck can kill my life
And my spirit along with it
So I sit and wait for you to come and take me away.

Long Lost Hamlin
Lisa Mahuron

They all march along to the very same pipe,
And they all strive to look just the same.
And although it's a death march, they are just alike
Right down to the very same name.

And I'm half sick of Hamlin, for all that it's worth,
And I refuse to be assimilated.
Oh, the mice—they've become the thing, from their births,
That they've loathed and claimed to have hated.

They line by the droves in their silly rows.
Like lemmings, they follow one sound,
And all through the lanes and alleys echoes
Their tiny feet hitting the ground.

Oh, they're so social–, and civil–, and mesmerized,
And self–righteous beyond even that,
And I'm weary of Hamlin, but they won't hear my cries
That somewhere, 'I smell a rat!'

So with cotton in my ears and chin held high,
I walk my own path and ignore them,
And though Hamlin is lost, I'll still get by,
And maybe be better off for them.

Window
Marilyn Ghilardi

A delicate view of lacy flowers
Blowing in the breeze

The tweet of yellow bird song
greets me

A red automobile squawks at me
as it parks its body

Seasoned ladies with black–creviced faces

Push their way out

Yellow polka dot hats and dresses
adorn their lofty bodies

They laugh and preen and scold
as they disappear from view

For I do not know where they go
I only see fleetingly

The world from my window view
that's all I see

One Day
Sheila R. Hall

I'll take her flowers, get her favorite book and read to her one day
I'll bring her muffins and coffee, I'll stay all day
We'll spend hours talking about old times one day
We'll laugh and we'll cry, about what was then, and what's now
But I'm so far behind, I have so much to do
I can't do it right now, but I'll get to it one day
I'll take the kids to see her, we'll go for a drive
I'll take her on a picnic, like she used to take me one day
We'll do all these things, it's so easy to say
Until one day you realize
It's a long time since one day

The Last Day Of School
Doris Ross

'Twas the middle of May, I was on my way
To the last day of school this year.
'Twas a time of war, the boys heard the call
Of home, planting time was here!
But for here and now on this one day
The community came together
Just to keep in touch and celebrate
The sharing of life and weather.
Each family brought a basket of food
To be shared by all who came;
As the mothers set food on the tables in rows
We kids got report cards, played games;
The men sat around in groups and discussed
The crops, the weather, and war;
And then we all met in the gym to eat food;
The best day of school by far!
Lunch time took 'bout two hours or so,
Then the school band hit the drums;
Our flag was raised high and the anthem was played;
Tears fell from most who had come!
The women cleaned up the mess that was left;
A ball game finished the day.
What a wonderful way to end the school year,
Start a summer of hard work and play!

The Chimes Of The Old Man's Clock
Don Fallon

The old man wound his clock
So diligently, it never came to a stop
He lived his life with such consistency
Just like his clock, ever so precisely

I still hear its chimes
Reverberating through the years
Thinking of old times
The chimes drowned away my fears

The chimes are forever in my head
So cozy I would lay in my bed
As they marked 1/4 and 1/2 past
Would fall asleep ever so fast

How I yearn for another stay—over
The chimes sweeter than coffee's aroma
Would gently awaken me in the morning
A wonderful day be it sunny or pouring

But now many a silent day
And yearning for old times I sighed
The chimes now only a memory
For the old man had died

Indecision
Erika L. Walker

I reached out to touch him,
but my hands only found the soft whirl of air.
I searched his eyes for the reasons why,
and saw a battle being fought.
I turned my back to him,
did not want him to see my thoughts.
Then I felt his breath on my neck,
it sent shivers down my spine.
I smiled, slowly turned around,
reached up to stroke the curve of his jaw.
I could feel his muscles quivering,
momentarily afraid of his decision to trust me.
For a fleeting moment we were one,
alone in this field of life
with the grasses dancing at our feet.
Then the clouds covered the sun,
and the indecision was back.
He tossed his head, mane flowing in the breeze,
turned and walked away
only to pause and glance back.
I could feel the power in his gaze,
this free and wonderful being.
We would come together again,
maybe for a little longer next time.

The Park
Ellen W. Hess

Her hair glistens, just like the winds make you listen.
She would engage as I contemplate each page.
Her eyes match the sky as the birds learn to fly.
As the pages become so few, I realize it is time for anew.
I decide to take a break and rest my eyes.
I can hear my body with all the sighs...
I then begin to reason why there are all the seasons.
Then as the day begins to turn to night,
I will ponder this wonderful sight.
And soon the stars will fill the sky,
As I will rise and say good by.

Seeing You
Krista Brown

I feel so lonesome, all
day long. I miss my loved
ones. Who have long been gone.

I wish they were here,
to see this day. So I
could give them my
love, in that special way.

It was their time, to
depart from this
earth. Who knows
how long, before
their rebirth.

Even though you are
not here. The presence
of your spirit, will
help me think clear.

Hopefully someday
our paths will meet.
when that day comes,
my life is complete.

A Painting
Linda MacDonald
A painting hangs upon a wall
for much of the world to see.
A new light is shed upon it
as everyone sees it differently.

One man sees life,
while one sees death.
One visualizes love,
the other remembers heartache.

One vast emotion,
four different lives,
seen in colors and shapes
through the heart of an artist.

A painting represents ourselves.
We see the hopes
of our dreams,
the wishes of our nightmares.

One man's perspective on life
just as it is to he,
that's all it is.
or was ever meant to be.

Forever Gold
James S. McDaniel
After the sun breaks a new dawn
Our soul touches the trees
Feel the warmth from our hands
Hold the birds in melodies
Our light bestows the picturesque beauty
For eyes to behold
While bathing with the flowers
Our world waves hello
And blowing as the winds
Our voices
Our voice of forever gold

Wondrous World
Phyllis E. Jackson
There are so many wondrous things
The Lord puts on this Earth.
And we take them for granted
Not caring for their worth.

Just stop and look around you,
Just open your eyes and see
All the beautiful things the Lord
Has given to you and me.

The birds, the bees, the butterflies
That flutter around the Earth,
The quite wondrous miracle
Of a mother giving birth,

The way the seasons change
Always fresh and new,
To walk outside on a bright spring day
And witness the kiss of morning dew,

The ocean, the grace of a waterfall,
The variety of flowers and trees.
There is such beauty that God gives to man
If he'll open his eyes and see.

Big Bad Wolf
Heidi Easter
I'm afraid of the big bad wolf.
I know where he lies.
I feel him watching over me.
I sense his boisterous cries.

I'm afraid of the big bad wolf.
He has bitten me before.
I see his weapons awaiting me.
I know he wants me to want more.

I ran away from him one day
and decided to cast him away.
He lurked about and searched for me,
yet hidden I would stay.

But then again he came around,
tempting my sinful ways.
In no time I was back in line,
receiving my last todays.

Yes, I'm afraid of the big bad wolf
I'm dying because of him.
All because I thrived on fun,
and he used fun to win.

Untitled
John D. Moore
Love that could not last,
Buried in the past.
True beauty will ever last,
With all thy frailties cast.
From all my lives in the past,
This one, I want to last.

The shadow has been cast.
I know, I will be dead too fast.
Please, hold me while I last,
And never forget our past.

Follow Your Dreams
Joel Williams
Some one once said, "You could not do it,
that opportunity had passed you by",
but you decided to
put forth another effort
to give yourself one more try!

So you aimed your energy
in the right direction,
despite the many challenges
you've had to face;
to maintain a winning spirit
you had to keep a steady pace.

Now you've accomplished one goal,
and we acknowledge you today.
We are all so proud of you;
so much more than words can say.

But remember, before anyone can win,
you must have the courage to begin.

You must believe in yourself,
and be the best that you can be;
only then your dreams become your reality.

A Scenic Journey
Hazel V. Kemp

There is a road that beckons to me.
It's long and winding with scenes to see.
Perhaps it will take me to a lake
There to entreat a picture to take.

Maybe it leads to a mountain high
To breathe the clean air where eagles fly,
Where majestic beauty makes you small
The loss of which earth couldn't recall

To the desert, a seeming wasteland
But one must look close over the sand.
In spring when cactus are in full bloom
Where horses and burros wildly roam.

Now to cities with skyscraper heights.
With houses and churches bright with lights
Full of people who scurry around
Like ants in a hill working the ground.

But out in the country life is calm
Pastoral pictures are like a balm.
The farmer, the sheep, the cows afield,
Fulfill all the dreams my road can yield.

Untitled
Troy C. Tunstall

Life is but a moments time,
maybe as long as the wind in a
chime,
and in that time we scarcely
know
the people who love us so.
Even though we hurt them bad
We never seem to feel so sad
as when the time comes when
they must go
The people who Loved us so.

Loving Infinitely
Cindy L. Ritchie

Loving infinitely!
Like the flower whose perfume permeates a garden in Spring.
Plant within, an understanding of Life,
lived and felt as Truth.

With all heart and soul give the true self to Life.
Peace, joy, love, and harmony is the path of freedom that
guides each footstep.

On lips, a tune of thankfulness.
Hands touch with gentleness, comfort and love.
This life lived in grace sustains and nourishes with such
bountiful blessings of beauty.

The kingdom of peace within. The mustard seed
has bloomed, and harmony moves invisibly All,
seen and known as Love.

Bow with a thankful heart,
and the whole universe smiles back in beautiful repose.
The warmth felt, is like a sun spiced day of
radiant beauty and light.

Loving infinitely!

The Ladies
Linda Jackson Chaney

I don't need your pity
What I want is help from you
Death is calling out my name
And there is much to do

My house must be really clear
Each dish should twinkle and shine
The bathroom needs to sparkle
So no fault they can find

Take good care of my plants
Give them tender, loving care
Trim, dust and wax each leaf
So no fault can linger there

Even though I've gone beyond
Surely there will be a way
To know such pleasure in the fast
That I've robbed "The Ladies" of their say

Though my halo will be on crooked
I'm sure to be filled with glee
Knowing that now "The Ladies"
Really will miss me

The Moment
Angela Gaut

The Moment
Passes quickly
Yet lasts an eternity
Unexpectedly
Becomes a memory
The fire, the passion
Quenched and kindled
Two souls
Merge and become one
But only for
The Moment

IMAGINE
Doreen Wilkinson

Imagine you awoke one day
To find that life had changed,
The scene you knew had disappeared
The world all rearranged,

Leaders from all across the land
Had clasped each other by the hand
And made a pact for wars to cease,
So all mankind could dwell in peace.

Brown and yellow, black and white,
Each acknowledging the other's right
To live without discrimination,
From city to city, nation to nation.

And everyone living by the golden rule
Which is found in the good book so true.
(Always do unto others,
As you would have them do to you).

No crime no hunger, no conflict no strife,
No blatant disregard for life.
No racial hate, no arms to call,
The hand of God had changed it all.

Life In The Valley!
Sandra Wolfe

Years spent at the bottom of a valley;
Striving hard to scale the rocky sides!
Groping blindly, trying to find a foothole,
To start the long unsteady, upward climb!

Progressing gradually, but sure I'll make it.
Confident the summit I will reach.
Avoiding every loose or falling boulder.
Determined not to give way to defeat!

Arising from the depths within the valley;
An arms length distance left to reach my goal,
But obstacles around me are surmounting,
And again into the valley I must fall!

I've lived for many years within this valley:
The ravine built of heartache, ruled by men.
A realm of constant fear, and pain and anguish.
A place where only women dare to dwell!

Does fate intend I never leave this valley?
Will the hand of destiny be poised to strike
Each time I take a step and move on upwards?
Will the unknown Force forever, drag me back!

My Heart
Sarah L. Sullivan

My heart is always longing
For your face to see
For your love I feel so deeply
Forever close to me

Tears I feel softly falling
From your face and mine
Like moonlight shining
from afar...
Calling us back once more
To the place where we met

Because You're Special
Kimberly Keill

This basket comes to you with things
that hold special thoughts.
They tell a story of
the magic that you brought.

The apple represents that you're the
apple of Kelly's eye.
The clock represents all the time
you've spent that has flown by.

The candy represents how sweet
and kind you have been.
The photo album is for you
to keep precious memories in.

The candle represents the brightness
you brought into her life like the sun.
The plant represents
the nurturing that you have done.

The champagne is for you
to celebrate your success.
Your caring and devotion
has helped make Kelly the best!

The Wind
Kay Whitaker

The wind when I was little,
It blew outside the door
And rattled at the windows.
I didn't like its roar.

Older, heard its soft whipping
Of clothes on Grandma's line,
And though it kept them snapping,
I liked its sounds sometimes.

When I was a young woman,
It always seemed a breeze
Which whispered through my hair and
Went playing in the leaves.

And it can still seem that way
When I feel well and free,
But when I'm down and burdened,
The winds no friend to me.

But just today I thought when,
My bad and good times gone,
From this place I have vanished,
Wind will be blowing on.

My Broken Home
John A. Webb

Stuck in this body of shame
feeling so hurt with a heart full of pain.
How much regret should one man have to live?
When all he wants is to start over again.
I'm not a loser. I don't care what they say.
My only regret was the love I made.
I've got to get over these feelings of pain.
Else they will only drive me insane.
Why? But why I say.
Why must it be that my children have to pay.
For my foolish mistakes of the love I made...

Cannibal Sea
Alexandra Hurrell

Crystal clear is the rippling tide
Clear as glass, nowhere to hide
Sea life spans the vast shoreline
The sea upon which all must dine.

To eat another is to live
Small meets bigger, one must give
Small most always loses out
To sharpened teeth or tapered snout.

Beyond the shore are hungry waves
A hungry fish upon these craves
For this is where the good meals dwell
Upon which larger fish do swell.

Being alive means being at risk
From one who's larger or more brisk
Hence each has to be aware
Fight the good fight if you dare.

No bargaining will save your life
A life so full of toil and strife
Waiting to be killed for tea
Do or die in the Cannibal Sea.

Speak Softly
Carolyn L. Holmes
Speak softly Love I pray thee
Let not anger taint thy words
For gentle sounds shall quickly find me
And thy wishes shall be heard

Utter not hurtful words that flay me
Leaving scars that cannot heal
Oh my fearful heart might betray me
Revealing doubts I dare not feel

Speak to me of tender things
In a sweet voice soft and low
Tug gently at my poor heart's strings
Tell me secrets I should know

Let not differences from the past
Tear apart the love we've shared
A love as deep as ours shall last
If two hearts have really cared

Many are the stars shining bright in the sky
And many are the drops of dew
Proof of my love shows wet in my eyes
Please say you still love me too

Heaven
Maria Meglio
I often think of Heaven and how it will be,
Peaceful, calm, and quiet, full of tranquility.
A scent of lilies in the air, sounds
of cannon that caress my ears.
Family and friends I love so dear,
For who I will shed no more tears.
Locks of golden angel's hair,
their skin so pure and very fair.
For now I sit and wonder,
How great it will be, when I am home
With Jesus for I know that He loves me.

Shiloh Before The Dawn
Brian Humphreys
Camp fires flicker their eery light.
Cold, damp earth of the moonless night.
Quiet men sit in solitary thought.
The coming day's battle to be fought.

Rasp of bayonets scraped and honed.
A sharpening stone borrowed and loaned.
Muskets checked, and checked again.
To fail this task a course profane.

All this done without a word.
Nary a blaspheme is even heard.
Comrades dead, appear as ghosts.
A quiet prayer to the Lord of Hosts.

Sleepless night and so to dawn.
Promise of sunlight in the early morn.
Tramping feet to greet the day.
Endless lines of blue and grey.

Protesting fate with silent voice.
Sad, weary souls who have no choice.
Soon to join in Heaven's glow.
Their final resting place...Shiloh.

Aids
Yvonne McElhone
Alone I sit and I wonder why
The way the world is and how young people die
For some its their fault they thought they were it
For others who are told they can't move they just sit
I am talking about an illness that is really the death sentence
Your life is in ruins and you have nowhere to go
You can't be a parent it's not fair on the bairn
If you go ahead and do it then you just aren't caring
You tell your family they don't know what to say
Mum wishes she could kiss it better and it would go away
Some of them believe it and some of them don't
It splits your family because of different opinion
They don't understand that there is not a lot of time to spare
Still they argue some for some against
One wants to kiss you the other one doesn't care
I have never taken drugs to the lot I declare
I can't really handle this its like a bad nightmare
But I have to live with it there is nothing I can do
I wish it was curable please believe me that's true
When your children are older make sure they know
The should take the protection wherever they go
I am sitting here thinking as he lies in his grave
He was one of the unlucky ones but he was brave
We now know how to educate our young and who to thank

As the Wind Blows
Nina Blake
As the wind blows...the trees come out of the ground and dance.
As the wind blows...the trains toot–toot as they ride on the tracks.
As the wind blows...people sing and dance.
As the wind blows...the river flows like a witch on her broom.
As the wind blows...the leaves glide through the air like a squirrel.
As the wind blows...the world turns like the train toot–toot.
As the wind blows...the roses bloom each day.
As the wind blows...the grass sways in the cool breeze.
As the wind blows...a mother scolds her child.
As the wind blows...people laugh and chuckle.
As the wind blows...it blows – it blows...it blows.

Historical Little Town
Robert A. LeRette
Stone wall 'round the cemetery
Flags on the poles
Policemen helping children cross
While the bell gently tolls

It's ten o'clock on a Saturday
Everyone's gone to bed
No liquors served in this town
It might go to your head

Sunday morning comes
And you walk to the big white church
You sing to the Lord, you raise your soul
And in your pocket search

Stone war hero in the center of town
across from the Town Hall
Standing on his pedestal
Granite eyes have seen it all

There's a red brick school yard
With a ball field in the front
Swing sets sway in the breeze
All empty in the summer months

The Contest Poem
Randy Rawls

I've written this poem just for you.
In the hopes you might like it too.
The words I used are clearly mine.
All I had to do was make them rhyme.

Writing it was lots of fun,
Disappointed when I got it done.
Wanted to add just one more verse,
This poet has never been terse.

For this contest, I penned these lines,
In the hope that the prize it finds.
Judges, please be kind as you read.
If it will help, I'll even plead.

Whether I lose or if I win,
It was fun, these few lines to spin.
It's fun writing what you might like,
Though I know the red pen can strike.

I close this now with this one prayer,
"When you call winners, I'll be there."
Judges, I gave it my best shot.
So please don't use it in the pot.

Remembering...
Glenda Victoria Waldon

In the silence I can hear you chuckle
In a breeze I can hear your laughter
In a cloud I can see your beautiful face
In the wink of an eye I can see how time flew bye
I can still recall your loving touch
Even though I don't remember very much
I long to feel your warm embrace
I long to see your smiling face
You were my mother
You were my friend
I wish I could see you once again

One In A Million
Arlene M. Howe

You're one in a million
I thought I'd let you know
Before the good Lord tells me
It's my time to go.

Through thirty some years of marriage
We've had our ups and downs
But when you say "I Love You, Dear"
That's all that really counts.

When we go to bed at night
and you're laying by my side
I hear you say "I Love You, Dear"
"As the day you became my bride."

Tho' my body it is broken
My spirits ebbing low
Remember that I Love You, Dear
And I wanted you to know.

You are ONE IN A MILLION
You never do complain
I love you the same today
As the day you changed my name.

A Garden Of Love
Barbara W. Oliver

In the garden of life
The flowers are friends
Filled with fragrance of love
That can never end.

The beauty in bloom
Is an unending rite
With each flower unique
In the Father's sight.

Gently kissed by the wind
And caressed by the Son
The Spirit will nourish
And strengthen each one.

This wonderful garden
Is more than a dream
Where flowers are friends
Binding love in each seam.

It's the seeds that we plant
And the fruit that we bear
A communion of love
That we're privileged to share.

Somewhere
Winnifred Parrish

Somewhere the sun is shining.
Somewhere the song breaks through.
Somewhere the cup's overflowing
by the deep blue sea.
Somewhere the North Wind's a howling.
Somewhere the night birds fly——
All appointed by heaven
in the vast mysterious sky.
You're the essence of Summer——
the quintessence of Spring
and always you're there with me, somewhere.

Heartbreak Cell
Brian Craig

So often it seems when love is at hand,
My fears well up and scream their demands.
Begging to be heard, pleading for reply,
Forging the tears which sting my eyes.

This terror I feel blinds me to all,
Sending me deeper into the caverns of my soul.
Back to the cell I've built all alone,
A cage within a cage I've come to call home.

In this cell of woe I have dwelt too long,
In perpetual darkness, ever seeking the dawn,
Drawn to a shade whispering hot rage,
I peer through the dark at my heart in a cage.

Upon a pedestal of tears, a small cage atop,
My heart lies within, its beating long stopped.
Broken yet safe in this cell of its own,
Bars of despair anchored in love turned to stone.

A lifetime it took for this sad place to form,
A refuge from heartbreaks fiery storm.
To hide, to heal until the next time we chance,
To seek salvation in the arms of romance.

Sayonara
Joan Yowell

Saying "I'll see you", "So long" or "Good–bye"; hard when you walk away, just as hard when you fly

A parting of ways, of minds and of hearts, and if it sounds simple, well it is 'til you start

You see, as life takes us our own separate ways, be it mind or your heart, there's a part within stays

Our memory recalls the joy and the tears, the many fun things we have shared through the years

Now I don't need to tell you, if you've once said good–bye, you will just keep things light, or break down and cry

And your heart might be breaking, your mouth says "Please write"; Oh, yes you're assured and we'll call you tonight!

Remembering last moments, days, and last hours; you recall and send prayers off, at times even flowers

After a time you're at peace with your sorrow, a rainbow is promised perhaps for tomorrow; from a nod of the head until the last word is said, "Sayonara".

Look
E. E. Garrett

Look for the Blue Skies, not the grey.
Look for the light, not the dark.
Look at the wonders around you.
Look at the gifts for all to see.
The birds the trees the flowers.
Do not seek what you don't need.
Be content with what God has given you
Life is such a wondrous thing
enjoy it while you may.

Dedication: My beloved husband

Why
Maureen Crimmins

Trees standing naked
Under a coat of white fur
Forming silhouettes
Along a roadside curve

I stare in amazement
Never weary of this sight
Exuberant in daytime
Disappearing into night

It's always the first snowfall
That awakens me in fear
Why do I wonder
Why I'm still here

As a lake to mirror
The image is the same
Like an answer to a prayer
That's calling my name

I cherish these moments
Dismissing my fear
For suddenly I realize
Why I'm still here

This World
Barbara Palmese

Can you find the beauty in each day,
Even when it's cloudy and gray?
When the day is steamy and hot,
Can you find a comfortable spot?

Do you try and find something nice to say,
To each person you meet that day?
Do you give a true compliment when it is due
And cheerfully greet people who pass by you?

This world will be a happier place
Because you put a smile on your face.
If they need a helping hand, you'll share,
And people will know you really care.

Keep smiling when things are tough
And circumstances are very rough.
You'd be surprised how a smile breaks the ice
And someone turns out to be very nice.

A smile works wonders in a business place
Where cold, calculating minds are running a race.
A smile is one thing people remember,
So liberally give them from January through December.

Faith In Rose Virtue
Kimberly G. Holt

As tender mercy reaps pure harmony
angelic concessions of the human spirit alter.
Sweet grace of ever present love
exceeds all treasures in existence.
Great benevolence—
if within essence was an ounce stronger
how blessed life would become.
Heaven's eyes see naught!
This evolution is yet to be.
Take the mind from the heart,
a transition will be seen.

Nature's Serenity
F. J. Dodge

Sitting on a tree stump in the woods,
Where once a majestic maple stood,
Looking around one can see,
Saplings sown by that tree.

Partridge berries cover the ground,
Food for birds year round,
Sphagnum moss, mushrooms too,
Excellent food for deer to chew.

Silently, I sit here and wait,
As a wood thrush calls for its mate,
Squirrels are running around
Looking for nuts buried in the ground.

Arbutus are in full bloom,
Violets, strawberries will open soon,
Odors of bloodroot fill the air,
Lady slippers scattered everywhere.

I travel to this spot each year,
A place my ancestors held real dear,
That old maple is long since gone,
Leaving the saplings to carry on.

The Indians
Laura Gauthier

All things were considered their friends.
Animals, Nature, the Universe.
They were peaceful.
Riding with the wind on a stallion whose power could be felt through the
    clothing they wore.
They rode bareback and seemed as one with the horse, the speed, the power.
They could guess what the horse would do, work with him, gentle in every
    way.
They were at peace with everything, including themselves.
Then the White Man came.
He brought weapons that took away the skill necessary for a bow.
He brought saddles for the horse, which took away the peace and grace with
    which they rode.
They became vicious, fighting amongst themselves.
Treating everything they had once respected with the disrespect of the
    White Man.
The White Man saw what he did, saw how evil they had become and, to cover
    all evidence of
what he did, the White Man tried to annihilate an entire race.
A race that had helped the White Man survive the long, cold winter and the
    starvation that
would have followed.
A race that, against all odds, had survived everything except the White
    Man's corruption.

Autumn Twilight
Diane L. Mirnande

I often dream of yesterday,
although it won't appear.

Of days gone by when we were young,
and didn't have a care.

But as the twilight softly sets
and days turn into years.

I'm thankful for your love and you
to kiss away each tear.

Grandparents' Thoughts
M. B. Stark

This seems to be a perfect time—
Your graduation day,
To write some things we always mean,
But sometimes do not say.

From the very moment you were born
And began your life, so new,
Through all the years that passed since then
You've been a part of our lives, too.

We shared your joys, and if there was pain
We felt that with you, too.
We gave you love, and were filled with pride
By the things that you could do.

There might be times when things get rough,
This will strengthen you, my dear,
To make your mark on this old world,
And make the world be glad you're here.

As years go by there will come a time
When we won't be here, it's true;
But please believe, wherever we are,
We will always be with you.

Miracle From The Sky
Anna Belle Staley

Beautiful, symmetrical wonders of nature's show,
Protectors of earth, conservers of heat,
Sparkling crystals pirouette from the firmament as snow.

They swirl and twirl as winter winds blow
And shining expectant faces at windows greet
The beautiful, symmetrical wonders of nature's show.

Forming in clouds both high and low
They perform a spectacular marvelous feat,
As sparkling crystals pirouette from the firmament as snow.

Transparent as glass they flutter to and fro
And crowd together in flakes as they meet,
The beautiful, symmetrical wonders of nature's show.

Sunlight shimmering on sheltering blankets below,
Twinkling like diamonds at the forest's feet,
As sparkling crystals pirouette from the firmament as snow.

The amassing, white, picturesque drifts grow
And the fashioning of God's phenomena is complete,
With the beautiful, symmetrical wonders of nature's show
As sparkling crystals pirouette from the firmament as snow.

The Flame
Anne—Marie Pratt

Around the circle they had sat ready.
Slowly it had come and the quicker.
A struggle at first as it rose
So the darkness seemed deeper.
Until a light so tiny glowed.
Breaking free from its prison.
Distorting the shadows as it pulled towards the sky.
One by one it was joined by other
And the night was split with light.
The fire was through and it stood guard
While they slept in their darkness.

The Unexpected
B. Bellini

Can I tell you the times not long ago
When I can remember the secure feeling aglow
A happy content every day was a new
A wondrous adventure enjoyed by us two

Let me remember – Oh no not again
These thoughts are so hurt feel from beginning to end
Everything changes too quick where have they gone
Out of my mind with a touch of a wand

Working hard I do try 6 days of the week
When my day off comes I'm tired and bleak
Now catch upon the chores as fast as you can
Sit and relax and start all over again

Can any one show me a new kind of life.
Where I could be happy, taste the spice
How do others get through it each day of the year
Don't they experience the routine of fear

I have asked I have prayed for some guidance and like
But now I respond with no glowing delight
I'll take what comes naturally if that's what I might
For my life is like a swift—flying kite.

Giving Thanks
Mavis L. Rasmussen
The turkey's in the oven
The dishwasher stocked up high
My aprons dusted with flour
From making pumpkin pie.

The buns are golden brown
Waldorf salad in its crystal dish
Sweet potato casserole oven ready
Now comes time to make my wish.

I wish all people everywhere were as fortunate as me
Sitting down to a feast and loving family
For those than have no shelter clothes tattered and worn
No laughing grandchildren, feeling hopeless and forlorn.

Our circle too is broken
Family members we miss so much
The phone lines have been busy
Each one remembering to keep in touch.

I bow my head in prayer
A tear slips from my eye
Thanking God for all my blessings
For without love and home, what good is pumpkin pie?

Untitled
James E. James
Are we swimming or
thrashing through the
sea of life?
If the mirror is our only gauge
of success, what be the fate of the children?

If "me" becomes the instant gratification, then we "are" the dying breed
the endangered species.
The temperature is rising.
Alas, remember the flash point of paper...
Fahrenheit 451

Grit
Phyllis Dannemiller
She came to me in an anxious state
Reconciliation with her husband was too late
Her tears showed a broken heart
but a willingness to make a new start

She told of tragic things unknown
but showed a courage that had grown
Her children were hastily gathered
even though her mind was scattered

To make it legal, she made the date
In her mind, she could hardly wait
Her doctor's empathy and support we did find
Our relationship would be of a special kind

A blended family were we all
Listening intently to God's call
God guided us through uncharted waters
Along with her son and her daughters

This lady whose courage is great
Is my friend and sister, that's no debate
We will always remember those days
That helped us grow in many ways

Visions Of A Dream
Tanya Kussrow
I dream of a vision
Not many, just one
A vision of a dream
In a place where all is fun

A vision of a dream
That takes me far away
I dream of a vision
Fantasyland we might say

Anything can happen
Just try it and you'll see
A vision of a dream
Is the place you'll want to be

How can we get there?
This question we do ask
Time and time again
The answer is the task

How to get to Fantasyland
You choose the decision
Just close your eyes
And dream of a vision

Jane
Karen Farmer
Jane fell to her knees last night,
it happened again; the fight. She
prayed, and prayed till she could
pray no more.

The tears fell from her eyes to her
lips and hit the crimson floor.

Jane said this was it I won't take it
anymore; She was right as she died
on the floor...,

Forest Road
Ron Steadman
I walk down the leaf—bedecked road
Slipping on the wet foliage
Chain saw in hand
To reap the Autumn's benefactors.

A little while elapses
And I find myself lost
Amongst the leafless shadows
Cutting and splitting and piling.

Time passes so quickly here
And I find that I must
Leave the slowly darkening forest
And my lonely chore.

I look at a drowsy forest stream
Made running gold in the gleam
Of the setting sun, through
Leafless branches, and I must go.

Chain saw in hand,
I walk down the leaf
Covered road and take one last look
At a fading ribbon of colours.

Ignoring the Problem
Tonia C. Severance
We stand, outside,
between walls,
blind and deaf,
seeing all.

a heap of rags,
the cold night wind,
burning fever
digging in.

cardboard houses,
paper sins,
eating supper
out of tins.

sunken eyes,
paper pants,
sky high ceilings,
the lowest rents.

We stand inside,
looking out,
our hands in our pockets,
hearts locked tight.

Untitled
Sandra Zobel
Will the past bring me closer
Or farther away to finding
The real person lost inside of me.
I look into the mirror and
See someone I don't know.
I look at photos and see the
Person I used to be.
I look to the future to see
The one I'd like to be.
Where do I look to find the
Person that's lost inside of me

The Magic Of The Rainforest
Deirdre Jordan
The sun sets softly over the rainforest
An inheritance which is yours and mine
As awe inspiring and majestic in beauty,
And as ancient and mystic as time

The rainforest beckons and sighs
Overhead a bird soars on the wing
Across the seeming endless sky,
Happy is he in His kingdom

Haven for creatures great and small
Damage may be done beyond repair
We should heed the animals cry,
We have no time to stand and stare

Maybe another sunrise will bring
A new understanding of this wondrous place
Animals birds and mankind can share
A new dawn before it is too late

The magic of the rainforest
Continues to weave its special spell
In the midst of time we stand
Shall we still have a story to tell?

I Will Trust In God My Saviour
Karen R. Young
I will trust in God, my Saviour
though fear is on every side,
I will trust when I'm uncertain
and in His love I will abide.

When Satan comes to torment
with my armor on I'll stand,
for my Captain and Redeemer
will deliver from his hand.

When in battle I lay wounded
and Satan comes to tear my soul,
I will trust in my dear Healer
for His promise to be whole.

My Jesus go before me
lead on through storm and gale,
for Your love is everlasting
and Your mercies never fail.

Lord Jesus, I will trust You
through fire, flood or foe,
I will trust You, I will trust You
when through unknown paths I go.

The Lie
Rebecca Brand
You go through difficult times in your life,
And the truth can be the one thing you may
Sacrifice.
The truth can get you in so deep,
And the mountain of lies can be steep.
You can hurt someone so bad and the consequence
Makes you very sad.
But a lie builds up so high,
And one day your true self will say goodbye.
Because of one thing you did which is you told
One single lie!!!!

Ancient Wisdom
Jason Burlbaw
In the shadowed forest,
lives a wise old shaman.
Giving all who enters a test,
not afraid of any man.

Going on a thorough search,
knowing each and everything.
Like an owl on his perch,
every word is piercing.

From his hidden home,
he roams the world of spirits.
Flees to lands unknown,
toying with death a bit.

Bringing visions to the weak,
lost in a world of thrill.
Allowing every ghost to speak.
escaping to all unreal.

In his mind are open doors,
some lead in others out.
Entering one just opens more,
showing ways for those without.

Cartography...Song For The End Of The Affair
Dorothy M. Hoogterp
The new maps told me
that the world is round

Nothing was said about edges.

Thus I did not know
or in any way foresee
one approaches the edge
and falls over
And the world is gone

The new maps told me
Of currents beneath the sea

ranges of mountains
caverns and canyons
volcanoes, rivers
beneath as above
endlessly connected
marching around the world.

The old maps would have
marked the edges clearly:
"Here be monsters."

Daydreams
Gracie Hernandez
What are daydreams?
A thought?
An illusion, or a
Fantasy?
Does anyone actually daydream?
Is it the ability to just be
able to daydream?
Daydream:
A thought,
an illusion, or a
Fantasy.

Nature's Pitiful Song
Jenn Kummer
As I stumbled into the garden
A picture came bright and clear
I hoped the creatures would give me pardon
from their quiet home frontiers.

I saw an eagle soaring
the wind beneath his wings.
A caterpillar mourning
in all the songs she sings.

A rabbit thumped right over
and sat below my toe.
A lion hung in the clover
to sit and watch the show.

All the creatures of the world
drifted to my side.
Chickens clucking, ducks a quacking,
I had nowhere to hide.

Then pitifully, sorrow came
Upon my heavy heart—
and nature showed me who to blame
For driving us apart.

The Caregiver
Judy Hamilton
Working with the sick and the old
Whose stories interesting but untold

Some restless, sad, and even a little mad
All looking for what they had

Days seem counted, uprooted, and slow
Leaving little, none, or nothing to show

Yet life keeps going to and fro
When one is waiting for it to let go!

Syntax
Burke Hilsabeck
(think)ing world,
what do you think of feel?

n(ever)mind.

you who sets limits and TIME on spring.
you who seek to define the endless.

what do you say to kissleepsmell
that is (of wonder rides
and jelly beans)?
take your (time) and...

smile and laugh,
to touch (whisper: not to reason) is
divine.
yesterday i found your soul
locked up inside a briefcase.

try to imagine my lamentation,
for i (living in this world of mine)
know not numbers,
(or combinations).

Soul's Kiss
Gracemary Antoskiewicz
She met him in the green forest,
Where a garden of ivory angels live.
His eyes were poetic as he took her
Hand in his, she caressed him with
Her voice as she spoke the words,
"Our souls have kissed..."

She left him in the green forest,
Where a garden of ivory angels live.
His eyes were poetic as he felt her
Hand leave his, she caressed him with
Her voice as she spoke the words,
"Our souls have kissed..."

She haunts him in the green forest,
Where a garden of ivory angels live.
His eyes are poetic as he remembers
Her hand in his, the caress of her
voice taunting him as she speaks
The words, "our souls have kissed..."

He waits for her in the green forest,
Where a garden of ivory angels live...

Rescue Me
Kim Wint

I rise up in the morning hoping to find love,
to find life's love stolen.
Deep wounds that hide within me,
starving to fly away once again.

The roadway appears to be smooth and clear,
sometimes dark and dreary.
The dark clouds hang and take my strength, for
I know one day my strength will be restored,
free me and come back again.
Rescue me and let me rise up and walk again.

To Edisto
Robyn Robley

He brought my heart to Edisto,
And eased my pain with the tidal flow.
The seabirds sang a song so sweet,
Shell–laden sand, nature's gift,
Laid at my feet.

The Palmettos stand so strong and proud,
House after house built amongst the clouds.
I feel the sand beneath my feet,
The splashing waves are such a treat.

He brought my heart to Edisto,
Now nowhere else will I choose to go.
I cleared my mind and eased my soul,
Along the shore on Edisto.

My heart it heals as dolphins dance,
The sunsets hold my eyes entranced.
The breeze, it blows my cares away,
I long to stay,
Just one more day...

Dedication: Cary, for showing me Edisto

A Saint Among Sinners
Jill Talley Hynes

She always knew her mother loved her.
She always knew that the Lord kept her.
She always knew there would be a better day,
She, always knew the right words to say.

A saint among sinners, yet she saw no evil.
She never cast a doubt, or felt reprieval.
Any day could have been her last...
Still, her face never held a disapproving cast.

The extra mile to most, was her least.
She never prepared a snack; always a feast.
She wouldn't hear of a brag, or a boast
She thought she was "common", she thought she was like "most"

She taught me how to love
She taught me to recognize gifts from Above.
All that she's done, she'll never see
Grandmother, please know how much you mean to me.

Ti amo siempre

Dedication: Barbara Livingstone, my loving grandmother

Free As A Bird
Troy Marshall II

Shoot them down out of the air
Look back and see they're not there
The birds don't do wrong
But you think it's right
To kill them in the blink of an eye
They did nothing
But you thought something
And shot them right out of the sky

Same with people who don't do wrong
Majority reigns and makes sure they're gone
Only God knows the truth
About those insane
That who kill for the fun of the game

So wipe off your tears
Cause God knows your fears
How the world has blinded eyes
Mockingbirds will die
And people will cry
But the innocent always come last!

Dedication: God and my loving mother

Untitled
Raven Wigginton

The day weeps with rain, laced through the trees the fog
turns to mist and soon is gone, I linger slightly in the forest,
the simple peace binds me there, to leave almost sinful,
how has life come this far without me even noticing, soon it
will be gone, like the mist of the morning,
I leave the forest, knowing of the sinful consequences, and soon
Find myself weeping at the edge of a large lake, the pool of
water is new, due to the fresh rain, I cry for the lake,
so beautiful, but soon to be gone, killed in its prime by the sun,
I wonder if it will ever know the short beauty of its life,
I swim to the middle as if to show appreciation, and wait for the sun.

My English Rose
Trish Donica

You call me love
Your English Rose
My petals you
have seen unfold.
Shall I be just
a blush of pink
that you will see
highlight my cheek.
Or shall I be
pearly white my
skin thou touchest
in the night.
A blood red Rose
just like my lips
that you, I know will
long to kiss.
The peach Rose and the yellow
are also part of me.
For nothing is so sweet
as when they are all together.
For now my love
that's all of me
Your English Rose forever.

Change
Monica E. LaFrancis
Are you ever in a crowded room
and you're sure no one sees you there
You sit and smile and talk to them
but still no one seems to care.
It's time for a change

Are you ever in a distant place
where you're happy and carefree
You wake up and find the truth
the hard times of your reality.
You've got to make a change

Are you ever down on yourself
and you think no one gives a damn
You have to be strong and say to yourself
I'm someone, I know I am.
Won't you make that change

You've turned your life all around
You're happy, but, life's still rough
You now realize that there are people who care
Their support and love is enough
Now aren't you glad you made that change.

You Are Not Alone
Judy M. Bertonazzi
Sometimes It's Only Us
As We Walk Through Life So Bold
No One That We Can Trust
Or So Our Thoughts Have Told

But Our Mind Plays Tricks On Us
When We Are Feeling Down
'Cause You Are Not Alone
You Have Love All Around

Dedication: Gary Hennel

Circumstances
Noel Darion Longboy
My Thoughts Are With You
As Days And Nights Go By
I Wish There's Enough Words
I Wish There's Enough Music
I Want To Hold You In My Arms
I Want To Be There For You
But Time Just Passes Me By

What If Times Were Different
Some Feelings Are Better Off Unsaid
Are You Afraid Of What You Want
And Why Do I Feel This Way

Tears Of Anger
Questions I Cannot Hide
Must We Deny Our Feelings
Every Time I See You Smile
I Feel I Can Do Anything

I Won't Rest Till I Know
Do You Feel The Same
If Only I Could Kiss You
Only If...

Senses
Michael Miller
I hear in the winds...
Their soft, cool song: singing out to me...
The day is come
The day is good
Dance upon the Mother Earth.
Everything hears even I,
and all begin to dance.

I see before me now, a bright crimson light...
Rushing within
Rushing without
Rushing all about
Everything sees even I and all are still with awe.

I smell upon the open air...
The scent of a storm,
it goes within.
Everything can smell even I and all are rejoicing

I reach out and touch as it comes,
within us all.
Everything touches even I,
and it bites at our senses.

The Change
Raymond M. Ross
I have found life is more of a trial period before you go to the
Heavenly Father. Life is twisted with swirls of a clouded view of love
and things that appear in plain view are clear to me from here on.
Things will never be the same for me and the people that know me for
when the rain falls in rapid orchestrated rhythm. When the moon ray
falls in a pulsating way on the dark blue tinted sky, I will be on a
journey far away from the worldly implication of what a man is.

Like they have plucked the strings of my heart and pierced the very
fabric of my soul. I regret with sorrow that when Angels sings I feel the
weight of guilt, and with this on my mind I want to say Thank You

Cry For The Children
Stevie Stevens
Cry for the children on foreign shore.
Cry for the children who breathe no more;

Cry for the children whose only crime
Was living at that place and time.

Cry for the children who once played free;
Cry for what was and will never be.

Cry for the children whom we all love—
Those who reside with the Lord above.

Cry for the children who live in pain;
Yes, cry for the children now once again.

Cry for the children who have no name
Cry for the children's unwanted fame.

Cry for the children we can't embrace;
Cry for the children in a better place.

Cry for the children who are bereft.
No, cry for those of us who are left.

Fade Away
Arthur H. White III

You've been dead inside for so long, others don't even notice,
That something is wrong,
Even now you're looking different, different than other night,
Like an eagle with broken wings grounded and can't fly,
Stop looking for the perfect place to die.

Even now I see you fading away,
Like the etching on weather worn tombstones, of forgotten graves.
Don't sit and wait for angels, angels that want you to fly,
Their price is high, they give you wings, only after you die.

Living to die, with no reasons,
Nobody cries for a forgotten soul,
That put its own self out to die in the cold,
Coldness that originates in one's own mind,
Those too afraid to face the journey, there is not borrowed time,
Afraid to live, to speak and be heard.

A distant memory is all that you'll be,
A familiar face with a forgotten name,
Just waiting to be erased, from life just the same,
Like the faded name on old tombstones,
Where only speechless bones remain.

High School Wake Up
Danielle Heggan

My alarm is set to go off at dawn,
I think of school, work and lawn.
My bed more comfortable than before I slept.
The dreams I'm having, that need be kept.

My mom gives me a third wake up call,
I can't get up, unless it's to the mall,
Reality hits...It's getting late,
Shower, make–up and homework won't wait.
It's out the door, lunch money in demand,
A quick check in the mirror, cigarette in hand.

Now I Know
Kathy Kester

I do not know what it is like
For my mother to hold me tight
And shelter me from life

I do not know what it is like
For my dad to wipe my tears
And calm my childhood fears

But God knows all about it
When I am cold, lonely and scared
He holds me close and shows He cares

When I am hurting and very sad
He is there to wipe my tears away
And to remind me all is okay

And now I know
He sent a dear friend along
To fill my sad heart with a song

Now I know what it is like
To be loved, cared for and treasured
By a true friend

Fatima
Tess Queyquep

You are most beautiful O Mary
And I'm your child most fortunate
Once more you call me to love
to peace
to simplicity...
I am humbled.

The Lady called from Portugal
Waited at the Cova da Iria
Here I am, Blessed Mother.

There she is
Most beautiful of all
Welcoming pilgrims from the world over.

At Residencia Alleluia
Her receiving arms soothe the weary traveller.

Mother, here I am
I kept our date
Inviting me to joy...

Dedication: Dearest Ma, our family inspiration

Gentle Breeze
Jayne Register

Like a gentle breeze you cannot remain
You come and go quietly
Spreading cheer throughout my life
When in your presence a smile arouses
Memories form for empty days
Outside the rain pours
Thoughts of you pass before me
A vacancy abides within
Bottles cannot hold these feelings
Only in dreams remain
A gentle breeze quietly fills the air.

Self–Induced Dementia
Holly Kestenis

On this cloud of illusion
our minds race.
Thoughts of you embedded
trapped in my head.

Lying here—why won't it end?
No sleep for hours.
My greatest pleasure
now desperate pleads.
Go away!

Every thought of you
a door to insanity.
Where is the morning?
With a swallow an eternity.
A straight jacket please.

I am afraid.
Trapped in a world of you.
Slow–motion. Never resting.
There has to be more. Anything.

Morning brings relief. Thank God.

Guardian

Michelle L. Whitehead

Constant companion
You offer me only a profound sense of despair, but your presence comforts me
Only when you sleep do I feel a muted sense of the mysteries others could offer me
Yet I resist
Because I know that it is you alone who care
You guard my heart like a black knight in corrosive armour
Valiantly slaying those who would dare try to nurture the dying red rose
It still pulses a dull crimson
You stand watch over my spirit like a faithful rabid dog
Heroically destroying those who would try to resurrect the comatose child
Still she slumbers in ignorant bliss
I feel your cold caress as you wrap my soul in your rotted rags with such tender care
Shielding me from those who would let in the sun
The shadows will never blister me
You stare silently through my eyes like a vigilante lover who knows no love
Pulling the blinds down against the miracles of life
So I never need witness anything of (deceitful) beauty
I shall never cry again

Dedication: My mother, Laura...she believed

Meadow Secrets

Leia Parker

I see a forest with a river flowing high,
I hear animal footsteps going by.
I see miles of green, green grass all around,
I hear crickets singing underground.
! see bees buzzing high,
Like a bird in the sky.
You would like it too,
If only you knew.
The secrets that fall behind it.

Dedication: The memory of David Parker

Spring

Katie Curlett

The cloud has cleared
There is nothing holding the sun back;
Animals awake,
Finally, the grass is a dark green, no longer
a dead brown.

People come out of their houses;
They take walks and enjoy the fresh air.
People are happier.

Flowers bloom.
You should have seen them along my road:
Pink, white, green,
Flowers of all colors imaginable!

Why do you cry when the rain comes?
You should rejoice;
It is helping things to live.

After the rain the flower's colors will
be more vibrant.
The sky will be ever so blue,
And you, you will be happy again.

The Book Of Afterlife

Tina Alvira

The page was turned and in golden letters read your name
It was time; the afterlife awaited you, and you received it
We grieved for you and we missed you
We were sad, your family and friends closest to you
But we knew each page has a name, then it is time to go
You were maybe sad at first, you knew you would miss us
But you were in a wonderful place
You had no more suffering, not any pain
The angels sang to you, the Lord comforted you
You have come to realize that you can still see us
You speak to us in our dreams, you visit us in our thoughts
And laugh with us in our memories
Parts of you are still within our hearts
We are not selfish, we do go on with our day to day lives
We miss you, but are happy you have deserved peace
We are grateful for our visits in our dreams and thoughts
When the page is turned and our names are read
We will be with you in the afterlife, together forever
In the meantime, I'll listen to you speak in my dreams tonight and
    I'll laugh with you in
my memories tomorrow.

Dedication: Dad, I'll always love you!

Untitled

Sandra Shelton

A lonely tree said on a hill,
It said O Lord why do I stand still?
I'd like to travel over this land of thine.
And most of all I'd like to behold,
Things of silver and things of gold.
The Lord said tree stand still and grow,
And I'll bless your arms with leaves to hold
The morning dew which kisses my lips
and falls to caress the ground under your feet.

Dedication: Shanna Bishop and Hunter Shelton

Untitled

Marilyn Woodham–Irby

So I was weighted by need,
Crushed by the will of others
into fine powder which,
Like ashes of a cremation
are sole remainder of a body
destroyed by fire,
Is all that remains.

And I became like bits of dust,
Cast upon the winds
of time and circumstance which,
Unlike ashes of a body which
lie in a treasured urn,
a special place,
Are soul remainder of me.

But I shall rise again,
Unfettered by circumstance,
need, or care, becoming,
As the body may resurrect
being not the same,
but better,
A glorified essence of me.

A Poem About Life
Phyllis Tremblay
Life is what you make of it,
You can either try or quit,
People are supposed to be trusted,
But in today's world, most people
get busted.
When people realize, what they
did to hurt others, they are
not even bothered, by this.
I believe that the most honest
people I met in my life, which
are few, should put their foot in
someone else shoe.
When people fight without thinking
of what they are saying,
They should kneel down, and start
praying.

I wrote this little poem,
Because, I myself have been hurt
by others in the past,
To all those reading this, if you
are in the same situation, then
by all means, get out fast.

An Attempt To Explain Why We Killed The Earth
V. M. Fry
First, we began the intimacies
By picking her flowers.

Then, we sat
By her good, windblown ears

And started with half–kisses.
Fingering her resources,

We muttered
"It's great to be rich."

Help Is On The Way
Mark Williams
When your boat gets tossed about
and the sky looks dark and gray

Just beyond the storm clouds
Help is on the way

If the answer doesn't come today
don't give up the fight

Keep your faith in God above
and everything will turn out right

Always look towards tomorrow
never dwell on yesterday

Do the best you can with what you have
each and every day

Just remember beyond the darkness
The light of day awaits

Don't despair, you're almost home.
help is on the way.

Daddy's Glow
Katherine M. Jones
A warm love security
no matter what the world gives

Whether a phone call or a hug
A dad is always there

Supporting, caring, never condescending
As proud for who we become as for what we achieve

The love is always there, it exists powerful and beautiful
strengthening with each day

Struggling to accept growing and absence
Happy when we show up, saddened as we walk out the door

Always waiting for the next visit
wanting to hear about new experiences and give
wise advice on whatever problems cross our paths
cherishing every moment

It is a love that shines brilliant and bright
A love that is often taken for granted
A love that illuminates from a Daddy's glow

Untitled
Gloria Pieretti
Time
Passing
leaves
me
behind.
Look
back!
See
me
making
tracks: : : : : : : : : :

Footprints of Angels
Mildred Capps Jerome
In the early morning hours
When the day is still brand new
When what you think is diamonds
Are just sparkling drops of dew...

You see the misty spots of vapor
Hovering just above the ground
That's the footprints of God's angels
Where they've been walking all around

They come in the depth of night
On moonbeams they descend...
To spend time in our world
To visit with old friends...

They stand silently beside us
Sometimes for minutes, even hours...
Their presence overwhelms us...
Like the fragrance of sweet flowers...
They go home on rays of sunshine
To return to perfect glory...
But they leave their tender footprints
Here with us to tell the story...

Peaceful Night
Vern Meyers
Alone beneath a quiet heaven,
Watching the moon as it glides along,
Making its way through the shifting channels of the sky;
Finding tiny starlets peeping through billowing clouds,
Twinkling lighthouses marking where shallows lie;
Seeing the clouds as, one by one, they slip by in silent reverie,
Not veiling the moon but adding a touch of mystery
To the steadfast light of that glowing disk;
Not hiding its beauty, but enhancing it.
As each cloud deeper than the others files in Indian fashion
before its queen,
Its edges take on a golden hue and its form is made to seem
A pyramid of dazzling brightness whose inner peak upholds the
moon.
And then it follows its fellows to float the moon in a sea of
color beyond description —
Not grey nor black, not blue nor indigo.

Walking through the rain–swept, starlit forest,
Finding once bare twigs decked out in lace and jewelry;
Crossing tiny freshets to gaze on nature's dowry;
The silent moon on high, the sparkling woods beneath,
Profound peace, serenity never to cease.

The Storm
Joan Goodwin
Beautiful, bountiful ocean,
rocking and rolling
to the rhythm of unseen musicians.

The sky darkens – the wind upbeat;
its tempo quickens.
The storm will warn, but offer no retreat.

Energy spent, whitecaps subside.
The cadence returns;
and the sea rocks on, rolling with the tide.

Future Shock
Pamela Block
Toward the merciless sun tall trees stretch,
Choked leaves gasping in the dusty air.
What have we done?

Desperate roots sink in the earth
Drilling deep for water
Don't they know there's none?

In the safety of darkness creatures venture forth
Pathetic survivors of the killing rays
Who will save them from the sun?

They search for the bitter waters
Waters that may refresh or kill them
They hope for rain but rain won't come

But along the banks of rivers, lakes, and seas,
Fish swim through city streets.
Civilization has been buried in a watery tomb

While here the wind blows the sterile dust
Off of the rocky skeleton of a dying planet.
Nowhere to hide nowhere to run

Summer Love
Felicia Susan McGillis
We had our time in the sun,
we loved
we played
we even fought a little along the way.
we did it for years
day after day.

Now the sun is not so bright
we lost our Love,
we gave up the fight,
why?
what happened to our light?

Peace
T. R. Wolfe
In the quiet of town
When there's no one around
One can find one's true inner self

In some far distant archives
There's a record of our lives
Like taking a book off a shelf

Some will read what is wrote
And make a mental note
To try and make themselves a little better

Yet on the very next day
Some will act the same way
As though they never read a single letter

Yet there are those lucky few
Who understood what to do
And they're the ones who'll really win

For those who didn't get to look
There's just six words in the book
"Peace without comes from peace within."

The Old People's Home
Stuart Cooper
In the old people's home
In a room, on a bed,
Lies my nan.

When I go in to visit
She doesn't know who I am
Her memory has gone.

I'm sitting there watching
Every minute of her life
Go by.

Looking at her silky white hair.
It reminds me of
A spider's web.

I'm at her side
Watching
Her die.

In the old people's home,
In a room, on a bed,
Lies my nan.

The Gentle Hand Of God's Diversity
Suzanne Elizabeth Chaney
Sweet scents infiltrate the sky
Look how lovely the flowers bloom
With their petals they intoxicate
Behold, how one can consume
Their entity of eloquence
Bound by, simply, their state of elegance
With beauty untouched
And intricacy immensely unfathomable
They reign with their magnificent perfume
Leaving memories – unimaginable
The Rose – the Poinsettia – the Lily
The gentle hand of God's diversity!

A True Friend
A. Joan Hambling
A friend is someone with whom you share
Your joys and sorrows
To show that you care...
Elation! When the news is great
Confide in each other
And decide your fate.

Companionship built up over the years
When happiness reigned with just a few tears
The outings together
Surprise ones more fun
The company joined
Enjoyed by each one

Time moves on, but we still retain
The link that binds us
In the friendship chain
Distance may hinder
But not break away
From those lasting memories
Stored from day to day.

Dedication: Pamela Hall, a very dear friend

Last Moments
Kevin Wilkes
An old man sits on a warm summers day,
Ignores all around him as his mind rolls away
His thoughts are of life, of birth and of death,
What might he have done before they lay him to rest.
His life's been of work, no rest and no play,
What's he achieved at the end of the day.

A tear starts to glisten in the old man's eye,
His emotions released and his soul wants to fly.
He feels so tired as he lies on his back,
The grass is his bed and the sky is his map.
It's to show him where's heaven, his new lead of life,
He's leaving no friends, no family, no wife.

His eyes start to shut, his heartbeat has stopped,
His soul is at rest, the tear has now dropped.
No longer a no one, no longer unneeded,
His spirit is flying, to Heaven conceded.

An old dog whimpers as he sits by his side,
The smell of his master will soon fade with time
His body is dust, He is no longer there,
But his existence lives on and still nobody cares.

Untitled
Sherrie Burling
Sometimes,
I feel like I'm standing
Outside of myself; on the outside
Looking in,
Not knowing who I see
Anymore...
Sheltered within a body;
Screaming to get out.
I stand, peeling off layers and layers
Of life,
Just until I can find the
Light again...

Untitled
Joan Bosher
There is a darkness in my life right now
For which there is no light
A loneliness that stays with me
All throughout the night
An emptiness, I cannot fill
As hard as I may try
"Move on, Move on" people say
"Don't let your life pass by!"

Move on to what? I ask myself
To pastures new and green
To new love and to happiness
What do they really mean!

My life is at a standstill
And I'm afraid, they'll have to wait
As I'm not going anywhere
I'll leave it up to fate

And as for love and happiness
I hope one day I'll find
A person who can give me these
Along with peace of mind!

Freedom
Dinah Pickersgill
The marshes stretch towards the sea
Grey wash joining paler sky.
The frantic song of a reed warbler
in the swishing bleached sea grass
competes with skylark's soaring scales.
Small black moorhens dart and dabble in reedy water.

Behind the marshes are wide green lanes
Heavy with heat and bees
and slashed with flashes of blood–red poppies.
Random tree–clumps offer shade and birdsong.

Far off, small waves gather like white frills
Breaking the sea's monotony
Its distant sound is like a train approaching
But never stopping.

Here, on the wet rippled sand
Feeling the ridged coolness under my feet
splashing through shallow pools
with floating weeds and tiny shells
Reliving a child's first thrilling seaside visit
The sheer expanse of sky and sea setting me free.

My Little Girl
Eleanor L. Olson
Holding and feeding you is how it used to be;
The whole world is yours to see.
Now off you go on your two little feet;
The world you are ready to meet.
School days seemed so far away;
But I cried as you caught the bus today.
You are growing up far too fast;
I remember days of the past.
The day you first walked; and the day you learned
to talk.
So off you go to discover the world around;
I'll stand back but my joy will abound.

The Dreamer
Jonathan C. Davis
Long I gaze at the stars
Thinking of you and
Wondering if right now,
You, too, have lost yourself in them.

They are so distant
And yet through them
They become reflections
Of our hearts and as such,
Are not far away at all.

Each star is a memory —
A few we've watched for a long time;
Countless others we have yet to notice.

Our dreams unfold throughout the stars
Making each point of light
Preciously valuable within the darkness.
It's as if I can pick out a single star
And say, "This star makes me feel young because..."
Or, "This star makes me smile because..."
Of you.
Of us.

My Little Dove
E. M. Gisiora
My Little Dove
With whom I share my love;
Allow me to hold your waist
And tease the succulence of your breast.
Let me mold my feelings into a song
And sing them to you all night long!

Smile giggle or laugh
But is that enough?
Come on, let's hold and roll
Hence Winter thru Spring, Summer and Fall.

Melt into my arms and feel warm
Lean o'er and listen to my veins hum
Count my heartbeat
And probe my feet
Show thy true affection
And from me will be a true reflection

Me is to love you always
In both and all ways.
I shall leave you never
'Cause I'll be yours FOREVER!

Shining Through
Danette Nigh
The sun is shining through my window,
through my eyes,
through my heart.
If only...
I was able to be as bright,
to be shining through the night.
Shining through your window,
through your eyes,
through your heart.
We would never be apart.
As the sun shining through with such light...
My love would be shining through the night.

The Procrastinator
William H. Keeling, Jr.
The days go by so quickly now,
I don't even know what happened.

I started out with good intentions,
But now my spirit's been dampened.

The time I set aside is gone,
Before I even started.

Maybe tomorrow will be a better day,
I'm thinking half–hearted.

Spring came, and spring went,
And I didn't even make a dent.

Summer's past, winter's here,
Maybe I could do it next year dear.

Projects pile, I'm in denial,
Maybe I'll get to it in a little while.

Where did the time go I set aside,
Excuse me dear, hand me the TV Guide.

curse!
B. J. Newton
curse the groove–daddy on simpleton street
for living by the beat of his drum
curse the filthy green notes
tampering with wholesome value

curse those who know what they are
when they don't

curse be to you
for not loving one and all
curse be to me
for not loving you
curse those wretch'd words that bleed
from cleanly scarred lips

curse the wicked window
that regurgitates my face

curse my tender lion cowardice
and titanical heart
curse the wet noodle
for mimicking my spine
curse love, curse hate, curse peace, curse war, curse!

Thorn
Eric Sudol
When life sticks you with a thorn.
Pull it out and go on.
Pain is most of life.
It stays when everything is gone.

Love is a temporary escape.
When it leaves, pain is there.
Love is another thorn of life —
It can be a blessing or a nightmare.

While I sleep, I wonder.
If I can escape the thunder...of life.

Generations
Annie Phillips Ewing
This too shall pass.
Things come, things go.

Past, present, future.
Yesterday, today, tomorrow

Father, son, grandson.
Mother, daughter, granddaughter.
In perfect order.

Life rolls on.
Today is yesterday, tomorrow is today.

The rivers must flow, the winds must blow.
We know not where they come, nor where they go.
Life rolls on

Farther on down the road, the rear view mirror
holds that which has past. We travel on,
and on, and on, and on out of sight, as
day turns into night
This too shall pass
As life rolls on.

The Man In My Life
Sharon Milward
I love you for being you,
For everything you say and do,
When I look at your smiling face,
I know that no one else can take your place,

I love you from the bottom of my heart,
I know one day we will never part,
All my dreams are for us to share,
For I know I will always be there,
I have wanted to find someone like you,
All your qualities I know are true,

I love you more as times goes by,
I feel I can touch the sky,
Without you my life seems incomplete,
I just can't wait until we meet,

I love you doesn't seem enough to say,
I just hope my feeling I can convey,
For I am here for you today,
To make you feel good in

Every way.

Music Of The Waves
Mike Garner
Music, tender 'mid soaring waves,
breathes sparkly shards of silver spray,
on salt–strewn, sun–warmed sails,
in darkling patterned, damp array;
'til starlight steals the sun away,
and watchmen stand and gently sway,
and guide their craft down moonlit ways
to far flung shores, where storm clouds fray
on sharp fanged crags of sky torn grey,
that rend the dark from clouds at play,
and Dolphins gambol in the lays
of music, tender, 'mid soaring waves.

Allow No Obstacles
Janet H. Peete
Learn to believe in yourself,
If you don't nobody will.
Your ideas could be as important
Like other outstanding achievers.
Words of encouragement might be needed;
To assure self–reliance in oneself;
Move forward to accomplish your dreams.

Excel above the occasion will lead to success.
Allow no obstacles to block your path;
Permit no hindrance to delay your course of actions;
Acknowledge no barriers to restrain your thoughts;
Consent to no deterrents that will influence your hope
Grant no obstructions that will impede your efforts.

Only authorize exaltations that will enhance your intention
Consider possibilities that will enrich your life.
Maintain a strong commitment for your convictions;
Be resourceful and secure about your concerns;
Let your insights become unlimited opportunities.

Now, be good to yourself for the better, surge ahead
And use your natural god given talents.

When We Are Young
Sarah Cote
It is the days
When we are young
When we learn to live

It is the pains
When we are young
That lead us to love

It is the friends
When we are young
That teach us to trust

It is the lessons we learn
When we are young
That shape our spirits

It is the life we lead
When we are young
That create our character

It is the days
When we are young
When we learn to live

Lost Horizons
Maria C. Layne
Far away, beyond the sea I left
New horizons to explore, new light to see
I carried my children, my soul, my life
My beloved inheritance for you to share
Years slipped by, day after day
And after all I come to see
My bright young face turned into shade
My hands don't hold my yesterday
Dreams sleep behind my thoughts
Far away, inside my soul
Another land, another sea
I came to share and died within.

Crucified
Joanne Dickinson
Thorns of pain in His head
Nails held flesh to wood
Vinegar to quench a thirst
Taunted...shedding blood and tears
Cause not one of them really understood

They left Him to die
Naked body nailed to wood
A sign upon reflection read
They in their ignorance
They never understood

This was a man yet no ordinary man
He however had understood
Their need to be saved from themselves
A reason to live and a way to die
He however certainly understood

Therefore He gave himself to man
A free gift yet still misunderstood
Even many have questioned this man yet no ordinary man
The Keeper of life and the Sustainer in death
'Cause the Lord Jesus...He's always understood

Hurt
Julie L. Isaac
Your son cried today
Because of you
And of things you said
That were so untrue

His soul hung heavy,
His heart was broken
He couldn't believe
Words he heard spoken

As he cried his tears
Along with mine
He asked me how
He could be so blind

'Cause he thought that you
and he were tight
And you were
until tonight
Someday you'll know
Just what you've done
And remember the day
You hurt your son

Untitled
Iris Brown
I see this light, this gentle dreamy
light unfold
Behind the trees like skeletons arrayed
with slightly caressing breeze.
The light gently becomes pure gold,
making all the world glow and the trees
like saintly beings – cold.
But wait – the sunlight wakens up the
earth – warming it.
Even the birds now become bold
they sing for joy of this sweet
happening – as yet untold.

The River
Matt Montesano
Life is a river, a passageway struggling ever forward.
There are dark cavernous times of doubt and uncertainty,
And rapids where everything seems to be happening at once.
There are gentle stretches surrounded by beautiful sights, passing
Mountain ranges and spacious plains under blue heavens above.
Many lives drink of the river; it is an intricate part of nature's
    existence,
Other life exists even within the very waters of the river itself.
On the journey, different rivers may cross its path,
One may even join it on its journey down the path of life.
Brooks veer off to follow their own pathway down a different trail.
The journey is a winding path, full of curves and bends.
There are straight stretches, shallow narrow portions, and wide deep
    sections.
There are bright spots, basking in the sun's warmth,
but also shady parts where the river takes cool rests.
There are falls where everything collapses, but the river struggles on,
    recovering.
In the end, the river fades away, flowing into the sea to become one with
    all its predecessors.
The river's origins cannot be traced; it is born of melted ice from
    mountain tops,
Rains from above, and grows from others of its kind along the way.

The Tears In My eyes
Irene E. Vennette
The tears in My eyes,
stains My broken Heart.

I am on the way down the road,
before I even start.

You treat me like a child,
when I think I am doing great.

For your actions are no relief,
as I believe the promises you make.

When My eyes start to dry,
then I think I am free,

You take me for granted,
and I am again out at sea.

The tears in My eyes,
stains My broken heart...

I am on the road again,
before I even start.

Fun Days
Betty Morgan

What fun we had when we were young,
No worries or cares, all halcyon days,
Hopscotch and skipping in the road without fuss
Just pausing for a while for the Red and White bus
Swings and Jacksies under the wood
Slides on cardboard when the weather was good
Whipping tops and pecky all in their turn
Bonfire night, with fires Auburn,
Roasted potatoes, half cooked and black
Katherine wheels and jumping jacks
Christmas time! with carols to be sung
What fun we had when we were young!

Don't Weep For Me
Phyllis N. Walsh

When the last page is turned
in the book of my life,
Remember only the best,
The good years.

For I saw the sun rise each day
And the moon slip silently into the ocean.
I've heard the sound of crashing waves
The lonely howl of the wolf

There was the scent of roses
A field of new mown hay.
The love of family and friends
This too was mine
I have held a newborn in my arms
Cradled the hand of dying kin.

Now I have harvested
The last crop from my tree of life.
It is time to move on.
Don't weep for me.

Dedication: My grandson, Roger Walsh

A Deep And Abiding Love
Walter Fiwchuk

It does unfold this day, a prodigious assembly, of little people.
You can see them, slowly marching from all their homes
To share in this late September's day, one good day left
A sunshiny autumn day, of a lovely summer gone by, forever gone
A day at their playground, this day left, of a day in their lives

They laughed, cried; played so very hard, glorious was the sun
They laughed, cried; needed this day to never, ever end
The children seemed to need each other, this interaction so much
Once again, oh boy without fail, that poor little chubby Tommy
has fallen off the high bars, crying lonely, on the ground

The children, gather around him; comfort him, they love Tommy
These children act, as adults should act, their need to love is deep
They all, individually; collectively, share a deep and abiding love

Over there, by the ever popular monkey bars, is mighty Jake!
He is Jake the homeless mongrel dog, worshipped by all
He is not treated like an outcast here, in this holy assembly
He is revered, honoured; respected warmly courted, fed by all
He somehow seems to watch over the children's safety, Jake watches
a flaming September's sun, slowly fades in a western sky, the inane
a deep and abiding love they all share, I myself was just passing by.

I Won't Cry Tomorrow
D. R. Materface

Through the patter of falling rain.
Autumn leaves are falling once again.
I wonder what this day will bring.
Will the birds forget to sing.
Will the sun fall from the sky.
Will the birds forget to fly.
I walk alone this country lane.
My heart is heavy filled with pain.
My eyes are moist. I want to cry.
Oh God. Please don't let my love die.
I promise I won't cry again tomorrow.
I promise I won't cry.

Old Tapestry
Beulah C. Brandstadter

The years weave patterns. We began the warp
With shooting stars of cadmium red
The glowing whites of love at twenty.

The raptured senses, the inmost being unfolded
Mind touching mind, sweetly, greedily,
Hand grasping hand, the body's haven.

The hearts strong sinews woven through,
Sorrows joined and feathered by the sharing,
Joy exalted by love's knotted binding.

Find the fractured space, grief's somber strands
Woven through the miasma of the slaughter,
The million threads centered to the one beloved.

Reknit, we added other shades of life.
The pinks and blues, the children's hues
Love's varied to ones patterned through the weaving.

Eons and a day slip by, our fifty years
Woven through with our laughs and tears
Thus my tapestry I chose to weave as your wife.

Darkness
Cindy–Lee Booher

Comes anyway
every day
even if we don't

want it to.

Tomorrow comes
for many
a new day
a new start
a new

beginning.

Totally unblemished
without mistake
clean and white.
Now how to keep
it that way until

darkness comes.

Anyway.

Welcome Spring!
Virginia Hammel

Good morning spring!
Come have your fling—
We're glad to welcome you,

With flowers bright
And days so light
With azure skies of blue!

With grass so green
You are a dream—
We all behold your glory

We now can sing
So welcome spring—
Come tell us of the story.

That life can be new again
Dreams can come true again
As spring leaves winter behind

We can look up and say
"What a wonderful day!"
And look forward to God's design.

My Bike
Autumn Marie Noah

My bike is what I treasure most
I like it more than breakfast for lunch,
including cereal, eggs and toast—
Though I admire this stuff a bunch
I can't ride my food around;
My toast doesn't have pedals or brakes
My eggs just sit on the ground—
(but they do go well with steaks)
Trying to go from here to there,
cereal can't take me anywhere
Now I think you see
why my bike is the only way to go for me...

Words Of A Depressed Poet
Vanessa Baladad

I remembered that day, when no one had anything to say
I watched the deep blue sky, turn into grey
I remember you going down, down into the ground
The tears never came out, and all was dry
Everything has sunk, into my memory
Do you remember that girl, that girl named Marie?

Sad as it was I'll never forget
The last day, the day we met, the day I'll never forget
Lived my life in this burning place, everything in my life has been
defaced. – But in the darkness there was a light, a light still burning
bright. The moon shines over this land, your soul slips through
my hand. Remember I said goodbye, remember it was all just a lie.

Thoughts come and go, my heart beats very slow
Does love take the pain away? Or will the pain stay?
How can things change? If we're so rearranged.
Every angel has wings to fly, every man lives and dies
The newborn child grows, like a sweet red rose
Your thoughts float down the stream, remember it's all a dream

I'm not alone, I'm not alone, I'm not alone
Thoughts float down the stream, life is but a dream...

In An Airport 10/29
Natalie Stephenson

every morning and night i come, one of many,
and see your wings waiting ready on the sky
and fly, i'd like to fly

though i am just a blank face in the still–running day
my heart is beautiful, longing, and my face is tired
i want to take myself in hand, and fly still higher

i want to run away from these empty crowds
from the man who stares at me cross–eyed and waiting
i see a dream in you, and still i am hesitating

if only i had the freedom to leave this every day something
if only i had the peace to come, and come and go
if only i could run, fly on wings of my own

inside my window, in the cold i see your waiting wheels
in the warm you call and settle, ready for air
you hold wax wings and promise of somewhere, anywhere

maybe i will not leave this today, people wait
i'd like to fly this place but i find i cannot run
i am landed, land bound, one of everyone.

You Are...
Victor J. Young

You're the dawning of day, a beautiful, sunrise,
Light filtering through my window, playing tag with my eyes.
You're the awakening of nature, the birth of a newborn spring,
Songbirds in flight, a chorus on the wing.
You're a fresh breeze on a summer day just before a rain,
The mist from a waterfall that flows without refrain.
You're that nip in the air, when out of nowhere fall appears,
A kaleidoscope of color, tree leaves shed like happy tears.
You're the purity of falling snowflakes, all different, yet the same,
Winter's blustery winds that lovingly call my name.
You're the peace and serenity that comes when night replaces day,
The course in which I follow and the light that guides my way.

My Mother
Darla Chevalier

Mother – how beautiful the name;
Day in, day out, always the same;
Loving, caring, forgetting herself; she forges onward,
Putting her needs 'on the shelf'.

Starting each new day with the Lord, radiating joy and love,
Bringing us a bit of heaven above.
She washes, she cooks and cleans,
All the while her face "beams".
She scrubs, and polishes; she sews and repairs;
Each piece being handled with loving care;
As with each life with which she is entrusted.

She molds, she teaches, scolding oft'times,
When so moved by the Spirit;
She shows by her example
The way that we should be,
She lights the path for us to follow;
That will take us home to God.

No matter where I go, or how far I may roam;
I will always return to my haven—
To my beautiful Mother at home.

The Family's Home
Gillian Gertridge

Walking into the old house,
The musty smell of furniture hits her face.
Faded patches of flower wallpaper
Where photographs of a happy family
Once hung proudly on the walls of the living room.

The navy blue carpet that held through many generations,
Now faded by the dust to a light blue,
Is sunken in the spots where the table once sat.
And in the corner of this once cheerful room,
A little blonde doll lies tossed aside

The furniture has the beginnings of moth holes
And the old wooden rocking chair,
Made faded by years of dust,
Still sits at its place near the window.
The window whose last view was of the marching soldiers.

Those unrelenting soldiers came and went with a fury.
They twisted through the town like a tornado,
Destroying everything in their path.
Including this house, this home,
Which was once the home of a happy and proud family

True Friendship
Amy Heenan

Through good times and bad
Through thick and through thin.
When I didn't belong,
You helped me fit in.
You gave me a place,
In a world strange to me.
Your sweet, smiling face,
Was all I could see.
In a world full of frowns,
Your laughter came through.
And that's when I found,
A friend that was true.

Whenever
Sheridan Anderson

Whenever you touch me, you make my body tingle
It's times like that, I'm glad that I'm single

Whenever you are near me, there's an aura in the air
Here, there, it seems to be everywhere

Whenever I am with you, I don't want you to go
I don't feel as happy, I feel ever so low

Whenever I see you, I think to myself 'Oh, wow'
'Get that sexy body over here, right now!'

Whenever I smell your smell, I know you've been around
I turn to look for you, but you cannot be found

Whenever I speak with you, my heads all of a muddle
Actions speak louder than words, so just give me a cuddle

Whenever I think of you, I feel the arrow pierce the heart
And hope deep down inside that we'll never be apart

Whenever you are far away from me, I think of you constantly
And look forward to the next time that you are here with me

Time And Forgiveness
Reina K. Guarnaccia

When time is on your hands,
and your world seems to turn so slow,
it seems as though the world – begins to glow,
and when this sight arises–there are
things good and bad,
and you never seem to realize just what
you had,
now comes a great darkness–and
this is what you see,
you watch the times you did wrong–
and wish that you did see,
and wish that you did understand–just
what you have done,
you wish that you could change
it – and make it all go right,
but all that you can do–is do
good in your future sight,
so please do try to stand – on
what you believe,
but remember that time – that
makes you want to grieve,
and don't forget to watch
yourself – from morning–then to eve.

Black And White
Forrest Campbell

I laugh just like you,
I cry and feel pain;
When you touch my skin,
we feel just the same.
But you were born black
and I was born white;
Our prejudice formed
because of our sight.
Yet if you were blind,
and I couldn't see,
just think of how nice
our friendship could be...

Aids
Betty Williams

I confused my hormones with happiness;
now my life is a big mess.
A lovely lady looking so fly,
I thought she must be an angel from the sky.
The two of us got together for one night.
Now I'll be paying for it the rest of my life.
I went to the doctor and was diagnosed with AIDS.
The doctor looked at me and asked when was the last
time you had sex and with whom. I thought the man
was playing; I said, "You need to stop doc just quit it."
The doctor looked at me and said, "This is not a game. Now I need
to know those names." So I gave a list of whom I had been with.
The doctor looked at me and said, "No wonder you have this."
Now I'm scared, this man is messing with my head; saying in
a month or two I may be dead. Now I'm down to eighty
pounds and my friends are nowhere to be found. My
brain is deteriorating fast and I don't know how long
this will last. The hair on my head is no longer there. My
healthy body is gone and I don't know where. Now
unprotected sex is what got me like this today.
I'm dying and that is the price I'll have to pay.

Dedication: My family, Paw Paw and Lois

The Daily Hour
William E. Sasso
There exists a daily hour
From my past year (very sour)
And an exorcist would fail to make it leave...

It's an increment of time
That is (to me) a heinous crime
Because it seems to last forever – No reprieve...!

I'd request from even Death
The single favor of His breath
Upon this Hour (with my hope that it would die...!)

It's an Hour holding sorrow
Which arrives again tomorrow
(Just a wee bit more severe in passing by...)

And I guess the only answer
To this minute–ridden cancer
Is to run and hide (though time you cannot flee...)

So for me, there's still an Hour
That projects remorseful power
And it's unrelenting in pursuit of me...

Light My Path
Cathy C. Daniels
I love the sun for what it does and all it has to say.
It speaks to me without words and brings lots of joys my way.
It says to me it loves me as the sunlight kisses my cheek.
It says to me I will be strong so that you may be weak.
It says to me stand still, quiet your inner thoughts;
Know that I have strength beyond which can be bought.
Know that every day I fight just to keep you warm.
Know that I am always here even in a storm.
Allow your heart to open invite my strength inside,
And you will find contentment like you have never tried.
For you see, I am not, a ball of gas burning in the sky;
I am God's heart...silently, beating, by and by!

Baby Angels, A Mother's Prayer Of Tribute
Lori Lutes Fields
Oh God, how very special my two babies
must have been...
For You to have called them to Heaven
so soon.
Before they even graced this earth...
Or became a reality to anyone...
EXCEPT to me their mother!

Oh God, each of my babies was so real to me...
To my body that carried and protected them, if only
for just a short while...
To my mind that imagined, believed and dreamed of
each of them, if even just for a short time...
And most of all to my heart, that still dreams
of them each and every day!

Oh God, in my heart I like to imagine...
That You took them because you were in such great
need of angels.
And with your help, I pray, that one day when
I too reach heaven...
That I will be able to recognize my two
very precious baby angels!!!

Mother
Gail Smith
You gave me life one
Winters day and cared
For me in your special way.

You taught me it all,
From A to Z;
But best of all you
Believed in me.

You said I'm special and
One of a kind, I seldom
Thanked you but you
Didn't mind.

You opened me up and
Tore down my wall,
You're the only one who
Knew me at all.

You've been there for me
My whole life through.
So in my own way
I'm saying thank you.

Heaven
John Kehoe
Come with me, step on the shoulders of Death
Or live meaningless on the flooding shore:
The prosaic land stealing life of breath
Tomorrow– the mist is calling for more
Tomorrow the wind will never rustle
You must choose now, as the tide overwhelms
Does not your mind cry: Ebb! Ebb! Audible–
–To your conscience alone, I fear it quells
I fear no one cares I fear no one dares
To barricade the rising flood of pain
The land to which the mind is made unfair
To sleep world, and only dreams remain.

Morning Sea
Tammy Huff
Morning sunshine washes over me in a glorious flood of golden light
White–capped surf envelops my feet, the foam whispering past my toes in a
dizzying caress
Rushing up the beach at the breakneck speed, then tarrying on the sand as
if loth to leave this
golden warmth of earth
Slowly back it fades, sliding under the next eager wave that rushes up
Softly calling its reluctant goodbyes to my toes

Farther out the waves break blue and white against the sky
The sea moves easily, effortlessly rolling; its great rippling muscles
plain to see beneath an
endless expanse of glittering blue
There on the rocks it shows its power, white foam leaps on high in a
mighty thunderous roar
The great cliffs are overpowered, disappearing beneath a towering
avalanche of frothy spray;
The sea has taken them as easily as it has taken me

But now – the swell fades, slowly back; the rocks again stand gleaming in
the warmth of day
The sea was only playing, after all, even with the earth's toes as it
plays with mine

Silencing The Chimes
Coreen Labarbera
I am a child waiting to hear the chimes ring,
but they are motionless in a musky, dark corner
of the house where no breeze can penetrate.
Grandma says she wants them to hang there so
she can see their shiny reflections on the wall.
It's not fair — chimes are not to be seen but heard.
Silent sleep seeks the sounds, unless where the wind
cannot stir them to their unique tinkling harmony
to scatter off the ancient dust from the silvery shells.
I grasp their strings and send waves of solace to the
singing bells only to find their tone flat.
Let them be free to ring — I'm just a child.

Typing
Inola M. McGuire
Typing, typing, oh how I love to type
This is no hype
Without this valuable skill
Our language stays at a stand still
Some take this skill for granted
But, it has its advantage

All sectors in life rely on typing
Whenever we produce something
Typing for a doctor is medical
Typing for an accountant is financial
Acquiring this skill will be a start
Formatting documents is an art

The manager needs his report
A typewritten copy gives him support
Typing at the keyboard is input
Printing the information is output
Proper typing requires dexterity
The rewards spell prosperity

Dedication: To Kathy–Ann, with love

Pack Rat
Angela Lei Brown
A virgin bag awaiting the thrill.
The thrills from life in which I would fill.
I grabbed disappointment and made it my friend.
I added past pains to insure I couldn't mend.
Other expectations, I just had to meet.
Wherever I went, I used other's feet.
I consistently helped others, when it wasn't desired.
Financially drained, and emotionally tired.
Throw in self pity, a little "woe is me".
Yes, the sorrows of life, please give them to me.

Finally, the bag was too heavy to bear.
I had to remove all the past pains in there.
One at a time, I laid them all down.
Oh, the joy and peace in God I've found.
Go unpack, pack rat, it's time to unpack.
No more these burdens can you bear on your back.
Use the time to reflect as you unpack.
But it's not your ticket to turn and go back.
You've acquired wisdom, that can't be denied.
It's time, your time to

STRIDE PACK RAT, STRIDE!!!

My Legacy
Nathaniel Bud Morrison
Let me spread my wings like an angel,
Let me swim like a fish in the sea.
Let everyone around me be better
Because they have known me.

Let everyone remember what Christmas
is all about
It's not just for having presents, getting
drunk, and falling out.
Christmas is the day to honor Jesus who
was born on this special day, to love us
and protect us and wash our sins away.

My Kids
Mary McKeller
God must have given His choice of jewels
When He gave my kids to me
And gave His special blessings to each one
All the love and care I had to spare
Was worth it all when I heard them call me Mom
The love and compassion they gave to me
Let me know how much they care

Kids do grow up one by one
And like kids do they leave the nest
You look around and they are gone
Scattered North and South East and West
Searching for a perfect place
To build a home of their own

When the evening sun cast creeping shadows
Sometimes I feel I am not alone
Echoes of laughter of familiar voices
Shouting Mom I love you I'm home
No amount of earthly wealth could buy
The joy and love together we share
That makes the joy of my life far beyond compare

You Act Like A Cheese
Sharon Kamara
You think you're so smart
But you can't even read
You think you can drive
Got 12 tickets for your speed
I tried to warn you
But you said you knew how
Now you live on the street
You big lazy cow
You bought your own goat
Dropped out of school
Now you walk it around
Not knowing you're a fool;
Get a new job
Hey! Get a career
Or you'll be back on the street
Selling that stinkin' beer
I'm sorry to insult you
Have a good day
You can pay me back
When you get your next pay

Dedication: My brother, David

Love
Lee Nells
Baby, Baby, Oh Baby

You look more beautiful
than the stars of the night

You are my angel and
my Goddess of love.

And when I first saw
you it was like a little
Cupid just shot me with
his golden arrow of love.

Ode To My Companion Warrior
Forrest Crawford
In the war we fought,
no one heard the cries of fear,
no one cared to see the tears,
no one wanted to feel the despair.
There were no reinforcements ever to arrive,
and there were no bastions of reserves
we were allowed to draw upon.
The only strength I received
in that ensuing conflict
came from my Companion Warrior.
We knew the Attack would come, for It always did.
It sometimes would assail us in a fury at the mid–day,
or steal in silently upon the wings of the night.
Towards the end, the bedchambers became a cell for torture.
The backyard became a POW internment camp,
and the living room a battlefield.
For as you'll see, my friend. The Enemy was my Father,
and my only ally, my Companion Warrior, was my Mom.
Therefore, I will raise my glass in a toast
to my Companion Warrior and say, "We fought well and won."

Dedication: My mother, Janice McCorimick–Williams

Grandparents
Kimberly L. Wertz
As strong as an Oak you can seem
to be. But when a storm blows you bend so
gracefully. I wish every one could see what
I can see. for you are the roots in our family.

Like the sun you shine warm and
true. You have done so many things no one else
would do. People who give so freely are so
far and few. We are a family that begins with you.

So no matter where we may chose to
roam. You are the guiding
star that brings us
home. Your love for us carries beyond letter or
phone. The knowledge of this covers us with
a warm safe dome.

I hope you can understand what
I'm trying to convey. Because you're there
for me come what may that presence in my
life keeps my fears at bay. And I thank
God for Grandparents like you each and every day.

Cracked Glass
Louisa Kenny
She looks upon their grave stones,
With great dismay,
One by one they were thrown into the caves,
But now there's no one to pay,
As solemn as Siamese,
They're all gone and dead,
And only now she's on her knees,
Have you been fed?
Now that I'm the last,
Who's there to catch you when you fall,
Can't push me to the past,
I'm just too tall.

An Angel Here An Angel There
Joan M. Sanginario
I see your smiling face
Hear your laughter, remember the fun.
My heart and mind cannot accept
That you're no longer here.
I want so bad to talk to you
I feel like you're so near.
Day after day we shared our lives
From the time that I was born.
No one knew, except for you
I'd be so sick, so torn,
I thank the Lord, he saw my pain
And sent my Amy Lee
He let you see her, hold her, know her
So you'd know, what was to be.
He gave me someone I could love
The way that I loved you.
I held her tightly in my arms
When we had to say good–bye
I'll love her, hold her and think of you
Until the day I die.

Dedication: My mom and special memories

Gate Of The Wisdom Angel
Christopher Kulovitz
The wind blew in
and so did she

Like that of feathers blown she appeared
Black curls swirled in delight of sunlight
and bending wings did flap at them in rhythm

She and all her gentile way sought nothing
but curious eyes did seek the gate at which she peek

Bold and bright she was
with boundless strides so young
that caring was obsolete to her trespass

Wisdom, she came upon with full intention
of her knowing and unknowing ways

Within her passing, kindness brushed against us
and clouds gathered darkness as she left a powdery stillness settle
into something that would be changed forever by her unharboured heart

Dedication: Norine Early

At One With God
Karen Copestick Moore
Raindrops fall like gentle tears,
Into a puddle they appear.
From a puddle evolves a pond,
Into a lake it will spawn.
From a lake a river grows,
To the ocean it will flow.
As Into the ocean the river runs,
All will then be as one.
God's love is like a raindrop true,
Pure and gentle through and through.
Like the river to the ocean runs,
In the end we'll be as one.

The Unwritten Poem
Marina M. H. Dib
Here I am, wondering, pondering at home,
Facing a blank page and an unwritten poem...
A feather quill in the ink is fully immersed;
Though weathered, this wishing well is usually well–versed.
With one thousand reasons to find a rhyme,
But none seem as pressing as the passage of time...
No chance of developing writer's cramp
Or a slip of the tongue on the envelope and stamp?
But sooner or later, I befriend inspiration
Which finally ends this writer's frustration!
Serendipity sails! Creativity flows!
Should the rhythm prevail or be drowned out in prose?
As the minutes fly by, I must get right on it!
If I draw the line here, I'll call it a sonnet!
To set one's thoughts and feelings free
With paper and pen is pure poetry!
To have it published, if you do,
Would be one of my dreams come true!
I'll hold on to Hope! I'll never quit!
For, lo and behold, my poem is writ!

Dedication: Family, friends, angels, muses, fairies!

Untitled
Joan Sanders
She's in there – the girl I used to be.
Last night while I was washing my face, I caught a glimpse of her in the bathroom
mirror, teasing me, daring me to come in and get her.
But I think I'll just leave her in there.
At least until we get through this "change of life" stuff.
We'll let it happen to the old woman who lives in our body.
She deserves it.
After all, it wasn't a friendly merger, it was a hostile takeover.
The young girl fought it as long as she could, but the old one was much stronger.
Now, the young one is a prisoner inside a body that doesn't belong to her.
But she's not dead.
One day when the old one isn't paying attention, and lets down her guard,
The young one will overpower her.
I'll help.
We'll execute some grand coup, and the young one will regain control.
We'll leave the old broad at home in the bed with her hot water bottle,
And go out and have some fun.
That's what we'll do.
We'll wait diligently, until just the right moment,
And I'll be young again.

The Lesson
Paxton Knight
I tore my eyes to sleep
to see you
I laid my love untilled
beneath you
I spoke of death
and ate four corners
to yoke your voice
in silence saying:
"Without you,
I look within you.
Within you,
look without me."

Because Of You
Karissa Anne Knox
Because of You
the textures of my life are changing,
the colors are brightening,
the lines coming into focus.
While the patterns of our minds intertwine
and the words we speak connect
and our hearts faintly begin to pulse at the same tempo
I hear the crescendo of
my spirit opening itself
as if it were reverberating saltwater waves laying themselves against the
        beautiful sand road.
And even if
the lines of my life were to someday slip into
silver shimmering mists again,
the moments of sweet
exploding
light
would continue to accompanying my spirit...

Because of you.

Dedication: For Andrew

Rose
Thomas Moore
I can see, the color of your rose,
It matches the color of my heart
My heart makes me cry,
These tears in my eyes.
I pray will water your rose–
That it my grow.
My hopes are in a tear dropped
From heaven,
As the morning mist; settles on your petals
bring you to the fullest of your bloom.
There I'd know your thirst
was quenched, And your day full of sun.
That's where we'd share,
in life's smallest moments,
our oneness under the son,
There is where we would be,
Taken in through the warm
glare, a breath of air
Sweetened by the aroma of your
rose.

Dedication: Erink, Love Dad

Harmony
Ka'eo Amado
Harmony is like a flower
Just like people's loving
power
To create harmony you
Say these things
And listen to the blue
Birds sing
Say hi, hello, how do you do
And don't forget the I love you
Harmony is like a rose
Those pretty things you
Smell with your nose

Speculations On The Uncertainty Principle
Richard Hannaford
Or, an Easterner driving the Clearwater Breaks
Oh, rolling breaks of Idaho,
Carved like a tub'rous PO–TA–TO.
Gullies and gulches, a sheer–sided wonder,
To ramble here often appears a great blunder.
Hunters for chukers, a coyote for rabbit,
But roaming here, surely, is not a sane habit.

Yet beasties abound (of sure–footed hoof?)
Afraid of nothing—but the collie dog woof.
Pies of their making litter the land,
And trails so steep—how on earth do they stand?

As I drive up the highway, I shudder and ponder
If others have fears, or do they have fonder
Recollections of stationary things,
never troubled by signs 'bout animal beings:
Of "deer crossings" or—terrible!—" cattle guard" ahead;
Such warnings—a nightmare—keep me trembling in bed.

So, I scan for those beasties and keep wondering how
Come there are no signs for "BEWARE, FALLING COW"!

Endless Stretch
Denise Miga
moving
over the roller–coaster road
green on left
green on right
black dividing
yellow thru black
splitting down the middle
day turns to night
headlights behind
taillights before
moving
faster
chasing daylight
rushing nighttime
flies on windshield
courageously dying
wash them away
moving nearer
towards city lights
our destiny...
Dedication: JoAnna, who always inspires me...

King
Irmadene Blankenship
Humming birds darting here and there
Seems like they are coming from everywhere.
Green ones, gray and black
They get fought off and they come back.
The feeder is a very busy place
They dart here and there and back up for a taste.
Then up and over the house they go to the
other side
Because there's another feeder on the porch,
besides
Who can win the race
To become King of the hummingbird place?

A Special Person
Gina Jirikowic
My Grandpa just died
But he gave us his pride.

I took it slow
though we must let him go.

He would always tell
How much he loved us so well.

Now he's an angel.

Just sit and lie
It's okay to cry.

I love him with all my heart
I wish we're never apart.

He loved his Cardinal birds
these are my last words...

Good Bye My Dear Grandpa
From your Gina

The Florida Girl
Nora P. Swackhammer
The sea and the sand and the sun and the beach
Make the Florida Girl a pretty swell peach
The Florida Girl is never a jerk when off to
school or off to work
Whether native born or transplanted her
ideas are never slanted
Like the rolling of the steady tide
Routine living keeps her in stride

Friday she yearns for the sound of the sea
She's warmed by the sun and her spirit is free
The sun and the beach are the weekend fare
She gets sand in her toes and sun in her hair
She's the picture of health wherever she goes
She's kid personality from her head to her toes

Travel the world over and you will find
The Florida girl won't leave your mind
One of the prettiest girls on earth today
She lives way down South in the U. S. of A.
The sea and the sand and the sun and the beach
Make the Florida Girl a pretty swell peach

155

My Dream
Tommie J. Gross
Beautiful roses white and
red smells better than done
said, beautiful green grass
down below, the soil and
worms help it grow, the
ray of sunshine shines
on my head, as I snooze
during the night, I dream of
a wonderful flight, I fly
around the world in one
night, when I return I say
"good night"!

Untitled
Valarie Wilson
i was / I Am
i would / I Did
i tried / I Succeeded
i lost / I Won
i stopped / I Started
i cried / I Laugh
i couldn't / I Could
i feared / I Conquered
i hurt / I Healed
i wavered / I Am Steadfast
i was uncertain / I Am Sure
i loved / I Am Love
i stagnated / I Have Grown
i attempted / I Triumphed
i feared / I Am Not Afraid
i am lonesome / I Am Not Alone
I am older / I Am Growing
i am a child / I Am A Woman
i exist / I Live
I am a dichotomy within myself

Dedication: Real love and family

Children
Cheryl W. Howell
Three children
seven, five and three
tumbled together in raggedy underwear
under army surplus
cling to each other for warmth and comfort
passing time until morning

they wake
slightly damp and smelling of urine
to scrape breakfast from last night's pot on the stove
and dress themselves from the clothes two sizes small
picked up from the floor
where they fell yesterday

trudging off
hand in hand
to life
knowing there will be no reprieve
nor early release
from childhood

Dedication: Mary Frances, my mentor

Promise
Susan Hargrove
You made me a promise
that promise I will
keep, the promise will be
with me even in my sleep
I will never forget
the promise you made
me, it's with me all
the time, that solitary
promise is permanent in
my mind, because the
promise of your love
is a promise for all time.

Over The Rocky Mountains
C. C. Negrete
The blue skies with cascades of cotton candy
rest on the peaks of the majestic Rocky Mountains.
In awe, I wonder can another sight
surpass this beauty I behold?
But alas! It is fleeting as the season changes.
Winter drapes the mountains and pines
with white snow that melts when
the sun shines the next early morn.
The spring heralds thunderstorms running
as fast as the Boulder marathon runner
to the finish line. Snow and rain evaporate
and leave the landscape quenched and fresh
as the sunflowers that grow year after year.

Our life parallels these continuous changes,
as we leave Colorado to our next destination,
we move but remain constant as we still
love each other.
Then, I see that there is another beauty
never to be seen except felt by you and I.

Dedication: To Alex, you inspire me

Poetic Psalm
Melaney McCroy
A beautiful day
A beautiful song
Flowing ever so gently as water through your palms
So beautiful, so pure, as my Poetic Psalm.

Sometimes your life may end up in turmoil,
Praying and staying together always is a cure,
so earthly and rich like the soil
Very cool, as you touch it with your palm
is my Poetic Psalm.

As this world goes round, I'm turning with it
Letting everything pass me over
Like a beautiful day,
A beautiful song

Water; flowing ever so gently in a beautiful place
As I try to grab onto it with my palm
Never to let go,
As my Poetic Psalm.

Dedication: Eternal Life

My Question
Erin Canady
I feel sorrow
I feel pain
I'm standing outside
in the falling rain
I want to talk
but no one is here
I live my life
in constant fear
What is my question
you do not know
It will never be answered
I know, I know.

Delaware At Night
Peter Mosiondz III
A cool and moonlit night we made of it, sitting
Along the passageway to freedom. You squeezed my hand
When merchant charters passed, or gasped as clouds turned gray
And pink, while amber lights tap–danced upon the draught.
Our bellies full of broth and beer,
We sought a sovereign bond sincere.

Six days have dragged, heavy with grief, for one
Wanting to bask in a smile's warmth, contented embrace, and
listening eyes.
I want no more of a concrete bench, or lapping waves
Where a bridge looms—great girders of gloom silent
Despite steel traffic sprawled across each end.
Only we two remain, she in my arms.
We link hands; a stately span connects two lands.

By this evening, shall I say I have loved her more
Than the river that had seduced me once before?
Dare I forswear a parabolic fate, or clap
A shrieking thunderclap of death between these palms?
With fortitude we'll rend elixir from the Gods,
Our affair a feverish fervor against their odds.

The Hero You Are
Holly F. Brantner
You fought in a war that no one won;
You gave up your youth to carry a gun.
Young and innocent, without a care,
And then they sent you over there...
To fight in a battle that should never have been;
A war of politics, not of men.
But you were strong and, oh, so brave;
You sweat blood and tears for the lives you would save...
And though the years have passed, the memories remain;
Times when you still feel the terror and pain.
The smell of death still sometimes lingers;
The stains of blood on your hands and fingers.
The cries of the dying resound in your head...
The words of comfort left unsaid.
Yes, the scars of war are etched on your face;
Scars that even time can't erase...
But try to remember the lives you saved;
That you did your best and that you were brave.
A hero to many, loyal and true...
You fought for your country—the red, white and blue!

Dedication: Tom, my hero and friend

A Loving Memory
Mathew Hackett
I remember your husky voice
With a loving tone
Your face was warm and soft
Like an old warm rug, cozy and gentle
I came to you and you gave me a bear hug,
With care and affection
Your wrinkled old lips gently touched my head
Your rugged hand grasped mine
Grandpa, though you're gone
That memory has been kept in my heart

Dedication: My grandfather (Paw), Eugene Hackett

Einstein's Nightmare
Melinda Mlynski
Looking at the face across the distance,
Smiling, its light speed lies
Like Einstein's nightmare,
Reflecting back the failure of our taking gift.

Possessed by the wanting to be all,
While not even being whole as one,
Always blaming, never admitting,
Scared to death of the relativity
That brings the blame back home.

Looking at the stars as foreground
Listening to the melody of time,
Groping at Albert's dream...
Filling the quietude left by noisy friendships,
Trying to let go.

As speed stretches thin the cosmic fabric,
We are blinded near the light.
So we succumb to our desires;
Understanding all in theory,
But doomed to the nightmare again.

Solution Needed
Brenda Elzey
What has happened to our youth,
So near, yet, so far away?
Going down, as fast as a shooting star.
They haven't been here for very long
Yet, their smiles have been erased
Completely, from their face.
No more laughter. No more joy
They seem no longer girls or boys,
But creatures, whose, distinctive features,
Are guns not toys.
Where are they, where have they gone?
Some sleep the deep, deep sleep.
Many sing the chain gang song.
Others stalk and prey on the old,
Just to keep their stories from being told.
So, how can we save them,
What can we do?
We've tried everything old,
It's time for something new!
Solution needed!!!

Dedication: Sharita, Shanay, Ashley, Marcus and DeAndre

Three Generations
Pat Harding

It came as quite a bombshell, the day they said to me,
There's something we've to tell you mum, a granny you'll soon be.
There's lots to do, things to buy, to make sure that we're ready,
A cot, a pram, bibs and clothes, and one cute cuddly teddy.
The weeks pass by, baby grows, tummy's firm and round,
A visit to the hospital, to have an ultrasound.
It really is amazing just what a scan can show,
The baby's head, look there's an arm, and even its big toe.
The day has come, the pains begin, hours pass slowly by,
At six fifteen and eight pounds three, she gives her first loud cry.
With eyes so blue, and hair that's fair, its plain for all to see,
A beautiful girl needs a beautiful name, we'll call her Stassy Leigh.

Reasons To Smile
Karen Stallard

Rainbows and waterfalls
Sunflowers and bird calls

Children's laughter
and happily ever after

fluffy white clouds
and crickets that aren't too loud

watermelon and windchimes
cool breezes and sunshine

Daddy with his sons
splashing and having fun

ladybugs and butterflies
and chasing fireflies

So, if you need a reason
here are a few
but in the end
the choice is up to you

The Burden Of Proof
Valeri A. Macharoni

Of all the times I thought to leave
There were just as many times
Something compelled me to stay
It's difficult to judge why this was the case
I like to think of it as Love.
At times it's as addicting as taking a pill
One is too bitter to swallow; the other is the cure
Hoping that the side–effects won't hurt you
When you doubt which way to go—
Go by what you know down deep
Don't be lead by what you feel
One frees us from lies;
One camouflages the truth
While the jury is out deciding the verdict
If you're released on your own recognizance—
Beware of your next move and the dangers ahead
For we are our own worst enemy
Yet, we can be our best defense
Maybe that's why
The Burden of Proof
That lies in this case
Rests on you.

Untitled
Barbara Johnson

I have found my bit of heaven, sadly not
in remaining a wife,
Through all the pain and sorrow, I still
had to get on with life...
The treasures I found around me in the
beauty of this Earth...
Joys and songs inside of me, indeed they
are my mirth...
So when allowing the pain and sorrow to
somehow take control,
Remember, all the gifts of Life are right
within your Soul...

God's Littlest Angel
John Woods

We never had the chance to know you,
We never had the chance to love you,
But we did.

We never had the chance to hold you,
to comfort and console you,
But in our hearts we did.

Though your spirit touched us so briefly
Its very presence changed us completely.

When your journey to heaven forced us to part,
With you, you took two very special pieces of our heart.

As God's littlest angel you'll spend
Your first Christmas teaching that love will never end.

And on this very special day,
We pray that God will let you hear us say,
We love you and miss you on this your first Christmas Day.

Dedication: Sylvia, loving mother and wife

Bloody Innocence
Marleen Stracener Lehr

Rest betrayed them for a merciful moment
The condemning crucifying crowd of Golgotha
Breathtaking mourning rushes, meek heartbeats await
His precious mother bewailing the affliction
of what was to come
Brutal death arriving, time known, scripture quoted
Precious blood dripping of godly innocence
"Crucify Him" they shouted without a seed of cause
Grievous tears of sadness seeped down
His pale sun–dried blood thirst desiccate cheek
Guilt–scenting cloud mixed, biblical prophecy unrecognized
Thorn–pierced head, side vanity absorbed
Anointed feet and hand abundantly nail driven
Upon eternal symbolic tree, beheld made cross
Lifelessly hanging, intercessionally drained
Culminated words sanctified crept through
destroyers of vexed crowd
"Father, forgive them, for they know not what they do"
Existence everlasting manifested, words etched
Proceeding resurrection of our precious Lord Jesus Christ.

Dedication: Carmen, my angel of song

The Plonker
George De Decker

"Who is that silly person who spoils life for us all,
by having aerosol in hand and spraying on the wall.
It may be him that throws his rubbish on the ground
and strews his cans and fag–ends and chewing gum around.
On the train you'll see him place his footwear on the seat,
he doesn't give a damn for things that are clean and bright and neat.
He doesn't want to pay his dues so looks the other way,
expecting us to keep him and support his lazy way.
To him a word called discipline is something he must fight,
because he doesn't want to know what's wrong and what is right.
He of course is stupid, although not quite insane,
but does he really realise he hasn't used his brain?"

His Hand In Mine
Lillis Cruz

I have to go, I have no choice.
Yes, I know, but not without me. For I am always besides you.
I'm so excited, I can finally set the record straight.
Yes, but not without me. You need me.

I rush out never hearing the words inside my heart.
Driving down in a traffic jam, I think isn't there something
I forgot? Did I lock the door, make the bed, take out the
trash? What did I forget to do?

What about me? Did you forget to seek me? Did you forget to
speak to me?

In my heart I heard the words. My spirit cried. My soul weeped.
I'm sorry father, I cried. I have been in such a rush.

Rush, my child? What's the rush? I did not make the world
in one day, nor did I do it while I was in a rush.

I stopped and wept, than I prayed, forgive me father.
I didn't realize until today how much I needed you.
All he wanted was his hand in mine.

Civilized Race
Leslie Greene

The face flashed only for a moment, but the headlines were clear,
another tragic loss of someone's loved one so dear.

I only saw your face for a moment, I got to know you by the end of the
day; how do you deal with the loss of a child so cruelly taken away?

I don't want to know how it feels, no hurt in my life could ever
compare; with the pain I see in these faces...the loved ones left in
despair.

Another search for the one who showed little care or compassion; once
caught...we try to deal with them in our own civilized fashion.

Opinions differ, beliefs on punishment...we hold strong; an eye for an
eye or turn the other cheek for the one that did the wrong.

But I think back on that face I saw flash across the screen; how do we
let these things happen to our fellow human beings?

So I'll once again watch with sadness as a loved one wipes the tears
from their face...and pray for God to have mercy on this so called
civilized race.

This Sad Day
Angie Easterly

They sang his praises in the
church today as those golden
chariots carried you away.
We all cried because it
was sad to know that
you really had to go. We
miss you a lot, maybe too
much because your face
will never again touch. But
we'll be strong and carry
on as will all remember this
sad day.

Spring
Essie B. Parker

I don't plant flowers in the spring any more.
I plant flowers every day in a different way
I plant a flower, when I smile and tell someone, "have a great day"
I plant a flower, when everything has gone wrong
In someone's life, and I tell them everything
Will be ok.
I plant a flower, when I stand up for what's right and tell
The devil, "to take a hike"
I plant a flower, when I tell a child you can be
Anything "you want to be"
Sometimes I plant a tree.
I plant flowers, everywhere, I love to see them grow
I plant a flowers, when I pray, Lord help us to love one another
The way we should
Teach us to take care of the earth, so we will have some place to
    be. Help us to
love and protect. And stop us from abusing and killing our
    child
If you think you will never plant flower in the spring anymore
Think again
You can plant flowers every day,
In the mind and heart and soul of men.

Rise Above
Samantha P. Freeland

We travel through this life on earth managing as best we can
watching time as it slips away
in hopefulness of one more day...

It's a complicated lesson, never easy as a rule
when reminded of our past mistakes
we feel we are such fools...

Yet in our darkest hour and as odd as it may be
we find kind memories of love
step in to keep us company...

It is there within love's warm embrace
we learn to give not take, to heal not scar, to push afar
all our worries, fears and hates...

And so we bow our heads with grace
we learn to trust in love
for in that moment we have the way to
...Rise Above...

Dedication: Jeffery, such warmth and light

The Family
F.S.O. Crawford
The family is like a book.
The children are the leaves.
The parents are the covers.
That protecting beauty gives.
At first the pages of the book.
Are blank are purely fair.
But time soon writeth memories.
And painteth pictures there.
Love is a little golden clasp.
That bindeth up the trust.
Oh. break it not, lest all the leaves.
Should scatter and be lost.

To John...From Eddie
Eddie Richards
Yes, He got down on his knees and he took a look at the River,
and said, I met you finally and you're just like I dreamed,
Will you save this last dance for me?

Yes, He practiced karate out in the plains of Kansas,
where he loved to feel the strong winds blow
and he loved to run in the desert of New Mexico, But most of all
what he wanted to see was the Colorado River.

Yes he loved to snow ski in Colorado and he danced with the Navaho Indians
  in Arizona
After climbing mountains out west
He figured he was at his best
But the Colorado River was his last dance.

John was as strong as an Ox and as tough as a Bear.
He didn't like the city life; the West was the place for him out there
Yes, He danced the Colorado River for he knew it might be his last chance,
Something I'll never forget and always remember, How he danced in the
  Colorado River

Dedication: In memory of John Stano

Blind Date
W. R. Rivera
Who do you see when you look at me
You only see what you want to see
The beautiful woman with big eyes, full lips,
A sensuous body and perfect hips

My mirror reveals
A fragile child, a sensitive heart,
Her soul tattered and worn
Love found, won and lost
Bitter from pain and scorn
Naivete and innocence nonexistent

Thirsty for compassion and warmth, she smiles
An empty smile, a desolate stare
Searching for truth and understanding
Unwilling to trust, forgive or forget
She looks away, content in her own solitude

Few words are spoken
Meaningless banter exchanged
When you realize her interest in you
Has faded

A Journey
Anthony P. Jones
Within a fleeting flight from morning to meridian night
Innocence arises whistling,
Unlistening to the parables of mourning,
Stood grey about in cries and shouts of purity's burning
Eyes follow the phoenix on an endless helix of sojourning
Ever upward on a silent cloud –
The proud departed lamenting
Through shrines and quarters of endless slaughter
Awakening forever the sleeping –
To airy shores where light implores pray enter this
Ethereal dream, pavilions of melody in regions of harmony
Sculpture and symmetry defined.

Young Men Marching
Richard Ezell
(On To War)
See the turmoil 'cross the land,
Hear the rockets roar;
No more laughing children,
Young men marching – on to war!

The age of man 'cross the land,
Will soon be no more;
As once again the rocket's flare,
Lights young men marching – on to war!

A flash of light, the quaking earth,
Brings mem'rys from before;
When this chilling tale began,
Of young men marching – on to war!

Why, oh why does man destroy,
All things that we care for;
All the laughing children
And young men marching – on to war!

Dedication: All the young men marching

Have I Set My Goals Too High?
Magdalene P. Balloy
Have I set my goals to high?
Or is life a foolish dream?
Or, am I a just child,
Reaching for a star, thinking it's not too far?

Have I set my goals too high,
Wondering if I should live or die?
I know to live I must keep trying
To make my life worthwhile.

But! Have I set my goal to High?
Should I awaken from this dream
Ending my belief that life is more than what it seems?

Should I stop myself from growing and wanting to unfold
And hoping that someday I may reach my goal?
Who can answer me? To be or not to be?
My true self is my quest, to peace and happiness.

If I have set my goals to high, life for me would fade away
I would just cease to be, but my soul would then be free
To find its rightful place in the sky.

The Fear Of Night
Margarita Ortega
Deep deep so very deep
I see a shadow about to creep
Hatred monster it seems to be
Its only presence frightens me
It creeps into the bush below
My red blood cells run a faster flow
It jumps about out of the bush
My heart now needs a faster push
I see it now as it's in the light
It only shows the fear of night
What you think that you see
Is what may not always be...

My Love
Vicki Stigall
Walk with me my love
Take my hand in yours
Give me your love
I'll give you mine

Walk with me my love
As the sun goes down
While the moon shines bright
All through the night

Walk with me my love
Till the sun comes up
Lighting up our hearts with love
For us to share for all times

Give me your love
I'll give you mine
Today and tomorrow
For all time
Walk with me my love

Dedication: H.W.S., the man I love

Do You Feel Free
Rachel Moreno
The gun is my smile, and the joy in my eye,
All result into one, great big lie. Do you know why
No of course you don't, you cannot see,
All the hurt and pain that's inside of me,
No one understand, and no one can guess.
All the food I eat, and drink, I drink, seems to be tasteless
Everyone thinks I'm a happy little girl,
They think I'm a diamond, a rose, or a pearl.
Or that's what I'm brought up to think.
but it seems like my whole life is in one big kink.
Tied in a knot, I can't choose what to do,
They say I'm as pretty as pink, but I'm as dull as black,
grey or blue.
The Question here is, do you feel free?
I can't say yes yet, but maybe someday I could be
I want to go where I want, and stay out all night,
but the decline of the answer, is like the sting of a spiders
bite.
Maybe someday I'll get to just roam, no one telling me who
to go out with or when to be home.

Dedication: My mother and to Katie

Thank You
Elizabeth Marston
I thank You for the many ways You've blessed me through the years
For the many times You took my hand and brushed away my tears
You never seem to tire of the way I lean on You
The way so many humans always seem to do
I don't mean to be a burden and take up all Your time
When there are so many others with needs greater than mine
So I'll count my blessings daily, o'er and o'er
And each day I'll find new blessings that I didn't have before
As I travel down life's highway with its lights all aglow
Just knowing that You're there for me is all I need to know
And as my journey ends and my life is nearly done
Again, I'm thanking You God, for I have truly won.

As If By Chance
Andrea Morley
Deep within and secreted away,
The trumpets roar and the world rejoices.
As if by chance, the miracle begins,
Despite the many choices.
And the guardians of life,
Watch over this fragile choreography,
And pave the way, as well they can,
For this contribution to humanity.

And the chosen one to bear this gift,
Is understandable hesitant.
To accept this privilege changes life for all,
And requires a total commitment.
And in disbelief, a pinch is placed,
As if to waken from a dream.
But day by day it becomes apparent,
The rewards are too many to redeem.

An time wiles by and it's finally learned,
What all these months have meant.
The time it takes is not for the development of the child,
But for that of the parent.

Death
Edward Blevins
I felt that cool sweet wind last eve,
and knew that death had just strolled by,
I feel his presence often now
and it makes my throat quite dry.
I know he lurks in each dark place
in the daylight and the night,
Like a lioness in an upwind hunt,
That makes her prey take flight.
I guess persistence pays quite well,
in the type of game he plays,
But his patience would be appreciated
For a few more precious days.
I grin at what this life has meant
and all the things I love, as well,
It been so long in great events,
Yet...very short from birth to bell.
Umm, I won't put up a grand last stand,
I will go quietly on out,
But if there is a life beyond,
You will know it by my...Shout!

Dedication: The one I love...completely

Holy Love

Veronica Medina

The gentle embrace of the wind is like being touched by His Holiness.
He embraces me through the wind; He smiles at me through the moon.
He cries with me through the rain. Everywhere I go and everything –
I see I see him with me, I can feel my Heavenly Father with me –
whenever I'm upset. He hugs me and takes away my tears; He–
calms me down; Ho soothes my soul. He keeps safe and strong.
Even when I'm wrong He still loves me. He makes me feel at ease when–
ever I feel alone. Heavenly Father you have my soul, my spirit and my
  body.
You are my Father and I am your child. There is no greater love than the
  love
of God.

Grandfather John

Patricia Besh

He was so close to eighty that day,
When he went away forever to stay.
I recall, so well, things he used to do,
His ways were good and at times funny, too.
He loved to work outside in the yard,
But many a time the work was so hard.
I would ask him to come, take a small rest,
He'd give me a look and call me a pest.
His clothes were always the biggest of size,
Never a tight thing like most the young guys.
He wore longjohns in every season,
And to my knowledge never gave reason.
Fore going to bed, I would kiss him good night,
On top of his head all shiny and bright.
He did not like getting kissed very much,
So his hand would wipe it off in a rush.
Now he's been gone for over a year,
I miss him so much, it's so hard to bear.
In my memory he will always go on
As one whom I loved named Grandfather John.

Dedication: Love to Larry, Dennis, Lori....

I AM

Judith Brown

The night was cold and rainy as I turned around the bend;
I saw a man just standing there and asking me to lend.

Please give to me some clothes, he asked, or some food to eat;
I cannot see, but I can feel, I need to rest my feet.

I looked at him and saw a tear rolling down his cheek;
I thought about how I would feel if I had been so weak.

I observe as people pass him by and do not look his way;
How is it that they do not feel, but think it is okay?

Once this man was someone's child whose heartbeat filled her womb;
Cold and lonely now he is, for no one's heart has room.

I ask for God to help this man, I don't know what to do;
He says, My Child, don't you know, I gave that strength to you?

I lay my coat upon the man and ask 'what is your name'?
He says, I AM, that's all to know, I am so glad you came.

Dedication: Jesus Christ, my Lord and Savior

Invasion Of A Dream

Laura Reuther

Innocent, like morning dew on a blade of grass
Images float like a misty cloud
Unable to grasp the meaning of a single red rose
Surrounded by a thousand points of light
I reach to touch it, to feel the prick of its thorns
It is only an illusion, a figment of my imagination
Then I see a flash, a spark, a dazzling light beaming
Bound by an unknown luminous presence
I want to know it, understand it, touch the core of its being
Just as we are about to become one, knowledge and I
You arrive, opening the door of dreams
Wrapped in my sleep I wake, never to find that world again

True Colors

Jennie Wysocki

So many moments, so many memories.
To you I have opened the window to my heart.
I let you in to see the real me;
The most vulnerable aspect of myself.
For this I am wary.
You are the end of my rainbow;
The sun after the storm,
And I don't know what I'd do
If this wasn't so.
Sometimes I am afraid to let the real me out.
I am afraid to remove the thin mask and reveal myself
To you, a virtual stranger
Whom I love more than I have any other before.
In time, the rain will subside,
The brilliance of the rainbow will shine,
And I will show you my true colors
So long as you promise to paint your life
As a beautiful picture
With your colors and my colors
Mixing in beautiful melodies.

Dedication: To my rainbow...my inspiration

The Transcendental Guide

Jonathan Blackstock

You know,
and you probably do,
that I once dreamed you were God.
Patient—
you were patient and determined, as nature, which is the actions of God.
And the advice you gave,
though difficult to accept as real truth often is,
was always benevolent and beneficent,
just as the wisdom of omniscient nature,
His nature,
is not easily seen on cloudy days
or on days like these.
Patience and faith confuse people like me;
I wish I could ask your advice one more time.
But at least we still hear your hearty and indisputable laughter,
which without words or logic,
naturally separated the consistent pretense
from the pleasure and missions of those who are truly alive,
as so few people are
and as you seem to be when we think of you.

Dedication: The memory of John Bennett

Lost Angel
Victoria M. Squier
She wanders around the world, in her own separate reality
She doesn't know where she's going, she doesn't know where she'll be
She dreams of a world, complete and without fear
She dreams of a world, where she will not cry one more tear
In their world, she doesn't fit in
She's an outcast, who they killed before she could begin
To begin her journey, to make her own choices
They made her crash, with harsh, cruel voices
Trying to break free, to break away from the pain
To stop staring at the world from outside in the rain
To move out of the shadows, to get away from it all
She's dying to leave, before she takes that one fatal fall
That unearthly scream, the fire in her eyes
She'll do it quickly, for she has broken all ties
She has no one left, she has no reason to stay
Why shouldn't she do this, why stand in her way?
Her reality's gone, the worlds all a blur
Her once loud voice will become a soft murmur
Laying in a coffin, staring up into the sky
Here she'll be at rest, here is her last good–bye

Dedication: My best friend, Brian Rudd

Darkness
Jeanie C. Hendrickson
As I stand on the bridge
and watch the current running so fast;
I try to think of the future and
let go of the past.

The North winds blow, icy and cold
Just like the feelings within me I hold.

To the beauty of spring, I must
think;
Before I drown in the dark,
icy drink.

Forbidden Love
Beth Willis
I imagine us on a sea of blue
Joining as one, me and you
The methodic sound of the waves
Reassures me that your touch saves
Me from every upset life gives
And that our love lives
For all the world to see
We belong together, you and me
The touch of your fingertips
To my trembling lips
Soothes my desire to run in fear
From the one person I hold dear
My life long mate
For whom I will always wait
Until the time is right
When the dark turns to light
Come and be with me
We were meant to be
In a land where dreams come true
Where our love is not taboo.

Dedication: Lance Hafer, my dearest friend

The English Rose
Rita Herbert
Oh Rose, the flower of England, you're there in glorious array,
In beautiful colours and perfumes to brighten any grey day,
You bush strong and vigorous, or you climb way out of reach,
Maybe stay near the ground, oh so perfect, in miniature close to my feet.

You can ramble all around the garden, or grow wild in the hedgerows and heaths,
Whatever your size or your notion, we know you're the flower of peace.
For you're given to patch up a quarrel, in saddened tribute you're there,
Perhaps next to a dappier's collar, to attract a lady fair.

Sometimes it's to say "I'm sorry" that you're feeling way under par,
What a beautiful versatile flower, so lovely, so fragrant you are.
The yellow one brings in the sunshine, maybe gives peace of mind,
While the pink one say we're thinking about you, for we're the thoughtful kind.

Purity comes with the white one, while orange flamboyancy shines,
Given in bouquets and posies relay messages time after time.
But the one that I think must be favourite, has a message all of its own,
It's the red one, that say's simply "I LOVE YOU" my darling, my dearest, my own.

An Evening Walk
Richard Rand
A silent night falls
as the sun casts its final flame
and clouds wander
through a crimson glow.

Whispering wind rushes
through bending grass
and a child's laughter flies away

as branches bow down
and leaves caress my face
while I walk in gentle stillness

Looking
Spring W. Parrish
Under a rock,
In a summer shower;
Or could it be...
in the gentle breeze?

I have looked at every petal
of every flower.
I've felt the wind
rustling through the trees.

It wasn't there
or was it ever?

Is it the sight of you
or the sound of you
or could it be your...gentle touch?

I don't know the answer;
But I'll keep looking.
Looking...for my lost love.

Dedication: My sweet Nikki

The Rights Of Animals
Gordon L. Perkins

Let the animals of the world unite
Its time for them to stand and fight
Let them show us, how to live together
And not to be hunted, and lost forever
Is there no haven under the sun?
Where nothing is safe, from the trap and the gun
Even fish and mammals under the sea
Have nets and boats, they have to flee
They kill, only to eat, not for fun
So why should they be on the run
They don't leave parents, without sons or daughters
Just because of mindless slaughters.
They live together with their kin
And they don't make coats of human skin
They have their own perfect genetics
So why test them for our cosmetics
God gave them the right, to be on this earth
Whether on land, or under the surf
Man is the animal, without a predator
So what gives us the right to be their regulator.

Dedication: Eve, Mandy, Trina and Grandchildren

Shadow
Ethan Dereszynski

The black emptiness of a lonely soul
is the consequence to a lover's goal.
Within the dark, the spirit wanders
empty of feeling, the darkness consumes
without thought, the shade ponders
without company, the loneliness resumes.
Black of heart, empty of mind
no sanctuary will this spirit find.
Filled with bleak and despair
no feeling in life can compare.

Dedication: To all who encouraged me

The End Or The Beginning
Paula L. Bamforth

Love is only a word—an expression that we use,
It has no true meaning—is to love to abuse?

Rock erodes to sand—the mists of time slips by
Life carries on, never standing still —
Noticing neither you or I.

We all lay apart within the game of life —
Tangled emotions lead to broken hearts—
And deeper sinks the knife.

A web of lies — a tragic end,
I want no excuses — too late for reasons —
Reasons unexplained.

I feel different —, stronger somehow
Experience has taught me — and the pearls of wisdom
Are with me now.

Soon I shall be leaving — taking to the sky
My troubles all behind me — leaving one last thing to say —
And that, my friend is...GOODBYE.

The Cost Of Pollution
May Scott

This — once a village, but a village still?
When ambulances, lorries, motor bikes,
Fire engines, cars all pound its narrow streets.

The old and young stand wavering at the kerb
And wait in hope for a brief lull in the flow
Of traffic. But, you ask, "No traffic lights?"
Oh yes, one set of lights. They're there alright.
But no expert worked out the time it takes
For elderly with sticks or mums with prams
To make the other side.

House walls begin to crack. Foundations shake.
Last month two children hurt in accidents.
Young and old alike live with pollution,
Walk to the shops tight–lipped. The smell is awful.
Can't open windows for there's no fresh air.
Only the diesel fumes, the petrol stench
As traffic pours from motorway to Bridge.
In what was once a place of peace and beauty
Are we condemned to live and breathe such filth?
"How long?" we cry. "How long?"

Untitled
Molly P. Eudailey

He said, "Turn to me, I'll set you free
from the bondage you feel inside.
I promise you I'd give you peace
abounding love and happiness.
I'll fill the void of emptiness
I'll give you joy unendless
My grace is yours just believe in me
and you will live for eternity
Jesus said, "I died for you."
"Would you have died for me?"

Dedication: My Lord and Savior

Someday
Nellie A. Kirkman

I watch the wait and hope and dream for a time that's gone.
I pray for a miracle, not just for me alone,
but for my son who was carefree,
full of life, handsome and athletic,
sometimes a little devious and even pathetic,
but always my son.
Now we struggle to find all these gifts
God gave so freely to us.
How can we find them again? We must.
Because of an accident, a second in time,
my son is paralyzed
and now his dreams are not only his, but mine.
We dream of good health, a simple step,
a walk together, even if its with help.
We resist the need to look into each other's eyes,
for we must hold our tears inside,
and wait for a miracle
that I know we will receive.
Maybe not today, but someday,
I truly believe.

Dedication: My son, Roger Jr.

Country Sounds
Ray Coles
Where meadows meet the wild pheasants call
Grasshoppers rasp beneath the poplars tall
The sound of sheep on far distant hill
Waterwheel turning on the old river mill
Silver stream running on pebbles round
All these things make the countryside sound

Sparrowhawk swoops on small frail mouse
Swallows build in the old farm house
Oaks and ash stand witness of time
Outlined like statues on the dawns skyline
The dipping flight of the woodpecker green
Trodden down track where the deer have been

The call of bats in the dim fading light
Screech of the owl in the far distant night
Bark of the fox at the break of the day
A signal to her cubs already at play
Bright line of foxgloves on faraway scene
Crisp morning air so fresh and so clean

Dedication: My late son, Neil

My Pair Of Shoes From Me To You
Misty Renee Rook
As my day unfolds into a single breath I have something for you
in my treasure chest,
Beneath the cloth lies a pair of shoes which, I feel, I must leave
for you.
With in this pair of shoes I wish for you to fill—
nothing but love and kindness from heal to heal.
My shoe laces are filled with joy and creativity, though my
frayed knots are a symbol of freedom and liberty—
Take care of the soul for it is thin;
one's heart is hard to mend.
So keep your heart in my old shoes;
Remember, child, I will always love you.

The Journey
Susan Yule
A long winter's journey in a crowded train,
Looking out the window and watching the rain.
Wondering, wondering, where will I go?
Following a train track, through the mist and the snow

Pulling into a station some children go,
But not me this time my worry still grows.
How many faces now do I know.
How many faces at the next stop will go?

At last I am wanted at last I rise,
And all over the train I hear children's cries.
Swarming the platform such friendly faces,
The fine country ladies in all of their graces.

Why do I wonder if they will take me,
Why else would they be here if not to see me?
Then I am chosen and I rejoice,
When I hear the woman's voice.

I look back through the window of the fine car,
And I leave my misery in London, afar.

Conscious Regressions
Jeff Taylor
One Friday evening
Decades ago
They sat comfortable,
Apart in the growing gloom.
The program's opening pages
They met with familiar,
Expectations.

Eyes opened simultaneously,
The chapter chimed
Its closing fears.
They shared a bonded slumber.
Unexpected
Forty five minutes
Dreamless oblivion.

I look back now
A worldly wiser adult.
Was that dual sleep
An innocent coincidence?
Where had we really gone
In that missing time?

Untitled
David W. Campbell
Heavenly father up above
Please protect the girl I love
Keep her ever safe and sound
No matter when or where she's found
Help her to know, help her to see
That I love her, let her love me
And then, oh Lord help me to be
The kind of man she expects me to be
Keep us now, keep us forever
Always in love, always together
Grant, oh Lord to my content
And thank you for the girl you sent.

Grail
Edwin Savoury
I just flew in from London.
Now we sit together here
this burning summer day
in your Toronto garden.

Neighbours on both sides,
friendly, honest simple people,
from Italy, from Portugal.
Peasants, they have brought
from Italy, from Portugal,
their peasant ways
into Metropolis.
Only the animals
are missing.

And what have we to bring,
my love, from anywhere
to anywhere?
Except ourselves,
our quest without tradition
for the trust, and love and peace
they have already.

Stan's Departure
D. C. Rees
They buried my old friend Stan today.
Celebrations now, he's on his way.
Eighty nine when he died enjoying life,
Trying to get pregnant, a teenage wife.
Two hours buried, but lives got to go on,
Now she's snogging his pensioner son.

The parlour is filled with so called friends,
Totting up the value of the odds and ends.
Drinks flow freely, for he was a generous man,
Tributes by the hundred, paid to poor old Stan.
Funeral cost thousands, new black for wife Lisa,
Two hours afore he died Stan paid for all, by Visa.

As Stan's best friend, we shared everything in life,
First, second, third, but not his teenage wife.
For I'm not up to it now, going on ninety four.
Never got married, shared with Stan next door.
Everyone will miss him in the passing of time,
Didn't go to the funeral. Well...he won't come to mine.

Dedication: To Stan Dowse, for inspiration

Brick Walls
Lorene Kuhl
Each day I build and build.
Each day I get more weak.
Weaker and weaker.
I keep on building and building,
Hoping to accomplish something.
Hoping to keep the dreams and wishes alive.
Dreams of a more peaceful world
Where nobody gets hurt.
Maybe one day I'll get too weak.
But I believe that if I just keep
faith, God will help me build a strong
and steady brick wall.

Matchstick Staircase
Glen Cambridge
The independence of quality
Bedrock the solid love
The wind lies dormant
On the Tulips of iron strength.

A candle's death shows presence,
Oriental chambers of music
Plays host to a Picnic of lust.
The loop of life straightens for death

Seasonal shelter of change
Forthcoming Punctured tone of uncertainty
Universal Depth of freedom

Religions of lust
Testify the proposal of reason,
An awakening of concerned guilt.

The jester rejoices in the gallery of mischief
Under the eye of description,
"The beholder of the eye and imagination"
I wish for the reality of fantasy to be brought forth.

Who Am I
Nona Pike
Sometimes I wonder
Who am I
I'm not the scared little girl
I used to be
Nor the confused teenager
That was me
I'm an adult, who wonders every day
An adopted child, given away
Found her father, what a waste
Found her mother, a little too late
Took her secrets, to her grave
Found sisters and brother
Who don't communicate
So many question unanswered
WHO CARES!
One day, I will die
To my heavenly home, I will rise
Maybe someone there will care
When I ask
Who am I

Dedication: My soul sister, Carol LaPorte

Beauty
Martha Garcia
Beauty is beyond a pretty face
It takes more than good looks to leave a trace
It takes beauty from within the soul
Because it's what's in you that makes like whole
It takes kindness, love and care
To make somebody want to stare
Someday you'll know that what I say is true
Because one day my friend I felt like you
I thought that beauty was a look
But what I know now would make a good book
That looks aren't always what they seem
Because true beauty lies within

Footsteps
Derek Harte
Alone, Isolated, Imprisoned
He walked free so recently
He walked to a podium more recently
A proud nation once again
United by two men
One Black, One White
Both united by victory
Victory over Racism, Victory in Rugby
For one day
Neither was separated.

For a long time I hated
I hated everything about them
I remembered Sharpeville, Biko,
Death, Violence, Hatred, Terreblanche.

A slow dawning
A grudging respect
My thoughts are with them all,
43 million,
For the future
Not just today...

Is This Love
Tim L. Miller

Is this love or just a plea of a broken heart?
I have felt the darkness that is closing in on my soul, it feels
cold, and dark then when I see her, it seems she gives off
some kind of light that warms my heart, and repels the darkness.
For to look in her eyes reminds me of the heavenly skies that are
above me. For to look upon her beauty could cause a person pain,
or drive them insane, For I have been caught in that beauty.
For now all I can do is to dream of holding her tight till we
see the morning light.

Could her kiss make me feel like I'm walking upon the golden
street's of heavenly bliss? Could the sweat from my hands be
the tears be from my heart wanting love to enter once again?
Could a touch of her hand make me be able to feel love
once again. These are the questions my mind are asking, as they
are trying to convince my heart to keep on trying, but now this
heart has come to realize it will never mend for the love it has
to share, for it has been shattered in so many pieces that only
her love will be able to pull it together again.

So can anyone tell me is this just a plea of a broken
heart, or the love I've been searching for?

Winter's Mask
Kathryn Jean McDonald

Winter's cold mask you cannot see,
It freezes you for eternity,
His loneliness makes him a prisoner,
Destined to solitude he cries,
If you look you will die,
But you hear the everlasting cries.

The wind blows when he's mad,
It snows when he's sad,
Snow melts when he sleeps,
But at last he wakes and winter strikes,
Again the mournful cries.

The Wing Clipped Bird
Gwendolyn Palmer Lowe

How shall I reach the other side whose arms will hold me up?
Wings clipped from the day of birth no love to fill my cup.
How desolate the land does seem and darkness fills its path.
Can't seem to know God's will or find the light for me He hath.
Then there are those He sends along the way to carry the wing–clipped
bird and give speed.
These beautiful people through God's grace the wing–clipped
bird they'll lead.
It comes natural to these to help others in this life.
They'll spend much time finding ways to relieve their strife.
Some don't know that their wings are clipped till God brings them down.
Waddling around upon the dirt its then they'll look around
To see the need for help in life no possible way to move about the earth.
Because not even wind can cause the wing–clipped bird to fly cause he's
clipped from birth.
Along comes some dear servant of God whose heart is moved
with compassion.
Their strength and speed give flight to a bird left without passion.
How wonderful are those who wait while others are slowed down.
You'll find they do God's will and you'll never hear a sound.
Thank you says the wing–clipped bird as he peers from the other side.
Thank you God for helping me though I did not know I'd need a guide.

Where Does Our Beginning End?
Alexander Pepple

paths crossed at the playground of night
two stranger souls in reach
any bitter weeds ignored in the hope for
a bountiful crop of sweet seeds
overshadowing all strangling weeds and

then from the excitement of newness in rosy plays
to the endless plain of daily sameness
from the constant search for new coupling thrills
to drowsing routine familiarity
from the zeal to change and mold and mirror to self
to the resigned tolerance of compromise
from the burning flames at the height of mutual discovery
to the cold embers of disappointing flatness

from the high–speed roller–coaster ride
at the crest of our tower of amusement
to this tied testing pedestrian walk
through the obstacle course of life then
caught in the Chinook whistling downhill
bent on decimating this sustaining tree of spring to
scatter the separated fruits towards the opening horizon

Angel
Yelena Khmelnitskaya

Hell, People from the Earth!
I am the One who was the first.
Who had experience the Love,
Who has been sent from above.
I saw the flame, I saw the fire.
I couldn't fly a little higher.
My wings were big, My heart was brave,
I didn't know how to pray.
But here it comes, my Death and Angel
They put me both in life's equation.
And no more wings and no more flying,
Once I was Born and now I'm Dying!!!

The Leprechaun
Gladys Cutler

The Leprechaun is a little man in a green suit
with shoes that have curled up toes.

He is always around in the month of March. When
you open a closet door, there he is in the corner, just
sitting there in his little green suit. When you open a
door to a cabinet, there he is on top of the sugar dish
looking very smug and right at you.

No one seems to know where these little men come
from or where they live but...look out when the
month of March comes because there they are!!!
These little men in green suits.

If you go outside on a cold and windy day, look
down and the leaves under your feet will be like
a whirlwind. Look real close and there will be one
of these little men in his green suit.

They bring happiness and joy to us all! Oh, what
would we do without these little men in their
green suit with shoes that have curled up toes.

Self

Sharon D. Patterson

Sitting, waiting, contemplating,
whether or not self should
talk or stay quiet.

Self needs significant
others in life.

Self sees pleasure and pleasant things,
as Self eyes wonder around the room.

Self wants to say something,
but Self is afraid.

Why must Self be this way?

Self wants to communicate
with other Selves.

Other Selves stare, glance,
maybe laugh, about what?

Self doesn't know.

Heart

Carolyn Brown

Dad died alone
in a distant home
where he lived
all by himself
Mom passed on
"Sweet one" she's gone
and now we three are left
Then one cold December day,
our little circle cleft
a harsh wind blew
like me never knew
and now we two are left.

Night Stalker

Joyce I. Saxon

Night Stalker, Night Stalker
Where have you been? I've seen across the map and homeward
bound again.

Night Stalker, Night Stalker
It's a lonely job you have, I've met people and been places
over this land

Night Stalker, Night Stalker
Don't you wish you could be a star in the Sky? No my love is
the road, seeing the land, rivers and the clouds in the sky.

Night Stalker, Night Stalker
Are you a happy man? Most times with CB in hand talking
to my brothers on the road

Night Stalker, Night Stalker
Are you a happy Man? I believe I am, I see the people around
me praying to the sky, and talking all in their time, I think I am.

Night Stalker, Night Stalker
God keep you safe and the quiet one too, Hurry home.

When First I Met Love

Marc Burrows

Sleepless nights, restless days,
tears of joy and pain.
In the spring of life when fancy free,
and hearts break again and again.
Each passing moment — thoughts of you,
nothing else really matters.
Cooing like doves, thanking heaven above
when first I met love.

Holding each other tight — until the darkened night,
Oh! why? must we part — let's hold each other tight...
...once more.

Why is it? without you, time just stands still,
entwined, wrapped in rapture, it's Adieu, Adieu.
Dreams of you, are heaven — such bliss,
hold me again — kiss me, let's kiss.

When looking back, I smile and say,
how foolish we were, how gauche.
When passing young lovers, cooing like doves,
how well I remember — When First I Met Love.

Nighttime

Doretta O'Hara

I toss and turn all through the night
And try to sleep with all my might
When sleep does finally come to me
I can't believe the things I see

I wish the morning would come soon
Then I wish to sleep 'til noon
For I'm so tired from the night
And all the things I saw in fright

Maybe something wrong with me
I can't believe the things I see

Hope

Kimberly Collins

She gave him her heart, she shared with him
her thoughts, her ideas, her hopes,
and her dreams.

He beat her and made her cry.
He gave her heartache and pain.
He treated her like an animal that needed
to be tamed.

Time after time she'd threaten to leave
and he'd promise to change. He'd say
his sweet little speech and again she'd stay.

There's been too many broken promises, too
many bruises to try and hide.
She was always afraid to leave.
She always hoped he would change.

Well he never changed, and she finally
walked away with her head held high, a
smile on her face, and a look of hope
in her eyes.

Kitty's Headache
Lesley Knight

Tiny Trevor the kitten thought he was human,
Into the cabinet he did stray,
For Trevor had a headache,
Silly kitten didn't know when to stop,
He ate the bloomin' lot.

Thirty tablets he did swallow,
Poor little kitty overdosed,
But as us humans know,
A kitty's tummy is hollow,
His owner she did fret,
She had to rush him to the vet.

The Vets they did panic,
To the hospital they took him,
Only an antidote fit for humans,
Would save poor tiny Trevor.

Out came the needle,
And into Trevor it went,
It didn't take poor kitty long to come around,
Now poor kitty is safe and sound.

Writing
Amber Snelling

Inspiration comes at a dark hour
Sometimes I cry. Pick up my pen and laughter finds my
tortured soul.
Sometimes I laugh. Pick up my pen and dark, gloomy,
unrealistic, mystical thoughts fill my room.
Sometimes I dream. Pick up my pen and fabulous, daring
thoughts sputter out onto the page.
But most of the time, I cry, and my pen comforts me
Cradles me
Allows me to fly...

Dedication: Roger, my superhero

In Memory Of Linda And The Myths
Susan R. Stern

When nightfall encased her room in an envelope of chilly air,
She followed the winding Pierian and scaled amethyst peaks
To glimpse lustrous Sirens and lusty gods,
The jostling throngs of sinewy mortals
Who aver obeisance to Tiresias' prescient tongue –
Whether sheathed in Flesh in vaporous swells as Shade.

Her dreams, flickering vignettes of jibs and thrashing seas,
Ceased the day Cyclops crossed their threshold –
Turning green pine to stone.
Long in drink, right hand bounded in leather,
He spewed his curses at those crushed beneath his heel.
All dreaded his deep rumble.
His dank, capacious den.

Though her prayers ascended to the bright hall of Zeus,
No dragon–drawn chariot swept her to Athena's shrine.
No screeching fury sought requital for her bloodied robes.
No guileful Odysseus the brute's crater eye.

Twice Linda waded in the shallow waters of the Styx.
Only once did she lack the coins to book passage.

Love Of Thee After
Rebecca Twichell

The day after you came back, things were as perfect
as virgin snow on a broad Maple tree.

The birds were alive with shining nectar
from the apple blossoms on their feet.

Fresh flowers on the table of our nook sat
still while the breeze blew softly and the melody
of a distant church rang with imperial charm.

Dew on the window was iridescent, as
the dawn was illumines and pure.

I felt so relaxed I was barely able to stand.
Along my bedside a lace nightgown
was laying, which you bought for me.

The color was as true as a soft cloud in the pale
blue sky, or a spider's web on the rose bushes.

Lady flies dance on the White Lily fair,
and love for us lingers with them.

Untitled
Kyle E. Messer

Hand in Hand
Arm in Arm
Together we
will fear no harm
Love it was
Right from the start
A perfect match
You touched my heart
With thoughts of you
A smile comes round
And flips my heart
Upside down

Untitled
Jacqueline Rowan

I feel like jumping off the train
slowing down and living again
To breathe fresh air to run downstream
To roll in grass and dream just dream
I'd like to wake in a beautiful world
Where life is sound not living hell
Not working till you nearly drop
Or running along without a stop
I'd like to feel the sand underfoot
See the highest of waves and stay just put
And live amongst the swaying palm trees
To feel the Mediterranean breeze
Softly brush my aching skin
To make me feel warm and to glow within
To make my eyes sparkle and my heart sing out
To see the song birds weaving and darting about
I long for my eyes to enfold and embrace
The wonderful sights of this tropical place
The swirling of clouds that bubble and boil
With life giving rain drops to quench the soil

Dedication: To my precious mother, Josephine

You Touched My Life

Marie Jaslanek

You loved me, you gave me hope
and inspiration
You helped me when no one else
would
You touched my life

You used to fill my life
But you had to go, it was your time
But one more thing before you're gone
You touched my life

You were my father
The best friend I ever knew, you always
helped me when I was blue
You touched my life

Why you had to die I do not
Know
But there will never be anyone
else who touches my life

Dedication: My father, John George Jaslanek

To The Mirror

Leah J. Utas

I stroked my beard
and shaved my legs
and said "I love you to the mirror"

I stood in the light
watching my body
unsure of who I was.

I opened my heart
and opened my mind
and said "I love you"
to the mirror

A Breaking Heart

Diana Calchi

My eyes are red, my face is pale
my body is shaking from all this pain.
I want so much to reach out to you
but you just turn me away.
My spirit is gone, my happiness lost.
My dearest soul is aching
My life is slowly deteriorating.
My heart quickly breaking.
"I love you" I whisper, a phrase with so much meaning
but you no longer love me,
or at least that's what it's seeming.
grasping tight to what we are or what we were.
Don't want to let go, not at all
or loosen up, none the less.
Don't want to face the pain
this suffering and sorrow.
What we were yesterday
won't be the same tomorrow.
So may I should let go,
believing true love forever always lingers,
But in reality, I now look,
You just slipped right through my fingers.

Summer Day

Clare Louise Heal

Summer Day
Summer Day
Summer Day
In the month of May

I sit in the shade
Lolly in hand
Picnic cloth on the ground

Hazy Day
Lazy Day
Daisy Day
In the month of May

Scent of Summer on the breeze
Blossom Heavy on the trees
Green grass stains on my knees

Summer Day
Sultry Day
Summer Day
In the month of May

Untitled

LeeAnne Lowry

A whisper
in a child's heart
Imagine magic
in the cool sky
Dream
a garden
that is light colors
growing in the night
The lake was blue
a day in spring
a silent cat cried
"walk with me"

A Look At Christmas

Tina Weglewski

This is Christmas, a time where you'll see "Frosty"
And maybe reindeers flying in the sky; one might even lead the way with a
     nose so bright
Followed by Santa, with gifts and toys to be delivered all through the
     night
You'll see shopping centers filled with people with bags in both their
     hands.
There will be decorations everywhere you look
And some who will spare no expense to be the brightest house on the block
There will be snow falling so lightly, but reeking havoc on the streets
There will be gatherings of family and friends,
exchanging gifts with smiles and laughs and tears
Some will be visiting with family they hardly see at all
Some will be far from home wishing they could be with their families
While still others sit alone missing those they once had
Some will be driving in their cars to look at the pretty decorations
While others will have to drive far to their destinations
BUT STOP and take a look!
There's a baby set before us He's so perfect and so true
A holy gift from heaven with many blessings too
This sight is so majestic and its so real to see
God's the giver of the greatest gift, life in eternity

Tyrone
Victoria Whitfield
Oh God we pray
Help us to carry on the rest of the way.

We loved our brother so dear
And we dare to ask, why did you take him away from here?

We know, everything is in your will
But, how our heart hurt and our body stand still.

Tyrone is at rest – God knows best.

He never meant to hurt anyone, how could he be gone?
The cause was a gun.

They may have taken your life, but they can never take your soul
That part of you Tyrone, we will always hold.

Yesterday we saw you, today you're gone.
But I know we will meet again at our other home.

It's so hard to accept, we are only borrowed to each other,
Our father, brother, sister, even was our mother.

A Lesson In Life
Doris M. Olson
Our walk through life is like a path
That shapes our destiny
For each of us can be apart
Of a page in history.
We don't have to accomplish miracles
Or reach our heart's desire
As long as we can do our best
Another person to inspire,
Because the world is such a worthy place
To share with everyone,
A special spot we all can have
Until our work is done.

Elders
Tricia Stalion
wise eyes
in a lined face
weary feet
keep a steady pace
wrinkled hands
a touch of grace
strong arms
feeling safe
soft voice
soothing words
whispered prayers
answers heard
attentive ears
do not discern
gentle hearts
acceptance near
loving thoughts
for troubled tears
His elders
for our years
Dedication: Devlin, Kim and Sue

R.C.C.: A Tribute To My Grandfather
Jason Vierck
R.C.C.– Robert Charles Campbell,
A man who treated everyone well.
He was my grandfather, you see.
And he loved me just because I was me.

A soft–hearted man of dignity and pride.
Upon his passing, I cried and cried.
I was ten at the time, that Halloween day
In 1987, when Grandpa passed away.

I was dressed as a vampire, but did not care
For I knew that Grandpa would not be there.
He was my best friend, and I his "big–shot,"
and this reminded me that he did care a lot.

I know he's watching over me every step of the way
And I still think of him, day after day.
Grandpa, if you're there, I miss you very much,
And I long for the day when again we'll be in touch.

You were the best grandfather anyone could ask for,
And I'll see you again when I too am knocking on Heaven's Door.

Prayer
Lisa Cagle
Prayer is the key that moves mountains and unlocks
Any door
Something you can do whether you're rich or whether
You're poor
It focuses your mind and prepares your heart
And brings joy which you needed from the start
Prayer is the answer for anything you do
And it's available for you and even me too
So remember to pray as you go through the day
For if you do, I promise the Lord will make a way.
Dedication: Community Deliverance Holiness Church, my family

The Last Piece Of Pie
Lillian Berman
It was I. I cannot lie.
It was I who ate the last piece of pie.

It lay there in the fridge.
I thought I would eat just a midge
but oh it tasted so good
and put me into such a happy mood.

Each bite led to another bite.
I really did try to fight
the yearning for just a bit
Oh, mother is going to have a fit
for the pie is all gone.

But, I cannot tell a lie.
It was the most scrumptious pie
and all I wanted was just a bit.

But once begun I could not cease.
Now the last piece
will bring me no peace
for I had finished the pie.

Gerard

Tara Marie Salvador

Baby Boy, Where did you go?
Into the ground, covered by snow.

Brother, you have been loved.
Now you shine like the stars above.

You will be passed down through history,
never to be lost from memory.

Though you left this earth and wander free...
your spirit is still here with me.

Mother misses and cries for you.
Dad and Tommy miss you too.

Your short life changed for so much.

Your absence causes pain
but your death was not in vain,

For in eternity we will meet
on a golden covered street.

An Old Wind

C. Joy Chafin

Haunting image comes to me
From somewhere, perhaps memory.
Not scary or dark, just familiar somehow.
I've seen before, been there; it comes to me now.
It swam to me, washed on my shore.
White wall, dark dress, friends hand; I've felt it before.
Wistful heart, I feel it now, I swim to meet it
I wonder how
I know this moment etched in time
How it came to me, is it mine?
Image flashes, I tread for awhile
It will swim to me, it's gone for now.

Mom

Sue Peters

I wanted life,
You gave birth to me;
I needed tender loving care,
You gave abundantly;

I wanted to walk,
You held my hand;

I needed to know right from wrong,
You corrected me;

I wanted to stand alone,
You stood by;

I needed to explore life,
You guided;

I wanted to marry,
You rejoiced;

I needed a friend,
You became my best one.

Untitled

Jennifer Boardman

When the wind blows against my face
I feel as though I'm in this demented,
deranged world all alone.
No kids, horns, or disturbances in my ear.
Not a single distraction to hear.
I'm in this demented hole alone.
Then the sun flickers down to me.
I begin to float...
Into the mild, mellow blows of the wind.
With no destination.
I float across the air alone.
A disturbance...
A kid screams, a horn honks...
Or an annoying, thundering, crashing sound.
The wind seems to cease.
My body feels as though its going to decline.
The wind no longer comforting.
Flickering rays no longer chasing my fears away.
I have to put the world on hold
The noises are making me delirious.
I'm not waking from this fantasy
My mind is too lazy.

My Success

Joseph Huber

I come in the wind as a plague of sickness. To justify myself
and curse your wickedness. I will claim your life without
hesitation, to poison all of God's great creation. I am unseen to
your eyes; that I know, so do not think that you may know me so.
I will watch you squirm till the last of your breath. And
congratulate myself for all my success.

I too come as a thief in the night. To overwhelm you with
pleasure's delight. Just outside your door step waiting for my
entry, to conquer all upon this century. My name will echo the
sounds of sorrow, I bid you farewell until tomorrow. And as the
Sun slowly fades, remain watchful for I am A.I.D.S.

Sounds

Tina M. Beatty

Listen, to the beat of a newborn baby's heart,
Listen, to the pitter—patter of feet running to jump in your arms,
Listen, to the voice of a child who knows no unhappiness,
Listen, to the talking of a young teenager on the phone,
Listen, to the cries of a young person's first heartbreak,
Listen, to your children while you can.

Can you hear, the hunger pangs in a newborn baby's stomach,
Can you hear, the rain falling outside as a child begs for food,
Can you hear, the voice of a child who knows nothing but unhappiness,
Can you hear, the sound of a shovel digging as a teenager dies,
Can you hear, the wind blowing as the stone is placed on the grave,
Can you hear, the pain in your heart as it cries out for the life that was
   taken.

If you listen, it can change your life,
If you listen, you could help someone,
If you listen, you can feel the pain,
If you listen, you can feel the unhappiness,
If you listen, you can see a change.

If someone would only listen.

Untitled
Lisa Seibert

Jesus Christ, my brother,
Keep my family, friends, and
myself safe from the cruelty
of this world,
Keep us warm against the
coldness of the world our
father made warm,
God, my unearthly father,
forgive all the people who made
your world cold, for they know
not what they do,
They did not see the beauty
you created as Earth.

I Am Not Born Today
Charles Strickland

I am not born today
But anyway
I have heard them say
That they don't let some stay,
That they throw them away,
I want to be,
I want to see
What's out there for me.
Don't cut me short,
Don't abort.
Don't stop my being
Without seeing
My love for you,
Because it's so true.
Don't kill me now
Because somehow
You will love me back,
And that's a fact.
At least give it a go,
And I will show
You the happiness will grow.

Memories
Betty Lou Miller

Memories are the only thing that can't be taken away
They live deep within you, day after day,
Drifting across your mind, like a song,
giving courage, the will to go on.
Enjoy them, the good and the bad,
while you long for things never had.
When you're sad, pull out a happy one,
to clear the clouds and feel the sun.
Use them on a rainy day.
Put them back and go on your way.

Memories are the hope that'll see you thru.
So, it's a personal choice—happy or blue.
If a parts missing, they'll make you whole,
by living in your heart and feeding your soul.
When looking ahead, just look back,
They'll guide you on the right track.
Search them, you're sure to find,
riches of happiness and peace of mind.
Worldly goods come and go and health will too.
But no one can take the past from you.

Eyes Of A Different Shade
Christopher Odeh

With woes
Come the blows
Ego questions self
Who is the worthy party
Path of doubt
Death
And life
Remind us
The mystery dwells around us
Ever past
Present
Future
Hold the vision

Liberty And Grace
Arleen J. Lindenmayer

In 1776 the pages of our constitution begun to unfold;
Formed by God's grace and by liberty made bold.
Becoming an independent nation living in the image of God;
In His Holy Spirit we are forever meant to trod.
In other nations there are people who want to be free;
So they come to America, the land of sweet liberty,
overflowing with opportunity.
When they get here, do we tell them the story;
Of Jesus, the cross, and the light of God's glory?
They need to find the right freedom and understand;
What makes America a free, independent land.
They need to take hold of the words of life;
And read about One man's toil and strife.
But what they really find in a land with plenty;
Are the wants and needs of many.
A coin with God's name on it cannot fill the need;
Of a nation that's filled with so much greed.
For true freedom is something we cannot buy;
No matter how hard we may try.
Liberty is the free gift of God's grace;
A grace that frees our hearts from the bondage of sin's embrace.

Everlasting Love
William Helton

I love to sit on the morning dew
and reminisce about me and you
as the fog subsides its dull bliss
and seals the night with a kiss

I love to hear the birds parched high upon the trees
as life opens a door that fits many keys
into its chamber of majestic glee
its made a space for you and me

As night overcomes what is day
have all hope our love will stay
as tears roll down the side of your face
I will wipe away all your disgrace

The force of nature fills in our heart
everlasting; never part
till fate takes us away to the other world above
there you will still be my love

Dedication: My long–lost love

Untitled
Katrina Kelly
Why am I so easily swept up
in romantic feelings.
Is it a curse to be so loving, so free?
I enjoy myself when I'm around others –
the real me comes out.
The fun–loving girl.
Where is she now?
Crushed under the oppression of you.
You're killing me softly. Smothering me.
Why?
Why kill my free spirit and love?
Just because you're dead in those senses –
doesn't mean I have to be too!

Yesterday
Victoria Denny Rose
It seems like yesterday when
happiness came without cause.

It seems like yesterday when
smiles were easy to find, and
frowns where rarely seen.

It seems like yesterday when
love came from holding hands,
a walk in the park, or gazing
into one another's eyes.

It seems like yesterday when
time was only a clock, and
freedom held no bounds.

It seems like yesterday when
life was more like living, and
today all but disappears.

It seems like yesterday...

My Daddy
Nancy Jo Ford Lindsey
I don't understand why he had to go,
The one I loved so dear–
The one who loved and cared for me,
Who always held me near.

My Daddy didn't realize
That he was soon to go
For, if he had he'd have told me,
I know he'd have let me know.

He always told me, when I cried,
That he would see me through–
He'd solve my problems easily
Like all daddies do.

I guess I'll have to help myself
In solving them from now on–
Because you see, he can help no more
For now my Daddy's gone.

Dedication: Bertha Ford, my beloved mother

Lead Us The Way
Chandler Rossignol
Lead us the way, We and They
Lead us the way to a better day.
Lead us the way so we can see that
prejudice and discrimination must cease.

Lead us the way, We and They
Lead us the way, and show us that everyone is just the same.

Lead us the way, We and They.
Lead us the way so that we can live in harmonious peace.

Lead us the way, We and They.
Lead us the way so we can see how the world really should be.

A Loved One Lost
Chris Trainor
To touch her silk like skin,
To hear her calming voice,
Our love we shared is irreplaceable,
My emotions distraught, for death she fought,
A horrific battle to the end,
A picture remains, but my heart is stained,
For her pulse exist no longer,
Memories are blind and provide a false sense of her presence,
An emptiness clouds my life,
The pain is great and its shadow I constantly fight,
I dream of the day where we meet again,
She was my post that kept me standing,
Without her I fall a wounded duck,
She was always there when I got stuck,
How can I ever replace the joy I receive from her smiling face,
Her beauty shined both in and out,
My anger prevails, my mind full of doubt,
What we shared was very rare,
She gave my life peace and meaning,
I can't let go, I loved her so,
She is lost and may never be found.

Hard To Hold
Tina–Marie Hesse
Billy Ray Cyrus,
A man of many talents
Sings many country
And love Ballads.

The songs he sings
Are tops on the country charts,
Though he has broken
Many hearts.

He made his big start
In 1992 with Achy Breaky,
And is adored by many,
Both young and old at Heart.

A hard working man,
I have been told,
Even though he's
Hard to hold.

Dedication: Billy Ray Cyrus, singer

The Love Of A Pet
Pearl McCartney
There's no way to express the love for my pet.
She made me feel so great in every way.
That way I could start each and every day.
When I came home she greeted me by what she said.
She met me at the car just like I was a star.
But now she's gone, she passed away and I feel so blue.
I waited for a while and then I got two.
They are so sweet and cute.
They keep me busy and make me laugh again at their funny ways.
Now they're like her, they start my day.
I'll never forget the love I have for her.
But I have more love to share with my new little pets.
The way they run, they're like two jets.

Life Is A Magical Gift
Peggy Wilson Thomas
Ask any mother, who has given birth, just how much is a miracle
    worth?
As you see the bluest skies floating down to earth,
Our most incredible gift, is our life on earth.
The beauty from the flowers, kind understanding from a friend,
Are precious memories that we can keep, forever, without end.
See weeping willows branches bend, magic is real, it's not pretend.
Tranquility you'll surely gain, from listening to the pouring rain.
Soft breezes blow gray clouds away, warm sun brings forth a
    glorious day.
Out in the garden, hear the children at play.
Don't cast your eyes up in the sky, wishing for things you want
    to buy.
Love, joy and creativity, these blessed gifts, are yours for free.
To love your life can be so grand. Don't plant your garden in
    sinking sand.
Make sure that your hours are wisely spent, smell the honeysuckle's
Pure, sweet scent.
Grow with sincerity, your loveliest bouquet, to appreciate it
    thoroughly,
Try giving it away.

Flood Tide
Phebe Alden Tisdale
Mindful of Wars of the Roses,
a toast to the House of York!
And to King Richard Third, knowing
why, on August twenty–second
of Fourteen–eighty–five,
that last Plantagenet's
courageous stance inspired
Sir Thomas Malory to encode
how a brave heart was linked to
Le Morte d'Arthur.

Hold high the rose of York,
the Christmas Rose, Whyte Rose,
Richard's white Lellebore. Truth is,
transmuted petals dissipate
as spray–soaked whitecaps surge
on deep blue sapphire seas.
Wind–blown across horizons,
Arthurs still holds the helm
of his white moonship, circling,
this Earth's flood tide of time.

Rain
M. M. Whitaker
The rain came down on our quiet little town.
Splashing on the ground.
It falls from the heavens up above
There where its quiet with peace and love.
Down the rain pours on the grass and the flowers
Its been raining now its seems almost like hours.
The grass looks shining bright and clean.
The flowers sparkle with a lovely sheen.
We need the rain to make plants grow.
We need the rain to fill our dams.
With water for us to drink.
Now sit back quietly and think.
How much we need the rain.

To Be a Mother
Pattie G. Snapp
I look into their eyes
And what I see
Are two tiny souls
Dependent on me

Made out of love
And born out of pain
In one single moment
Life is never the same

Watching them grow with caution
And living in fear
Hoping for something better
Than the life I see in the mirror

A human you are and
A human they will be
So I must teach them the morals
To pass on through eternity.

Dedication: Justin and Chase

Autumn Eyes
Steve Sprigg
The sun rests soft upon the hill, there's a cool and drifting breeze.
It caresses softly the darkening land and gently sways the trees.
But in this hour of evening shade I know that there will be
Happiness with you always as long as you're with me.
The days pass by so quickly now, life seems to rush by.
There's never time to think too much no matter how I try.
But in these days as Winter nears there's warmth within the air
For you're the sun within my soul, the dreams I long to share.
And Autumn eyes you're always here for me, you fill my days with cheer.
I never feel afraid when holding you, so please stay always near.
For my treasure lies within your golden smile and the soft touch of your
    hand,
And Autumn Eyes I love you more than you'll ever understand.
You'll never know just what it means to be standing by your side.
You'll never know how my heart feels, how it suddenly opened wide.
The love I have comes pouring out and I give it all to you,
And Autumn Eyes the love I have will remain so pure and true.
Now Winter comes and Winter goes and soon turns into Spring.
Life has blossomed with Winter's pass, there's a new song now to sing.
But the memory stays within my head, for memory never dies;
I'll never forget my season of love, my days of Autumn Eyes.

Spun Glass
Lorie Beardsley
Strong, spun cords of caring
Form a transparent figure of friendship.
When the light from a smile
Falls upon it,
A rainbow of personality
Breaks into its various shades.
Don't hold the figure
Too tightly,
For the shadow of your grip
Will blot out its colors.
Hold the figure carefully,
For it is so beautiful
Yet so easily broken.

People Will Talk
Muriel Joshua
The little red rag that's behind our teeth
will spread gossip fast whether lie or true
It's busier than bees and faster than feet
False report victims don't know what to do.

People just like to run their mouth
They whisper and chat and like the melee
Sometimes they don't know what they're talking about
Their tongues keep a–wagging most of the day.

If you hear something that you want to repeat
Don't add to it, there will be no end
Whether public, private, or on the street,
Refrain from back–biting your very best friend.

No matter what you may say or do
Negative words make you worry and squawk
Never let it cause you to be lonely and blue
Always remember that People Will Talk.

Dedication: My unforgettable Granny, Louisa James

Our Love Was Meant To Be
Tammy Hewett
How many days have I gone without
knowing our love was truly
meant to be?

How many times have I watched you sleep?
The look upon your face
is one I know and love.

How many times have I wondered
where I'd be now if we
had never met?

How many times have I looked
into your deep blue eyes
and realized that you are my true love?

How many times have I realized
that our love was simply
meant to be?

Dedication: My dreamlover, my husband, Tony!

Telly
Christine Mary Whitehouse
Telly ho telly come to me.
Coronation Street, Brookside, what do you see.
The films can be fun.
The time is so right.

Emmerdale, Neighbours nothing is left out.
Home and Away, is here and afar.
So put your telly on, to tell you how far.

The news is not grand it can be sad you say.
The weather is wrong so we understand.
Cilla, ho Cilla tell us some more, or find us our family.
We lost years before.

Love Slave
Patty Pilkington
I never knew what love was until you
You turned my world around, made me happy instead of blue.
You've made me your slave of love to do with as you wish.
And also we both like to fish.

I am now your LOVE slave that none other can touch.
Your loving is sometimes too much.
No I'm not a "slave" as to be captive, but you
hold of my heart, body, and soul.
My love for you will never grow cold!

SLAVE of love that is what I am.
To what others say or think I don't give a damn!
I wish you could take me far, far away
My love and desire for you grows
stronger every day!

My one and only, I LOVE YOU so very much.
At times I just can't wait for your sweet and gentle touch!

Dedication: To Jeff, whom I adore

Tear Drops
Jennifer L. Barnett
Every tear I shed is for you,
an every night my heart has
bled for you.

I cry tear drops for the love I've
sacrificed; to give birth to a new life.

I cry tear drops for dreams
that never came true; since I lost you.

I cry tear drops for the years
that have gone by; since you
left me for the heavenly sky.

Even though I know you're
looking down on me, forever I
cry tear drops for the love I lost.

I cry tear drops for the pain it cost.

Dedication: Bryan, I will never forget

Rain Of Pain

Scott Shaw

Somberly staring
I seem to be
Precariously perched
Upon the verge
Of a weeping urge
Why they do not fall
I cannot answer
But I can say
Just because they
Don't moisten the flesh
Doesn't mean they're repressed
On the inside
Continuing the slide

The River

Diane Hatzes

A river is the wrinkled fingers
of an elder, it flows through the
stream as the wrinkles flow through
the skin.

A river is a tree with its branches
flowing in all directions.

A river is a thought flowing in
your head.

A river is a dream that is never
forgotten.

A river is a mirror that reflects
on your life.

A river is an idea that keeps
circling in your mind.

Dedication: Dedicated to my parents

The Midnight Moon

Shanna Belyeu

The change I knew was coming but I didn't
expect so soon. I sit sadly alone thinking of you
working under the midnight moon.
I lay in bed and squeeze my eyes real tight and
try to fight the lonely tears from my missing
feelings for you. For now my husband works
under the midnight moon.
I understand you're working real hard to make
things good for you and me. It's just a lot of
time away from my one love, I believe hung
the moon in the sky. Our time together is truly
special and more sacred than we'll ever know,
We get a chance to turn our lives around and
keep that everlasting glow.
You have pulled a lever deep down inside of me
I never knew was there. My love for you grows
stronger each day. You must know I desperately
care and I'll always be there for my one and
only who now works under the midnight moon.

Dedication: My loving wonderful husband, David

Clothesline

Peggy Ray

Torn apart like
worn–out jeans
Together pinned by wood and tin
Time permits more
passing wear
Time has made the threads
grow thin
Brilliant blue will not replace these
faded, tattered shreds I wear,
For once upon a clothesline past
the brilliance
turned to fondness
there.

Teen Years

Minerva Martinez

Seventeen years old! Full of young life.
Seventeen years old! Fall of my youth.
January 1st 1975! I took a fall, that ended my
life. Five years I lost, what could I say
It was my fault.
Forever I thought! When will I walk, for a
second chance, for a skip, or maybe a hop.
Jump rope I tried, running was hard.
My family was there to endure, the
greatest pain we ever knew, they cared for me;
They washed my hair with love 'n care; they
bathed my body with tender care.
The walker cast, and body brace, the Harrington
steel rods, that kind of stuff, will always be a
part of me and my past.
As years have gone by, I wonder and cry,
Will I ever get up from this fall that ended it all.
I'm now 21! I pray to the Lord, look down
from above, and have grace and mercy on me.

Dedication: Martinez's, Pastor's Sam and Bea Torrez

As I Gaze

Angela V. Cunningham

As I gaze upon my reflection in the mirror
I see a little girl, daughter, a sister
girlfriend, wife, mother
lover, confidante, a friend...
And I sigh

I sigh at the remembrance of my past joys
and my past pains
Then I lovingly embrace myself as I realize
just how much I have endured...
Yes, I have endured

And I see myself clearly
I see the laughter in my eyes
Feel the joy within my heart
And a peaceful smile comes upon my face

You see, as I gaze upon my reflection in the mirror
I realize (oh how I've come to realize)
Just how important it is for me...
To simply and completely love ME!!!!!

Kalee
Nina Walden

The day you arrived, was a wonderful surprise.
We loved everything about you, even your cries.
You melted our hearts and captured our souls,
with the miracle of life that never grows old.
Your smile is more radiant than the brightest sunny day.
That little smile takes all our fears and worries away.
Blue cannot come close to describing your eyes.
They're filled with so much light and wonderment and sunrise.
Your happiness brings us so much pleasure.
The love you give back we will always treasure.
You've pulled us together, even closer than ever.
We look forward to the days we will all have together.
Sharing our love, with each other, forever.

When Demons Die
Matthew D. Winkle

The darkness without fuels the darkness within
The void draws me near, shadows pulling me in
A child of light, brother to sun
Emptiness hides me, my death has begun

This hell passes slowly, or doesn't at all
The shadows torment me, I stumble and fall
I lay on my face in the darkness of night
The demon is in me, I no longer fight

The sun rises brightly, a hope in the sky
It drowns out the shadows, I see demons die
I stand on my feet, my face covered in mud
My tattered soul weeps, caked in stable blood

Rain falls to earth, warm and deep red
The mud washes clean, the darkness is dead
The sun takes my soul, a husband to wife
Hell moans behind as I step into life

Dedication: To Nicole, with my love

Have You Ever Seen An Angel?
Frances Hutson

Have you ever seen an angel?
Do you wonder how one looks?
Do you suppose they all look like
the ones we've seen in books?

I've never seen an angel,
at least not too my knowing,
But I've heard some are spotless white
With feathery wings and glowing

Some looked like the feminine kind
Some were big and strong.
Some appeared with others
Some were all alone.

I believe God sends them,
With messages from above.
To guide, protect, comfort and help
All revealing the depth of His Love.

Dedication: To Buddy, who has seen

A feeling
Jason Bateholts

I felt as if I was a bird flying into a summer sunset, so free and full of life. Without warning it all changed to black, soon I began to feel fear and loneliness. I was no longer a bird soaring threw the summer sky. I now felt like a spider dark as night and so alone, soon the pain was so great I could no longer bear it. Suddenly there was a bright shimmer of light at the end of the tunnel. It was a pretty face with eyes blue as the sea that cry out for true love, a heart pure as sterling crystal, as true as a mother to her cub. Her voice was like a gentle breeze passing threw a meadow of fresh blossoms. She made me feel whole again. Now I pray for a way to tell her that I feel that I love her.

As A Family
Sharon Fulkroad

We are told that mankind should be;
As a family, full of happiness, laughter, and glee.
Yet look around and I'm sure that you,
Will find many a reason to feel quite blue.

For where is the happiness, laughter, and glee?
Has it been buried beneath the sea?
Who has it? Or where did it go?
Please tell me if you do know.

You say we all hold it inside.
But we all feel too much pride.
Release it, let it out of your heart.
We all need to do our very own part.

Please heed my earnest plea.
For then you will find happiness, laughter, and glee.
Then we will no longer feel blue.
For mankind will be as a family, fresh and new.

Dedication: My late husband, Harold Fulkroad

A Lesson Learned
Rick Robnett

Along the wooded stream we'd ride,
My grandfather and me.
A small boy proudly at his side,
My hand upon his knee.

There was so much to see and learn,
The world was new to me.
I marveled with each way we'd turn,
At all the forest trees.

Where did they all come from?
Was the question in my mind,
I looked to Pop, he was the one
With the answer I would find.

Forty years have come and gone
And still his words ring true
"Son, the Good Lord planted one,
and then they all grew."

Dedication: My grandfather, Noel M. Owens

Grandmothers
T. D. Jones

G is for giving love and understanding
R is for the rock on which a family is built
A is an added spice of life she's always there
N is never giving up on us.
D is for her daughter by blood or by marriage
M is the mother of us all.
O is all of our dreams and wishes put first by her
T is her strength to bring us 2gether
H is happiness and home life with her
E is for eating and the cookin' of our favorite food
R is for rightness of her vision
S is the standing power of her backing
Or standing behind us in what we do.

Sweet Dreams Of You
Kelly Hodges

The stars cannot match
the glow in your eyes
when you're in my arms
underneath a moonlit sky.
The softness of a rose
doesn't compare to your skin
when it presses close to mine.
In the gently blowing wind
you slightly tilt your head
softly our lips do meet
and we close our eyes.
As we kiss — a kiss so sweet
your tongue meets mine
in a soft gentle way.
The tenderness of your kiss
ooh I love so much.
We're not in a hurry
as the passion begins to grow;
we've got a lifetime to enjoy it
and it gets better as we grow
into each other.

Can't You Hear Our Kids Crying Out
Tammy D. Jones

Our kids are killing, robbing and
dying.

One more brother from the ghetto
and a weeping mother crying.

What's the matter with our race
Can't we learn to love one another
And stop the killing pace.

We're letting our kids get away
when we should punish them for the
things they do day by day
you don't have to punish them with
abuse that will be the time when
your motherhood will step into use
So don't be afraid to show your
kids whose boss, Because in the long
run you'll pay the cost. So wake up!
This is what it is not all about
Can't you hear our kids crying out.

Me, Myself And I
Charlisa Thomas

I love my Mother,
I love my Father,
but I sure love me, myself, and I.

I love my Grandmother,
I love my Grandfather,
but I sure love me, myself, and I.

I love my kinfolk,
I love my pets,
but I sure love me, myself, and I.

And I Do!

I Stood Among The Roses
Donald E. Hopkins

One day I stood among the roses,
just taking in the breeze, so
I asked God, answer me one thing please,
if the roses are so beautiful!
Then why don't they have more leaves.
God answered me without hesitation.
So they cold grow clear across the nation.
and the thorns protect them from most any thing,
drugs and snakes and even human beings.
The roses grow in a variety of colors
to distinguish one rose from another.
The red rose is meant, from the heart.
The yellow rose of Texas is meant, will never part.
and all the other roses are meant for you.
and that's the beauty of the roses too.
That's why I stood among the roses
just thinking thing through.
and hoping that the day would come,
I'd give a rose to you.

Dedication: My daughter, Jackie and son, Jeff

Hugs
Ardys M. Olsen
For My Mother

Hugs feel so good.
I sure wish I could
Give you one each day.
But I'm so far away.
Then I had a good thought.
So these candies I bought.

Now, when you're feeling blue
Need a hug, maybe a kiss too.
Fill your coffee mug
Reach in for a kiss and a hug.
Sit down and know I'm of you thinking
Though I'm not there with you drinking.

Because every day, many times
I am thinking of you.
And the candles are signs
Of the very thing
I wish I could bring
Every day to you.

In the dark Of The night
Mary E. Beck
In the dark of the night.
Spooks goblins, and witches
Cavort on the 31st!

Beware of the spooks
The goblins might get you!
The witches will flavor their
stew!!
A spell will be cast
You'll dance to their tune
—except.
Those born on Halloween
"They are immune."

Pandora Had A Box
Michael J. Ruggiero
Monsters and Ravens,
Taunters and Guides,
Watchdogs and Sentinels
indwell and hide.

Called into open;
breathed into life;
dethroning legends
which locked them in
strife.

Well—behaved
to injurious fault
adds bitterness and sting
to grains of salt
sardined in wounds
beneath the skin;
gaping wide open yet
dark and closed in.

Dedication: The healer of wounds

Little Bit Country
Emma D. Shadrick
Every morning before the sun comes up
He saddles up his Nordic with his coffee cup;
He showers out, suits it up, goes off to earn a buck
Lasso's up his Auto van, pretending it's his truck.

He saunters in the house saying, "Evenin'" to his bride
Grabs his Hopalong Cassidy gear, his horse and off he ride
He's off to hear the Country, forget the Rock and Roll
Forget it Miles, he's forgotten Jazz and Heavy Soul.

He's become a little Country in his black ten gallon hat
His Texas blackened boots and silver buckled belt;
He does the Texas two—step, sings along with Bonnie Rait
Cries in his beer to Tanya, dust and denims now his fate

But we love our cowboy Buddy
All dressed in his Texas black attire;
He is now ready to do "Country"
Even if be by an open fire!

Dedication: George – my dearest nephew

To My Kourtney
Emma M. Zanetti
I'm glad there's you to
smile at me
And brighten up my day,
To share my thoughts and
understand the things I do and say
I'm glad there's you to laugh with me
at ordinary things,
To show me what is special
In everything life brings
I'm glad there's you to be with
And I think its time you knew
Just how happy you have made me
And how glad I am there's you

Flashes Of The Mind
Michael Hatter
The surge of the mind, lighting bolts strike,
a murderous scene,
and one screams with their might.

There's a toss, maybe a turn,
walls crashing in, a house in mud,
a flash of reality with a thud.

The child cries, confused, and scared,
mother abandoning, and all she wants is,
someone who cares.

Destruction of things, items.
privacy of lives, statues, furniture, and jewelry.
Again in the background,
a child cries.

The dawn rises, the wind is warm,
she tosses the sheet.
Was it reality, or flashes of the mind?
Maybe even a mental state, eased with the passing of time.

S. S. Otseago
Lester E. Frum
The ship slid silently forward, in the blackness of the night,
The deep, wide channel in the middle, but the Pilot steered too far right.
With the shocking suddenness of a big gun's wild retort,
She struck, wedged herself and listed far to Port.
The men in the Hold below went momentarily mad with fear.
They grabbed their life—jackets and went hell bent for that upward stair.

They gained the Deck and stood there, waiting for that fearful cry,
"Abandon ship, lower the boats", but still they heard no word from the
     Bridge on high.
No word from the Bridge, but the deck lights came on just the same –
What was the Captain doing? Was the Pilot alone to blame?
Now, before the boats were lowered, the men went down below,
Some for their personal papers, Others needed clothes, you know.

Oh, what happened that night so still and clear?
Had the Pilot fallen asleep or had he been drinking beer?
Or, perhaps a naughty gremlin had helped him steer.
Oh yes, it hasn't been mentioned, but the men all made shore safe and
     sound.
After all, why shouldn't they? The ship had only run aground.

Untitled

Margie A. Soden

My name is Margie, let me take you
back in time the year was "1969."
"When" September 22, 1969
When the sun still rises here at home.
Our boys in Vietnam are left to roam.
We know they are fighting
for something very strong. Who has
the right to say they are wrong.
When the wives and loved ones are left to wonder—
Will they come home again soon to ponder—
Someday soon they'll be home once more
never more to leave our home side shore.
So now all we ask is "When?"

A Smile

Rebecca Bound

A smile can be happy or sad
Depending on who gives it,
Especially coming from a loving Dad
When he asks you the question, "Who did it?"

A friend has a smile that's warm and bright
When meeting you for the first time,
A baby can give a smile just right
And its darling face seems to shine.

It doesn't cost a cent and is easy to do
Whether happy or sad, warm or bright,
And will make your life pleasant and happier, too,
A smile's a special delight!

So start to practice every day
And never, ever cease.
Without much effort, everyone will say
"You've made a good start on PEACE."

Dedication: Jessica, whose smile is my inspiration

Mother

Wilma Hathcock

Mom always knew what was best
and how to rise above the rest

She seemed to be able to read your mind
knowing what to say and what to leave behind

She knew you like a book
all your memories hidden in every nook

Life will never be the same
for a long time it will feel like a game

Only you play alone

Your best friend has gone Home

She's left you with the best
memories of her wit, wisdom, love and caring

Your heart, her memory and God above
will help you carry on for the ones you love.

Another Day

Eva Langford

Another day in the life of me
To rise and shine, "perhaps to dream"
Of love fulfilled and tasks completed.

Another day in the life of me,
What will I do and who will I be?
I do not know, I cannot tell,
In what I've chosen will I do well?

Another day in the life of me,
To be the best of what you see,
Give some thought to the days endeavor,
Then preserve each moment like a priceless treasure!

Happy Ending

Warren L. Foster

Hearing the news
Brought me the blues
Feeling down
Brought a tear to this clown
Please God if you're listening
I'm depending
On a happy ending

Friends grow cold
As they're told
Memories are all that's left to hold
Loneliness is a wind
Too often heard

Footsteps from behind
So much on my mind
Trying to stay one step ahead
Trying not to lose my head
Please God if you're listening
I'm depending
On a happy ending

Faith

Frances Dew

There are times when the changing aspect of my life seems threatening. But
    during those times, I
reach higher for my keep–on–keeping power and I rely on my FAITH in GOD
    and my BELIEF in
His WILL. That's enough in itself to enable me to see the good in whatever
    adversity I am
experiencing. Also, I try to keep a positive attitude because I realize
    that setbacks and stumbling
blocks are really opportunities to do or receive something better. Then as
    I center myself in
GOD's divine Order, I can be at peace knowing that I am more than equal to
    any change of
condition that may come upon me. I seek a quiet time to commune with my
    Heavenly Father
which helps strengthen me with faith and courage. The one thing I can be
    sure of is that I do not
have to face any "change" alone. And, whatever I desire for the betterment
    of my life, as long as
it is aligned with the will of GOD – I have but to seek his face and trust
    the outcome to be in my
best interest.

The Cat Dance
Dorothy W. Hicks
The lamp burned dimly in the hall,
As shadows cast upon the wall
Pose quietly for plans unknown,
Like stately figures on a throne.

Suddenly the shapes twirl round and round,
With tail unfurled to soft musical sounds
Graced the hall with leaps and bounds
Success as a ballerina had been found.

When all was quiet too tired to move,
My cat paused, leaped on the bed for needed rest
He knew his performance was the best.

As A Mother
Athena Nolen
Teenagers overdose by a strange pill;
Young boys sent off to war and are killed;
As a mother my heart pains within;
As I see children worldwide struggle in the world they live in;
Aborted babies cry;
Oh why, mommy, did I have to die?;
Their flesh torn from their lifeline makes me want to cry;
In my soul there is a mournful groan;
Some mother's son shot down only blocks from his home;
Prostitution, child molestation, drug addiction, and cult suicides;
These are things which cause the mother's seed to die;
Searching for answers and glancing up to the sky;
As a mother I will constantly wonder and ask the question, why?
So much starvation, disease and evil in the land;
I know this couldn't have been the Creator's original plan;
Even though I enjoy the beauty of the flowers in Spring;
And at church I am often moved to sing;
As a mother the question still remains why?
Why, oh why, must mankind so early die?

Dedication: To my loving husband, Cedric

Races
Henrietta Gumpert
Years ago each morning going to work, a
man I did see
He got on the train several stations
ahead of me
It took almost an hour to NY for us both
to ride
He tried to save a seat for me, by his side
He asked if I ever went to the races to bet
Told him so far I hadn't done it yet
Told me of a horse at New Orleans to race in a
few days time
Thought it a hunch (Hazel Gompers) similar name
to mine
I bet on Hazel, she ran and didn't make it, but she
sure did try.
How was I to know she was a mudder and
that day the track was dry.
About 6 months later she came in first on a muddy day
But I hadn't bet again you see.
It was good old Hazel didn't win that first time
and she never made a gambler out of me.

Life's Journey
Doris McKenzie
A long winding journey's lingering procession
through the varsity of life we must go.
Stepping stones, a bridge to cross, its up to you,
you have the choice.
He who takes the safest route can go beyond the
little brook, but he who dares the stones to cross,
opens up Pandora's box.
The mysteries of life enfold, each one a story
to be told.
So when the bridge or stones you meet,
the choice is there, there at your feet
Whichever you decide to take, there it is
you seal your fate.

Healing Heart
Shari McCollum
It's not the end
that's what I've been told.
My hearts on the mend
so broken and cold.

My direction's unclear.
My road I will seek.
If I look in the mirror,
could to my future I peek?

I feel so alone,
so scared and unsure.
The further I roam
my way is a blur.

Soon I will see
come into my sight
the me I will be.
For this I will fight!

Dedication: My parents and my children

The Winding Road
Philip Arthur Burton
There is a winding
road that will lead
me home it may be hard
I will find that road
some day alone, every step
Is worth the journey
I have walked other passages
and found to my own surprise
That many paths have deceived me

Along the way adventures might
wait but I will continue each step
with pride and hope one day to
Travel that road home and

not wander a stay any more
It will be a good journey a long one
I have to agree you should know that
for it will make me happy knowing
that I will be home again giving
a good feeling of lasting joy

Dawning
Wendy Danielle
First, there was the solitary warble – heralding the break of a new day.
A cuckoo woke to the iridescent light.
I sat and watched the garden colours slowly brighten
as light lightened.
The bird's song became a furious crescendo,
Their day had begun.
Two cats played on the dewy grass, their stealth silhouetted by the new
    born day
And gradually the sun dawned with a peachy glow –
Colours now full of light paraded before my eyes:
beige clouds in a pearly blue sky
And the perfume of summer drifting in the warm air.
...Beauty...Peace...and time to reflect.

Windows
Amy Linden
When I was young, and until today,
I was fascinated with windows I passed on my way.
When I took the train home late at night,
I'd look in each window there was a light.

I'd imagine a family – different than mine,
And hoped I'd see some tangible sign
Of a loving mother with little children around.
I wondered if they the secret had found,
To exist together in a happy family setting
Where there was never anger or any fretting.

These many windows never showed me much,
But in my imagination I was almost able to touch
The lives of those I never knew –
As the train rumbled by and they passed from my view.

I still love windows; big apartments are best.
New York City and the buildings are a great test
For my imagination to fly and soar,
To think of good things, happy families and more.

Daniel's Special Day
Sandra Pierce
Brought to you by the letter D and the number 2.

There are Dozens of things that you can Do,
now that you are turning 2.

Walk, talk, jump and run,
things you learned when you were one.

Looking ahead to turning 2
there are more things to know and Do.

Potty training, snuggies and a Youth bed for you.
A swing set, new friends, lots of words,
and music too.

D is a letter, blue a color and 2 a special number.
You'll grow even taller and Dress yourself
before this time next summer.

We look forward to sharing next year with you,
now that you are turning 2.

A Boy's Dream
Cloamae Suiters
He sits in the morning sun
Not a care in the world has he
along a babbling brook
he passes the time, a fishing pole
By his side
Then a large sigh as the little guy
Drops his line in the water
Just a few more days to enjoy
The lazy, relaxing ways for school
Begins
With his dog at his side, he dreams
away the last days of summer fun,
Just sitting in the morning sun.

Home
Christopher D. Reagan
When you were very troubled
and far away from help,
God was there by your side
when there was no one else.

He comforted your heart
and never left your side,
He humbled your stubborn spirit
when you filled with too much pride.

He's been with you in times
you could not handle pain,
He lifted all your worry
and put down all the strain.

He will always be with you in spirit
and never leave you alone,
whenever you feel lost and afraid
ask and you will be HOME.

Dedication: My family and friends

Untitled
Marjorie K. Morehead
One evening as I was all alone in thought
I contemplated thus...
What if all of a sudden there was no one on this earth but me...
How would I feel?
What would I see?
Where would I turn—
with no one but me...?
Then I realized there would still be One—
Whose presence I would feel so mightily!!!
He "could" be counted as Three...
Father, Son and Holy Ghost, the Precious Trinity!
So don't worry about me when I'm gone,
Only a worn out body will be alone...
He will have taken "me" through the sky—
and then I'll be at "home"
He has claimed me for his own.
How do I know this to be so?
It's what I feel—It's what I've heard—
It's what God teaches in His word!!

Dedication: My Father in Heaven

Valentine

M. Hunter

This is to beauty and also to
Class, one to whom I would love
To make a pass.
But if this act would cause
Offence, then on my way I may
be sent, then never more to be a
Friend
But if this act does not offend
Then I could be your lover and
Most of all a very dear friend
Forever and ever.

Dedication: My wife forever, May

Hardrocker Of Time

Olivia S. Snead

In an ancient city
Where the crowd is strong
And life strives on its
Famed and would be glory
Of the struggling great
Yet to be:

He came toward me from
The midst of people,
The hardrocker of time,
Alive and glorious.

His hair of luxury length
And dark as the raven
Flowed upon his shoulders
Famed,
Identifying his name
Only yet whispered,
Powerful within the confines
Of the secrets
In the mind.

With God As My Guide

Deborah Ann Murray

With God as my guide
I have nothing to fear
He walks by my side
To make my path clear.

He guides me each and every day
Making sure I do not stumble
God helps me find my way
So that my world does not crumble.

He teaches me right from wrong
What is good and what is bad
Not to be weak but strong
And not to feel sad but to feel glad.

He lets His love shine on me
No matter what I do or say
There none greater than He
To my Almighty God, I pray.

Dedication: Sister Marie Cordata SSJ

First Bloom

Rebecca Brand Lunsford

Peace lily peace lily I waited
For your bloom,
Oh the day you came I was
Crying in my hearts room.

The window in my heart only
You can see through,
Peace lily, peace lily, this,
Pain you must have knew.

Family death is why you were
A gift. He was gone three years
When you first bloomed.

Sunglass Talk

Kathi Raymes

Contentment comes easily, awakening
Fully immersed in your arms,
I quietly pray time would stand still
At this very moment
Catching your glance I quickly look away
Fearing you might see
The secret in my eyes...
Let me tell you.
Your kiss intoxicates me
Having me at a disadvantage,
Questioning if I really want to be in control
After all, loss of reality
In your presence is my delight...
Let me tell you
Words can be deceiving
But hearts don't lie
Let our smile be our common ground
I will meet you there...
Come here, let me tell you
I long to be close...
As close as a "Butterfly's Kiss".

Dedicated To The Souls Of Flight 800

Diane M. Perpetua

A void remains within my heart
For those I had known
And those I had not
A sadness keeps me earthly bound
To cry a tear for answers unfound
I see the faces of one and of all
The smiles, the fears, the why's
I hold within my heart the years together we
did fly
I hold within the friends of old
The friends of new as well
I wonder why I wasn't there
Instead of here to tell
A fatal flight for all to bear
A day that's been long set
A tragedy for all to hear
A day we won't forget
But God is kind and has a plan
Although we know not what
We must relinquish to His hand
For He forgets us not

Seven Oaks
Pam Thompson
Thunder roared as lightening flashed;
the rain came down in a tremendous splash.

The wind exploded in the sky;
swirling everything in sight.

Many trees fell that night; all of different size and height.
Oak trees, Pine trees, Poplar Too;
Some as old as one hundred and two

Seven Oaks is not the same; since that night of wind and rain.
Six oaks fell that very night
Only one remain in sight.

Lover's Tryst
Ralph N. Smiley
Oh warm Summer night
'Neath full moon rise
Forest awash in golden glow
Lovers into the others eyes
Fuse their lives.

The wine chilled
The cheese soft
Baked bread 'neath a bough
As to each vow
Lingering they there.

The food eaten, wine deplete
A cock crows thrice
Sun on horizon rise
Sparkling dew of morn
Heavy on grass adorn
The couple to their tryst
Bid a fond adieu.

Dedication: Future wife, Merlinda Asis

I Am Because You Are
Deborah Beliveau
When I am laughing
It's because you said something funny
When I am crying real tears
It's because I feel your pain
When I am as happy as I could be
It's because you're in my life
When I have a thought of you
It's because I feel you near
When I am feeling hurt and down
It's because of the miles between us
When I dream about real things
It's because the dream is of you
When I am glad to be alive
It's because I have you to love
When I feel warm and fuzzy
It's because you give me happiness
When I think of my future
It's because I know you're in it
When I think of a best friend
It's because you are mine
always and forever

Untitled
Judy Curry Squires
When I was a little Girl,
I always knew that when I picked
That special someone you would be
There although you cannot be here in
person I know in my heart that you
are here
Walking beside me holding my hand.
I love you Grandpa so very much,
Thank–you for all you've given me
Throughout the years.
If I shed a tear today and smile a million
Smiles, I smile for you Grandpa I smile
For you this very special day.

Gentle Grin
Aaron Jones
...Standing at the Threshold–
and about to sink in.
Teeth held in gentle grin
not sinning, never sinned.
Standing at the Threshold about to sink in.
At once alone, yet guided
from tender moments chided.
Taken from thee...standing, waiting, patiently.
Stretching as far as the eye can see.
Go no further, do not surrender
then cover lost worth,
the battle will be for naught.
And naught will only agree,
that this moment with all of its tranquility
falls listlessly away.
Standing there, alone, unaware.
At the Threshold, about to sink in,
with teeth held in a
gentle grin.

Dedication: For my dear, Andrea....

Yesterday
Roberta Brunell
In twilight I see you,
The last rays of the day
Dancing round your feet.
As we work together
Making life complete.

The children now grown
With lives of their own,
Like leaves in the wind,
Slowly blowing home.

Murmurs of yesterday
Softly edge in mind,
Of Summer play
And the mountainside.

As the river
Captures the silence
Over the noonday hill,
A glimmer of yesterday,
Standing Still.

Encore
Martha A. Hethcoat
In the final gloom of September
The butterfly turns to her last
Audience, the roses.
She tells them that she will
Meet them again.
Where there is no yesterday or tomorrow.
Just a bright green, eternal spring.
And I will perform for you there,
My loves, and kiss you forever.
The cold winds of an old yesterday
Will have vanished and faded away.

Dedication: Amalia, Charlie, Gale and George

A Lover
Celeste Cabibi
Meeting my love right then and there.
Awake for my dreams to come true.
Releasing my strength I have left to bear.
Realizing I'm lucky to have you.

Happiness has taken over my tears.
The sadness has drifted away.
Now I have nothing left to fear.
Because you've given me the brightest ray

Receiving the wonderful gift of love.
Seeking within my soul.
Lifting my spirits the distance above.
Still trying to stay very bold.

Exhaling the memory I've left overcome
Being needless to say.
Relaxing my reflexes that are cold and numb
Dealing with glee every day.

Dedication: My lover, Joshua Randall

A True Friend
Sandy Keith
A true friend is a treasure
Far more precious than gold
It's someone who's always there
Through the years, as we grow old.

In sad times and in glad times
When there's doubts and fears
And we need a shoulder to cry on
To rid ourselves of our tears.

A true friend is a rarity
And so very hard to find
But when we meet someone special
It's the ties of both hearts that bind.

For to have a friend that's true
Means being one in return
It's not something that's easily given
But something we all must earn.

Dedication: Sue; a shining inspiration

Always Something Human
James Peters
The last time our winter was green
The grey rain dropped in swirling lines.
In the yard all the green leaves
Remained still, so as not to miss a drop.
The green world outside breathed in the water,
Without once exhaling, maniacally focused,
Yet still calm and receiving, and I thought
Them healthy and happy because it rained
Long and lean like we ourselves together rained
Falling in curves from the corners of our eyes,
Our smoothness gathered in pools of soft pleasure
While the rains fell and our green winter
Let loose with one last sizzling sigh.

Change
Myska Petrash
In the garden I can see a little girl that once was me
Free and full of life is she
She smiles, laughs...free of fear
She runs, she plays, and hides and sings

In the garden I can see an older woman much like myself
Troubled wrinkles crease her face
She wrings her hands
Prays for change

No longer is the garden green
The wind picks up and chills the air
A change must occur within herself or
Forever more the wind will blow

In the garden I can see a flower bloom, the change in made
The woman I see is myself
She lives a life she has chosen
No more wrinkles indented within her face. Smiles and joy and peace

In the garden I can see, the little girl I'll always be

There Is A God Somewhere
Pauline Wright
I can see the raindrops falling.
I can see the sun shining, I can
feel the wind blowing in the air, I
can see the birds are flying, I can hear
the waves dashing, there must be a God
somewhere.

I can see hills and mountains, I even
see lovely fountains, I turned around
and look and there were beautiful
valleys and colorful birds singing sweet
melody, it causes me to pause and think
"how do we get these beautiful things"?
There must be a God somewhere.

Though we have sorrow, though we have
pain and we feel like all of life is vain
take a look around and great peace you will
find. There is a God somewhere and he cares.

Dedication: Monique, Latoya, Beulent, Hyasinth and God

The Old Goshen Road
Virginia L. Walker
The historical white church, on a well–known hill...
when as a child...I remember...
tables were spread under the trees
every one would eat their fill,
families would write in the book so huge
Father telling us of days of old...
the front wooden bench...was where he sat,
so he told,
the small stones toward the back...mark the place
of dear ones laid to rest,
many years have gone...the Church still stands
nothing seems the same, except the stones at the back
and the historical legend that goes on.

When I Was Young
Robin O'Connor
...I used to fantasize
about spending my life with you
Imagine looking deep in your eyes
A part of me even thought it would come true

...I used to long for
our wedding day
My heart would have soared
to hear the words you would never say

...I used to yearn
For much, much time
All disdainful words would burn
When people heard the wedding bells chime

But then I grew and sighed
My youth has died
My soul has tried to keep you alive
But now there is too much to strive for
And I don't dream about you
Anymore

Mama's Tears
Jerrianne Lindekugel
They were slowly streaming down her pale,
yet Beautiful face

With a quiet fear and bold, brave grace

Her eyes, they held a deep, helpless sorrow, that
Seemed to be searching a release from
All tomorrow

I knew right then, I could plainly see,
Mamma's life, her smile, was up to me

My little hand raised her quivering chin,
As I told her I'd protect her from hurting again

I'll never forget my life at three,
Or the lesson I'll carry all my years
The child of courage I have grown to be,
Planted and nourished by Mamma's Tears.

Dedication: Mom, my endless source of strength

What Is Hate?
Keith M. Estes
I am hate,
I like to blame people for my mistakes,
I am disorderly conduct without being
provoked,
I am jealousy and envy,
I am the thief who is poor and hates
working hard,
I am reverse psychology/used to present
everything I do wrong as something right,
I am the excuse for not being loyal,
courteous,
honest,
I am peer pressure because I hate
to see you do well,
Though it may not seem,
I do have a conscience
and I hate myself for having hate,
I am what America will soon become...
HATE!!!

Dedication: All negative people

Nothing Stays The Same
Jill G. Shipp
Little red caboose, have you come loose
from that train upon the track?
It doesn't seem fair, 'twasn't long you were there,
the last car on the back!

I used to sit having fit after fit;
At the crossing I would wait,
And then I'd cheer because you were here
the last to pass the gate,
But now radar has come to replace the fun
of waiting for that last little wave.
So life passes by, tears are futile to cry
I guess I'll have to be brave!

In You I Trust!
Bob Cates
Please forgive me for what I said,
Teasing you only made you mad.
Please forgive me for what I've done,
I didn't mean it, it was all in fun.
I love you Cheryl with all my heart,
Please don't let this tear us apart.
Trust is an important part of life,
Without trust we'll never become husband and wife.
My time is close, I'm almost thru,
Soon I'll be out, and I'll be with you.
I'll never doubt you ever again,
Please forgive me, and be my friend.
I trust you Cheryl with all my heart,
That trust will keep us together, even if
we are many miles apart.
Please forgive me for what I said,
I'll make it up to you in a nice warm bed.
Please forgive me for what I've done,
My world without you, would be a world with out fun.
I love you Cheryl with all my Heart,
When we are together, I'll never want to part.

She Was Dreaming
Janice March
Pain flowed into her dream.
Landscapes of wounds behind her eyes.
Sorrows pierced her heart.
She was dreaming.
Oh, so much grief, so much sadness.
Blood—scarlet rivers, she saw.
She was dreaming.
Was there an end to her woes?
Suddenly, dawn poured its light into her slumber.
It washed her pains away to a pleasant peace.
Her wounds are healed.
Grief melted from her heart.
Morning light shimmered her eyes.
Alas! Tears of joy trickled from her eyes.
"Good riddance, pain," she said.
No more grief.
No more scars.
No more pain.
She stopped dreaming.

Dedication: My church (spirit and truth)

I Am
Amy Cordon
I Am the link that science wants to find in that old cave.
I Am the whale, the Spotted Owl, the one you try to save.
I Am the star you wish upon, I Am the songbird's tune.
I Am the scent you long to smell around the month of June.

I Am the sparkle in his eye, the one you hold so dear.
I Am the grin on your child's face, I Am who put it there.
I Am the very breath you breathe, and when you take your
last, you will see the all that's me but finally, face to face.

You do believe and do perceive the all that you want me
to be, but I control the He that's me; I Am the all that ever
be. I am the great I Am.

Untitled
Rosemary Duffy
The sky is a blue – like crystal
The trees are coated in colors so bright –
The air snaps and crackles
From the leaves showering fitfully down.

The valley is preparing, for winter
Its harvest all but done –
The fruits of the earth are gathered,
Hints of apples, corn, and pumpkins
wafting through the air.

Mother Nature is holding a party –
Her annual good–bye...
Her children pause and enjoy –
Joyous, playful, exuberant –
Ready to savor; not ready to let go.

Time has a way of displacing –
Things now – end, and are no more.
Yet, with that final, glorious burst –
The promise of the future is here.

A Mother's Prayer
Sandra S. Van Orman
Heavenly Father, hear my prayer
Take care of my boy while he's up there.
Guide him to your loving arms,
Keeping him safe from all harm.

Let him know we miss him,
And love him so very much,
And how at times I know I feel
His warm, loving touch.

Heavenly Father, watch over him
He meant the world to me.
And grant that I'll be good enough
To see him in eternity.

Help us, Lord, to bear this pain
And make our burden light.
One more thing, Lord, could you please
Give him a kiss goodnight?

Dedication: To Paul with love, Mom

Our Little Girl
Evelyn Kinsey
On your wedding day, when you walk down the aisle,
behind tears of joy your dad and I will smile.

Cause although we do not always see eye to eye,
honey, we were once children and now we understand,
that we should not let these precious memories fly by.
Let us choose to walk into the future hand in hand.

For when we look upon your glowing bridal face,
we will remember you in a different time and place.

Clumsy young parents who fussed and fixed a curl,
knowing then you would always be our little girl.

Please God...
Ginger Lee Patterson
(For Police Officers)
He wears his badge with honor and pride,
Handcuffs and gun hang from his side.
His hours are long – his rewards are small,
But there's never a time that he doesn't walk tall.
If he gets into trouble and things look grim,
Please God...place Your hand on him.

He can get tough and he can be strong,
When he is pursuing those who do wrong.
There are times he is gentle – times when he's warm,
His concern is protecting, keeping others from harm.
If he gets into trouble and things look grim,
Please God...place Your hand on him.

His life is filled with danger, everywhere,
Many times, aimed at him, bullets fly through the air.
He has had quite a few narrow escapes,
surviving with bruises and cuts and scrapes.
If he gets into trouble and things look grim,
Please God...place Your hand on him.

An Angel Present
Isabel Ortiz
I saw an angel today
as I was on my way
He stopped to say
to take a moment to pray
When I thought that harm
would come to me
There were watchful eyes
helping me...see
I have a constant friend
in them
they reach your heart from within
They often remind us to be kind
to be helpful to others
who are blind
I have no fear
when they are here
I can feel their presence everywhere
They are sent to us
from God above
through them he
offers to us love

The Battle Eternal
Merle Kinder
Up, slowly it rises
Waves of heat rolling in its wake
Moment by moment it lifts
Shards of light washing away the darkness
The moon receding as if in flight
Onward, upward it pushes towards its zenith
Bathing all within its pervue in its fiery glow
Until there upon it begins its decent at last
And the moon returns to claim its starry throne
Cooling, soothing darkness putting all to peace
The moon reigning proud in all its glory
Till once again its morning
And the battle starts anew.

What Is A Mother
Margaret Poston
What is a mother,
Like a soft gentle breeze.
She touches her young,
Kisses bruised split knees.

She's always there
to dry the tears
and ease the pain
of childhood fears.

A Mother is blessed
and so full of love,
Sent from the Father
in Heaven above.

Touch her Lord
and keep her near
to all of those
who hold her dear.

Dedication: Florence Adams– my mother

The Miraculum Gift
Virginia G. Bailey
There stood this old lady
With shoulders stooped,
Head held high
As high as she could hold it.
Stretching and straining was she
To see the Grand Priest pass by.
Miraculously he stopped before her.
And, "How old are you?" He asked.
Then anxiously awaited her reply.
"Sir, I am eighty–nine years old,
I will be ninety soon."
"Wonderful! Wonderful!" exclaimed he.
"Wonderful — Wonderful it may be." Said she.
Echoing his words without thought.
"Age is something that cannot be bought."
Words of wisdom the priest gave.
As he raised his hands toward the sky.
"Oh how very true that is kind Sir," she agreed
And with a heavenly gleam in her eyes,
So full of love for her Master to see
Replied, "but it is God's gift to me."

Untitled
Anita M. F. Fischer
Like tears from a weeping heart
Falls the rain;
And the rush of the wind is the soul's lost cry
Along dark passageways of despair.
Where can one turn? to whom?
To God? He answers ne'er.
For God can only help the ones who help themselves.
So where to start? – in soul's dark depths, alone and quiet
with thoughts that drift as the surging tide
Hope may come,
Quickly, with one golden ray of sun.

Dedication: My beloved father, Bertram Smith

Childhood Memories
Lorraine Helen Prehart–Fourcaud
During the quiet moments of a long and
busy day, I turn to memories of my childhood
when there was also time for play. School was
fun, a wonderful place to learn; patient
teachers encouraged our creativity and helped
in each and every turn. At home, Mom
would be cooking dinner and Dad came
home from work. Slowly, we ate, and talk
at the table was cheery. (No one had the
look of today, a look of one so weary.)
And life was a great deal simpler, most
everything was done by hand–this was
no great chore, today I understand,
And love, love at our house, there was
so much – a gentle hug and kiss, my
childhood memories consist of all this.
I sit and smile as I go back in time –
for I'm relieving my childhood, in that
special corner of my mind.

Dedication: Beloved parents, Helen and Joseph Prehart

Tears Of Love
Emmanuel U. Iloabuchi
I once boasted that I would not cry
when one so loved departed from my side
but when it happened and took me unawares
it was then that I confirmed my greatest fears.

I closed my door and shouted "WHY?"
as torrents of tears cascaded down from my eyes
and in my mind the scenes flashed by of moments
spent together so cherished in time.

I then remembered her last words on earth
which she struggled to say with her dying breath.
"No matter how hard a man may seem, he has a heart
which lies beneath and when the man loses someone
so dearly loved, those tears shall flow freely from above"

The days have gone by and the years have past
her words come back clearly I smile and then laugh.
and deep down inside me I now know for sure
that those tears shall flow freely forever
in love.

Why
Wanda Wandersee
Why is the sky blue?
Why is the grass green?
Why is the sun yellow?
Why are flowers different?
Why is there violence?
Why is there alcoholism?
Why is there abuse?
Why does love have to hurt?
Why do parents have to say "I told you so"?
Why do children always ask "why"?
Why is there a rainbow after a storm?
Why is everything why?
Because we would still ask ourselves why?

Dead March
Jeannette Oatley
In regimental ranks the dead now lie
Silent, at coffined "attention",
Their faces to the sky.
And none "fall out" and none "desert"
Their grim eternal posts,
And for the sentry duty
There can be only ghosts.
And now and then a new recruit
"Falls in" to join the line,
A little mound of fresh dug clay
Provides the only sign
Another soul has signed their hand
Upon Death's dotted line.
No medals these, no cheering crowds,
No bright parades, no trumpet sounds
No "discharge" now, no going home
Just uniformed in Essex loam.
Now, "at ease" beneath the ground
They evermore must be,
The only march left to perform—
Into eternity.

The Dancing Leaves
Anetha Hunte
The tree that stands
outside my window
stands tall and proud
silently it cleanses the air
I watch its leaves
being danced about in a breeze
on a summers evening.

Day is leaving slowly drifting away
But still a yellow light
between the branches of the tree
gleams bright
And then as night navy blue creeps in steadily,
so the yellow gleam between the branches
will leave.
and I, my eyelids growing heavy
I feel sleep gripping me tight
as I drift into dreams
still watching the leaves of the tree that stands
outside my bedroom window,
casting shadows in the night.

Shadow
Fancy Cuevas
Walking through the night
I see a shadow
Is it a stranger or it's only you

When I walk or run
I can still see you
Sometimes I think it's in my mind

Sometimes I feel like looking back
But I'll be afraid it's only you
My shadow.
Dedication: My daughters, Diana and Gabriella

Moments
Richard Anderson
The sun impales the clouds and so our souls.

We could weep hopelessly on matters grave;
there are so many acres yet to save.
There are so many battles to be won,
but solipsists write treaties in the sun.

We wipe away unrest with beer—cold hands,
and shield our eyes, reframing galaxies.
We walk with excellence in cloudless lands,
erasing dark and bloody histories,
and will not justify our quiet partying,
or even hear the righteous angry mob
that cackle, sad and mad, at smiling sinners,
(their foaming envy posing as morality).

I raise a glass to Summer and to moments,
to toast this true, if fractional, ascent
and wave away two—fifths of their dissent.

Dedication: To the late Kevin Crowther

Thoughts And Desperation
Christian Newman
Maybe, you were just a dream.
No: Nightmare, rings clear, and truly
Echo's the pain; the cruelty
The attends a vision so serene.

Speak! Give life to this dream,
Give me a sign of your physicality;
Banish these thoughts, of fearing my reality:
Creases upon mind's gentle stream.

Maybe, you were just a dream,
For I begin to doubt;
My mind, a mind without,
Created you, a vision so serene?

Speak! Are you my imagination?
Then why, in my mind,
Can I no longer find
You? Oh! Thoughts and desperation!

Dedication: Maria, dreams come true...

Algebra
Anthony J. Coak
Algebra. I can't do it.
My pencil won't work,
I sit and chew it.

Monomials and polynomials,
the degrees of and dividing,
they haunt me and taunt me
and force me into hiding.

Algebra, the whole concept,
what's it all worth?
I wish the man who wrote this book
had never been given birth.

Little Orphaning Annie
Eli Konsistorum
"Life is just a bunch of rotten cherries", Annie kept saying in Angry
daily protest to her destined lot
"What good is living", she would reason "For any one who's got the
troubles that I've got"?
Continually tortured in body and soul, with pills and booze she
lullabied her mind
And through distorted thoughts of escape, she tried to leave her
troubles behind.
But we mortals cannot alter fate, no matter how hard we try
For 'tis written by the phantom hand where, when and how each must die.
And so poor Annie died many times, whenever she came to the brink,
She was led to the waters of eternal sleep, but she was not allowed to
    drink.
Until one day her time had come, and she went and did her thing,
She courted death and teased him till, she felt his final sting.
I visit her flowery grave now and then, and my heart begins to pain
When I think of poor Annie, so young and so pretty and I wonder if
she died in vain
For although her eyes can no longer see trouble, they will equally never
again see
The beauty in a flower, and good friends like you and me.

Silence
Chris Pagan
As darkness falls
Over the sky,
I'm laying in bed.
Too cold to get up,
Too warm to be dead.

As darkness falls
Over the sky,
A deafening silence
Breaks the stillness
In the air.

As darkness falls
Over the sky,
A cold wind breaks
Over the city.

As darkness falls
Over the sky,
A dimly lit sun
Shines one last time.

Where Is The Bird?
Jenni Forrest
The light hits a dogwood tree
Through my window
Its branches swaying in the wind
So gracefully
So effortlessly
It stands alone
In all its beauty
I want to be the dogwood tree
But I am that tiny flower
That fell and drifted away
As I sit on the black pavement
I wait patiently
for a bird to carry me home.

---

15 Jan 91
Yvonne Johnson
Listen...
Do you hear the history?
Way above us
Now it's fading...now it's gone

It was there
Just for a moment
Mighty, streaking, silver death
What a perfect night it is
To start a war

There's another
Do you hear it?
Who needs words with such a sound?
It's a statement in itself:
'No mercy here '

Now they're coming even faster
No more fading, just a rise
First melody...then symphony...now building to cacophony...Crescendo!
Stunning prelude to a war.

Paradise Grounds
Andrena Milligan

As we open the gates in Mersey Street.
We see the oval grounds
A place of sport and laughter
As the people come in crowds
But a place that's known to all
Is the dug out at the side
Where all the players' managers
Always seem to hide.
One that will be missing now
Is a man that did them proud
His name is Davy Roberts
A name we often heard aloud
He was a man of character
Of love and spirit too
If players were in need of help
He was there to see then through
Davy is in different grounds
Called paradise
A place of loving care
One day his friends at the oval
With them paradise he will share.

Another Day
E. Langford

Another day in the life of me,
To rise and shine, "perhaps to dream",
Of love fulfilled and tasks completed.

Another day in the life of me,
What will I do and who will I be?
I do not know, I cannot tell,
In what I've chosen, will I do well?

Another day in the life of me,
To be the best of what you see,
Give some thought to the day's endeavor,
Then preserve each moment like a priceless treasure!

One Fine Day
Stephen Morgan

We came out from the shadows,
The rain clouds cast upon that sunny day.
The sun breaks through the silver edged
Clouds; a mist so fine peaceful thoughts
Beautiful day,
You walked on by

Sunny day a warming breeze,
No words to speak we know
Each thought. A look, a smile,
The sun breaks through,
A flower grows, sweet sound
A bird in song, that mist so fine,
You walked on by

A tear of gladness rolls on down
A distant sound of river's flow
We are here life so fine
Do we deserve, as beauty surrounds
This body mine
You walked on by

Untitled
Margaret Tasnier

I was dreaming
going no place
while I was waiting
for your eyes to find me.
Hypnotised by sunshine maybe
Singing at the gulls along the beach.
Much too wise for sandcastles
my castles were across the sea
or still within my mind.
I must have thought
the night could save me
as I went down into pillows.
But I was dreaming
before you.

Stay within my darkness
just a while longer.
Come to me
our collective ocean
will wash over all our days
and troubles.

Untitled
Marjorie H. Robley

Mr. O'Possum is cutting corn
Mr. Raccoon is a hauling
My little dog is sitting on a stump
Killing himself a bawling.
Yonder is a brick house sixteen stories high
Every room in that old house is lined with chicken pie
Violet's are blue
Roses are red
Little John is a sweet boy
Everyone thinks he is a toy
Swing your partner to the right
Swing your partner to the left
Dance, dance, and dance and do your best

The First Fish
Joyce Anlezark

A new adventure, down to the lake to fish
with grandchildren.

Maggots, fishing line and picnic to hand.
Silence, patient contemplation.

Gentle lapping of the water, birds singing,
cows mooing;
Mounting excitement.

Sandwiches passed down to the expectant
fisherman;
Ripples on the water, is it a catch?

"Quickly, Grandma, Grandpa, Philip's caught
a fish", cries Richard.

Grab the camera to record the catch for posterity.
THE FIRST FISH.

Dedication: Philip and Richard

The Tie Which Binds
Christina Marie Mulchandani
As the sands of the hour glass flow,
The murkiness of time dilutes the present;
Only memories linger,
A passing shadow of time;
So when life's heavy iron takes its toil,
And but the bitter winds and the silence greets your woes;
Your struggle will not be attended alone,
For beyond its strangling hold;
Lies the tie which binds the present to the past,
It does not give way to the drug of forgetfulness;
Nor does it disappear like the morning dew,
This desert flower of rarity awaits;
Amid its own turmoil;
Taking heed to your cries,
Soothing the sting of your torment;
For the tie which binds is nothing more than what you give — to a
    stranger...
Gaining strength within the breathing of time,
A seed nourished by laughter, tears, and secrets;
Living beyond eternity,
And it is the same bind that I have already given to you — my friend...

Self Esteem
Courtney Carleton
The early morning sun shines into your room.
You can already feel the impending gloom.
Here comes the pain forever felt, into the darkness of your room you would
    like to melt.
You wish there could be shelter from the heartache, and the pain.
Sometimes you pray for clouds to come, for thunder, and for rain.
You start to cry, then wonder why life has to be this way.
You grab your blankets, hide your eyes, and then you start to pray.
You feel you're ugly, that you're fat.
You've lost your friends imagine that!!
You'd like to leave, you'd like to run, but you pray for joy, and for sun.
Put up your guard, and hide your eyes
Someone's coming, put on disguise.

Mom And Dad
Kimberli–Ann Wohlman
Such a distance away
but still in my heart
I think of you always
although we're apart

I know you'd be proud
if you saw me today
striving to follow
the Lord and His ways

I'm raising my family
with love and assurance
and living my life
in a positive way

Thank you for teaching me
life's little lessons
it is God and your love
that make me go on
knowing I can
face today

If I Could
Mitzi N. Perez
"Mom, can you catch a cloud"?
If I could, I would catch a cloud
All for this innocent, precious child
Anything for that smile!

"Mom, can you fly to the moon"?
If I could, I would fly to the moon
All for this innocent, precious child
Anything for that smile!

If I could, I would lasso the sun
So we could play ball
Scatter the twinkling stars around
So we could play jacks
Slide on a slippery rainbow ride
Swing on memorable moonbeams high
All for this innocent, precious child mine
Anything for that smile!
If I could

Dedication: All of my children

Angels
Gladys A. Sullivan
Are there celestial beings? I'll tell you how I feel,
I've never seen an angel with wings that fly in air.
But here on earth, I've seen my share, and they don't fly or just appear.
A voice that reaches out to say, I'm right there for you, all the way.
A little child to show us, we forgot to say "Thank You",
Or the elderly remind us the very precious, "I love you!".
A day can never be too long, or a night so filled with strife,
that we cannot remember, the angels in our life.
They come in various age and size; in jeans and fancy clothes,
yet it seems as if our angels always finds the time and knows
that today has been a bad day,
but least we should forget, Thank you God, for life is good.
For we have had the best.

My Daddy's Poison
Danielle M. Rygh
The weekend I am to see my daddy,
he promises me he won't drink one drink.
He thinks I'll just forget, but I don't.
He knows I won't say anything, and I don't.
To him the alcohol is his best friend, but
It's really his enemy in disguise.

The next weekend I'm over to see my daddy,
he says he won't drink his poison.
He thinks I don't remember what he promised what he said.
Then I go and cry the cry that everyone can hear but him.

Again, I am coming over.
The promise is now nonexistent.
And while I'm put through slow and excruciating
pain, the poison continues to go down drink
by drink.

And just then I begin to hear my daddy's silent cry
for help, that no one else can hear;
painful cries that not even my dad himself can hear.

Betrayal
Glenda Darlene Tharp

Why is it so hard?
Where did it go wrong?
Will I ever be able to find where I belong?
Why is it so hard to see
That all I want is respect
And love?

Why do we go though this?
Is it worth all the hurt?
Where does God want us to be?
Why can't I see His plan?
Does He have one for us?
Am I wrong to feel hurt and betrayed,
When everything we should share
is shared with someone else?
How am I supposed to feel?
I try to find my way
But is it wrong?
How will I know?
When will I see?
All I ask is to be told.

Jealous Daughter
Winifred Spector

She wants to be me, but she is she.
She would like to have been born
Before me, to slaughter her daughter,
Deliberately.
She loves my clothes, but loathes
Them on me.
In the same room we cannot be,
She directs her jealousy always
Toward me.
Her hostility she does not hide,
I finally cannot abide,
I slaughter my daughter,
Mentally.

Brides Of Snow
Marion R. McManamy

The falling snow adorned the trees like brides,
They're all aglow in veils of virgin white;
A slowed car on the highway dips and slides,
While fields and lawns reflect a wintry night.

See how they stand, all dressed and beautiful,
The maple and the pine and all the rest,
A gentle couturier calm and dutiful,
Spreads ermine at the feet of those he dressed.

So there in winter world of moonlit dreams,
We see their flowing soft magnificence,
"The hunter of the East" with golden streams
Will bathe their hearts in his beneficence.

The morning sun will kiss their veils away,
While nature's jewels on their branches dance,
And bridegroom fill their hearts with his embrace
As they awaken from their bridal trance.
And we in gazing thus recall our goal,
To greet the loving Bridegroom of our soul.

Untitled
Linda Lohrengel

My mother my friend
My mother my friend
You could always change
Sadness to joy within.

My mother my friend
You were always there
for me, on you I could
Always depend.

My mother my friend
Love, understanding and
faith was the message
You would always send.

My mother my friend
I will always love you
To the end.

My mother my dear
friend

Turning Point
Wendy Cook

I look at the moon, the fat, round, golden, iridescent moon,
Once a symbol of our love and everything that was good about it,
And I think of you.
Your face and memory are intertwined with its beauty.
When did your memory silently slip away and the moon become
just the moon again?

The night fades into morning and the nameless void shadows become
familiar objects again in the light of day.
Life awakens! When did the darkness become light? When did the
sun slip in?
At what point did it cease to be night and turn into morning?
When did I start living again?

My Days As A Teacher
Nina Levorn Hasty

Distress and disappointment is what I feel when I walk helplessly
    through those two
unwanting prison door.
The hall walls close in as if I was in a gas chamber as I walk on
    the worn out floor that
shows its age. The ceilings cry for me for me from every direction
    as they leak day after day.
Words are spoken and some days I hear them. Like a knife they
    cut and like a rubber band
they bounce off of my frozen up body.
My emotion system shuts down to the worldly atmosphere.
You can't hurt me—I'm in my own world with my own rules.
Long live peaceful smiles and cheers.
You can't win my spirit—
you won't, I've worked to hard to be able to walk through those
    challenging doors
that no one seems to want to challenge anymore.
When I close my door, you, you and you do not matter.
I'm in my own world with my own rules. You do not and cannot
    matter to me.
Only for my students will I take the unwanting looks and words.

Love Pain Hate
Lauritz Dieckman

Love me with your hate
With the pain I can inflate
Cut me with your razor blade
My hate for you will never fade
I want to be your whipping boy
Abuse and hurt your little toy
Hate me with your love today
To keep my only thoughts away

A gift from you my noose of thorns, to keep around my bleeding neck
Tied to the feet of others you loved, hear the pain and rip of flesh
Down pour of raining blood, drenched in your love for many

With every nerve you overfry
You will never ever see me cry
Love pain hate all are one
Take your time and have your fun
Prick my heart with your twisted knife
Drain from me my poisoned life
The pain is always right here
I carry your love entwined in fear

Three Roads
Chris L. Baker

Three roads there are to life;
That is what I say.

I have traveled only two.
One that lead me wrong;
to sorrow, trouble and hurt.

The second I still travel.
My path, it could be wrong.

The third I've yet to see,
and the path, right wrong
is really up to me.

Senior Years
Beryl Pauls

He's not as spry as he used to be
Many years ago,
His joints are getting stiffer
And his movements all are slow;
Gray hair is getting thinner,
But he still has quite a crop;
But he will keep going as long as he can,
Until he has to stop.
His sight is slowly failing,
And he doesn't hear as well,
But he still remembers farming days,
And many stories he can tell.

He can't do the things he used to do
Many years ago,
When he tilled the soil and planted seeds,
Or used a garden hoe;
But he still enjoys a tasty meal,
And a pleasant country drive,
He is a friend to everyone.
And he is glad to be alive.

Plenish
Peter K. Horne

The dozen things mankind must do
to live this life and see it through
happily with God's Creation;
life and structures; the full nation:
to exchange gross for things that shine,
like Health, Contentment – Milk of kine.

Starting unskilled they first must LEARN
to combat ignorance then turn
to whole life business and its grind;
many new learning modes they'll find.
COMMUNICATION; for without
the Word of life there's no redoubt.
ATTITUDE too, for with this strength
rightly applied there is no length
nor height can't be attained as said
by HIM who knew, who taught, who led.
ASPIRE; DEVELOP; DO; then FEED
the noble two of law and creed.
DILIGENCE; KINDNESS; PRACTICE TRUTH;
BEHAVIOUR; CONCORD: (s)age from youth.

Battle of the Bulge
Denna V. Marvel Felix

Every day it's constantly
The battle of the bulge
I dream of all of the goodies
I'd love, so much to indulge,
It's don't eat this and
It's don't eat that
If you do, you will get fat
It is simple as all that,
If you indulge
You will bulge
and
If you don't,
You won't!!

I Know Not Why?
Eva Langford

I know not why,
So blue the sky?
Why grass is green?
Why mountains high?

Why breezes blow?
Why flowers show
Their colours bright?
We do not know!

I know not why
God's birds can fly
When man must walk,
To soar we try!

When raindrops gentle
Cleanse earth's mantle
A rainbows aura
Covers all creation!

I know not why!

Inspiration
Elizabeth M. Crellin

A poet uses his
imagination.
Love of nature
is his inspiration.
A poet is sensitive
to colour and beauty.
Making it almost
a duty.
To express feelings
by willing in prose.
A birds sweet trill
and the excitement
grows.
An unexpected pleasure
a badger on the lane.
Foraging on his
moonlight trail.
A shaft of light a
glittering water fall.
God's love is revealed
to one and all.

The Legacy
Donald G. Mongrain

Forget me not.
My story, I must tell.
Death! Death! Death!
The blood of many
lie upon the hands of evil.
For the love of a
Sister,
a lover,
my only friend.
I must stop the kill.
For the legacy must end.

Dedication: Deborah Borg, Carolyn Brown, D. Morrison

Cleanliness Is Next To Godliness
Julie Blake

Nooks and crannies
No dirty dannies
Or feet face and fannies

Niches and bolt holes
Crevices and plug holes
Noses even ear holes

It's a sterile environment.
Mother's a wiz
With the bleach, soap and Jif
No sign of a whiff

She scrubs us all over
Given the chance
If we start to scream
She applies the cold cream

I just want to leave
And once, just once
Wipe my nose in my sleeve.

Remember
David V. Maddren

Remember the times when we were kids
Of whitewashed steps and dustbin lids
Of hoops and sticks and whips and tops
When sweets were rationed down at the shops

Remember the times when we were boys
Of leaden soldiers and wooden toys
Of football boots and a leather ball
We really thought we'd got it all

Remember the times we were in our teens
Of pointy–toed shoes and drainpipe jeans
A night at the pub drinking bottles of Brown
When a packet of fags cost half a crown

Now we're grown up and getting old
We've rheumatic pains and we're feeling the cold
We don't go out much, no one invites us
Can't go far anyway we've got arthritis
We live day to day from January to December
All we do now is sit and remember

Mietka
Tim R. Bridges

The truth for these so many years
lay buried in a sea of tears,
that holds such sad and lonely fears.
The sadness that she never hears
nor feels the pain inside that sears.
Would that sunlight near
and with it darkness clear.
This truth to all appear;
a sound that is so dear.
I hear Mietka cheer...
Your little girl is here.

Dedication: Mietka, my little girl

A Love Story
Apikia Shaw

To mold your face in brass,
And place it at the crossroads of
the earth
Where little men could stare
with–wonder–ment!
A tribute, "this", he calls!

Lo, Dear;
Were I gifted with the art
of fashioning,
I'd form your face
with dust of distant stars.

And then, my Dear,
I'd place it on the Highways of
the heavens,
where the Gods of all Universe
might see,
and understand
why mortals
Love!

We End In Your Guilt
Maricarda Ortiz
With every stroke
He shortens my breath
As the time between us
Lessens.

His hands in my hair
Bring tears to my eyes
With memories of what was—
Or of what I thought was
Due to living in his illusions.

With every touch
He gives way to our death
Bringing rebirth for us both
In the arms of another.

And my memories in grief
For my childish belief
That he and I
Would live an eternity
Together.

I Am The Lost One
Jennie Schaefer
Banish soul that no longer sees your face
hides behind the dark shadows of your love,
While my heart roams the earth endlessly calling for you
but the message gets lost in the circling wind,
Our dreams are now exile dreams left behind in the broken dust,
Just leaving me with the memories that holds me prisoner
where I stand,
And I wonder aimlessly searching for answers about those forgotten
kisses,
As the whispering promises drag beside me through time,
I can feel the world ending beneath my feet with an eternal torture
of loving you,
And I am forever cursed because I AM THE LOST ONE without YOU!

Dassie
Philip Kiberd
There sits the Dassie,
A little stone bun.
Eager for warmth,
Quick for to run.
Rocks for your shelter,
Heat from your sun.

Teeth ever gnawing
Eyes ever keen
The leopard is cunning
The eagle is mean

Friend of the elephant,
Small bundu troll.
See me approaching,
And bolt to your hole.

I spy you in the evening,
And in the morning light,
You know I am watching,
And squeeze out of sight.

You
Lynette R. MacMartin
You say you've found the answer, this time you
know you're right.
You patiently pursue him so you can stay the
night.
You wake up in the morning thinking he just
might be the one you dream of to love and hold you tight.
You need to find the answer, to help you through
The night, as sure as morning wakes you, you're going to see the light.
All my fears release me as you hold me here just right.
Longing for some ecstasy, you bring me sheer delight.
Reaching out for destiny to turn the wrong to right...
You're looking for some company to fill your lonely night...
It's time to say goodnight now. I want to be with you...
Tell me that you need me the way that I need you...

Thanksgiving
Debbie Auen
I am extremely grateful for my health
And that I have been spared both poverty and wealth
For these precious gifts I thank GOD above
The capacity to give and receive love
Hearing your distinctive voice
My mental ability that enables me to comprehend and make a choice
Emotions that indicate how I feel
Having a best friend who is faithful and real
Possessing a conscience that ceases to ache when I am wrong
Having a caring family to whom I belong

All of life's heartache and sorrow
The stumbling blocks today transformed into stepping stones tomorrow
The privilege of just being alive
I am grateful for GOD'S Grace peoples help my determination
To do more than merely survive
I appreciate every man and woman who served (serves) in our military
In an effort to preserve our country's freedom then and now
At the foot of Christ's Cross I humbly bow
For the greatest gift presented to me
Is GOD'S unconditional love poured out at Calvary

There Is A Song
Christle Gray
There is a song I sing;
of colored dawns and clear blue skies,
of sunlight sparkling in your eyes.
There is a song I sing.

There is a song I sing;
of windswept beaches, grains of sand,
walking with you hand in hand.
There is a song I sing.

There is a song I sing;
of rainstorms lasting for a while,
making rainbows like your smile.
There is a song I sing.

There is a song I sing;
of onyx skies and starry light,
of lying in your arms all night.
There is a song I sing.

It is a song of love.

Morning Haze
John Merry

Again sleep eluded these tired weary eyes,
Exposed to the mercy of star speckled skies.
To ponder on thoughts of previous days,
And marvel the splendor of morning's soft haze.

Birds sing cheerfully from where they perch,
Soon to wing in flocks, for food they will search.
As creatures who've stirred from their underground maze
Will forage and frolic, in the morning's soft haze.

People who've rested arise from their sleep,
Ready themselves for the jobs they keep.
Oblivious they are of the cattle that graze,
In the vast countryside, in the morning's soft haze.

When One Of The Family Goes To Jail
Virginia A. Hague

When one of the children, of a mother out there goes to jail,
this child doesn't think of the pain he puts his mom through, how
much her heart breaks into, or how much mom wants to hold you.

This child doesn't stop to think all mom has gone through, just
to have someone else to judge you, and mom knows all the pain you
go through too, mothers always sheds a lot of tears for you, just like
when you were a child, and when she used to hold you.

You have a family that really loves you, and what does mom
say when they inquire about you, there's that little niece who really
misses you because you're not there to give her a hug every time she
saw you, she loves and misses you.

This little blonde headed blue eyed girl who when she was a
baby used to cry every time she saw you, now sheds tears, and prays
for you, and son I want you to know your mom does too and I'll
always love you.

Dedication: To all single mothers

Christmas Is Coming
Marcella M. Kilby

Christmas is coming
Cheer, cheer, cheer,
Soon there will be presents to last all year
And one thing I know,
There will be snow,
Too shine so prettily, of colored lights that glow.
And during the night with snow a falling,
Howling winter winds a blowing
While sitting by the fireside, so warm and aware
Where friendly voices, singing everywhere
I'll lift my glass to wish everyone good cheer.
Too take a glance at such beauty from the tree this year.
With the wrappings of gifts such a glorious site.
Loving by my loved ones so near
And too, dear Santa Claus, who will be arriving soon,
Some will be seeing Him, on new white snow.
Or as if going by the moon
As from the fireplace, such crackling sounds
Too wait for Christmas this exciting night.
Cheer, cheer, cheer, was all I could hear
Christmas is coming

Untitled
John Dalton Emery

Yesterday I saw my old friend Mike
In his day he had so much fight
Now his shock—clouded eyes look the other way
Too many wars lost
Too many dreams tossed
Like the character he used to carry in his eyes and walk
Lost to the passing of times reaction brings reaction
Other's own selfish needs and
The inevitable inability of our being able to handle
Life's crushing pressure

Where have my old friends all gone away
In their faces strangers stay
In our youth so strong and brave
Only to be worn away

Until We Meet
Lorinne Izquierdo

To my sister, the one I've never known
I hope in my heart you're not alone.
A pretty little girl, who left too soon
to a place full of flora and in full bloom.
You left behind a family so sweet,
and we're all anticipating the day we meet.
So sister, sister the one I love,
someday I'll meet you in that place above.
Until that time be patient my dear
for I'm longing too, to be ever so near.
So remember my sister, my special friend,
you're in my mind and heart until the end
So keep a special place just for me
to frolic with you and live happily.
Sister, oh sister be you ever so kind
as you can see, you're always on my mind.
I hope one day we will be together
and our hearts will float just like a feather.
Happiness is still in the future to come
when finally we meet and our hearts become one.

Love Hurts
Rachelle Shapiro

You look at me but you don't see,
Exactly what you mean to me,
The love, devotion, pride and pain,
the sorrow, loneliness and disdain.

Your eyes are cold, heartless and mean,
are things always as they seem?
I long for the warmth and for the glow,
But that, of course, you already know.

I love you so dearly I think I could die,
Does it hurt you to see me cry?
A future together is all I could hope.
even without you I know I could cope.

Won't you give us another chance?
Our lives together will be greatly enhanced.
Love me again as you did in the past,
and I guarantee you that this love will last.

Honeysuckle Lane
Harold Werner
The honeysuckles are budding and breaking into bloom
spreading their rare and delightful perfume
for spring has come again into honeysuckle lane
above the moon shines bright
and the prayers seem not so in vain
thought I sit alone tonight
you haunt honeysuckle lane
your shadow comes slowly down the trail
you stop and lean on the old bridge rail
your frail hand holds tight the cane
dear girl, your last walk in honeysuckle lane
we sat that day where I sit tonight
loving our life so plain
never dreaming a world so bright
could bring sorrow to honeysuckle lane

Passing Seasons
Donna Quellette
Her promise to stay forever drifted away with time.
You watch her walk away, never turning to look into
your eyes to see the hurt.
The summers and winters passed with haste.

The seasons are passing you by
still you wait for her return
Knowing that day will never come.

Spring is here now, quietly the snow melts.
Can you hear it dripping off the roof?
Can you hear the birds sing?
Listen, you can hear the birds sing?
Listen, you can hear the flowers slowly opening?
Do you know that you are a sparkling jewel in the sun?
Did you know I have always loved you?
Can you see the smile on my face?
Don't you know, I love you daddy?

Dedication: The fathers in the world

The Man In The Glass
Nancy Leigh Bryant
When you get what you want in your struggle for life
And the world makes you king for a day.
Just go to the mirror and look at yourself
And see what the man has to say.
It isn't your father, your mother, or wife
Whose judgement upon you must pass.
The one whose opinion counts most in your life
Is the one looking back in the glass.
You must satisfy him far beyond all the rest
For he's with you right up to the end.
And you know that you've passed your most difficult test
If the man in the glass is your friend.
You may be the one who got a good break
Then think you're a wonderful guy.
But the man in the glass says you're only a fake
If you can't look him straight in the eye.
You can fool the whole world as you travel the years.
And get pats on the back as you pass.
But your final reward will be heartache and tears
If you've cheated the man in the glass.

Wanting
Barbara Binder
Why is it, what we have we do not want,
And we want what we do not have.

Can happiness really exist, or is
Happiness only that of wanting.

Wanting possessions, love, contentment and peace.

Is wanting real or a striving of our imagination
That keeps us living.

Striving for the day the wanting will be fulfilled,
And then,

When we want no more, will we be?

An Angel In Disguise
Colleen Ducke
Sweet little baby girl with your eyes so bright.
You came to me to help with your plight.

I was aware of your pain and despair...
I wanted to hold you and tell you I care.
I had no idea of the role you would play...
in changing my world for the better that day.

You came to me so quiet and scared...
Your tired little body so in need of repair.
I was the one you chose to help you that day
You slipped into my heart where forever you'll stay
The story you told through only a doll...
Made me aware of the fact that I had been called

A miracle, a presence, a sign from above...
You gave me the gift of unconditional love.
The gift that you gave took me by surprise...
You sweet baby girl are truly...
An Angel In Disguise.

Old
Nicole Carrell
They have seen many changes
They have done many things
And now they have to stop.
They cannot see anymore changes
Or do anything more.
All they can do is sit and wait.
What are they waiting for?
Death. Silence. Peace.
They have come so far in life.
He was a lawyer, she was a school teacher,
And him, he was a farmer.
Now the lawyer, the teacher, and the farmer
Have no more clients, students, or cross.
All they have are memories.
What has happened to them you ask?
People say it is the worst fate – they are old.
People don't realize something though.
The skin may wrinkle, the hair may grey,
And the eyes may go blind,
But the heart and the soul still shine.

Game of Life
Lavon Prahl
Life is sort of like a ball game
We can't all be winners
We can pitch in and do our best
Sometimes we foul up when put to the test.
Catch what opportunities we can
Until we have run our course
Not always batting 100, and we
Kick a little too, and sometimes show remorse.

The final score if how well
We have played the game,
How many rounds we have gone
And taken our part of the blame
We never strike out but continue to play
And just keep bouncing back until that final day...

Love
Margaret D. Cross
Unseen — though visible to kind eyes
everywhere
Heard in loud happy laughter
and quiet weeping
Felt in a mother's touch
and a lover's strength

Elusive — but held in our arms
with each small child
Remembered when the music plays
a sweet reprise of the past
Know as fragrance from petals
faded but still dear

Light as a breath drawn in surprise
a respite for weary hearts
Constant as the seasons
making their yearly rounds
With frosty leaves and fireflies
designed to delight our minds

Firepond
Bianca Mihalik
Sarah, in flowing cotton frock,
Hostess at bloom,
in Summer's crisp garden
of babbling brook descending
the hub
of the greenhouse room
at Firepond...
In elegance and powdered youth,
intoxicating through eclectic domain,
Native to the blush
and primal splendor
of the perennial artistry
of Maine...
Reminiscent
of the Wolverine
with eyes to stare
in teakwood wonder...
tasting, seeing,
the vast significance
of Being

Old And Lonely
Wanda P. Christison
Here I set in my lonely room,
Listening to the cold wind blow,
When I awake to the morning
light, I will likely be looking at snow.
Its winter now, not much
sunlight, mostly just cloudy and
cold, soon spring will come and so
will the sun, to warm these weary old bones.
I wait for the day I can sit
outside, watching the birds build
a home, enjoying their songs, along
with the sun, content, as the days drift along.
With all God's creatures, so busy
with life, I no longer will feel so
alone.

Tympanic Thunder
Edwin Gibson
Rolling cadence in the sky.
Stroboscopic lightning,
Soothing sounds of rain,
Patter of drops
On leaves and roof.
Sweet trill of birds
After the storm.
Tempo of crickets.
Time to think.

"The future we dream,
The past we rue;
The world is old
Yet ever new.
What is — has been,
Will be again.
Cycle in cycle
Forever more,
What is now
Was before."

God's Gift
Gladys Collins
The beautiful Christmas tree a reminder each year
The sacrifices of Jesus and why he is was here.

The star his crown that adorns the sky.
The glitter his halo no one can deny.

The white gentle dove for one as pure.
The sparkle of purple for the robe he wore.

The deep red garland for blood he shed.
Brown of the bark for sandals he tread.

The tree that wears all of these things...
whispers peace on each that he alone brings.

We worship the tree OH! NO! Never no.
It's only a gift on Christ we bestow.

Please accept dear Jesus this day, your birth.
We abide in glory of your humble mirth.

At The End Of The Day
Bess T. Hinchcliffe

Isn't it sad at the end of the day
To look up to heaven and sadly say
Dear Lord I hurt someone today
I made someone's heart a little bit weary
Someone's eyes a little bit teary
Instead of a smile I gave them a frown
Turning their lives upside down

Isn't it nice at the end of the day
To look up to heaven and gladly say
Dear Lord I helped someone today
I made someone's heart a little bit lighter
Someone's eyes a little bit brighter
Instead of a frown I gave them a smile
Making their lives more worthwhile

The Man In The Moon...
Cherylle Burton

Made Love to the
Man in the Moon
The pale iridescent view
Nature's orgasmic splendor
Peering into the radiant
hue of the Moon
I felt it through and through
A Silent Seduction that
filled the very depth of my Soul
Transcended by the suns
reflection glow; So eloquently
designed...Casting Shadows
upon the darkness of night.
I am enveloped apart
the essence of its Spontaneous beauty.
Such Wonder and delight!...
Awed beneath the moon's light
The little things in Life...

Dedication: My mother, whom I love ...

The Inventory
Linda A. Freeman

We walk from room to room, not knowing where to start
How do you inventory what's left of a broken heart?
Well I'll take that and you'll take this
A towel marked hers, and one marked his
The pots, the pans, the silverware, well how do we decide?
The glasses that collected dust, one was groom, the other bride
The furniture that took so long for us to agree upon
The Lamps, the plants, the pictures, of memories that are gone
The chair there by the window, where I used to watch the storms
With lightning flashing in the sky
On nights that were much too warm
And there the bed where we made love, and sometime we would fight
It really doesn't matter who was wrong, or who was right
All the words are said, no tears are left to cry
Just kiss me once before I go,
And say your last good—bye
So you go your way, and I go mine,
The start of a brand new story
When all is said and done
We finished our inventory.

Wonder
Tiffany Haren

As I watch the waves crashing into the shore
The wind suddenly whips up my hair.
The sun's brightness reflects off the glimmering water
Making it transpire into something special.
Even though I am in reaching distance
I can still taste the salt,
Feel it burn on my body,
And smell the freshness of it.
In the distance two sea gulls, probably mates
Are playing in a cat and mouse chase.
And slowly when my eyes drift back to the endless water
I wonder what it would be like
To feel the strength of it,
Be the beauty of it,
Yet, show the peacefulness of it.

Lonely Can't You Tell
Thomas Smihula

I'm so very lonely you can tell,
I'm like the penny who never made the wishing well.

At times I wonder if I should go on,
because all I hear is pro and con.

Yesterday I was a tree,
today I'm just the deep blue sea.

I walk a road not knowing where,
its time to think do I really care.

Sometimes I wish upon the earth,
the rest of the time I'm in the turf.

I've been stepped on I know not why,
and inside myself I begin to cry.

Now tell me why if you understand,
I walk alone in this lonely land.

Hope And Sadness
Sarah DanKenbring

In my life of sadness
I try to break away
but no matter how hard I try
I can't seem to break away.
Nobody understands
Nobody cares
I feel their looks
I feel their glares.
I'm scared of people
I'm scared of school
I'm tired of trying to keep my
image, who am I trying to fool?
Sadness controls me
I have one true friend
each day I wonder if
tomorrow's really the end.
I'm tired of trying and I
can't seem to cope
but one word keeps me going
and that one word is hope.

201

Do You
Shawna Rhynard

Do you wonder when life will treat you well?
Do you wonder if it will always hurt;
Even after returning to the dirt?
Do you wonder about heaven or hell;
What will become of your mortal shell?

Do you believe love is always well;
Or sometimes leads you straight to hell?
Do you believe the world is calm;
Or ready to drop the bomb?

Do you believe you are tied;
To Jesus who died?
Do you believe he died for our sins;
So we ourselves might make amends?

The Sea Shore
Frances Helmold

We went to the sea shore long ago,
many times in the days of my youth,
The scene is etched in my mind, and so
I recall as a moment of truth.
Wave after high wave comes frothing ashore,
bare feet planted in the warm sea
feel the west sand slipping away ever more
in an endless rush to be free.
With each returning wave comes Neptune's gift
to compensate for the loss of the sand,
of seaweed, shells, driftwood to lift
high and dry on the everlasting land.
If I were to go back this very day,
since that time, it has been fifty years,
I would still hear happy voices at play, laughter echoing in my deafened
    ears.
It looks, smells the same in its broad expanse,
like unrequited love it will remain,
each wave pulling sand in its wild dance,
only to deposit its gift once again.

Where Did Love Go
Georgia Richard

Where did my love go?
The one I needed so.
Did it fade because of the silver in my hair?
And the youthfulness is no longer there
And the lines and wrinkles that have increased?
Brought about the reason your love ceased?
Has the slowness in my step caused you to look around?
And could it be that my voice doesn't sound
As it once did when it attracted your attention
That has brought about this indifference and tension
All of these things maybe true
But I did not stop loving you.
My heart is the same, maybe a bit tired
To bring back what we once had, I've really tried
But it seems to make things worse than they are
And I sometimes wish I was away and so far
That maybe you'd think and long to see
Someone who loves you and remember me
But I suppose this happens to some who grow old
And yet love gets sweeter for some I'm told.

Days And Dreams Gone By
Jenifer Harrison

Strange, sorting through her belongings,
Deciding what to do with another's treasures
Now they are no longer needed.
A little blue bow, bright with expectancy.
What memories did it bring to her
Of happenings long past?
A golden fifty on its yellow ribbon
A silver twenty five on its silver bell
A porcelain cherub holding a golden ring
Where the white dove perches with
Outspread wing.
Such treasures, from days and dreams
Gone by, fill the tiny plastic box
With its blue opaque lid.
What shall I do with another's treasures?

You, My Daughter
Patricia Stair–Hensley

You spoke to me before you were conceived and
You opened the Mother's Heart in me.
When you were born, You fired the heart of my being
And the sunlight in my life.
As you grew from infant to woman,
You brought the knowledge of pure Love to me
By the lifting of your infant hands to my cheek,
By the Vision of love's light in your eyes
And the enfolding of my self into your child arms.
You have held me thus in reality and in my thought
Through the days and nights of life's time and eternity.
You and I, together, have born a Love for each other
That can be known only in the heart of
You my daughter and me, your mother.
I love you –my forever child– without limit.
Thank you for Teaching me what pure Love is.
Thank you for becoming the Woman you have chosen to be
While remaining my child in the heart of me.

Dedication: Dawn Vanessa and Tahnee Denee

Nostalgia
Bernadette Tovar

A memory is a gnawing feeling inside,
a sense of remoteness,
a yearning for what is gone.

A memory is the breeze running through your hair,
a soft whisper sprinkling on your face,
a curious tinkle of small bells.

A memory is a mirage in the horizon,
a translucent prism,
an effervescent bubble.

A memory is a scrapbook of cut–out newspapers,
of yellowing photographs,
of impromptu sketches.

A memory is a moment captured,
but forever gone.

Dedication: Mom, Dad, Tere, and Toby

The Final Silence
Philip Michael Jenkinson
I am the final existence, the last thing on earth,
Man made me in his image, man made me to serve.
Computers he built to control his destruction,
The end of his world at the push of a button.
Man made himself God so divine in his power,
But ended it all in a nuclear shower.
So crazed was man in his obsession to rule,
Not man the inventor but man the fool, who took
On himself the decision to die,
Who destroyed all his cities and blackened
The sky.
I am the final existence, but I shall soon be no more
My circuits are dying I fall to the floor.
Now nothing is left, no last sound in my absence,
Nothing is left, but the final silence.

I...Us
Nicole M. Blair
When I am alone, thoughts of you keep me company...
But now my thoughts are not merely reminders of happy times as
Friends—
They are secret yearnings borne of the emptiness, the distant
places between us.
I see things differently now...the love I thought I could do
Without, the care I convinced myself was unnecessary to be happy—
I now find make a difference I never understood before.
This, all a way of admitting the self—deception I never realized
until now.
Before, I never could admit I needed anyone as much as I need
You—
Now that I've found you, I so urgently long for the time when we
Can be together again.
Does this mean that I am not what I used to believe I was—
Strong, independent, happy in my own right?
Or does love, while inspiring me to be open, reveal another part
of me?
Love childlike and honest allows me to admit the simple truth...
I need to be Us.

Albuquerque
Angel Flores
The moment that I saw her, I knew she was for me.
The beauty she possesses, it's so plain to see,
When I get around her I'm as happy as can be,
She's the beautiful Albuquerque.

Among the scenic mountains, that seems to touch the sky,
When that sky is cloudy, there's a teardrop in my eye,
The weather doesn't matter, she's as lovely as can be,
She's the beautiful Albuquerque.

There's Old Town, Cliff's Amusement Park,
You can dine on a mountain top.
You can drive right on route 66.
There's art work, Indian culture and natural history,
She's the beautiful Albuquerque.

If you're there in October, you will see her at her best,
Come over and join her, at the International Balloon Fest.
So if you like the sunset, fresh air and scenery,
Visit the enchantment of Albuquerque.

Our Private Hell
Verlin H. Stevens
Come, my friend said to me
and we together will top this hill,
for on the other side he promises
are greener grasses still
and to myself I think, Oh, you are such a pill!
But still I go, and why I do not know
for there is no way out
and this I do not doubt.
We put forth our hand
and quit the life of an unknown man
his money we take and then we run
but never from this deed that's done.
No one comes to go our bail
for like all others...
We've made our private hell.

Nature Answers
Petronella Dowell
I stroll through a field full of clovers
A green valley beyond me I see
A day dream of future tomorrows
What will they turn out to be
I enter the valley of colors
Green, Yellow, Gold, Crimson, clear Blues
The water running beside me
In this babbling brook I see clues
I think of that brand new tomorrow
I rejoice in the love for today
While tossing pebbles in the brook
The clear water turns echoing waves
The waves hitting one to another
The reflection of self disappears
A cool breeze wisps across my face
The thoughts and the feelings are clear
We live on for one another
We give of ourselves day by day
With lessons of love and guidance above
We'll all surely find our own way

Granny And The Whippoorwill
Charles R. Harper
The whippoorwill calling
Midnight falling,
Granny called me to her room,
The window open
A summer breeze
So rare; so soon,
Her eyes full of love.
She whispers in my ear
Take time my young grandson,
To hear
The whippoorwill,
There in the silence of the June night,
I sat with my Granny
Just for a while,
Many years have passed
I remember her still
Every time I hear,
The call; of a whippoorwill.
Dedication: Granny Jordan, stern but loving

Love
Mary Honomichl

Love is a gift
Sent down from heaven.
Love is cherished
by those who have it.
Love is shared
by many people.
Love is wanted
by those who are alone.
Love is needed
by those who are neglected.
Why is love
the way it is?
Love it the way it is
because love is powerful
and love keeps growing.

This Is Not My Home
Tonyah Thompson

What is happening?
I don't understand.
We used to be free.
Smiles were on the faces of our women,
Children ran free in the sunshine,
Men were free to be men.
We bravely hunted buffalo and brought food to our families,
were proud of the care we supplied.
Now we are led to this place.
This is not my home.
Who gave these people the right to tell my people we are no longer free,
to tread upon ground that has always been our home?
How can they make me live here?
This is not my home.
I cannot care for my people this way.
What will happen to them?
They are not getting enough to eat here.
It is because of this, that I had to steal away to hunt.
And now they lock me up,
Don't they understand, that I, too, am a man?

Jailbreak
Rachel Amanda Reis

We are all just prisoners here,
Stuck in tiny cells,
And set behind the bars of life.
We are our own Jailers.
Our employers are our Wardens.
There are no keys,
To the locks on our cell doors.
Bread and water are our Attorneys,
And law has no justice.
We did not get our trial by jury.
We did not see the judge.
We do not get time off for good behavior.
We will not be paroled.
Life is the Death Penalty,
And living is our crime.
There is no escape from the prison
Of this planet Earth.
There is no escape.
THERE IS NO ESCAPE.
No jailbreak.

Second To None
Heath Shawn

You were my second to none,
The one I counted on.

At any give time, right by my side.
No mountain too high, no river too wide

Any obstacle I would try, to keep
You by my side.

Your spirit keeps me high,
Your words tell no lies

With you I feel pride...

A reason to be alive...

Cardboard Boxes
Markanne T. Rouse

I saw a baby Robin bird today
that had been pushed out of a tree
living in a cardboard liqueur box.
Cold Turkey's not for me.
I wished the little birdie "good luck."
I hoped the little birdie wished the same to me
I took the empty sturdy boxes
that held that evil brew.
I knew it was true
that even the birds are resorting to
living in cardboard boxes, too.
A box – A castle
in the hood – in the woods
it matters not where we plant our roots
as long as it grows into a shade tree!
Fore, the next little bird —
who — has been pushed out of the tree
in the hood — in the woods
fore, we all end up hood ornaments
in someone else's hood in the woods!

Dear Lord I pray
Leeann Perkins

Dear Lord I pray
I love you more each day

No matter what the task
You're there when I should ask

If ever I turn away
I will find you again some day

You are always there for me
How can I help but worship Thee

Your son came from above
His message filled with love

All you ask from us all
Is to simply believe His call

How wonderful a lesson
Our reward will be great in Heaven

Our World
Athena McKay
Crime is rising, education is declining. Oceans full of oil,
air full of pollution. Fists are clinched, hearts are broken,
and heads filled with hate. It's not too late, but our world
is dying. Tears run down a mother's face as she holds her only
son in her arms dead, without a trace, of the one who could
burn down a church or set off a bomb. All of this in a place
that we call home. Our world is dying. We see it on the news
and read it in the paper. Violence and Ignorance are the
problems, but what is the solution? How long do we have before
it is too late? Do we even care that our world is dying? People
are being senselessly killed day in and day out. The age of
mothers is getting younger, graduation rate going under. People
are loaded with fear and eyes full of tears. It's a shame how
people can love to hate one another, and that is why...
OUR WORLD IS DYING!!!

Our Love
Shelley Rogers
Our first glance I will never forget, the look in you eyes was so intense
February 14th came and there was your name on my calendar in hearts
You found out and our romance starts
Our date to the movies, Our trip to the mall
You took my hand and stood tall
You didn't want to lose me you call
The days we spent together were so much fun
Then the time had come March 19th Our wedding day,
I was so happy I would have to say
The love we share
The way we care
We've had good times and bad
We've been happy and sad
We've both been hurt
But our love we could not desert
The message was sent
That we were meant
To be Together Forever
Our loves so strong
WE BELONG!

Burning Memory
Garland Moore
A beautiful smile flashed across my
memory,

Belonging to a very sweet woman who
meant so much to me,

The smile awaken a flame in my heart
that has burned for her love since the very start.

Over the months while she was lost to me,
the flame grew small but burned with intensive heat.

Now that she's close the flame has rise into a fire,

My heart burns for her love and melts with desire.

Every part of my soul screams out her name
every part of my heart is engulfed in flame.

Dedication: Donna and loving daughter, Santanna

Mother
Jennifer Milstein
The one that makes me
better when I am feeling sick.
The one that's always
there for me when I feel like
ick. The one that's gonna be my
friend for the rest of my
life. The one that married
my dad and they became
husband and wife.

I would like to tell you
more but there's nothing else
to say, Except my mom is my
best friend and I can tell you
that any day!

Fragile Handle With Care
Sherry L. Rutter
Angels from heaven,
children are born.
Blessed and tender,
never to scorn.
Tears on a pillow,
milk spilled again.
Momma cries helpless,
too young still, sweet one.
Daddy could help but,
he's walked out the door.
Baby Blues, is that what
you call it?
Social disposition lost,
in society's storm.
God bless the children, no
age restrictions endowed.
Just keep them protected.
No Violence Allowed!
Remember the little Angels...
Fragile Handle With Care.

Untitled
Anthony M. Kalota
Oh God! it's a hard road we walk.
Times of fear we really need to talk.
Changing minds and fulfilling life.
It's an uphill climb with strife.
We battle, we struggle and we fight.
Then look to others, then ourselves to find what's right.
Through the pain, the confusion, growth we find.
With the work, comes an empathetic change of mind.
We'll see our world as it be.
Then we can accept and pay the fee.
We sacrifice old lives for new.
For true happiness there's nothing else to do.
Being content with the ills of our ways.
Only keeps you and people at bay.
Relationships are of humanity.
Becoming fulfilled, becoming real is reality.
Chip away at your fantasy day.
Then build your love and life with new clay.
Work and work and work to grow.
Remember what's negative is your foe.

I Will
Theresa L. Cofarella

how do I survive
in a life of fear
all I feel are the tears
coming down on my face
someone put me in my place
where I'm supposed to be
so everyone will see, the real me
because I don't wanna change
like me for me and who I am
there's nothing else to explain
just help me be sane
for nothing can stay the same
a world of thanks I'd give 2 you
some day this will come true
this will be what I will do.

My Favorite Place
Juanita Kay Morgan

My favorite place is a place that
I dream of often.

A place that is quiet, with a
breeze that is as soft and fresh
as a baby's breath.

There is a waterfall in this
place that is forever spilling into a
cool and clear shimmering pool.

The fragrance that is in the air is
indescribably wonderful,...it is so
pure that it gives you the feeling
of being an innocent child.

My favorite place is a perfect
place to be,...I only wish that
it existed in reality instead of my
dreams.

Urgings
Kathryn J. Davis

Gray fingers caress
And probe into tender
Hidden shoals as early
Morning fog lingers
Unwilling to leave
The night tide's sweet
Rhythmic callings
Laden with promises of
Feasting, twining of souls
And an everlasting pleasure
Wrapped in her limped
Kelp hair. When mist and spray
Mingle, coldhearted boulders
With their imperfections
Inflict mortal wounds
Heard in the crying of
The attendant gulls—
While the unrelenting sea
Absorbs all love offerings
And awaits tomorrow.

Life's Lonely Road
Mildred Smith

We are only passing through this world,
We haven't long to stay.
We must be careful of the things we do —
And the things we say.

I know I've failed to see the flowers
God has made for my delight.
I've squandered many precious hours
Turning wrong instead of right.

Remember a word of love, a kindly smile
Will help someone you walk beside
Carry his heavy load
As he travels down each weary mile
Upon life's lonely road.

Untitled
Heather Trimble

Tonight I walked through a wilderness of snow.
All was silent except for the crunching sounds
Under my big, black feet and the constant
Pounding of thoughts in my head.
I stopped.
Stood in the center of a road.
Snow fell and met with tears sliding down my numb face.
I whispered, "I love you. I do."
And bit my lower lip to keep from screaming and to
Contain a torrent of tears that would have washed
Away that white stuff at my feet.
Soon my hair became ice and I started walking again.
In circles.
I pictured us roaming among the hills, arm in arm,
Laughing as the snowflakes hit our eyes;
Cleansing them of their impurities.
Before I turned to enter my house
I looked back and said goodbye
To the snow
To you.

The Stockmarket
G. Milton Luttrell

Who can pull the Dalai's Lama
and soar up high on wings of gold?
Wall Street is no guarantee.
The bull runs wild, bloods run hot.
What one knows, a panacea?
The bear shows up, bloods run cold.
The Fed has raised the interest rates,
stocks go down, some hold on, but some are sold.
Some ride the tide on debenture, others
anticipate their next adventure.
Some folks jumped when the market fell
from second stories, others held then
recovered and survived to tell of other glories.
One should look for better days.
Prices catch all, catches catch can.
Wings doth jump for today's cadaver.
Mainstreet market's gibberish done.
Can two walk in paths undone?
Life and law leave much unwon.
This planet turns before the sun.

What Lies Within
Estevan Vela
If eyes are the gateway to a person's soul
Then what's most beautiful to me
Is peeling back the layers of superficiality
To reveal what's underneath

When I think about what's in our brain
I wonder how intricate a master painter was to design
All of the wonders of the world
And create the myriad of schema
that's in our mind

When you look into a person's heart
What do you know?
It's either darker than the darkest night,
Or pristine as waters off the glacial snow

Our Special Child
Mary Lee Powers
There was a little boy in our house
Who was different from the rest.
He could not talk so well
Nor run around with zest
He learned to do a puzzle,
A crayon he could hold;
Take off his shoes and sweater,
His paper he could fold.
Once he got to know you
He'd creep into your heart.
He'd give himself completely
If he trusted you from the start.
He made us very happy
And made us understand
That he, as all the rest of us,
Need a friendly, guiding hand.
Sometimes he was quite determined
And sometimes passive, mild,
Vulnerable and defenseless.
He was our small retarded child.

Desert Sand
Robert Labescat
The city spills over with the tears of winter;
Dense mist covers the moor;
In the distance the desert screams,
Desert of love in a country of plains.

The sandy wind obscure his vision
Or is it the crimson spot that overflows?
Useless misery covered with medals,
Are we a toy for demented monarchs?

In our world what are two pebbles of sand
Howling in the desert and speaking laser?
The wind rolls and then disperses them,
Puts them back in their place in the universe of time.

O time that hurls men into hate,
That gives them life and doles out death,
Give them the wisdom to wait,
To search, to understand
That the dunes of sand have greater powers than these birds of fire.

My Little Pro
Debbie J. Warren
She tries real hard
Not as good as the rest
But follows her guard
And does her best
"Catch the ball y'all"
the coach said with plea
They all tried And she caught it...With glee!
She's not very tall, At least not yet
But she's mine, all mine
And soon she'll get taller, I bet!
All that matters to me, is
She's my Little Pro,
My cup–o–tea of whom I'll never let go!
Dedication: "The miracle of life", thanks God!

Untitled
Heather Pitts
Emptiness is in my heart.
Someone's missing,
It feels as though I'll fall apart.
In my mind,
I can still hear your voice,
I can still see your face.
Why does it seem I was blind sometimes?
I never knew it would hurt this bad, or
When I found out you were gone,
That I'd be so sad.
I thought I could be strong,
I thought I could handle it,
But the emptiness was just too great,
For my heart to bear all alone.
It'll be a long wait, till I ever forget
Your smiling face or your sparkling blue eyes.
I love you so much, that I can't say goodbye.
You belong to that special place,
In my heart, and in my eyes.
I'll never forget you and our wonderful times.

Family
Jennifer Miller
I remember the old days out at Grandpa's cabin.
When every summer day something interesting would happen.

Grandpa and I would go to the lake to fish.
And each time I would make a simple wish.

I'd wish that all of us could be together,
today, tomorrow, forever, and ever.

Mother could crochet her doilies like lace.
Everyone could enjoy life at a slow pace.

But I realized it was a just paradise dreamed.
Winter lasted forever it seemed.

What I didn't realize is in the summer we could play all day.
But why not enjoy winter, and take a ride in the family sleigh?

The seasons are great anytime of the year,
but it's family and friends that make life so dear.

The Tall Ships
J. J. Jones

Oh, how your sails whisper of glory,
if only the men in your life,
would really relate the story.

How far would you have gone,
if the Captain was not there,
to lead you along.

Maybe to Brussels, maybe to Spain,
down with the sails men,
we've ported again.

Yet another stop, in another time,
to expose your finery,
a proud sailor could only see.

What Matters?
Arne H. Hansen, Jr.

What matters that hundreds of millions
of years ago— no humans
Walked on the Planet Earth.
What mattered at that time
Was decided by Dinosaurs
Of every size and shape.
What matters, that 65 million years ago,
Dinosaurs became extinct—
Wiped out by a Comet,
But "Lo", a lowly mammal survived
And as a consequence
Men, women, and children
Are in every nook and cranny
Of the Planet Earth.
What matters at this time
Is decided by the "Super–rich",
The 10% of the population
That owns 91% of the wealth
Of the Planet Earth—
Is this really "What Matters?".

Respect
Carla Landes

Respect was grand when I was young
Your elders, your teachers, almost everyone

Respect was granted without second thought
Only when trust was broken was respect lost

Now it is perceived, to receive, respect needs earned
How sad for our elders for respect they do yearn

Yes ma'am and no ma'am are rare nowadays
As times have changed for the children we raise

In my youth there were consequences for disrespect
The spankings and groundings were meant to correct

But now the consequences of disrespect are society's big disgrace
The youth of our nation are rampant with violence, gangs, and hate

We look around at lack of respect and say "what a shame"
All we have to do is look in the mirror and see who's to blame

Jason
Melissa Sutherland

He was said to be the one to let us all have our fun
But we all came crashing down by the time the snow turned brown
He did not deserve to die We did not deserve to cry
Sacred, blessed, and holy he was and this all happened just because
All the lights they were too bright on that dark and hated night
He must have been the chosen one to have God end all his fun
The boy in the car is one we knew and now he was crying too
We all felt so bad for him and we all were so mad at him
For he had hit our dear friend and everyone should know the rest
He was so kind and nice to see that everyone loved him endlessly
It's not hard for me to say that in our hearts he'll always stay
By our side he'll always be and I hope everyone can see
For even on that fateful day Jason did not go away

Dedication: The memory of Jason Kaemick

A Dark Night
Robert S. Harvey

On this dark night and in this strange place
We have shared a compressed lifetime of
Emotion and passion, learning and confessing only
For these few hours—these few short/long hours.
Now you sleep soundly and vulnerably beside me.
And I know that I will soon leave you forever.

Passion, like pain, is never truly recalled
But on some dark lonely night I will remember
Your laughter and your hidden sadness. I will
Remember the ocean/woman smell of you and the
Taste of your skin and your lips. Most vividly
I will remember your need to be held.

On some future lonely dark night all that we shared
And felt will become more alive and vital. You will
Be more beautiful and vulnerable. You laughter more
Lilting and your sadness more touching. In that moment
I will realize that holding you so closely had
Filled an aching emptiness in each of us.

Our Flag
Nancy Everett

Our flag is a symbol of freedom waving over each sea
It is there to remind us that by God's grace we are free.

The red strips remind us of the blood that was lost
By those fighting for our freedom at any cost,

The white stands for purity of a new nation under God,
A land where no earthly king could trod.

The blue stands for the bruises taken by others for us to view
For without the scars of many, we would be so few.

The stars remind us to look to the sky.
For with God in heaven our true victories lie.

When we look on the flag waving against the bluest of skies,
I fear we forget why our grand old flag flies.

She was designed so we could recall,
"One nation under God, with liberty, and justice for all."

The Sun
Diego Rail
If the sun shone at night
Would the night be dead?
Would the stars die,
Or would they hide themselves from our eyes?
Would it still be night,
Would the moon come out,
Casting a glare on the water?
When would bats fly,
And when would stars fall,
And to where?
We would lose the sunset,
We would lose the dusk.
The twilight
And the silent unforgiving darkness,
If the sun shone at night.

As Joy Melts Away
Amanda Carroll
A shimmering pink,
A glowing purple,
A calming blue
The sun,
a glowing orb, still shining
as it melts beneath the waves.
The sea is calm, silent, still.
Then suddenly, a crash sounds, like
a waking storm!
The humpback breeches, water cascading
about him like a sea of diamonds.
And for one, brief moment, the world is sane.
For one brief moment, the world is peaceful
and serene.
Then it goes, and
the stillness hangs in the air.
The world is empty again.
Empty.

Dedication: For Katy and A.K....because

Light Of The Dawn
James Dimare
I've been waiting all night for the dark to reveal the dawn
Trying with all my might to deal with the fact that you're gone
The heartache, the tears, the taste of the salt
Are there to remind me just who is at fault
Though I can't remember just how to be strong
Here in the light of the dawn

I can still see your face in a world that surrounds me
Where I'm caught in a place of illusions and could be's
The thunder, the lightning, the claps and the flash
They echo and shadow like ghosts from the past
Some memories are faded while others live on
Here in the light of the dawn

I could sit here forever and wait for your return
But I know you'll come back when hell no longer burns
The laughter, the smiles, the look on your face
Are all things I've lost and can never replace
Though right here in my arms is where you belong
Here in the light of the dawn

The Journey
Georgina Jacobs
It's not where you're going
Or what you might find
At the end of the road
Or the day.
It's the journey that counts
The path that you choose
The living you do on the way.
Each step is the journey
Each word is a path
It's not what you might do
But how.
Tomorrow may not be
What you'd like it to be,
The journey that counts
Is the now.

Children Be Obedient
Laura Armstrong
Children be obedient, even when life seems unfair
Children be obedient, God loves you and He cares.
He sees your every problem, He knows your every need.
Children learn to be obedient and stay on bending knees.
God gave you your parents to guide you through the
years. Yes, sometimes there will be problems and some
times there will be tears!

Your parents know what's best for you they've been that
road you see? Children obey your parents! by doing so
you show Honor To Thee.

Children obey your parents, don't rush to grow up —be
a child. Enjoy life while you can because with every stage of
life comes responsibility at hand!

Children obey your parents in all you say and do.
Children obey your parents a long life is Promised to you!

Dedication: Felicia, Annazette, Deanna and Art

Flying Saucers
K. L. Sobrero
Just alone in a room,
So lit, to barely cast a shadow.
Eyes take on a mind of their own.
Taking care to make one's body,
to follow suit, lay themselves
upon every view.
Softness like no other could compare.
Likens to only a sour mash
Whiskey stare, or is it just a
sentimentalist journey?
Waiting to climb on board
As the train leaves,
this kitchen en route,
to the kitchen I once befored.
Stood mother and her mother and
her mother before.
Its cabinets hold treasures
of cups and saucers so handed
down, it means much more to me
than photo albums all stacked and stored.

What A Beautiful Life It Is
Denise Brown
What a beautiful life it is.
To smell the flowers to see
the green grass and blue sky.
To awaken to a new day some
What different than yesterday.
Life is like a merry go round
never knowing what tomorrow brings.

We have so much to do
and see, can we do it all
in one life time? We don't
have to be rich or poor to
enjoy life to it's fullest. Reach
out and grab what life has
to offer. What a beautiful life it is.

How Can I Tell You?
Viola V. Hayes
I cannot put in words the things I want to say.
I cannot put in words the way I feel today.
My heart may gay and carefree be
But yet for words to say I have no key.
With sadness my heart may be filled
And yet for words my lips are stilled.

How can I express the way I think and feel?
I have the thoughts but words do not from me steal.
How can I speak what is in my heart today,
When I have the thoughts but have no words to say?
My tongue is tied for want of words to tell
You how I feel. Will silence do as well?

By silence can I rightfully impart
What this day is in my mind and heart?
How can I say just what I mean?
How can I tell you of each dream?
How can I explain each thought and sign?
When words to tell you are not mine.

Passion's Sweet Pain
Debbie Gillotti
It awoke me like thunder
Invading the night
Her touch, enticing my soul
Who was this woman, did I dare to ask
Yet circumstance would not allow

Was there a message unspoken
Being shared between hearts
With a gesture so simple as this

We hold back in fear
of disrupting the calm
Putting all temptations aside

The night fades to day
A moment long past
Yet a lingering presence remains

An image embedded in memory
A joining of passion's sweet pain.

Ode To Adam
Mildred Z. Lawrence
From the first time I felt your arms around me.
I heard you whisper,
Don't get scared, it's only me, dear.
To the second time,
With your whiskers, on my cheek.
I still feel you near.
I don't know what it means,
When you come to me, in my dreams.
Since I'm so relieved,
Maybe you believed,
How much I love you, still.
I hope, the third time, you take me with you.
Every day, without you, is too much to bear.
So, before I get old and gray,
Come take me away.

Spider In The Web
Patricia Anderson
As it spun and weaved its web
So intricately, so divine
Who would think such a small creature
Could weave, plan and intertwine

I watched it carefully as it spun
It let its web out one by one
And then it weaved and wove its nest
It appeared to be at a final rest.

Then I watched and waited
As the enemy came by
It swept it away, as a silent spy
As if it didn't matter how much time was spent...
Weaving and creating its special nest.

Time has gone by and all I see
Is the spider in the web caught carefully
In an invention that it designed
That was destroyed by mankind.

A Child Needs
Flora Flinders
A child is not a pet.
That you feed and then forget.
A child is not perfect like.
We all want them to be.
They all grow up just like you and me.
A child has needs and wishes that sometimes don't come true.
Some of us know because it has happen to us too.
A child might be angry, and have a lot of hate inside.
Do something about it don't wait because of your foolish pride.
A child needs both parents to talk to him, or her.
They need to know that they are loved, that is one thing that is
For sure.
It doesn't matter if you are rich, or poor,
If a child has your love they should not ask for no more.
They need respect like you and I.
And someone beside them when they cry.
They need to be taught manners, and be the best they can be.
After doing all of this maybe they will see.
That we love them and need them very much.
And that we all need a little loving touch.

210

Red Wine
Heather Coble
The glass tips over
staining the carpet,
like blood.
Forever,
like memories.
Maybe the time was wrong.
It almost seemed right
in so many ways,
yet wrong
in so many more.
But which ones
really matter?
Just the ones you think of.
You should have thought
a little longer.

Little Cabin In The Woods
Martha Edwards
There's a little cabin in the mountains of New York State,
Crying out with loneliness because of it's fate...
The wind comes around it with a cry and a moan;
The little cabin cries out, "Please, folk, come on home".
"The lake by me is froze; And I have a cold nose...
I need a fire built within the midst of me,
I'm so unhappy without my fam–i–ly".
"Why did you leave me alone", he sighs, with a groan...
"Is it something I did to make you faraway roam?"
"I'm sorry you left...I felt so bereft;
Did you take all the birds that to me did sing?
Oh, please come back and your violin bring;
I miss all the music you and the birds did make...
Why, oh, why, did me, you decide to forsake?"
The little house cried and the tears rolled down,
Leaving many icicles around his crown.
"Now don't you feel bad that I have no hope,
Because you left me all winter and I sit here and mope?"
But thinking of spring, he knew they'd be back in a while,
And that brought to little cabin's face a great, big smile!

Prayer Rock
Mindy Hobbs
I'm your little prayer rock and this
is what I'll do; Just put me upon your
pillow until the day is through, so when
you turn the covers back and climb into
your bed...Whak...your little prayer rock
will hit you on your head, then you will
Remember as the day is through to kneel and
say your prayers as you wanted to.
When you finish, just dump me on the floor
I'll stay there through the night time
to give you help once more;
When you get up the next morning...
oops, I'll stump your toe so you'll remember
your morning prayers before you go and
start the day, put me back on your
pillow when your bed is made, and the
clever little rock will continue in your
Aid.
Dedication: My loving and cherished man, "Robert Blount"

Angels
Carmon Wells
Angels "oh" Angels it's not all in vain,
You give us the courage to endure all the pain,
We live here on earth, just waiting the day,
When our Heavenly Father will come to us and say,
"This earth that holds heartache, trouble, and strife,
Is only a very small part of your life.

The best part is coming, when you will come home,
Where you and the angels are all part of my throne"
For now they'll be with you, whenever you need,
To know there's a place away from the greed.
They'll listen, they'll hold you,
They'll love you, they'll cry.
And when it's time to come home,
They'll teach you to fly.

Lonely World
Annie B. Arbuckle
As I walk in this lonely world,
I can only walk alone,
I can't stand to see the suffering and
Pain in people faces young and old
So I'll walk alone.

As I walk in this lonely world, seeing
People shifting in and out,
Young and old, from far away places.
Never knowing how far to roam,
Knowing they'll walk alone.

Now I walk in this lonely world.
There's a shadow that walks behind me
One that will never fade away,
One that will take my troubles away
And in my footprints He will stay
In my heart (Jesus) He's always there
With Him in my world,
I'll never walk alone.

My Unspoken Words
Bill Benhardt
For the many chores I take for granted
but done by you most every day.

For the many nights you waited up
and worried in that motherly way.

For the apologies not said
the times I let it slip away.

For all the times you helped me out
these debts that I cannot repay.

For the times that I upset you
but you loved me any way.

For all these things
and all the things I never say.

Thanks Mom. I love you.
Happy Mother's Day.

Why?
Scott Douglas
Tell my why
I stand by
and suffer the
worst there is or could be.
I wonder how
I came to this time now.
For I see,
can it be
death at the
door of me.
As I die
while you stand by
I ask myself, "Why?"

Dedication: To Tinna, and my friends

Sylvia's Smile
Charles K. O'Meara
When I see Sylvia's smile
I see a sun–speckled, radiant rainbow
After a sudden Hilo rain.
Hair of gold
White flashing teeth, lips of rose
Sapphire–sparkle in her eyes.

When this smile is turned on me
My heart turns over
And becomes full–
Time stands still.

Her dazzling smile
In her pink batik dress
On the Pacific ocean terrace
In far–off, mythical Raro
This vision I keep deep
In my heart– always.

Dedication: Sylvia G. O'Meara, my love

U.S. Marine
Lori Dearth–James
For her I will stand tall and proud.
I will hold my head high.
She is in my blood; have no doubt,
I'll fight to my death for that flag in the sky.
To her I am loyal and true
And have dedicated my life.
Every day I will defend that red white and blue
For it holds every ounce of my pride.
I will proudly represent this land.
I will bravely fight for freedom.
Human rights I will defend.
The enemy—I will courageously defeat them.
For her amber waves of grain,
And purple mountains majesty;
Courage and pride I was trained,
And I'll give my life to keep her free.
I believe in my country's heritage
And I will never let her know defeat.
She is the United States of America
And I am her marine.

Reaper's Time
Shannon Thompson
I'll let the reaper tell my vengeance, for I see in my eyes,
your fear.
Executioner and witness, may my journey cease to appear?
Disguised sins, cloaked the black veil abridged my mortality.
With reverence, and trembling, I'm marked with heaven's
siege or a proposed fallacy.
Shield my soul, from the demons sovereign, as I embark upon
flight;
Or shall I dance now, with the wind drawn, by autumn twilight.
Snow blind in agony, I share my infant eyes veneration;
Cleave from a womb, bound by my own creation.
Imposed separation from my known entity, I pray for winter's
retreat.
With an insight openly revealing, time alone, to hold the
reigning judgement seat.

Coming Full Circle
Sue Reinhart
Learning to smile and then to
giggle;
Watching his toes as they wiggle.
Learning to crawl and then to walk,
wishing you could help as he struggles
to talk.
Learning to skate and ride a bike;
teaching him to drive – he's no longer
a tyke.
Learning to choose the right girl
for his wife;
praying he'll be happy for the rest
of his life.
Now HE'S about ready to become a Dad;
jotting down so many notes on a pad,
At last he will truly understand;
all the joy and love a son brings
to a man.

Dedication: My son Ken, with love

Regal Beauty
Tomesa Colwell
In all of her regal beauty she stood
Done in colors of pearl, ribbons streaming down.
I have passed her many times stopping only for a glance
Knowing that I will never sit upon her smooth harness.
Knowing that I alone will never hear the music playing from the speakers.
I think of the horse, dream that she is mine,
Everyone would watch me go around and around and around as my laughter is
    carried off by the wind.
For the time I'm pretty, dressed in such finery.
No rips in my clothes, no holes in my shoes,
My face scrubbed to a glow,
And there is happiness in my every smile.
People would turn to look, not turn away.
I let go of the pole and spread my hands to the sky, I feel so free.
The other horses would be jealous of my beauty.
Jealous that they had to take a ride with empty saddles.
She is my horse and I am her rider.
I look down at the rags that clothe my body, and open a dirty hand
With heartbreak in my eyes I look at the pennies that I clutch.
She is my horse and I am her rider...If only in my dreams.

My Dad
Sheena Watkins
I dreamt all last nights of you
It was so real so true I knew
You lived
Although they said you'd died.

I dreamt of all the fun we had
Laughs we shared
I felt a glow inside
Although you were dead.

I know now you are alive
I cannot see you, but you are beside me
In my heart and soul
My love will carry on for you
like the memories in my head.

Sometimes
Ronald L. Reece
Sometimes, it's hard to find the words
For the things that I want to say:
To describe the flight of the birds,
Or the sunset at the end of the day.

Sometimes, it's harder to show gratitude,
Or say thank you for the things that you do.
Too often I give a bad attitude
And hide the feelings I hold so true.

Sometimes, when life seems so depressing,
And nobody I know seems to care,
I fail to recognize the blessing
For the moments that you're willing to share.

Sometimes, I overlook the opportunity,
And feel that I've committed small crimes:
When I fail to show you the sincerity,
And to thank you always:
Not just, sometimes.

Behavior Impaired
Sheila Boerner
Behavior impaired is the label he wears
Who understands and who really cares?
Certainly not his mom or his dad
Who abandoned him when the going got bad.
They heard society's message:
"If it feels right, its gotta be good,"
Drink and take drugs if you're in the mood
Live for today, don't think of tomorrow
A child is a burden so leave him behind.
Now what chance does he have?
Foster parents, will they adopt?
Fetal alcohol syndrome,
Attention deficit disorder,
What do they mean to the school?
Restructure and accommodate
For what his parents caused and forgot.
Provide an aide, a special work station,
His own schedule and positive rewards.
Special funds and caring personnel,
But what happens as he goes on through life?

Hugging
Mary Jacobsen
"Hearts at one" is that sacred something lost
behind walls we build to keep ourselves ensnared
within perimeters of misconception.

Who dares teach who dares not hug a distraught
child suffering from shock or pain? Hugging
is mother Earth, enveloping humanity:
father, mother, sister, brother.
Not to understand its goodness, or be shy
of its spontaneity, is to deprive
or be deprived of that magical essence,
integrity, given into safe hands by our Lord.

Not to caress, but express and transmit
the ability to comfort, soothe and heal.

Who's In Charge
Ted Dickerson
As sunlight fades and shadows creep
Across the forest dark and deep.
Night sounds, sharp as tinkling bell
Chime through forest, mount and dell.
When mortal tires of daytime chores
And rests through slumber, dreams and snores.
Night creatures capture habitat
Where, erstwhile, man sublimely sat.
Thinking he were king of all
But needing rest, in sleep doth fall.
Yielding world to other realm
Where someone else is at the helm.
He passes night without a clue
To what God's other creatures do.
His arrogance makes heaven smile
Because he thinks that all the while
He is in charge of what surrounds
Ere he, in pride, wears maker's crowns.
He is but cog in wheel so grand
That turns without his puny hand.

Friendship
Saturnino Noriega
Tell me, exactly when
winter turns to spring.
Or, precisely where
a bell ends its ring
Pinpoint the very spot
rain starts in a cloud
Or, where a sound is softest
or most completely loud.
You can't for they occur
with very subtle blends.
Quite like discovering
we've become friends.
It may take a million years
or the slightest glance.
Matters to it not
time or circumstance.
It can come heavy as stone
or as light as a feather
One day it's just there,
like the weather.

Celtic Dawn
Lee Jobson
Crescendos of colour,
Adorn Celtic hills,
Powerfully silent,
Yet, beautifully still.
Except for the song of a bird in the trees,
Or the gentle hush of a cool summer breeze,
Memories of winter,
Fade like the night,
The sun arises flexing its might,
Flaming gold orb burns azure skies,
Colours the day amidst waking sighs,
Mystical shades of violent pinks,
Chase the moon as if wounded it sinks,
Beyond the ocean the moon slips away,
The Celtic Dawn greets the virginal day.

Rain
Timothy Nelson
And as I sit and watch the rain
Falling to the ground
I realize nothing is the same
A new begging is abound
What lurks beyond the horizon?
Mysteries left untold
Feelings that one would impression
Are now, not so bold
Left to personal revelation
What I would deem impotent
Now, aids in my creation
Bringing forth what is imminent
Carried away by a thousand voices
Enchanted by their call
Traveling back to their sources
Their faces demonical
But alas, They are salvation
Eternal guidance
Releasing me into temptation
With nothing left but admiration.

Not Lost
Joan McCraw
My love for you didn't last, that didn't make it wrong,
I felt each day I loved you more,
so why was it less strong
Why must we pledge to live each day involved in only us,
when every day that we did spend,
we cherish, held in trust.
Of course we're more than passing ships,
and that will always be
We learned to tell when love is love,
without changing you or changing me.
Lover, what I felt for you no one else will feel,
Promises I made to you will never be less real.
Maybe years of what we had could sometime be a bore,
but tiny things remembered now still make my senses soar.
No one gives a guarantee
to live for you or live for me.
So as the clouds of time roll by,
please, keep me there in your mind's eye,
When years like coins have all been tossed,
I'll know you're gone, but you're not lost.

Automaton
Patricia Garrigan
A hidden key turning, into the body of time,
Arms and eyes flailing, windmills of design,
Are they pointing straight at me?
Hidden key, winding, winding ferociously.

Twisting and turning, a bee in the bonnet of time,
Set on a course of destruction, uncertain,
No method, is it madness they sign?
Mechanically structured, but alas, given a mind.

What enemy of justice created such a being,
A thing of such corruption, no one can control.
Defying all, it rattles on a path of no direction,
Lost to all but providence, no vision, no grace,
Nothing but awkward derision, a hidden key turning.

My Mask
Bradley Carlock
My love has left
And gone away
Ne'er to return
Here to stay.
I loved her so
With all my heart
And hoped that we
Would never part.
Time has gone;
Love has passed.
I reach and pull
Down my mask
Of happiness
And gleeful joy
To hide the pain
And keep my poise.
For if I don't,
Someone might see
The hurt that's deep
Inside of me.

Look Into The Body
Adam Shepherd
The doctor is reading the patient's thoughts as she starts
to pick at his brain to know what he's thinking.
She takes the brain out of his skull; as she takes it apart
and puts it together like a model car just to see how it works.

He sees the doctor's long lanky legs that are beautiful,
along with her knees, ligaments, bones and joints.
The sight of her legs keeps him distracted from the experiment.

There was a woman who snatched a guy's heart out when she
puts her hand through his chest as she takes his heart out
and eats it like a raw piece of meat.

He looks into those beautiful brown eyes as he can see the
cornea, lens, pupils, and the rest of the eye socket.
He recommends that she need glasses due to her bad eyesight.

The organs inside the body are graphic and amazing.
Look into the body for more than just the appearance.
Look into the body parts to know what makes it tick–tock.

The Blackbird's Song
Michael S. Orchard

On Summer evenings, it can always be heard;
The sweet relaxing song of the Blackbird.
Perched on a post, or a chimney high;
He'll lift his head and sing to the sky.
For a while, the worries you've gathered all day;
Are soft and gently serenaded away.

It has to be one of my favourite birds;
With its song so pleasant, it needs no words.
Though I've heard it so very often before;
It will always be one I truly adore.
So, listen this Summer and be quite still;
And you'll surely hear the blackbird's trill.

Dedication: Dearest Sylvie, my wife

Day Break
Laura Olson

Today I see the sunrise
It rises slowly up the pass
The glistening rhythm radiates my chest
pounding my heart with fire
Could I be mistaken? This feeling intensifies my need to breathe,
to flower,
to live.
I must be intoxicated by the light
It must flourish within me as if it never left
Why must I resist such love? It doesn't have to be
Please stop my temptation to go forth without a sigh
to have never loved in my life, to have never exasperated
Oh sun, you are so glorious, majestic and still
You seek my will and all my power that is within me; yet, I will
not totter, I will not crumble within your glow...
You truly are beautiful...
I do need you
I do want you

Dedication: My grandparents, you inspire me

Fairytales
Miranda Jordan

When I was young they told me fairytales
With beaches of white sand
and lovers strolling into sunsets of faraway lands.
Or a prince rescuing his sweetheart
on a gallant white horse, Taking her away with him
to love her forever, of course

They said to wish upon a star
or a coin in a well was as good,
then my dreams would all come true
when I was young, I thought they would

but growing up through heartache
I cried my share of tears
and I have learned the lessons
of many empty years
I found no happy everafters
hello is always followed by goodbye
there are no happy endings
fairytales are lies

The Boy
Bernadette George

He always rushes.
In and out of the doors he goes,
like the wind.
Quiet as a hurricane.
Not a moment to waste.
Never slowing,
ever changing.
Passing through childhood like a train,
visiting stations.,
making stops.
But always he's off again,
down the track.
Things to do,
places to go.
The world to meet, head–on.

Leaning Tree
Belva Bodner

Leaning tree don't lean
On me
But lean toward
God's great
Heaven.

Open your arms to enclose
The wind and expose
Your bountiful branches
To all mankind.

Leaning tree be good
To me
And bear your fruit
Once again—

For God's great gift
To all of us
Is within which
You are given.

Confession Of The Heart
Linford A. Wray, Jr.

Today I stare as I did yesterday and the day
before that; and as I will tomorrow and the day after.
I search for that gracious smile, that warm
hello, that sparkling laugh, that gentleness
which defines your femininity.
Even though I'm physically distant I'm so near
spiritually, I feel the rhythm of your heart
and the harmony of your soul.
My mind races with images of you and abstract
thoughts of you overwhelm my consciousness.
My shyness conceals my hearts intent because
I realize my limitations.
My conversations are design to puzzle you so
you can't figure my unspoken language.
I dare not stare into those heavenly eyes
because I'll reveal my true identity.
So therefore I study my fantasies, maintain
my self control and try to rationalize this obsession.
Even though I'm content with this distance,
I'm eager to capture the closeness.

Untitled
Brandy Mitchell
We loved and lost a child so small,
Our precious Tyler was loved by us all.
He was smart, beautiful, and happy too,
On that June 10 our lives turned so blue
He stepped in the road to get a toy,
When a van drove by and hit our little boy
We'll never know or understand why;
You took our baby boy to your home in the sky
We know now he's well taken care of
by our friends and family who are up above.
One day soon we will be together,
And we'll laugh and play always and forever
I Love You, Tyler.

Dedication: The memory of Tyler Suggs

A Black Child's Hope
Flynn Pryor
I am a black child
and I'm proud of who I am.
I've been taught to love
and respect my fellowman.
Be he red, yellow,
black or white;
I'll pursue peace with all,
for I know this is right.
I've been taught that knowledge
and truth will set mankind free...
to let "You be You"
and "Me be Me."
I have hope in the day
when my color and my race,
will not be the excuse
for prejudice and hate.
That day is coming
and how joyful I will be;
to live and learn with my brothers,
in complete harmony.

Free Fall
Curtis M. Mook
i look up to you
as the august afternoon drips hot and salty
from our testosterone chins
slow motion fear in my squinted eyes keeps shouting
come on just do it
from the cool blue rocky pool below

i look up to you
as we try to wipe away the anxiety
from our adolescent brows
a well—timed blink of my excited eyes keeps whispering
he just did it
from the peak where i stood before

i once looked up to you
instead
i race you up the cliff to do it again
to splash into what some might call suicide

Dedication: Ben – my brother, my friend

Babysitting
Jessie Demers
Sammy Litter
was always the sitter,
she claims they were rough,
musclemen and tough
they complain and whine
always says, "That's mine!"
Barbie dolls cover the floor
Joie leaped hard into the door
big and fat they want to be
so they can wrestle with Marie
they love to sit and watch cartoons
chewing, bubble gum and blowing balloons
peanut butter and jelly they want
I say if you don't eat a ghost will haunt
running here to there very hyper
but not one has a wet diaper
they bring every toy downstairs
lining them up in perfect pairs
outside they love to run
oh ya, what great fun.

Leave Me Not Alone Now
Jennifer Ravalli
Leave me not alone now,
for my love has not been lost.
Young and fickle fantasies can so easily be tossed.
Leave me not alone now,
to sit in shades of gray.
Let our love not be wasted,
it has not yet been tasted,
while rainbows shine through my window pane.

Love me for another day,
and do not hasten,
for tomorrow you may not know what you wasted.
Love me for another day,
and let our love be basted,
with stitches neat and tiny, of water color laces.

Gentle Rain Falling
Chad Burris
Gentle rain falling,
Tap dancing from the sky;
Trying to be happy
But can only cry.

Gentle rain falling,
Cleaning sky and earth;
Trying so hard
To give hope a new birth.

Gentle rain falling,
On the roof overflowing;
God is watching over me
Falling asleep and knowing.

Gentle rain falling,
No longer to roam.
Under His wings
love and happiness
When at last I'm home!

Welcome The Night
Morris A. Alire

Kiss the day goodbye
Let night surround you with its
Cotton soft, black, sweetness.
Oh! Look! The starwinds of the heavens
Stirring up glistening stars to greet you
For night shines its life of stillness
And bids you sweet surrender.
Dream, perhaps a dream of love and let
The angels guide you for sweet is the
Nectar of a dream in sweet surrender
Kiss the day goodbye
Sleep in its total darkness
Rest, strengthens and prepares mind and body
Another day arrives. Face it.
Sunrise. Sunset. Day is done.
Kiss the day goodbye
Let the dark surround you
Welcome the night.

Dedication: My sons, Mark and Christopher Alire

Our Blue Christmas
Michele Bartucci

This time of year, I wish it would just pass me by, if Christmas is
    supposed to be so
joyous, why do we sit and cry? A time that was so precious and dear, A
    time we took for
granted, now we're left with faded memories, somehow unclear. The twinkle
    in his eyes
as he opened his presents we miss, we wish you were here to hold, to love,
    to kiss. We
thought you'd stay forever and never go away, but now we sit together not
    knowing what
to say. On Christmas day we come together acting happy and kind, but we
    know what's
on everyone's mind. And so we dedicate the same song to you as every year
    because it's
so true we'll have a blue Christmas without you.

To My Granddaughter Morgan Jade Mejer
Judy Italiano

The day you were born God was smiling down on me,
He placed in your hand a special key.
The key that would open all the love in my heart,
and let me adore you right from the start.

I love the way your smile at me,
your kisses, your hugs, your chubby knees.
The way your lip quivers when you're about to cry,
the gleam that is always in your eye.

The way you play peek–a–boo,
the way you always untie your shoe.
the way you cuddle so close and sweet,
how you look like an angel when you're asleep.

God gave this grandma the best gift there could be,
when he gave a granddaughter like you to me.

If ever you need me I will try to be there,
just call your grandma from anywhere.

Life's Sunset
Myra Sandy

When my life is over
and my days on earth are done
let my passing be like that
of the setting sun
Brilliant colors fill the sky
signs of God's wondrous worth
and the glows not an ending
but the moment of night's birth
Like the day our life contains
a morning noon and night
and the darkness is not an ending
when preceded by the light
The flaming glows of sunset
serve to comfort and reflect
to soften all the years
filled with pain and neglect
And as the day cools
and the colors fill the sky
I cannot help but think
what a beautiful way to die

Never Be A Part
Bridget Jameus

Beyond a shadow of a doubt,
I will always be there,
Look over your shoulder,
Listen in the wind,
Look up in the sky,
Do you feel it?
I am there,
With you sharing in all these things,
Open up your heart,
Take a deep breath,
And I will become a part of you,
Forever and always,
We will never be apart again!

Dedication: Claire, my wonderful mother

Wooded Area
Rebecca Bigelow

The wooded area undiscovered its beauty,
the changing leaves bright red and yellow,
a few hanging to their luster green splendor,
the lifeless tress bowing to nature's cause
others twisting pretzel–like,
toward small pools of water.

Selfishly hiding nature's workers,
a spider busily spinning a web,
which glitters in the morning light, giving off beautiful rainbow of
    colors,

The warm sun shows a golden case around a lonely daisy,
as if to show off its splendor's beauty,
each petal so delicately placed.

The bee doing its daily duty,
drinking the pollen from the generous flower,
all nature's beauty there for everyone to see and share,
only if we took the time to care.

Best Friends
Holly DiBenedict
Once in a lifetime if at all
you may find
A friend that is trusting,
understanding and kind
One who has shared with you
great laughs and heartbreaks
and truly gives love
never white washed or fake
that treasured best friend
that shares secrets forever
makes you laugh when you're down
and applauds you when clever
knows how to tell you with tact
and with grace
when you've done something stupid
or have food on your face
honest yet witty
when you need some advice
and you trust in the answer
to be just and precise

Narry A Cloud
John Comadoll
A whirl of wind unleashed,
Across the field of drought,
Girth of trees they oxidize
And nary a cloud aloft.

Versatility of the people...
Seems to be the Augury is...
the Cloudless sky...
Shall reign supreme
The drought for a season remain

What went wrong that did debase
Where once, Nary a cloud aloft?
Nothing!
Destiny in Control.

Memories
Jamie Bower
We fell for one another,
and I thought it would always last.
But I guess I was wrong,
because now it's all in the past.
I never will forget,
that one special night.
When I laid in your arms,
and you held me so tight.
My eyes fill with tears,
when I think of you still.
No one can comprehend,
this feeling that I feel.
Sometime when I lie awake,
you feel so far away.
Yet you're always in my heart.
Where I want you to always stay.
I'd like to go back,
to the way we used to be.
But I know that we can't,
so it will remain a memory...

Nourishment
Jane Gilbert
The day is still, with a heavy feeling in the air.
The humidity challenges the sun for rain.
Everyone and everything is running in low gear,
In anticipation of the predicted storm.
You can hear the foretelling silence.
The wind picks up, and the fluttering of leaves is heard.
They turn their faces upward looking forward to the deluge.
The robin chirps for the oncoming rain,
As if announcing its needed nourishment.
Your eyes drift upwards with expectation.
The breeze becomes a churning wind,
Tossing branches in its wake,
And still the air is dry and brittle to the touch.
When suddenly the sky opens its doors,
And the nourishing water pours forth drenching all in its path.
At first the land refuses to drink,
Then like magic it consumes with an unending thirst.
The greens of the earth are brilliant,
And our universe seems to cry out with joy.
We are renewed, we are again ready for the sun.

Maybe I Should Alter The Route
Megan King
If I walk on the road they have chosen for me,
Where will I be?
Will I follow someone else's path? Tracing another persons steps?
Or my own.
They are the map makers, they have traced out my path. I could let them
    guide me in the
direction that they want me to go.
Or, I could erase their marks, making a new path.
I could let them take me and sculpt me into their own, molding my every
    move the way
they please.
Or, I could mold myself.
I could go with their dreams.
Or, I could ride my own and see where they take me.
Maybe I should alter the route.

Follow Your Dream
Ida B. Seaborn
Sometimes when my head is hanging low
Not knowing which direction I should go
I see a ray of sun behind a cloud
Why then can't I be just as proud?
I open my mouth wide and try to sing
Wondering what tomorrow will bring
Uttering sounds with much disarray
Should I shout or get on my knees to pray?
My thoughts just flash like they're on fire
Churning, burning with constant desire
I hold my hands up to my face
What stance should I take to make my place?
Suddenly sounds are whispered in my ear
Spoken softly only for me to hear
Stand tall and walk make no mistake
The path is narrow but walk up straight
When you decide what you want to do
Follow it closely, make your dream come true

Dedication: My daughter, Yolanda

The Sky That I See
Jennifer Henry

The sky that I see is a faint blue
and I look up in wonder at its picturesque view.
There are no hindrances in the sky to see,
not even drizzle or heavy raindrops to fall on you and me.

As I look up at the sky and just stare,
I know that it could only really be,
My God's unique handiwork that,
I can see right up there.

I see God's white clouds in my vision's view.
His gleaming and radiant sun I see too.
I see rays of God's sunshine, shining through,
Blessing me and blessing you.

I give God the glory for the sky that's a faint blue.
I give him praise for magnificent clouds and a
beautiful sun too.
Knowing it's only His hand that can draw,
this scenery, that I am expressing in poem to you.

Untitled
Ruth C. Peters

Oui Marie, ever shy
Held in Daddy's arms
Looking at the night sky.
Twinkle on little star,
But that round thing
Shining in her eyes.
"Ball, Please, in my hand"
And of course, she remembers
Each time she paints
The sunrise, a sunset,
Or the moon bouncing
A silver path on the lake.
He gave it to her
In her hand.
"Have a ball, Daddy's girl!"

Last Lap
Harry Hays

The scrawny cat with age laid bare
As her every strike found nothing there.
At the gate the old horse of slackening pace
Just gazing glumly into space.
Fast falling scores in the cat and mouse game
And birds simply flying away,
Flying away as had eight of those nine lives
To which the cat alone lays claim.
Time was prowling; the predator now prey.
The horse curled back his lip and neighed,
Gone twenty read discoloured teeth displayed.
Then he stumbled as he tossed his mane—
Silly old boy! Shouldn't try that coltish fling again!
Sometimes through muddled minds most rove
Images of those who'd given care and love;
He, who once the horse did ride
She who'd fondled the cat by the fire–side
Both now in the old folk's home by the sea.
He like the horse, giving back a bit
She, still a bit of a cat at eighty three

It Used to Be No
Cathy Perritt

No bombings to make us cry
because we had to say goodbye
No killing or gangs
to make us hear the bangs
No stealing to use the money
for dealing
No drinking or dope because we
think it will help us cope
No beatings to make us feel
life has no meaning
No fires to have us lose
what was ours
No rape no matter if it's
family or a date
No taking from the poor
just because you want more
No dying just because you
are tired of trying
No! where did it go?
We all know. We just let it go

My Rose
Velishia Fletcher

My rose full of pride and grace, once
Standing tall glistening in the morning
light, keeps my day full of warmth.

My rose once full of life and love
withered away one day; as her petals
fell one by one.

Seeing my beautiful flower lose hope
and space thinking another would
take her place, but it was the
love of my rose that left behind
another rose that I call mine.

Dedication: My mother Rosa Little–Nannan

Cyber–Tiger
Philip Murless

Listen. Out there, beyond the Earth's curve,
The Screech and rumble of man's endeavor
Blend, hum slowly on the air.
All this occurs at my behest.

The sap of life is ruled by me:
The calendar, tick of clock, commerce,
The orderly procession
of movement following will.
Without me now all this would cease.
Wait for the millennium, where
a hundred equals nought,
Where the end of the World is nothing,
and the Apocalypse is nigh.

Think, 'Destruction', and I reply in kind.
Such is the life–force in the pathways of my mind,
Learned with a rapid, patient application,
A million times more speedy
than human brains can find.

Don't Cry
Desiree Laughlin

Remember me as a good soul,
for my life is no
longer whole.
Remember me for
who I am.
for no one gives a
damn.
Don't shed a tear
if I die.
I'll be in a better
place so please don't
cry.
No one cares for me
anymore.
It's time to knock on
heavens door.
If Jesus doesn't answer
I'll go to hell.
People want me to
die so I might as well.

Stepping Out
Florence Brown

Much inside has been destroyed.
I am insanely annoyed.
I've grown to be just like you
but at this moment
I don't want your point of view.
You taught me much,
you gave me all and
we've all been part of the whole.
It was you who stepped out of your role.
I am violated,
I am incinerated,
I am torn and so cold.
How could you be so bold?
Pronounce me dead, for I feel as such.
From me, don't you dare expect so much.

Splash
Michael Muellerleile

Quietly swimming the two young hearted lovers splash
Slightly tense, they are aware of how the sound goes hence
Across the water to waiting ears
Those ears only hear the sudden startled laugh,
The only evidence of the off–shore dance
The lovers are shrouded by dark water below and stars above
Building wet memories and Love.
But the lover's views are oh so different, as they float and bob.
They remove the burden of weight from their mate.
Their hearts begin to throb.
'Tis not from work though, rather a labor of love
and of coarse they pay some attention to the stars above
There's a tactile reason for this aqua bliss
and also two souls are exchanging a kiss.
Exchanging gifts meant only for each other
as the drifting music from across the way
prompts them to add rhythm to their stay
Rippled reflections of on–shore lamps
Lay out an electric carpet that enhances this willing trance.
Quietly swimming the two young–hearted lovers splash...

Rosalie
Lionel J. Gittens

Rosalie, a fair rose with such a sweet name,
A person whom we found without blame.
I reminisce the days gone by
of such a charming lady by my side.
In sorrow or joy she was there,
Which strengthen me, and left me without fear.
Oh' Rosalie, your time was best spent
caring for us, even if it caused inconvenience
You showed no indicator for gain for oneself.
Rosalie, though you are not with us anymore,
we miss your antiphony.
For when it is heard from the living
You are re–constructed within.
Rosalie how sweet a name
A person whom I found without blame.
May the angels take care of you
And bless you amongst the few
'Tis my Grand Mother I speak Off
Who had given us the precious gift
Of care and unending love, you fair rose.

The Darkness And The Night
Jessica De Angelo

The night drifted in with awaited presence
of the beauty found within the morn.
The darkness interceded like the passing of
wind that gently danced through the trees.
It seems as though the distant crying was the result
of a life so brutally torn.

The darkness acted as a cover to hide thee undignified,
secrets that we bury away deep within our soul, and as always
we can secretly consider ourselves not worthy, unholy.

So do we cry out into the lonesome of night? Or do we wait
for the beauty of the morn in the so cherished light.

Dedication: My loving mother and sister

Auschwitz
Justin Velasco

I'm in Auschwitz about to die,
So weak I cannot even cry.
At any moment the gas will leak,
All the men start to shriek.
My family is in Heaven waiting for me,
Right now I'm a prisoner but my soul is about to be set free.
It is winter but ashes fall instead of snow,
The exact number of Jews nobody will ever know.
I know I'll be ashes in just an hour,
We were given soap and told we were going to take a shower.
To the Nazis hair meant more then lives,
Thousands of men will never again see their living wives.
Jews were shot left and right,
We were led to the gas chambers without a fight
Heaven is now within my sight,
No longer will my life only consist of nights.
My family is waiting just inside the gate,
There is not much longer for me to wait.
The gas is now starting to come out,
No longer does anybody shout.

Old Age In Disguise
Valerie M. Cubitt

In my head – I'm not so very old – Childish things
I still do – So I'm told
So why! Oh why! When ever I stare
At my reflection in the mirror there –
The image I see, I do declare – Is my Father looking back at me.
In my heart rears – a dashing young lad – Wicked thoughts
Well, a hundred I've had –
Then why! Oh why! As I walk uphill – My heart
Beats fast – But my legs stand still – And even
Young lasses pass me, as they will – To chase other sweethearts.
In my inner thoughts – I plan out – each grey day –
But soon forget along the way – And I
Cannot always hear what's been said – With distant bells
That toll in my head – And with the sun
I slink to my bed – Weary and tired be I
In my mind's eye – I still race with the hare – So
Look in that mirror – And who leans there? – Bent
In back – and snow white on top – A wrinkled
Gaunt face – and fit only to drop – I'd love
To weave a spell to stop – Me aging – Just like my old Dad.

Endless Love
Dominica Presley

I count the seconds we're together. The
minutes I long for more. The hours become
my blessings. The days I do adore.

The months are filled with romance. The
years with true delight. My love for you
grows stronger every day and every night.

A rose can't describe my love. A peach is
not as sweet. A cherry topped with you
and cream is a special treat.

My heart is filled with passion that
burns for only you. This my love is real
and I swear that it is true.

A Chair With A Cynical View
R. Wood

I sit here inside my human frame,
watching a world go by so full of shame.
It hides its face from the view,
of all that is honest, all that is true.
It preys on our fantasies, deep in our minds,
so deep, it would take a year for a "Psychiatrist" to find
It covers up the horrors of death caused by "War",
by reporting it on the "News" until it begins to bore.
It even promotes "Rape and Murder" you know,
by showing them as "Entertainment" on "Television"
every hour or so.
We all lie, cheat and steal, no matter how small, as routine,
Honesty is looked on as a weakness, yesterday's scene.
We allow people in the East to starve every day,
While others, in the West are throwing good food away.
GREED, is our watch word, "I must own more than you",
"Do unto others as they would do unto you".
"So we taught all our children disrespect, disrespect for almost
everything
Little did we know, they would grow up, to threaten our very being".

You And Only You!
Horatio Lawrence

Your arms are long and slender,
To caress my body with ease,
Your hair is light and bouncy,
Blowing gently in the breeze,
Your lips are smooth and sweet to kiss,
Even your bow legs...I do miss.

I miss being next to you at night,
Lying beside you – holding you tight,
The warmth of your body and your tender touch,
These are things I miss so much,
Our love, is as solid as a pound,
You and only you, makes my world go 'round.

You are the one that makes my day,
Oh so special in every way,
You give me hope to see my time through,
You cheer me up when I'm feeling blue,
I said "I love you and I always will"
You fill my life with joy – What skill...

Cocaine
Sara R. Karnish

White as snow, the children know, how it took
many lives one day. They say come and play,
build a snowman, out of its white sand. Its
like a powder, that freshens the life of you. It
can blow you off, or light your fire, it can cause
you to commit your suicide. Its not like all the
rest, it can make your family hate you, make
your friends leave you, make you money, or
leave you poor, it can even turn you into a
whore, so don't mess around with it, unless you
want its deadly disease. Drug addict, little
witch, twenty in one town, forty in another,
you could end up a hooker, or dead in a gutter.
So back off, get away from it, or you'll fall in love
with it, because it's cocaine.

Delphinium
Teresa Booth

Long slender stems rise from the earth,
Tightly tipped with compact green buds.
Reminders of small unripened ears of corn,
Poised, waiting, weathering sun and rain.
Time passes, the buds separate slightly.
Stems lengthen lessening the bud's compactness.
They fatten and swell with growth.
Their outer casing thins to near transparency,
What colour their hidden petals? Blue or white?
No clue yet given as to which. Patience! Time will reveal all.
Casing stretched beyond its limits, petals break forth.
Deepest of deep delphinium blue.
Open clusters of bells reaching outwards,
Bright splashes of colour against coniferous green.
Time passes, the blue fades, petals wither, shrivel and die.
Hold. Wait again! For forming next are pods of life,
Newly formed seeds waiting to ripen and fall,
Dormant in the ground till next spring
When tender shoots will once again seek light,
Life revolves full circle to recommence again.

Praise Of Remnant Acoustic Prohibition
Doug Tolley
Collections of apathies raw in Neptune's admiration
scold the horizon with a secret but transient glow.
The tied provincial enhancements
worked by countless souls
falls by its side
and the fairer being is condemned
to an adverse contentment
ripe in glory.
The convention of representation
thus falls as the shallow ebb of humanity
eaten by starvation
never healing to reprepare
the Gods of self contamination.
Repaired secretions mark the sunset with guilt
but it is already smeared
by the envied wrath of gold.
Haloes from the everglowing eye
cause distant reminders of a past never lived
once forgotten
but infinitely remembered.

Victim
Arlene Libuser
Pain, sorrow, rage and anger
Trials grand jury, hearings –
All I see is blood and murder,
Kill him – hurt him – revenge!
How would it feel to do this
to him – as he did to her – kill–
Nowhere is there relief –
The jail sentence isn't long enough
To close the hole in my heart
My world has changed – never
to return to normal.
I've survived but my love
my angel waits with God.

Dedication: Al Libuser, my love

My Pride And Joy
Amanda Jane Johnson
Perfection in nature is sweet yet so rare,
A dream I had missed until you did come there.

Such joy felt on hearing those very first cries,
One born to me, a twinkle in mine own eyes.

Precious bonding expressed throughout each new day,
Every progression so memorable in its own way.

Years filled with love, although too sometimes pain,
Not knowing at times we're their sun after the rain.

Each moment is cherished when I think of it all,
Your first word, your first step, each stumble each fall.

My love has grown stronger you taught me to share,
No burden too heavy for my love to bear.

My pride is my weapon against all who challenge thee,
For you are my pride and joy daughter and you will always be.

A Poem For Autumn
Jane Wall
Morning mists swirling gently,
Like a snowstorm.
Falling leaves earthward bound,
A kaleidoscope of colour.
Air full of prickling frost
Making your cheeks glow.
Bonfire smoke scents the air,
It is burning nostalgia.
Wild boar grunting in the undergrowth,
The dominant male, dangerous as a bull
Protects his herd.
Striped piglets squeaking with
Autumn youthfulness.
In the distance, the roar of stags,
A strange, haunting sound
As they challenge each other,
Like ancient warriors to be the new King.
Pine cones to collect for winter fires.
Chestnuts and berries, fruits of the earth,
A last gift, before winter sleep arrives.

Horse
Hal Cutcher
"Which one to pick 'n choose t'day, hmm? Do I let others
go' n try for her ag'in? (Swings loop, widens hoop, then
casts with flick of wrist and misses)! "Damn! That wrist just
won't hold. Aw what th' hell! It hurts and yellin' won't do
no good." (Drags line back in to catch up loop, swings wrist
to make it just a bit more wide, watches mare trot slowly by.
She nickers soft, bares teeth in grin). "Doncha walleye me,
old gal or I'll bang yer nose!" Then swings arm wide and
high, wrist flicks and hoop drops soft around her neck. He
gently pulls her into him and sets the halter. Coils rope up
and leads her with an ambling gait to where gear lays close
on ground. "OK, old gal," (he soft says as tack goes on),
"let's take our time and settle down, lots to think and do.
(Pats neck). "So, Bess m'love," (he climbs and sets), "let
us gitup and go." (Heels touch sides, ears perk up, she goes).

Nights Of Torture
Cadell Beasley
Whilst awake in the midst of night.
My mind quakes and my heart yearns.
No more the rested soul!
Never easy to fall to slumber.
Swimming in hurt and drowning in grief.
Fearful of the future...The uncertain.

The night stands still but my heart beat quickens.
Once more the realisation of horror fills my thoughts.
I shake and cry as distant memories consume my being.

When again will pleasant dreams coax me.
I cling to hope of tranquility once more.
Yet the reality is harsh and cruel.

The morning slowly creeps upon me.
Another night of tortured sleep.
Tormented images invaded my dreams.
Will I ever brake this cycle of pain.
Ever to fall in love again?

My Dad

Tammy Lynn Roberts

You have always been there for me,
It might be hard for some to see.
You show your love in many ways,
You've helped me through the worst of days.
When I was young, you were a dad,
Who never showed that you were mad.
As I've grown up you've helped me know,
What direction I should go.
You're a quiet man with a big heart,
I should have seen it from the start.
Through the years, you've been there,
Showing me how much you care.
You've listened to all of my fears,
And helped me through many tears.
On the occasion of your birthday,
There's something that I want to say.
I appreciate all you've done for me,
I hope that someday you will see.
You give me hope and make me glad,
I'm proud to say, you're my dad.

Dream

Diane Appling Kelley

A sleepy encounter on a rainy dark night
Drifting above clouds arms stretched in flight
It may be a movie yet I am the star
Apparitions of ancestors echo afar
This night is of sorrow – last night of joy
The night before rejoicing a new baby boy
Some say its a thought shadowing my mind
Elders say its God's cinema "a view into time"
Sometimes I awaken expecting a change
Shrouded in mystery wonderfully strange
The sun shines a new day of refreshed esteem
Whether God's cinema or thought
I know it's a dream!

Dedication: To my big sister and friend – thank you Madeline

In My Dreams

Lyndsay Jayne Shaw

My castle in the clouds, of which nobody knows,
Its walls of shining silver, its towers of shimmering gold.
The windows, oh have you seen?
Are diamond paned, 'tis true,
The couches, chairs and stools,
Are yes, a deep rich blue.
I have a horse, a beautiful horse,
All silver with wings on his back,
With a toss and a neigh, he flies me away,
Always bringing me back.
Around my castle are crystal stars,
And fairies shining bright,
Who sit on the moonbeams and talks to the stars,
In the dead of night.
Sometimes the fairies have a ball,
And invite the Dryads, Imps and Gnomes,
And all the stars gather 'round to watch,
Sitting on diamond stones.
Sometimes I am invited too, but only when I'm asleep,
For I dream of the castle, the horse and the fairies, only in my dreams.

Grieving Heart

Heather Julian

Sadness overwhelms my thoughts,
Totally consuming my heart,
I had never prepared for the anguish it would bring,
When the one you love departs.
Sometimes I can feel his presence,
As I am walking down the street,
A warm caressing effervescence slowly envelops me.
My heart knows that this will never replace,
The feeling of his actual hand,
As he would gently hold my face.
Each night my inner tranquility grows,
As I visit the place where he rests.
Laying a single red rose upon my loved one's chest.
Beside him in the glow of candlelight,
As I look up to the sky,
I know he must be listening,
By the way the stars twinkle and shine.
I know in my mind I should not despair,
Believing deep within my grieving heart,
He will always live vividly there.

The Madman

Jim Dodok

When the mighty have fallen
and the weak start to rise
never neglect the madman's cries
he'll tell you of pleasure
and he'll tell you of pain
too much of one is what drove him insane
he'll tell you of life
and when you'll breathe your last breath
because of those visions you'll condemn him to death
he'll tell you of wonders and never a lie
and when you hear of his passing no one will cry
for it's hard to shun
and it's hard to deny
the truths that are told
when the madman cries.

Wendy

William Henry Smith III

Here I am again
but this time I'm not crying
Walking in the sand
hear the ocean's calm
this time I'm smiling.
I've got Wendy on my mind
She's my peace in troubled times
and I love her.
I see her bright blue eyes
filled with warmth and laughter
hear the ocean rise
got my feet in the water.
I've got Wendy in my heart
God knows we'll never part
and I love her.
I feel a gentle breeze soft against my skin
I'll climb the tallest trees just to be with her again
I feel Wendy touching me
She's a calm and gentle sea
and I love her.

Lee
Shana Sloan

He polished up my emptiness
With memories of light
And helped me remember
Who I truly was
Inside
Deep down, under heart
And pain and
a steam—roller cylinder that seemed to have crushed out yet
Not smoothed
my inner world
of so long ago.
He told me to write, to type,
To get it out there somewhere
So she could read it
And not leave it
Alone
in sticky paper stacks and moldy boxes
musty and fading away, never to be seen,
in the basement
of my soul.

My Prayer
Mary E. Sykes

Inspire my heart, dear God I pray
The perfect words that I might say
To each and every soul that will hear
Especially since I hold them so dear.
Our truth, our very nature is that of love
A Gift we all share from God above
Loves vibration goes forth from
Coast to coast
And is received by those hearts that are open most.
Let love mercy and forgiveness pierce the dark side of thee.
And with the dawning of this truth
Love will truly set you free.
If you will practice this truth each and every day.
Your life will be transformed,
and it's for this that I pray.

Without Words
Eric J. Kridle

Cool winds blow as the night
hides under city lights —
hazy white and golden glimpses
of love behind closed doors.
Soft clouds touch the sky
and quietly the trees cry;
silenced by rustling leaves,
because there is love no more.
Delicate autumn flowers
sway sadly while the showers
of love are swept away
on the wings of yesterday.
To recapture what was lost;
years of hopeless dreaming cost
years of endless pain,
now the showers turn to rain.
Rain to sleet, sleet to snow,
till there is nowhere left to go
but to turn within yourself
and bring out what is locked inside.

Growing Old
Vicki Hendrix

The old house seems empty now
An old couple live within
No one comes to visit
Except an occasional friend.
They seldom come outside now
They spend their time alone
And somehow seem much older
Since all the kids are gone.
The house once rang with laughter
Within and without
And the pitter patter of little feet
Could be heard all about.
The children all are married now
And have homes of their own
They seem to have forgotten
The old folks left at home.
It's sometimes easy to forget
The kind folks you once knew
So don't forget your parents
For they gave life to you.

River Song
Helen Grummett

A stirring in the grasses,
startles the curlew
into flight,

A soft footfall,
in the morning dew

As the breeze, snatches my song,

And whispers it to the trees,

The gentle murmurings,
of the lonely river.

Speak to me of you.

The Bond
Heather Hargrave

Your friendship is a precious gem
That I admire and cherish from deep within
Shining brighter than the sun's most powerful ray
It is ever—present from day—to—day
It is warmer than a winter fire's glow
More pure than a mountaintop's new fallen snow
It carries more memories than Santa's sack
Gives one way, then gives right back
Exchanges joy, laughter, sadness, and tears
Fights battles, distance, change, and fears
Builds confidence and character, trust and love
And fits separates together like hand and glove
It creates time when there is no minute
In a barrel of bad apples, it finds the good one in it
Your friendship is the icing on the cake
Making each new day worth the wake
My Friend, as we grow older, we may not live near
Thus may only visit once each year
But you dwell in such a strong place of my heart
That ne'er our bond of friendship will break apart.

Heart
Ruth Shaw
Lovers passion
Cools too quickly.
Yearns for a kiss –
a touch – a caress.
Seeks understanding.
Receives ignorance.
Of feelings – of cares –
of misery.
Abandons hope,
for bliss – for pleasure –
for joy.
Looks to others,
desperately – wearily –
ceaselessly.
While the heart expires,
doomed.

Love Is An Ocean Contained In A Tea Cup
Sean Bigard
Millions of drops formed into one,
Thousands of thoughts made from none.
A billion good things and a couple bad,
Moments of happy and of sad.
Bad things come and bad things go,
But in the end, Love will show.
It fills everything fuller than seems fit,
It lights every candle that needs to be lit.
It carries the moon and all the stars,
It cannot be stopped by miles or bars.
It knows no bounds, its limit, shall exceed,
It's found not in money, but lives in deed.
Softer than down, harder than stone,
Love is there when you are alone.
It's in the dark, it's in the light,
It's to be found when nothing's right.
I'd hate myself if I'd never known Love,
For the lowliest creature, I'd rise not above.

Dedication: Lisa and Dusty, I'm sorry

Pitch Black Sky
Meggie Munley
As I look at the pitch black sky
When, in my bed, I lay
You are like the sunshine
I look forward to seeing the next day

When things are going pretty rotten
And life is going pretty bad
You are like the pillow I cry on
When I'm weak and sad

If my life were a pitch black sky
You would be my twinkling star
And I hope your starlight will never fad
Because I love you just the way you are

I know I often make mistakes
But you teach me right from wrong
And as long as we stay friends forever
Your light, in my pitch black sky,
Will keep on glowing strong

Defeat
Megan McKnight
Despised tear,
I bid you leave.
Your presence implies
victory over me.
Visual evidences
of interior pain
show lack of strength
in inferior men.
The downward trek
of one salty tear
leaves an irritated trail
to be hated and feared.
Despised tear,
I bid you leave.
Pride detests
implied defeat.

To A Lost Soul
Anna E. Maloch
This is not your milieu—
This is not your way of life.
Go where you belong,
into the world, artistically.
Your mind is caged, yet free.
You want to burst loose
but somehow feel
You do not dare – not just yet
You are as old as Methuselah;
still you are as a child.
You are self–sufficient, yet insecure.
The searching, the restlessness
that is part of you, does not last forever.
You are reaching out for whatever seems
beyond your reach – but it is there.
So bend, perhaps, as the twig is bent,
and then, maybe your horizon
will come into view, and you'll know –
But you will never know, never know
unless you try.

Beveled Glass Windows
Shelagh Raphael–Hall
I shall always remember,
I was admiring
The beveled glass windows
When I first saw you;
Your beauty dazzled the glass and me.
I love old houses,
They are so special.
You were special,
Standing there;
You seemed to be
A part
Of all the things,
One seeks,
But so seldom finds;
Creations of Beauty
By master craftsmen;
The craftsmen are disappearing,
Their arts becoming rare.
Where are those beveled glass windows,
Where are you now?

225

Pride and Joy
W. Haynes

Me and my wife in our little red hot shot
It's not fancy but we like it a lot
No big engine and that's no lie
When we come to a hill we surely die
With a '48 trailer trailing behind
You can sure bet you can't turn it on a dime
But we gear down and get over the top
Far behind the rest and not worrying about the cop
Some call us a hazard to the lane
But on the level we're just the same
We're just out here trying to make a living
With the LTL's we've been given
So next time you big rigs pass us by
Wave, blink your lights and say "hi"
We wish we could afford your big Mack
We can't so we'll just say, see you on down the road Jack.

Living Angels
Alaouise A. Moore

You are so very weary
As when you first came
Into this world
Your skin so thin it tears
But weathered as is the bark
of a tree
Hands and knees knurled as the roots
Your eyes may no longer focus
Your ears no longer hear
You may know my name one day

But not the next
But a familiar voice or face
I may remain
Yet I cannot forget the good years
You must have shared.
So, I silently, tearlessly, wearily await
That you the living angel.
Greet and meet
God's choir of angels high

Pain/Love
Renee Cox

Deep in my heart there's a terrible pain
I never want to feel this pain again.
Being hurt by someone you love very much
Is a pain that no one needs to touch.
Feeling the pain inside their heart
Knowing that inside they're tearing apart.
Knowing that you're part to blame
Can drive a person extremely insane.
Words that shouldn't have been said
Keep filling and bouncing around inside your head.
Actions that shouldn't have been thrown
Are differentiated from the love usually shown.
You remember back to a special day
When everything was okay.
You go to that person and try to explain
How you're partly to blame.
An apology is given from the heart
And now neither one of you are tearing apart.
But the love for each other that is deep and true
Helps both of you say "I Love You."

Dreams
Harold L. Christison

Dreams are just dreams,
that sometime comes true.
Death is a fact,
that happens to you.
Death is just part,
Of the common man's dream,
Some time it comes early
that's how it seems.
I sit in this cell,
here all alone,
No paths to walk
No trails to roam.
Death would be easy,
my dreams are the same.
I dream of death,
I'm going insane.

Dreams
Holly Hubbard

Dreams are made of,
Things that are good.
Sometimes dreams,
Can't be understood.
Dreams are made,
In your mind.
Dreams can fade,
Within time.
When you dream,
You dream a while.
Your dreams can go on,
Mile after mile.
They can be short,
Or last all night.
They can be happy,
Or give you a fright.
Dreams can be good,
Or even bad.
When you think about it,
Some can be sad.

Inconstancy
Clyde Dotson

I saw you as you slipped away
Stealthily, silently as a wraith
And as you went, my dying faith
Mocked me as a bird of prey
Plays with its captive ere
It slays it. My heart, I fear,
Went to be with you to be for aye
Your captive: to be a thing
For your fancy as it turns
To that for which it yearns,
Or in a sudden move spurns
The very one who would bring
His all in all to sacrifice
In the cold ashes of your love.
What then could be the price
That places your value above
The sacrifice that I made today?
Am I not now as I was when
You gave me your love, then
Without warning slipped away?

What
James Corey

What the hell is going on
I don't know, do you?
It feels as if we're in a storm
No more skies ablue.
Darkness is at once upon us
Desperation fills the void.
Never saw the damn thing coming
Its strength I can't ignore.
Loneliness and helplessness
Are feelings I have known.
I do not know what I'm to do
Give the dog a bone.
Desperate times and desperate measures
I haven't got a clue.
What the hell is going on
I don't know, do you?

The Ways Of The Winds
Irv Feldman

These are the ways of the winds:
softly caressing, tender, mild,
light as the early laugh of a child.
Brushing so gently the golden–crowned grain,
spreading the scent and the seed of the plain.

These are the ways of the winds:
Fresh and exciting, briskly gay,
playfully slapping and slipping away.
Hinting of hidden whimsies of will;
dancing one moment; the next, standing still.

These are the ways of the winds:
Brutal, destroying, grimly wild,
sharp as the unhappy shriek of a child.
Violent walls 'round a turbulent tower,
churning up fury with uncontrolled power.

These are the ways of the winds.
And how like the winds we are.

So Very Loved
Veronica Winslow

Before my eyes
I saw you go
Before my eyes
I truly didn't know
Before my eyes
how minutes could change
a life so
Before my eyes
you hardly let it show
Before my eyes
I saw you go
Before my eyes
you said so little, our hands
clasped tight, no time to woe
Before my eyes
you had to go
It must have been so hard for you
to know
Before my eyes I saw
you go.

Life's Cascade
Heidi Bigelow

Juggling reminds me of life,
everything has to balance out,
or it will all soon fall apart,
and you'll regret it, no doubt.
But pick up all the pieces,
and please try it once more,
you'll soon get the pattern,
and continue it for sure!
If you want something different,
want a change of pace,
then take it slowly,
don't treat life as a race.
Try it again and again,
until you get it right,
then your future will glow,
shimmering new and bright.

The Mullberry Tree
Carole A. Weems

Millions of stars were out that night
As I lay backward with delight.
Cuddled beneath the hovering arm
With leaves about me–I sensed no harm
At first it was a place to run
When I would hide, having some fun
Then it became my safety zone
Where I would climb to be alone.
So young I was, it seemed to me
To grasp the branches of that tree
But high I'd climb, so high above.
To find the place where I felt love
There I'd find those outstretched arm
Those branches shielded me from harm
And held me tight so I'd not fall,
Then love, I felt, even so small.
It became my confidant,
I told it what I need and want.
My only friend, I loved that tree
It was always there for me.

Her Memory
Rodney Eberle

She's a soft gentle rain
a cool breeze at night
sunsets on water
stars shining bright.
She's a flower at bloom
the first sign of spring
Aurora Borealis
the song that birds sing.
She's midnight swims
an old rocking chair
campfire's glow
and now teddy bears.
She's wild horses running
a mother's lullaby
warm embraces
why I sometimes cry.
She's no longer with us
yet always with me
for these things serve
as her memory.

My Mind And Heart
Derek Brown

My mind sees more, than ever my eyes,
The truth, the tricks, the wicked lies.
My heart touches more, than ever my hand,
The lows, the highs, feelings, noble and grand.
My mind hears more, than my listening ears,
Silent cries for help and unseen tears.
My heart feels more, than its pulsing feed,
The seeking hand, of a hand in need.
My mind tries to be constant, as my heartbeat,
In the love, you give, the most valued treat.
You taught me well, of the treasured prize...
That tarries and dwells, in fond disguise,
Till time is right, to show its face,
When the hour arrives, to make pulses race;
Stretching out fingers, removed from the glove...
The caring hand, of sharing love.

Where Are You Mama?
Holly Williams

Words dry up in my mouth
So it's easier to say you are away
Say you went south
Better that then to receive pity for pay
I have no answer to reply
for you are gone
Life without you is like a sigh
Or like the end of a song
Wishing the song was still on
Just one more time, I want to say I love you
But you are gone
My heart broken and bent tears on my face like dew
Death the perpetrator
came unto you one night
stole you away, like a true terminator
not a word as to where, was it right?
Mama where are you?
Is it nice there where you are?
Nicer there then here with me? Mama will there come a time when my child
    will ask the same of me?

A Fire's Touch
Dan Noble

Flaming fingers stabbed at will,
the tinder–dry trees beneath.
While smoke and haze teared the eyes
and searing heat the feet.
The inferno raced towards the town,
fanned on by wind, its soul.
And countless animals fled for life,
while three men teared and toiled.
They chopped and dug to save the land,
while balls of flame rolled by.
They quickly lost all track of time,
beneath the burning sky.
They shortly found themselves entrapped,
by flaming walls of heat.
They quickly perished, to save the land,
they fought so hard to keep.
The fires cooled, the winds died down,
the town was scorched but safe.
A sign was cast beneath the sky,
God thanks their souls this day.

His Own Hand
Jane Jackson Balay

When a man takes his life by his own hand
You wonder why, and ask, Who was this man?
What or who hurt him so bad
That he was willing to forget
That he was a Dad?

A girl and boy who love him and are left to feel so sad.
They cannot understand what happened to their Dad.
He was handsome, intelligent, brave and true.
He fought in a war for all of us, too.

Now who was the person who hated this man?
Who did not care if he died by his own hand?
Deep down in their heart they know they are to blame.
I think from now on the one who is guilty
Will forever feel the pain.

Fairy Tale Dreams
Deborah Bailey

Before I closed my eyes at night,
Mom read me stories and tucked me in tight.
Way back then I was too young to understand,
That the feelings of love were so bold and so grand.
I never thought that "Happy ever after..." might come true,
But as I learned about life and about love,
I met you.
I remember Cinderella with her glass shoe so small,
I remember Rapunzel with her tower so tall.
I never expected feelings, strong like this,
Yet there was Sleeping Beauty
And her Prince's loving kiss.
No play ever written
On Shakespeare's finest day,
Could possibly explain
Just why I feel this way.
"So once upon a time..."
And "In the days of Kings and Queens..."
Could never cure my lovesick heart
Because of those fairy tale dreams.

Raging Calm
Catherine Hicks

I am a storm
sudden and fierce.
At times I'll say words
that frighten and pierce you.
I speak without thought,
later, wishing we had not fought.
I feel regret,
not knowing yet,
what will come of this.

I hope and I pray
that I will say,
what is right
to start taking the flight
towards a new happiness,
just between us.
The smiles start anew
first me, then you.
Forever Happy,
Forever Friends!

Untitled
Craig Griffin
They only came to watch a game
That will now never be the same
They only came to sing with joy
Each man, woman, girl and boy
On a day when the sun shone high in the sky
Many lost friends, the only noise was a cry
On the terraces we watched, men kicking a ball
When suddenly death roared its terrible call
There was nothing we could do
Though we wanted to try
There was nothing we could say
Just stand and cry
And now though we can't reach
Into every home
The supporters of Nottingham forest promise
"You'll Never Walk Alone"

Spring
Francine Bergeron
Pluto's wrath unfolding:
Spring,
Playing hard–to–get.
Weather notwithstanding,
A big–city newspaper offers
A chef's tribute to the season:
A golden caviar of pomegranate seeds—
Vegetarian variation on the theme.
A snowy mass
Carpeting the greenhouse rooftop
Goes into rewind.
A bouquet of blossoming pin cherries
Set upon a lacy tablecloth
By an anxious host,
Awaiting guests—
Despite a foot crushing
By a temperamental cow.
A far–off forest fire
Perfuming the air:
Senses titillated by danger.

Communication
Sara M. Anderson
"Do your children go to school?"
Asked the baker who was standing on a stool.

"Yes," replied the librarian who was looking through some books;
"They go to school willingly, and take with them good looks."

"Good," replied the baker who was putting in some rolls,
And in the heat of the oven, accidentally spilling them on the coals.

A teacher then came in with a smile on her face;
She said to the librarian, "Your son just won the race."

"Yippee!!" shouted the librarian, bursting with joy,
"I will praise him, my little son Roy."

"Good for you," said the baker with a smile.
"You and your son may stay for awhile."

So after school, Mr. Raft and his son
Went to the bakery and had some fun.

Emptiness
Krista Molnar
There's a feeling in my heart
of emptiness,
Where something some day
will fit there.
But I don't know what will fit
there, or who.
Perhaps it's like the pages
of an unwritten book.
I don't know if it will ever
be filled,
But someday I will find
out what fits there, in that
empty spot in my heart.
Emptiness
in my heart,
empty, so empty.

Take Heart
Daisy S. Aldridge
When the skies look dreary:
When the head is weary,
And it seems there's naught but pain
The Lord stands by
To hear the cry
Of a soul with Heaven to gain.

When words so sharp
They pierce the heart,
Making all seem over and done
The Lords takes heed
Of every need
Of a soul with Hell to shun—

When the heart is still
List'ning for God's will,
Though it seems nobody cares,
The sun WILL shine
In God's good time.
Each deep concern He shares!

Spring Time From A Hill
Allison Papineau
As I lay here looking at the sky,
the wind is silently passing by.
Blowing the grass every which way,
not knowing if to leave or stay.

The clouds above are large and white.
The perfect day for flying a kite.
The birds are flying high above.
Could that be a dove?

One by one the flowers pop up.
All over the ground they can be found.
In the valley below, the children sway to and fro,
on swings made of rope and wood.

Near the pond the frogs are jumpin' here and there,
there and here, catching all the flies they can.
Do ya understand?
The moon is high in the sky proud of its show.
So now it's time to go.

The Peace Of Love
S. M. Bailey

Words on scraps of paper,
For you my love I write,
And when darkness closes in,
It is you who lights my night,
For this poor man, he can be rich,
This fool he can be wise
By finding rest and peacefulness,
In your tranquil loving eyes,
You see me stripped of burden
Of the cross I have to bear,
You see me without battle,
Free from the troubles that we share
And simply just by being there,
You bring to me a peace
Tranquility and comfort,
All fears of mine have ceased.

My Step Sister
Christine S. Tenney

When I was little and in pig–tails,
we were introduced.
With dozens of different emotions building up inside of me,
I had no idea that I had just met a friend for life.
So many things to get used to and in such little time.
Our family extended and our lives became full.
we shared part of our childhood
growing up together.
Through laughter and tears,
there were many years.
The time came when you reached
the age of maturity and we eventually slipped away.
You went in one direction.
I went in another.
We were brought back together in happiness
and you received a new name and a family as well.
Now there is only the future ahead
and in it
I predict one thing will never change–
and that's the love we'll always share.

Judgement
Elizabeth Baker

Don't judge me by the color of my skin, judge me for being me.
People on my street say I can't play with their children for
I'm different. No I'm only being me. Affirmative action says
Hire me for I'm a minority. No I'm only being me.

I was brought into this world a human so shall I leave as one.
Don't judge me by my race judge me by my actions. I learn, I
read, I play as you do. So please stop judging me. Racism
such an ugly thing, causes people like you to hate people like me.

My skin is dark, my heart is pure, yet you still judge me.
Today I say to you love me for being me. Stop, stop
judging me. We were brought into this country not by
choice. We tended your crops, raised your children,
cleaned your homes and yet you still hate me.

If God had wanted me like you he'd done so. Stop
judging me. Look at me look at me I say am I not a
man, a woman, yes a child? Do I not bleed if you cut me?
Today I take my stand and say to you. Stop, stop judging me

Find Yourself A Special Friend
Cherylta C. Cruz

If there's someone you can talk to
Someone no one else can replace –
If there's someone you can laugh with,
Till the tears run down your face –
If there's someone you can turn to,
When you need a helping hand.
If there's someone you can count on,
To advise and understand –
If there's someone you can sit with,
And not even say a word–
If there's someone you can trust,
To keep each confidence he's heard –
If there's someone you think more of,
As each year comes to an end –
Then you're a lucky person,
For you found a special friend.

Love Made In Heaven
Tammy Hodges

I took his hand,
He took my heart.
Two people together,
Never to part.
Because Lord knows I love him,
And he knows it too.

United together,
Until death do us part.
Forever and ever,
Heart to heart.
Because Lord knows I need him,
And he needs me too.

He took my heart,
And we're never gonna part.
Love made in Heaven.
United together,
Gonna stay that way forever.
Love made in heaven.

Untitled
Kathy Gustafson

We began dating in high school.
A couple young, new love our tool.
On bended knee, hand in hand.
You asked me to wear your wedding band.
Your wife you wanted me to be.
Share our life, with you raise a family.
In November we were wed.
So special to share a wedding bed.
We were young, didn't know.
What it would take for love to grow.
Mistakes we made, from choices bad.
Not realizing the special thing we had.
Our love withstood test after test.
Then with three children we were blessed.
Memories precious we hold in our hearts.
As we look back, to our young start.
Thru the years, loved ones lost.
Love doesn't come without a cost.
Twenty–seven years, soon to be.
As we celebrate our Anniversary.

Untitled
Jennifer Wilber

Upon a shooting star I glide
Gleaming with joy I have nothing to hide.
The others have stopped in their place,
Frozen and dazzled by all of my grace.
I shine uniquely and unlike the rest
My glow comes from within; my heart in its nest
Comfortable and confident I shall never fall
Many souls watch over me; I accept them all.
As my journey proceeds to drift
I'll keep my head high only to lift.
For if I look down, I see only debris
Of paths and courses not meant for me
Way up there over by the moon
Is where I am destined so very soon
My dreams have been planted; yet the seed remains dry
I must nourish my hopes; so I continue to fly.

Empty Pockets
Alexandra Shirley

With a pocket full of dreams
I set out to take on the world
Feeling I will conquer all
Forgetting I'm just a girl
My mind runs rampant
As I plan and scheme
Working feverishly day and night
To fulfill all my dreams
One step forward
Two steps back
Can someone give me a break?
Cut me a lil slack?!?!
I've given all I can
To make my dreams come true
I'm running out of ideas
As I search for clues
My dreams begin to dwindle
And my time is running out
I had a pocket full of dreams
Now its a pocket full of doubts

The Way Of A Dream (Revised)
Michael Mills

And all was a silent child
He, smiling with no teeth, lit the room
A mother's eyes glowing with tears of joy,
Love reigned over the moment and I reasoned...

Could one begin to believe?
Something moaned silently and rushed forth
It was still and serene, yet all around
and none could see what it was.

Naked souls and bare desires
Knowing only lust and labor
Softly caressing with a firm hand, then scattering
in the darkness of bright lights.
Singing like angels with golden chords,
chickens clucked the remains of a mute song.
The wind hummed and then shouted.
A world laughed,
A baby cried,
All in a silent dream.

All My Life
Michael Gizzi

All my life I wanted to touch the sky,
like it was the ceiling.
All my life I wanted to touch the sky,
Oh! What a feeling.
All my life I wanted to touch the sky,
but it's really not there.
All my life I wanted to touch the sky,
it's nothing at all except air.
All my life I wanted to touch the sky,
that would be the most perfect thing.
All my life I wanted to touch the sky,
maybe all I need is wings.
All my life I wanted to touch the sky,
but so many things get in the way.
All my life I wanted to touch the sky,
that's what I'm going to do today.

My Child
Faith Wapachee

My thoughts and dreams are for you
You're the life inside of me
You're a part of everything I am and anything I do
I will try to be the best I can be

To me you are the reason the sun, moon and stars all shine
Right now you are only but a stir
but you're a part of me, an unbreakable bind
A mother's love is one that endures

I can't wait to hold you close in my arms
And count your tiny fingers and toes
See your smile so sweet and warm
And through the years, watch you grow

You are my pride and joy, my everything
You are a special part of me that I could never replace
I pray that we will have that understanding
And you will feel the love that I'll carry for you
...always

A Candle In The Wind
Bridgette Denise Tillman

A–A person we will always love

C–Cause you're in heaven with the man above.
A–Always and forever you'll be in our hearts
N–Now and forever we can never part.
D–Do your best and take a stand
L–Love will be there to guide you through the promised land.
E–Even though you left this world and couldn't say good–bye

I–In our hearts we cried, so much deep down inside.
N–Now the Lord is there to guide you, you may now sit on the throne

T–The time has come to officially announce, that you finally made it home,
H–He will guide you with His wisdom and also His fame
E–Enter the kingdom of heaven and you'll never be the same.

W–With the help of God you will succeed
I–In heaven He's all you'll ever need.
N–Now take the Lord's hand, as He welcomes you in
D–Don't never doubt His word Tony, you're "A Candle In The Wind."

231

Whose Child?
Roseann M. Saltzsieder

A newborn baby, whole life in front,
Who will you be? What will you want?
This baby could be the heir to the throne,
Or maybe the victim of the slumzone.
If you looked in his eyes
What would you see,
Could you tell by just looking
Who he will grow to be.
The man who cures some awful disease,
The man/child who may never get off of his knees.
The education so different
Home life heaven or hell?
One parent or two?
Sickly or well?
This child is a clean slate
But before he can crawl,
Has his life been decided
By the luck of the draw?

Dedication: My niece, Shannon Rose Saltzsieder

Idyll
Marsha G. Ellis

Perfumed ballads in flat shallow chords
And rose crusted porcelain nothings
You have drowned and sedated me in such white noise,
Such bitter, blatant mistrust.
Rain tarnished rings on love–trembled fingers,
Feather kisses on sleep black eyes
Dangerously close to truth
I'm dangerously close to you.
I've fallen asleep to the music
Of leaf tumbled lanes
And snow–patched houses, chimneys
Spilling October from brick,
Fresh dew grass on bare toes
And summer drummed out on warm backs.
This smooth, smooth treason
Is too much for me.

Emptiness
Rachel Pearson

That black abyss of life that people find,
the darkness of men conformity.

The vacuum that creates this nothingness,
Creeps into the lives of the unsuspecting.

Panic starts to set in as people clutch
at tiny pieces of hope,
scraps of life, scraps of anything.

Yesterday seems a lifetime away,
tomorrow always comes too soon,
another night beside the fire wondering
where it's all gone.

Slowly things unfold, in the middle,
hope, that final straw waiting to be grabbed.

That black abyss grows smaller
day by day, will it ever fade and go away.

Soft, Warm Seductions...
Mary L. Poll

– Soft, warm seductions
Tight embraces – two shadows
become one –

– Soft, warm seductions
move down the neck;
envelope the monotony.
Deep breaths – silenced,
shaking...

– Soft, warm seductions
move to Venus – tingles,
hearts leaping; gasping...

The Higher One takes over –
He enters and observes the cradle –
One cell, two cells, three –
Wide, gaping eyes stare honestly back.

– Three souls joined one lonely night...

I Remember
Cathy Panaccione

I remember how I felt when
you left.
I remember your father standing
in my living room telling me
you were killed
I remember the loneliness in
My heart knowing I'll
never see you again.
I remember the flag draped
box wishing it wasn't so
I remember my tears
Watering the flowers
I remember your
Smile, your laugh and
most of all I remember
You!

That Time Of Year
Angela June McEvoy

Lobellia hanging from the baskets,
Cascading to the ground.
Petunias proving glorious colours,
Protruding all around.
The fountain singing nicely
As water drops into the pool,
Competing with the tranquil sound
Of the calming waterfall.
Two turtledoves fly to the birdbath.
Splashing around, they seem to say
Oh, what a beautiful garden,
Oh, what a lovely day!
The dragon fly that visits,
And what a sight to see,
He brings, oh, so much pleasure
To all my friends and me.
Tomato plants in flower,
Hoping for some rain.
Indeed we really need a shower
For the beauty to remain.

Where Do You Go To River?
John Brogan

Twinkling river, where do you go,
When far out of sight, in valley below,
To the ocean cloaked in shimmering blue,
Tell me river, where do you go to,
Do you trickle to nothing and run out of steam,
With nowhere to go, only where you have been,
Have you a plan, or does fate take a part,
Do you meander, to where you depart,
Do you grow larger or smaller, divide into two,
Get angry, torrential...tell me, what do you do,
When torrid and parched and not to be seen,
Where do you hide...where have you been,
Have you an option on which way to go,
Who makes the choice on direction of flow,
Do you live eternal, or perhaps fade away,
Do you think of tomorrow, or just of today,
Is there a meeting place only for you,
And that's where you go, and that's what you do,
Questions unanswered, that I'll never know,
Tell me your secret...river, where do you go?

As We Were
Diane Wagner

Joy and sorrow,
Life and love,
Brings me to a high.

Where people meet,
and people greet,
to wine and dine affairs.

So here we are,
here we come,
We want to say good–bye.

The times we're shared,
the times we've cared,

Shall now just pass us by

I Was Always There
Stephanie Baumgarten

One night you put our love to sleep
Since then I lay and weep
I gave you my heart
You tore it apart
I would love you forever
If we had a new start
You're on my mind and in my heart
Since the night my heart fell apart

I thought you were the one
The one who would last
But I know now I cannot compete with the past
I hear our song we once knew
I'll never forget the dance with you

I loved you then and I love you now
I just wish you were still around
Wrapped in your arms
My fingers running through your hair
Just remember I was always there

The Burglar
Maisie Feary

Oh, how I hate that guy,
The guy who burglared my home,
He walked in without a care,
And took the things I own,
Some of the things I really loved,
They meant a lot to me,
He probably just sold them,
Or gave them away for free
How could he just walk in
And take my house apart,
And take the things I really loved,
That were closest to my heart,
My hate for him is really strong,
I want to hurt him, like he hurt me.
But I know that would be wrong,
That's the difference between him and me.
Doesn't he know the hurt he caused
When he searched through all my drawers,
Because now, I just want to leave,
This is not my home anymore.

The Magic Of The Moonlight
Lyndee Caldwell

As I stepped into the forest,
There was magic all around.
I unleashed my wild spirit,
And let my guard down.
It was not the first time I'd been there,
I'd been there many times,
Feeling the magic of the moonlight
Running up and down my spine.
I played with the babbling brook,
And flew with the wind through the trees.
I bathed in the silky soil,
And inhaled the fragrant Lilies.
And then...the sun came up,
And I sadly shed a tear.
I stepped out of my wonderful forest,
And the magic disappeared.

Letter To A Distant Love
Astrid Ellie

I close my eyes at night to sleep;
Instead I see your face.
Instead of snoozing 'tween the sheets,
I long for your embrace.
Most times, I lay upon the bed
And gaze an empty gaze,
While in my mind I see the past
And all its pleasant days.
At times I seem to smell your scent
And it brings me close to tears,
It makes me long to have you near,
So my tongue may revel in your taste.
Oh how I miss your warming touch
That held such gentleness,
How I miss your caring treatment
That showed such immense kindness.
I am no longer close to tears,
For cry is what I do
As I lay and reminisce,
And write these words to you.

Waterloo Rd
Patrick Doyle

Rain falls around their feet,
For them life is never sweet,
Cold wind, pulled up collar,
They walk by, do they ever bother?

As I ride through London's Streets,
1.8 beneath my feet,
Life for us is ever sweet.
No rain to damp, no wind to chill,
Someone to tend us when we're ill.

The reflection of colour, rain has made,
as the day begins to fade,
Life's not a problem for me and you,
for him depends on this ISSUE.

When we're home smug and dry,
will he laugh or will he cry
Not a problem for me and you
we don't sell the ISSUE!

Hannah
Wendy P. Frost

I saw you born my little one
The wonder made me weep,
And all the glory of that night
Kept me from my sleep.
I never thought to hold the pride
Of sharing these first minutes
And know our lives were turned about
Just by your presence in it.
What else could prove the beauty of
This world we take for granted
Then the birth of one small child
A precious gift untainted
And so my little granddaughter
I watch with special pleasure
The progress of your little life
With joy I cannot measure

Children Of Dunblane
Michael Moran

My tears are stinging softly
My eyes are red with sorrow
My heart so full of sympathy
There is no more tomorrow
With tomorrow take from us
Today will last forever
Every day is March 13th
The last day we were together
No more just popping to the shop
To spend their hoarded penny
No penny chews, or sherbet dabs
Too small, too young, too many
I'll say goodnight now children
Though it will never feel the same
No "cuddle me daddy" or "kiss me mummy"
No childish bedtime game
No nunnite to you my babies
No coldly, cruelly slain
Nunnite to you my children
Children of Dunblane

The Phone Call
John Brookes

Once upon time
An eel named Jo,
Lived in a lake,
And he lived all alone,
One day he had a brain wave,
And got himself a telephone,
He soon made friends
At the other end of the line,
And arranged to meet one,
At ten to nine,
They hit it off right from
the start,
How nice to meet you.
After all this time,
And he found she really,
Captured his heart,
And so all fish,
Be of good cheer,
And come to the wedding
of the year.

Where Are You
Susan Grivas

I see where you go
close to my heart,
but! Very far from my grasp.
I see you when flowers grow
in the spring of my most desires.
In the winter phase you start to fade,
but! "Where do you go from there?"
I wonder where your presence will be
when I turn the corner of my confusion.
Maybe if I look I will see
your twinkling eyes among the stars.
Fading in and out
going, going way beyond.
I see, I hear you somewhere
but! Unknown to me,
You happen to be inside of me...

Raincoats
Lauren Perez

you have eyes but you cannot see
you won't take time to listen to me
the world goes by but you're oblivious
Time does fly and it is mischievous
no one know 'bout what's inside
no one knows 'bout what I hide
feeling of bleakness lurking away
my biggest weakness is I don't say
I am all alone and I feel betrayed
this endless drone of times that strayed
now asking I am for help I need
my soul is sore and hard I plead
we walk in silence side by side
lacking guidance but I can't confide
in you my secret of pain well hid
and wonder how we met or why we did
and inside I look for empty answers
while my hands shake from this wretched curse
so now I leave and you sit there
I see you grieve for this maiden fair.

A Prayer To Our Lord For Our Brother Joey
Janice Napier

Dearest Lord it's been since
November ninth, we ask for and
since then my brother has been
in a coma, with no changes in his
condition, with the exception of severe
staph infections and weight loss.
Dearest Lord our 88 pound brother
has no chance, please help and
guide us to accept this he's only
twenty—eight. At this rate he
belongs with all the angels and
saints, his heart is strong, but
our hearts break, please Dearest Lord
open him to heaven's gate. He
will always be loved and never
forgotten, for our memories will
live on. So please Dearest Lord
take our brother home. It's hard
to accept, but with the love of
our Lord we will never be alone.

Executioner
Lucas Williams

Confusion sets in
As my mind goes blank
Swimming not in the river
But in the riverbank
The voices in my head
Won't quit screaming at me
I try to Chase them away
But they know what I can't see
In the corridors of my mind
Are the cobwebs of the night
Lost is the battle for day
But still I stand and fight
A warrior falls my brave soul dies
Now I can laugh without feeling
Look into the executioners eyes
Who takes my head while I am kneeling.

Untitled
Susan E. Pope

If you're ever going to love me
Love me now while I can know,
All the sweet and tender feelings
From which real affection flow.
Love me now while I am living
Don't wait until I'm gone,
And then chisel it in marble
Warm love words on ice cold stone.
If you've dear sweet thoughts about me
Why not whisper them to me,
Don't you know 'twould make me happy
And as glad as I can be!
If you wait till I am sleeping
Ne'er to waken here again,
There'll be walls of earth between us
And I couldn't hear you then.
So dear if you love me any
If it's but a little bit,
Let me know it now while living
So I can own and treasure it.

Deep Inside
Rebecca Tijerina

Looking into your eyes
I see a light to my surprise.
I come to realize
It is the love I feel for you inside.
I don't know how
you took me, by your side.
I've never told you at anytime
But Deeply I think you knew
It's you I want and only you
I wish you felt the same way too
It will be hard but worth the fight.
Can't you see
I'm in love with you
And it is out of sight.
But in due time
I will say those words
That will make my dreams
Come True
Just to say
I Love you.

The Myth Of Namby—Pamby
Gary K. Roussel

This morning I awoke again
My colour disappeared
No longer was it visible
The reflection in the mirror
No longer pink or white
No longer black or red
No longer jaune or olive
No longer brown or cream
No longer life's confusion
No longer any spite
No longer quick to judgement
No longer grief with life
No longer any frantic looks
Upon the colour of my race
The feeling of rebirth again
The world's a whole new place

Sarah Jean
Patricia L. Backlund

She was always special, this curly—haired little miss,
forever smiling and throwing all a kiss.
To everyone she seemed to dance down the street,
greeting happily all she did meet.
To oldsters she took time to visit and ask,
if she could perform some helpful task.
At school she befriended the timid and shy,
encouraging the slower to give one more try.
So popular was she, this Sarah Jean,
that her classmates selected her as their Prom Queen.
But then her steps seemed to slow,
causing concern for all she did know.
Her smile though sad always was still there,
but people knew she was ill and felt great despair.
When she entered the hospital her friends knew fear,
realizing for her that the end was near.
There on a grassy hill that is kissed by the sun,
they said a last good—bye to this precious one.
Heaven is the final destination for Sarah Jean.
Please send Angels to escort our little Prom Queen.

This Is What You Shall Do
Sara Andrews
Always love me.
For I have done nothing to offend you.
Don't try to stop me.
For if I'm determined, I will succeed.
Laugh at me.
For if I'm funny, I will laugh too.
Do not be afraid.
For those who fear are destined to fail.
Be nervous.
For it means you really do care.
Listen.
For you may miss important things said
Remember.
For memories are keys to my heart.
Look into my eyes.
For they are free passage to my soul.
Have fun.
For without fun life has no purpose.
Love life.
For if you love life, life will love you.

Seeing One's Heart
Michael A. Powells
shapes of illusioner dreams
paint
heavenly scenes of the
immortal
love that I have
for you
my heart stands motionlessly
like
Carved images in Stone
and
has more unwritten words
That
will Forever Care your
name
Dedication: To Bonita, whom I love

Where Is She Now
Fern Wilkins
A goose once laid a golden egg,
or so I have been told.
And all my life I've wondered
if that egg was ever sold.
Now, did that goose lay just one egg,
or did she lay a dozen?
I wonder if she hatched one.
That would keep the hen house buzzin'
Was the goose the main attraction
at a fair or in a zoo?
Did someone pay the income tax?
Did she pay her union dues?
Whatever happened to that goose?
I'd really like to know.
She's had so much publicity
she's probably lying low.
If anyone should hear from her
and someone surely should,
Please tell her I'd be Oh so pleased
to meet her — if I could.

Shadow Lace
Beverly J. Smith
Shadows dancing on building walls
In the west, the evening sunset falls.
After an overnight, frosty, freeze,
The leaves remaining on the trees
Gently dance, casting shadows of lace,
As time and sunset seem to race.
Before the dusk comes once again
To bring the night and maybe rain.
The time is short, to catch this scene,
When sunset glows against the green
Of grass that hasn't yet turned brown
And leaves have not fallen to the ground.
Like sunsets on a mountain top
Or as the sky just seems to drop
Into the ocean, and its wake,
As on the rocks the great waves break.
The moments pass so swiftly when
The sunset signals daytime's end.
I count my blessings as I see
This glorious painting God created for me!

Time
Maria S. Thompson
The past is beautiful.
It is good
to remember the past.
However,
we must not let the
past
take away from the
future,
nor must we think of the
future
so much as to forget the present.
The present is
now
and it will be gone tomorrow
never to
come back again.

The Hunt
Rebecca Domigan
Thrashing through the darkness of the forest,
The smell of fear and sweat fills the air.
Cold rain quickly pounds against your skin,
And in your mind you know that with one wrong step,
and down you shall go.
The cry of hellhounds constantly ring inside your ears,
Their fiery eyes in constant search for blood.
The forest floor shows you no salvation,
for it is all but bare.
The scream from trumpets fills the air,
Only the storms thunder brakes their sound.
You know that you cannot beat the odds.
A snap of a bow, a screaming arrow,
Warmth slowly drips from the shoulder.
The trumpets, the hounds, the thunder leave
the depths of your ears.
Nothing remains but the sound of the rain.
No pain, no joy, no sorrow, no fear.
You only feel the heaviness of your own body,
And carefully you fall to the ground.

Peering Through
B. J. Weesies
Peering through the darkness
in this world of make–believe
the sun sank from sight
as the moon rose, white and bright
and the snowdrifts dazzled like crystal walls
as the winter winds embraced me
I felt a little faint
I knew Mother Nature wasn't pretending
as the snowdrifts, were surrounding me, piling high
I put my mittens on and pulled my cap down tight
this wasn't a laughing matter
so, I prayed, to make it through the night
then heavens, moonbeams
shown a light so bright
guiding me through the blinding storm
and the winter winds
whispering in my ear
Son your fears
will soon be gone
your home is very near.

My Best Friend
Essie Nicole Hickman
I love her so much
And I know she cares
No matter what has happened
She's always been there.
She is my best friend
The closest thing to me
And I'm sure that's the way
Things will always be.
When she talks about me
She does it with pride
For the last fourteen years
She's stood by my side.
So here's to you, mom
My best friend
I hope our friendship
Will never end.

Clouds
Dora Brock
I love to see the fleecy clouds,
A sailing in the sky
Their shapes are wonderful to see
As they drift noiseless by.
But sometimes this pleasant sight
Changes from white to grey,
Raindrops fall and down they splash
To cause a rainy day.
Then black clouds bring the thunder
And there is a mighty crash
A streak of vivid lightning
An awe–inspiring flash
But then there is peace in the golden sunset
When night clouds form around
And one can see a silver lining
That glorifies the ground.
Yes, these are clouds of all descriptions
In all their fine array.
Thank God we have eyes to see them,
At any time of day.

Untitled
Stephanie Soto
Cute, with lips like his mother.
Handsome, with looks like his father.
Angel in heaven with God
Now watching over you.
Complete as a baby could be.
Everyone misses him, too.

Died not to bring you sorrow, but to watch after you,
And as he watches over you, he blows you kisses.
Kisses and love all over the place.
Over and under you
Toe to head filled with "Chance Love",
And brother to sister to father to mother.

More love comes down from the heavens.
On the day of his death you wept.
Reverse it now, think happy thoughts.
Today and tonight he's in a safe place.
On again tomorrow he'll blow you a kiss.
Now blow him a kiss back and sweep the sorrow away.

Untitled
Nicole M. Hodge
I want to breakdown and cry
But I can't shed a tear
Instead I drown my sorrows
In another bottle of beer
Listen to sad songs as I smoke
A cigarette
Remember our times together which
May only cause regret
Lie in my bed trying to sleep
Not catching a wink
Take another sleeping pill
To allow myself not to think
Wake–up with a love hangover
And take an extra long shower
Think about each minute we shared
Regret each meaningless hour.

The Sagebrush Ocean
Sharon B. Miller
I never thought I could live away from the sea.
Yet now, the open desert calls to me.
Early morning sun on frost–covered sage
Tells me it's time to begin a new day.
So much to do, yet always there's time
To stop and see beauty on the land that is mine.

I look to the hills and know that one day
I'll wander their slopes and watch rabbits at play,
Smell the warm pine and lie in its shade,
Know that this earth is both cradle and grave.
Here life is subtle, not easy to find;
Because life is struggle, only the tough can survive.

The sound of the waves is now far away,
Their unceasing surging and endless play.
I feel a moist breeze upon my face,
The kiss of the ocean in a new place.
Here also is life and constant motion:
The wind on the tops of the sagebrush ocean.

Untitled
Mary Fitz Edwards

Born with a shadow hanging over my head,
A child of Great Britain, with a milk box for a bed.
When I was just nine months old,
Great Britain said I need you no more.
My fate was put into the peoples hands
And Canada adopted Newfoundland,
A title to add to its collection of land.
Bread and molasses is what I was fed,
While shadows still hung over my head.
Then the Americans showed that they cared,
They built me a hospital to rest my head.
Having never seen a hospital before,
I was unconscious when I went through its door,
Upon awakening I could have swore,
That I had landed on God's shore.
Thank you America, for aiding me, I'm multi–country.

Autism Sam's World
Wendy Turocy

"Sam." A mother whispers.
He looks up. He looks down.
He maliciously picks at his fingernails. He echoes.
"This is a test. This is only a test of the emergency broadcasting system."
He shifts violently back–and–forth.
"Sam?" She calls.
He removes one of his shoes.
He swings the shoe by one lace like a pendulum.
"Uhmmmmmmmmmmmmm. Beeeeeeeeeeeeeeeeeeeeeeep."
He starts to sway gently.
"Sam." She pleads.
He stands up. He sits down.
He lifts his shirt and gnaws the bottom seam.
"This concludes our test of the emergency broadcasting system."
He looks up.
"Sam,
I just wanted to say I love you."
She sobs.
"Had this been an actual emergency..."

In My Dreams
Cliffia L. Harra

Often in my dreams, it's your face that I see,
And your tender lips that have kissed me.
Kisses that made my passion flow,
And set my body all aglow.
In this dream, the touch of your hand,
Thrilled me like no other can.
And between us, there was no shield,
To you, my body, I did yield.
I'd never knew love like this,
As I got lost in all its bliss.
You gave to me, such desire,
When our bodies met, it was like molten fire.
And we made love like never before,
When we were done, I could take no more.
We were tired, and needed to rest.
So I laid my head upon your chest.
When I awake,
The dream was gone.
But my love for you,
Still lingers on.

The Old Tin Box
Charlotte C. McLaughlin

There's an old tin box in the attic
Holding secrets from the past
And memories that last
I found mother's graduation ring
And dad's old boy scout pin
Grampa's old copper tie clasp
Then grannie's picture locket last
That old tin box in the attic
All that's left of a family tree
They could be junk to someone
But they're like gold to me
A lock of hair in a plastic bag
The faded words "Eddie" on a tag
These are the things left to me
Items of my family's history
I took the box and closed the door
Now I'm the keeper of that memory store

Alone
Timothy S. Carlton

Sometime things start to turn out bad
And I find myself feeling down and sad.
Then I realize by myself is where I belong
As long as I have me I will never be alone.

I have associates; with my happiness and joy I share
But when it comes to sadness and tears I know I'm the only one who care
What I feel is right for me, to you it may seem wrong
I don't care what others say because I'd rather be left alone.

Not to say I don't appreciate some of the associates that I have
It's good to have them around to share some happiness and good laughs
As I listen to the radio, sometime I hear that special song
Then everything comes together and I'd rather be alone.

One day everyone will be happy for all the things they've done
That will be the day to pat yourself on the back because you have won.
Now that I've got my point across people I'm gone
I might be myself but I am never alone.

Decisions Decisions...
Jean Sorenson

Confusing at best
Is hard to say
Shall I leave it till tomorrow
Or decide today?

Maybe I'll leave it
Just put it aside
Play it by ear, and
Let it ride

The problem with that
If it's left too long
Many things can happen
It could all go wrong

It'll play on my mind
Through the day and night
But when I decide
The decision will be right.

Valentine's Day
Shirley A. Phillips
On Valentine's Day (1945), when we were seventeen,
You gave me a gold heart–shaped locket at school one day.
We were sweethearts then, as we are today.
The tears, joy and happiness we have shared along the way
Are more dear to me than I could ever say.
Forty–two years have passed since that Valentine's Day.
The locket is still a shiny gold heart, stored away,
And if you opened it you would find
Two small pictures of sweethearts that were put inside.
TODAY, on Valentine's Day (1987), you send red roses
to my desk,
And today, once again, I realize you are the very best!
For no one could ever take your place,
We have grown older together and closer as the years have passed,
But who would have known they could pass so fast!!!
To me, we were sweethearts only yesterday–
Still hold me close to your heart through each year, day by day.

A Bunch Of Dreams
Monica Villarreal
Every time I fall asleep
I dream of you. There is not
A night that doesn't pass by
When I don't dream of you.
I dream we are together
and happy. I dream we are
so much in love with
each other. I dream I see us
holding hands, walking in
the park, or sometimes just
hanging out. The dream I
especially remember is when
we are alone in my room,
making love, and all I can
remember is it was beautiful. I
dream we could be together
forever. But, then I wake
Up and I realize it was
All but a bunch of dreams...

Butterfly's
Judy Derflinger
Butterfly butterfly
you are so sly you can fly up to
the sky.
in a wink you fly one place
to the other, no one knows if you
are a father or a mother.
touching everything gracefully
as you go, you look like the falling
snow. Showing your different shapes
as you flow, you really put on quite a show.
Your colors are so bright that
you don't pale in the brightest of
light. Might be you even come out at night.
Flowing with the wind as you
drift in and out again and again.
I hope you will always come
to visit with us again and again.

Dedication: My darling grandson, Cody Feaster

Don't Judge Me!
Kindell Keyes
Don't Judge Me!
Because the color of my skin.

Don't Judge Me!
Because of the way I speak.

Don't Judge Me!
Because of my style of dress.

Don't Judge Me!
Because of my occupation.

Don't Judge Me!
Because of the way I walk.

Don't Judge Me!
So that you won't be Judged.

Two – So Richly Blest
Bonnie H. McErlane
You've sent Your Angels to take our Mother away.
None of us had time to really say good–bye.
If we could have had only a minute, this is what we'd say:

"Thank you Mother for helping us grow,
For all the things you did that only we know.
For kissing our bruises and bandaging our knees,
For rescuing our cats that climbed all our trees,
Thank you for always being there, to hem our dresses, fix our bows,
iron our clothes and clean up our messes.
Thank you for showing us how to be wives and mothers,
For in our hearts, You out shinned all others."

You've left us with a will to keep living, even when it seems not worth
    trying.
And, when God's Will is done, to have no fear in dying.
He has seen fit to wash away all pain and cleanse your spirit with this
gentle rain that is falling, as God takes your hand and lays you to rest
in the earth beside Daddy—Two, So Richly Blest.

Experience Polio?
Clara F. Taylor
I know a woman well,
Continue living in this normal world.
Since Aug. 1953–age 14, to tell,
When polio took her strength, was told.

Four months a bottle to walk,
But Sister Kenny treatments worked.
To continue her sacrifice walk to talk,
When asked "what happened to you", unquote.

Victims of polio are a dying breed,
is sad no interest to cure.
Someday an herb, a pill, or a seed.
to cure polio, all so pure.

This woman lives struggling to be,
In this fast hectic world pace.
As normal as allowed, it's me!!!,
Someday we may meet face to face.

Broken Crayons
Tamarah Vandergriff
I bought a box of crayons,
and brought them home to color.
I stayed out of the lines
and tried to match them perfectly to the color of the sky
as it is in my world.
Red, brown, black, and yellow
were shaded in the corner of my hope.
I colored dreams of wedding dresses,
children and success.
A special place with happy faces
and hearts— bright flowers
with straight green stems.
But the crayons broke in my hands,
and melted wax dripped from the walls.
There were no wedding dresses, no children.
no bright flowers worth straight green stems,
just a mirage of colors all condemned to black.

Runaway Billet
Robert L. Mitchley
Lodged, since a tiny acorn into the
side of a mountain's scape, He stands
far above the winding road.

One crooked old oak long since dead and
split with limbs storm broke...

The logger fells it low, sawn to length,
one billet veers down hill, bumps and
smacks against his peers crushing tinder under tow.

Never stopping at his nook where laid, the stump
bounds head first onto the main road.

Cars and trucks rend their nerves of steel
as the billet commands their scold.
And to those drivers swerving and honking
He's just a stumbling block, but to
the logger His partial load!

I Love You
Sarah F. Thompson
I've tried so hard to replace you in my heart
But no one else is the same.
I know that since I couldn't see this before
I am the one to blame.
Now all I have are the memories
Of all the times we went through
And of all the precious moments
I should have said that I loved you.
If I should die alone.
With no one else to love
I know that I will continue to love you
As I'm looking on from above.
And maybe then one day, when I see you again,
You'll gather me in your arms
And my pain will come to an end.
I just wanted to say I love you
Since I could never say it before
And with each day that passes.
I love you even more.

God In The Elements
Henrietta Smith
On a hot summer day the trees serve as fans,
Swinging and swaying all through God's land.
Then I heard thunder roaring across the sky,
I feel it's God voice, and I know why.

He's trying to tell us all to pay attention,
Remember everything in the Bible that was mentioned.
Now the lightning appears and send down bolts,
That's the blinking of His eyes giving us a jolt.

That's His way of letting us know He's still there,
And we better remember, He's going nowhere.
The rain is His tears coming down from overhead,
Crying over us about the blood that's begin shed.

Satan, is doing his best in trying to destroy us,
Remember, Jesus is sunshine, in him do trust.

Old Memories Never Die
Esther Ruth Wilcox
It's a lonely life without you
My eyes are dimmed with tears
As I walk this road alone
Through long and empty years
When love is gone forever
We go our separate ways
I try to leave the past behind
But old memories never die
They just slowly fade away—with time.

Those memories that we shared
Down through so many years
Oh, there were good times and bad
But still life goes on
We must not look back
So, with the passing of time
Forward is the path we must take
But old memories never die
They just slowly fade away—with time

Friendship
Brenda T. LaFerriere
Friendship is a very special kind of word
Friendship is always having someone, who needs to be heard
Friendship is something which is not easily found
Friendship is always having someone who will be around.

Friendship is having someone there through good and bad time
Friendship is having someone to help you when you're in a bind,
Friendship is having something special between two people to share
Friendship is knowing that there will always be someone near.

Friendship is having someone who will listen to you
Friendship will always take away your lonesome blue,
Friendship is having someone there in a case of need
Friendship is not only having one person to lead.

Friendship is having someone you can lean upon
Friendship is having someone in which you can depend on,
Friendship doesn't always come very easy
Friendship is never saying that for that friend you are too busy.

Misunderstood

Brenda L. Warren

Shy,
quiet and lonely.
Nervous,
anxious and afraid.
Observant,
listening and watching.
Boring,
with nothing to say.

SNOB they say of her,
but if they only knew,
that if they got to know her,
they'd see her heart exuding,
kindness and
tender
loving
care.

Tell Me Darlin'

Alice W. Klos

Tell me darlin', when your fingers glide softly across my skin,
Is it me you're thinking of, or is it him?
When you gently smile and look down at me,
Tell me darlin', whose face do you see?
Tell me darlin', why the frown?
Are you wishing my hair black instead of brown?
When you look into my eyes, what do you see?
Are they soft warm brown, or grey troubled seas?
I can't make the choice, you will have to choose.
Either way one of us will have to lose.
Tell me darlin', I've got to know.
Is it me or him who has to go?
You can hold his memories there in your mind,
or a flesh and blood man till the end of time.
You know I've always loved you.
I can't darlin' compete with a ghost.
So tell me darlin'.

Dedication: Arlene and Terry

Grant Me Eyes

Julie B. Harper

Grant me eyes
That I may see
All the hurt and need
In a moments time
Let it disperse
Upon my head
But not the curse
The love, the love
Unconditional I seek
So I can help
The wayward and meek
To understand with vigor
The thought
Of this dream I've caught
The simplest of man's needs
Oh' Grant me eyes
That I may see.

Dedication: Joseph, my son with love

The Faces Of Man

Judiann DeBella

How sad it is the faces of man, the untold
stories of our own desolate lives and feelings.
How sad it is we obsessively gorge ourselves with
too much of life's selfish, destructive and
unnecessary needs, how an ugly and ignorant face
is turned toward the ailing and the insane, the
destitute and hungry. Is it we are all just
hypocrites towards an unstable world or is it not our
problem? Is it we see more clearly with our eyes
shut or is it just convenient or is it that there
isn't enough money to show some kind of decency towards another?
We cannot simply close our eyes to wish our
problems and fears away because someday, something
will open them and we'll find that a web has been
spun around us. Instead we have to unite together
and work through our own self-defense and morals,
work with our minds, our hearts, our souls and our faces.

Colors Of Love

Marilyn J. Blank

Love casts many colors as it cascades through our life.
Its hues reflect from others as they cause our joys and strifes

Faith, innocence and purity transcend their whitish glow.
Giving unto life security and peace to the soul.

Happiness, laughter, carefree days of childhood fun.
Are captured in our hearts like rays of golden sun.

Caring, sharing, loving feelings, warmth that inspires happy dreams
Create a carefree joyous glowing and fills the heart with reddish beams

Sadness, losses, trouble, loneliness, anger, fear.
Bring on shades of blue, gray and black that make our sorrow clear

Love is like a rainbow with colors shimmering through.
Ever revolving around us to make each day brand new.

Dedication: My family and friends

Hidden In Silence

Susan Doty

Rain falls from the sky,
Like tears from a child's eyes.
Gray clouds cover the sun:
A bright day turns into a dreary one.
A chilly autumn breeze causes trembling in the trees.
The sun's rays blend and fade as the mountains provide shade.
Children that fall victim to fear
Scream loud, but no one can hear.
All their wishes narrowed to one—
The wish for this life to be done.
They see no where to turn
As the hunger inside them starts to burn.
They run away from the pain,
Away from the hunters searching for prey.
They hide in the darkness, silently crying out for help.
They are lost, only because no one searches.
They are right in front of our eyes,
If we only cared to look
At more than the pouring rain.

Gone From The Nest
C. M. Diehl

I miss the kids, now that they're away...
Especially cheering and watching them play...
Football, soccer, volleyball and lacrosse,
Living our lives with each coin toss.

Watching them grow, their failure and success...
Helping them out of each and every mess...
Being useful, that's what it was...
Or maybe it was the feeling of love.

Whatever the case, as older I get
It is those things I cannot forget...
Happiness, sorrow, gladness and cheer,
Now when they visit, we sit down with a beer

They relate their memories, their point of view
It's nice to know they remember you, too.

Happiness
Carol Greco

The warmth of the sun on a crisp spring day,
The sound of the birds as they're singing away.
The hug from a child when you're feeling down,
That moment of quiet when no one's around.

The feeling of sand so cool beneath my feet,
The sound of the ocean when I lay down to sleep,
The moon and the stars on a clear summer's night,
That moment you realize that this love is right.

The innocence of children as they laugh and play,
And they take me back to my younger days.
To lend a helping hand to those in need,
To watch a flower grow from a planted seed.

The cry from a baby after just giving birth,
knowing this is God's greatest miracle on Earth.
When I arise in the morning and greet the new day,
I know I will find happiness in many new ways

And You Say I'm Selfish
Nigal C. Wagner

remorse
floats
away from you
with
quiet moments
i never had
to own
i borrowed them
from you

i have no
recollection
of myself,
tell me again,
who was
i
before you
defined
me?

Hey Mary
Athina Tsouros

A tiny figure shrouded in white, trapped and displayed
behind a wire screen like a rare revered bird.
Still and humble your hands held close together
fingertips meeting, a prisoner bound to obedience
the chains strong but invisible.

A stone cross tall and proud lords over you
like a stoic sentry on special duty
You appear unaware of your majestic surroundings
Your eyes a piercing blue as the deepest ocean
do not seem to see before you
Your mouth gentle like a butterfly's wing is closed

You long to be left alone to mourn in peace
Your pain still as sharp as a poisonous arrow
Yet all around we cry out to you
But you know there can be no response, only silence

Winter In Nevada?
Kerry Brooke

There's that huge red moon
Peeking over our handmade woodshed.
You would think it was August,
But it's mid–December instead.

There's no snow on the ground yet,
Nor hardly any on the mountain caps.
I don't foresee snow for Christmas
When January marches in, perhaps.

So strange to have the back door open,
Especially this time of year.
Usually there's snow to our knees
And we are bundled warm in winter gear.

With houses shut tight because of chill,
Fireplaces and stoves going...
It leaves one confused...
MY CATNIP IS STILL GREEN AND GROWING!!!

To The Love Of My Life
Karen M. Pelkey

Oh, Heart of My Heart, these words I write.
You're in my thoughts, both day and night!
I love you more than a million words could ever tell,
The moment we met, for you I truly fell!

Your eyes, so dark and piercing – so full of love,
Make drops of ecstasy fall from above
Upon my body, trembling from your gaze and from your touch,
Knowing my Love, that you Love me as much!

Yes, My Love – the Woman in me needs the Man in You,
To be embraced by your Love so warm and true.
To return that Love is so easy to do, ever in your arms,
Your breath upon my skin, giving to me all your charms!

We've shared tears and laughter, so many times together,
Just you and I, sharing our dreams together.
My Dearest Sweetheart – a Legend You are,
I'm Yours – Yes – Yours Forever!

A Monkey
Ashley Winter
In the jungle, there's a funky monkey,
He grooves to the disco beat.
He dances to his heart's content,
Just look at his groovie feet.
Can you hear the Tarzan's call?
The monkey stops, dead still.
He swings in the trees, on
The breeze.
Until he gets to Tarzan's
window sill.
He jumps in the air, on
To the floor, then into
Tarzan's door.
He starts to dance, and
Then to prance.
Then starts a break–dance
On the floor.

I Wanted...
Orri D. Brown
I wanted to see you just one, maybe even twice
without all of the cover–up.
I wanted to see the man, inside the exterior
come out for a while
I wanted so much for a second, maybe even a minute or two,
for hours of fun.
I wanted so much just to be, to exist in your world,
be one with you.
I wanted to see what it is like, just to experience,
your place.
I wanted to be a part, if only for a night
maybe even a day.
I wanted you to know, to let it be understood,
how it was I felt.
When for that one day, for those minutes and seconds,
it was you and I,
no one else.

Dedication: David, thank you for love

Angels Of Satan
Elmer Lovan
We see them at work, day and night
Tempting people, with big houses and yards.
Filled with cars, boats and trailers.
The children, have no place to p lay.
They are in the big house, watching
Violent TV, with a teenage baby sitter.

Mother is at work, the bills tax and insurance to pay
And clothes closet to fill.
She's not home to kiss and hug their hurt away.
Children, never smell, hot bread, cakes, cookies or pies,
As we did, when from school we came.

But Satan is pleased with the work of his angels.
Many children, will be his some day. Mother was tempted
To work, the bills to help pay for big houses, and
Yards, full of cars, boats and trailers

Dedication: To my wife, Ella Marie

The Moonlit Woods
Suzy Morton
As I walk through the moonlit wood,
I see shadows and shapes ever merging.

The wind whistles through the skeletal trees,
With branches grasping at unseen forces.

The sounds of the leaves underfoot break through the eerie silence!
As I walk along the darkened path.

I start to hurry as the trees bend and sway,
As though alive yet dead inside.

The dense trees ahead look dismal and gloomy,
I feel as though I'm being followed yet nobody is there.

The moonlit wood sends a shiver down my spine,
I hope I get home soon.

Untitled
Crystal L. Howard
I lie awake at night, waiting for the
morning light. Will today be the same?
Will people see me as insane? I went
thru my days thinking I lead a normal life.
Soon someone came and changed all of
that, I felt I was stabbed with a knife.
I wish that person would never have
come around. Now every day I wait for
that familiar, yet unfamiliar sound. You
may wonder what I'm talking about. I'm
talking about the death that makes you
scream and shout. The icy cold fingers
of death that grip your soul. Pulling and
yanking till it swallows you whole. You'll
never wake up but feel you are forever
falling. You will hear someone screaming
your name and calling and calling. You think,
Surely we're almost to the end, but what
you don't know is that you've only just begun.

The Timid Bridegroom To His Bride
Anthony Telschow
Why am I
so fond of dancing?
Because I cannot move.
My legs are caught up at the joints.
My arm movements are crude.

Tensions mounting right the way
through my spine
and higher.
My poor flesh cannot translate
what the rhythms
have inspired.

But clear the benches.
Sweep the crumbs.
Bring along the drums.
Let us see what shall become.

O let us have this dance.

Untitled
Amber Gapinski

As I look up into the sky I realize that the dream we once
shared is gone.
As I look out into the ocean I realize that our waves will
never meet again.
As I see the sunset or rise I realize we will never see it
together again.
As I roll over in the morning I realize you will never be
there holding me in your arms again.
As I walk around our favorite lake I realize I will never
hear I love you again.
As I sit here and look upon the walls that were once
covered with pictures of us,
I realize we will never be again.
As I sit here and write this poem I realize I wasted three
words on you...
"I Love You!"
No more will you hear it again!

Land Of Make Believe
M. D. Moss

Where is this land called Make Believe?
Where live the wounded hearts to grieve?
Where time and passion have passed them by
So to Make Believe they come and cry.

Into the land of Make Believe
Travel the shattered and bereaved
Where heavy spirits can heave a sigh
No more to groan with the burden of life.

So won't you come and join me?
In this beautiful land of Make Believe?
Where we can live among sheltered dreams
Planning the future with hopeful schemes.

Your fondest wishes will be commands.
When you journey to this land.
There are no liars to deceive
Because its only Make Believe...

Dusty Spirit
Melonia Williams

The feelings I endure and
The sorrows I encompass
Keep floating to the surface
While I am mesmerized

The path of life is dusty
From misuse and from doubting
I want to find a windy gust
To help me clear the way

That horse so full of spirit
Could be my ride to freedom
If only I could free my fears
And ride the path with life

Don't tell me to uncloak myself
For I will only shadow
And wither to a lifeless stone
Of fiery depth within

How I Wish She Was A Little Girl With Her Toys Again
Mary I. Houchins

It have been years since her
Life began,
She was as brave as a soldier
Her life in God's hand.
But I wish she was a little
Girl with her toys again.
The terrible pain, that burned inside
Of her like a flame, like showers
Of falling rain.
She heard a trumpet, than a roar
And a burst of tears
It was more than she could bear
Looking back, wondering what's there
She knew it was near
Her life ended with no fear
How I wish she was a little girl
With her toys again.

Terminal Love
Peggy J. Klinge

deep inside me the tiredness lies,
heavy as wet snow
cold as dry ice.
deep within i want to give up
on so many things
and sleep without awakening;
but the need of you
holds me here.
the necessity of my breathing
becomes clear as you hold me;
i linger now to hear your voice;
to feel your love in the touch
of your eyes to mine;
yet sometimes i pray
you will not come again—
then i cry when you do,
for i am ashamed of my need
and just too tired of living alone
to tell you to go home to her.

Franklin Street
Cheryl Smith

Going back to Franklin Street,
Wish it could be memories
of sweet yesterdays, come
slowly back to me.
on Franklin Street, once it was
a dream, a beautiful dream
for me.
thinking of the happy times
the moments we shared
dreaming of summer nights
I once spent there.
Franklin Street, wish, I could
be there. on Franklin Street,
I see you waiting there
smiling without a care
on Franklin Street. Wish I
Could be there.

Dedication: To Joseph, I love you always

Dreamers
Chris Mickel
Fifteen Years down the drain,
I know everything,
Isn't it a shame.
Mom says,
Get a job now,
Make my millions,
But I don't know how!
Drive my Porsche or my Jag,
Oops, I think mom's
Starting to gag.
Back to school,
I can't be late,
The school bus will not wait.
For fifteen year old dreamers,
It's not too late,
To learn the golden rule,
So life will be great.

Trees
Jeanie M. Grace
Oh for the trees that sway
in the breeze.
White birch excellings my
favorite you see.
Magnificent its beauty standing
Tall and lean, with so much dignity.
Incredible it does seem,
stretching to the sky as the birds
fly by who occasionally land to rest in
their nest.
With leaves that wave their color
to change.
Succumb in the fall and new birth
in the spring.
White bark shines in the night
from emission of moonlight.
Oh 'tis lucky we are having nature's
fine trees to make our life's
excursion a pleasure indeed.

Walking
Michael R. Doyle
On the road that I have taken
One day, walking, I did awaken
Amazed to see where I had come,
Where I was going, where I was from

For this is not the path I thought,
And this is not the place I sought,
And this is not the dream I bought
But just the same, It's all I've got.

I've changed my road with a sad smile
Only after the pain of many a mile,
My path is lit by my desire,
To put behind me heat and fire.

Because on the road that I have taken
One day, walking, I did awaken,
One day, walking, I did awaken,
After all I loved I had forsaken.

The Beginning Or The End
Jewel Bachmeier
Mother nature has been stripped bare
Now, people slowly stop to stare
It's too late man has gone too far
The Garden of Eden has been replaced with tar

The once sweet clover and the babbling brook
The breath of life, man himself took
The greed of man nothing could be sadder
For it was given to him on a silver platter

Money has no value, Mother Nature has no price
Nothing can save us not even mans mechanical device,
The creator is looking downward with a sigh
For the time is coming for all mankind to die

The beauty and the home of the brave
Look again my friend — it's only a grave

Shine
Brian Michael Payton
Deep within my heart lies
the unspoken words.
Silence is drifting, wanting to
speak the feeling of love.
Freedom has come afar to deliver.
Tender love is swayed in the wind.
For the dawn of the new day
brings feeling of gay.
For the night brings tender
kisses, for love is all around—
Thy tenderness speaks forth
unchanted sweet love.
Thy tender breasts are like
grapes from the vine.
Thy love will shine like
the moon, so beautiful like the star
Forever more you will shine again.

Dedication: To: Sandra, friends forever

God Blessed Me With You
Melanie Brochu
God Blessed me with you
to
love me for me

What I mostly need
is
monogamy for security

If you take the time
to
love me for me
through
conversation
gentle touch
truth

I will love you for you

You will love me for me

Fading Away
Michele Szymanski
The T–shirt from Jamaica, crumpled in the drawer,
colors faded with all the memories.
Calvin Klein bleached from endless washes;
Frayed and tattered at the ends, its newness gone forever.
Sunlight fades the curtains, and creates a
barren hole on the vintage brown shag rug.
Notebooks filled with hopes and dreams, collect dust,
slowly turning yellow, as do the dreams.
Photographs hang from the wall, with faces that are
barely recalled in my aging mind.
Man's best friend lies on a withered couch,
black hair turning grey.
Things around me are gradually slipping away, losing their
brightness, their importance, their color.
Then a friend calls to say hello, and I realize this friend still
has brightness, color and importance in my life,
and they have never faded away.

Strength For Today
Dorothy Kuxhausen
Give me strength for just today.
A hopeful heart for tomorrow,
Forgetting the things that happened yesterday
Making the best of whatever comes my way.

Whatever God has planned for me,
May I never question,
Though it may not be my desire,
May I accept it readily.

Sometimes it is hard to think,
That all things work for good
When everything looks dark and gray
And you are weary from a long day.

A God that knows when the sparrow falls,
Is surely watching over me.
I know that in the end
I'll be ready when he calls.

Plea Of A Street Child
Jewell Castro
A crust of bread, please
pangs of hunger remind me
how long it has been since last I ate
A small cup of water please
to soothe my parched throat
A pair of shoes, please
to cover my bleeding feet
A warm coat, please
to stop the shivering, shivering so
strong that I sometimes think it will
separate the flesh from my bones
A kind word, please
a reassurance that I am alive
that I am still here
that I am still me
If none of these can you give me
look not me with scorn
I do not need your pity
I simply need your help.

A New Beginning
Helen Shady
This is a day of new beginnings,
A span of time to shape and mold;
Let us treasure memories of yesterday
With its joys, woes and lessons,
Realizing they are now beyond recall.
Tomorrow is but a dream – a hope – a mystery; nothing more.
Today beckons with twenty–four hours of uncharted living;
Let us use each moment with gratitude and faith.
With yesterday's lessons to guide us, let us concentrate only on today;
Knowing that each must first feel grief and pain
To fully appreciate the blessings and joys of life.
So with shadows to soften the glare of the sun, help us
To challenge each passing hour so that with love and faith we can
Face today's setting sun with satisfaction of a day well spent,
And with happy anticipation of another day to come;
Another new beginning.

A Taste For An Angel
Johnna Bridwell
Fine wine has a special quality of
taste as well as class, Rose or a sparkling
White, the flavor gives itself applause
as the tongue craves more.

The beauty of a string of pearls are
defined by their classical simplicity, art
and nature, a timeless combination,
tasteful yet rare.

True pleasure starts from within, a
tremor passes as a blush searches for
a hiding place. I long for you, flavor
gave me a reason, and a taste for
an Angel has me humbled before
you in your deliciously romantic
concoction of love.

More please...

Key To My Heart
Malissa Mercer
I had closed the door upon my heart
and wouldn't let anyone in.
I had trusted and loved only to be hurt
but that will never happen again.

I had locked the door and tossed the key
as hard and as far as I could.
Love would never enter there again.
My heart was closed for good.

Then you came into my life
and made me change my mind.
Just when I though that tiny key
was impossible to find.

That's when you held out your hand
and proved to me I was wrong.
Inside your palm was the key to my heart
you had it all along.

Lois
Marilyn Faye Smith
My mom was Mother Nature, at her best.
Her face was like the sun's rays, warming you
from inside out.
Her hair was the color of wheat, ready for harvest.
Her arms could hold and sway you, as the wind
did to the trees.
Her eyes could reveal in a glance, if you were O.K.
or on her list.
Her legs had to be made of stone, otherwise,
how could they have stood such long hours.
Her mouth was smooth, and rich, and from it poured
words of wisdom, warmth, and power.
Her frame though short and slim could and would
do whatever, to provide for her children.
She was the giver (of so much) and the receiver
of so little.
Yes, my mom was Mother Nature at her best.

My House Of Memories
Kay Koontz
Pictures on the mantle
Pictures on the wall,
Each a golden memory,
Of my love, my life, my all.

Shadows by the window,
Shadows by the door,
All bring back the happiness,
Of times now gone before.

Snapshots of the garden,
Snapshots all around,
Wedding pictures glowing,
For future pathways found.

Tears of joy and longing,
Tears along the way,
Are memories left of a lifetime,
Which no one may take away.

Born Again
Diane M. Sawyer
After rebirth,
the flames of fire run high.
Christ beating solid now,
throughout my stoic silent flesh.

He stands with me strongly amongst the tides.
He moves with me stealthily amongst the waves.
His perception beyond my perseverance.
Satan's deception calmly at His side.

I raged and seethed the fire.
I burned and died in the flame.
I covered and shadowed the ember.
Until I rejected Satan's mold.

Now I glow and burn the ember.
I live and breathe the flame.
The Holy Spirit guides my fire.
For Christ is in my Soul!

Rainforest
Kevin Harris
Birds and bees fly through the sky,
as the evening wind blows by.

The bright green leaves on the trees,
waving in the breeze.

Birds fly high into the sky until they disappear,
into the misty air.

Snakes on the ground slithering around.
In the crisp air the sound
of buzzing bees,
flying through the trees.

Animals on the ground
make beautiful sounds.
The canopied ground, echoes the sound.

God Only Knows
Rebecca Carey
Sometimes I wonder
What is the meaning of life
Is it just to grow up
And to become someone's husband or wife?

Or is it to explore
And find out what you can?
Then share things we know
With every child, woman and man?

Is it just an accident
That we are here on Earth?
And is it an accident
That women were made to give birth?

Is it also an accident that we have
Summers, Falls, Winters and Springs?
God only knows
The answer to these things.

When Troubles Come
Ondray B. Ladia
When lightning strikes, are you scared? Do you think of the consequences impaired? In the night under the darkened sky a single strike catches thine eye. And just as I throw up my head to see, the Heavens begin to rain down on me. Cover thine head and go for shelter, to a place of warmth in this uproaring weather. I wish I was back home in my mother's protection. The way she helped me in my time of need, but that has passed. I'm just another one of my Father's seeds in the world's grasp. Raindrops heavily hit the ground. If you listen closely, you can hear the sounds of crying children seeking love, when their guardians are out doing drugs. Not mowing their lawns as they should. Their seeds will grow up like weeds of a garden, and deprive them of their livelihood. The rain stopped, and the night grew still. Yet the rain thereafter had given me a chill. The clouds rolled back and the stars shined bright. Throughout all that has happened, this turned out to be a good night. So in life, when you feel that your troubles have got you in a maze, keep the faith, because trouble doesn't last always.

Untitled
Marissa G. Mooney
Let us be careful with "our" children;
with all children...
that in our effort to teach
responsibility, proper etiquette, good behavior, etc....
that we do not strangle the life in them...
kill their spirit and their spontaneity, their creativity,
natural instincts and spirit!
It is our responsibility to help shape them—
NOT to force them all into the same mold.
Perhaps instead to "groom" them... to keep them within the same garden,
but allow them the freedom to be their very own, very special,
very beautiful flower or plant.
With sunshine and water and care they will grow and blossom,
and they will learn to weather storms and rough terrain,
cold seasons and even... overwatering.
Hopefully, they will grow together but not at the expense of one another—
always reaching for the sun... but deeply rooted.

You, Or Myself, Or I and We?
Charles Hearn, Jr.
And this person said "Speak to us of self-knowledge."
And he answered, saying: "To thine own self be true."
The way you understand this, it's up to you!
Your heart's knowledge...
You would know in knowledge,
That in which you've been taught, and learned...
Or, which you've gathered within thought
You would touch with your fingers,
The naked body of your dreams, or; so it seems!

And it's well that you should!
The hidden self knowledge,
Of yourself, that's true to your soul...
You need not run, although that's your goal!

When your treasure,
It's revealed to your eyes
It shouldn't be a surprise...
Because this is real, with no disguise!

Kathleen
William G. Aragon, Jr.
As I climb the mountain road of life,
I pause from time to time,
To gaze upon the curves I've passed
And wondered when I'd find,

The trail that leads straight to the top,
The summit that seems so far,
And if my path were lit
I'd find our shining star.

And though you are a curve I've passed
I cannot help but see,
You were a shortcut to the top,
A love and a smile for me.

So when I think of the love we knew,
I smile through broken dreams.
For I see the mountain next to mine,
Is a mountain for Kathleen.

Just Wondering
Priscilla McShane Moore
Did you ever watch a frog jumping with delight
As a glistening shower of water bathed him clean?
Or see a raven watching at the side
With the hope a worm was waiting as his meal?
And what about the marigolds and soft pink roses too,
Blushing from the first good taste of the morning dew?
Did you draw a breath of wonder as you found a baby bird,
All pink and naked, deserted on the grass,
As you listened to the music all around you
On a woodland path?
What would happen if a rainbow broke and tumbled down?
Would the pink and blue and gold be soft to hold?
Or, like a broken promise, disappear?
If the grass were gray or purple
Would it really change a thing?
Would the sun still keep on shining bright and clear?
And will there be tomorrow and tomorrow and next year?

Untitled
Pamela Martin
Misty darkness
Cold still night
No warmth or sunlight.
Where have the days gone
The nights just pass on.
The way our lives did
That Monday night.
We understood
We never knew why
But we couldn't say
Goodbye.

That last kiss
Seemed to go on forever
And that hug will always
be in my heart.
No matter how hard we try
We just couldn't say
Goodbye.

The Lungs
Florence Williams
I didn't know, I would ever see,
The lungs compared to a tree.
The trunk, the branches and leaves do show,
The many things we need to know.

A tree was strong not long ago,
But now its loss its power to grow.
The "winds of time" blow hot and cold.
Soon we find we are growing old.

The path we take to heal the lung
Is with us now, the bell has "rung".
We look at it, and it is me,
What does it take to heal a tree?

If you believe, it can be done.
Like a "well oiled clock" it will start to run
God's grace to all on "Mother Earth"
My prayers for all, and the lungs rebirth.

One Love Shared By Two
Barbara S. McCann
Borrowed from a song,
One love shared by two –
Sometimes time between visits long,
yet, it is if time stands still.
My life's always brightened by you.

Soul mates, friends, and lovers
Maybe now, maybe later, maybe never...
Sometimes alone, sometimes with others –
We just never been so clever...
To know how to put it together.

Only the future knows what lays ahead,
Easy or hard, life's passions bind us together,
For we always seem to use the same thread.
Whether apart or together, life's better because...
We have one love shares by two.

Searching
Melva Chandler
Pardon the intrusion but I didn't know what else to do
I've misplaced some thing; it may be here with you.
I looked away for a moment and it just disappeared
If you don't mind will you look to see if it's here.

I held on to it tightly, it was never out of my sight
I placed it beside me each and every night
In the early morning hours I could feel it near me
It seems I've lost it; I don't know where it can be.

Often times through my window the moon would shine
Reflecting the radiance, the beauty of what was mine.
It brightened my days when they seemed dark or black
Please help me find it, I desperately want it back.

The warmth I felt as it entered and embraced my soul
The inner strength it gave to help me become whole.
What I am searching for is as pure as a snow white dove
Somewhere I lost you and your precious love.

Counting Time
Onin–Age Iron
? What is it that is but isn't?
That ends the very moment it starts?
That has no beginning nor an end?
And even mends broken hearts!

'Tis time of course, whose toll
the movement of the planets tallies
to keep all things from happening at once
in history's peaks and valleys.

A time to live and a time to love
A time to work, and yes, to play
And only death requires no time
For 'tis not followed by another day.

So, keep in mind when counting time
The only time that counts is now
For to touch eternity all one needs
Is a kiss and love to show you how.

Lady
Guadalupe Lee
I rescued you from the traffic street
big brown eyes and curly sprig,
You sit there starring at me
while I eat, spaghetti without meat.
My lady, my lady
you are sweet
Real tears you cry
and I wonder, why?
If you could talk
What would you say?
Oh! go ahead have some
of my spaghetti
My lady, my lady
Not your real name
but all the same, you
are a princess to my
sentiments indeed.

On Human Knowledge
Tom Dahl
Infinite sand grains
Slowly sifting eternal Time
Cross for an instant the life of Man
And etch, so finely
On that lubricous clay, the human brain
A delicate pattern
A picture of life.

The writer
Poor musing scribe
Dreamily traces with blunted quill
Each finite line
For the moment impressed
But soon gone.

Thus some resemblance of Life is held
Thus we think
We know
What we are.

Right By Your Side
Debra E. Garrett
I will always be there by your side
Whenever you may need me,
No matter the situation, by your side I'll be
There ain't a chain strong enough to hold me
Ain't a breeze strong enough to slow me,
There ain't a road too rough to ride,
That will keep me from getting to your side
I will ask nothing in return
Or feel you'll owe me a thing.
I just hope it will help, just the comfort I bring
I have an ear to listen, and arms to hold ya near
I'll have the shoulder to cry on, to shed that tear
I'll always be by your side, and try to be somewhat of a guide
I can't promise I'll make things better and right
Can't promise days thereafter sunny and bright.
I can promise and guarantee you, I'll always be there
By your side when you ask or just need me to...

Dedication: My husband, that I love

Untitled
Sara R. Anderson

Trees all over this world
Stand together.
They are of different shapes and sizes
Yet, they all stand together,
Through rain, storms, winds and snow.
Wouldn't it be something
If we could all stand together
Red, yellow, black and white,
Turn this world of prejudice and hate around
Try a bit of caring and understanding
And swallow the pride that blinds us.
Our Creator, put us here just as he put
The trees here.
Wouldn't it be beautiful
To live as one
Through winter, spring, summer and fall
Like the trees do.

Hope
Kevin Smith

From the first time I saw you with
that everlasting smile I didn't
have a clue that I would be
with you for a while.

Your beauty is expressed and your
mind is so sincere when it comes
to you there's no contest for you
keep my heart and soul clear.

Oh how I linger for your touch
and from your lips a kiss
I never wondered how much of
your sweet company I missed.

Trapped in a world that's full of
despair with no room to cope
I look to the heavens to find care
and with you I have hope.

Leaving
Lucille E. Teats

How would I leave a home I have treasured?
A love that is lost and cannot be measured,
By the hours I have toiled to make
this a home. I have cooked and cleaned.
I have sewed and mowed. I have papered
walls and painted doors. I have scrubbed
and waxed many floors. But, what can
you say when love is out the door?
The children you've cradled and sung
to at night. All have grown up and
have taken flight.
Where is the love to make it right?
The vows that were taken have been
carelessly strewn. To another
woman you have closely grown.
How can I leave what seemed to be
ideal? How can I believe it was never real?
The thirty four years seem like a day.
The palace, the king, have all gone away.

Secret Lovers
Amy Hudson

We met as two souls hoping to find love. Each looking for that missing
    link. Our worlds are so different yet we long for the same things,
we feel the passions and desires...
We know that we may never have each other but here we can share our deepest
fantasies...
We long for each other's soft lips and touch, hunger for the mind, body and
    soul...
though flesh never crosses the line. We close our eyes and our worlds
    collide. In our minds we have kissed, touched, and left the desires
    and passions which burn deep within.
Our hearts feel the heat between us. A hot, brilliant, fiery, burning
    desire... It grows
deeper with each secret shared and every thought that unfolds... Each time
    our minds
cross that line our souls wash over each others taking in the embraces
    feeling the
tenderness as our bodies entangle and become one... aeh aka LADYHUDSON

Leaving A Shade
Jerry W. Ogburn

She must have liked the one red rose
That I got her on Sweetheart's Day
They say it's in the same place
And if you move it, you would see
A shadow till this day
Because my baby loved her one red rose
That she got on Sweetheart's Day
The pretty flowers that grew around this one red rose
Have grown used to it now and probably think
That is where love is, but the small flowers wonder why
The one red rose doesn't grow and doesn't cry
She will talk to them, and play sweet music
So they will grow to know, how special one red rose can be
The morning sunlight still shines on it
Though knowing it will not grow, but it still has its place
And remembers that Sweetheart Day
Her friends that stop by don't ask why and do not try
To replace the one red rose
A shadow till this day

Break Your Heart
Fenn Morse Starratt

Cosmic pied piper comes out of the past
Blasting through orbital structures so fast
Collision course altered, attendant debris
Connect the dots in eternity
A million miles of spangled tail
A cataclysmic cosmic hail
Collecting dust, star births on high
Comet Hale—Bop thunders by
Ancient time traveler transects the sky
Inspiring awe, some people to die
Their deaths put a blight on this beautiful thing
A gross bid for greatness, this Sapien Cling
To the alter of yearning, we bring broken things
Our slack—lipped forms cast shadows slight
And Comet Hale—Bop rules the night
It's questing brightness, showery light
Paling slightly in the stark moonlight
Ancient time traveler transects the sky
Don't leave us...please...come back...goodbye.

Someday
Karen Devereaux
You said you almost loved me and my heart sank to my feet
For fear that inch between what you feel and love might never meet
I waited for your love to come to hear your heart sing out
But on and on it never did come my dreams were dimmed with doubt

We laughed and sang together as the days passed on in turn
The secret held within your heart was not for me to learn
Suddenly things seemed to changed my heart could feel the chill
Emptiness stood just outside waiting for the kill

That night you found it difficult to look into my eyes
I knew the end was very near I'd soon hear your good–byes
I held my tears I would not cry, your eyes began to fill
You gently kissed my forehead then we both stood still

I knew that you had loved me in your own special way
I still hold my breath and wait for you to come back to me someday

For You
Regina Calton
The sun rises and sets for you.

The winds shift to the West for you.

The trees remain at ease when you pass by.

The flowers open every season for you.

There are never any sounds when you

shout in a empty tunnel. The songs that you

love always play for you. Never take any of

these events for granted for nothing is

possible without the Lord who sacrificed his life

just for you.

The Magic Swamp Boat
John W. Bryant, Sr.
And so the small swamp boat was built,
At my homestead by the river.
By the flowing black swamp water,
By the mighty gum and cypress trees.
All the magic and mystery of the swamp was built into it.
Into its strong light fir wood body,
Into its smooth–curved design.
Built a thing of worth and beauty.
Like a Stradivaris violin,
And it floated on the water.
Light as a wind blown feather,
Quiet as a dark swamp shadow.
Built for many years of pleasure,
Built for many miles of service.
Built the Cadillac of swamp boats.
A witch dwells in black swamp water
Who will cast a spell upon you.
If you linger too long on this water
You can never leave the swamp.

Memories
Enid Ross
Memories are treasures no one can steal,
Deep down inside us always, so real.
The thrill of a newborn baby's cry,
The sadness of a last goodbye.

Childhood days full of laughter and fun
Holiday snaps in the summer sun,
Shimmering leaves in a woodland scene,
A tall handsome figure bronzed and lean.

A much loved pet loyal and true,
Memories return like the morning dew,
A special present – a tender kiss,
A brother who called me little sis.

A sad life this would surely be
Without a treasured memory!

Believing
Yvonne Clement Rolling
I hear the trumpet sound,
to the beat of His coming,

The sun is shining bright,
I look to the Heavens,
clouds heavy and white,

There is a part,
shining so bright,
I know, our time is near,

So fear not,
believe,
and have faith,

We'll all be together,
Love, Hope, Faith!
Dedication: In loving memory – Lucymae Alford

Majuk Leaves
Debbie Hagen
The leaves swirl in the wind
and carry me over different lands
I smile and remember
through each page of trees

I call out to every character
but they continue smiling
plastic eyes and mouths
I'm unknown to them

Try as I might
I can't enter their realm
and I leave them behind
as they keep on smiling

It's hard to recall
the lands I once traveled
on my leaf of
tree pages...

Missing You
Kim Wainwright

Love is stronger than before
Pain is deeper growing more
Time has gone for me and you
I know the things you're going through
Love for you will never go

Your words mean more each passing day
My heart stays true to what you say
With my love I think of you
about the things we used to do
Love for you will never go

You could be lonely, feeling bad
Thinking of the times we had
Or with another girl instead
While you are here inside my head
Love for you will never go.

Well Worn Paths
Mary R. Howell

What convoluted pathways led us here
From distant lands and townships near,
To live our waning days in friendships newly found
And know the bonds by which each life is bound?

The griefs we need not speak of for we share
The same scarred resting souls in poor repair.
The terrors of the wars that we have known,
The lifted hearts for those returning home.

The wins and losses and the peace and strife,
Are all the fabric of a common life.
The scars and bruises, tears and smiles in mass,
All mark the years and decades as they pass.

We sometimes feel that life clings on too long.
It loses all the flavor, all the song;
But memories linger on. The heart can hold
New loves beside the treasures now grown old.

The Beggar's Imprompt
Jacquelene Sue

Within the walls of much oppressed,
Were those half starved and barley dressed,
The meek and stately beggar bared his soul.
To all the prisoners there he bared his soul.

"While free men roam this world tonight,
I stand in ponder of your plight,
And know your crimes will surely take their toll."
"I'll witness that your crimes will take their toll."

"But I, poor souls, endure the time,
With begging as my only crime,
There's comfort here and I'll not cry for home."
"Yet I will hear your wailing cry for home."

The beggar's imprompt was met with contempt,
His worn face bloodied, his clothes were rent,
They left his dying body all alone.
His quiet dying body all alone.

Untitled
Veronica Coleman

I am his puppet, he has always controlled me
He comes in my sleep and wants me again
I never push him away like before
Is it him that I want or something disguised
I want what I used to have, what I have now
and more
I long for him because I don't have him, because
I cannot have him
He has no idea that he is tearing me apart
I shouldn't let him affect this way yet I am
powerless against him
He comes when I am most vulnerable, when I can't deny
the thoughts I try to make myself stop thinking
He fulfills my darkest thoughts when I am utterly
alone, when no one can witness my betrayal
I do not want to go back but I cannot seem to move on
I do not want to go back but I cannot seem to move on

Temple
Tiffany Brantley

We for me was you alone
Hiding lies in hazel eyes
Telling gospel with the slip of a pink rag tongue
Foreign to me behind slick, salty lips.
Your languid hands – lithe, without line, but hard
from human labor – tempt me.
Ghosts greet us in the corners of the sky
on humid, fragrant breezes.
Upon this grassy wildflower–strewn knoll
where we two sit
silent, violent, poetically inclined.
Gravestones in the valley rise as countless grey
cathedrals. From where we are sermons are
forgotten fables without morals. Hymnals are thunderstorms,
lightning, and flash flood fires. Burning me
with the dry hot chill of our desire.
Bathed in dreams of dew
we rise to tell the stars
of silence, violence, and poetry.

No Surrender
Timothy Ryan Yeager

Inspired by pain,
On my knees in the rain.
All is lost and nothing gained.

My spirit is bear down,
I'm hearing this meek sound,
Begging to stay where I lay.

I must stand and rise,
It's time to be wise,
Fight off this poor sadness,
Or this my demise.

I felt myself stronger,
Stay will I no longer.
The strength I had stole,
Came straight from my soul.

Dedication: Clifford Albert Yeager, Sr.

The Poacher
Kathleen Just
In the heart of the wood the animals stirred
The stealthy footsteps as yet unheard,
An owl hooted once from the branch of a tree
And the sound that it made echoed eerily
Beneath the light of the hunters moon.

At the first of the snares the poacher paused
Not giving a thought to the suffering he'd caused,
He looked down at the creature, and it stared back
With an unseeing eye as it was thrown in the sack
Beneath the light of the hunters moon.

The poacher thought of all the people he knew
Who were willing to buy a cheap rabbit or two,
So as long as they continued to purchase his wares
He would go on poaching and emptying his snares
Beneath the light of the hunter's moon.

Dawns Break Through
Cheryl Pedraza
Toward the dawn, I linger,
Where Solitude abounds,
Unencumbered moments,
Refrain, with nightly sounds,

Window seat, my matting,
A means to indifferent dreams,
While country side, beyond me,
Spins starlight on simpler things,

The nights alone, lacking a hold,
Twine introspection's depth,
From sadness to various forevers,
Each, attend the tears I've wept,

The dawn, with basking sparkle,
Casts nebulous blur before my eyes,
For now, my rhythm is rich for rest,
Assured, secured, I am yet alive.

Losing Weight
Wray Senter
Exercise, Weight Loss, Muscle tone
Clothes tight
What is life telling me?
Do I look a fright?

Gathering diets, Buying Scales, Denial
Looser clothes
It's off to the weight bench
In the attempt to lose an inch.

Sweat, Aches and pains, Day dreams
Jogging suits
Things I now do during my break
Just to make my body ache.

Pounds, Inches, Sweat
Aches
All seem to go away
As I struggle through my day.

Old Sweep
Jean Chisholm
I remember the day you were given to me,
A little black pup with no pedigree.
And right from the start, you quickly made known,
The best chair in the house was to be your own,
The children adored you, and shared all their play.
In the long summer evenings, or old winter's day.
And a wag of the tail for each one you met.
With just one exception! You hated the vet!
But now they've all gone with homes of their own
There's just you and me "Sweep" left here on our own
And two wise old eyes are looking at me
Your face is all white where the black used to be
Your legs are unsteady I note with dismay
My faithful companion grows older
each day
Who care's if you never won best of the breed?
My dearest old mongrel is precious indeed!

Helping Others
Karen K. Diveney
Sorrow and pain are with us each day
Some hearts are so heavy they can't even pray
We cry...we struggle...but continue to live
How much more of ourselves can we give?

no, "don't give up," take a day at a time
and Let God help you up the mountain to climb
The valley of sorrow is dark when alone.
and our heart's feel cold, and heavy as stone.

A problem so great with no end in sight,
we mush encourage each other, and "not give up the fight"
don't ever simplify what for other's we can do,
Little to us, could see a friend through.

Yes, show just one person each day as you start.
Reach out just once, with love in your heart.
Let them know someone does really care,
and our Heavenly Father is always there.

Jesus The Savior
Rosie B. Murphy
Jesus was born of a Virgin
In a manger in Bethlehem
A Star of the East led the wise Men
To where the Babe was born.

Do you believe in Jesus?
He can save you from all sin
He is the Savior of the world
Do you believe in Him?

Blessed be the person
Who will come to Jesus today
And give his heart to Jesus
As Christians earnestly pray.

Then you will believe in Jesus
So come give your heart to Him
Go out to work for Jesus
And stay away from sin.

Stephen, Dear Brother
Graham Taylor
With my head in my hands as I look up to the sky,
Watching the clouds drift slowly by,
Thinking of the good times that we had,
Treasured memories, when we were happy, not sad,
But to have you back would be my wish today,
But I know I can't whatever I say,
To hear you laugh,
To see you smile,
Just to chat or play games for a while,
To play in the park if we had kids,
Or to hear your friends just call you "Tidds,"
But not having you around I often cry,
Why were you taken from us, why? Oh why?,
The pain of it all will never fully go,
But now and for always, I love you so.

Dedication: Stephen Mark Taylor, dearly missed

The Police Officer's Badge
J. E. Warhurst
It is polished and shiny and looks so fine.
Once you earn it you have to tow the line.
The minute you wear it upon your chest
it becomes a symbol that you are the best.
It means honesty, integrity, and fairness to all.
You life is never your own, but at the public's call.
Night or day, any hour, it makes you a mark.
It doesn't protect you from a shot in the dark.
Over the years the shine starts to fade,
but brighter still is the man its made.
It is often what separates you from the crowd.
It is a second family of which you are proud.
So now comes your time, you can't be denied.
When you pin on your badge wear it with pride

The minute you wear it upon your chest
it becomes a symbol that you are One of The Best

Dedication: SGT. De Warhurst, APD

90's Teen
Christine Lilly
A little girl
growing up fast,
from toys to boys
leaving cooties in the past.

Her crush is now boyfriend.
Her love for him strong.
She spends the night at his house,
His parents are gone.

The next days were great,
They drive each other wild.
Until he finds out...
That she is with a child.

He leaves her to care
for the young one alone.
A common life of a teen
On this Earth we call home.

Little Bit
Gina M. Kunz
You're very special to me. You give me support when I need it.
    You're my best friend, and you listen to me
and my problems. I wouldn't trade you for the world. We've
    been together a year and a half now and we
just get closer every day. You're always glad to see me and
    I'm always glad to see you. We don't live at the
same place, but my wish is that one day we will. That way we
    can see each other more, even though I'm
out there almost every day. It's just not enough time together.
    If anything ever happened to you it would
crush me. We play together, we play chase and throw stuff and
    when you need to you lay your head on my
shoulder, like when you get your shoes put on. The best thing
    of all, I can trust you with my kids, and that
is everything.
LITTLE BIT there is no other horse like you in the world.
I LOVE YOU.

Help
Dottie Helms
Lord please help me
I don't know what to do
I'm sitting here tonight
feeling empty and feeling blue.
I need for you to guide me
through a wondrous path
and take away this pain
this pain, that's from my past.
My heart is broken
in so many pieces
broken totally in two
Lord I'm really glad
I have a love as wondrous
as you.
Lord please help me
to have a better life
and help me feel that
love from you
through all my pain and strife.

My Little Friends
Eilleen W. Spence
I have two little fish of gold...
Their names are Moe and Min
I watch them swim round and around
To see which one will win.
From early morn to late at night
They are together, but ever fight...
They swim and swim with lots
of pleasure...
When I feed them food, it's a very
small measure...
Now Moe has a very charming
black mustache,
Which he shows me
When he makes a splash.
But, Min, not to be outdone by Moe—
Has big black eyes that she
sure does show!

Dedication: My children, Deb, Byo, Tom

Feelings
Ben Tran

Throughout the countless full moons that we have witnessed
Throughout the countless stories that we have created
You and I
From start to finish
Let the heavens and earth be our witnesses
Let's not try and guess the inner feelings that we've
Shared and created
There are many wonderful things that came to
Me in life
But there's nothing in the world that can compare to you
Not even close
You're always in my heart and in my mind
And every time I think about you — Boy, you're so fine
You've got to be mine
You're always in my heart and in my mind
Boy, you're the only reason for me that's worth living
From time to time

My Heaven
Deborah Woods

Illuminated skies of vibrant rainbows,
golden daffodils beneath hovering monarchs;
never ending splendor of emerald fields and sparkling beaches,
frolicking pandas near brilliant pink flamingos;
I hear classical melody and trickling brooks,
glorious chatter of playful youngsters;
I smell fragrant wild flowers and gingerbread,
the essence of cedar gently lingers;
I feel fine ,warm sand cushioning my feet,
I wade through crystal clear springs;
there is no pain, I feel no fear,
no misery or suffering to endure;
I will never before have known this elation,
encountering familiar loved ones once lost to me;
surrounded by endless caring faces, smiling, laughing,
unconditionally, I feel that they love me;
in this place I won't find wickedness,
only peaceful embraces, tranquility, love;
this is my heaven.

He Failed Her
Kuran Anne Brown

Just when trust was at its peak, and hope within
Filled her soul...he failed her.
Just when his friendship meant the most and she
Needed his tenderness...he failed her.
He could have grown their friendship into something
Even more "tried and true", instead...he failed her.
He could have loved her and cherished their
Great relationship, but...he failed her.
How did he fail her? He "took" her, he wanted her;
So he "took" her, with force and no thought for her feelings
Or the outcome of such an act,
And in "taking" her...he failed her.
Then he denied that he "took" her and this crushed her hope,
Her faith, her trust, and with the pain of denial in her heart,
And in her soul, she suffers in knowing...he failed her.
Why does this have to happen? Why can't he see that in
"Taking" he has ruined all the "giving"?...he failed her.
He failed her, he failed her, he failed her.
God be with her if she is to ever trust again.

Untitled
Shannon Gregoire

Maybe death is an opening to another world
A world of floating images—
With friendship and love blooming...
Or even a reunion.

A place to be loved...
And accepted
To start all over,
To change.

I often think about death
And I'm not afraid.

No one to hate,
To never be bored,
To never cry,
Everything is fine.

Love Poem
Patricia A. Davey

Never thought
you had it in you
The way you swung down
after Ganymede
o what about
what we did on Mars
sliding along
making love
it drove me mad

Now here you are
making those moves
you know how
to do it
if we don't stop soon
all the stars
will surely wink out

Dedication: Joseph Lanham, my grandson

Always With Love
Barbara J. Mizzell

When I am at last called home, weep not for me.
For I will be with our Father rejoicing.

I will be dancing on the clouds with the Angels.
Hearing the most beautiful of music.
Seeing the ones I've loved through my life in a brand new light.

Don't weep for me,
For I will always be close to you in spirit, in love.
You will see me in your dreams.
You will feel me when a gentle breeze touches your face.
You will hear me in the rustling leaves.

I will be with you always.
In your thoughts and memories,
You shall carry me forever in your heart with Love.
Always with Love.

Dedication: In Remembrance – William Ray Sapp

Good–bye
Yvonne Emerson

Saying good–bye is never easy, especially when you're only nine,
Especially when you're saying good–bye to your father,
As I looked at you...so still,
All I could think was...this isn't real,
My daddy's not gone,
Not when all I wanted was for you to stay,
No more kisses goodnight,
No more hugs, when I'm hurt,
No more singing together,
No more silly games,
No more nothing...except...silence,
But daddy the hardest part is...
No more I love you,
So here's one to take with you,
I love you daddy...
And I still miss you, I guess I always will,
So all these years later,
I'm finally able to tell you...Good bye,
With love, your daughter.

The Light That Shined
Valerie Helton

In a life full of adventure and experience,
Loneliness plants itself and grows rapidly.
It creates a sadness of pain and insecurity.
Unsure of which direction to travel
Only adds to the insecurity of each decision.

In a body of inner beauty with no shame,
The far away look and slow movements
Expresses the insecure thoughts buried within.
Lost in a world of lonesomeness and pain,
Everything shrinks to a dark hole in my life.

Then there appears a blurred light ahead.
Like a moth, I am drawn to that light.
The closer I get, the more clear it is.
In full amazement, the light is no longer blurred.
That light I see is my life.

Untitled
Kim Gastineau

Childhood Memories
Time lost and gone
Sadness and sorrow, go hand in hand

Love desired
Trust never found
Conquering fears bigger than the universe

Jealousy and contempt
Stolen kisses at a glance
Unerasable footprints on the heart

Love finally found
A troubled babe born
Journeys ahead, future unknown

Sunsets, lullabies from the heart
Friendships never made
To succeed is triumph over evil

Dawn
Pamela J. Hickman

This morning as the sun began to
Climb slowly over the horizon
I saw the day break through the
Puffy cotton clouds
With glittering rays of sunlight
Filtering, reaching and grasping the sky.
The bright gleam of light turned
the dark dreary sky
Into the most beautiful color blue
I had ever seen.
The clouds formed fingers, pushing the
Darkness, separating it
So the bright sun could make its grand entrance
Slowly in anticipation of the warm glowing light
the small swift fingers
of the puffy white clouds
Pulled back the curtains—
The brilliant sun hit center stage
As the sky applauded it.

You
Roselle Pomeroy

The sun was shining that day you died
I saw its brilliance and didn't know
That the Light–of–my–Life had just gone out
Leaving me with
an afterglow.
The birds were singing that day you died
I heard one just outside my door.
And never dreamed that The–Song–of–my–Heart
Had faded away
To be heard no–more.
The earth was steady that day you died
I walked on grass so fresh and sweet.
And I stepped out firm...as silently
The world slipped away
From beneath my feet!

Dedication: My daughter– Carol Ann– beloved

A Child
Melanie Bruce

A child living in a never ending nightmare,
A child having no winter coat to wear.
A child getting no hug or a kiss,
only getting an angry hiss,
Wondering if he'll hit or miss.
A child waiting out in the snow,
Waiting, waiting for him to go,
and feel lucky for now that she
missed his blow.
A child wondering what she did
wrong today,
from a beating she got and didn't
deserve anyway.
A child waiting to be loved,
not getting slapped and shoved.
A child not knowing what to do or say,
Does anybody really care anyway.

Dedication: For my children, Cori and Travis

Tears
Ethyle M. Cummins

Midst joys and sorrows through the years
I've tried my best to hide my tears
While others can control it all,
Against my will, the tears do fall

I tell myself that through God's grace
That surely I can change my pace,
And whatever happens in my day
That I'll respond the perfect way

With no red eyes, no sweaty palm
My heart so light, my face so calm
With poise and grace, but with concern,
This frame of mine just must hold firm!

But then, as I awoke today,
This single thought was there to stay;
"Be not ashamed, but just accept."
This fact, that even "Jesus wept."

Angel Wing
Monica Iroegbu

Angel wing on puff white cloud, poor Angel lost her wing.
Searched high and low, she found a soul, trembling in his boots.

Angel embraced this shattered soul, in her one wing that remained — administered tender loving care to the bruises on his heart. Then Angel firmly nudged soul back on the road to destiny — an envisionment of life fulfilled, blessed, and unburdened by a troubled past.

Finishing her work, Angel soared up high through the clouds that reached to Heaven. She came upon that puff white cloud where her gossamer wing shone bright.

Angel sewed her lost wing with a thread of light. Happy with a job done well, Angel flew right on to her home in Paradise.

It's Up To You
Hattie V. Ramos

As dull as it might seem, we see
nothing as what they are. As we have only
one life, you can only do the things that
you drive on. Indulge in the desires that come to
you. Believe what you are doing is right, the
beliefs that hold you to the wrong on the
things in life you haven't done, but regret as you
age older. The fantasies are a cloud of smoke,
and the daydreams are a vision of what
can happen, either could or not, be made into
something. In the course of life, we develop,
grow, mature, and realize we have to find
the direction of our life. We motivate, we
lunge into our destinies that are below each other
Hearts race. Skin touches, kiss drives, into our
life. We realize that sometimes you can't
resist temptation.

Dedication: Harold Truman

Easter Morning Thoughts
Lou Chance

Easter is here for all to see
And remember the Lord died
For you and me.

He hung on the cross for all to see
And died for our sins,
Yes, you and me.

The Lord loves us all — both large and small —
It makes no difference who we are —
And it makes no difference
If we're from afar.

The Lord loves us all in a very special way —

He touches our lives
every single day — lives
and wishes us well on life's
pathway—

A Bomb In Oklahoma
Donale Bryant

It came across the TV one day,
people were hurt, and some passing away.
April 19, 1995 a day some people were
praying to stay alive. It hit America
like a storm, especially Oklahoma City
where it did the most harm. How could
someone do this kind of thing, in such
a horrible, horrible way? The news media
come on and said, "most of the people
they were finding were dead." Many children
and adults too, were lying there on
stretchers right in front of you. It
wasn't a movie that comes on at 8
and then goes off before it gets too
late. It was something real, that
happened that day. The day the
Murrah Building was blown away.

Dreaming Natures Way
Kathy Herdman

Bend with the breeze
Taste the brightness
The color of the sun
Oh flowers and trees

Sway gentle yet firm
Savor the moment now
Unfold your greenest
Give way to the worm

Caress the moment so
Wrapped tight around
Forgetting your want
Remembering your own

Touch with the heart
Grow strong in faith
Let your thoughts go
Stay near never part

Wild Flowers
Val Gordon

In early Spring, before the last frosts are over
And the winds are still chill,
There appears a small golden petalled flower.
It is the brave little Aconite
Before the much vaunted Daffodil.
Yet it receives little attention.
Next, another tiny flower appears,
St. Veronica's Handkerchief.
With deep blue and white colouring and its touching legend.
Shortly afterwards comes the cool and sedate Primrose.
This flower seems to stand aloof from the others.
Other varieties come fast.
Then come Shakespeare's selection,
"Daisies pied and Violets blue and
Ladies Smocks all silver white."
Perhaps the most attractive of all our wild flowers
Is the tall and stately Foxglove
With its rows of bright red bells.
In a soft breeze you can almost hear the bells chiming.

Dive Into Me
Alejandra Aguilar

Sometimes you wonder, what you're going to
say, to the ocean breeze and the quiet bay.
The fear stands before you, right in the face,
when suddenly your pulse begins to race.
Should you dive with splendor or should
you dive with fear?
The tide begins to ripple, the ocean seems
to sneer.
I clutch my hands together, pointed up so
tight and I dive into the water with all
my daring might.
The water starts to rise and fold me of
some sort, but then I float so high with
the ocean's kind support.
I return to the shore, at the far end,
and I thank that mighty ocean, that great
caring friend.

The Sound Of Death
Rene Salazar

Just walking 'round deeper in the night.
Looking for one reason; to believe, to feel, to live.
Maybe the love played old trick on me.
And hold my heart in the top of heaven; now broken
In a thousand pieces, make up to breath.
Put my fingers close to the sun, need some warmth,
and light.
My eyes saw many things terrible when the earth
belonged to the moon.
That time, my body was beautiful like the eagle.
Flew in your memory, ran in your desires.
But never love you.
Only played the game like other humans; it was good
My poor eyes closed the future seeing the past.
Crossed the river, can see myself in the mirror of the life.
Alone with a big stone for a head, and the rest
Of my body is feathers, perhaps it's a dream.
One part of my soul lives forever, the other half is over the soil.
And dying, and died, only with the idea of seeing, you again.

Pa–Pa
Sheena Kennedy

Pa–Pa, you're my hero
I look up to you,

You helped me through
bad times encouraged me
through good.

When you left I
cried so hard I
hated you for so long,

But now I realize
you're not really gone,

You're here every day
in spirit but especially
in my heart.

Dedication: My Pa–Pa, I love you!

Expressions
Joanne Hansen

When I discovered poetry was a way to self–express,
It seemed so natural to write my feelings to profess.

Some thoughts that haunt me deeply, some words that were never said,
It's time I put on paper whether or not they're read.

I think that it will help me and blessings then I count,
Remembering where I've come from and trials I've had to surmount.

The joy's in life so numerous and overwhelming to believe.
The miracles that God has worked so my troubles I dare not grieve.

One's life can be so very full that it's difficult to see it.
I pause to see the little things that help me live each minute.

When I discovered poetry as a way to self–express
My cup of blessings overflowed, it's wonderful for stress!

Family
Jan Murray

I started off in married life.
When I was very young.
Though life was hard I struggled on,
And had myself a son.

Life didn't get much easier, and much
To my surprise.
I had myself a daughter, with the most
enormous eyes.

I thought that was my life complete,
But it got even better.
Another daughter came along, I'm
Really glad I met her.

Each one has made me very proud,
To say that they are mine,
Cause from these three, my Grandkids.
Have totaled up to nine.

Speaking Of Mountains
Nena C. Walsh
Mountains are plenty
On God's forsaken earth,
with anticlines and synclines
Upon HIS molded turf.

Accumulation mountains
Of Original or Tectonic type,
Regurgitate their lava
After sudden volcanic fright.

Deformation mountains
With many forms adrift,
Consist of Dislocation,
Folded and Laccolith.

With all their breathtaking beauty
HE excluded none, it seems,
But to top it off completely,
"Check out" the mountain streams.

Winter
Martha R. Pohl
The winter sky of leaden gray,
Cold wind that takes your breath away,
Means: by my fireside I will stay!
From winter hide!
At times the sun is shining bright,
Beguiling me with warmth and light.
But is it really warm? not quite!
I'll stay inside!

But if I need to venture out,
My freezing form I'll wrap about,
Till just my eyes are peeking out.
I hate the cold!
In yester–year I loved the snow,
And didn't mind the wintry blow.
But frolicked on the ice! I know:
I'm getting old!!!!

We Are Them
Lisa Naylor
Our children are so innocent their beauty so unique
But this world no longer offers, all the wonders that they seek
There is evil there is danger fast encroaching on their truth
And we are them their parents, building walls around their youth

This race of little people, grow fast towards the day
When their innocence and wonder is life's to take away
When their only taste of freedom, is soon enough to be
A bitter taste of what's to come, the things they need not see

And we are them their parents, building prisons to ensure
That what this world can offer, is what they're searching for
And the truth behind that vision, the innocence they see
Is the evil and the danger, of the things that shouldn't be

Our prisons can't protect them, our prisons can't defend
The wars that they are running to, the truths that never end
And we are them their parents, preserving what they see
When this world no longer offers, the beauty they can be.

Answer Today
Jacquelyn Custer
My days are all empty,
Empty and blue—
My heart is broken,
Broken for you.

In vain I have written,
Written each day—
Wondering how long
You'd be away.

Each day I expected
A letter from you;
Each day you neglected,
What can I do?

My tears would vanish,
Vanish today:
If you'd but answer,
Answer today.

A Mother's Work Is Never Done
Carollyn Harris
Mother's always on the run,
Her work is never done.

There's laundry to wash,
And piano lessons to get to,

There's floors to mop
And dishes to do.

Bills to pay
And beds to be made

There's shopping to do.
And dinner to cook,

As you see,
Mother's work is never done!

Joy
Valerie J. Sullivan
Gently he took her in his arms
Caressed the softness of her skin
Gazing into the blueness of her eyes
Heart thumping with joy

His fingers touched her soft golden hair
A smile upon his face
His to have, his to hold
He felt such bliss, such joy

Eyes filled with tears
His love so immense
He trembled at the thought
A future full of joy

Such feeling, such fear
Such pain, such joy
In his arms So small, so perfect
Seven pound of NEWBORN JOY

Best Friend
Sabrina Axt
I am so lucky
to know someone like you.
When others have deserted me,
you've stayed with me through and through.

I can tell you anything
and know that you will care.
I never have to be alone
'cause you are always there.

You are delightfully funny
and full of good cheer.
You can always make me laugh.
With you, I have nothing to fear.

We haven't known each other long,
but this message I must send.
You have always been nice to me.
Thank you for being my friend.

The Contemplation Of Lovemaking
Tatiana Burgess
The scent of musk is all she needs to smell
For her to spew her aromatic dust.
The bull will gallop hornless to the well
As hidden depths persuade him to trust.

A bucket midway down contains a fruit.
Whose red appeal gives cause to stamping hooves.
His muscles burn within his leather suit.
As coaxing waters cause the pail to move.

To get apple, he need only leap.
For his shear weight would snap the main support.
And there within his waters deep,
His prize he can enjoy, and her for sport.

And so, he takes the deadly plunge therein
And signs in blood is debt to cardinal sin.

The Fear
Jonathan B. Touchstone
The fear comes and goes
It flutters my heart, chills my soul
The fear of living for nothing strangles my will
This fear is so strong it is destined to kill.
And escape with my last breaths
That come so soft and calm
In the midst of the stormy night
I feel the coldness of its cool embrace
That can only be warmed by the hot rushes
And gushes of its mortal stream
A piercing, agonizing pain embraces my mortal being and
leaves a chill, alone, to run its course down my spine
And the tears come and fall into the puddles of my mortal being
The soft, calm breaths become ragged, choking
And they become the last as the realization
of death closes in on my mortal mind
and I am left cold, in the darkness of
the cool, damp abyss
as my soul departs...and...fades...

Their Family
Eileen M. Colvin
Their family comes
From around the world:
Their hair is straight,
Their hair is curled,
Their eyes are brown,
Their eyes are blue,
Their skins are different colors, too
We're girls and boys,
We're big and small,
We're young and old,
We're short and tall.
We're everything that we can be
And still we are a family.
They laugh and cry,
They work and play,
They help each other every day.
The world's a lovely place to be
Because their family will always
Be a happy family.

One Dark Night
Michaela Knot
In the dark I lost my path,
and all I could see were the words upon my epitaph.

The branches are thick and cover the light,
I am falling – deep into the night.
A mist enshrouds this maze of trees;
it makes me feel weak, and I stumble to my knees.

The mist recedes;
but the trees remain there
and I find myself fighting –
against odds unfair.

There seems no end, it eludes my sight,
but my hopes and dreams are burning bright.

Even in the darkness on this one night.

Wherever We May Go
Jean H. Hoyle
There is a sense of wonder and we must surely know,
The work of God's creation wherever we may go.
Travelling down the highway in all kinds of weather,
We see the beautiful mountains with flowers and trees together.

In summer the trees are green and beautiful as can be.
In fall the leafs are changing colors all for you and me.
We ride over a long bridge which crosses the river wide
We know man built the bridge with God at his side.

We see fish swimming around, and God's animals on the ground
The seashore is so beautiful along the ocean deep,
I walk along the seashore with sand on my feet.
The birds are flying in the air, we see creatures everywhere.

I love to search for seashells, to see what I can find;
I find them so beautiful with different shapes and kind
You see it is a wonder, we must surely know.
The work of God's creation, wherever we may go.

Nora
William Greene
Dans le microcosme de sa chambre rose, la porte fermee, fenetre close,
Comme pendant cette nuit de juillet, moi, dans son lit, je me le pose:
Pauvre Nora, ayant tant et pendant si longtemps lutte, affrontait la mort –
Avait–elle peur ou soulagement devant l'abandon subit de son corps?

Elle plongea seule – nous autres l'on continue ensemble notre chemin –
Laissant sa brosse porter les derniers parmi ses cheveux perdus, son
    parfum,
Ses lions et oursons, glaces fruitees, seringues et aiguilles, ses
    lunettes,
Son armoire remplie de derniere mode, reves de sante et de vie complete.

Cette annee–ci septembre parait froid plus en avance que d'habitude,
Comme si la fin d'une vie accompagnait une fin d'ete brusquement rude.
La plage se vide d'enfants, la mer n'attire de baigneurs sauf un chien;
Les grottes se font noires et sans echos: seuls restent les rochers,
    au guet du terrain.

Dedication: My parents

Untitled
Karie Weber
this is just her body, sunken six feet underground
this is just her body, her soul cannot be found
she died a lazy Sunday, the church bells rang so cold
the sound filling the air, so confused, yet so bold
tears filling eyes, none dropping, not just yet
my friend is in her grave, this is as close as I can get
as I touch the newly filled grave, I remember how she said
she would never forget me as she lay in her eternal bed

her dark eyes so sad, so tired, so dry
her body so weak, so sick she couldn't cry
she claimed that it's her fate, that she would be okay
I believed her, until that fatal day
my hopes of her recovery had evaporated with the tears
those days I had spent with her, wishing they were years
the memories will never fade, as so that's what she said
and how I will miss her, as she lay in her eternal bed

The Door
Sheila B. Roark
I stand before the mystic door
Not knowing what to do.
Should I just quickly walk away
Or seek a world brand new?

This door that stands all by itself
Holds secrets dark and deep.
But do I dare go through the door
And take this drastic leap?

Why is change so very hard?
Why do I feel such fear?
What stops me from just walking through
This door that's standing here?

I finally know what I must do
I will not try the door.
I'll walk away to things secure
And all I knew before.

A Baby's First Christmas
Iris A. Peterson
Christmas trees, fairy lights, the home with warmth aglow,
Gifts, Toys and Fun for a little one
From those who love you so.

A silver star shines so bright upon the tree so tall,
It's your very first Christmas, baby newborn,
Just like the one so long ago.

When Baby Jesus was born, in a stable all forlorn
In a tiny town called Bethlehem,
The world was filled with joy
For news had travelled around the world of the birth of a Baby Boy.

That's why we celebrate at Christmas time,
It comes from Heaven above
To fill everyone with happiness
And fill their hearts with love.

Dedication: Baby grandsons, Michael and Nathan

Restless
Victoria Thompson
You were always the one with
the restless will
So afraid of growing old if
you dared stand still
The words that tumbled from your lips
were never in your heart
Saying things you didn't mean
for you was the easy part.

You're the one who used to say that
love's a game for fools
For those without the guts to live
a life outside the rules
The tenderness felt in your touch
was never in your soul
Your eyes betrayed the game you played
like your heart they're as black as coal.

Untitled
Andrew Walmsley
My mind drifts back to that weekend
Everdreaming of the thundering skies
Roaring burns and misty glen
There in my arrival awaited a lady
So fair in grace and pure in heart.

Through the days and evenings together
as one
We held each other close in our arms
I thought of her as a rose
So fresh and natural
How much I again long to be close

The Isle of Anan so beautiful
Compared to you 'tis naught
A place in peace and quiet
It is what I sought
And the rugged scenic mountains
The peace I got couldn't be bought.

Nostalgia And Aspirations
Debby Pickles
Our dreams are better than reality,
We live our lives for the memory,
The sun shines brighter when the day is done,
And we love more strongly when our love has gone.

We always yearn for something more,
Then mourn behind the ever–closed door,
For something which has begun to rot:
Always wanting what we haven't got.

Sunshine would be welcome on winter nights,
To thaw our limbs and ease our flight;
But love changes fast, as does the weather,
And the time before is always better.

Why do we long for something else?
Why never content to be ourselves?
Because good times are better when they are recalled,
And a life without dreams is like no life at all.

A Day In A Wheelchair
Gwen Wright
Morning comes it's very clear
A dull dark day is here
The just hides its face
And every thing is still
It is a cloudy summer day
The sun has lost the race
With time to begin the day
With everything in place
No children passing by to school
Or folks who go to work
It is the summer rule
With holidays for perks
But yesterday was bright and clear
Tomorrow is another day
Dear sun you will be here

Dedication: My late husband, William B. Wright

Chalke Downs At Dawn
Andrew Hope
I walked along the Bridle path,
The blanket mist enveloped me,
When suddenly I stepped into
A clear patch both warm and sunny.

The sun shone down upon the corn,
But I discerned another form,
Slowly forming from the mist
And saw a sight not to be missed.

A Fallow buck, and then his doe,
Walked through the mist with fawn in tow,
They walked so very close to me.
That every detail I could see.

Their soft brown eyes, their dark brown coats,
Long graceful legs, white fur at their throats,
Then suddenly they noticed me,
Their fleeting forms at treasured memory.

Days For Living
E. Blagrove
In age you have reached the zenith
Yet still to unfold those tales of Ypres
Then, to be no time for weeps
However much it is put behind
It ever stays fresh in the mind,
The memory plays many tricks,
As time passes and the clock still ticks
You can speak of beauty abound
As the south coast you wander around
Now happier stories of which to boast
Swans to feed with breakfast toast.
Still the channel stretching for miles
Brings back quite a few smiles
When those many friends you meet
Always fresh, the memories of Ypres.
The strong bonds you have made
Lasted to this day, A decade.

Dedication: Monica Holmes (daughter) Australia. JP. MP.

One And Only Love
Stephanie Alder
You walk in the front door to
find that you are all alone. Your one
and only love has departed.
The only thing that she left
behind was a single white rose and
a note saying that she could no longer
take the loneliness and emptiness.
And as you read this it brought a
single tear to your eye.
You know in your heart that
this is not the real reason she left.
You know she found a new love.
Although you are hurt, you
cannot be mad. You're just glad
she finally found someone who
could give her what she needed...
Love, caring, happiness, and protection.

Man's World
Valerie Morrell
This world has become a manmade place,
Full of worry and strife, and away from grace,
Wars and destruction, famine and starvation
Man is creating his own situation.

When will he realise his own devious deeds,
Is ruining the world for his own endless needs,
He destroys it, pollutes it, this beautiful earth,
A wonderful creation, a God given mirth.

Oh God, open man's eyes, let them see,
That peace can only come by being free,
Learn them to love and understand,
That love can bring brotherhood upon this land.

Then maybe in a short time to come,
They'll realise that "thy will" must be done,
They will tread on the pathway of truth and love
And be aware of the blessings that come from above

Abandoned Ship
Colm Brook–Gibbs
Can you recall the ill that heaped you here?
Skin torn free, ribs now standing clear,
Midst your haul of oaken chest and sack;
"Lost, with all hands," I fear.

Did a squall arise to spill and sweep you here?
Or change of wind devise your shambling veer?
Was it the gruel, broke your tested back?
Or these sands your master failed to clear?

Too close a call that will always keep you here;
No more reins or lashing rope to steer,
Nor Moorish strains of hashish dope to pack;
I've seen too soon the entrails of your career.

The grossest sprawl, well suited sheep or deer;
Bleached bones in jackal's sweeping leer,
Trammeled again, this Ship was rash to hope for slack;
Poor camel, slain amidst the desert sere.

Untitled
Tammy Gilbert
It happened so fast
without any warning,
one minute they were happy,
the next they were scared
The roads were wet, he did
everything right, but being so
young couldn't keep the car just
right, the other car hit, flew
my son in the air while metal
wrapped around him and everyone
else there. A man lost his fight
to live, and left this earth, my son
lost a part of himself that will never
be repaired, if only we could go back
till that Christmas Eve, when everyone
was happy, but it happened so
fast. Without any warning.

Midnights Hour
Phoebe J. Laing
In the stillness of a velvet night
Through spacious windows, myriad's of lights
Shine like strings of little stars
Along a dark beach, seen from afar

Muted rhythm of sea waves, pervades
The quietness with a sweet refrain.
Lulled in peaceful, gentle slumber,
Hushing all the busy strain.

A whispering ticking of the clock,
Wings its way through sleeps time–lock
Easing in, the new days dawn amid
Trilling song birds, heralding the morn.

Daylight of its own accord
Brings in its wake a bustling horde.
Sweeping aside dreams fancied flight,
Until the next short hour of midnight.

Untitled
Laura K. Vannah
"Sometime again" keeps running through my head,
Spinning and swirling, wondering why you fled.
Whatever happened to the love we shared,
What made it so you no longer cared?

When will you stop running away from the past,
When the present and future is all that will last?
If I am the best that has happened in life,
Why did you cut me out with a knife?

Life is full of mystery and doubt,
What made you take the easy way out?
Where have you wandered that I am not allowed,
What has made you so callous and cowed?

You need some time to sort things out,
"How much time?" I want to shout.
In hopeless surrender, I am waiting to begin,
that precious moment you've called "sometime again".

The One Who Raised Me
Robert D. McCully
You're my mother,
the one who raised me as a child.
The one who fed me,
clothed me,
and tried to tame me when I was wild.

I guess that wild side turned to evil,
and it gave me a bad name.
I wanted to make you proud,
but it seems I brought only shame.

The things I do,
and the things I have done.
I am trying to put behind me,
'cause the future has just begun.
Dedication: My mother, Patricia Jones

Winter Of '97
Lori Jo Berk
Nineteen hundred and ninety–seven
Little snowflakes fell from heaven.
They fell over the seven seas
Freezing ponds and covering trees.

Nineteen hundred and ninety–seven
Little stars shown down from heaven.
Lighting up the new–fallen snow
While the cold north wind did blow.

Nineteen hundred and ninety–seven
Little icicles froze in inches to eleven.
Glistening and glittering in the bright sunlight
Casting long shadows by the moon at night.

Some people think that snow is a curse,
Bringing hardships, colds or even worse.
With glee I'll think of pure snow from heaven
And the beautiful Winter of '97.

Into Emptiness Sincere
Joshua Brubaker
It was the Wondering...
The heartless thoughts and plans that decided my Fates
As the needle runs out of Destiny

Inside that hidden World
Micro–second wars lay Waste
Spreading the disease of Logic
To peaceful enemy Battlegrounds

Wandering though Planes
Flying at Midnight
But hiding at Crescent–Hour
I believe in Nothing...
And it has shown its faith in Me.

Through bared beliefs and clouded Eyes
I watch the legacy of a Child
A novel of a life, fall into Curtain
Into Emptiness Sincere

When All That's Left Is To Believe
Jackie Sutterfield
Sit back and I'll tell you a dream.
That came from two girls, who were
Not what they seemed to be.
Nobody understood them yes, it's true
But wait I've got more to tell you,
The girls had something deep inside.
A dream was to be expected, this is
All they had to look forward to.
There were doubts but never to be anticipated.
Schoolmates and enemies made fun, but
That didn't care.
They knew there was someone who loved them
Someone who was higher then any king or queen
Or empire.
"If God's love is in you then who can be against you"
Their motto now
Today's dream just might be tomorrow's reality!

Dark Dreams
John DeLaurentis
Deliver me from these deep dark dreams.
Resolutions crumbling, torn at the seams.
Day in, day out, all seems the same.
Desires inside, hard to tame.

Capture the spoilage, throw it out!
Don't let it win another bout.
Sin runs rampant in dark times;
Minds and hearts filled with crimes.

But there it is—the glowing light,
Piercing through the darkest night.
Shattering illusions of lost hope—
Making me strong, so I can cope.

Point the way to eternal life,
Free from this world of pain and strife.
The lion is tame, lambs by its side;
Unveiling has come, no place to hide.

Joy
Seena M. Cesefske
Teach me, oh teach me, My God how to pray,
To kneel in sweet retreat at Thy feet each day,
And as the spring rains bring life to the ground
Let my Soul's growth in Thee be found.

And in the hushed stillness of the morn
When life again each day is reborn
Forgotten are the clinging troubles of the night
As the world is again bathed in morning light.

And when grief and tears are out of hand,
Oh God give me a strip of thy woodland.
Grant me a moment by a babbling stream
The song of a bird or a meadow green.

With the sun on my face and the wind in my hair
Oh God Thou dost answer my most fervent prayer.
And when each day again comes to silent rest
With humbleness I come to Thee to be blest.

Mornings
Mary C. Mitchell
The sounds of early mornings
Are so different than the days,
The skies are dark but glistening stars
Can show us all the way.
Sound of crickets – a hooting owl
In the distance coyotes play,
These sounds I hear each morning
As I walk alone and pray.

Not many folks get up and watch
Those colorful morning rays
But He alone, each day can paint
Those dark skies all away
Sometimes I'd stop and wonder, and watch
The sky above – turn shades
Of red and yellow, a kaleidoscope of love
As He our gentle Saviour watches from above.

Christmas
Emily Miller
Christmas is a busy time of year
Shopping in malls
As Christmas draws near
We will deck the halls

When we are busy decorating the house
And the Christmas tree
I hope I don't see a mouse!
There is so much to see.

We better get to sleep
For Santa comes this night
We won't want to make a peep
Mama, won't you turn out my light?

Today is Christmas day!
Gifts under the tree
So happy and gay
Look, a doll you see!

I Watched You Die
Gina Clark

I sit by your bed and fight back the tears.
trying to hide the confusion and fear.
I hold your hand and silently pray
that you will hold on for one more day.

I feel the time tick slowly by
as I watch you close your eyes,
I knew that you grow tired and weak
and I wanted to cry as I heard you speak.

"Take care my friend I love you, now it's time for me to go
but I promise I'll watch over you and I will always know
I'll always be inside your heart, as long as you believe
Please try not to cry for me, I don't want you to grieve."

Once again you closed your eyes, and that's how they would remain
At that moment I knew I would never see your smile again.
As the last breath rose from you chest, I broke down and cried
you were my best friend, and I had to watch you die.

Your Loss
Linda Diane Markwell

You kept me on hold–your "sure thing".
How many nights did I sit home, waiting for that phone to ring.

You thought you had me all wrapped up on hold.
I kept begging you to stay—you just had to go.

Every day that passed kept hoping for more.
All I got was another closed door.

But now that I'm through, you're knocking it down.
It's a little too late for you to come around.

You were always looking for someone new.
I can't believe how much time I wasted on you.

You'll never get back–my love–that you had.
Please move on—I know I have.

The Wind
Suzanah Ewing

The wind whistles by my adobe wall,
wending its way towards the mountain.
There it meets a greater force
that slows its fury.

Sometimes it is ferocious,
stirring all that is in its path.
At others, it is little more than a gentle lamb,
nudging against Mother Nature.

In the still, summer, late afternoon
the wind sends blast of hot air
Over the desert plateau,
like an oven fan.

On milder days it freshens the atmosphere
with wafts of cool breezes,
Enlivening the lazing lizard on my garden wall
and my lagging spirits.

All My Child Has Learned
Corinna M. Davis

Not knowing much of anything,
My child entered into your class.
For I saw one day his progress
Never knowing he'd learn so fast.

Not much outgoing or independent
That, it changed as time went by.
He remembers all you taught him.
Even the question mark after "why".

Sometimes he would come home bragging,
that his teacher, she cares so much.
The difference that she made in his life
By her sweet and gentle touch.

So...Teacher, We'd like to thank you
For the credit you've rightly earned.
And thank you for the teachings...
For all that our son's learned.

What Is Blue?
Nichole Lemonte

Blue is...
...A balloon floating in the air
...A T–shirt drying in the sun
...A butterfly soaring in the wind
...A rainbow leading to the pot
   of gold
...A pair of blue jeans folded–up
   in a basket
...A ribbon tied to a box
...A sucker wrapped up
...A house sitting on the grass
...A river flowing through a tunnel
...A crayon sitting on a desk
...A note book lying in the sun
...A marker drawing a cloud
...Blue is a pencil drawing
   the beauty of earth.

Beefsteaks On The Grille
Glenn Rochon

In morning's light, all dressed in white,
I wield my weary knife,
And drawn across the sharp'ning steel
The blade comes back to life.

The mid–day meat is cool and dark,
A patient lying still,
For vivisection, thick and slick,
Beefsteaks for the grille.

The evening lures the legions forth,
Hordes of hungry hounds!
Who tempted by the sinless flesh,
Devour it in pounds.

The night sends scenes of gristle, blood,
Of sizzling, scorching Hell.
Lord tell me how a soul's to sleep
With beefsteaks on the grille?

My Hope
Joseph Henry

I so want to meet you,
And hold you in my arms;
To be with you for just a few,
And be beguiled by your chains.

I think of you quite after
In the night when it is dark.
Your face is passion softened.
To your sighs my body harks.

I feel your presence so near,
Even throughout the day.
Your sweet entrancing voice I hear
With the love it wants conveyed.

Little time is left to me
In this obscene childish place.
In a little time I will be free
To kiss that smile back on your face!

Love
Paula S. Boyd

Love, who knows whether or not
they have it.
Love, who knows how to get it?
Is love an automatic thing,
Can anyone experience it?
Love, why does it hurt so much?
Can someone please explain?
Can someone give an answer to
this question?
Can there be life without love?
Can you live without it?
I wish we could, then we'd never
have to worry about this feeling.
Why does love have to exist, can
someone please answer me
this question?
Love, what is it?

A Time In My Life
Michele Good

If there has been a time in my life when I cared,
It was that summer day when I gave you my heart with my love so free and
    bare.
The happiness and memories will always be there.
If there has been a time in my life when I gave,
It was when I told you a place in my heart I would save.
And forever for you my soul would crave.
If there has been a time in my life when I was obsessed,
It was that night when your loving hands so softly caressed
And a certain enchanting feeling that the night possessed.
If there has been a time in my life when I was in love,
It was when I realized our love was sent from above.
And how our togetherness fit like hand in glove.
If there has been a time in my life when I let my heart pour out,
It was from the moment I knew we were no longer going out.
Everyone heard my aching heart cry out.
If there has been a time in my life when I tried to gain,
It was when I stopped trying and forgot the pain.
I want your love and you again.

Untitled
Thomas Hinz

Life is more than work alone
You work all day and then come home
You can't forget to care, share
Love someone when you're not there

Someone's at home they sit
and wait and really
Hate to see you go 'cause
They would rather
Have you home
You hug them, love them
and adore but then
You must walk out the
door and count the
hours till you come home

For this is what we must do
To bring our
Family their daily bread.

Togetherness
Debbie Brown

T...Together
O...Oklahoma
G...God
E...Enters
T...The
H...Heart
E...Enlightens
R...Reality
N...Nationwide
E...Exits
S...Spiritually
S...Superior

Together Oklahoma, God Enters The Heart, Enlightens Reality
Nationwide, Exits Spiritually Superior.

Dedication: The people of the United States Of America

Love Your Enemies
Patricia Austin

Every morning when I start each day.
Satan tries to stop me from doing things
God's way.

But my Lord gives me armour and Guidance
from above.
And instructs me to love my enemies.
To be worthy of God's love.

It's really hard to do sometimes, to leave
vengeance up to HIM;
Patience, patience, patience he says to me,
your cup is to the brim.

Timing is so important and I'm the only one
that knows.
The exact and perfect time, each person's cup
just over flows.
Amen

Am I Afraid To Die?
Michele Blanck

Lying on the floor in a dark room
I sucked in all my breath
It would only be moments before panic sets in.
I close my eyes to picture death.
Walking through a sheet of glass,
I am holding my breath
I can hear the crash.
I can see no light,
As my head starts to throb.
The air re escaped from my lungs
I gasped and breathed hard to recover.
I loved him, I held his hand when he died.
He didn't look scared,
He looked peaceful.
So why did I cry.
As much as I miss him, I don't want to die.
I would again hold his hand maybe paint...
sing...fly.
I am not so afraid, it's just not time.

Little Turkey
Marie MacDonald

Thou art the ominous, yet alert creature
From which all great intellects have been born.

Your proud mandible, with whimsical skin roll so
Sore to the eye

With feathers perfect for a mattress stuffing
And claws as graceful as a prima donnas

Your stamina, courage, and bravery is to be
Commended and condemned

May thou and thou comrades, be at peace
In our freezer, and feel elated as we

Warm you to a steamy 400 degrees.
You little turkey.

A Wondrous Love
Carolyn Marie Strubberg

The lightning lightens,
The thunder roars,
As the earth trembled and shook.
Time goes by,
We laugh, we cry,
The night finally came,
We would never be the same.
Love sent to love,
A blessing from heaven above,
Hopes and Dreams are now coming true,
Now that there's a me and you.
The lightning lightens,
Our lives are brighten,
The thunder is still roaring,
As the passion is pouring.
The earth still trembles and shakes,
This love we found is no mistake.
A miracle happened by God,
He created such a wondrous love...

Birth Of A Memory
FranceAnna Arriola

Vibrations of sound bumping together
or by variations of color to a parchment are tethered...
Whirling, swirling, tumbling, gliding
then into a mysterious aperture sliding...

Suddenly, out of space or from the parchment arises...
images of the mind with their many disguises...
Fragments of visions joining as a whole
to give birth to stirrings from deep within the soul...

Ethereal, enchanting tropical isle,
promises of warmth and love beguile...
Dark emotions leering grin,
depicting the worst of all possible sin...

On a palette of essence of life intended...
repertoire of colors, carefully mixed and blended
to shades of evil or divine manifestation,
until in the heart a new memory is made a creation...

Silent Cries
Rena Lundmark

Silent cries no one hears,
A heart filled with dried up tears.
Reached out arms empty and bare,
No one's there, no one cares.
A mind filled with hopes and dreams,
A shell is shattered to bits and things.
A lonely soul an awful thing,
A big dark hole with no ending.
Aches and pains so deep inside,
Makes you want to run and hide.
Silent cries – dried up tears
Empty arms – no one cares
Shattered dreams – bits and things
A lonely soul – a big dark hole
Pains inside – run and hide
Because no one hears
Your silent cries.

Summer Scene
Stuart J. Kent

The trees sway in mental limbo,
Speaking to each other in the gentle breeze,
As silence is halted,
By the rustling of leaves.

The grass makes waves,
Like the oceans of blue,
Flowers acknowledge,
With a gentle bow.

The breeze starts to calm,
The silence is once again,
No more breeze,
Just summer rain.

Dark clouds float on by,
Exposing the summer blue sky.

Dedication: To Dad, whom I miss

The Big Apple
Clover D. Morris
New York is fine in the winter time
But when it is summer...oh boy!
No heavy clothes no runny nose
It is time to jump for joy.

No snow around you can sit on the ground
And don't even think twice about it,
But try it when it's cold and your body just seem old
Believe me...it make no sense to doubt it.

Party all night until broad daylight
Or just stay home and have lots of fun;
You still have to work even if you are a jerk
And you'd rather laze around like a bum.

The state that never sleeps where people play for keeps
New York is a fine place to be.
In the rain or in the sun you can always have fun
New York is the place for me.

Where Has Mommy Gone?
Karen Rosseland
Oh God, sweet God, where has Mommy gone?
For we've cried for her and needed her
It has been so very long
We wanted to surprise her
And show her what we made
But she was late again tonight
And after time, excitement fades
We felt we must discuss with her
The choices that we faced
But tired and stressed when she came home
Demands we had erased
We placed our dreams on hold you see
For Mommy disappeared
She was busy being Daddy
For all those many years

Dedication: Tiffany, Neal, gifts from God

Dictionary
Daniel Castelline
My dictionary tells me things that I never knew,
he is like a wise old owl,
its pages are like the words he's saying,
he tells me everything that I want to know,

I ask him questions,
he gives me answers,
he tells me how to spell a word,
he also tells me what it means,

he shows me what something looks like,
if I want to see,
he's always very happy,
and is filled with lots of glee,

he's always there for me,
sometimes he gets mixed up though,
I say I need a word,
and he'll give me a picture of a bird.

Pow–Wow Pride
Sheri Pashe
Clad in buckskin leather,
The dancers sing aloud,
Singing up their praises,
As they begin to draw a crowd.

Eagle whistles blowing,
As energy builds in all,
The beat of the drum is going,
Making us stand tall.

This is how it should be,
Time to capture back our pride.
Culture is in our corner,
You no longer have to hide.

So, dance with all your gusto,
Show all the world to see,
Life is such a beautiful thing,
When your spirit's free!

Imagine
Sherrie Berrian
On a cool spring eve above in the sky,
I saw a sea gull soaring way up high.

Waves rolling in, their caps against the shore,
The sun setting low, my eyes searched for more.

I stopped and looked, my feet in the sand,
A lovely young couple, I saw hand in hand.

They were so in love, you could look and see,
Hearts beating, eyes meeting, a love that was free.

My day was now over, so I went on my way,
But I'll always remember such a beautiful day.

The things I saw, such beautiful scenes,
I awoke and realized, it was only a dream.

Grace
Jeralyn Toben
When dreams come true
And you learn to fly
On wings of faith
You'll feel Heaven's high
In that place.

When dreams come true
In a special way
And the sun comes out
On a cloudy day
You'll know grace.

When dreams come true
And bring a strong light
That you never knew.
You'll not see the night
Or dark place.

Dedication: The clients of gompers

A Memory
Lincoln E. Wood
What is a
memory?
It is a glistening lake,
Soft green meadows,
A deep blue pool of thought

It wanders, whispers, crawls
lackadaisically
Around the tendrils of your mind
Caressing them –
Flowing.

It is a cat
A cat that purrs
meows, rubs your ankles
Jumps in your lap, kneads your flesh
And suddenly

Disappear–

Alone
Margaret Bates
Another argument we've had
just like so many before
I wait for you to say, "Don't go"
before I close the door.
Those words I long to hear don't come,
I guess this means we're really done.
I know this way the fights will end
And the tears will fade away.
But God to end it all like this—
Please ask me, love, to stay.
The doors now closed as I know are we
with memories forever to live.
Our future is gone, there's no you and me
with no togetherness to give.
In my heart your loves forever strong
And with that inside me, I'll carry on.
Alone

Memories
Lillian M. Seidel
Sun so bright. The sand hot upon
my feet. The ocean so calm and deep.
A place to get away, with many memories
to keep. My children so excited
And so sweet to see, the great
ocean so big with waves so high.
Look Mommie, I can ride the waves
up to sky; watching their faces
so happy with smiles, eyes that
glisten, hair blowing in a soft
breeze while feeding sea gulls,
And their chatter they listen.
Then again I hear, look Mommie,
I can leave my footprints in the
sand; I replied yes you did,
And now the ocean waters
will take them to another land
Oh! the joy of lots of memories
of my children running in the sand.

About A Grandkid
Patricia Thompson
When my own kids were born,
I was...delighted.
But, when my first grandkid was born,
That...was really like being enlightened.

Because, a son or a daughter,
is something so pretty.
But a grandson or granddaughter,
that...no doubt is prettier.

And you know, seeing my son or daughter,
it is a great feeling of joy.
But looking at my grandbaby,
That...is happiness, no matter if girl or boy.

For my kids, I can do
anything, anytime, always, ever.
For that sweet grandbaby,
something impossible? No...never.

Wandering In My Mind
Vernon D. Verdades
Sometimes I wander (in my mind)
Sometimes the places I visit (in my mind)
Are not there at all
They're only (in my mind).

Sometimes I lie on the sands of Carolina (in my mind)
Sometimes I roam the lowlands of Scotland (in my mind)
And smell again the dung–sweet soil (in my mind).
But always wherever I go (in my mind)
And whatever I do (in my mind)

You are always there (in my mind)
You invade every fantasy I've ever had
Or tried to have (in my mind)

I guess that's why I don't often need to wander (in my mind)
'Cause you are always here–and there (in my mind).

i am
Hillary Shirey
i am a mad girl who wants to know
i wonder why he left me so i hear his voice in the back of my mind
i see families so happy all the time
i want to know why that could never be us
i am a mad girl who wants to know

i pretend i'm feeling fine even when i'm not
i feel like punching him even though i cannot
i touch his picture imagining it is him
i worry because the pain will never end
i cry because i can never let him know
i am a mad girl who wants to know

i understand you, but in a way you are my foe
i say i still love you so
i dream of the day i can let you know
i try not to let you hurt me so
i hope you can hear me say
i am a mad girl who wants to know

The Threshold
Brid Wynn

Now in the twilight of my life
I stand before the door
And fear to knock and enter here
Where throngs have gone before.

I think of friends now dead and gone
And wonder if they'll meet me
I conjure up each dear old face
And hope that they will greet me.

My eyes grow dim and through the tears
Some memories come fleeting
Some just flit by — some still are clear
Of laughter and of weeping.

The door swings back and I see in
For this moment I have waited
And I join my friends of bygone years
Will all my fears abated.

Life
Sandra Maddalena

Life is filled with ups and downs
Like a frown on a clown

Life is full of heartache and despair
It's full of laughter and sometimes fear

Life begins with a baby's cry
It also ends with death, and why

Life is complicated and can be unfair
It something that everyone shares

Life has a beginning and an end
It's full of families and lots of friends

So be happy and try your best
To make your "life" the most memorable yet

When He Came He Brought Fear
Geraldine Leach

And he fell, and he fell, and he
fell and he fell, until on this
earth he came to dwell;
he and his unholy caravan
speedily moving
deceiving man.

Using principalities, power and might,
committing dastardly deeds
both day and night;
working undercover and out of sight
keeping man in a state of perpetual fright.

Mans afraid to live and afraid to die
afraid, afraid, is his constant cry.
He's afraid of tomorrow
and what it might bring,
mans afraid, afraid,
of everything.

Trails
Robert Summers

There are many trails that go back home and many trails to roam.
Trails that lead us East and West to oceans white with foam.
Trails that lead to Canada; trails to Mexico.
Trails that we may walk someday and trails we'll never know.

There are trails that take us wandering to where the cold winds blow.
Trails that lead to mountaintops where few will ever go.
Trails that lead to valleys; trails that lead to caves
Trails that anyone will walk and some only the brave.

There are trails that wander all around through deserts and through towns.
Trails that lead us here and there and trails that can't be found.
Trails that go to everywhere; trails that lead nowhere.
Trails to travel by ourselves and trails that we must share.

We must follow trails that are not safe—we don't know to where.
There are places filled with loneliness and trails to lead us there.
A trail that has no ending; one we must walk alone.
Trails we all must take someday to our eternal home.

Peace And War
Robert A. Carroll

Peace and war go hand in hand
Just another bullet to kill a man.
Who is bigger, who is smaller?
who is shorter, who is taller?
Peace and war go hand in hand.

From the beginning of time 'til its
Infinite end peace and war go hand in
hand. It takes war to make peace.
To keep peace we wage war; where will
it end? Whichever we choose it's all
around you. Near and far, whether at home
or in your car, for that matter, wherever you are.

Peace and war go hand in hand.

Dedication: Nora T. England (Mother)

A Heart Of Gold
Denise M. Allison

My life was touched in a wonderful way,
I thank God for the miracle, every day.
I had the chance to know a man,
Who stood above others across the land.
In his eyes you could read a book,
It only took just one look.
In his face you could see the years,
Oh what joy, pain, and tears.
In his hands you could feel the love,
Truly heaven sent from above.
On his lips you could hear the words,
Although not always spoken, but surely heard.
In his hug I could feel his soul,
Touching mine and taking hold.
For the rest of my life I will always know,
I was loved by someone special,
Someone with a heart of gold.

Dedication: In memory of William McMullen

To My Church Family
Cheryl Jorgensen
Not too long ago, you were all strangers to me
I walked through these church doors and that all changed
The love from your hearts poured out in a smile
And I knew I'd found a home.

You truly are my family in every sense of the word
I can laugh with you, cry with you
I can depend on you and you can depend on me.

You have nurtured me and cared for me
You have helped me in my Christian walk
You have prayed with me and you have prayed for me
And I know that you are genuine.

Each night as I pray I thank God for this family
And I thank Him for His Son Who's shed blood made it so
There are no words to adequately describe what's in my heart
All I know is the love and joy is deep and pure and real.
And I can only say, "I love you family."

To My Special Childhood Friend
Patricia L. McLucas
Today, I say goodbye to my special childhood friend
When we were young, we thought out lives would never end.
We grew up together in the peaceful setting of Blyn.

We laughed and played, we fished and swam, life was clean and pure.
Our friendship would always endure.

He baited my fishhook and held the barbed–wire fence
Being the gentleman he was; He was my childhood prince.

I don't ever recall a cross word from my friend,
Even as spoiled as I'm told I might have been.
Richard's kind and thoughtful ways continued on,
Even though through our teens, our friendship wasn't quite as strong.

I'll never forget my friend, the memories will always with me abide.
And so I say goodbye to him, until we meet again on the other side.

Looking For The Place That We Called Home
Patricia Brumfield
While I was traveling down the lonely country road,
I saw a field of flowers growing wild and free.
And as I stopped the car to take a closer look,
I knew this must be where the old house used to be.

As the fragrance of the flowers filled the air,
I thought I saw a young girl playing there.
And then I heard a sweet voice saying soft and low,
"You must be looking for the place that we called home?"

She said you're standing where the front porch used to be,
and there's the rocking chair that once held you and me.
The birds were singing their old songs of long ago,
And while I listened, soft, warm tears began to flow.

Then, in the distance I could see the old oak tree.
It was standing proud and tall, as if to welcome me.
And just below the tree I found the stone.
And knew I'd found the place that we called home.

Missy
Laurie Sobczak
I have something to say
dear lady
I have a living breath
inside of me
It is you
It comes from me
yet it was
born deep
within
you
We became
separate
yet
You live within my
soul
You make me
grow
Don't ever
go

Harp In The Wind
Hazel F. Donaldson
Tall Eucalyptus, harp in the wind,
play for my singing heart.
I will remember:
Tall grasses swaying,
embowered by love
and encircling arms—
Violet shadows on sunlit hills—
Midnight lakes with drowning stars.
Play for my singing heart.

I am a wanderer longing for home;
play for my aching heart.
Help me forget:
The years swiftly passing—
Frost on the hills—
And winter winds calling.
Play for my homesick heart.

Even Then, Even Now
Mozelle W. Rivers
It was over forty years ago
I fell deeply in love with you.
My heart went a fast pitter–patter
Whenever you were passing thru.

Although you are now married
I know not to interfere
But my love secretly for you
Has lasted all these years.

I wonder how many people
Are having this same encounter too.
This feeling – then and even now
Has me still in love with you.

If something should happen
That makes your marriage fall apart
Look quickly over your shoulder, I'm there
With a love abundantly in my heart.

Imagination
Jamie Jensen
Round here the mighty king,
Fears the joker's tricks.
While the wild jungle
Is nothing more than
A mad hatter's dream.

Round here queens in rags,
Dance in castles of sand.
The tide washes away the royal reality.

Round here angels lost their wings
As the verdict falls.
The courtroom is corrupted
By acid judges.

Round here the rainbows fade quickly
And the pot of gold in never found.
The clover lies in wait.

Cascades And Profusion
Pamela Tamplin
What a sight, oh what a scene
The prettiest place I've ever been
It fair took my breath away
Such colourful beauty on display

Flowers stand tall, the heads held high
Their glory reaching to the sky
Little flowers look up and say
Look we're down here, don't move away

Have you seen so many greens
Bushes, fir trees, leaves and things
Velvet faces, silky spines
English gardens of all kinds

We stand in awe, we stand and stare
Its human hands, it's love and care
There's happiness here, its all aglow
At the Chelsea flower show

Carry Me
Margaret Boulay
The body tired and aching,
I dare not close my eyes.
The enemy will surely see,
My weakness should I try.

The days are never ending,
I long to see my home.
Simple pleasures are my desire,
In the jungle there is no phone.

The men who share this journey with me
All feel the way I do.
That one day we shall all be home,
How wonderful to have dry shoes.

Carry me along with you,
Pray that I shall be.
Tomorrow home with family,
In a land that's free.

To Be Alone
Barbra Moran
It is not sad to be alone
or bad to be alone
I am glad to be alone
Less laundry to do
More things to do
for less money too
Fewer groceries to buy
Less cash to get by
No reasons to lie
I can walk when I want
Talk when I want
Travel when I want
Where and with whom
I want
I can stay as long
or as short as
I wish
when I'm alone

First Glimpse
Shelia Montgomery
He entered with a frown that bespoke of his struggle.
There was nothing within reach to grasp or to snuggle.
It was cold, it was loud, it was very bright!
He would liked to have returned to the quiet of his night.
There was too much openness and he felt he would fall,
To add to his displease was the incessant maul!
What was this place he had passed into?
After safety and security, was this his due?!
How had it happened and who was to blame?
There was not even one he could put to name.

The discomfort he suffered gave rise to voice.
Wherever he was, he was given no choice!
Then, there it was, a familiar sound.
He chanced a peek to see what he'd found.
Through a misty haze and radiant light,
He discovered love in his mother's sight.

Dedication: To Daniel Long, my inspiration

Wild Geese
Irene Lynn
Night was closing in on me,
The cold winds blowing 'round,
Yet I stood listening, breathlessly,
To the old familiar sound.

Overhead the shadows slowly passed,
The "honking" sounded near.
Wild geese were flying south at last,
A sign that autumns here.

I stood and pondered, as I gazed,
Up at the wavering "V".
I never cease to be amazed,
At this miracle I see.

Who tells them, how do they know,
It's time to start their flight.
Who directs them which way to go?
I watch them, wondering, in the night.

Grandmother
J. L. Taylor
When I see you
with your shoulders bent
walking with your head tilted to the ground
because your pale eyes aren't so sharp
or
when I see you
with your crooked fingers
like gnarled old bark on a tree
trying to just make them grasp
for the keys deep in your purse
I'm sad
when I see you
with thin white wisps of worn out hair
cradling the sweetest old lined and wrinkled face
I'm glad that you are my grandmother
I respect you
for all of your wisdom
I love you.

Melody Of Spring
Lola W. Wesson
With soft, green carpet covered, 'neath a ceiling of azure blue,
The daffodils and hyacinths have slept their long night thru.
And now they stretch their tiny arms and pry thru sun warmed earth
To brighten all the countryside, and revel in Spring's birth.

The tender leaf buds open, on maple tree and quince,
And gently, softly, flutter, when by the raindrops rinsed.
The new—green sword is punctured with colors, fresh and rare,
And flowers shed their fragrance upon the balmy air.

The joyous songs of birds, those harbingers of Spring,
Are heard from across the meadows, where tree—tops fairly sing.
Small wonder 'tis that Cupid goes hunting then for hearts,
And that, with aim so sure, they're pierced with every dart.

The earth so bathed in beauty is wondrous fair to see,
And sorrows seem a long way off, amid such ecstasy.
So who is there to say, that Spring with so much glory,
Is not of all the seasons, most beautiful and Holy?

Ether
Sarah Bowdidge
I am all that was
I am everything that is
I am all that will be.

I am dead
I am alive
I am not yet born.

I am past
I am the present
I am future

I am prophecy
I am fulfilled
I have yet to occur

I am everything
I am nothing
I am.

Shadows
Jacqueline Hayman
Shadows in the wind
dance with reflections
of a new day's beginning.

Often times forgotten, they
dance endlessly to the
rhythms of the wind.

Their presence is forever,
changing ever so briefly
as the moments slowly
move forward in their
pursuit of day.

Shadows in the wind,
blending slowly into the void
of darkness, only to dance
once again to the rhythms of the wind.

Drop
Shasna Ali
What kind of fate is this
That I should be so brittle
And I must recoil in fear
At the hand raised at me
I am not soft
I am hard and do not cry
At the pain of the hit
It is at the fear
Which causes me to shudder
And to hide in the shadows
Crouching in corners
What kind of fate is this
That my mistakes must be eternal
And drown me
And listen to my gasping for breath
One day I shall stay down
And then I'll show you
It wouldn't be fate
But me, coming into me

Someone Else
John K. Campbell
Look at him look at her
They go through life without a care
That's what we think of the other guy
Why me why me is the lonely cry

Negative thoughts come and stay
How can we make them go away
No one else seems to worry this way
Or so we seem to think

And as we share our lives with friends
We soon find out we are not alone
So ease the problem help is at hand
On your own it is hard to stand

Be united one and all
Don't leave the weak behind don't let them fall
Help one another to help themselves
Don't wait forever heed the call

You
Bethany Wilson
I saw you standing by yourself
Gazing at the wall as if something was there;
Maybe a window to your thoughts
Or a mirror to reflect the structure of your face.
There's some yellow in your brown eyes;
Pretty shades of color
Tantalizing your moods and past times.
I want to reach out and grab hold of your hand
To maybe feel what you do or to see what you see.
The blushing of my cheeks when you smile at me;
The shortness of my breath when you come close.
Your smile means the world to me;
Your laugh makes me dream.
You understand my moods and bear them with me.
When I cry, you hold me close and say all the right words;
You make my heart murmur your name.
Over and over three words are repeated;
I love you.

Song Of The Seasons
Nancy Jackson
Unyielding as a Women scorned, the seasons come and go.
Cold and bitter is the mantle of January.
Her grip extends to February, causing the month of
March to fill her cheeks with the North wind.
So even April will shiver under a pale sun.
But soon the mood will change,
May will show her garlands of pretty buds and flowers.
the trees will stretch their branches inviting us to feel
their new vibrations of life.
The full crescendo arrives with June and July causing nature
to burn beneath the high hot globe above us.
August will smother us with standing heat, the beautiful
song of September sings of Autumn's mellow fruitfulness.
October will paint the vivid colours of nature, bronze, yellow,
red and green. Soon to be hidden by the mists of
foggy November.
Sending us scurrying inside to the warm, bright fires of
Winter where we can watch the cold light of December
and tune into the never–ending song of the seasons.

Untitled
Vincent Dudley
Come to me and face the fear
come and breathe your final breath
walk into the darkness I hold so dear
and know that I am your death

Within my mind your thoughts become perverse
as I squeeze the life from your soul
this anguish I cause could not be worse
for life has become a bottomless hole

Condemned by the weakness that shows
I become stronger in their shame
he who hides their fear knows
it is I who will bask in muted fame

And pity the soul that feels naught for life's demise
For the pain must live deep inside
To hide in the shadows of the one who cries
And because every day, a little more of me has died.

23rd And 1/2 Psalm
Geri Roberson
(An Expression Of Trust)
The Lord is the captain of my ship,
I am guided by his righteousness, I will not slip.
He calms my anxiety, He restores my soul,
I exalt in His love, seeking goodness as my goal.

Even though I walk in the shadow of grief and despair,
I will not falter knowing my Savior is there.
For the Lord is strong, compassionate and mighty,
His rod and His staff are of great comfort to me.

He prepares a table before me in the presence of my foes.
My plate is full, my cup overflows.
Surely goodness and mercy shall follow me all of my days,
Oh Lord, show me your paths, teach me Your ways.

I will survive the treacherous waters and go safely ashore,
Where I will dwell in the house of the Lord forevermore.

The Love In Our Life
Michael R. Jackson
Love brought to Earth life
in it are many wonders
Love is life our greatest gift
for we know that love is Christ

In holding all these truths
I must show this love to you
as we adventure through our life
His love will keep us tight.

Bursting with expectation
though there be a foe
we advance in bold experiences
for Christ's love is in us both.

Love's the center of this world
consummated by God's Son
Our commitment to undying love
and cause is everlasting.

Clogs
James R. Watson
Clattering irons on frosty mornings,
Hard–packed pads in winter snows.
Rainwashed cobbles show reflected,
Burnished leather and brass capped toes.

Flash of gilded nailheads gleaming,
Buttoned strap or leather lace.
Elm grown pattens, iron protected,
Bestowed therein a humble grace.

Children's slides in icy winters,
Sparks struck bright from flinty kerbs,
Youthful pranks and games remembered,
Oft my pensive mind disturbs.

Humble symbols of an era,
Gone with pinafore and shawl,
Forever vanished, ne'er forgotten,
Live on in Northern memories all.

My Song
Laura M. Scheuermann
I heard a song today

Soft muffled music of a blue flower
opening petal lips

Or was it the gleam of a silver
stone reaching for the sea

Perhaps the shrieking gull
above, playing king

Was it the wind's rhythmic
rock across the grass

I heard the song and
needed to make my sound

A small, discordant note.

Inside My Mind
Norah Clappison
As I lay down to sleep
I look inside my mind so deep
Searching for answers
To questions I need to explore
Turning the handle and opening the door
Looking to find out
If I'll be remotely normal,
If ever and when.
My thoughts run off in circles again
Twisting and turning,
A frightening ride
This way or that way
And will I collide.
No matter how much I try to resist,
My mind always wanders off
Into a cold, dark mist.
I'll have to get up,
I can't stand anymore,
I'll just turn the handle and open the door.

Welcome Home
Nancy L. Brown
As the pearly gates then opened,
A fanfare it did play.
for the angels and the cherubs,
Came to watch your judgement day.

The Lord he came to meet you.
And he looked upon your face.
Within your eyes, he searched your soul.
And found a gentle loving place.

The Lord He then embraced you
Saying "In this man I see no fault.
For on earth this man was kind to all,
and is truly worth his salt".

A burst of joy, came over you.
The Lord said "That's alright".
"For only men, with hearts of gold".
"May walk within the light".

In Praise Of Scotland
Jeanette Sloan
When you visit Bonnie Scotland
You'll see heather covered hills,
There'll be Lowlands, well as uplands,
With their rivers and their rills.

You will see a lot of islands,
With their harbours and their bays
And the peats, all stacked and ready
For the colder shorter days.

All the forests with their pine trees,
Standing straight and green and tall,
Interspersed with beech and larches,
Making man feel very small.

So come and see our people,
Our mountains, streams and deer,
And the welcome that you get here
Will be heartfelt and sincere.

Interwoven
Shirley L. Borthwick
You were born to me – I am music
Flinging me afar, clamoring for growth
As goldfish in bowl, struggling for identity
You will chant my melody eternally.

You were born with me – I am clothing
You altered me for bright oranges and yellows
Musing as prospective bridegroom, you surged
toward perfection
Death claims no garments
Your soul will shroud in my apparel eternally.

You were born in me – I am home
You deserted me for the expanse of road
As a toddler bereft of family and fortune
Eternally, I will be where you roam.

Dedication: Blake– jumping jeans

Brother O'Mine
Alice Gadd
He was a gentle soul
This man of eight decades and more
With a pretty wife, nine years his junior.
A Lady with an unquenchable thirst for perfection.
Which this Dear Man tried his utmost to satisfy.
And so the story goes.
"I can see it all now", he says one day with
conviction.
It is raining, You are holding an umbrella
over your head.
The diggers are digging a grave
"I want him here," you say,
"No, I want him over there."
But in the end, the scene changes.
And Fate has a role to play
He is leaning over a coffin
He whispers softly.
"The wrong person will be holding the umbrella."
And so it goes.

Unwelcome Guest
Twilla Mae Brewer
The Santa Ana blows outside,
A mighty lady she.
She lifts her head, she churns the tide,
Fights fiercely, remains free.

Tall trees bend low and kiss the earth,
Nothing stands in her way,
She sighs and cries, and laughs with mirth,
Yet knows she cannot stay.

She comes from deserts far away,
Blows sand filled skies before her,
She rumps and stumps like kids at play,
Steals hats and kites, and sails Sir.

Her stay is brief, and as she leaves
She turns and smiles in knowing
She's been our Guest, has done her best,
And we're so glad she's going.

If
Terry D. Stovall
If dogs were granted their wish to fly
As fast, as far, and as high
As the feathered bird who desired to be
Finned and scaled like fish in the sea;
And fish began to walk the land
With the gracefulness of superior Man;
And the sun so longed to give birth
To trees and flowers like mother earth;
And finally life, in the blink of an eye,
Mimicked death and decided to die;
Man would yearn to see his best friend soar,
But would dog be his best friend—or
Would his new best friend be the bird,
Which is now the fish that walks the world?
If by chance all opposites switched,
Man's reputation guarantees this:
Gas on the sun, he would eagerly pour;
Infinite love Man would make, and very little war.

Soulmates
Jan L. Shahan
I was always brought up
to know there was love
in this world of confusion
it's what dreams are made of.

I thought I'd never find it
as the years slipped on by
then you came into my life
and we saw eye to eye.

Our love started blooming
like a beautiful rose
now I know that it's true,
in this life that we chose

We are lucky to have found it
within each other's heart
the key to everlasting love
Soulmates 'til death do us part.

The Man Who Told It The Way It Was
Walter Wallace
In retrospect I do recall—
One of the most likable boxing men of them all
At almost every veteran boxer's affair
I seem to sense his presence there, the man who told it the way it was!

He covered "the beat" for his boxing friends
At almost every bout or social affair
With pad and pencil in his hand, he was there
The man who told it the way it was!

Babe "O" was the fighter–writer's name
He gained his fame, writing about the boxing game
In his "Reporter" a tabloid perhaps by some, deemed as small
He reported all the news, about the most exacting sport of them all

As a boxing writer, we all rated him with a big A plus
Because lovable Babe "O" was a man who told it the way it was!
And we all love him now as we did back then
But we may never ever, see the likes of him again.

Roommate
Paul Ubbelohde
She is tantalizing in an old black fedora
matching tennis shoes, Goodwill vintage

I listen, halfheartedly, as she sings
(off key)
a song she wrote and dedicates to me

On Saturdays we search junk shops
looking for a used guitar
end up getting stinko, in a shot and a beer bar

She disappears for awhile
returning with that (let me stay) smile

Lies about a job interview

Would you remain acquiescent—
and continue to pay her share of the rent?

Angel In Disguise
Amy Grace Wharton
As I felt the tears fall down my cheek;
my courage became one of those among the meek.
Until one day, to my surprise;
I met an angel, in disguise.

Then, this woman took me by the hand;
and she tried to help me understand.
Then she dried my tears away;
and told me the pain, was not to stay.

She knelt down beside me, and bowed her head;
with tears in her eyes, she quietly said.
"God, love her, protect her, and ease her pain;
for her love for you is an eternal flame".

To me then said, "God's strength was within my soul;
and that as long as I had faith, I'd be in control".
So now with this woman by my side;
I realized she was, – My Angel In Disguise.

Untitled

Luke A. Brown

So many times I take
This pen in my hand.
Hoping to be inspired,
Wanting beauty and truth to run out
Of me in this ink
Onto this field of virgin white.
I want my thoughts and ideas
And dreams to come, to interest,
to inspire. They will not come
However, they are stopped by something
Some unrecognizable force.
Could it be fear of criticism?
Could it be shyness?
Maybe they are just lazy.
Maybe the truth, my truth, is not ready.
Maybe it is not complete.
The frustration mounts, it creeps
In slowly, pushing my love out.
I sit and wait for the light of day.

A Grandma's Lament

D. M. Weyrauch

God bless a grandchild
in the teens
help keep them clean
both soul and jeans
Polish the halo
'round their heads
make them holy
(let them make their beds)
God bless and love
the girls—the boys
instead of heartache
let them bring joys
A grandma's prayer
when at life's end
My grandchildren are
special
My joys to them I
lend.

In His Wake

Jessica Lane

Eyes of blue, and cold as stone,
Hair blond as sand.
Smell the Autumn breeze in his breath,
Hear the birds sing in his voice,
Feel the leaves tremble in his touch.

Listen to his whispers,
Listen closely, his sound is lost
Within the roaring, amber waves;
Lost behind the clouds of night
In the blanket of darkness.

The stars glisten like shattered glass;
His eyes pierce like a needle.
He paces the beach as if he was at
The world's edge,
And could walk no further.
The waves pass under his feet;
Empty shells pulled in by the tide.

A More Colorful Sunset

Lester V. Andersen

Sunsets paint a clouded sky
with colors never found in dyes.
We watch with awe such lovely views.
but most of us have eyes to use.

But what of those who cannot see;
Who miss these wondrous scenes.
They can only then be told
what we, with eyes behold.

We falter, with un—guided speech,
our sightless fellow men to reach
these wonders seen in tree and sky,
but some day God will mend their sightless eyes.

But yet, though seeing, we miss the goal.
while they are searching with their mind,
with fine tuned senses and thought more kind,
feel greater beauties in their soul.

Vows Made In Wine

Kristina DeAnn DuBerry

She looks out the window into the rain,
Remembering the heartache, remembering the pain
Tears stream down her innocent face
Crying for another time and place
For a Mother who cared to think
of other things besides a drink
Mommy said she would be here at one o'clock
She knows she is late though she can't read the clock
the click of the clock blows away dreams
of dinner with Mommy, among other things
She crushes the hopes of her only daughter
Sifting through them as if they were water
She looks out the door and says, "she's not coming."
The rain on the windows continues its drumming
drowning the hopes of one little girl
who already thinks the worst of this world
but the moment is forgotten in mother's mind.
For no one remembers vows made in wine

He's Not Romantic

Joyce Coffee

He's a shoulder to cry on when things get rough
A hand to hold when the going is tough
My back—up when the kids get satanic
But he's not romantic

Gives me no compliments but no insults either
Takes over for me when I need a breather
Makes no comment when I grow gigantic
But he's not romantic

He treats my mother as if she's his own
He's crazy about his children even though they're all grown
He is calm and sensible when I start to panic
But he's not romantic

Waits patiently when I talk and linger
Lets his grandchild wrap him around her finger
He's a rock when I'm feeling frantic
But he's not romantic

Pretending

Sue Fulkerson

I'll run like a child
all breathless from play,
and smile at the sun
on this Summer day

I'll rest in the shade
of an old oak tree,
that survived Winter
just like me

I'll leave my cares
for another day,
watching clouds build castles
while winds blow them away

Then I'll dream of tomorrow
and days yet to be,
carefree as the child
who still lives in me.

Awakening

Elizabeth Eisner–Thompson

Awakening
I feel a gentle breath
caress my face,
no more
than a fleeting whisper of peace.
Motionless I lie
wondering . . .
is it the spirit
come to guide the day?
. . . or hovering
in protection from the night?
No matter.
The peace it brings
yields ceaseless joy
in brightest day
and deepest night,

and promise of eternal bliss.

The Challenged

Patricia Anderson

When young I practiced runs and scales
While sitting comely and straight,
Rehearsing my recital piece
For Mother and my aunt Kate.

Piano keys responded not
To childish finger's fumbling,
Along with sweet and soothing tones
Discordant notes came tumbling.

Years later, now–arthritic bones
Perch on the piano seat,
Still encouraging stiff old hands
To keep in sync with the beat.

Trifocals placed, buttocks pillowed,
Striving at every measure,
Never becoming accomplished
But venture's such a pleasure.

First Glance

James Booth

Wood and oiled lands ascend to water
Ground
aquatic dreams

Robbed of tenderness in fitful strife
Open
without remorse

Hinder those fish catcher's nets
Adrift
answer Poseidon

A wretched, glass–enclosed heart
Worked
absent again

Feminine contentions realised again
Smoke
and water

The Battle

Debbie Higgins

They say they can tell
by the thinness in her face.
She gets angry
and demands her space.
She questions why
they're doing this to her.
She says it's for torture
and that's the reason, for sure.
She can't pay attention
or even carry on a conversation.
She always goes back
to eating or her weight.
To get on the scale,
She just can't wait.
Why can't she see what others can see?
She sneaks around things so carefully.
When will she stop or will she be able to?
What should I do or should I send her to you?

My Body, I Surrender

Heather Williams

My mind thinks thoughts of you
My heart sings songs to you
My soul does long for you
I give my love freely
My body, I surrender
Made as your complement
In you, I am complete
Together we are one
I am not my own
I give myself to you
Learning to love you
I grow stronger each day
I rejoice with you, I struggle with you
I stand with you
Learning to love Him as we go
Together we are whole
I am not my own
I give my love freely
My body, I surrender

By The Light Of The Moon
Barbara Roraff

I saw a dark cloud with a silver lining,
by the light of the full moon.
It surely took my breath away,
For it reminded me of you.

I didn't believe in fairy tales,
But you've shown me they come true,
By the twinkle I feel in my eye,
Whenever I smile at you.

I once lived in a darkened land,
Which only your gaze could see—
But your love unlocked the door,
That eventually set me free.

And now I've shed those darkened years,
And as I gaze at you by the light of the moon,
I see a dark cloud with a silver lining,
Slowly gliding across the full moon!

The Tempest Most Foul
Ann E. Meritt

Roaring blackness soundless terror
engulfs our fears.

Swirling clouds tear and chip mercilessly
at all we hold dear.

Soon this villain has past with its thunderous
roar; as it rips up winged shutters and tears off
empty doors.

What's left behind is quiet and still, but soon a
cry peals out— "Is anyone alive?", it shouts!

Slowly the limpid mankind rears its head
to see what everyone doesn't wish but dreads.

The tempest most foul has passed on ahead and
left not but a few scattered torn up tiny shreds.

Woes And Sorrow
Joshua Daniel Archer

As the tears roll from my eyes,
so do my woes and sorrow.
I can't take it, all the lies,
I have no tomorrow.

Nobody understands me,
because nobody cares.
Won't anybody ever see,
my emotion is a pack of bears.

They look at me through despise,
they hate me for no reason.
I might as well wear disguise,
they think that I am treason.

So as of this, I hide my life,
I am but a dead rose.
I might as well take my knife,
and drown all my woes.

Untitled
Carlinda Gooday

Missing you is something
I feel every moment
It's like a little piece of sadness
that I carry around with me
When I stop what I am doing
to take a moment to think of you,
there is an emptiness
that fills me up inside,
But along with the sadness
there are wonderful memories
And when I think of all the
Special times we've had,
I can't help but smile
in spite of the sadness.
It is then that I realize
that I would rather feel
the pain of missing you
than lose a single
Memory of you.

Dream Of A Fool
Pamala Oltmann

When you were young, still wishing on stars...
Did you wish to be a doctor, lawyer or a famous rock star?
Did you ever dream to be rich? For surely not poor...
Or did your dreams ever go that far?
I had but one dream, a dream that finally came true...
A dream of a love, which came true with you.
Straight out of a dream of a young lonely child...
Searching for her love, to live that dream for awhile.
Yearning in her heart to be wanted and needed...
Being pushed back away...words gone unheeded.
Such is the luck of a poor lonely girl,
Such is the luck of a dream of a fool.
To give all her hope for that love and a dream...
Her search of a lifetime, yet so it seems.
Ever so faithful, standing nearby...
In hopes of a dream, yet dare should she try?
Waiting for the words she so longs to hear...
Spoken by someone, in her heart, she holds dear.

And The Thunder Will Roll
Ross Runnion

When the lightning flashes,
And the thunder rolls,
Creatures of the Earth hear the crashes,
And men feel it in their souls.

For we must know our own true worth,
Within the concinnity of this world.
The trees, sky, and rocks are indifferent to our birth
And our death, no matter what flags are furled.

When the sun sets on our time,
And the clouds of salubrity hover over the land,
To many tenants of field and stream will it seem sublime,
After mankind is gone, like a dune in the sand.

Quiescence of nature will our absence not dash,
For even after the smoke clears and our last bell doth toll,
The lightning will flash,
And the thunder will roll.

Life Hits The Gold
JoEllen Dee Crispin
In an exhibition of quiet waters life portrays a peaceful calm,
So soothing to mankind's spirit: even as Gilead's Healing Balm;
Till suddenly on vast horizon there's display of turbulence role,
To cause frightening confusion which overwhelms serenity of soul.

Like an observant soaring sea–gull we may questioningly survey,
Such startling appearance of turmoil infringing a comforting day;
This is improper time to "dip wing" lest raging billows overtake,
We must serenely abide the winds current: in an expectant wait.

We can only subdue conflicting torrent when not becoming hostile,
In retained assurance thriving hope will bring reward in a while;
If truly believing a given situation and circumstances shall pass,
We will remain in constant control: the perpetrator to outclass.

Willingly recall from memory many virtuous victories of the past,
Feed hope faith for survival: knowing tumult must obey its avast;
In quickening of truth faiths eye will again faithfulness behold,
Hope of Love through faith will triumph; then LIFE HITS THE GOLD!

Being Unwanted
Dorothy Kamler
It wasn't always that way
but, at some point when I was quite young
no one really cared about me.
Stay out of the way!
Don't cause problems. (Whatever that meant?)
Don't talk to anyone!
I no longer had a room, a place of my own.
Not even a dresser or space for toys.
Whatever space I used, it was too much.
Whether I ate or not made no difference.
Just don't get dirty!
(I guess that would've
acknowledged my existence.)
So when I ran away, I wasn't missed.
Even though there weren't others
in my place, it didn't matter.
What little impact I had,
was the cause of all misery.

The Turtle
Elizabeth A. Cherney
As I rushed home one busy day, a turtle caught my eye.
There he was beside the road— I can't imagine why.
I saw his face, wrinkled and green; he seemed to wear a smile.
But every time he budged an inch, it seemed more like a mile.

"Where are you going, little friend?" I asked the turtle green.
He looked at me, perplexed and asked, "Whatever do you mean?"
"I see you're walking down the street; you must be going somewhere.
But at the rate you're traveling, you never will get there."

"Parrumph! Nonsense!" The turtle laughed, and slowly shook his head,
"If I hurried like you do, I'd probably be dead!
And, while I wander down the road, you pass much beauty by.
You don't take time to see the earth or look up at the sky."

So from my turtle friend I learned
to slow things down a tad.
Since then I've been enjoying life—
and I am rather glad!

Letters To Grace
Loretta K. Full
My Dear, Dear Wife,
You are my own true love,
Always kind, always true.
Your calmness and serenity
Does guide us, daily through.
Your unselfish love, your unbending faith,
Makes your presence so special
No matter the place.
In the kitchen, you are an artist,
As a wife, a perfect mate.
As a mother, you are ever–loving,
As my best friend, you are truly great.

Untitled
Barbara Bernard
If I Should Die Tomorrow
Then let me go alone
Of me erase all memories
And all affection shown
In dreams I will return to him
A comfort in his sleep
A small untouchable part of me
For him alone to keep
In dreams I will be real to him
In reality I'll be gone,
But listen closely to the wind
To hear my sad love song

Flowers On The Ground
Amber Rivard
Flowers on the ground
Clouds in the sky
I leap with a bound,
But I cannot fly
Flowers on the ground
Leaves on the trees
I hear a sound,
But I cannot see
Flowers on the ground
Such different colors
Oh how I would love
To be those flowers on the ground

Daddy Was A Wonderful Man
Norma Childers
As my daddy traveled his last mile, into his new place,
Daddy did not take things with him my heart will never erase.
Daddy did not take pain, tears, nor pride,
Daddy walked with the Lord as, his guide.
Daddy traveled down that old White River for many of miles,
I knew daddy loved that old river as, he showed it with his smiles.
Now daddy has traveled that last long mile to our Lord today,
I still have one last memory I would like to say.
My daddy was a wonderful man,
He could not work from, his shaking hand.
His ten children was, his pride and joy,
No one made him happier than, his three boys.
God has been with daddy for 85 years,
When he was sick, we all shared his tears.
As I prayed for my daddy each day,
I would, thank the Lord for, his long stay.
Dood, Bob, and Bill, there is one thing I can say,
You were so special to our daddy until his last day.

Heavenly Minded And No Earthly Good
Lydia M. Rogers
Lord, help me not to see the skies
And miss this rod that's in my eye.
Help me not to "shout" and "run"
And not give a hand shake when I'm done.
Give me wisdom in all my ways
To do good and give someone the time of day.
I need to see that there's work to do.
Not just at church but on city streets too.
Cause me to seek out the lost and blind
To spare someone that extra dime.
Be with me Lord, so I'd do as I should
And not be heavenly minded and no earthly good!

Untitled
Kathleen Keane
My life ended today
But I am still here
The doctor told me;
My dreams and goals have disappeared
You've come so far to start over
What am I to do?
I've tried to meet my goals
My health is bad
I'm scared
Who wants someone who can't reach their goals?
My life ended before it started
I can't turn to anyone
They all look to you to make the difference
I can't disappoint them

Morning Drum
Jessica Cammaroto
On the middle of a morning through impending noonday sun
if you stay with the rhythm of the steady beating drum
to the point of tomorrow where the future drinks its fate
like the dew on a leaflet as the sun is getting late
to the sweet anticipation that you'll put your hand in mine
as the sky closes the evening where horizon red hawks fly
through the fire heat of passion as their wing tip feathers burn
till they're lost amid the skyline to await the sun's return
fading rhythm cuts the darkness and is lost within the black
giving warning to the evening that the sun is coming back
and it turns away triumphant and yet distant is the hum
of a laugh amid deep shadows and the steady beating drum.

Modern Poetry Lesson
Mina S. Siegel
Write of philosophy, politics, flowers,
Freudian theories, pondered for hours,
Put your whole being, your heart and soul to it...
Chances are few will even plod through it.
But
Write anything
And—space—it—
Be careful how
you
place it;
I think
you'll
concede it...
Everyone
will
read it!

There Are No Limits
Anthony Wolfe
There are no limits in time.
Never give up, always stand tall, and make me proud!!

You know where I am, I've gone fishing.
There are no limits on the lake in heaven.
I'm here fishing from dusk to dawn as I always do,
I am a thousand winds that blow over you, trolling
along in my boat.
If you ever want to talk to me go to the lake, and just
call out my name, that's where I'll be.
There are no limits in love and devotion to all my family
and friends
Look and Listen!! I'm not far from you.
Just at the lake, me and my boat...fishin'.

The Wonder Of The Light
Linda Stewart
Deep in my heart there is a strength
So powerful and strong.
That if you believe in God's "White Light"
he will heal you, and make you strong

It may require changes that you did not anticipate
But if you let him walk with you.
He'll guide you all the way.
So trusting be and open up your heart.

There will be days when the going is rough.
And you will want to turn and run
But hold on tight, with all your might.
Until that loving healing light make you new again.

The Deer Hunt
Kimberly S. Schuh
In the misty morning of dawn's gray light,
stands a deer alone, frozen in flight.
Its eyes lock with the man drawing near,
the man lifts his gun, aims at the deer.
A shot rings out but the bullet goes wide,
the deer takes off through the wooded hillside.
On and on through the woods man chases his prey,
the deer is swift, and he runs further away.
Through the dense woods and valleys he'll flee,
running ever faster, for he must get free.
The thudding of footsteps, the shouts he can hear.
feelings of panic, being trapped set in, total fear.
A gun is fired, the deer drops to the ground,
the hunt is over, the life is gone, there is no sound.

Sister Friend
Shirley Becker
You've a VERY SPECIAL friend to me
Someone I love most dear
You're so much a clone of me
Like a twin to cherish and hold near

You're a "sister gift" God gave to me
And I just want for you to know
That I'll be here for you forever
No matter where you go

Friends like us will never part
Or distance take away
The lifetime special bonding
That we share today

Untitled
Kristen Tackett
i wanted a memory—you gave me a dance
i needed a star—you gave me a chance

to play in the time—and twirl in the words
creating a rhyme—in a blue ribbon

i tend to tie in my hair—but it still wisps in my face
tickling my cheeks—avoiding me grace

it's a beautiful dream—the life of a thought
all too real it seems—even the music

thanks for the memory—of a wonderful twirl
a breathtaking ribbon—for a mediocre girl

Seaside
Barbara Fehner
Lights shining bright on the sand
like sparkles of a glistening rain as, we walk
hand in hand. Laughter all around us people humming
softly in evening light... a far off whisper of a
merry go round by a seaside long ago far away,
thoughts drift to a carefree day,
a scent of lavender fills the air,
my life will never be the same... our path will cross
someday, in a circle we will dance and sing
leave messages in the sand. I miss you.
Our light will shine again... by the seaside.
Stars in the night sky, twinkle by...
I'll hear you laugh, see your eyes so blue
Only then I'll know it's you...

Your Life With A Knife
Gary Pesti
Waiting for life to begin.
You open the jar and then drive right in.
It's getting hot,
the air is just too damn thin.
You take another breath,
but slowly feel death.
You try to tell yourself a lie.
It's worthless, you're gonna die.
You make up a fantasy,
like it's the end of me.
You begin down the stream,
it's a deadly dream.
It starts out as a story about your life,
but now you're dead by a knife.

Thou Shalt Not Kill
Sylvia W. McGhee
"The tears fell as I read and my heart ached of what it said;
They had turned him around so he would come out just right,
They could see his heart pounding and he wiggled about,
Until the doctor crushed his head and took his life out.

Thou shalt not kill didn't mean a thing,
Murdering so many without even a blink,
Killers of babies, our President, too
For not putting a stop to what they do.

I wonder if it would be different
if he were made to watch
As those shiny instruments ended the lives
of so many tots."

The Road Of Dreams
John G. Fuller
Where stand I today on the road of dreams?
Taken with reverent joy in the past
When its lure streamed long but not overcast,
Shining forth its wealth of exotic themes
If I should but set my feet to follow.

So, step by step, I strode along its way
Enchanted by the uplands growing green
And sometimes sad to leave where I had been
But knowing the road did lead me away
If I would reach that horizon aglow.

And standing here to check the road ahead
It seems to wander far, so far to tread.

My Thanks
Adele Pikus
Lord, I can always count on You.
Whether, I am happy or just plain blue
Each day, you gave me a new treat
Pleasure and happiness that
can't be beat
No matter what cross I have to bear
I know that You are always there
How Lucky to have You by my side
Through stormy weather You
Always guide
Make me strong and make me good
Teach me to do what I should
Thanks for being with me today
Thus making my life a golden ray

A Letter Of Good–Bye
Vicki Ann Roehrick
I find I have to leave this letter here on our bed.
I find my voice unable to speak those words, needing to be said.

I just couldn't face, you to say my good–byes.
I just couldn't bear, to see the pain in your eyes.

I'm off now to chase, some of my resting dreams.
I'm off now to discover, some of those missing things.

The pieces of me, that I find you can't console.
The pieces I need, that will help to make me whole.

Perhaps, I will come upon your life again someday.
Perhaps then, I can truly give my heart... and stay.

From The Eyes Of A Child
Roberta D. Bowen
Among the tall, enchanting flowers,
are curious eyes that stare for hours.

Where fairies flutter from lily to rose,
wearing fancy gold hats and satin clothes.

Where beetles converse and ambitious ants answer,
and busy bees learn to become belly dancers.

The most charming of all, the lady bug,
chatters amongst chums while tidying her rugs.

But curious eyes will soon begin to roam,
for sunset is approaching, it's time to head home.

Call Me Jackie
Pamela Lee Kopack
Engulfed
In shadows
Mystique
Draped her soul
Like a regal necklace
Without a crown.
In the heart
Of history
Among
The peering eyes
She became
A single flower
In the garden
Of eternity.

Stagnant Waters
Steven Paul Tidcombe
The stagnant water with rainbow pools,
Amidst a concrete plain.
The scars of a black gold era,
The wealth ironically vain.

An epitaph to past, are slag hills black,
Half a century worth of rape.
The healing touch of British gratitude,
Are mountains of red tape.

Although the past, my youth forbids to touch,
I inscribe with no bitter ink.
I can see why prejudice exists,
And how the injured think.

Red River
Muna Al–Harhara
My inner thoughts were mute
The house that waits return
My face had changed its colour
Like the leaves in summer
I had change a lot from childhood
But I had not changed mature
Tired mind were wondering
The lies I had told were becoming
The friends I knew accepting
And the red river screams
The trail of blood is changing
Its weak energy drowning
Regaining strength was over
Dried out like the Red River.

My Imaginary Friend
Sheena Pattni
My imaginary friend you can't see,
Only, of course if you were me.
He's got brown scruffy hair which he hasn't washed for years,
And has still got potatoes growing behind his ears!
He's got funny clothes striped red and green,
And I must mention he likes to eat beans!
He has one black boot and one white boot,
But I don't think I have ever seen him wearing a suit!
He comes with me everywhere,
And if he falls over he doesn't care!
My friend, he gets me into trouble,
Like a witch going hubble bubble!
If he wasn't there?
I don't know, would I really care?

Oldham
Sheina Burns
I came in search of paradise,—
I'm not too young, I'm not too wise,
I didn't find my paradise —
Just Oldham.

It isn't grand, — it isn't great,
It gives you nothing on a plate, —
But it befriends you if you wait —
Does Oldham.

And so I'll stay in this fair clime,
You've given me a gradeley time,
And I'll say thank you with this rhyme —
To Oldham.

Untitled
Shareen Widder
Does red, white and blue,
mean anything to you?
Does the American way,
mean anything today?
Everything has gotten way out of hand,
all across the United States land.
As anyone can plainly see,
it's not as it used to be.
We're not "One Nation Under God" anymore.
Most of our people are at war.
If we try harder to get along,
to help one another and sing one song;
Born in the U.S.A.
Things may change for the better today.

Who Scores
Cathy Deak
Here I am, lying in bed,
With my pillow under my head,
Wondering and thinking,
While my thoughts and eyes are sinking.
Will tomorrow be?
The world may never see!
A war may start across the oceans,
As everyone has those notions.
Or will it be, that we will never see a tomorrow as
good as yesterday.
But, we may live in sorrow.
Today, Tomorrow — We will Pay.
Our Children may go to WAR—
And Nobody will ever SCORE.

Looking Back
Sherry Ellis
I look back at all I have done,
To only have pain and agony.
I try to understand what has happened,
To only know I am hurting.
The love we had, was so short and quick
There are so many words but,
none to communication.
So many looks but, none to see.
No touching, no love making,
No kiss to turn to in the night,
I feel dead inside, with no hope.
The love I once knew is now gone,
I don't understand the pain that I have,
It came so fast, left so very slowly.

Shades Of Autumn
Joseph W. Lauretta
The teacher told the class one day —
To bring in leaves of autumn
So they hurried quickly through the woods.
And everywhere they sought 'em.

They picked up many from the ground
And in the air they caught 'em
Placed them in a paper bag
And to the school they brought 'em

The teacher sorted out the leaves,
Contented as she taught 'em.
How leaves change color in the fall.
To many shades of autumn.

284

Untitled
Claudine E. Hunt
If you want to feel you're doing
something really worth your while
Just help a man in trouble
and watch him start to smile
Lift his burden on your
shoulder and relieve his weight
of care and stick until you
have helped him from the
valley of despair.
When he turns to thank you
with a gratitude that's real
surprising, at that
minute just know how good it
makes you feel.

I'm A Beautiful African Queen
Roberta D. Coleman
I'm a beautiful African queen.
With many goals...many ideals...
I'm a beautiful African queen, with
lots of pride, standing tall, I'm that
African queen! that's going places ,,,
Standing up tall looking over my
African kings...and queens!

I'm here to stay...I'm determined
to reach my goals. I'll not let my
pride stand in my way! Cause I'm
the beautiful African queen...with —
dark brown eyes and reddish brown braids.
Standing tall for my African kings and queens!

As She Walks
David Maybury
As I watched my sister walk the aisle to meet her spouse–to–be,
I recall the days of yesteryear when we were nearer three.
We disagreed, and yes, we fought, as siblings tend to do;
But through it all, it will never change, the love we carried through.

I pray for both their happiness as they journey on the way;
Oh God, may they be blessed of you as they journey day by day.
They travel now to warmer lands to celebrate their love;
Keep them safe, and bring them home, peaceful like a dove.

How do you let a sister go when she marries one young man?
How do you ever realize that they're walking hand in hand?
How do you release that hold on her as she leaves the family nest?
You turn to God, and bless his name and remember how you're blessed.

It Began With A Kiss
James V. Swanson
It began with but a kiss this relationship of ours.
Which left an impression on me that lasted for hours.
I'll refresh your memory of that special day.
At least, I recall it happening this way.
Your eyes slowly closed as we began our embrace.
And your hair hung down just touching my face.
Then our lips met and my body began to glow.
This feeling for you it started to grow.
I held on to you firmly not enough to offend.
Just enough to let you know that I didn't want it to end.
Then it finally had to happen our lips split apart.
Our embrace slackened as we began to depart.
We both took a breath and looked at each other.
Nothing was said, as we embraced for another.

Soul Searching
Tamara Hubbard
How many nights will I cry
How many full moon risings will go by
Before the great spirit heals my soul
When will it soar and be free like the eagle
When will life come back to me
I cannot forget the night we became one
And you touched my soul
When you left I thought you took it with you
But I only locked it away
I couldn't let you have it
I couldn't let you destroy me
Even though you may always have my heart
My soul is all I have left
All I have is me.

Heaven Is The Dwelling Place For Angels And Mankind
Hildegarde Willson
Our destiny! The heavenly country
Wondrous gathering! Forever free
Jesus Christ! Within God's kingdom
Preparing a place! For you and me
Great comfort! The love of God!
Outreach! Forgiveness! No more sin
As the hymn just a closer walk with thee
The kingdom of heaven for eternity
Christ within

Heaven is the dwelling place for angels
And mankind

Amen

Grandmother's Backyard
Dorothy I. Evans

When I think back today of those
Yesterdays. Grandmother's back yard
was just like a PARK. Then I had this
Little doll. I'd dress up and we'd
PLAY among the FLOWERS ALL THRU
The day. There was LILY of the VALLEY
The sweetest one of All and honeysuckle
And hollyhock the tallest of them all
When the peonies were in blossom it
was a sight to behold. You would want to
Pick a armful just to hold
Oh how lucky I was when I look back
Today to have had grandmother's back
Yard to play in all the day.

The Lonely Man
Kathy Pilkey

A man with no one of his own
so sad and small he seems.
His children lost before they were grown,
now he lives with just his dreams.

Wandering around, he's always low,
not a soul he ever sees.
Long ago his tears ceased to flow
and he thinks only of what used to be.

To have a friend to talk to,
when things are hard to bear
could bring him joy so very new
and maybe a reason to care.

Eternal Friend, Good–bye
Denise Wier

The day is almost gone
and the sadness still remains

I will no longer see you
only in my dreams

I will no longer hear you
only in my thoughts

The many memories I have of you
will live on forever in my heart

Until the day we meet again
To my eternal friend I say good–bye

The Complexities Of Life
June Petrie

Oh how I crave the simple things;
A long arduous walk in the woods,
The warm caress of the summer air,
Or the fragrant smell of flowers.

In the simplicity, love shines;
Dreams become reality and complexity, unnecessary,
It is here that one can reach into the very
depth of our souls and relinquish the beliefs that
chain us to the values of a materialistic world.

Oh how I yearn to seek out the truth and grow in love.
For it is here that the true value of life lies,
And it is here that I wish to stay.

Killer Whales
Siobhan Brennan

They rule the ocean, free as a bird
Diving and swimming, not saying a word
Fishes and creatures and coral galore
Each day an adventure, new things to explore

Waltzing downward through the bottomless sea
So smoothly, so graceful, so elegant and free
Through strong waves and storms, as soldiers they fought
And in the end, they are hunted and caught

Thrown in a pool, the key tossed away
Separated from family, filled with dismay
So leave them alone, just leave them be
For killer whales deserve to be free!

Cleopatra
Ian Maclennan

My maids have done their magic work at last,
and I in all my glory as a queen
look through the shadowed gloom to mirrored night,
where Anthony, my lord, has reached his throne.
I long to be the regent of his eyes,
and stretch my wrist toward the gentle fig.
I feel a subtle sting,
and chill flows up;
then great bird's wings take forth my golden soul,
like noon's high sun in heaven's priestly hands.
And I for Anthony cry out,
wanting his lordship like a yearning child
to see my beauty coming from afar,
arrayed by light in my soul's shining dress.

Lonesome
Lynne Donahue
It's a word hardly ever heard aloud,
which is one reason to believe
that it's around all of the time, only
to creep up and hit us from behind.

It's a word sometimes heard over and over
again, only to bore you to tears and
make you feel even more so, and it's
probably the one thing you don't need
right now in your life, but probably the
one thing that keeps you half sane.

It's a word hardly ever heard aloud
which is one reason to believe
that it'll be yours forever, and will have no
need to creep up and hit you from behind.

Dedication: Anyone that relates to it

Heaven Diamonds
Selene S. O'Dell
Shining diamonds
falling from the sky
falling drops of rain
under the moon light.

Diamonds of water
disguising my pain
mixing my tears with
diamonds of rain

I saw you leave
I kiss you goodbye
heaven diamonds
Tears from the heart

Reality The Depressing Face Of Living
Matthew A. Caldwell Hooper
Death pleasing to many
Fate a simple fact for living.
Happiness the truth behind dying.
Thinking death as a new beginning.
For those who die are they
really unhappy?
Destiny strikes as the forgiving.
Life the test of our own
morality.
Hate cuts a deep wound
of reality.
Death striking is never the
ending.
You must find your living in
the dying.
Let your soul do its searching.

Dedication: My mother, Sally and father, Mark

Love Thy Neighbour
S. Connell
I saw a man lying down,
People thought of him a clown;
Stretched out on the pavement hard,
For his life had been scarred,
Drinking was to be his pain,
Never to be himself again;
The crowd stared with open eyes,
He just lay there to their cries;
"Leave him alone – he's just a drunk",
"He's wet himself – The dirty skunk",
Then for a moment, I saw his face,
Eyes of blue, so full of grace;
Maybe he's been somebody's dad,
Perhaps some awful life he's had;
I lean't into the pram I pushed,
Taking a blanket from the babe I hushed;
"Rest his head upon this sheet",
To make him comfortable whilst on this street:

Black Forest
Elizabeth Anasir
They're spooky but real,
The tall ghostly trees.
Black night's closing in.
I'm lost, and I feel
There is no return.
But all of a sudden,
There is a light,
And over the branches
The moon smiling bright.
I'm finding my path,
And run home fast,
The frightening woods
Behind – at last.

So many times in life,
Darkness do we fight,
Only to be rescued
By a guiding light!

Friend
Vanice Guidry
The sun was shining all so bright,
I stared at it with all my might.
It was hot all that day,
I couldn't go outside just to play.

Then all of a sudden it started to rain,
Down came drops against the pane.
It hit the glass with a ping,
Then all of a sudden the doorbell rang.

It was my friend across the street,
I was so glad we got to meet.
Now I'm not alone anymore,
Because my friend was at the door.

Desolation
Vidya Chandran
Lush green grass
rolling plains
sparkling rivers
meandering close
No wonder this
God's creation as it was
Man's accursed hand
a cruel blow did deal
to render asunder
the fabric His power had wrought
Today parched denuded lands
stand forlorn
Silent reminders of man's haste
to make better todays
for himself
Sparing no thought
for the rest that live
or the tomorrows yet to come

Proud
Adrian L. Diekson
We are not branded cowards,
We're a very peaceful type,
Just a true American,
Who for our land will fight.
If Hitler thinks the power
In his hands does lay,
Just let him try to enter
The good old U.S.A.
He'll find we're not so peaceful
Once he makes us mad,
Wondered why he entered
And wished he never had
I'm so "happy" in this "land"
And also proud to say,
I'm a fully blooded "American"
In my home, the U.S.A.

Wondering Why
Annis L. Mann
Why, Lord
Why my son?
Did he deserve to die.
You loaned me this child of mine
To love, to teach, and then return.
But Lord, I had only just begun
He was only 12.
You gave me three more sons.
When I look at them my heart
Is filled with love and happiness.
I see laughter, pride,
I see strength, Love,
I see life.
Then – I look again
and I am filled with sadness.
Wondering –
If not again you'll take my
Three sons from me.

Space Shuttle
Vevarine I. Brown
The space shuttle took off in a blast.
Only God knew it was the last.
it exploded right after take off.
it was a great tragedy and a great loss.

Seven people lost their lives,
Husbands daughters and wives,
it was a great loss to the space shuttle
But God in his wisdom knew it was a muddle.
Children lost their parents men lost their wives
Wives lost their husbands,
But God sees all and knows all.
He knew before the blast, that that would be
their last.
I pray that they had found God in all their
space glory.
So when the blast went off they were on
Their way to see God in all his glory.

Waiting
Susan Glodgett
I told you I loved you.
I gave you my life.
I thought that you cared.
I thought that you'd write.

You never wrote back,
or said the same thing.
I had to go on living on dreams.

The dreams are getting old.
My life is getting dull.
It seems like I'm always
waiting for your call.
But, the phone never rings
and if it does it is never you.

I just can't go on feeling so blue.
I just can't keep living my life without you.

Gentle Silence
Sandi Smith–Neil
Still the morning
no breeze that blows
no birds that sing

Traces of dew
so newly formed
ring so loud so clear
yet silent so sweet
visit one from another
with glistening ease

Only hours to live
so futile the try
so long, intriguing the song

Lingering quietly
Whispering gently
words only the eyes can hear

The Life We Live
Evabel Thomson
Thank you Father for the night
Thank You for the early morning light
Thank You for Your love
That comes to us from above
Thank You for the life You gave
For all of us, our souls to save
Thank You for the psalms we sing
Thank You God for everything
Thank You for the life we live
Thank You for the love you give
Thank You for the fish and foul
Thank You for the wise old owl
Thank You for the driving rain
Thank You for taking away our pain
Thank You for the wind that blows
Thank You for the lights that glows
And when this earthly life is over
May we live with You forevermore.

Untitled
Sunny Barnhart
Were I granted one earthly wish today
It would be that I could devote
The rest of my life
To learning what makes this sweet man
Fly
And setting about to become the best
Thermal any bird has ever ridden.
For in becoming
The wind
Beneath his wings
He
Would become
The wings
That would carry me
Aloft
As well.

My Donna
Charles A. Elkins
When I think of love,
I always think of you.
You are so loving and kind.
When I think of love,
You are the one on my mind.
I heard love is blind,
In our case this is not true.
I can see clearly that love,
Like ours is rare to find.
It has survived the ravage of time.
You're always there for me,
Through thick and thin,
No matter what the problem,
Or where it's been.
I'll never want any other.
My love for you Donna will never end!!!

Box Of Pain
Tanya Wise
A tear falls from the eye,
Just a silent cry it falls down,
To the ground with out making a sound.
Doesn't anyone hear it does anyone care,
Everything is passing by people watch
not knowing why.

I've lost someone dear and kind,
I guess everything has its own time,
People don't know how it is to feel so bad and be trapped in a sea of sad.

It's like being in a box having no way out,
Locked in pain and this is how it's about,
One day it will come that I will go without telling anyone.

Untitled
Sarah A. Hostettler
He is possibly hidden,
May be forbidden.
Could be older,
Of course broad shouldered.
Once you find him,
Don't let him go.
If you love him,
Let him know.
He may not feel the same,
But who is really to blame?
A good thing will last,
If it's difficult— let it pass.
Find whom you hold dear,
Hold him close— keep him near.
Your man may be cold,
But stand tall— remain bold.
For if he is true— he will not make you feel blue,
And he will always, always love you.

Good–Bye
Pearle Hoda
I didn't get to say good–bye, I feel her presence still.
Perhaps it's best, but tho I try, the thought returns against my will.
She really didn't like good–byes; I clearly remember this.
She preferred to say, "So long," with a warm hug and a kiss.

I must be satisfied, I guess, for the love and harmony we shared:
A glance into each other's eyes was proof enough to show we cared.
Although we didn't say it often, I think that we both knew
A closeness that was special; experienced by us two.

Her leaving was so sudden. I wish that I had known
The last time I saw her...that before long she'd be gone.
I hope I let her know, somehow, with words or deeds, or anything...
How much I love her so, and the emptiness her loss would bring.

I miss her very much and she wouldn't wish for me to cry.
Yet, still, the thought resurfaces: I didn't get to say,
"Good–bye."

Weird Holiday Poem
Toni Todd

A yule's a log, but what's the tide
at Malibu? There's no sleigh ride
here in LA. It's tan-n-balm.
Spread it thick—just swipe your palm.
Donning duds and decking halls,
the best we've got is light-strewn malls.
In tinsel-town there is no snow,
just December lawns to mow.
A Santa hat atop pierced youth.
Yes, it all seems quite uncouth.
Hollywood holidays are unique.
Take them sort of tongue in cheek.
Although the winter scenes are fakes,
we've really got our share of flakes.

Memories
Margaret A. Smith

I see her hand lying idle on the arm of the chair
My heart twists and aches to see the truth showing there.
For these are the hands I've known all of my life
They've sheltered me through joy and strife.
I've always expected to feel them near
At times when I've needed them be banish all fear.
They've held me gently and held me tight
They've stroked a curl, soothed my forehead at night.
They were vital, busy, firm and strong,
Their work often accompanied by a song.
Now the fingers are thin and veined with old age,
The hands are shaky and weak.
I want to hold them and kiss them gently
For my heart is too full to speak.
Oh my Mother, I give thanks for the life I see there,
Lying idly along the arm of the chair.

Clouds
Carla J. Smith

Clouds are soft cotton,
All puffy and white
You can see them for miles,
even at night.
Cotton clouds absorb water
from grounds down below,
And when they get full,
they squeeze it all out
and let it all go.
Black clouds expressing dirty water,
White suggesting pure,
The black are squeezed out,
sooner than white,
So we humans can find its cure.

Grace
John Johnston

My feelings of love for you are true
I enjoy all the fun things you do and say
I'm very lucky to know someone like you
I hope our love will last forever and a day.
You're always happy, never sad
For you there are never any gray skies
You bring out the good in me, not the bad
I hope your love for me never dies.
You're sweet, caring, and kind
You accept me for who and what I am
You hold a special place in my heart and mind
You're fragile, gentle and meek as a lamb
You're soft and delicate like fine lace
I'll love you forever, my special Grace.

Untitled
Lily Marconi

I wish we could have a happier world today
Spend more time caring about each other
Get rid of all the hate and graffiti on the streets,
Keep loving our father and our mother.

Let's have more love and a lot less hate
Children, love your relatives and your parents
Help them all you can
Before it is too late.

Make the World a happier place to be
By doing good deeds every day.
Laugh, dance and communicate
Please give this wish to you and me.

I Know My Child
Shelby Andrews

I know my child how it feels to
be human,
I know my child how it feels
not to be loved by someone,
I know my child how it feels,
I know my child how you feel
you can't trust anybody,
I know my child how it feels
when you cry,
I know my child but you just
have to put your hate and tears
As far as they can go and love again,
I know my child but just give
people a chance,
I know my child what you're
going through,
I know my child how it feels
to be human.

Lord Take All My Trouble Away
Joanne Stampley
Tonight in my bed, I gently lay
Lord take all my troubles away
in the mist of my distress
wrap me in your caress.

As I leave my burden in your care
bow on my knees in prayer
remove the dark clouds as I live
help me to learn to forgive

in the morning when I rise
help me get through the day with no surprise
let your light shine on my sorrow
as your words brighten my tomorrow
for tonight in my bed, I gently lay
Lord, take all my trouble away

Suicides Light
Wanda C. Fisher
We're like moths, around an outside light, the attraction,
is that brilliant light. Some get too close and are lost
in the light, others fly by and look at the light, never
getting close enough, to suicide's light.

Everyone, I think, has been attracted one time, to that
brilliant light, that wonderful shine. When we go where
like moths, to the light, zap, and were gone from sight.
some will never know the attraction to the light, some will
die by the glorious light.

Some will be saved by beckoning moths, don't fly too close
or you too will be lost. The light is the end and a beginning
you see, for the ones, who couldn't stop, the beckoning.

Dedication: For Lynne and Gynnie

Hold On To The Night
Chad Kite
If you don't understand it slips away, and
you'll not see it go. It's gone forever even though
it'll come back tonight after the passing of the light.
Into its arms you go because of the memories,
but it's gone, and memories
they last forever, but not into never
can you take something so fake
as a moment unhappened,
a moment you so wish to be true
so understand my friend,
You must hold on to dark, to blindness.
Hold on to the night.
That sweet midnight when nothing is wrong
and the day is forever long.
When love is strong and ignorance is gone
Hold on to youth and faith
Hold on and fight.
Hold on to the night.

Just One Touch
Robert Gwin
Just one touch if only it could be
Every day I see her I wonder does she see
With a passing glance or a whispered wish
I weaken a little more for her kiss
Her hair of auburn colors the fire in me
While her eyes cut my soul's desire to be free
She is and she is not what I need and what I want
She is real and she is a phantom that loves to taunt
If I reach would I fall
Would she hear my hunger call
What would I gain who would I lose
I can never know I can never choose
Every day I see her I wonder does she see
Just one touch if only it could be

Lonely
Candie Mueller
Can you hear me cry,
Lonely
Can you see me when I smile,
Lonely, Lonely
I wish you were here by my side,
Lonely
Can you feel the knife's blade,
Lonely
Can you see my heart bleed,
Lonely, Lonely
It's not time to say goodbye
Can you hear my aching heart
cry
Lonely

Yesterday's Gone
Sharina Mears
Though my soul has left these native plains, my feet never to walk this
     earth again,
My eyes shall never see the tears, you will shed throughout the years.
Though my heart shall feel no pain, or my body feel the rain.
Mama I know, this is going to hurt, to lay this body, in the dirt.
I ask you please, don't ever forget, my heart has stopped, my love...not
     yet.
I shall be with you till the end of time, though you cannot see me, my love
     is alive.
When you need to talk, I will always be near, though my words you cannot
     hear.
I shall fly upon eagle's wings, no more bound by earthly strings.
So please don't cry for you must go on, even though my life is gone

For you see, my soul is at peace, rest Mama set me free.
Now close your eyes as I drift from this land, and know someday we will be
     together again
Turn around Mama, walk away, yesterday's gone, live for today.

Mom Said
Veronica L. Kirk
Mom saw a fluffy cat.
Mom said pick up that hat.
What did I find...
That fluffy cat!
Mom saw a cute dog.
Mom said look behind that log.
What did I find...
That cute dog!
Mom saw a ugly mouse.
Mom said clean up this house.
What did I find...
That ugly mouse!
Mom saw a toad.
Mom said go sweep the road.
What did I find...
A smashed toad!...(OUCH)

Self
Rita Cunningham
Try not to stand long before someone
Who keeps your faults hidden

The friends like true love, looks pass the surface
World—power means nothing. Only the unsayable,
Jeweled inner life matters.

Search me and find yourself
love tucked a way like the world under a winter blanket
Will surface with warm arms to hold thee
The sun shines will make a jewel sparkle
A fool will never flee the sun.
Do not fear love, for without it we only exist, look
into my eyes, see the love there. Reach out touch, lest it flee.

Dedication: To Don Kirk, love you...

She
Brad Potter
The snow begins to fall again,
And again two foolish lovers clash in its wake
They float through the fields of white
Paying no attention to needless things
They embrace and follow through with a kiss
Each second seems like eternity
She is beautiful in her parka and mittens
He is dashing in his sweater and hat
Each knows how special these moments are
And they are not willing to forget them
She falls to the soft fluff below and
He follows embracing again they stare into each
others eyes and see a future destined for them
A soft flake, unlike all others falls onto her face
Melting instantly, as he did at first sight of
her
She knows he thinks pure thoughts and that
She is part of them and always will be.

Our Love
Kimberly Batiste
Roses by day
Violets by night
Our love for each other glows and shines so bright
We've had good and gone thru bad
Still our love is so strong, others wished they had
We've traveled up the road
Down the road
And around the block once or twice
Still it's you I lay beside at night and the
Feeling is so nice
I love you now
And I loved you then
The bond we share together
Will never end

The Death Of Myself In Third Person Plural
Adam Hamilton
My, Myself and I
Sat down one day to cry
The sun at its lowest
and clouds in the sky
For Myself of the three
That night had to die
All three remember
what all three have seen
Myself is now gone
the other two green.
Me looked forward
and whispered good—bye
I turned his back
While they softly cried.

To: Grandma
Phillip Crawford
Grannies are the best thing
to ever Grace the earth.
But you are the best one
I got after my birth.

I hoped you liked the poem
and the poem is true
and I just hope you know
that I...Love...You...

To: Grandpa

Grandpa's are really neat
He come in lots of sorts
but why, I do like this one
Its because he can play sports.

I love You guys.

The Golden Years
Geraldine R. Prasser
The Golden Years find people around the earth
I call them Rusty years for what it's worth
My joints seem like they should be oiled
My skin looks like something someone boiled
The size 9 clothes are long past
And in any race, I'd be last
I do get the senior citizen's discount price
But being able to go without a cane would be nice
The Social Security checks keep me perking
Since they say I'm too old to be working
I do plan a trip or two
They're getting further apart and very few
I do still drive a car
Not very fast or very far
Yes, the Golden Years do have a certain flair
Full of memories, grandchildren, and friends everywhere
Maybe the rust isn't so bad
The rust seems normal now and shouldn't make me sad.

A Special Day
Dianne Ker
Your voice sounds soft, kind sincere
So why did I write of things I fear?
I'm glad you let your feelings out
I told you mine and without a doubt
We seemed to be on the same plane
Each one nervous to explain
What we hoped could transpire
If our meeting set us on fire.
Some private place for us to be
If you wish to make love to me
Whatever happens just let's say
This is our extra special day
No rules, set pattern, to adhere to
From one another, we'll take our cue.

Dedication: My Mr. Valentine

Death Of A Planet
J. Cassidy
Mysteries solved, truth to sell
Shall we face a foretold hell.

Millennium beckons, closing prediction
Prophecy, truth, reality, fiction?

Esoteric teaching contest religious dogma
Why choose, no choice, no option.

Life's too long —
For philosopher and seer.

Play the hand,
Embrace what's dear.

A Spinster's Regrets
Connie G. Ford
I am old my life will be ending soon
As I sit on the porch and look up at the moon
For in my life I made no promises and shared no dreams
And now I miss all those wonderful things
I think of the little things that gives meaning to life
For I was never a mother nor was I a wife
Of someone across the table to share a meal with me
Someone who laughs when I cry about an old movie
Of someone I'm proud to say has stolen my heart
And when I go shopping will push my cart
Of someone who comes in and says "what's to eat"
And when I'm tired will rub my feet
Of someone to share life and make me smile
Someone to lie close or just sit awhile
Of someone to fill that empty chair
Who would gently stroke my face or brush my hair
And when the day is done and I'm in bed at night
To have a gentle kiss and hear "Honey, good–night"

In His Name
Margaret L. Hernandez
When we live in Him,
we have power to win.
If sick and lame,
all ages know His Name.
When the cards fall,
on His Name we call.
When in a bad place,
we call for His Grace.
As the end draws near,
who will we fear?
Some may believe not,
but look what happened to Lot?
Descending He will do,
but will He call you?

Ode To A Day
Jean M. Arthur
Some people face the East
to greet the early rising sun.

Some people ring bells and
bring flowers as a sacrifice
to their Gods

Some people chant and sing
to invoke blessings from on high

Some light fires and pour libations
as symbols of their thankfulness.

Everywhere people know that
a day is special and that
it is a gift to be cherished.

Michael My Angel
Kevin Rolfe
Is this going too far?
Michael my angel
Has this gone beyond?
Michael my dear
It won't seem to end
not that I want it to,
should I call you an angel
In black Northern wings;
should I continue to suffer,
Mike my assassin
should I bleed on my own
and tell you I'm fine,
Will you say what I want to hear
when pushed for an answer
Say you still love me
But refuse to come near
I'm waiting
to claim the head of Goliath.

The Old Oak Tree
S. J. Shore
As a tear starts to form in my eye
I know that soon I'm gonna die
So please will you accompany me
To my favourite spot beneath the old oak tree.
Here I used to sit and look at life
And cherish the love given to me by my wife
In life I've had a lot of fun
I've a grown up daughter and a lovely grandson
But now my time is nearly done
And there will be no more fun.
I've often taken risks and been a chancer
A man finally brought down by cancer
So please don't feel sorry for me
But just cherish this moment beneath the old oak tree.

The Strongest
Daniel Haynes
At lessons he was best,
And he was different from the rest,
So they'd mock him in the hope that he would cry,
His soul the crowd did rend,
Because they could not comprehend
That a boy like him
Was human just like them,
So they teased him on and on,
But I knew that he was strong,
Because his smiling face
Would never let them win.

And ironically he knew,
As he gave a patient stare
That the pain they gave him
None of them could bear.

Juanita
Yvonne Paxton
J is Juanita, a sister so dear,
U is Unique, a girl without fear.
A is Accident, which need not have been.
N is Never to be nineteen.
I is Isolated on this lonely spot.
T is Tears, for her, such a lot.
A is Alone as we all are without her.
JUANITA a sister, daughter, and auntie;
an adventurous, talented, beautiful, young woman.
Too good for this world.
But why did it happen?
For one moments thought
She'd still be here.
Living and loving without any fear.

Dedication: Juanita Newcombe – 1971 to 1991

Eternal Life
Philip J. Blackmore
I have not gone, I am still here,
You cannot see me, but I am near,
Just think of me and you will feel,
Sensations that will feel so real,
Do not grieve me, don't feel sad,
Just remember the good times we had,
I'll always watch over you, You're in my heart,
And when your world you do depart,
Together again as one we'll begin
When this new life you enter in
Eternal life there is you see
And here I'll wait, until here you'll be.

Dedication: Peter Blackmore, beloved father

The Derelict House
Michael Gair
Bleached bones that glare into a winter's night
And yet do ring the moon in fitful style,
Who but a giant could embrace awhile
So sweet a form and yet rise up to fright
The tender soul with hard reflected light.
Soft desolation, feared by some who might
A different picture paint than that they see.
There is a perfume, is a sound yet still;
There is a breath, a sigh, that breathes anew
That magnifies the beauty, tones the view,
That time can never alter, never kill,
For time but adds the beauty to fulfil
The glory; but the vision seems to chill
For this sad shape was once a home to me.

What Does It Matter
A. Presland
If tomorrow I was to die
What would it matter
The sun would shine
The birds would still chatter
The morning dew would still appear
A new born baby would cry
I may be gone, but don't shed a tear
For life goes on when I die
The flowers still open in glorious bloom
The trees continue to grow
A peacock with its glorious plume
A farmer with seeds to sow
New beginnings every day
So death you should not fear
Just rejoice in life's beautiful way
And I will always be near.

Dedication: J.B., my inspiration

Untitled
Derek Ashcroft
Was there light in the sky
Before you came into my life,
Was the grass green
Before you became my wife,
You turned darkness into daylight
Each time that you passed by,
All the love you gave me
Seemed to make the years fly by,
Every minute spent with you
Were certainly from heaven sent,
My life is one of happiness
And all the misery went,
Each moment you are away from me
And not here by my side,
Makes life so dull and lonely
I count the tears I've cried.

Dedication: My darling wife, Brenda

The Beachmaster
David Rooke
I enter into my dreams each night
My key unlocks the gate
As soon as I am in I search
Hoping I'm not too late

My dreams begin my search
Some buildings, look a church
Suddenly I'm on the beach
With you in front just out of reach

Try as I might in the night
The gap between us grows and grows
Will I ever hold you tight?
Only the Beachmaster knows

Dedication: To my darling Jane

The Gift
Elsie Rutherford
God gave a star
As it shone in the night
And said, "I give you light."

He gave me the sun
As it rose with the dawn
And said, "A new day is born".

But I'll give you a gift
More precious than all
A gift beyond compare
A little girl with shining eyes
And lovely, soft brown hair

He kept his promise
His words were true
For the gift he gave me
Alison, was you.

Lost Within Love
Stephen Burnett
Although you may not love me
Although you may not care
If ever you should need me
You know that I'll be there

Your love may all be taken
Although you are sincere
If ever you're forsaken
You know that I'll be here

For that day when you left me
You knew my heart would die
And all the oceans could not hold
The tears that I have cried

What Is Love
Madge Spencer–Smith
Love is not getting–but giving,
Found in a dream or a thought,
It comes from the sheer joy of living,
Of companionship happily sought.
It doesn't remove all mountains,
Or paint skies an azure blue.
It doesn't even dry your tears,
But it gives you the strength to get through.
Love isn't painted with glory,
It isn't all riches that's rare.
Love is an age old story,
Found anyplace– anywhere.
Deep as the deepest ocean,
Bright as the stars high above.
Clear as a crystal fountain,
This faith, this hope, this love.

Unwanted Lover
Marie E. Neil
Sitting, waiting, anticipating, willing the phone to ring
Yet when it lets off its piercing thrill, you know it isn't him.
Look back on time, the tears and laughter, always on your mind
Three years later, grown apart, that love you cannot find.
You sit and wonder what went wrong, and did he really care
It makes you wonder if true love was ever really there.
Browsing through old photographs, brings memories flooding back.
Positive, this is the one, but then the love turned slack.
Feeling blue, unwanted, unloved, you begin to blame yourself,
I loved that man for being him, not his possessions or his wealth.
So now is the time to give up hope for he will never all be mine
Strong love and passion I felt for him, will love again in time
But, until that time, when I feel strong, and learn to love again
I'll sit and wait, anticipate, and battle through the pain.

Thoughts In Separation
Barbara Brolan
Drained of emotion.
Driftwood washed up
By the ocean shore
Hoping to be with you.
One day more.

The acoustics of my heart
Never want to part.
With the words
From your heart.

We never had yesterday
Today or tomorrow.
But we had
everything.
So no sorrow.

A Mother's Love
Kate Brown
Love can fire us, and like fire, consume.
Love can intoxicate, like wine or heavy perfume.
Love can drown, drag us into deepest despair
Yet still fill us with desire.
But this love can shrivel and die, be reborn,
Flourish, fruit and yet wither at dawn.
The one love that endures is cherished within
It fills us with pride, a sense of doom
and fear of all we know will come, too soon.
It overcomes the bitter feuds,
fans the flames that fate eludes.
It binds us forever and swells us with fulfillment
Albeit tempered with anguish, laughter, shame,
frustration, hope and enlightenment.
That love, that love that conquest all
Is the love for a child.

My Garden
J. E. Flood
My neat, small, plot of land.
Planted, and tended, by my own hand.
Tubs, and hanging baskets, a mass of flowers.
Petunias, pansies, lobelias, hang in bowers.

Red, blue, pink, orange, and yellow.
This riot of beauty, makes you feel mellow.
The lawn needs some immediate attention.
My choisa, and dwarf conifers, deserve a mention

Patio with table, umbrella, and chairs,
Where you sit and forget your cares.
Watch the clouds and birds go by,
Happy, and contented, I give a sigh.

The Golden Ring
Linda Milton
Points against or a knock out
or will we throw the towel in?
Sweat and tears, get ready for another bout.
A contender in life.

Jabbing, jabbing blow after blow
breaking all the vows.
Emotions building, emotions low
A contender in love.

Ducking, diving, bob and weave
there are ropes in a golden ring.
The bout is over. Is it time to leave?
A contender for happiness.

Untitled
Ann C. Younger
Golden promises, broken dreams
Sometimes this life is not what it seems
Human nature is open to err
Left to count the cost of care
We need an anchor on stormy seas
To feel the gentleness of summer breeze
There is a wisdom we're free to learn
The fragility of our human terms
Given freely we have choice of will
The small voice of calm beckoning be still
We may not know if decisions are right
But with eyes forward to follow that light
Its the journeying on meeting these strifes
And in faith trusting injustices are part of life
Learning experiences, the suffering the pain
Teach us new growths spring forth wisdom, your gain

The Dandelion Fragments
Jack L. Insch
The dandelion fragmented,
teeth, float off – on the heavy
summer's breath
fleeting and dancing –
Parasolling down, one settled
in your silken auburn hair
I picked it, cupping it
gentle in my hands.
Squeezing eyes dark shut
I made a promise, and a wish
Then, puffed her from my palm
She rose and drifted,
high – high, with eager
childish expectations,
floating off – on the heavy
summer's breath.

A Place For Hunters Of Dreams
Margaret Gardner
The forest is the ideal place–
For hunters of dreams,
Beautiful trees and cool valley streams.
Enjoy the sounds of various kind,
Many things in your dream you'll find

Birds will fill your dream with a happy sound,
In the hunter's forest,
Your dream will be profound.
It is not unbelievable, enjoy your dream,
It will be so clear, real it will seem.
No need for a bow and arrow, never a gun at all
You're the hunter in the dream forest,
Cherish your dreams, They will be easy to recall.

Forgotten Son
Dominick Herrald
with dark of night creeping into his head
he journeys back to the site of the dead
with shaking hands and uncertain mind
the same existence he was at that time
one horrible night in a foreign land
but the blood's in his soul, and not on his hands
for what he has done he will never forget
now his heart weighs heavy with the regret
he'll open his eyes to find them still there
the faces all looming off in the air
torn without help he holds them all in
no valid reason for his mortal sin
hundreds of questions, he asks only one.
How could a mother do this to a son?

Good Morning
Idella Edwards
'Twas an ordinary morning just like any other,
And I'd really have preferred to stay under the cover,
But early, to the chirping of birds I awoke,
As the sound, on the rain–sweetened breeze, did float.

At first I rebelled to this interruption so rude,
My tired achy body seemed to fuel my surly mood.
But as I lay there and listened to the marvelous sound,
My soul was inspired by a song so profound.

Such chirping! Such tweeting! Sweet music to my ear,
My spirit began to soar as God came near.
I praised Him and thanked Him for all His loving care,
And for the song of the birds on a morning so fair.

Circle Around
Mary Gunzburg–Vitkowsky
Rodeos and Lassos
Circles and stars.
Skeptical cows
Musical bars.
Vicious circles
Lassos hurled.
A flag unfolds
Life is sold.
A life retrieved
A life relieved
Circle, score
Throw, encore
Never free
Stupid sap
The circle of life
Eternal trap

Dedication: Win, Tory and Mother

Untitled
F. G. Hayman
Memories play such special parts
Of things that's dearest in our hearts
The games we played and all we did
When we were young, just a little kid
School days, holidays, Christmas time
Are all locked in this heart of mine
Where we went, the places we've seen
Things to treasure, of what we dream
Family's gathering to celebrate
We danced, we laughed, we would meditate
Going on your first special date
Getting married, Boy did you feel great
Life must go on and some depart
That's the hardest pull on your heart
But you reflect and carry through
Your memories, Your Treasures, That's You.

Love You Forever

Tracy Mitchell

You said you'd love me forever
Until the end of time, that I
Was so special; yet you broke
This heart of mine.
How could you "forget" to tell
Me that you'd been untrue
You have lied and cheated
On someone who "meant the
World to you." So please
Forgive me darling if I smile
when you say you'll love me
Forever, always and a day
For in my heart I know
You could never be true
Not even to someone who put
All their dreams in you.

Dedication: My dearest grandfather's memory

Words Of My Heart

Ravinder Kaur Rehill

With my Heart,
I am writing my first letter of love.
I am writing the true words of my Heart.

All I ever think about is You.
My loneliness has brought me close to You.
I am crazy about You, and only You.

Who gave You the right?
The right to steal my Heart.
You have stolen my precious Heart.

Hatred lead to friendship.
The friendship grew closer.
This closeness is now Love.

It must be love, says my Heart
You are the first true guest of my Heart.

Window Of My Heart

Patricia Ratcliffe

My hearts a secret window, though no one else can see,
Where flames of love are burning, deep down inside of me.
The flame of love is a garden, where flowers grow so bright.
From seeds that you first planted there, one very special night.
Although I did not know it then, the seed you planted there,
Took root and started growing, into our love affair.
And now if you look closely, through the windows of my heart,
You'll see those flowers blooming, although we're far apart.
A flower for each season, that flowers every year,
Growing that much stronger, for the one I love so dear.
The flowers there will flourish, from the love you gave to me,
Spreading little seedlings, that only I can see.
And in the years that follow, they'll bloom within my heart.
Reaching out to you with love, until the day we part.

The Taj Mahal At Dawn

Vyvyen C. Jenkins

I saw the Taj;
I saw the Taj Mahal
In all its shining beauty, gleaming white
Against an azure sky. I saw it then
As others see it – try to catch its charm
In pictures, yet it quite eludes them.

But then I saw the Taj;
I saw the Taj Majal;
As the train ran across the misty plain,
The dawn–red sun shone on the silver vapour;
The burning light broke into coloured prisms
Upon the pearly cloud. And rising like
An insubstantial dream, appeared the Taj;
Its dazzling whiteness baseless seemed to float,
Seen through a rainbow haze.

Oh yes, I saw the Taj!

The Race Is On

Buford L. Horner

the race is on through the bush and
through the grass some going slow
some going fast

they make their turns with great
ease—you would never guess they
could with all that speed

the hoofs fly they jump high faster
faster they really try—the riders feel
great they've done their best

they pushed to win—they didn't hold,
to ride like this you must be bold

As they come into home stretch—the cameras
flash and the people scream "there's my
winner I've got my dream".

Love In One Blade

Donavin Tsosie

Half my life is fading here
Like nightmares breathing near
My mind is turning blue
Life is short, and birth is new,
I hear the bells of death ringing clear
Gaining hope and loosing fear
My dreams of you are strong at heart,
Angels would crush my soul if we fall apart,
Our love is tempted and going on
How could we have kept this quest going strong.
The drugs are soothing, yet my brain drains,
Alcohol is my help, but filled with pain,
Now it comes to my time that fades,
All our love in one blade,
So don't count on being the one saved,
All over love is beneath my grave.

Sonnet K–1
Kandice Carter
Only two days have passed
but it feels like two years
a wish for time to last
to stop the pain and fears
with family we blame ourselves.
Why are you so hard to manage?
It is so hard for us to care.
I wait...wondering what your mom will so
Hoping in fair health you will be.
All you had to do was call me.
Though I probably wouldn't have listened
Too much into my world, only thinking about self.
Until then I hope and cry waiting – by the phone.
Hoping that you'll soon be home.

Buckinghamshire Morning
Chris Watkins
Whiteleaf Cross lies buried in mist,
Clenched within this steely grey fist,
Rolling slowly across the Chiltern hills.
Red eyed sun, bids me good morning,
Shards of daylight carry the dawning,
Dispersing the mist, while dispelling its chills.
The woodland awakens from slumber, gradually,
Birdsong fills the air with instinctive melody,
Greeting the new day with its cheerful sound.
Nervously, fallow deer, peer through the trees,
Dancing gracefully away, with consummate ease,
While sugar coated frost drips onto the ground.
Breaking silence you could cut with a knife,
By degrees, Prince's Risborough comes back to life,
As I look down on the town, from my hilltop view.
Buckinghamshire is beautiful at this time of day,
I pray that it shall always remain in this way,
Glistening with sunshine just as if it were brand new.

Forgotten Words
Gail P. Harts
Yesterday we said good morning, each time we passed someone
Today we don't even say hello, we respect no one,

Thank you is a forgotten phrase that we don't find time to use
I'm sorry are two words that most of us abuse.

Whatever happened to respect like yes sir, yes ma'am and excuse me.
We have become so displaced these words we hardly speak.

Where are those words and deeds that once kept neighbors friends
Whatever happened to nice things that were life's little trends.

We should go back to yesterday, recapture Faith and Truth.
We were happier then, we lived longer we had trust and roots.

Well! Good Morning God and Thank You,
I'm sorry if I offended you today.
Excuse my fellow man, He's just forgotten how to pray.

My Special Good–Bye
Amy York
On the day you left me
You called out my name
The very next day
The feather came.
Between you and me
That was our good–bye,
And, your special way to say
Babe, "it's time for me to fly".
You're not very far from me,
I've found this to be true
By the way things happen
Honey, only you would do.
When God so chooses
That we meet in Heaven,
Each day that passes
I will love you, Kevin

Now And Then
Jason Haley
That was then, this is now
and it is so weird how
so many things have yet to change
all the new seem so strange
we quickly adapt to our needs
we all change to give in to greed.
Just another day
but everything can't stay.
Its so easy to forget
the many things we really regret
but memories and friends fade away
as we turn to go a different way
A new beginning, or a different end
my life's over as another begins.

In Praise Of Volunteers
Kathy E. Kinser
When I consider one vast human force,
Which aids the noblest causes of mankind,
I see an image of our rich resource,
The helping hands of those with civic mind.

They give of time apart from home, career,
To mentor, nurture, lift a life in need.
Absorbed in work humanity finds dear,
A force to help a worthy cause succeed.

They come from many walks of life, to give
Unique experience to every task.
They labor so that others better give,
To make a difference is all they ask.

Dedication: Sandy, Cheryl, Sue and Jack

Eternal Love
Elizabeth Miller
As we walk through this world hand in hand,
Reminiscing back, when we wrote our names in the sand.
I thank the stars, which shine above,
For sending down, someone like you to love.
You were the wind, beneath my broken wing,
Now just the thought of you, makes my heart sing.
With each tender kiss, you take my breath away,
Each tender touch, my heart knows you'll never stray.
Our love will stand the test of time,
And though all eternity, you'll always be mine.
When I lay me down to sleep,
I pray the Lord, your love I'll keep.
Without you, life would have no reason,
With you, our love will last longer than each season!

Un–Wedding Night
Judith Grant
They discovered
Who they were
That afternoon,
Post champagne
And cognac
And flaunted caresses.

Now One,
They saw the two
Too clearly
To contain the fight
Over who they are
Each in the light.

Ah, Love —
How quickly your flight.

Squirrel
Alice O. Harbison
A Squirrel with a bushy tail,
Scampering up a tree,
Storing food for winter,
As busy as can be.

Winter winds are here,
Please hurry and prepare,
There is no time for playing,
Just feel the cold, cold air.

With cheeks puffed out so full,
Of all those nuts and seeds,
Store them in your cupboard,
For all your winter's needs.

A Scent Of You
Jamie A. Barchuk
I'm tired, I'm bored
I'm lying here alone and suddenly I
realize something beautiful
I'm wearing your shirt
It smells like you
And now I'm smiling, I'm comfortable
It's so wonderful! I feel so lovable
God I need you
You're so bright
You're so meaningful
I'm lying here alone collecting sweet
thoughts of you.
Our memories will live
Our future will grow
Tomorrow our dreams will definitely
Come true—
I feel so refreshed — with just a
Scent of you

Functions Of A Mother
Dana M. Cooper
She cooks your breakfast, lunch, and dinner
And you can be sure they're all winners!
She cleans the house, and washes clothes,
And sometimes even wipes your nose!

She picks you up when you are down,
And puts a smile where there was a frown.
She makes you well when you are sick,
Yes, Moms are the trick!

She's the person who we all love,
That was sent from Heaven above.
She is the angel who came down to earth,
To give your life a special worth.

Friends
Jackie Webb
People, people everywhere
And not a friend for me
Dripping personalities
Sliding on past me.

Reaching, stepping, grasping
I caught one up for me
But much to my surprise,
I ended up with me!

Imagine that, I heard me say
Imagine my surprise
Reaching down, I found —
My own best friend is me!

The Doe
Pat Gabriel
Her eyes held mine
across a narrow stream
her feet hesitated
she did not run

I stood transfixed
by her beauty
her innocence
her trust

I walked away
she did, too
my morning blessed
by her presence

The Unknown
Robert Messina
Distant hatred
Unknown wrongdoing
Dying lust
A creeping from behind
An endless path of emerald
Insane body, fading away
Surrounded by the unknown
All directions, endless as time
Vision inside a closed door
Opposite locked by truth
A repeating flame
A wanted vision, unseen.

Dedication: Ruth Naomi Smith, in algood

Stealth
Margaret K. Baum
Softly, by stealth
Love creeps in,
Its cat paws
silent,
Its whiskers tickle
in surprising ways,
Its steady gaze
of brilliant flecks
mesmerizes,
Soft fur caresses
while kneading flesh.
Impossible to resist – until...
Submissive to its spell,
I succumb, stretch, savor
the pleasure of its purr.
The pain of its coarse tongue.

Children In The Dark
Casey Alvey
Eyes in the dark,
glare through the cold,
young children die,
they're lost and alone.

'til men come,
giving their time,
to save these kids,
from certain demise.

These innocent children,
no longer sit in gloom,
the love of men,
has saved them from doom.

Dedication: To my sister Melissa

Untitled
J. B. Rodgers
When I build my house, as I will someday,
It won't be of brick, or mortar, or clay
But it will be built of ambition so high
To attain it I'll undoubtedly have to fly
And if I succeed, as I hope I will,
I'll sit atop my lonely hill
Patting my back and thumping my chest
Smugly saying "I did my best"
But if I miss, as is easily done
I'll still feel sure that I have won
For I'll have lived and loved and lost
So that no matter what the cost
When the journey's over and my number's up
You can bet your honor, I've drained the cup

The Sand Of Time
Jennifer Vandersteen
She looked up into the clouds above,
twisting and turning like a wind–blown dove.
The waves beat upon the shore,
and with every strike, her heart tore.
The wind blew her long, thick hair
tossing it about without a care.
Oh, how she longed to hold him once more,
and run with him along that golden shore.
The sunset cast a lonesome glow
upon the mountains, both high and low.
With misty eyes, she turned away,
and made a vow to herself that day.
As long as his memories with her remained,
upon those grains of sand she would never walk again.

The Lake
Robert M. Pflug

The lake is smooth and peaceful tonight;
I am waiting for the bull frog to croak.
I am waiting on the shore.
A school of fish breaks the surface of the water.
In the background, are the crickets,
Composing a song with the hoot owl.
I have a comfortable seat on a rock,
As I listen to the echoes of the day,
Bouncing off the canyon walls.
The moon reflex off the surface of the water;
And I prepare for my night's rest.
Hoping, no, almost knowing, I am safe,
Until the dawn;
As the bull frog begins to croak.

For Ricki
Kathleen E. McKissock

"What makes the sun shine so bright?"
"Don't owls ever sleep at night?"
"Where did the turtle go when he died?"
"When I run real hard how come I get a pain in my side?"

The queries keep coming, year after year,
With answers elusive, I'm not ready I fear,
For the big questions coming,
For the next things I'll hear.

I'll tell what I know, help all that I can,
But there are no rules, and I've no set plan,
To love and to teach and to care and to try
To do what I'm able, then to kiss you good—bye.

Independence
Ronna H. Saunders

Independence, what does it imply?
Responsibility, an awesome will to try.
Courage, to stand. To fight.
Valor, defending truth and right.
Honor, Hope, Glory,
Values of old...
Stars and Stripes in colors bold.
"A dream," the world says with a sigh,
"Reality," replies Miss Liberty as she holds our beacon high.
Men and Women, taught at mother's knee
To cherish freedom and value liberty.
God, in whom we put our trust,
Faith in Him, may it ever be thus.
Freedom, what every soul craves,
Found in America
Land of the free – home of the brave.

Heaven's Gate
Sharon C. Hunter

As I look up to the stars of old, my mind
Begins to expand dreaming of wondrous stories told.
Looking for faces of those I know or ones of
yet to meet.
I strain to hear the glad voice cry of my
Maker soon to greet.
The trumpets blare to make all aware, the
Flood light shining bright.
Chorus sings, all round bells ring, the time
Will soon be right.
Sudden darkness blinds my eyes, my ears
No longer hear,
The crashing cymbals, the pounding drums.
I now begin to fear,
It is not my time, it is not yet my fate to
Pass through – Heaven's gate!

Dedication: To Mom and Dad, love

In Loving Memory Of Boe James Keller
Betty Lou Pollestad

I lost my little friend, Boe today
He was so sweet and brought much joy.
Polite, mannerly; always wore a smile
Cowboy hat, boots and in real style.

Not just Mom and Dad you made happy
But everyone who crossed your path.
The training given by your parents, Boe
Made everyone wish you were their boy.

You lightened all our lives, Boe
More than you ever know.
We know you are in Heaven
Where there's Peace and Angels sing forever.

My Prayer!
Kristi Treanor

Dear God I hope You'll forgive me,
For all mistakes I've made today.
And please Lord help me see,
All you've got in store for me.
And let me use my talents wisely,
Although you know Satan tries me.
Lord you knew what I was when you got me,
And I'm trying hard you see,
To be like you in every way,
And follow you day by day,
Dear Lord you know I love you,
And to you I'll always be true.
And Lord I know you love me too,
By the things you say and do.

The Future Is Now
Michele Miller
Welcome to the future, Yes, you heard me correctly. Today
is the future. Forget about holding things back because
the past wasn't so great.

Do not fear the future and do not weep for the past. Time
waits for no one, so move on with your life. If you do not
like the direction your life is going in learn from your
mistakes and change that.

If you don't you are stopping yourself from getting the
best out of your life and later on you will regret it. So
break free, live and make a difference in what is to come tomorrow.

Dedication: The Sun Coffee Shop People

Street Cat
Luis W. Osorie
He is my only friend. Comes and goes as he wants.
Not asking or demanding. I feel his caresses when I sleep.
The concrete underneath me is cold, the wind blows hard
against my body. Yet he remains with me.

He is my friend.

Not like the others.

Always demanding. Always screaming. Always
touching. Hurting.

My friend loves me just for whatever I am.

For what I will always be. Nothing.

This is his street. He is my friend. My only
friend. A cat

Burning Children
Paul W. Watkins
Watched by the glow of my footsteps
across the cold night ground,
Seeking the enfolding darkness
my mind clothed only with shadows,
Badges of honor, hardly, killers of spirit
and slayers of children.
Attitude fine honed by years
open eyes and spirit,
They burned the babies because parents believed,
My party, smiled the Babylonian whore.
Silence is joining, soul gagging.
Will they come tonight, the masked ones?
Will I feel the foot on my neck
and make dust bunnies my dinner?
Is it just in my mind and when will
they try to follow me here?
Now that they burn children
because parents believe.

Save For Victory
Muriel Marceau
Save! Save! Save! Save!
Bang a nail in Hitler's grave.
Every penny, every pound
Sinks it deeper in the ground!

Buy less sweets and buy less ices,
These are little sacrifices
Compared with those who leave their wives
To serve their country with their lives!

We must have guns and ammunition,
Seeing this, stop! look! and listen!
Save for freedom, save for right!
Go to it! Save with all your might!

She
David Tornstrom
Her eyes burned blue
like the hottest flame
they saw right through me
I've never been the same
She spoke like the rainbow
and gave me the gift of her name
the breath parting her lips
a fresh Spring rain
her slender beautiful figure
toward me came
flaxen hair brighter than gold
about her face a frame
she gave me a choice between her
or glory, fortune, and fame

Panther
Cherie Reed
How often have I thought to be
a creature half as sleek as thee
with surety beneath my foot
and claw to deal with thug or crook
How often have I wondered at
the way that God has provided you
with velvet garment ever new
A coat of pitch
as oil from the depths of earth
your strength embodied in its hue
And I imagine that to walk with such calm
such grace through twisted trails without a trace
must make you feel above the rest
A splendid vision forged in bone and flesh

For Jessica
Glen Hudson

"Promise me you'll never leave", she said.
I smiled.
I pledged everything I knew, passed on all I possessed,
shared everything I embodied, and she has forsaken it all.
Yet, my attempts are feeble and insignificant, she takes
no notice of me.
I helplessly long for her, but in her life I play no greater
role then that of a pawn.
Then it was her that looked away and left I all alone.
I gave chase after her, screaming "I love you."
I ran faster, but still made no gain. I screamed "I love
you." Yet, she could not hear me, or possibly chose not to.
I yearned to stop, to turn back. I knew if it ended my heart
would shatter.
Possibly someday I shall reach her, possibly she shall hear
me, or possibly I shall forget this all ever occurred.

Love Notes
Kimberly Irvin

Come with me;
We'll build our life
A fairy tale come true.
Love with me;
We'll experience passion
We'll learn what lovers do.
Stay with me;
We'll share our love
We'll raise our children too.
Grow with me;
We'll trod life's path
We'll unleash our love anew.
Live with me;
We'll remain best friends
Memories of skies so blue.
Fade with me;
Time marches on
In heaven, I'll stay with you.

Save The Children
Stacey Burns

Save the children from all the guns
and fighting they see, for this would
not be a problem if we set good examples
you and me.

If we don't save our children no one
else will, they will grow up warped and
think it's cool to kill.

Parents take the time to love one another
that's the main objective you see, because
they learn what they see from you and me.

So give them all your love please don't
hesitate, our children need us now before
it's too late.

No Answers
Amber Landini

Sometimes it is hard to tell
reality from a dream.
Is life a one–man sport,
or do we all make up a team?

Do you stop to sniff the roses,
or focus on the thorns?
Is life a perfect puzzle,
or are the pieces slightly torn?

Is there life on other planets,
or are we the only to exist?
With so many questions left unanswered,
could we ever end this list?

Wendy The Butterfly
Bill Christy

Wendy, Wendy, you are an elusive Butterfly,
and it comes to me as no great surprise, you will
unfold your wings at first sunrise.

Though I'll try to catch you with all my
might, you will spiral upward in magnificent
flight.

I will follow you through meadows, forest
and streams, and catch you often, but only in my
dreams.

I'll never stop trying as we cross this land,
always returning home with an empty hand.

But when the sun goes down and the night
grows cold, you will flutter back home and be
mine to hold.

Rhyme Is Sublime
Thelma Hull

When I write a poem, I want it to rhyme
(though the trend is to write free style)
To me it seems I have to keep time,
Get the rhythm and beat then compile.

When I write a poem, I want to convey
Feelings from deep within
As they bubble and surface, what I wish to say
Flows out at the end of my pen.

When I write a poem, the genre I choose
And the stab at poetic refrain,
May gladden or sadden, or simply amuse
As I strive for the poet's domain.

Calloused Hands
Connie Kleiman

On calloused hands he laid his head,
to rest from burdens heavy still.
Tho' night has fallen and peace abides,
his heart grows weary and yearns for solace.
In distant shadows, life's faint memories
slip between the threads of sorrow.
Dreams now dulled by passing years,
avail themselves in taunting wonder.
Oh what clinging presence this,
residing in the darkness ever.
Hope flickers not for youths swift exit,
but abides within the heart eternal.
With reverence now he bows his head,
in peaceful prayer as comfort nears.

Dedication: For my loving husband, Bill

Broken...
Keith Breedlove

Moonlight streams through roof top cracks,
and falls upon their broken backs,
huddled together, no hope, just fear...
in their darkest dreams never thought to be here...
broken hearts and shattered minds...
all love and hope left far behind...
a fix, a score, one vein—full more...
was this all worth walking out that door...
lost in a sea of humanity...
victims of our own hypocrisy...
youthful minds so weak so dry...
no more tears left, not one to cry...
through roof—top cracks the moonlight streams...
and shines its light on broken dreams...

Life
Anita Kister

The space of time will always be,
As will the depths of sky and sea.
The darkened sky cries out for light
And daylight sinks into the night.
The sun will set for lover's eyes
And morning comes to watch it rise.
A rose will bloom and petals red
Will soon be faded, withered, dead.
A planted seed is soon to grow,
And then will come the rain, then snow.
A snowflake small, but beauty great;
And roots are crushed with snowflakes weight.
The rain can fall like dead man's blood
And bring sweet life, or death in flood.
A cloud will pass by overhead,
And change its form, or so I dread.
For every new—born babe that cries,
A dying faith and love revives.

A Teenage Mother's Heartbreak
Linda E. Estep

I hear their words, I have no choice.
I speak out loud, but I have no voice.
I want to keep you, they say I can't.
Why won't they listen, to what I want?
I already love you, so very much.
I want to hold you, to see you, to touch.
My heart is broken, so deep inside.
The emptiness is a void, so deep and wide.
"If only", I say and quietly pray.
"If only" they'd give me just one more day.
I promised myself I'll find you someday.
Where there's a will, there's always a way.
My only hope, and my only prayer,
Is that you'll want to meet me, and see that I care.
Through all the pain and all the tears.
Maybe together we can make up the years.
I will always love you,
Your Maternal Mother

Untitled
Joan Hannah

Our lives are but a moment
Caught between a cry and a sigh
Reaching unsure to something
And never knowing why
Riding through the darkness
Together and then alone
Forcing the clay to mold
Into the texture of a stone
And then like ancient statues
Beneath a headstone cold
We crumble to hereafter
With promises of gold
And if that promise holds
To be a legend true
I pray my darling love
I'll forever walk with you

She Waits
Joe Bonham

With tear stained cheeks she feels the unloving thrusts.
Her soul falling deeper into a hole she tries to visualize a man with a
     great soul,
who only wanted to caress and to hold.
She did this in hopes to withhold the knot in her throat from letting go
     the cry
that she so much wanted to let explode.
With a quiver of her chin she realized then what would happen next would
     happen again.
When he was through, he would return her to the place where she felt so
     subdued.
Back to that darkened street corner with walls of concrete left alone she
     would be,
to feel that pain which she did not envy.
Cold dark and empty she would wait until the next man came and took her on
     a "date".

A Thing Called Fate!
Ashleigh Liles

Loves soft whisper across time, the power is yours and mine,
Rainbows, shooting stars, children and lovers these are a sign.
Fate finds lonely people and gives them this sign,
Making a couple whose faces glow and shine.
This shining comes from the soul of answered dreams,
Falling from the tails of beautiful moonbeams.
Undying love and faithfulness is the key,
To dance in the gardens of love for eternity.
When you're with this person it's as if the world pauses and heaven sings,
Or it's as if you're flying on angel's wings.
When you find your special person you will know,
By a look, a touch, or a kiss a love can grow.
If you're lonely you just wait,
Look around you have some faith, it will find you a thing called fate!

Dedication: Patrick, the person I love!

A Look Into My Heart
Rocco C. Spears

The sun shines across the land.
The tears flow down my cheeks and into my hands,
My heart is breaking from the cold hard fact,
that you've left me and you're not coming back.

As I sit here on the bed we shared,
I think back to the time you cared.
I realize now what I lost.
It's never worth it when you count the cost.

So take my advice and play it smart;
don't take risks with your heart.
'Cause there's nothing on earth that can ease
the pain.
And no one on earth can bring them
back again.

Undying Love
Sharon M. Pierce

I called him my best friend
To the girls I knew back home
On me for love he could depend
But he left me all alone
Every time I saw him
My body went into shock
Now all I can do is cry for him
Twenty—four hours around the clock
My heart was filled with so much love
All of it true and only for him
Now he must watch me from above
Since alcohol tool over, and suicide stepped in

Dedication: My beautiful angel: Daniel RJD LeBlanc

Subway Dreamer, Solitude
Jennifer Frank

concrete, it can be so cold: the cement hearts under stone faces
big cities dancing underneath the smog and you're always trying to escape
    places
big cities are so unpersonable; they remind you of the way you feel inside
cold and hard and lonely and drifting, there are no laws by which you abide
wherever the subway takes you while you lose track of the track
always make your independence your strength; let nothing hold you back
do you find solace in a subterranean quiet and in your deep solitude
peace in a corner, as a face among many, you sit in the bustle and you
    brood
on silly things, like lava lamps, and why people bother to smile
and why are you here living, anyway, and how will you make it worthwhile
wherever the subway takes you, no matter how rough the ride seems
you'll always have your solitude, your bus tokens, your dreams.

My Love
Calvin Woodall

My love for you is great
No matter how my heart aches
As I see you walk by
it make me wanna cry
And wonder why this had to be

I love you with all my heart
why can't you see
or even acknowledge that about me
I love you still even tho
you don't even notice me

Maybe one day
Just maybe you would say
I Love you
That would make my day

Apron Strings
Violet Langland

The Apron Strings are now being cut
so you can finally grow up. Some may say
I've cut them late, but I'm your mother
and its one job I hate. I've cut the string
four times before and watched each one
walk out the door. I know I should have
cut them long ago, but I didn't want to
see my baby go. Now the day has finally
came for me to cut those Apron Strings.
As you open the door and walk on thru
my heart proudly beats for you. The
time is right and baby you look great,
the rest of your life is yours to mold
for in my heart you'll always be and
memories I'll always hold. Happy birthday
daughter the Apron Strings are now
cut, I wish you every happiness and lots
and lots of luck.

Miracles
Patty Smith

Aspen trees with green and silvery leaves
Swaying, rustling in a summer's breeze...
Those tiny yellow flowers that top
The weeds choking my garden...
Pinks and purples and blues of sunset skies...
Button–nosed newborn mewling kittens...
Hurts–the–throat cold lemonade
On scorching hot summer days...
Miniature rainbows caught in dewdrops
Suspended in a perfect spider's web...
All these – and more –
Twang the heart with their miracle of being...
Yet all would I trade for just...
One more gentle touch on my face,
One more loving smile,
From my beloved departed mother...

The Tunnel
Michelle Eckert

The tunnel of life is dark and dim,
with no chance of finding end.
The walls around me are closing in.
Help!
Suddenly I hear a voice.
A clam, gentle voice.
That voice is you.
With you as my guide I can
see the light.
When you leave, my light leaves too.
When you're back, my lights back too.
Without my light, I'm lost with no
hope.
With my light I look through
the darkness,
Only to see my light leave again

Roller Coaster
Kiley Thibodeau

Love is like a Roller
coaster
you have your ups and
your downs.
You have your smiles
and your frowns.
It's sometimes bumpy
and it's sometimes
smooth.
But you'll have to choose
what ride is right
for you!!

Dedication: Phil Jr. and Philip III

Honest Enjoyment
Dawnita Ransom

Lights From heaven up above,
gates from which we all can love.
Crystal clear streams and birds
in flight, help us enjoy dawns
early light.
Walking green pastures,
smell the scent.
God's creations, the times descent.
Dusty fields, full of grey,
hollow pastures, work filled days.
The times of honor and of praise,
before the rumble, the worlds craze.
Smile so softly as you daze,
Remember sweetly these good days.

As We Celebrate
Sharon Scheff

As we celebrate the day when we became one, let us reflect
on the laughter, the happiness, the fun.

The tears we've shared, the joys and the fears, I shall
cherish these memories for the rest of my years.

You are my strength and my guide, my calm in a storm. With
you by my side, I shall never feel harm.

We've overcome hardships, and our love stands so strong, for
the day we were wed, we said from now on;

Is shall love you and keep you all the days of my life, and
I shall thank the Lord daily for making me your wife.

Dedication: Tony– always and forever

Mom
Lauren DiDonato

One fine day a bunch of angels wanted to find
something sweet
So, they went past the good things to the special
treat
They went to the deepest part of the heart, but when
They found nothing they had to depart
They went deeper still to the best part of love and
Finally found what they were dreaming of
She was hiding under some beautiful stars and next
To her sat golden bars
The angels knew their dream came true and that, Mom
Is how they found you

Dedication: Anna DiDonato (mom)

God's World Help Save It
Amelia Garcia
God made this world for us with love,
But we're not doing a very good job of taking care of it.
We need to clean up our world and make it a cleaner and
    safer place to live.
We need to stop the violence and drugs.
We need to stop littering.
We need to stop graffiti
We need to stop cutting down trees in the rain forest.
We need to stop all the bad things we are doing to our world,
The world God made for us.
We need to clean up our act or there won't be a place we can call clean.
There won't be a place we can call safe.
There won't be a place we can call Home.
Help clean up your home,
Because I care and
So should you!

Love Of The Universe
Linda D. Browder
Ultimate Source:
Dancing to the divine rhythm
of creation, everything balanced
and planned at precisely the
right moment.

We move in the direction
the ultimate source
takes us; not always knowing
when or why we will go
Here or there – or
Who we will meet on the way.
Everything at precisely the right moment.
Calculated not by us but by the
Creator of the Universe.
He writes the scripts, we play the roles,
with free choice to publish or edit
the scripts designed for us.

My Doctor
Marion Hitsman
Dr. George Renton D. O.
Is my Doctor you know.
He hears and sees, and listen to me.
I cry a little, and I die a little, and
Dr. Renton is always there for me.
You must meet my Doctor he's really
something to see.
What's inside of him, comes out,
And reflects upon me.
The love, the care, the compassion
And understanding he gives that all to me.
Dr. George Renton D. O.
Is my Doctor you see,
What a Doctor, What a Doctor.
He is so full of life, what a joy to see.
As I am dying, he puts Hope in me.
To live, To live and to Believe
Without pain there is no life for me.

Pain
Phillip Butler
My Pain soothes:
My pain reassures:
My pain builds confidence:
It takes me to places I've never been:
It makes me strong:
It hides and exposes my weaknesses:
I thank it:
I curse it:
My pain...
I need it:
It calls to me, beckoning, and eternally steering my path, leading me down
    the wrong trail, forever
showing me the way.
My pain...
My pain took my wife:
My pain ruined my life:
My pain destroys:
My pain, my friend, my lover, my companion, my...Bottle

My Pal
Ruth Mulcaster
She was my pal, my life
I lived for her day by day
I know she is gone from my life
She was soft and lovable
I miss her day by day
She always stood by my side
Never a whimper always love was there
I miss her day by day
The pain I felt on that day she left me
I'll never forget the love of this
Pal of mine as its ever there
It's hard to bear the loss
But the love is always there
She was my pal my life

The Secret In My Garden
Ruth Pearson
As I was in my garden the other day.
I knelt down to plant a flower, and to pray.
I noticed the different earth there was, brown, yellow, white, black, and
    red clay.
I said, to the Father above,
This is the earth we were fashioned of.
So why should being brown, yellow, white, black or red.
Ever go to our head?
Why Father, would some think being black is bad?
When it is the richest and best earth you had.
I've noticed that white earth is usually sand.
Why would we think, out of only this, you would create your man?
I think you took a little of each one.
Mixed them all together so we could become just like your Son.
So why then, being a little more or less of one color or the other.
Ever keep us from loving our sister and brother?

Fathers Do Sometimes Go Away
Serenity Gordon
Seize the moment cherish the day, Seasons change and people go astray.

There was a man that I once knew who loved me so true.
Until up, up I grew and away with part of my heart he flew.

Now the man I used to know as my father is still alive but
dead to me on the inside.

I don't understand why he tried so long to be a part of me
only to leave me much denied.

Why did he attach me to his heart only to rip mine apart...
Thus I will never know but to go on strong and from life's course learn
to grow.

Untitled
James J. Meyer
Is there any nicer way to start a day
Than with a thought of love
And with that thought a memory
Of someone beautiful

I suppose there are those who claim
it waste
To dwell upon such thoughts
Because of more important things
For which to spend their time

But to me all the money, wars and games

That they are won't to do
Are not as important even
As a fleeting thought of you.

Dedication: Margaret

Imaginary World
Leo J. Flores
In a world that one's mind can carry, a herd of toy horses
gallop through a forest of fake plastic trees. Nothing
can go wrong in this imaginary world that a young girl
carries in her mind. The air is fresh and the water is
crystal clear. Porcelain people love one another and the
parents in this imaginary world don't abuse their own
children. The problems the girl faces in the real world
are abuse, neglect, and fear which you can see in her eyes.
This girls own parents don't see the creative talents that
that this girl carries. They see the girl who stained the
living room carpet, after spilling her drink. These parents
only see the girl who had a little bit of dirt on her dress
after playing at the playground at school. Her parents don't
seem to realize this girl is just nine years old. The
expectations they have of the girl are those of a nineteen—
year old. Whenever the girl feels lonely, she can escape to
her imaginary world filled with her own imaginary friends,
sunshine that appears only for her, and joy.

If Life Was Easy
Janice E. Petros
If life was easy
We would all have it made;
There would be no bills
They would all be paid.

If life was easy
No one would hate;
We would accept each other
At any rate.

If life was easy
We would all be free;
To live our lives
With faith and glee.

Shelter Me Beneath Thy Wings
Helen Brooks
Blessed Saviour, thou shalt lead me lest my feet be led astray
Blessed Saviour, thou shalt feed me heavenly manna every day
Oh lamb of God who died at Calvary, by Thee my soul has been redeemed
When by storms of life, I'm threatened, shelter me beneath Thy wings

I gaze into the blue horizon, filled with awe at what I see
Poised above in clouds of glory Jesus watches over me
I am ready for Thy coming for Thy blood has washed me clean
When I need a blessed haven shelter me beneath Thy wings

I will keep Thy holy edicts avoiding evil like the plague
I'm just an ordinary person, not a prophet nor a sage
In return, my Blessed Saviour, heavens all I hope to gain
When at times I'm weak and weary, shelter me beneath Thy wings

---

For Now
Kathi Serr
God saw that he was tired,
And a cure was not to be,
So with loving arms around him,
God whispered "follow me".
And we, who saw him suffer,
Watched him slowly, slip away,
As he followed God to heaven,
To awake another day.
And we behind that mourn him,
Believe that God knows best,
And take comfort now in knowing,
He is finally at rest.
He has gone to prepare a place,
Where all of us will dwell,
And one day again, we'll see his face,
And know that all is well.

Dedication: Dad, thank you for staying

Untitled
Vivian Barraza

Mom, just a note to say, how many times throughout my
days, I'll stop and think to myself, how very fortunate,
proud and how very blessed I am to be your daughter.

On this very special day, when we celebrate Mother's
Day, I just want to remind you, how very special you
are and how very much you're loved.

Mom, you're the best and if every mom on the face of this
Earth, would nurture their children with the abundance
of love that you have, the world would be a much better
place. You are my best friend, I love you and Happy Mother's Day.

Dedication: Margaret Barbara, my mom

I Want
Bloody Feathers Mayo

I want to live and love with you and be one forever
To be near you so I can reach out and touch you and make love to you
I want to talk with you and hold you close and tight every night
To wake up with you each morning and see your smile
I want to share my secrets with you and be honest with you
To understand and respect you and accepting you as you are
I want to find shelter in you when I am afraid
To hold you when I need warmth and to be with you through all the seasons
I want to walk with you in the sunshine and cuddle with you in the cold
To care for you when you are ill and be joyful with you when you are happy
I want to grow old with you and be with you until the end of time
I want all of these things with only you
I would do all of these things for only you
To you only I give all of my love

Dedication: My beautiful singing Dove

Life
Walid Issa

With tears and rage I welcomed you, o life
With laughter and joy you welcomed my life
With four legs I crawled away from your bosom and your door
With open arms you waited for me on the next shore
With my dawn of knowledge I rose to seek the treasures of your wisdom
With your golden key you showed me the way to your kingdom
With a wounded heart I praised the mystery of love
With a loving rose you set my heart free like a dove
With pride and courage I fought your battles
With gold and silver you jewelled my medals
With justice you crowned your measure
With fear I obeyed with pleasure
With three legs, a dimmed light guided my eyes once more to you
With the same loving arms you welcomed me and I you
Naked I came to you life
Naked you buried my life.

Dedication: Fr. Andre, my brother

Who Has Seen The Gentle Wind
Frank Seerattan

A gentle spring breeze blows
merrily through the trees.
It brings with it rebirth and new life,
after winter's long cold spell.
Today's gentle breeze brings fragrances
to titillate the senses.
Yesterdays gentle wind blows into
tomorrows boisterous storm.
It wrecks havoc all around us
as we hear the death knoll sound.
Buildings and lives are strewn about
like leaves in a cool fall breeze.
This gentle wind, this fragrant wind
has left a bitter taste in the air.
Tomorrow we begin the arduous task
of putting together our broken lives
left by the once gentle breeze, the fragrant
breeze that once permeated our senses.

River Of Life
Hope Hathaway

You try to blind us—
we'll look all the harder.

You try to bind us—
we'll struggle all the more.

You try to silence us—
we'll scream all the louder.

You try to break us—
we'll kick a little harder.

You try to ignore us—
we'll come back with brute force.

The human spirit will triumph,

As the River of Life flows its course.

So Like The Stars...
Hazel Firth Goddard

I watch the stars, each bending to the bind
of continuity, in sequence of repeat...
Moon, it too, climbs at earth's insistent
call, consistently to rape prized privacy
beneath a forest's black laced limbs.

Alone, I answer to a universe made up of
chiefly silent song...the love nest
we once shared is dream's delight...
So like the stars, I fondle night's black lace.

Old habits haunt me yet, for strangely still
a caftan's chiffon fold falls willfully,
to offer blood warm flesh that does not flinch
from your remembered touch now cold in Time.

So like the stars old memories repeat...
they light Capellas in a hurting heart.

Heavenly Angel Wings
Dorothy R. Sirois
Heavenly Angel wings delighted in my soul,
Oh heavenly Angel wings, guide me
across the stream of all my Blessing
We behold, through our Burdens
We must Bear.,
Our Guardian Angel, is always near.
Give me strength overcome fear,
of this trouble world,
Oh Heavenly wings, let your light
Guide me across the stream:
Oh mine Angel come to me, your
wings of love and comfort guide
me, for all the world to see.
To, carry me, to my eternal Home,
For God's Love He gave to me
My Angel's Wings.

Dedication: Brian J. Sirois, my son

The Bleeding Heart
Linette Lawlor
The bleeding heart,
self—sacrifice to your unknown god.
The Mater Dolorosa
extending her arms
and her still beating heart
to him.
He accepts the heart
of the Lady of Sorrows
and offers his sacred organ
to her need.
Neither die,
for he is her God
and she is the mystical lover;
each other's salvation

At The Bookstore
Amy Sadanaga
The treasure of today
Was sitting next to you,
While sorting through each book
'Til nearly half past two!

Where did each hour go?
As we ventured out to see,
How many stories we could find
To keep us company!

Now that we are finally home
And you are sound in bed,
I wonder how many storybooks
Are dancing in your head!

Dedication: My daughter, Kimberly, with love

Precious
Allegra Leigh Clark
She sits at play looking so precious

The intent expression of curiosity on her face

Her long blonde hair

Her beautiful blue eyes

Her perfect features

She looks like a small angel

Then I realize, though at times I can
hardly believe, that she is my child

Dedication: My daughter, Sarah

Racizm Is Not A Joke
Pamela S. Leonard
It's my turn to speak out so listen up close,
Isn't it time to realize racizm is not a joke.
The color of a person's skin doesn't come close to fazing me,
you could be pink, purple, or green, but I would still treat you equally.
It's time to look towards the future and forget the past,
we've got to stop this now,
we can't let it last.
We've put up with the slavery,
we've put up with the fights,
now it's time to forget all that,
lets make this world right.
We've got to look after our people and
stop caring about the color of the skin,
the outside doesn't matter,
what matters is the person within.
so let's stop the teasing and stop all the fights,
let's start working together,
because we can't get peace overnight.

Friends
Margaret Wright
Friendship is a special thing
shared between two friends
It gets you through the bad times
and the good times never end.

It's someone to confide in
when others you can't tell
They'll always stand beside you
Even when you fail

Your friendship's unconditional
Respect is always best
Add all these things together
and you've each been truly blest

Wishes
Cassie Cox

I only wish I found you
before, the way you make
me feel I adore. The way
you treat me makes me
feel like life will never
stand still. You treat me
like I've always wanted
someone to. You make
my life feel brand new.
I only wish you knew how
very blue I was before I
found you. So now I pray
that me and you can hopefully
be true. Because, I never
would of known of you if
life was still so blue.

Dedication: John Taylor, I love you

Thursday Night Homecoming
Tina Widell

Six shining eyes,
Chubby cheeks,
And three golden smiles
Will meet me at the door tonight.
A week's silence will vanish
With loud hello's,
And plenty of giggles.
Then it's pj's and stories,
Hugs and kisses.
"Good night, boys.
Sleep well tonight
For tomorrow I can play."

Dedication: My sons, Duaine, Andrew, Kevin

Heaven So Blue
Cheri House

I know some day we will be leaving
This old world for the new
And we will be with our Savior
To walk across the Heaven so blue
So you can fill your eyes with glory
And praise the Lord for the light
For He will be standing beside you
To walk across the Heaven so blue
Now all of the angels up there
Will be so happy with you
Now you can see all your loved ones
As you walk across the Heaven so blue
So have you saved your soul for Jesus
And will you be ready to go
When He comes calling for you
To walk across the Heaven so blue

Nineties Kind Of Guy
J. Robert Evans

I don't spend my time sitting in the bars.
Hanging out with the boys.
Talking sports and talking cars.
And male posturing, it really ain't my thing.
I give my time to my family.
And reap the joys that it brings.
I'm caring, and I'm sensitive.
And at times been known to cry.
Categorically speaking, I'm a nineties kind of guy.
I care for my children, I clean and I can cook.
And when the kids are bathed and ready.
I read their favorite bedtime book.
I'm attentive to my wife, I listen while she talks.
And I love holding hands, on romantic moonlit walks.
I'm happy and I'm blessed, no need to ask me why.
Categorically speaking, I'm a nineties kind of guy.

Winter Moon
Elizabeth M. Verbeck

Palely, coldly, she looks disdainfully down
On her reflection in the Black River water
No warm, golden rippling of soft pure light
Just a frigid silver glitter that will shatter
Into glass–like shards with the river's movement
Callous, unsympathetic –
Remote from the lance of pain around my heart
I stood bathed in her triumphant, gloating light
And I knew. I knew!
She has taken you–this cold, cruel winter moon
And I am dead.
Without you, I am living dead!

Dedication: To Paul, my only love

Hands
Tracy Talbot

Small, big, slender or fat. Rough, smooth, white or black.
Yellow, purple, red or blue. Stories are what they tell you.
Truth, lies, troubles and pain. Never are spoken.
But written...engraved. Lined throughout.
Telling the beaten paths of our hearts and souls.
Telling us exactly just how old. Descriptions of who we really are.
Parts that we cannot escape or hide.
Love them, hold them, touch them, caress them.
They feel so much so deep so true. Souls unite through and through.
Sending us vibes we cannot deny. Hands should be praised.
For they give so much. Love, affection, a gentle touch.
Clap for happiness or a job well done.
Write a meaningful word, phrase, poem or tongue.
So much our hands do each day. Never resting or going astray.
Thank you God for my hands in which I have two.
I promise I'll never take for granted all that they do.

We Care
Patricia J. Capansky
To help someone along the way
As we go through our life each day
Can be a most rewarding thing
And oh what joys it can bring
I know that it is in God's plan
For us to help our fellowman
And if the help we give today
Can help a child to run and play
We let them know that we are there
And show them that we really care
Our helping hand and giving grace
Is something time will not erase
And nothing on earth can ever replace
That happy smile on a little child's face

Times
Patrick Giguere
When we sit and when we wonder
We end up thinking of times
Times we had and times we didn't have
But then there are times that we wish we had
and moments we wish that would linger
And then there are times that we wished never happened
But within all those times we forget to think
To think of all the pleasures we had during those times
There will be a time when we remember those times
and when we remember is it too late to share
To share the joy and laughter that one should
Or will we ever share those wonderful times we had
with someone we love or trust or...
Do those wonderful times die with us, too

How Do You Do?
Barbara Littlejohn
My name is Mr. Lee.
I wanted to know your name
So I got down on one knee
Wherever you go, or whatever you do
Remember, someone is always watching you.
I like your eyes and I like your hair
I really do think we would make a great pair.
Let's go down to the river
And take a swim
Be very careful right there, it's pretty thin.
Do you think we will ever
Be friends?
Well if you don't want to
I guess this is the end.

A Fence
Jean S. Sweetapple
A fence is meant to be
A meeting place where friends
Can lean on either side and share philosophies.
The chain-link pattern's consistency
Encourages an ordered flow to what we say,
Sometimes at length, although
We only meant to pass the time of day;
But birdsong leads to music talk,
And butterflies to marveling
At the utilitarian ways of fragile things;
Sweet blossoms lead to fond remembering
Of long past greening years
And youthful springs.

Stance on domestic soil lends confidence
And we explore
The powers-that-be and trivia.
That's what a fence is for.

Soar To Perfection
Kris Gregson
I want to fly so far from here. I cannot
wait any longer. I watch the clouds so
high. I long to soar to Heaven, to perfection.
If I did maybe they what He already knows
I can and will be. They want perfection
here, but it is not possible. Perfection of
this world is worth nothing and is not
true perfection. Very few on this world
can visualize or even comprehend true
perfection. Only in Him is there perfection.
Only in Him is there no exception. He
is unconditional love. Therefore, I wish
to fly, to soar, to mount upon eagle's
wings and ascend to Him.

Dedication: The wonderful, gracious father God

Circus Babble
Eileen Moritz
Cornered cloth, shield ancient guide.
Confusion tamed, as lions laugh.
Future told in turning card,
Ring-master points enlightened staff.

Angels walk a line above;
The ring of fire, desired gate.
Court Jester spins the mischief moon,
Illuminating beasts of fate.

Curtains close, as words unite;
Meaning driven back by force.
Emerged in blue, a mirrored mind;
The milky way, on dancing horse.

Dedication: To Mickey ... My Odyesseus

Ginnie
Amber Breezee

"Oh" how I love my friend Ginnie,
She is as bright as a new found penny.
She makes me laugh and smile.
Makes me forget my trouble and trials.

When together we giggle and laugh
like two school girls,
You would think we came
from different worlds.

She makes me happy all day long.
And in our hearts we sing a song.
I thought of all the blessings,
My friend do impart.
I tied them well with memory thread.
And tucked them in my heart.

Dedication: Dedicated to my friend, Ginnie

The Weight
Gretchen Bakies

The weight on my chest crushes my heart
And makes it hard to breathe.
It brings sobs that crush me to the ground
And tears that make it hard to see.

Oh if only someone would reach out a hand,
To pull me up and shove the weight aside.
But only two kitties come to see me,
Rubbing against me and purring their concern.

How can I learn to let that be enough?
How can I learn not to want more?
If I don't, the weight will crush me to dust.
And who will care for the kitties then?

Child
Denise Grassa

She looked at me in her own way.
As if to say, will you hold me today.
Not a word does she speak.
Yet I held her, I held her to my cheek.
Each time, I came to say "hello"
She seemed to be saying, do you know...
Do you know the love you have given.
You do know, for Christ has risen...
For no longer do I see those empty eyes
staring back at me...
For the love that was given
Now makes this little girl's life now worth livin'...

Dedication: Dana, Shellie, Ken, Darrin

Untitled
Andrew Burke

Pure fear of that one touching touch;
The touch of life
Or the touch of death.
The demons haunt her dreams,
The angels live her life.
An existence of paradoxes—
Hypocrisy to its fullest.
Her life is one of torment,
Her soul cannot rest.
She knows what is right,
But wrong seems so much easier to do.
Dance with the Devil and die,
Or take the forgiving hand of God and be forever his.
What will it be?
What will touch her?
That one touch, of life or death;
The dread, the anxiety,
The pure fear of that one touching touch.

A Quiet Place
Warna J. Gaddy

With the easiness of a peaceful
trust with one another
Trust born of a yet unknowledge friendship
They move closer together, exchange greetings,
smiles for they have become friends of hearts.

He opens his arms inviting her in for
what turns into a warm embrace
Holding her to him he searches her face, her eyes
finding no resistance, ever so softly he touches
his lips to hers.

Gently, they explore, meeting in a
place that has no color, no barriers
A place where there is only the eternal nature
of male and female.

A quiet place.

Moonstruck
Kyra A. Harr

She felt threatened,
until she turned her head
and saw him standing there.
Their eyes met
and he signed her near.
He then leaned down
and shielded her with his kiss.
Her troubles disappeared.
Embraced, tears rolled down her face,
as emotions filled her soul.
Reminiscing, she remembers...
How his strong arms make her feel safe.
Then, once again, the time has come...
They part, Forever Friends.

Walking Through The Valley Of Life
Cheryl LynnHeart
Life is but, a vapor on this earth,
here this moment, and gone the next

This is your time to live every
moment of your life to its fullest

A time to sing, and a time to dance,
a day to share and a day to care

Time to give, and time to receive,
moments to love, and moments to be

Oh Father, Mother, Child, and we
Is there anything we've left undone

Dedication: Jesus loves you and me

The Winding Staircase Of Life
Deirdre Thompson–Moser
The winding staircase of life
Taking each step
I wish to go no further
Just jump off and end the journey
There is no way back
Only forward
Can't see what's ahead
I don't care anymore
Like the little dog who
Chased the rabbit off the cliff
They fell to their death
I hope my staircase sways
And causes me to fall
Never to come back up again

Forever
Margaret E. Bates
I hang up the phone with hot tear in my eyes
I can't believe we've just said, "Goodbye".
Not to the talking but to all that we were
I thought together forever was us for sure.
All the laughter and fun and joy that we had
Was I fooling myself, was it really that bad?
I know there was anger, tears, I did shed a few
But it breaking up what we really should do?
Our future it held many beautiful dreams.
My love was for nothing, on so it does seem.
Now you say its all over, I have to let go
But I'll hang on forever with my heart hoping so.
And maybe in time you'll call me and say,
"Us forever, my darling, beginning today."

Incandescent Light
Jane Bell
Teach me to love by loving
Teach me to forgive by forgiving
Teach me to endure through endurance
Teach me to trust by trusting

For who can know love except he is loved
Who can forgive unless he is forgiven
Who can endure but having endured
Who can trust without having trusted.

Let me like a planet be
Living in eternity
Shining by reflective rays
Receiving, giving all my days.

Little House
Julia L. Hasell
There is a little house,
Resting on a hill,
By a country lane,
I remember still.

We used to live there,
When we were small.
Now the trees around the house,
Have grown big and tall.

The little house is empty,
Everyone went away.
But we still wander back,
Where we used to stay.

Husband, Father, Grandfather
Abby M. Holman
As we come here today to say goodbye
We all want you to know how much we love you
Memories of a strong man
Yet so weak
Your great laughter
Yet so quiet
You suffered much
Yet kept your spirits high
Now you have gone to a better place
Where you can watch over us
And guide us in our lives yet to come
As we leave you here today
In this beautiful place
You can have peace
We will always know that you will be with us
In memories and in spirit

Dedication: Memory of my loving grandparents

Biology
Angela M. Willis
It is a place that sometimes shivers
with goosebumps
or it can be prone to feverish flashes
this place has a mind of its own
where thoughts and memories are thrown
rooms are plentiful here
one is for feelings
which contains a heart
the walls in this place are thin
skin
and are used to keep unwanted visitors
from getting in
everyone has a place like this
although no one has one exactly alike
welcome to biology 101
class dismissed.

Untitled
Theresa D. Kelly
Night time is my favorite time
For that's when I can dream
I'll dream about you and me
About how things ought to be
You'd hold me in your arms
Kiss me gentle, slow
You'd tell me that you love me
And will never let me go
Then suddenly it's day again
And you are nowhere near
I begin to hope today's the day
The day when you'll appear
To tell my heart and soul
The words they long to hear

Dedication: For M.J.C.

The Thoughts Of A Soldier
Billy W. Youngblood
I was that which others did not want to be.
I went where others feared to go and,
Did what others failed to do.
I asked nothing from those who gave nothing
And reluctantly accepted the thought of
eternal loneliness...
Should I fail.
I have seen the face of terror,
felt the stinging cold of fear, and enjoyed
the sweet taste of a moment's love.
I have cried, pained, and hoped...but most of all,
I have lived times others would say were best forgotten.
At last someday I will be able to say, I was proud of what I was...
A Soldier

Dedication: All soldiers past and present

Love Is A Feeling
Kirk K. House
A special feeling
Love means caring
Courteous, considerate and
kind, when you love
Someone you will know it
Because you feel what they feel,
You feel their pain
Love can be mistaken for
hate.
Could you love someone
you hated?
Can you hate someone

You love?

At The Cross
Layne Lucas
As Jesus hung on the Cross,
He paid for our sins.
By the shedding of His blood,
Even though He hurt within.

As He paid the price for our sins,
Shows that Satan can never win,
And how powerful Jesus is
When you accept Him.

So, as we become Christians,
Let us not forget His love,
And the way He set us free,
So we could fly like a dove.

Dedication: Shawn Colvin, Michael Peterson

Life
Michelle Hipsky
My children outside, playing in the snow
Having the pleasure of watching them grow
My lover, as he wraps me in his embrace
The feel of his fingers caressing my face
The soft touch of a breeze as it kisses my skin
The sound of the birds as the day does begin
The sun and the flowers, the smell of spring
Oh, that is such a wondrous thing!
These are the things that I think of now
As I sit in my rocker and wonder how
Life passed by so quickly, so steady and swift
And I hold in my mind each precious gift
Tears fall from my old eyes as I take my last breath
But I am not sad, or afraid of death
I am remembering and thinking as I give one last sigh
How wonderful life was, and how fast it goes by.

Dedication: Rob, Amanda, and Erika

Live And Learn
Laura Greene–Patton
We had to make our choices,
And all without a plan.
If we did the same things over,
Would we change, or let them stand?
"If I knew then, what I know now,"
As the old folks used to say.
Could it have made a difference,
Saved the strife of many a day?
We learned to cope, to go on ahead,
That's how it was meant to be.
Handle the bad, enjoy the good days,
And make a difference along the way.
If the tall, steep ladder of success,
Evades our giant steps and timing,
Just be glad we all had a chance,
To have so many tries at climbing.

Dedication: All my children

The Room
Sandra Glassman
In the dark and dusty gloom
I retreat to the solace of the room
should I allow the sun to shine in
I say to myself with a grin
Bright picturesque paintings adorn the wall
this room is mine even though small
No one can receive so much pleasure
as myself, when I retire to my room during my leisure
Maybe a poem or a symphony I'll ponder
It's so peaceful there I just let my mind wander
aside from my family with whom I feel the strongest bond
the room is the place where I create without a magic wand
sometimes even as I sleep, ideas begin to fester fast
Into the room I run so my ideas will last
everyone should have that special place
so ingenuity won't go to waste

Sweet Memories Of Love
Janice Mills
Long ago love, lost to all but memory.
Love perhaps lost in haste, never to be.
Never to know what might have been
Just sweet memories of a love that was then.
Shared dreams and hopes of a life to come.
Are those dreams now shared with another one?
Dancing until dawn to a favorite song.
Walking hand in hand, as we strolled along.
A sweet, gentle kiss under a harvest moon.
Never knowing it would all end too soon.
A picnic lunch in the warm spring sun.
Laughter shared together, life was such fun
Young love never spoiled by life's daily grind.
Rather, love that forever remains sweet in the mind.
Such a pure love haunting my memory.
Forever in my heart, never to set me free.

Untitled
Ladele M. Buckman
Power–pure brute force crashing, bolting across the Sky:
Nature's laser show.
The majesty and wonder of the tempest both amazes and
    astonishes the bystander, filling them with a sense of awe
that can only be expressed through the storm.
The torrents of water pummel the Earth with unceasing fervor, and the
Stars hidden in a blanket of black.
As the Wind carries the Thunderclouds to the next demonstration
    of might, the
Nightlights of the Blackness flicker as if blown by an unseen breath
    coming from far away.
All is calm.
The quiet of Night has set in and the Morning Birds wait patiently to wake
    the Sleepers from their night of undisturbed slumber.

The Doll
Amanda MacLellan
The doll sits there unmoving
She doesn't blink an eye
She doesn't look real happy
But you know she will not cry
The doll can't be made fun of
If she likes a real strange boy
The doll doesn't have feelings
Can't feel sadness can't feel joy
The doll doesn't have to worry
If she looks pretty or not
She'll always wear the same expression
And stand in the same spot
The doll doesn't have to worry
Her life will never fall apart
For since she can't move on her own
No one will break her heart

Our Wedding Day
Marcia Gilmore
Memories of our wedding day
Forever in my mind will stay
That beautiful day, the 27th of June
That for me could not come too soon
So tall and handsome was my groom
By far the most wonderful man in the room
My bridesmaids in their dresses of pink
So pretty they are, everyone did think
My parents were so very proud
That night their sky had not a cloud
The ceremony was double ring
My heart could do nothing but sing
The wedding kiss was quite divine
Romantic and long, not out of line
The love that we knew was there to stay
Has continue to grow to this very day

Do Your Best
F. Richard Schneider
Each day is a new chance
To really learn, really grow;
Mistakes of yesterday past,
Do what you can to correct
Then quickly move on to now;
Don't worry about tomorrow,
Think on how to do the best
With what you have, who you are;
Hold true to what means most,
Look up, not backward nor forward;
Do what is right and true
Always with the best effort;
Try once, try twice, even more,
Try to keep the line straight;
Work not just to finish
Work to do your very best.

Lonesome Love
B. J. Wood
If I could take you in my arms, and tell you how I feel,
there would be no uncertainties, and nothing to conceal.

For I would give my heart to you, and all the love in me.
And I would tell you what it means to share your company.

Because you are the happiness of every song I know,
Wherever stars bestow their light, or flowers start to grow.

Wherever there is beauty in the picture of a day.
Or memories are soft enough to wash the tears away.

If I could gaze into your eyes and hold you close to me,
I know our dreams would all dissolve—into eternity.

Dedication: My sister, Quin Reece

Green Memories
David R. Templin
Scattered,
as fallen leaves,
they've gone
their
separate
ways.
one here,
one there,
one somewhere—
as if
they were never mine.

Yet,
green
in my
memories.

If It Wasn't So Hard To Say Goodbye
Rebecca Keyes
If it wasn't so hard to say goodbye, I would be done and over with you but, my heart doesn't seem to want to let you go. If it wasn't so hard to say those words my eyes wouldn't have filled up with tears. You were my world but, it is gone. You forgot how important my love was to you. If only I could say those words, maybe my heart wouldn't be so broken. I try and try each day but, the words can never seem to say goodbye. I wish it wasn't true, your love for me is really gone. I try to understand what I did wrong but, as I drift away it seems so has my love for you. Each hour, each day, each week seem to just slip away not knowing how you feel. You say you need time and space, how much more do you need before you hurt me like I have been hurt before? My world seems to shatter as each day passes by without a word or sound from love. Oh, how I weep trying to understand. If only it wasn't so hard to say goodbye...

Dedication: Those who broke my heart

Lexicon
Brandy Tapscott
These words are mine,
Are yours, are ours
We own them
Each
They represent these thoughts
All tied
Of mine, of yours,
Of ours
So pure
So sweet
Touching hearts
Like little feet
Released by tongues,
Erased by guns,
Bone brittle
These words
Of mine, of yours
Of ours.

Time
Henry Peters
The only thing we have in common
is time.
like the sea, it's not enough all the
time.

We came together like the water,
and part with the tide.

Though we're not together long, the
sea is on our side.

And in the morning after, we go
our own way.

And wait for the time, we will
be together another day.

Mind Games
Kelly Olver

To live, to dream forever
Release all your thoughts for the world to see
Believe in yourself; keep dreams together –
Make life worthwhile so your soul is free.
Take from your dreams the courage that's needed
Remember the way to give of yourself.
Be ever proud and the word is heeded
Try to be more than a mere little elf.
Stay true to your heart and always be sure
Let life run its course; whether good or bad
The mind is a tool that opens all doors.
Strive for the best so you'll never be had
Live for today; let tomorrow be still
Ev'rything happens when you know your will

The Garden
K. T. Blue

Your children each different
You gave without limit
Secrets you kept
But at night when you slept
You must have suffered
Yet you were the buffer
This may sound just fine
To make something rhyme
But I know for sure
You opened the door
'Cause when we Fought
It was love you taught
You planted the seeds
And removed all the weeds
For the garden that grew
All the love that we knew

Dedication: In memory of Regina & Harry O. Kline (my parents) 1911–1997

Where The Children Play
Jessica Garton

Outside where the children play,
There is one face missing today.
A face of innocence, beauty, and trust,
Her portrait hangs with a slight hint of dust.
She's not at school where she should be,
And not outdoors where the eye can see.
Have you rechecked her house, looked under her bed?
She's not at the library, or behind the old shed.
"Not under here," you said with a sigh,
Maybe she's at the store for something to buy.
Where are those blue eyes, that face slightly round?
We've searched all the places where she should be found.
Still, outside where the children play,
No one's seen my friend Jon Benet.

Easy To Remember
Carole M. Erickson

Easy to remember
Never shall I forget
That warm summer evening
When we first met.
Your eyes so blue
Your cheeks so red
I knew from that moment
Some day we would wed.
Many years have now passed
As I look in the mirror
Remembering precious times
Will sparkle a tear.
Through good times and bad
Sometimes happy,
Sometimes sad
Our life together
Will always be
Easy to remember.

The Coming Fall
Tammy Smith

Summer days with friends brand new;
Times like these are all too few.
Love and laughter shared by all;
Good times won't end with the coming fall.

Fishing poles and music shows;
Every day the friendship grows.
Plans and dreams made by all;
Friendships won't end with the coming fall.

Summer days soon will end,
But friendships like these will never bend.
Good memories cherished by us all;
Friendship lives on in the coming fall.

World Peace Could Happen
Frederick A. Hassell, Jr.

World peace could happen if we don't fight,
World peace could happen if we all unite,
World peace could happen just you wait and see,
World peace could happen if you follow me,
World peace could happen it might be hard to do,
World peace could happen love will follow you,
It's all about everything, God knows what you are doing,
It's about world today and all we are choosing,
We should be here for one another and treat each other like sister and
    brother,
World peace could happen if we try with all our might,
World peace could happen then we would not have to fight,
World peace could happen every single day,
World peace could happen in a special way,
World peace could happen if we all try
World peace could happen then so many would not have to die,
World peace could happen and this is no lie,
World peace could happen if we just BELIEVE!

Our Great Sin
Jennifer Slaughter
They ripped His clothes
and took a whip and sliced it thru the air,
flesh, it ripped, and blood, it poured,
they took no thought to care.
Then they took a crown made of thorns
and crowed Him like a king,
the blood ran down His brow
and yet He spoke not anything.
Then they placed around His shoulders the finest of any linen,
all of this they did and not realize they were sinning.
Then a heavy cross He carried up a hill called Calvary
and three nails; two placed thru His hands, and one put thru His feet.
"It is finished!" are the words that make us see our great sin.
He did this for you, would you do this for Him?

Once I Had A Heart
J. Lee Bragg
Once I had a heart. That
I gave to you.
Now I have none, and you have two.
When I leave this old earth. To
heaven I will go. But you
Will have my heart. And I none
to show.
I will give back my pretty things.
On my fingers will be no rings.
Oh, my darling, please be true.
If I had a million hearts. I would
give them all to you.
Then we could hear sweet angels sing.
And we could show our wedding ring.
Then we would be so happy. Just
me and you. I would have back
my heart and you would have more
than two,...

Angels In The Sky
Kim D. Sallis
In the beginning, there was my father,
my mother, my brother, and I.

Father soon would have to love and
nurture us over a distant sky.

Mother's love grew stronger and delicate
as a dove. Together, our love my
mother, my brother, and I, grew as high
as angels in the sky. Never thought one
or more of us would die and fly as
high as angels in the sky.

First, mother then brother, and yet it
will be another. I, alike will fly
high as all the other angels in the sky.

The Lover's Red Rose
Mandy Monroe
Red Roses;
it sits there in its vase
with tarnished water.
you stop and smell it
every day.
but the longer it sits there
the more it dies.
the beautiful blood red
petals begin to wilt and
dry up, leaving them
darker then before.
it's almost like the lover's
love after time.
it begins to fade away.

Anne Frank
Nicole Nesse
Anne Frank, the most courageous of them all.
Hid from Nazis; Winter, Spring, Summer, and Fall.
She hid for several years,
With a great many fears.
She befriended a man named Peter Van Daan,
And wrote in her diary from her Dad.
She tried to be cheerful,
And not be so fearful.
Talked a lot to hide her fears,
Tried her best not to shed tears.
In her dream, saw her friend Lies,
And all she could do was cry.
When I think of how she tried,
It brings a tear to my eye.

Life
Kevin D. Bynum
At once I was at peace
With no clutter in my brain
Suddenly the hustle of social life
Fiercely driving me insane

Trying to reach for what was lost
Never acquiring a fair chance
Always feeling left behind
But that's all in the past

As I sit wondering when it all will come
Not understanding totally
where it all has gone
I simply realize, we must press on.

Dedication: Tasha, Brooke, and Little "O"

Standing On The Corner Of The Third World

Audrey Nadine Smith

We shall eat fear tonight
The taste sour and electric
It is bitter on our tongues
But more bitter in our bellies
No child should appease hunger with this
Our appetites draw us
To stand on the shore of tomorrow
To pray for a brighter dawn
To pierce the darkness that has crept
Through the souls of our nation
But tonight
We shall eat fear
As bullets sweep past our ears
Falling into the dust
We crawl upon bloodied dirt
Wondering, wondering
When will fear be kept at bay?
When will this mad hunger of intolerance stop?

The Broken Sword

Nicole L. Jordan

A gallant rider on a white horse overcome by darkness
Hears the moaning lisping wind.
The trees crying out in fear hiss
As their trunks and branches twist and bend.

The frenzy of the lapping waves continues
As they crush the fragile shells of the shores.
The swiftly moving deep black clouds
Encompass the heavens like a series of closed doors.

The rider weeps with sadness and wonder
As he prays in vain to save all above and beneath.
The brave valiant rider in a dark world of power
Is like a broken sword in a golden sheath.

Life

Karen Shipes

Sitting by a stream
Content to watch it flow
Birds singing brightly
Plants beginning to grow.

Relaxing in the shade
Happy just looking awhile
Children's happy times
And a baby's first smile.

Laughter and pain
Tears and smiles
All of these things
Make life worth while.

CHAPTER THREE

Personal Profiles

The following pages comprise concise personal profiles of the poets featured in this book, including pen names, occupations, special honors, other published writings and even personal goals and philosophical viewpoints. You will find that some are professional published writers, while others are appearing for the first time ever in print. But all of these poets have one thing in common: they are all compelled to reveal their feelings about life through creative expression in the form of words and verse.

EDITOR'S NOTE: *Please keep in mind that not all poets who have contributed to this book will appear in this chapter. All biographical information presented is specifically at the behest of each person listed.*

Author: Robert Abbate; **Birthplace:** Lansdale, PA; **Occupation:** Teacher; **Hobbies:** Camping; **Spouse's Name:** Sue; **Education:** B.A. Penn State 1982, M.A. U.S.F. 1994, University of San Francisco

Author: Anita D. Abbott; **Pen Name:** A.D. Abbott; **Birthplace:** Newport, VT; **Occupation:** Private Nurse; **Hobbies:** Writing, studying, crocheting, reading and traveling; **Memberships:** Hearts on Fire Ministries – Outreach Worker; **Children:** 4; **Grandchildren:** 3; **Education:** High School, Nursing, Course pertaining to my Nursing Career; **Personal Statement:** My goal as a writer – to touch another soul by my inspired writings.

Author: Alejandra Aguilar; **Birthplace:** Union City, NJ; **Occupation:** Student; **Hobbies:** Creative writing, painting, soccer, etc; **Personal Statement:** Writing poetry is my form of expressing my inner thoughts and feelings. I admire all poetry through its vibrant imageryand creative expression.

Author: Monica Regina Alston; **Pen Name:** Miss C. Brett; **Birthplace:** Prince Georges, MD; **Occupation:** Pharmacy specialist; **Hobbies:** Reading, writing essays; **Memberships:** Member of US Army; **Education:** Graduated BA/english from North Carolina Weslayan College; **Personal Statement:** All my 23 years of life, I have been at a struggle for words in conversation, but it has always seemed to come clear through denotation quite liberally. Writing freedom gives me that.

Author: Eva Anderson; **Birthplace:** Orlando, FL; **Occupation:** Registered nurse; **Hobbies:** Hand–crafts, reading; **Memberships:** NAFE, elder– 1st Presbyterian Church in Shawano; **Education:** BS/MS–nursing administration and health sciences; **Honors:** National honor society– high school; **Awards:** Nat'l nursing award for quality care plans from HMSS in TX; **Personal Statement:** Poetry is a release of emotions for the writer as well as an extension of themselves; for the reader it puts emotions into perspective.

Author: Jesus J. Arambulo; **Pen Name:** Susara; **Birthplace:** Manila, Philippines; **Occupation:** Professor of English and literature; **Hobbies:** Writing, reading, listening to classical music, tbn programs; **Memberships:** Association of Christian educators of the Philippines; **Spouse's Name:** Sylvia Martinez– Arambulo; **Children:** 2; **Education:** Finished associate in arts, bachelor of arts, master of arts (candidate PH.d); **Honors:** Honor roll listing; **Awards:** Professional and academic awards; **Published Works:** Poems published by "Caracoa", "Likha", and "The Paulinians"; **Personal Statement:** Writing poetry is not only to transcend the facts of earthly life but also to give glory to God's divine creation.

Author: Annie B. Arbuckle; **Pen Name:** Annie; **Birthplace:** Huston, MO; **Occupation:** Retired; **Hobbies:** Writing poems, songs and sewing; **Spouse's Name:** Robert Arbuckle, Sr.; **Children:** 5; **Grandchildren:** 11; **Education:** 7th Grade; **Published Works:** "Lonely World", my daughter published it in a small paper where she worked; **Personal Statement:** Don't let anyone talk you out of your dreams. Remember dreams do come true. You just have to believe and pray to the Lord.

Author: Laura Armstrong; **Pen Name:** Helen Archer; **Birthplace:** Elizabeth City, NC; **Occupation:** Education aide; **Hobbies:** Cooking, exercise, reading, travel, writing; **Spouse's Name:** Art Armstrong; **Children:** 3; **Grandchildren:** 1; **Education:** 1 1/2 yrs. college; **Personal Statement:** Children are our future and how we raise them will determine how our future will be.

Author: Gila Ashtor; **Birthplace:** Toronto, Canada; **Hobbies:** I enjoy Judo; **Memberships:** Private Martial Arts Club; **Education:** Entering Grade 9 in a Private School; **Honors:** 4 years in a row, Ontario Judo Champion; **Published Works:** National Library of Poetry, Poetry Institute of Canada; **Personal Statement:** I held my husband's hand so tight I soothed my newborn's whine, Now, the gift of yesterday is night and tomorrow's day – not yet mine!

Author: James Atkinson; **Birthplace:** Leeds; **Occupation:** Engineer; **Hobbies:** Travel and music; **Spouse's Name:** Margret Atkinson; **Children:** 1; **Grandchildren:** 3; **Education:** Secondary Modern; **Published Works:** All Involved Don't Say; **Personal Statement:** Writing makes me relax, also I can express myself. In words and verse. Special influences Captain Joe, Roy, Mick. Dad's Army.

Author: Magdalene P. Balloy; **Birthplace:** Grenada, British West Indies; **Occupation:** Cosmetics sales; **Hobbies:** Gardening, writing (book in progress; "Beyond The Darkness"); **Memberships:** International Society Poets– International Poetry Hall Fame; **Spouse's Name:** Arthur J. Balloy; **Children:** 3; **Grandchildren:** 2; **Education:** Self–educated; **Awards:** The National Library of Poetry, Editors Choice Award 3 times; **Published Works:** Beyond The Darkness, A Vision Of Hope, My Awakening; **Personal Statement:** In 1963, I was transformed by death–like experience, when Jesus appeared to me. Since that life changing event, I have developed a hungering need to express myself through poetry.

Author: Vivian Barraza; **Birthplace:** Indio, CA; **Occupation:** US postal service employee; **Hobbies:** Golf, reading, basking in the sun, entertaining friends/fami; **Memberships:** ly; **Education:** College of desent, management program; **Awards:** Athletic; **Personal Statement:** I have a real life story to tell and I want to do it in the form of a book. Expressing what I feel, through writing, isvery therapeutic.

Author: Angele Bassole–Ouedraogo; **Birthplace:** Ivory Coast; **Occupation:** Student/Free Lance Journalist; **Hobbies:** Reading and travel; **Spouse's Name:** Yvon Bassole; **Children:** 1; **Education:** Ph D Women's Poetry (Africa) Ottawa University plus a Degree in Journalism; **Awards:** French Foundation's Poetry Award (1993); **Published Works:** Burkina Blues (1997)/Freedom for Nelson Mandela (1986); **Personal Statement:** There are two things that make me feel at peace with myself–reading and writing. Doing only that, such is my deepest desire.

Author: Michele A. Bayer; **Birthplace:** Long Island, NY; **Occupation:** Elementary School Teacher; **Hobbies:** Writing, reading and fishing; **Memberships:** Professional Child Care Registry; **Education:** Bay Path College, M.A., B.A. in Psychology/Education Cum Laude; **Honors:** Maroon Key Honor Society; **Awards:** Suffolk County Writing Award, Student Leadership Award; **Published Works:** Children's Illustrations, Poetry, Suffolk Life Paper; **Personal Statement:** Writing helps me to reflect on the simple pleasures of life, helps me to nurture my soul, and is a creative self expression of my feelings.

Author: Tim Beck; **Birthplace:** Richmond, VA; **Occupation:** US–2 Missionary– United Methodist Church; **Hobbies:** Poetry, weightlifting, billiards and basketball; **Education:** BS– business administration from VA Commonwealth Univ– May 94; **Personal Statement:** My inspiration for this work comes from all of God's children and the special light they all have to share...in contribution to our world.

Author: Joseph Bertalan; **Birthplace:** Dante, VA; **Occupation:** Retired Music Teacher, Golf Coach, Church Music Director; **Hobbies:** Golf, gardening; **Memberships:** Methodist Church; **Spouse's Name:** Joyce P. Bertalam; **Children:** 2; **Education:** BM (WV University 1943), SMM (Union Theological Seminary, New York City 1953); **Honors:** Nat'l Boys Life Jr Golf Champ,'35, Who's Who Coll Studt '40; **Awards:** Tri St Golf Champ, Ashland KY '56, Who's Who in The East '50; **Personal Statement:** With all the hard fighting in WW II, I thank God for seeing me through it all "without a scratch".

Author: Judy M. Bertonazzi; **Birthplace:** Vineland, NJ; **Occupation:** Marketing Manager; **Hobbies:** Biking, camping, reading, writing; **Education:** Bachelor of Arts in Communications, Pre– M.B.A. Student; **Published Works:** What Glows At Me? 1997 The National Library of Poetry; **Personal Statement:** There is nothing more satisfying to the soul than seeing someone deeply moved by the written word.

Author: Philip J. Blackmore; **Birthplace:** St Albans, Hertfordshire; **Occupation:** Parts Manager (Motor Trade); **Hobbies:** Most sports and photography; **Spouse's Name:** Moira; **Education:** Secondary Modern; **Personal Statement:** Writing poetry is a way of giving my thoughts life and expresing emotion.

Author: E. Blagrove; **Birthplace:** St Pancras, London; **Occupation:** Retired Florist, Self Employed; **Hobbies:** Dancing, letter writing, verse jottings, reading, handy work; **Spouse's Name:** Alfred Charles (deceased); **Children:** 2; **Grandchildren:** 3; **Education:** Elementary; **Personal Statement:** Writing of the real world. Seeing life as it once was, can be, today and tomorrow. Peoples interest influences me with inspiration.

Author: Nicole M. Blair; **Birthplace:** Elmer, NJ; **Occupation:** Home Health Aide; **Hobbies:** Reading, writing, computers; **Memberships:** Library of Poetry Int'l; **Education:** Nursing School, Graduate – Vineland High School; **Published Works:** Lew, Mother and Dad

Author: Marilyn J. Blank; **Birthplace:** Portland, WI; **Occupation:** Quality control worker and real estate agent; **Hobbies:** Dancing, reading, gardening, writing, poetry; **Spouse's Name:** Raymond Blank; **Children:** 3; **Grandchildren:** 1; **Education:** High school and tech school; **Personal Statement:** I love to write poetry because it gives my mind a challenge to create and put my deepest thoughts and feelings into words.

Author: K. T. Blue; **Pen Name:** Misty Blue; **Birthplace:** Wilmington, DE; **Occupation:** Writer/Photographer; **Hobbies:** Pondering the mysteries of life; **Memberships:** Smithsonian, Nat'l Conservatory, Library Of Congress; **Spouse's Name:** Kevin; **Children:** 2; **Grandchildren:** 1; **Education:** St Elizabeth High School, Goldie Beacom College, Neuman College and Writers Digest School; **Published Works:** Cover of "Purpose", August 17, 1997; **Personal Statement:** My work is a journey through difficulty, loss and acceptance in the hope that others may more easily find their own path to understanding and hope for the future.

Author: Jamie Bower; **Birthplace:** Winslow, AZ; **Hobbies:** Writing poetry; **Education:** Cave City High School; **Personal Statement:** My only way to express what's inside is writing what I feel.

Author: Rebecca Brand; **Birthplace:** Hanford; **Occupation:** Attend Riverdale High School; **Hobbies:** Writing poetry, reading poetry; **Education:** Attending 11th grade; **Personal Statement:** I think the best way to share your thoughts without speaking is writing; poetry is within your soul.

Author: Teresa Brereton; **Pen Name:** Teresa Lynn; **Birthplace:** Hagerstown, MD; **Occupation:** Mother and Student; **Hobbies:** Loving those around me; **Children:** 3; **Education:** Currently in College for Nursing; **Honors:** Dean's List; **Personal Statement:** God's love and the Book of Romans has been my inspiration, not just for writing but for how I should live my life. Thank you Lord!

Author: Sharon A. Brown; **Birthplace:** Memphis, TN; **Occupation:** Teacher; **Hobbies:** Reading, writing, traveling, dancing, piano; **Memberships:** International reading assoc. TN ed assoc, Memphis ed asso; **Children:** 2; **Education:** Univ of Memphis BS home econ, MS community health, Med curriculum and instruction; **Honors:** Intro into kappa delta pi education honor society; **Awards:** Heroes and homefolk, favorite teacher, pathways to teaching; **Published Works:** Nutrition ed article published in the Tri–State Defender local newspaper); **Personal Statement:** Writing says all that I ever wanted to say but could not say out loud. It is my soul speaking.

Author: Kuran Anne Brown; **Birthplace:** Mobile, AL; **Occupation:** Territory Mgr – Alpha Photo; **Hobbies:** Photography and travel; **Memberships:** National Parks Assn and Nat's WildLife Assn; **Spouse's Name:** Julius Dale Brown; **Children:** 1; **Education:** Graduated – Memphis Tech High School; **Honors:** Celebrated 30th Wedding Anniversary! 1967–1997; **Published Works:** Tennessee Fall In The Smoky Mountains, – Nat'l Library of Poetry (in; Anthology – A Sea of Treasures 1995); **Personal Statement:** In my poetry, I want the reader to "see what I see" or "feel what I feel" as I express scenes or emotions.

Author: Judith Brown; **Birthplace:** Keyport, NJ; **Occupation:** Fleet Manager, The Hertz Corporation; **Hobbies:** Gymnastics, writing poetry; **Memberships:** Amer Assoc Motor Vehicle Admins, US Gymnastics Federation; **Education:** BS – Michigan State University, MS – Keyport, MS; **Honors:** HS–Senior Edition YrBk, Nat'l Honors Soc, MSU Var Athlete; **Awards:** 1929 Jr Olymp Championships, Wash DC Nations Capt Cup Gymn; **Personal**

Statement: Jesus Christ is my inspiration and the Bible is the greatest book I have ever read!

Author: Debbie Brown; **Pen Name:** Pretty Woman; **Birthplace:** San Antonio, TX; **Occupation:** Professional fashion model; **Hobbies:** Garage sales, buying anything for resale, writing; **Children:** 2; **Grandchildren:** 5; **Education:** A "Mazin" modeling school; **Personal Statement:** Writing is an expression of one's most personal inner thoughts. Only those who write enjoy and understand the depth of these heartfelt emotions.

Author: Orri D. Brown; **Birthplace:** Miami, FL; **Occupation:** Substitute teacher/full time student; **Hobbies:** Writing poetry, dancing, basketball; **Memberships:** Order of the eastern star, heroines of jericho; **Education:** Florida State University; **Personal Statement:** Jealousy, Come Home

Author: G. B. Browning; **Birthplace:** Forest Gate; **Occupation:** Retired; **Hobbies:** Gardening, darts, painting, writing poetry; **Spouse's Name:** Victor Hugo; **Children:** 4; **Grandchildren:** 7; **Personal Statement:** My poetry comes from my heart.

Author: Melanie Bruce; **Pen Name:** Melanie Earleywine; **Birthplace:** Atlantic, IA; **Occupation:** Waitress; **Hobbies:** Reading, writing, crosswords, and cross stitch; **Spouse's Name:** Divorced; **Children:** 2; **Education:** High School; **Awards:** For Volunteering (YMCA and Ball V Fire Dept); **Personal Statement:** Writing is the best way for myself to express how I'm feeling and what my thoughts are. My inspirations are my children.

Author: Ladele M. Buckman; **Birthplace:** Newport, WA; **Occupation:** Student; **Education:** Currently a junior in high school; **Honors:** Made the honor roll my freshman and sophomore year; **Personal Statement:** Let no one depise your youth, but be an example to the beliefs in word, in conduct, in love, in spirit, in faith, in purity.

Author: Tatiana Burgess; **Pen Name:** Tatiana; **Birthplace:** Brooklyn, NY; **Occupation:** Nurse; **Hobbies:** Reading, music; **Memberships:** Nat'l Student Nurses Assoc, Amazing Grace Choir; **Education:** B.A. in Political Science, BSN degree from New York Univ 1999; **Honors:** Who's Who among Students in Amer Colleges and Universities; **Personal Statement:** I thank and praise my Lord and Savior Jesus Christ. He has always been my inspiration.

Author: Laverne E. Burns; **Birthplace:** Canada; **Occupation:** Real Estate Associate; **Hobbies:** Writing, crafts, gardening; **Memberships:** Lake Elsinore Chamber of Commerce; **Spouse's Name:** Russell E. Burns; **Children:** 3; **Grandchildren:** 1; **Education:** High School Grad, 2 Years College; **Honors:** Charter Member Wom Club; **Awards:** Dept of Human Relations, L.A. County, Others from 15 Years; **Published Works:** Many News Articles, Active Charity Works; **Personal Statement:** My son has been disabled since the age of three. Presently, I am trying to publish a children's series. Let's know God's special gift!

Author: Nancy Bursik; **Birthplace:** Sierra Vista, AZ; **Occupation:** Sales Associate and Housewife; **Hobbies:** Writing poetry and reading; **Memberships:** National Poets Society; **Spouse's Name:** Matthew J. Bursik, Jr.; **Children:** 1; **Education:** High School Graduate; **Honors:** National Honors Soc, Who's Who among Amer H S Students; **Awards:** Editor's Choice Award, National Library of Poetry; **Published Works:** Memories, Feelings, Time to Set me Free; **Personal Statement:** My goal as a poet is to have my own book published. My writing is a part of my life. This poem "Love" was written by myself for my wedding. Each guest received a special copy, now I'm pleased to share it with all of you.

Author: Celeste Cabibi; **Birthplace:** Cedar Rapids, IA; **Hobbies:** Poetry, drawing and writing; **Education:** High school (sophomore); **Personal Statement:** I know when I get older, I want my career to be based on one of my arts. To me an art is someone's talent, their art. I was taught to make use of any talent that I had. My talents are poetry, drawing and writing.

Author: Lisa Cagle; **Birthplace:** North Carolina; **Occupation:** Teacher's Assistant; **Hobbies:** Bowling; **Spouse's Name:** Thomas Cagle; **Children:** 1; **Personal Statement:** I will always give thanks to the Lord for all the knowledge, wisdom, and abilities that he gave me. I enjoy going to church, and being with my family and loved ones. I'm just enjoying Jesus!

Author: Robert Calco; **Pen Name:** Andrew Carnes; **Birthplace:** Cleveland, OH; **Occupation:** Financial Planner, Entrepreneur; **Hobbies:** Writing, reading, traveling, study of economics, history; **Spouse's Name:** Olga Calco; **Children:** 2; **Education:** Obtained Autodidactically, experientially and despite 3 yea rs of Liberal Arts; **Personal Statement:** The phenomena of daily life do not stare out at us with an obvious meaning: they must be interpreted. Good fiction of whatever genre or form must illuminate this process in some meaningful way.

Author: Matthew A. Caldwell Hooper; **Pen Name:** Matthew Albert Caldwell; **Birthplace:** Palo Alto, CA; **Occupation:** Cashier; **Hobbies:** Writing, poetry, basketball; **Education:** High School, passed with G.E.D.; **Personal Statement:** My poems deal with reality through my eyes and from what others tell me about experiences they have had. My failures have helped in life.

Author: Glen Cambridge; **Birthplace:** Barking, Essex; **Occupation:** Deputy Night Manager; **Hobbies:** Travel and listening to all types of music; **Education:** Mayfield High School, Dagenham; **Personal Statement:** Thoughts are like oxygen, we need them to survive, so when painted on by thought remember, "The harm in trying cost the air we breathe."

Author: Mary Jeanne Carlin; **Birthplace:** San Francisco, CA; **Occupation:** Road maint worker; **Hobbies:** Fishing and camping; **Memberships:** NRA; **Spouse's Name:** James Cook; **Children:** 3; **Education:** High school; **Awards:** Parent of the year '96; **Personal Statement:** As a single mother raising 3 boys in the middle of the 'hoodthis tree has weathered many a storm and still stands tall and strong.

Author: Timothy S. Carlton; **Birthplace:** Griffin, GA; **Occupation:** Quality Auditor at NACOM (Griffin); **Hobbies:** Writing poetry, listening to music; **Education:** Griffin High School Graduate; attended Griffin Technical Institute; **Honors:** Desert Storm Vet; **Awards:** U.S. Army – Army Commendation Award, Army Achievement Medal; **Personal Statement:** Thank God for the special talent that I have, also thank everyone who has inspired me to strive for success.

Author: Aleata Carpenter; **Birthplace:** Port Alberni, BC, Canada; **Occupation:** Secretary; **Hobbies:** Hiking, swimming, and all aspects of nature; **Children:** 2; **Personal Statement:** Thank you to my brother, Bad Piatka, and Walter Collins (wild life artists) who combined their talents on canvas with mypoetry, in tribute to the eagle.

Author: Robert A. Carroll; **Birthplace:** Columbus, IN; **Occupation:** Production Associate; **Hobbies:** Fishing, camping; **Memberships:** North American Fishing Club; **Spouse's Name:** Mary Ruth Carroll; **Education:** High School and Computer Programming Training; **Personal Statement:** When I fish alone I have all the beauty around me, to think and write. I also have a wonderful wife to write poems to and to inspire me to write.

Author: Kandice Carter; **Birthplace:** Cleveland, OH; **Hobbies:** Writing poems, plays, songs, singing, dancing, talking/phone; **Memberships:** Member of Pilgrim Church of Christ; **Education:** High School Graduate of Martin Luther King L.P.S. and entering College

Author: Barbara L. Celello; **Pen Name:** B.L.Sea (AKA); **Birthplace:** Merced, CA; **Occupation:** Ex Secr, Model & Instruct, Cust Serv Rep, Caregiver to husb; **Hobbies:** Writing, reading, gardening, dance and exercise, tennis; **Memberships:** SCBW Society of Childrens Book Writers; **Spouse's Name:** William F. Celello Sr.; **Children:** 3; **Grandchildren:** 2; **Education:** College–Major: English, Secretarial Science; Minor: Music; **Honors:** Sealbearer(HS), Las Madrinas(HS Merit Org), Scholarship Soc; **Awards:** ICL(Instit of Childrens Lit) Graduate –Advanced; Comm Serv; **Published Works:** San Fernando Poetry Journal; Diet Journal; Community Publications; **Personal Statement:** As a longtime caregiver to my paraplegic husband, I deeply appreciate life's gifts, both physical and spiritual; external essence begins from within ourselves.

Author: Melva Chandler; **Birthplace:** McAlester, OK; **Occupation:** Cashier/Waitress; **Hobbies:** Writing and needlepoint crafts; **Children:** 2; **Education:** High school diploma – semester at vocational school; **Published Works:** "A Letter To Heaven"; **Personal Statement:** My goal, as a writer, is to find a publisher to review all of my poems and create a book of poetry.

Author: Gerald Chokas; **Pen Name:** Lone Wolf; **Birthplace:** Bowie, TX; **Occupation:** Self Employed; **Hobbies:** Guitar, seclusion; **Children:** 1; **Education:** High School, 25 years everyday experiences; **Personal Statement:** Infatuation is easy; true love takes time. Yes, thank you for this one vision of truth. I shall most surely forget.

Author: Allegra Leigh Clark; **Birthplace:** Arlington Heights, IL; **Occupation:** Homemaker; **Hobbies:** Reading, movies, baking; **Memberships:** Sigma Alpha Chi and Good Shepherd Hospital Auxiliary; **Spouse's Name:** Thomas T. Clark; **Children:** 1; **Education:** BA in sociology at Carthage College, Kenosha WI; **Personal Statement:** As a writer, my main inspiration has been my daughter, Sarah. I try to express intense emotions through my writing that are otherwise difficult to express.

Author: Roberta D. Coleman; **Pen Name:** 82804–Sexy–Dee; **Birthplace:** Chicago Heights; **Occupation:** Homemaker; **Hobbies:** Reading, writing, cooking, meeting people, taking walks; **Children:** 3; **Grandchildren:** 1; **Education:** Finish grammar school, three yrs in high school; **Awards:** One award for poem, "Lonely–Lover"; **Personal Statement:** Yes I'm getting back in school, so that I can become the writer that I know one day I will become. Did two yrs. and half of a nonfiction writing.

Author: Eileen M. Colvin; **Birthplace:** Dillion, SC; **Hobbies:** Cooking, writing and cross stitching; **Personal Statement:** Writing poetry or just writing at all is what I like to do best, besides cross–stitching I am good at too.

Author: S. Connell; **Birthplace:** Liverpool; **Occupation:** Customer Service Tele–clerk; **Hobbies:** Decorating, gardening, bird watching; **Children:** 2; **Education:** Litherland High School; **Published Works:** Alpha and Omega; **Personal Statement:** If "every picture tells a story" – then "every poem reveals a thought." Poetry enables memories to exist forever.

Author: Dana M. Cooper; **Birthplace:** Hot Springs, AR; **Hobbies:** Horseback riding, reading, swimming; **Education:** Attending Second Baptist Christian Academy; **Personal Statement:** I would really like to thank my sixth–grade teacher. She was the one who first saw that God had given me this talent.

Author: Ida Corradino; **Birthplace:** Brooklyn, NY; **Occupation:** Legal Secretary; **Hobbies:** Writing poems, painting, bowling; **Spouse's Name:** Angelo; **Children:** 2; **Personal Statement:** Since high school, writing poems has been my own personal way of keeping a diary of events in my life. I enjoy writing, and feel it gives me the opportunity to put on paper my innermost feelings.

Author: Regina Anne Cosenza; **Pen Name:** Regina Bianco–Consenza; **Birthplace:** Elmont, NY; **Occupation:** Bookkeeper; **Hobbies:** Loving my children; **Spouse's Name:** Vic Consenza; **Children:** 3; **Education:** B.A. Speech/Theatre/English, St John's University 1975; **Honors:** Sigma Alpha Eta Speech Honor Society; **Personal Statement:** I believe every writer's soul has been touched by some special person responsible for inspiring the dream. My heartfelt thanks and prayers to George Cevasco.

Author: David A. Crawford; **Birthplace:** Cuba City, WI; **Occupation:** Concrete Construction Worker; **Hobbies:** Fishing; **Memberships:** Poets' Guild; **Education:** B.S. Social Science; **Published Works:** Approved for publishing in the anthologies Treasures and Best New Poems; **Personal Statement:** It is my goal to be the author of poetry books and the author of the lyrics of popular songs.

Author: Forrest Crawford; **Birthplace:** Wyatt, MO; **Occupation:** Social Worker; **Hobbies:** Writing, KEDO; **Spouse's Name:** Margreite; **Children:** 4; **Education:** B.S. in Social Work; **Honors:** Four times on the Dean's List; **Personal Statement:** "Coming of Dawn", an anthology

Author: Patricia A. Creem; **Birthplace:** New Haven, CT; **Occupation:** R.N.; **Hobbies:** Writing poetry; **Spouse's Name:** Charles William; **Children:** 3; **Grandchildren:** 5; **Education:** University of Bridgeport; **Honors:** Magna Cum Laude; **Awards:** Nurse of the Year – '96; **Published Works:** A Grandmother's Gift; **Personal Statement:** Different situations in my life have inspired me to express my thoughts by writing poetry. It has proved to be relaxing and creative.

Author: Lillis Cruz; **Pen Name:** Abigail Sean; **Birthplace:** Salt Lake City, UT; **Occupation:** Laundry Production; **Hobbies:** Homemaking, writing, arts and crafts, painting; **Spouse's Name:** Tom; **Children:** 2; **Education:** High School, Some College; **Published Works:** Only One Touch – Sparrowgrass Poetry Forum; **Personal Statement:** I have divine inspirations, for my works. I write what I feel or how I can feel from someone's viewpoint. I give glory to God.

Author: Katie Curlett; **Birthplace:** Princeton, NJ; **Occupation:** Student; **Hobbies:** Soccer, skiing, volunteer work, ski instructor, music & art; **Education:** Presently a 10th grade student at Lawrenceville School; **Awards:** Science; **Personal Statement:** Accept the challenges so that you may feel the exhilaration of victory.

Author: Hal Cutcher; **Pen Name:** Hal Cutcher; **Birthplace:** Buffalo, NY; **Occupation:** Retired; **Hobbies:** Tennis, hiking, swimming; **Spouse's Name:** Phyllis; **Children:** 2; **Grandchildren:** 2; **Education:** BC Math, Unv of Buffalo, 1949; **Personal Statement:** Writing is my portrait, in words, of life.

Author: Samuel Dartey–Baah; **Birthplace:** Ghana; **Occupation:** Geodetic Engineer; **Hobbies:** Travel, writing and debating; **Spouse's Name:** Sandra; **Education:** Graduated University Of Science And Technology, Ghana, Bachelor of science engineering; **Published Works:** May It Be, Flow Out, Beauty–Step Magazine (Ghana), Radio Reflections, Ghana Broadcasting Corportation; **Personal Statement:** If we write understanding our hearts, emotions and thinking of the people, we shall have many readers.

Author: Patricia A. Davey; **Birthplace:** Portland, OR; **Occupation:** Retired; **Hobbies:** Photography, gardening; **Memberships:** Astara; **Spouse's Name:** Fred G. Davey (deceased); **Children:** 1; **Grandchildren:** 1; **Education:** Lewis and Clark College –3 years, U of Wh (Night School), St U (Night School); **Honors:** Honored by Lewis and Clark College for poetry 1985; **Awards:** Listed in current "Who's Who In The West"; **Published Works:** Assay, Prospor's Cell, EPOS, Cedar Rock, Venture In, NEXOS, etc.; **Personal Statement:** Writing for publication has been my life's ambition. For me there is no greater thrill. Poetry is the highest form of language.

Author: Pauline Davis; **Birthplace:** Colfax, LA; **Occupation:** Education; **Hobbies:** Writing, reading, concerts, travel and plants; **Memberships:** Little Cypress Baptist Church, TCTA, 55 Plus, AARP; **Children:** 1; **Grandchildren:** 2; **Education:** High School, Business College, Some College; **Honors:** Outstanding School Service; **Personal Statement:** Now that I am approaching retirement I hope to write and would like to write songs and a book about the life of my family.

Author: Mark Dawson; **Birthplace:** Evergreen Park, IL; **Occupation:** Physician (M.D.); **Hobbies:** Music, guitar, piano, harmonica and composition; **Spouse's Name:** Grace; **Children:** 2; **Education:** College, Univ of Illinois (Urbana, Il), Medical School, University of Il (Chicago); **Honors:** Eagle Scout; **Personal Statement:** "Twins" was inspired by premature twins I tirelessly cared for at Cook County Hospital in Chicago. After surviving two weeks they died 30 minutes apart.

Author: Lori Dearth–James; **Pen Name:** Lori Dearth–James; **Birthplace:** Lima, OH; **Occupation:** X–ray Tech in Lander, Wyoming; **Hobbies:** Writing, reading, playing with my children; **Spouse's Name:** Mike James; **Children:** 3; **Education:** Graduated Parks Junior College, Thomton, Colorado; **Honors:** Dean's List; **Personal Statement:** Poetry entered my life following the unexpected death of my sister, Cheryl. Writing gave me a freedom to express my feelings; I've been writing since.

Author: Martha–Claire Denniff; **Birthplace:** Chesterfield; **Occupation:** Student (University); **Hobbies:** Horse riding, reading; **Education:** Currently studying at King Alfreds College, Winchester; **Honors:** BA in English and Drama; **Personal Statement:** Writing poetry is my way of making sense of this world and escapism from long lonely nights when my boyfriend is away at war.

Author: Paula Denning; **Pen Name:** Paula D.; **Birthplace:** Ilminster; **Occupation:** Student; **Hobbies:** Music, cooking and drama; **Education:** Wadham Community School; **Personal Statement:** I usually do not write with a goal in mind. I just write how I feel from what I see and what I believe in.

Author: Frances Dew; **Pen Name:** Frankie; **Birthplace:** Preston, GA; **Occupation:** Banking and Customer Relations; **Hobbies:** Writing, singing and traveling; **Memberships:** Speakers Club of America and Business/Professional Women; **Education:** Business Professional, Pasadena City College; **Honors:** Writer's Forum List; **Awards:** N.A.A.C.P.; **Published Works:** Columbus Times Newspaper and Naz Baptist Church, Co, Ga; **Personal Statement:** Writing is my kindred spirit. It is healing for the "Soul." It keeps my energy flowing. I have great admiration for poets Maya Angelou and Nikki Giovanni.

Author: Marina M. H. Dib; **Birthplace:** Cairo, Egypt; **Occupation:** Singer/Composer/Lyricist; **Hobbies:** Music, theatre, mystical studies, travel, dance; **Memberships:** Var org that save animals' lives, defend & encourage respect; **Education:** Foreign Languages; **Honors:** V Principal's Honor Roll and Home Economics Cert of Merit; **Awards:** Best Comedy Actress in College Talent Competition; **Personal Statement:** Singing in twelve languages, various styles. I hope to be offered a recording contract soon and realize my dream of being a successful international performer!

Author: Lauren DiDonato; **Birthplace:** Manhattan; **Occupation:** Student; **Hobbies:** Piano, softball and writing; **Personal Statement:** I enjoy piano playing for the last 4 years. I have been writing stories since the day I learned to spell and hope writing is in my future because it's what I love.

Author: Deborah Dietrich; **Pen Name:** Deb–a–Roo; **Birthplace:** Cincinnati, OH; **Occupation:** Customer Service, Human Resources; **Hobbies:** Writing, country music, movies, dancing, entertaining; **Spouse's Name:** Cary James Bush; **Children:** 3; **Grandchildren:** 2; **Education:** Graduated High School, College, Business Training Courses; **Published Works:** Have wrote others to submit; **Personal Statement:** My writings are the best way for me to communicate my most inner feelings to those I care most about. These are inspired by my faith in God and my love for life and people.

Author: Jigme Dojee; **Birthplace:** Kham, Tibet; **Occupation:** Tibetan Translator for Tara Coll of Tibetan Medicine; **Hobbies:** Poems, stories and reading books; **Education:** At College at present Physical and Life Sciences/Previous Schooling in Tibet and India; **Personal Statement:** Having left my homeland during the Alhral Revolution, I am very fortunate in being able to be of service in preserving the Tibetan tradition.

Author: Beverly Dollarhite; **Birthplace:** Kalamazoo, MI; **Occupation:** Homemaker; **Hobbies:** Writing, sewing, traveling; **Memberships:** Maple Grove Baptist Church; **Spouse's Name:** Ted Dollarhite; **Children:** 4; **Grandchildren:** 4; **Education:** High School; **Personal Statement:** My high school English teacher taught through several poets. Then on essay day she said we could write a poem. Thank you Mrs. Eiserman.

Author: Lynne Donahue; **Birthplace:** Providence, RI; **Occupation:** Self–employed, food business; **Hobbies:** Boating, animals, country music; **Education:** Seekonk High School, Seekonk, MA

Author: Susan Doty; **Birthplace:** Anchorage, AK; **Occupation:** Student; **Hobbies:** Gardening, crochet, reading, sewing; **Spouse's Name:** Jeremy Doty; **Children:** 3; **Education:** Palmer High School, City College of Chicago (pursuing AA degree); **Published Works:** National library of poetry; **Personal Statement:** My poetry has been inspired by my life and the lives of those around me. My favorite poets are Robert Frost and Conrad Aiken.

Author: Scott Douglas; **Birthplace:** Fort Worth, TX; **Hobbies:** Soccer, tennis, collecting dalmation stuff; **Memberships:** FFA,

NHS, choir; **Education:** 11th grade; **Personal Statement:** You must go for things even if they seem impossible to win.

Author: Petronella Dowell; **Pen Name:** Joyce or Peachie; **Birthplace:** Sioux Falls, SD; **Hobbies:** Reading and writing poetry; **Spouse's Name:** John Pack; **Children:** 5; **Grandchildren:** 8; **Honors:** To be living a life God set forth for me.; **Awards:** To be loved unconditionally by God; **Personal Statement:** We all are rich in God's love. For it is He who gave us life and the opportunity to learn from it.

Author: Angie Easterly; **Birthplace:** Sequatchie, CO; **Hobbies:** 4–wheelers, music, friends; **Awards:** Two Poetry Awards; **Published Works:** She, Love Lost, and You; **Personal Statement:** To those who helped me see the light through the eyes of a rainbow. I love you! Community Baptist Church. (J.C.M.B.C.)

Author: Lisa Edwards; **Birthplace:** Ft. Oglethorpe, GA; **Occupation:** Supervisor at K–Mart; **Spouse's Name:** Kenneth Donald; **Children:** 1; **Education:** North Cobb High, Acworth GA– graduated; **Personal Statement:** My poetry is a window into my soul

Author: Sherry Ellis; **Pen Name:** Ashley Norton; **Birthplace:** Bell; **Occupation:** Medical Billing; **Hobbies:** Writing, painting and decorating; **Spouse's Name:** Loyd Ellis; **Children:** 2; **Grandchildren:** 3; **Education:** College student; **Published Works:** Dreaming in Metaphors – National Library of Poetry; **Personal Statement:** I have control in what I write and to see the accomplishments in my writing is a reward in itself.

Author: Kimberly Elmore; **Birthplace:** Charleston, SC; **Occupation:** Server, King Charles Inn; **Hobbies:** Reading, writing, my pets and skating; **Spouse's Name:** Jeffery A. Elmore; **Education:** 9th Grade; **Awards:** Several for poetry and writing in my school days; **Personal Statement:** My influences comes from my mother, Josephine House, who overcomes any tragedy in her life, and has taught me to be strong and stand alone.

Author: Brenda Elzey; **Pen Name:** Ebony Timbers; **Birthplace:** Salisbury, MD; **Occupation:** Computer technology teacher; **Hobbies:** Computers and traveling, writing poetry; **Children:** 3; **Grandchildren:** 5; **Education:** Master's degree in Urban Education– Rowan University; **Honors:** President's list, Dean's list; **Personal Statement:** To be able to share one's thoughts and feelings through poe ry, is God given. To God be the glory.

Author: Donna M. Erickson; **Birthplace:** Kearny, NJ; **Occupation:** Beautician and School Bus Driver; **Hobbies:** Reading and punch embroidery; **Spouse's Name:** Joseph Erickson; **Children:** 1; **Education:** Natural Motion School of Cosmetology; **Personal Statement:** Life is so very short. Live every day as if it was your last and always keep love in your heart!

Author: Keith M. Estes; **Birthplace:** Elmira, NY; **Occupation:** High School Student; **Hobbies:** Basketball, writing; **Education:** Honor Student in High School; **Honors:** Honor Roll; **Awards:** Student of the Month; Math Award, Language Arts Award, etc; **Personal Statement:** I got the idea for this poem from things I've seen and been through in my life. My only goal as a writer is to write a lot of good poems that aren't published.

Author: Nancy Everett; **Birthplace:** Chattanooga, TN; **Occupation:** Registered nurse; **Hobbies:** Golf, martial arts, cross stitch; **Spouse's Name:** Van; **Children:** 1; **Education:** Associates degree in nursing

Author: Karen Farmer; **Birthplace:** Laurinburg, NC; **Occupation:** Student; **Hobbies:** Writing, reading, cooking and gardening; **Children:** 2; **Education:** International Air Academy–1989–1990, Central Carolina Community College–1977 – currently; **Personal Statement:** My inspiration comes from everyday experiences of life. This poem is an acknowledgement to all the "Janes" in the world who have encountered domestic violence.

Author: Sarah Fausett; **Birthplace:** Stuttgart, Germany; **Hobbies:** Reading, writing, and music; **Education:** Entering the 7th grade in the fall of 97; **Honors:** Presidents award for education excellence; **Awards:** Civic oration award; **Published Works:** "Our Courage", in anthology of poetry by young americans 1997 edition

Author: Anita M. F. Fischer; **Birthplace:** Ipswich, England; **Occupation:** Biophilian Bodywork Specialist; **Hobbies:** Travel, reading, writing and dance; **Memberships:** American Soc of Alternative Therp; Assoc of Bodywork & Massg; **Spouse's Name:** Wilbur G Fischer; **Children:** 5; **Grandchildren:** 1; **Published Works:** A Summer Journal, 1969; **Personal Statement:** Regarding the soul's search for God, life's road having brought me understanding, my lifework now is sharing my balancing philosophies of body/mind/spirit integration.

Author: Flora Flinders; **Birthplace:** Ashland, KY; **Hobbies:** Writing and typing; **Spouse's Name:** Glenn Flinders; **Children:** 4; **Personal Statement:** I write poems because I love to write them. They all come from the love within my heart.

Author: Angel Flores; **Birthplace:** San Antonio, TX; **Occupation:** Gas Plant Operator; **Hobbies:** Writing poems, short stories, collecting sports memorabilia; **Spouse's Name:** Sandra Flores; **Children:** 1; **Education:** Some College; **Honors:** I consider getting this poem published an honor; **Personal Statement:** My goal is to write a book that makes it to the top 10 on the best seller list.

Author: Warren L. Foster; **Occupation:** Banker; **Hobbies:** Travel; **Memberships:** Global Network for spiritual success – Deepak Chopra; **Awards:** N. L. P. Editor's Choice Award; **Published Works:** "Peace of Mind", "And In His Dream"; **Personal Statement:** Our friendships in life are gifts to be cherished.

Author: Samantha P. Freeland; **Pen Name:** Samantha Priscilla Freeland; **Birthplace:** California; **Occupation:** Health care worker and artist; **Hobbies:** Composition, poetry, songs, stories, music, gardening; **Children:** 1; **Education:** High school honor grad, business college honor grad, english, accappella, art, junior college honors; **Awards:** English scholarship, business eng. overall excellent student; **Personal Statement:** I am thankful for all that I have met in life, for I have learned to love and express love through my heart and hands.

Author: Sharon Fulkroad; **Birthplace:** Reading, PA; **Occupation:** College Student; **Hobbies:** Writing, sewing, music, reading, painting; **Spouse's Name:** Harold Fulkroad (deceased); **Children:** 2; **Education:** High School, Pursuing Degree in Medical Assisting; **Personal Statement:** I have been inspired by my late husband who told me to believe in myself and that I could do anything.

Author: Debra E. Garrett; **Birthplace:** Mt Camel, IL; **Occupation:** Waitress; **Hobbies:** Volleyball, crafts, drawing, poem writing; **Spouse's Name:** Bryan Garrett; **Children:** 3; **Education:** GED; **Honors:** Beautician License; **Personal Statement:** I can write my best poems when I'm alone and going through a situation that I'm at the time of really feeling what I'm thinking and writing.

Author: Sandra Gaulke; **Birthplace:** Sac City, IA; **Occupation:** Work for the state of IA– dept of human services; **Hobbies:** Writing, reading, sewing, singing, cake decorating; **Memberships:** American business womans assoc. past treas, past sec; **Spouse's Name:** Kevin L. Gaulke; **Children:** 6; **Grandchildren:** 10; **Education:** High school, teaching certificate from Wilton College; **Honors:** Top Eleaenta in my class; **Awards:** Woman of the yr in 1994 for american business womans assoc; **Published Works:** Personal for friends for them to present as gifts; **Personal Statement:** As a single parent for quite awhile, I discovered words exp ressed in writing mean more than those verbally spoken.

Author: Edwin Gibson; **Birthplace:** Lubbock, TX; **Occupation:** Retired Early; **Hobbies:** Writing and gardening; **Memberships:** Kappa Sigma, Rotary Club, Charter Mem, US Horse Calv Assoc; **Spouse's Name:** Frances; **Education:** College Degree; **Honors:** Other Published Works in Hard Bound Books; **Published Works:** Music Lover's Cook Book, Collected Stories and Essays (some Poetry); **Personal Statement:** Even in Grammar School, I wrote poetry as easily as I breathed. I spend my time gardening and writing. I have a novel and screen play in production.

Author: Jane Gilbert; **Birthplace:** Dexter, ME; **Occupation:** Retired; **Hobbies:** Gardening, crafts and painting; **Memberships:** GFWC Dexter womans literary club– sunshine club; **Spouse's Name:** Graydon; **Children:** 4; **Grandchildren:** 8; **Education:** High school; **Personal Statement:** Writing poetry is a form of meditation for me.

Author: Sandra Glassman; **Pen Name:** Melodee; **Birthplace:** Brooklyn, NY; **Occupation:** Piano Teacher; **Hobbies:** Reading, writing poetry and stories – composing music; **Memberships:** Amer Coll of Musicians–NAR–ABI, ISAA, Intnl Soc of Poets; **Spouse's Name:** Stewart; **Children:** 2; **Education:** High School; **Awards:** Numerous Awards from Sparrowgrass, Iliad, Press, etc.; **Published Works:** 9 Editors Choice Adwards NLOP – Poetry on the Internet, poem/music in Holocaust Archives, Washington, D.C.

Author: Linda F. Grace; **Birthplace:** Kingsville, TX; **Occupation:** Cook; **Hobbies:** Reading, writing poems, cooking; **Spouse's Name:** Scott R. Grace; **Children:** 3; **Grandchildren:** 1

Author: Judith Grant; **Birthplace:** Sioux City, IA; **Occupation:** Clinical Nurse Specialist; **Hobbies:** Horses, computers and travel; **Memberships:** Nat'l League For Nursing, 5 nat'l councils for nursing; **Children:** 1; **Education:** Master's degree in nursing administration and clinical nurse specialist in gerontology; **Honors:** Who's Who In American Nursing, Who's Who Of American Women; **Awards:** Expert Nurse–1991 CA Nurses Association; **Published Works:** "The Reverend's Tear" (short story) in Siouxland: an anthology 1995; **Personal Statement:** Writing has been integral to my clinical work and also a powerful tool for dealing with personal trauma. Pen is mighty when I feel not.

Author: Laura Greene–Patton; **Birthplace:** San Bernardino, CA; **Occupation:** Retired secretary; **Hobbies:** Reading, writing, computer; **Memberships:** AARP senior center; **Spouse's Name:** Hubert (Pat); **Children:** 3; **Grandchildren:** 9; **Education:** High school, computer– adult education; **Published Works:** Life Is A Day, Do You Remember?, local newspaper; **Personal Statement:** When I write a poem, I share my thoughts.

Author: Nancy S. Gregory; **Birthplace:** Reno, NV; **Occupation:** Retired; **Hobbies:** Travel, gardening, grandchildren, animals; **Memberships:** The nature loving club; **Spouse's Name:** Ernest C. Gregory; **Children:** 2; **Grandchildren:** 7; **Education:** High school, some college and just living life; **Published Works:** "My Prayer", "A Dream Or A Glimpse Of God" and "Life's A Bea"; **Personal Statement:** Life is hard, but we should strive to live it to the fullest because it is just one stop along the way toward a great beyond.

Author: Kris Gregson; **Birthplace:** Newton, MA; **Occupation:** Artist; **Hobbies:** Writing music and poetry; **Education:** I am a senior in a high school with country gardens; **Awards:** Won an essay contest for a piece called "Oil Spills"; **Personal Statement:** The inspiration for all that I do is my father in heaven. I praise him for these talents, also the support of my parents and fiance.

Author: Stan Gresswell; **Birthplace:** Cottingham on Hull; **Occupation:** Retired; **Hobbies:** Writer of novels; **Children:** 7; **Grandchildren:** 5; **Education:** Elementary secondary school; **Personal Statement:** I get inspiration in writing my novels and would love to have one published, if only I could find a good publisher.

Author: James Gribben; **Birthplace:** Coatdyke, Coatbridge; **Occupation:** Retired C.I.S. Agent; **Hobbies:** Fishing, gardening; **Spouse's Name:** Letitia Gribben; **Children:** 9; **Grandchildren:** 16; **Published Works:** A Walk in Memory Lane, Coatbridge, Why; **Personal Statement:** Long may the poet's dream, for therein lies mankinds desires...

Author: Diane Groth; **Pen Name:** Diane Dalum Groth; **Birthplace:** Clintonville, WI; **Occupation:** Retired; **Hobbies:** Crafts; **Education:** Metropolitan College of Business–University of Wisconsin; **Personal Statement:** May these few words touch the hearts and lives of others. No poet could ask for more.

Author: Wanda Hancock Rohman; **Birthplace:** Salem, AR; **Occupation:** Teacher (Retired); **Hobbies:** Oil painting, reading, church and writing poetry; **Memberships:** Historical Society, OK Retired Teachers Assoc, Art Assoc; **Spouse's Name:** Deceased; **Children:** 2; **Grandchildren:** 5; **Education:** Degree from OK State University; **Awards:** Writer's Conferences Awards; **Published Works:** Poems in Reflection, Anthologies; **Personal Statement:** Life's flame plays briefly upon times's stage. Rugged country life,

caring parents, teachers and grandmother Pearl influenced me. Inspirations – life experiences and God's beautiful creations.

Author: Richard Hannaford; **Birthplace:** Seattle, WA; **Occupation:** English Professor; **Hobbies:** Golf, camping, water gardening; **Memberships:** Rocky Mountain Modern Lang Assoc; **Spouse's Name:** Mary A Hannaford; **Children:** 4; **Grandchildren:** 3; **Education:** Ph. D. Indiana University; **Honors:** Ford Foundation, Woodrow Wilson Fellow; **Published Works:** Scholarly articles on Dickens, Richardson, Scott, Hardy

Author: Julie B. Harper; **Birthplace:** Rose Hill, NC; **Occupation:** Housewife; **Hobbies:** Cooking, gardening, reading; **Spouse's Name:** Charles R. Harper; **Children:** 1; **Education:** High school, 1 yr college; **Honors:** Dean's list; **Personal Statement:** Poetry is a beautiful form of art I've always admired. With God all things are possible. Thank you for the inspiration, Charles

Author: Charles R. Harper; **Birthplace:** Rose Hill, NC; **Hobbies:** Painting, writing, collects antiques; **Spouse's Name:** Julie B. Harper; **Children:** 3; **Education:** High school grad 1971; **Published Works:** "Time", A Tapestry Of Thoughts, What Will I Leave Behind, "The Long And Winding Road"; **Personal Statement:** Poetry is an expression captured to give the reader the complete thought, not to be misunderstood by ignorance nor kneel at the dictates of peers.

Author: Michael Hatter; **Birthplace:** Washington, DC; **Occupation:** Sales/Marketing; **Hobbies:** Music, weightlifting, reading and fishing; **Memberships:** YMCA; **Education:** Graduated Oak Hill Academy; **Honors:** Dean's List; **Awards:** (Poetry In Print) honorable mention; **Published Works:** Quill Books, National Library Of Poetry, The Amherst Society; **Personal Statement:** Writing has always been a way of expressing my thoughts and feelings. The heart and mind are the food for creative activity.

Author: Viola V. Hayes; **Pen Name:** Vi Hayes; **Birthplace:** Corfu, NY; **Occupation:** Housewife; **Hobbies:** Knitting, quilting and crafts; **Memberships:** 1st VP society of military widows chpt 6, Western Hills Ch; **Spouse's Name:** James R. Hayes (deceased); **Children:** 2; **Grandchildren:** 2; **Education:** High school and 1 yr of college at Arizona State University; **Awards:** Many 1st, 2nd and 3rd place ribbons for knitted articles; **Published Works:** Morning and My Country– National Library of Poetry; **Personal Statement:** When life gives you scraps– make a quilt.

Author: Joan E. Hayes; **Birthplace:** Washington, DC; **Occupation:** Supervisor, AT&T; **Hobbies:** Writing, working with children, drawing cartoons; **Spouse's Name:** McKinley Mann Hayes; **Children:** 3; **Grandchildren:** 4; **Published Works:** A short collection of poems on internet "Beyond the Waterfall"; **Personal Statement:** Conversations only last a brief time but written inspirational words flourish to develop the mind.

Author: William Helton; **Pen Name:** Charles Dahmer; **Birthplace:** Seymour, IN; **Occupation:** Journalist; **Hobbies:** Reading books by Dean Koontz; **Memberships:** First Southern Baptist Church; **Awards:** Solo 1st Class Award; **Personal Statement:** Life is on the threshold of non–existence, as we chop down another enemy and use it as shelter.

Author: Sandra Hernandez; **Birthplace:** Bronx, NY; **Occupation:** Biller, coder; **Hobbies:** Painting, writing, reading (scripture); **Memberships:** Church, union, hispanic cultural committee at MMC; **Children:** 2; **Education:** H.S.; **Personal Statement:** "Peace radiates from within and illuminates its surroundings".

Author: Tina–Marie Hesse; **Birthplace:** St Petersburgh, Fl; **Occupation:** Insurance Broker; **Hobbies:** Reading, knitting, arts/crafts, pen–paling, coll. dolls/mask; **Memberships:** s Billy Ray Cyrus Fan Club, Leann Rimes Fan Club, Double Day; **Education:** Graduated High School 1985; **Honors:** Junior Varsity Tennis in Jr HS, Honor List in Senior Year; **Personal Statement:** Billy Ray Cyrus was my influence for this work as well as another poem that I wrote about him and his musical career.

Author: Gareth M. Hogg; **Pen Name:** Gareth Miles; **Birthplace:** Bury St. Edmunds; **Occupation:** Semi Retired; **Hobbies:** Gardening, reading, D.I.Y.; **Spouse's Name:** Phyllis; **Children:** 2; **Grandchildren:** 2; **Personal Statement:** I used to find some poetry difficult to grasp. I try to bring everyday situations to all people with my poems.

Author: Sue H. Horn; **Birthplace:** Milford, MI; **Occupation:** Certified Medical Asst/Homemaker; **Hobbies:** Crewel embroidery, singing in my church choir; **Memberships:** LWML, at my church; AAMA, medical affiliation; **Spouse's Name:** William; **Children:** 3; **Grandchildren:** 6; **Education:** Associates degree in applied science; **Honors:** Laude notation on diploma; **Awards:** Golden Poets Award & honorable mention for 2 other poems; **Published Works:** "Words From My Mind And My Heart", book of poems I wrote; **Personal Statement:** This poem and the others from my book are dedicated to God, who gave me the ability to put my thoughts and feelings down on paper. He has shown me the beauty of all things. I am thankful I can leave these poems for my grandchildren.

Author: Peter K. Horne; **Birthplace:** Newport, Monmouthshire; **Occupation:** Retired Seafarer & Personnel Manager; **Hobbies:** Work practises and their relevance to life; **Spouse's Name:** Ivy Claire Horne; **Children:** 2; **Grandchildren:** 2; **Education:** General and Nautical; **Awards:** 1st Mates Certificate F.G.; **Personal Statement:** "In the beginning was the word"; ie communication and practice giving life to all things through affection of purpose; the anima mundi; as relevant today, as ever.

Author: Derrick Horner; **Pen Name:** Conbrad Colt; **Birthplace:** Akron, OH; **Occupation:** Warehouse manager for the Akron Beacon Journal, actor/model; **Hobbies:** Songwriting, listening to hard–core, honky tonk county music; **Memberships:** Tennessee Songwriters Assoc. Int'l & Nashville Songwriters; **Education:** Grad from Garfield High School 1988, attended Univ of Akron, Got a diploma in broadcasting from Ohio center broadcasting; **Honors:** Merit and honor rolls; **Awards:** 1st in city wide accounting test, 2nd in internat'l acting; **Personal Statement:** Behold, Jesus is coming quickly, as his reward is with him, to render to every man according to what he has done. Revelation 22:12

Author: Cheryl W. Howell; **Birthplace:** San Francisco, CA; **Occupation:** Legal Secretary; **Spouse's Name:** William J Howell; **Children:** 2; **Education:** B.A. Sociology and Psychology – Loma Linda University; **Personal Statement:** I am fascinated with the process of children using their genetics and environment to create the people they become.

Author: Stephen D. Hunt; **Birthplace:** Dayton, OH; **Occupation:** Correction Officer; **Hobbies:** Scuba diving, travel and fishing; **Spouse's Name:** Linda; **Children:** 1; **Education:** High school graduate

Author: Sharon C. Hunter; **Birthplace:** Port Washington, WI; **Occupation:** Licensed Practical Nurse; **Hobbies:** Reading, cooking, crafts and painting; **Memberships:** PTA, Parish Nurses of Zion United Church of Christ; **Children:** 5; **Education:** Graduated Evansville School of Practical Nursing; **Awards:** Volunteer of The Year, Lincoln Elem 1995; **Published Works:** Several Civic Articles in Local Newspapers; **Personal Statement:** It is my belief that reading is the cornerstone for life. To expand your mind with the written word brings joy to the world.

Author: Christina Hurst; **Birthplace:** Danville, IN; **Occupation:** University student; **Hobbies:** Music, writing (poetry and music); **Education:** Business finance undergraduate; **Honors:** Homecoming queen; Who's Who, a honor roll; **Awards:** Senior high faith and practice award; **Personal Statement:** I want to say thanks to two very big influences that I've had. Mom and Dad– you guys are the greatest – I love you!

Author: Frances Hutson; **Birthplace:** Columbia, SC; **Occupation:** Wife, Mother, Foster Mother; **Hobbies:** Collecting angels, writing songs, poetry, photo albums; **Spouse's Name:** William F. (Buddy) Hutson; **Children:** 2; **Grandchildren:** 4; **Published Works:** Some of my poetry has been published in Foster Parent Publications; **Personal Statement:** The inspiration and influence that guides me is a spiritual one. It comes from God!

Author: Onin–Age Iron; **Birthplace:** Chicago, IL; **Occupation:** Writer – Journalist; **Hobbies:** Writing, philosophy, history, poetry, fiction; **Memberships:** Chicago Council on Foreign Relations;

Spouse's Name: Feliz Tormenta; **Education:** Law Degree – LaSalle; **Published Works:** Hundreds of poems in small presses; **Personal Statement:** Poetry is the ultimate art form, for it absorbs and conveys the essence of all other art forms—music, dance, art, sculpture—into clearest thought.

Author: Walid Issa; **Birthplace:** Lebanon; **Occupation:** Actor; **Hobbies:** Writing and reading; **Education:** BA in theater; **Honors:** Dean's List three times

Author: Mary Jacobsen; **Birthplace:** Manchester; **Occupation:** Royal Norwegian Emigre Government – British Embassy–retired; **Hobbies:** Music, opera, literature; **Memberships:** WRVS, NADEAS, O50, U3A, Are Council; **Spouse's Name:** War Veteran Herbert Jacobsen; **Education:** Girls High School – Cardiff College; **Honors:** Presented: H.M. King Olay of Norway 1980; **Awards:** Arthritis and Rheumatism Council for Research (21 Yrs Awrd); **Personal Statement:** Education as a liberator is beyond price.

Author: Bridget Jameus; **Birthplace:** Elliot Lake, Ontario, Canada; **Occupation:** University Student (major; french and psychology); **Hobbies:** Creative writing, drawing and dancing; **Education:** I have a degree in developmental services worker and now enrolled in Algoma University; **Personal Statement:** Through all my hardships I write. What I cannot tell peopl e I write down. Writing is therapeutic for my heart and sou.

Author: Cody A. Jennings; **Pen Name:** Zio; **Birthplace:** Shreveport, LA; **Occupation:** Computers/ games; **Hobbies:** Writing to good music; **Personal Statement:** This is but 1/3 of the original, influenced by everyone who helped me realize who I am. I hope to write screenplays among other things.

Author: Anthony P. Jones; **Birthplace:** Oswestry, Shropshire; **Occupation:** Unemployed; **Hobbies:** Reading, writing and arts; **Personal Statement:** On the passing of a child from a world where little has been learned, to a place where even less is known.

Author: Aaron Jones; **Birthplace:** Dover, DE; **Occupation:** Student; **Hobbies:** Music, art, hard work; **Education:** Savannah College of art and design– current student; **Honors:** Governor's school for excellence in art; **Personal Statement:** Poetry is more than just linking words together. It is a representation of all that encompasses the human condition.

Author: Stephen L. Jones; **Birthplace:** McGehee, AR; **Occupation:** Student in College/Justice Wielding Vigilante; **Hobbies:** Baseball, writing; **Education:** Graduated McGehee High School, May 9 1997; **Awards:** Beta Club Ar Creative Writing & Nat'l Writing Champion 1997; **Personal Statement:** I appreciate The Poetry Guild for having a contest that opens up to new, unpublished poets and places the emphasis on creativity and originality.

Author: Tammy D. Jones; **Birthplace:** Albany, GA; **Occupation:** School; **Hobbies:** Basketball, softball, track and field, writing poems; **Children:** 6; **Education:** High school; **Awards:** MVP for basketball, best short story writer; **Personal Statement:** Before I read about poetry guild, I used to just let my poems sit, then I decided to send one of my poems in, and because I live in a place where people think they can't make it,ithad me down, semifinalists came, I felt I could do anything

Author: Nicole L. Jordan; **Birthplace:** Mobile, AL; **Occupation:** Student (High School); **Hobbies:** Writing and reading poetry, coin collection, pin collection; **Education:** College Bound High School Senior; **Honors:** Murphy HS Nat'l Honor Soc., Who's Who Among Amer HS Students; **Awards:** Honor and Merit Awards throughout High School; **Published Works:** Stars, Anthology of Poetry by Young Americans; **Personal Statement:** Poetry is my way of expressing my feelings or creativity. Thank you Mom, Dad, Marirose, and Kevin for all of your love and support.

Author: Muriel Joshua; **Occupation:** School Monitor; **Hobbies:** Knitting fishing nets, poetry; **Memberships:** Central SOA Church, ADRA, St Croix Red Cross; **Children:** 5; **Grandchildren:** 8; **Education:** High School; **Honors:** Certificate of Recognition, USA Copyright Registration; **Awards:** Toastmstrs Intern'l Poetry, Fund of Acct, Intro to Cmpt, typ; **Personal Statement:** Poetry is like a sweet intensifying music of the soul of all who appreciate its worth. I am anticipating a brighter future because of it.

Author: Matthew R. Jubak; **Birthplace:** Huntington Beach, CA; **Occupation:** Bartender/sales promotions; **Hobbies:** Extreme sports; **Memberships:** LA boxing/North American Fishing Club; **Education:** Edison High School graduate, certificate of mixology; **Awards:** Honorable mention (iliad press); **Published Works:** What Did I Do?; **Personal Statement:** Philosophy; Life is a never–ending experience. Goal as a writer: Touch people so they will remember me. Inspirations: Younger brother Joshua Jubak; Jim Morrison.

Author: James P. Kass; **Birthplace:** Dubuque, IA; **Occupation:** Professional Driver; **Hobbies:** Traveling, meeting people; **Personal Statement:** My goal, is to reach into the hearts and minds of millions of readers. Their feelings of awe and admiration, is my greatest reward.

Author: Sandy Keith; **Birthplace:** Conway, SC; **Occupation:** Nurse's assistant; **Hobbies:** Writing, walking; **Spouse's Name:** Robert (Bob) Keith; **Children:** 2; **Education:** Harry Georgetown Tech College; U.S. Army; **Honors:** Dean's list; honor grad– U.S. Army Morse Code School; **Personal Statement:** At present, I plan to continue writing for the fun and further my nursing education. I would also like to try writing stories and children's books.

Author: Diane Appling Kelley; **Birthplace:** Washington, DC; **Occupation:** Accounting Clerk; **Hobbies:** Reading, writing, bowling and camping; **Memberships:** Emmanual Baptist Church; **Spouse's Name:** Gregory; **Children:** 1; **Education:** High School Graduate (1973); **Personal Statement:** God has given me a sister with a heart of gold who encourages me to put my thoughts on paper in good and bad times, and to one day fulfill my goal of being a novelist.

Author: Gregory L. Kelly; **Occupation:** Warehouse Manager; **Hobbies:** Writing poetry; **Memberships:** Co Flemings President Club, International Society of Poets; **Spouse's Name:** Leona Kelly; **Children:** 4; **Grandchildren:** 4; **Education:** High School; **Honors:** 2 Editor's Choice Awards for 1996; **Awards:** Employee of the Year for 1985–86, Copy–Right Award for 1996; **Published Works:** A Tapestry of Thought, Best Poems of The 90's and Spiritual Messages of Hope; **Personal Statement:** I live only to serve God and to do His will, in everything, that I do and to bring the lost souls to his church.

Author: Hazel V. Kemp; **Birthplace:** Whitehall, WI; **Occupation:** Homemaker; **Hobbies:** Lapidary, seamstress, beadstringing, crochet and knitting; **Memberships:** Order of the Eastern Star, Royal Neighbors of America; **Spouse's Name:** Chester R (deceased); **Children:** 2; **Grandchildren:** 4; **Education:** High School; **Honors:** Worthy Matron, OES, Eagle Scout, 2 Editor's Choice Awards; **Awards:** U.S.A.F. Wife; **Published Works:** "There's A Whole World of Happiness", "After Fifty–Three Years", "My Mean Parents"; **Personal Statement:** I believe in strong family ties, God and the opportunities in this country.

Author: Diane Kennedy; **Birthplace:** Pennsylvania; **Occupation:** Elementary School Teacher; **Hobbies:** Writing, cross stitch/needlework; **Spouse's Name:** Thomas Kennedy; **Children:** 4; **Grandchildren:** 2; **Education:** Bachelor Degree – Summa Cum Laude – St Leo College; **Honors:** Phi Theta Kappa – International Honor Society; **Awards:** Phi Theta Kappa Hallmark Award – Poetry; **Published Works:** "January", "Little Sister"

Author: Rebecca Keyes; **Birthplace:** Fort Smith, Ark; **Occupation:** CNA, PCA; **Hobbies:** Poetry, singing, dancing, crafts; **Education:** Attending Lincoln School Commerce (medical assisting); **Awards:** Singing and crafts; **Personal Statement:** I want to thank my parents for all their support and love and God above for the gift I am about to receive, my baby.

Author: Yelena Khmelnitskaya; **Pen Name:** Yelena Khmelnitkaya; **Birthplace:** Russia, Moscow; **Occupation:** Student; **Hobbies:** Playing piano, violin; **Education:** 2nd year in college, John Jay College; **Personal Statement:** I think life would become easier if people would share their thoughts with each other, and poetry is a very interesting way to do that.

Author: Kathy E. Kinser; **Pen Name:** Kathy Kinser; **Birthplace:** Detroit, MI; **Occupation:** Homemaker, writer; **Hobbies:** Travel, photography, reading; **Memberships:** PEO, womens symphony guild, medical alliance; **Spouse's Name:** David E. Kinser; **Children:** 2; **Education:** BA Illinois State Univ; **Awards:** 1987 Kodak photography award; **Published Works:** Co–author of book, Puppy Stuff; **Personal Statement:** I enjoy pulling words out of the air that best convey my thoughts. What better way to succeed than through poetry?

Author: Alice W. Klos; **Birthplace:** Rochester, NY; **Occupation:** Retired; **Hobbies:** Sewing, Art Pastel Pictures, Crafts; **Spouse's Name:** Deceased; **Children:** 5; **Grandchildren:** 12; **Personal Statement:** I have written poems since I was 13. I sent one to my cousin, she insisted I enter your contest and so did my friends.

Author: Tadeusz T. Kosnikowski; **Birthplace:** Inowroclaw, Poland; **Occupation:** Translator (redacteur–traducteur en quatre langues); **Hobbies:** Gardening; **Memberships:** Veterans association (World War II); **Spouse's Name:** Teresa Kosnikowska; **Children:** 2; **Grandchildren:** 4; **Education:** MBA (London–England); **Personal Statement:** Inspired by ASOP's. "Wise people don't trust flatterers"s

Author: Christopher Kulovitz; **Pen Name:** Corin Amick; **Birthplace:** Chicago, IL; **Occupation:** Advertising Copywriter; **Hobbies:** Poetry, nature, theater; **Memberships:** A Hopeful to the Poetry Guild; **Education:** Always continuing; **Published Works:** Black Hands, (Xpressions Journal); **Personal Statement:** My philosophy on life transcends into my writing; think loud, speak soft.

Author: Grace Ellen Kurth; **Birthplace:** Tomahawk; **Occupation:** Homemaker; **Hobbies:** Crafts and poetry; **Children:** 2; **Education:** 12th High school; **Personal Statement:** My poems come from my heart and soul. I base them on moments of inspiration and events in my life time.

Author: Robert Labescat; **Birthplace:** Capbreton, France; **Occupation:** Medical Doctor; **Hobbies:** Travel, photography, poetry; **Spouse's Name:** Divorced; **Children:** 2; **Education:** Graduate, Medical University of Bordeaux, France; **Awards:** 2nd prize, poetry, U of Populaire of St Nazaire/96–1st 1997; **Published Works:** Un Hiver Au Fond Du Puit (a collection of poems); **Personal Statement:** Live for today, for tomorrows are illusion and yesterdays are only the stones that support the present.

Author: Brenda T. LaFerriere; **Birthplace:** Lowell, MA; **Occupation:** Assembler; **Hobbies:** Writing, painting by number, arts and crafts; **Spouse's Name:** Raymond G. Comtois; **Children:** 1; **Education:** Graduated in 1982 with honors from Greater Lowell Regional Vocational High School; **Personal Statement:** I have always written poems and I would like one day for someone to read them besides myself. People told me that I should become a poet. I love to show my feelings but have a hard time, through poetry this is my way to show how I feel

Author: Violet Langland; **Pen Name:** Granny Heart; **Birthplace:** Indpls, IN; **Occupation:** Disabled; **Hobbies:** Writing; **Spouse's Name:** Martin (deceased); **Children:** 5; **Grandchildren:** 10; **Education:** 8th grade

Author: Nancyann Laroche; **Birthplace:** Richford, VT; **Occupation:** Paraprofessional for two years; **Hobbies:** Writing poems/fiction stories, drawing, painting, singing; **Memberships:** "HomeTown Follies", raising money for meal sites/elderly; **Education:** High School Graduate; **Personal Statement:** Two fiction stories for future publishing. The characters are my family and friends by their personalities. My present work is the sequel to the first.

Author: Penny Lawson; **Birthplace:** Dayton, OH; **Occupation:** Laborer and CMA; **Hobbies:** Reading, writing, listening to music, collecting miniatures; **Spouse's Name:** Divorced; **Children:** 3; **Education:** GED; **Published Works:** Poem – Reflection of Me; **Personal Statement:** Philophscial viewpoint – survive and be an overcomer. Goals as a writer – to be consistent and profitable

Author: Wilson P. Levron; **Pen Name:** Wilson Paul Levron II; **Birthplace:** Gulfport, MS; **Occupation:** Maintenance pipefitting, steel fitting, welding; **Hobbies:** Writing–reading–auto mechanics–tape player–small appl repair; **Memberships:** Lifetime member NRA, lifetime MS Gulf Coast, comm. college; **Spouse's Name:** Diane Levron; **Education:** Harrison Central Sr High

School–1974, MG.C Comm College 1976 sophomore class rep. Perkinston MS–1978, Long Beach, MS; **Personal Statement:** Thanking God for my education, I have always enjoyed reading many different types of books and poetry, I recommend this to anyone.

Author: Jerrianne Lindekugel; **Birthplace:** Marshfield, WI; **Occupation:** Housewife; **Hobbies:** Poetry, music, glass engraving, horseback riding; **Spouse's Name:** Travis L Lindekugel; **Children:** 3; **Education:** High School and 2 Yrs Technical College – Associate Accounting Degree; **Personal Statement:** "Mama's Tears" is a recollection of a very difficult memory for me and my mom, which has now become a symbol of triumph and courage to us both, and hopefully to others.

Author: Amy Linden; **Birthplace:** New Rochelle, NY; **Occupation:** Office Mgr, RTC for Retarded/Handicapped Children; **Hobbies:** Learning to enjoy life and discover myself; **Education:** Graduate NRHS, Berkeley Secretarial School; **Personal Statement:** I began writing poetry in June 1997 and in two months, 90 words spring forth; my memories and goals. It's not too late to live.

Author: Arleen J. Lindenmayer; **Pen Name:** Arleen Jeanette Lindenmayer; **Birthplace:** Guntersville, AL; **Occupation:** Sewing Machine Operator; **Hobbies:** Drawing and writing; **Spouse's Name:** Divorced; **Children:** 2; **Grandchildren:** 2; **Education:** GED at Wallace State College; **Personal Statement:** Without a doubt I know the words I write come to me on the wings of the Holy Spirit. For I write for Him, for the purpose of spiritual healing.

Author: Barbara Littlejohn; **Birthplace:** Itasca, TX; **Occupation:** Housewife and Part Time Child Care Provider; **Hobbies:** Arts and craft, plants, flowers, reading; **Spouse's Name:** Robert L LittleJohn; **Children:** 3; **Grandchildren:** 5; **Education:** Graduate; **Honors:** Good Grades – Teacher's Helper; **Awards:** Ribbons – Plaques; **Published Works:** I write Rhymes; **Personal Statement:** I wanted to be an artist, but that didn't work out too good for me. I said I am going to keep trying until I find something.

Author: Elmer Lovan; **Birthplace:** Willow Springs, MO; **Occupation:** Retired railroad engineer; **Hobbies:** Gardening, travel; **Memberships:** First Baptist Shawnee, KS, Brotherhood Locomotive engineers; **Spouse's Name:** Ella Maire Lovan; **Children:** 5; **Grandchildren:** 11; **Education:** High School; **Honors:** Learn how to obey God; **Awards:** Good health for 80 years; **Personal Statement:** I can envision a wagon with the 3R's riding in state. But we need 2 more R's to pull. I name responsibilty & respect pulling the other and reading, writing. Teach our children the 5R's and be proud of them at school, shopping mall & home

Author: Layne Lucas; **Birthplace:** Madrid, Spain; **Occupation:** Student; **Hobbies:** Song writing, poetry, guitar, piano; **Memberships:** Nashville songwriters association; **Education:** Starting 10th grade; **Awards:** Perfect attendance; **Personal Statement:** My writings are my testimony, I hope to touch the hearts of all. Influences are; Pam Rose, Pat Bunch, Maryann Kennedy, Katrina Kontol and Michelle Naylor.

Author: Damon E. Luke; **Birthplace:** Bronx, NY; **Occupation:** Student at Lincoln University; **Hobbies:** Poetry, reading, sports collecting; **Memberships:** Young Entrepreneurs Program (Columbia University); **Education:** Junior at Lincoln University, graduate of Manhattan High Sc hool; **Honors:** 3rd place Lincoln University poetry contest

Author: G. Milton Luttrell; **Pen Name:** G. Milton Luttrell; **Birthplace:** Brooksville, FL; **Occupation:** Environmentalist and Structural Masonry Specialist Contr; **Hobbies:** Woodwork and old car/truck enthusiast; **Memberships:** Florida Water and Pollution Control Operators Association; **Spouse's Name:** Betty A; **Children:** 2; **Education:** B.S. Florida State University Med University of Florida; **Honors:** Distinguished Member International Society of Poets; **Awards:** Golden Poet Award, World of Poetry, Sacramento, CA 1988; **Published Works:** Several poems in National Library of Poetry Anthologies; **Personal Statement:** "Conformity is the glue that holds society together, while non–conformity is the catalytic agent that inspires originality."

Author: Cheryl LynnHeart; **Pen Name:** Yvonne Lynnheart; **Birthplace:** Stayton, OR; **Occupation:** Home Computer Business and Writer; **Hobbies:** Writing, singing, creating pretty objects; **Memberships:** Inter–Faith Ministries, Writers Di, Full Gospel Bible Coll; **Children:** 2; **Education:** Graduated Associate Degree in Business and Communications; **Honors:** Business Scholarship, Americorp, Service to Comm Scholarship; **Awards:** Poetry Contest and Publishing in Poetry Guild; **Published Works:** Church of God of Prophecy – Newsletter; **Personal Statement:** It is my goal as an Inspirational Writer to passionately share the sweet love, of Jesus as I reach out to others in my writing!

Author: Julie Mahoney; **Birthplace:** Framingham, MA; **Occupation:** Adminstrative asst; **Hobbies:** Horseback riding, hiking; **Spouse's Name:** Thomas Mahoney; **Education:** Associates in small business, Dean College– Franklin MA; **Personal Statement:** A writer can be inspired by many different people and places, but a good writer writes from their heart. Gods gift to all poets.

Author: Peggy Marasco; **Birthplace:** Altoona, PA; **Occupation:** Homemaker/Retired Hair Stylist; **Hobbies:** Crafting and community theatrer; **Spouse's Name:** Ralph; **Children:** 2; **Education:** Bishop Guilfoyle High School, Altoona Area Vocational Technical School; **Personal Statement:** Of all the handicaps that we face daily, ignorance is the most debiltating.

Author: Janice March; **Pen Name:** Linda; **Birthplace:** Chester, PA; **Occupation:** Receptionist; **Hobbies:** Bike riding, art, reading, traveling, writing; **Children:** 3; **Education:** High school grad, (GED diploma), certified secretary; **Awards:** Certificate (completed writer's digest school of fiction); **Personal Statement:** The movie industry inspired me to become a fiction writer someday. I want to express myself to the world through my stories of mystery, suspense and drama.

Author: Troy Marshall II; **Birthplace:** Catlett, VA; **Occupation:** Student at Liberty High School; **Hobbies:** Soccer, marching band, Christian fellowship, writing poems; **Memberships:** Marching band, J.V. soccer team, winter guard; **Education:** 10th grader; **Personal Statement:** Writing poetry is a way to express the true feeling from inside your heart. Poetry comes from anywhere and everywhere. To all poets, "Good luck".

Author: Inna J. Martin; **Pen Name:** Joy Carter; **Birthplace:** Bloomington, IL; **Occupation:** Wife, Mother, Writer; **Hobbies:** Writing, reading, arts and crafts and sewing; **Memberships:** National Honor Society, U.S. Army Veteran; **Spouse's Name:** Ronald Carter; **Children:** 7; **Grandchildren:** 1; **Education:** Herzing Business Institute, Jefferson State Jr College; **Honors:** National Honor Society; **Awards:** Upward Bound Program (Miles College), Youth Tutoring Program; **Personal Statement:** Writing poetry is a gift of the spirit. I have always valued heart gifts of expressed words. To write is uplifting to my soul.

Author: Minerva Martinez; **Birthplace:** Haskell, TX; **Occupation:** Asst Manager (Ranchito Restaurant); **Hobbies:** Travel, photography, camping, walking; **Memberships:** Worland Community Concerts; **Education:** Graduated Worland Senior High; **Personal Statement:** I give all praise and glory to God's Kingdom. My family made it possible, encouraged and believed in me, that I would be fine in the end.

Author: Bloody Feathers Mayo; **Birthplace:** Merced; **Occupation:** Tattoo artist; **Hobbies:** Drawing, tattooing, and making Indian jewelry; **Memberships:** AIM– american indian movement; **Spouse's Name:** Dancing Moon Mayo; **Education:** 11th Grade; **Honors:** 2nd Place in spelling bee contest in 2nd grade; **Awards:** 1st Place diarama contest; **Personal Statement:** I'm hoping to have as much success with my upcoming book I'm writing, as I have with this poem. Thanks to Dancing Moon , I have learned to write, understand, and appreciate poetry!

Author: Norma Jean McCann; **Birthplace:** Wuerzburg, Germany; **Occupation:** Dairy Queen; **Hobbies:** Reading, writing, skating, fishing, playing pool; **Spouse's Name:** William J. McCann, Jr.; **Education:** GED, Air Force, Life

Author: Shari McCollum; **Pen Name:** Shari Lee; **Birthplace:** Great Lakes, IL; **Occupation:** Nursing assistant; **Hobbies:** Playing saxophone, reading, spending time with my children; **Memberships:** Manitowoc marine band, green bay camera club; **Children:** 3; **Education:** Grad 1993 from Marion College of Fond du Lac (BS psychology urrently attending Lakeshore Tech College for nursing; **Personal Statement:** Sometimes it is easier to sort out the confusion in your mind by writing it down on paper then move forward a clearer goal.

Author: Kristina S. McCreary; **Pen Name:** Kristina Sally McCreary; **Birthplace:** Illinois; **Occupation:** Housewife and Mother; **Hobbies:** Drawing; **Spouse's Name:** Billy A McCreary, Jr.; **Children:** 2; **Education:** High School Graduate – Served in the Army; **Personal Statement:** My writing has never been any good until I married my husband 3 years ago on July 20, 1994. He's written many poems and inspiring letters to me over the years. So I give thanks to my husband, Billy Alton McCreary, Jr.

Author: Inola M. McGuire; **Pen Name:** Maureen McGuire; **Birthplace:** St Vincent, West Indies; **Occupation:** Business Education Instructor; **Hobbies:** Writing, travel and cooking; **Memberships:** Nat'l Business Educ Assoc, Intn'l Society for Business Educ; **Children:** 1; **Education:** Graduated Lehman College, Bronx, NY; **Personal Statement:** Writing poetry and short stories are forms of relaxation for me. My desire is to write an Oscar winning screen play.

Author: Arieona R. McKune; **Birthplace:** Eugene, OR; **Occupation:** Certified Nursing Assistant; **Hobbies:** Writing, travel, painting woodcrafts; **Spouse's Name:** Alfredo B. Munoz; **Children:** 1; **Personal Statement:** My loving, supportive fiancee Alfredo, the father of my beautiful young daughter Samantha, is the inspiration for most of my work.

Author: Sandy Meloche; **Pen Name:** Sasha; **Birthplace:** Windsor, Ontario; **Occupation:** Housewife, mother; **Hobbies:** Writing, walking; **Spouse's Name:** Terry Meloche; **Children:** 4; **Grandchildren:** 1; **Education:** Grade 12th; **Personal Statement:** Words make or break a person. I enjoy putting my thoughts into something that satisfies the soul, mind and heart.

Author: Ann Hunot Mendenhall; **Occupation:** Retired; **Hobbies:** Reading, writing, gardening, genealogical research; **Memberships:** Husband is a memb of Ellington, Mo Genealogical Research Soc; **Spouse's Name:** Bobby G. Mendenhall; **Children:** 12; **Grandchildren:** 33; **Education:** Completed 8 Yrs of Elementary and 4 Yrs of High School; **Personal Statement:** Six children with husband William Hunot. Widowed. Married Bob Mendenhall who has six children. Written short stories, children's books and poetry. Feel like Grandma Moses!

Author: Lolita Arreola Mendoza; **Pen Name:** Fernando Poe; **Birthplace:** St Maria; **Occupation:** Grandmother; **Hobbies:** Arts and gardening and dressmaking; **Spouse's Name:** Enrique A Mendoza (deceased); **Children:** 8; **Grandchildren:** 14; **Education:** Graduated: Divine Word College; **Personal Statement:** Writing poetry is a way of developing one's talent, expressing our love of nature and uplifting one's spirit. To me, I admire poets Henry Wadsworth Longfellow, Alfred, Lord Tennyson and Edgar Allan Poe.

Author: Elizabeth Miller; **Pen Name:** Dixie Dallas; **Birthplace:** Chiuhua, Mexico; **Occupation:** Housewife and Mother; **Hobbies:** Writing, painting with Artex paint; **Memberships:** Church; **Spouse's Name:** Jack Miller; **Children:** 2; **Education:** Grade 8; **Personal Statement:** I started to write stories at the age of 14 then poems shortly after that. I've had many inspirations in the years that I've written. Eternal Love is one of many of my inspirational poems!

Author: Michele Miller; **Birthplace:** Chicago, IL; **Occupation:** Student/Sophomore at Mother Guerin High School; **Hobbies:** Piano, writing and recital; **Memberships:** Cast member of the Sun Spots; amateur recital group; **Personal Statement:** My poetry and music are my attempt to explain and understand life's circumstances. My inspirations are family, friends and nature. My goals are to act professionally, while maintaining my writing and music.

Author: Sharon Milward; **Birthplace:** Eastbourne; **Occupation:** Housewife; **Hobbies:** Swimming, driving, writing poems, gardening; **Spouse's Name:** Dave Milward; **Children:** 2; **Grandchildren:** 8; **Education:** 5 GSES; **Personal Statement:** I was very pleased to get my poem published. I really didn't think I would do it. But I have.

Author: Melinda Mlynski; **Birthplace:** Lake Forest, IL; **Occupation:** Advertising sales; **Hobbies:** Poetry, music, movies, literature, travel, museums; **Memberships:** Bahai House of Worship; **Education:** B.A.– University of Evansville, IN; **Honors:** Honor roll, directors award for band

Author: Shelia Montgomery; **Pen Name:** Shelia Wiggins Montgomery; **Birthplace:** Pelham, GA; **Occupation:** Retail Business Owner Computer Graphics & Freelance Art; **Hobbies:** Golf & Travel; **Spouse's Name:** H. Frank Montgomery Jr. P.G.A., M.P.; **Children:** 2; **Education:** Jefferson County High, Monticello, Fl – Berry College; **Published Works:** The Tee Times (a golf publication); **Personal Statement:** The written word has the potential to live forever, influencing and touching lives, where as the spoken word can die upon its birth.

Author: Garland Moore; **Pen Name:** Bucky Moore; **Birthplace:** Dyersburg, TN; **Occupation:** Carpenter; **Hobbies:** Reading and writing poetry, hunting, fishing, camping; **Children:** 1; **Education:** High School; **Personal Statement:** I hope to write and publish my own book someday "For poetry so ever cleanses the soul, touches the heart, and broadens the mind."

Author: Juanita Kay Morgan; **Birthplace:** Gastonia, NC; **Occupation:** Manufacturing; **Hobbies:** Crochet, cross stitch, soft ball and my children; **Memberships:** New Vision of Hope Outreach; **Children:** 4; **Education:** Graduated High School; **Honors:** Graduated High School on A & B Honor Roll; **Personal Statement:** To me writing poems is a window to a person's innermost feelings that can bless another person's heart, mind and soul.

Author: Mary Jane Morrison; **Birthplace:** Akron, OH; **Occupation:** Housewife; **Hobbies:** Travel in USA and abroad, piano, writing; **Memberships:** Church (Heights Baptist-Richardson, TX); **Spouse's Name:** Charles B. Morrison; **Children:** 4; **Grandchildren:** 7; **Education:** Buchtel High School, Akron, OH (1942); **Personal Statement:** Our grandson, Chase Walton, graduated from Berkner High May 31, 1992, Richardson, TX. Chase was killed by a drunk driver March 16, 1995... forever remembering.

Author: M. D. Moss; **Pen Name:** Morgan Scarborough; **Birthplace:** Paris, TX; **Occupation:** Struggling writer; **Hobbies:** Music, aerobic dancing, animals; **Education:** BA in english arts-minor in psychology from East Texas State University. Commerce, TX; **Personal Statement:** My dream come true would be knowledge of having entertained or uplifted someone's heart and mind with my poetry and stories I write.

Author: E. Murphy; **Pen Name:** Tom Edwards; **Birthplace:** Bury Lancashire; **Occupation:** Security Officer; **Hobbies:** Long distance running, reading and writing; **Memberships:** Bow Street Runners Athletic Club; **Spouse's Name:** Divorced; **Children:** 4; **Grandchildren:** 6; **Education:** Secondry Education; **Personal Statement:** I often wondered, about writing, but thought I lacked talent. I saw your competition notice and thought why not? As a schoolboy I read poems by Keats and Longfellow.

Author: Saturnino Noriega; **Pen Name:** Onin; **Birthplace:** Alamogordo, NM; **Occupation:** Management Consultant/Business Manager; **Hobbies:** Reading, writing, history, philosophy, fiction, poetry; **Memberships:** Chicg Counc on Foreign Relations, Acad of Political Sciences; **Spouse's Name:** Merry Gale Stuart; **Education:** Law Degree, LaSalle; **Published Works:** Hundreds of poems in small presses, hundreds of newspaper articles; 4 novels, two musical plays and one screen play; **Personal Statement:** All art is captured by poetry, for it transends the gamut of human thought and emotion — it liberates the human spirit.

Author: Robin O'Connor; **Birthplace:** Langhorne, PA; **Occupation:** Busperson, server at a banquet hall; **Hobbies:** Singing, painting, writing, photography and tennis; **Education:** I'm still in high school, I wish to attend Dowling College when I graduate.; **Personal Statement:** I'm only 15, but I've done a lot of growing up in the past few years. My dream is to sing, I don't care to be famous. Just singing and writing on the side of any job, and I'd be happy.

Author: Charles K. O'Meara; **Birthplace:** Tarrytown, NY; **Occupation:** Naval Officer/Aviator (Retired); **Hobbies:** Birding, hiking and photography; **Memberships:** Elks (BPOE), Retired Officers Association (TROA); **Spouse's Name:** Sylvia; **Children:** 2; **Education:** Masters of Int'l Mgmt; BA econ/business; **Personal Statement:** Life can be challenging. Being a career carrier aviator, drew a fine line between life and death and made life very precious.

Author: Doris M. Olson; **Birthplace:** Minneapolis, MN; **Occupation:** Retired; **Hobbies:** Writing poetry and knitting, working puzzles and reading; **Spouse's Name:** Donald E Olson (deceased); **Children:** 4; **Grandchildren:** 12; **Education:** High School; **Published Works:** Reflections of The Soul, "Heavenly Thoughts of Angels"; **Personal Statement:** Writing poetry gives me the opportunity to express my innermost thoughts and feelings.

Author: Kelly Olver; **Birthplace:** Waymart, PA; **Occupation:** Credit Specialist; **Hobbies:** Pool, writing, tennis; **Memberships:** American Poolplayers Association; **Children:** 1; **Education:** Western Wayne High School, Bloomsburg University; **Published Works:** No Place – "Windows" at The World National Library of Poetry; **Personal Statement:** All of my poems come from the heart. Writing gives me a chance to express my deepest emotions without the fear of being judged.

Author: Margarita Ortega; **Birthplace:** Del Rio, TX; **Occupation:** Whse wkr; **Hobbies:** Swimming, hiking, camping, writing poems; **Spouse's Name:** Jose F. Ortega; **Children:** 2; **Education:** High school diploma; **Awards:** Choir trophy

Author: Isabel Ortiz; **Birthplace:** Paterson, NJ; **Occupation:** Leasing Housing Technician; **Hobbies:** Poetry, music, reading, letter writing, going to movies; **Education:** Eastside High School (class of 1977), Sawyer School Of Clifton, August 1981; **Honors:** Typing, shorthand, attendance awards; **Awards:** Mayors award leasing housing specialist, May 1990; **Published Works:** How Hearts...Move and Jesus; **Personal Statement:** I am inspired by faith, hope and love. My dream in life is to be an achiever; determined in whatever field I desire and to influence others with my poetry and works.

Author: Luis W. Osorie; **Birthplace:** New York City, NY; **Occupation:** U S Army Medic; **Hobbies:** Tai Chi; **Spouse's Name:** Sarah Osorio; **Education:** 2 Years College EMT; **Awards:** Combat Medical Badge – Desert Storm; **Personal Statement:** I don't let pain or fear immobilize me, instead I draw my strength from them and continue on.

Author: Ronald L. Overfield; **Birthplace:** Barberton, OH; **Occupation:** Retired public school superintendent; **Hobbies:** Grandchildren, writing, reading; **Spouse's Name:** Helen I. Overfield; **Children:** 3; **Grandchildren:** 4; **Education:** AS– Kent State Univ, retraining and MS– Univ of Akron; Doctorate– University of Missouri– Columbia; **Published Works:** Numerous professional articles; The Secret Place; weekly newspaper columns (several yrs ago); **Personal Statement:** I am currently writing a book of anecdotes taken from my 35 years in public education and in search of a publisher.

Author: Robert A. Palmer; **Birthplace:** Barnettsville, IN; **Occupation:** Retired; **Hobbies:** Poetry, songs, languages, holistic medicine, cooking; **Memberships:** VFW; **Spouse's Name:** Bonnie L. Palmer (deceased); **Children:** 5; **Grandchildren:** 4; **Education:** College Graduate Culinary Arts, Chef, Honolulu Com College; **Honors:** Honorable Discharge, US Navy; **Awards:** Asiatic Pacific Ribbon; **Published Works:** I love to write poetry and songs to my girl friend. It was because of her, I wrote Butterfly Love. I wrote lots of son; **Personal Statement:** gs to her, one called Sugar Lips.

Author: Cathy Panaccione; **Birthplace:** Newark, NJ; **Occupation:** R.N.; **Hobbies:** Reading, writing and doll collecting; **Memberships:** Assoc Critical Care Nurses; **Education:** Winfred Baldwin School Of Nursing; **Published Works:** The Day You Left For Nam, Our Special Angel, Why; **Personal Statement:** I thank my parents for their love, support and belief in me. I miss the both of you very much.

Author: Karen M. Pelkey; **Pen Name:** Karen Pelkey – Love; **Birthplace:** Ontario, Canada; **Occupation:** Secretary; **Hobbies:** Poetry composing, sewing, sketching, and photography; **Education:** College Degree in Micro Computers; **Awards:** Gold Pin Award for Business Proficiency; **Personal Statement:** Writing poetry makes me feel warm inside and allows me to express my heartfelt thoughts on paper. When I write, my whole heart and mind are deep in thought.

Author: Gordon L. Perkins; **Birthplace:** Watchet, Somerset; **Occupation:** Chef/Catering Manager; **Hobbies:** Writing, socialising; **Children:** 2; **Grandchildren:** 4; **Education:** Secondary Modern School; **Published Works:** A Somerset Scene, 1994 Anthology, Poetry in Motion, Southern England; **Personal Statement:** I enjoy writing poetry because it helps me to relax in a very hectic working life.

Author: James Peters; **Birthplace:** Merced, CA; **Occupation:** English Instructor; **Hobbies:** Reading, writing, Latin; **Education:** B.A. English, San Jose State University, M.A. English CSU*F; **Personal Statement:** Poetry is the arrangement of indelible. Emotion upon time's parchment .

Author: Iris A. Peterson; **Birthplace:** Hull; **Occupation:** Retired early, ill health; **Hobbies:** Writing, reading, computer studies, quilling, Italic writing; **Memberships:** Humberside Writers Beverly, New hull Writers at Hull; **Spouse's Name:** Divorced; **Children:** 2; **Grandchildren:** 2; **Education:** Elementary; **Honors:** This is an honour having my first work published.; **Personal Statement:** I enjoy expressing thoughts, feelings and love through my poetry. My goals as a writer to get varied works published. My inspirations are my grandchildren.

Author: Glenda K. Phipps; **Birthplace:** Leatha, KY; **Occupation:** Office of John V. Heutsche, atty; **Hobbies:** Building birdhouses, music, gardening, refinishing furniture; **Children:** 3; **Grandchildren:** 3; **Education:** High school grad; **Published Works:** Poem "In Search"

Author: Sharon M. Pierce; **Birthplace:** Berwick, Nova Scotia; **Occupation:** Student; **Hobbies:** Reading, writing (songs and stories and poems); **Education:** High school graduate Grade twelve honors; **Personal Statement:** To all the suicide victims of the world. You are never alone, and should not ever think so. Love can span the world so whoever crosses over will always be with you. Forever.

Author: Patty Pilkington; **Pen Name:** Darlene Rains; **Birthplace:** Johnston County, NC; **Occupation:** Machine operator; **Hobbies:** Riding, writing poetry; **Children:** 3; **Education:** 12 Yrs high school; **Personal Statement:** Inspirations are the laughter of children and the love of my heart Jeff R.

Author: Sally Ploski; **Birthplace:** Gloucester, MA; **Occupation:** Business Owner/Painting and Wallpapering; **Hobbies:** Many types of crafts, sewing, stamping, stained glass, etc; **Spouse's Name:** Bob Ploski; **Children:** 3; **Grandchildren:** 6; **Education:** High School; **Published Works:** I Believe in Angels; **Personal Statement:** I have found that poems are an excellent way to express my feelings to those I care about. I have written three poems, all of which are for people very dear to me. I hope to expand on my writings in the future.

Author: Martha R. Pohl; **Pen Name:** Abigail Deborah; **Birthplace:** Topeka, KS; **Occupation:** Licensed practical nurse; **Hobbies:** Writing poetry and songs, plastic canvas needlepoint; **Children:** 2; **Grandchildren:** 3; **Education:** Some college; **Awards:** Graduated 5th in nursing class; **Published Works:** Friends, The Good Shepherd and other writings; **Personal Statement:** I love to write but haven't done much with it. My poetry comes to me as I'm falling asleep and I get up and write it down. I have taken yrs to finish 1 poem. My favorite poets are Henry Wadsworth Longfellow and Edgar Allen Poe.

Author: Roselle Pomeroy; **Pen Name:** Roselle Pomeroy; **Birthplace:** Bemis, TN; **Occupation:** Retired; **Hobbies:** Reading, writing, crafts, bible study; **Memberships:** First Baptist Church, Bemis; **Spouse's Name:** Deceased; **Children:** 3; **Grandchildren:** 2; **Education:** High school, business college, computer classes– Jackson State and Union University; **Awards:** Silver poets award– twice world of poetry; **Published Works:** Poems in Dollar Gen. newsletter, stories in Bemistory poems, "The Corridor" 1982, Edward A Fallot poetry winners; **Personal Statement:** My writings have always been a part of me. Natural as breating. I enjoy it very much. It is a gift from God to be shared.

Author: Margaret Poston; **Birthplace:** Los Angeles, CA; **Occupation:** Self employed; **Hobbies:** Art and crafts; **Spouse's Name:** Daniel; **Children:** 3; **Grandchildren:** 3; **Education:** 2 yrs college (medical assistant); **Published Works:** 6 other poems published; **Personal Statement:** The Lord is my inspiration. Many times in the middle of the night he wakes me with the words he wants me to write. This really is his work.

Author: Michael A. Powells; **Birthplace:** Washington, DC; **Occupation:** Security Officer; **Hobbies:** Martial arts; **Memberships:** NRA; **Education:** Cardozer High; **Personal Statement:** There are so many things we give away and I give away my words. I hope they find a home.

Author: Belinda Jean Proietti; **Birthplace:** San Bernardino, CA; **Occupation:** Human Services; **Hobbies:** Writing poetry; **Memberships:** New Beginnings Christian Church; **Children:** 2; **Education:** AA/Certificate – Human Services; **Honors:** Dean's List; **Awards:** Hall of Faith – New Beginning Christian Church; **Published Works:** World of Poetry; Nat'l Library of Poetry; Fine Arts Press; The Association of American Poets; **Personal Statement:** My desire is to be faithful with the talent God has given m e; to be given to others as a means of comfort and encouragement.

Author: Tess Queyquep; **Birthplace:** Philippines; **Occupation:** Librarian (Houston Public Library); **Hobbies:** Traveling, reading, gardening; **Memberships:** American library assn, Phi Beta Mu; **Education:** M.A, MLS (master of library studies); **Personal Statement:** God's gifts are many, just open your eyes. Fatima is the fulfillment of a lifedream.

Author: Christopher D. Reagan; **Pen Name:** Christopher Darin; **Birthplace:** McAlester, OK; **Hobbies:** Listening to music, writing, singing and computers; **Spouse's Name:** Heather Marie Reagan; **Children:** 3; **Education:** McAlester High School; **Personal Statement:** My goal as a writer is to touch at least one life, and give them hope. I can only achieve this by doing what God gave me talent to do.

Author: Cherie Reed; **Birthplace:** Washington, DC; **Occupation:** Administrative Assistant; **Hobbies:** Running, swimming, music and writing; **Spouse's Name:** Frank E Reed; **Children:** 2; **Education:** Studying to become paralegal; **Published Works:** A Rose 1996 Nat'l Library of Poetry

Author: D. C. Rees; **Pen Name:** Clire Rees; **Birthplace:** Herfordshire; **Occupation:** Retired; **Hobbies:** Motor caravaning, gardening; **Memberships:** Monmouth Writer's Group; **Spouse's Name:** Sheila Rees; **Children:** 4; **Grandchildren:** 6; **Education:** Priory Street, Boys' School Monmouth; **Published Works:** Question of God? Closet Poems, Poetry Now 1996; **Personal Statement:** Started writing in 1996 at the age of 63, stimulated by a creative writing course and the encouragement of the tutor. Carol Jenkins

Author: Marjorie H. Robley; **Birthplace:** Rossville, TN; **Occupation:** Pageheatrics, Mental Health; **Spouse's Name:** Deceased; **Children:** 1; **Grandchildren:** 1; **Education:** 2 Years College

Author: J. B. Rodgers; **Birthplace:** Pittsburg, PA; **Occupation:** Insurance Broker; **Hobbies:** Golf, tennis, theatre, travel; **Memberships:** Burlingame Country Club, Olympic Club – Elks Club; **Spouse's Name:** Deceased; **Children:** 2; **Grandchildren:** 3; **Education:** Stanford Univ Grad

Author: Jessyca Rodriguez; **Birthplace:** Miami, FL; **Occupation:** Private Investigator; **Hobbies:** Reading, movie watching; **Spouse's Name:** Henry Kirkland; **Children:** 1; **Education:** Criminal Justice Major; **Honors:** Graduated with top of class; **Published Works:** If only 1, Miami Herald, Miami Times; **Personal Statement:** Poetry allows me to release my stress, overcome my fears, express my joys, and relive my passions.

Author: Yvonne Clement Rolling; **Pen Name:** Yvonne Clement; **Birthplace:** Augusta, GA; **Occupation:** Housewife; **Hobbies:**

Writing, crafts, decorating, floral designs, sewing, art; **Memberships:** Notary public; **Spouse's Name:** Steven J. Perry; **Children:** 1; **Education:** H.S. grad and tech school; **Honors:** Perfect attendance; **Awards:** Art– American history; **Published Works:** Paintings On Show; **Personal Statement:** I enjoy quiet time to do my thing– no matter what it is.

Author: John Rose; **Birthplace:** Sheffield; **Occupation:** Radio Presenter; **Hobbies:** Theatre, cinema, tennis and songwriting; **Education:** Eleven "O" levels and four "A" levels from Kingsthorpe Upper School; **Published Works:** "The Sycophant"– Poetry Today

Author: Victoria Denny Rose; **Pen Name:** Victoria Denny Rose; **Birthplace:** New Albany, IN; **Occupation:** Display; **Hobbies:** Golf, reading; **Spouse's Name:** Douglas; **Children:** 3; **Grandchildren:** 8; **Published Works:** National Library "Best of the 90's", Walk Through Paradise", Poet's of the 90's; **Personal Statement:** I haven't begun to write. With the passing of cruelty to my sisters I use this as a healing process. Within these next years I hope love takes what fear has found.

Author: Raymond M. Ross; **Pen Name:** Raymond M. Ross; **Birthplace:** Clovis, New Mexico; **Occupation:** Full Time Student; **Hobbies:** Football, basketball; **Memberships:** Army Reserve; **Spouse's Name:** Kathy; **Children:** 1; **Education:** Working on Degree in Physical Education; **Personal Statement:** The movie "Dead Poet's Society", inspired my interest in poetry and the desire to change my life.

Author: Karen Rosseland; **Pen Name:** J C; **Birthplace:** Jacksonville, FL; **Occupation:** R.N.; **Hobbies:** Creative writing, discovery, adventure, travel; **Children:** 2; **Personal Statement:** I know God breathed life into the gift of creating words as descriptive tools to decorate his handiwork and encourage the hearts of his people.

Author: Jacqueline Rowan; **Birthplace:** London; **Occupation:** Basildon Market Trader and Shop Proprietor; **Spouse's Name:** Anthony Joseph Rowan; **Children:** 2; **Grandchildren:** 1

Author: Michael J. Ruggiero; **Pen Name:** Mikol Josant; **Birthplace:** Syracuse; **Occupation:** Writer, artist; **Hobbies:** Backpacking, playing clay and wooden flutes; **Memberships:** Writers and books literary center, arts and cultural council; **Spouse's Name:** Carolyn Hastron–Ruggiero; **Children:** 1; **Education:** BA Philosophy/art wadhams hall; pastoral counseling, University of Rochester; **Published Works:** Encounters (short stories, poetry, art); Rochester Catholic Worker (articles); **Personal Statement:** Poetry gives a voice to the life beneath the surface, introducing us to unseen forces that are nonetheless constant companions for everyday life.

Author: Amy Sadanaga; **Birthplace:** Baltimore, MD; **Occupation:** Illustrator/Writer; **Hobbies:** Poetry, songwriting, singing, playing clarinet and painting; **Memberships:** Artsbridge, F.E.M.A.L.E., Mothers At Home, symphonic band; **Spouse's Name:** Kenneth; **Children:** 2; **Education:** Pennsylvania Academy Of The Fine Arts, Hahnemann University, master's in art therapy; **Honors:** Dean's List; **Awards:** Scholastic Magazine Scholarship, best portfolio in nation; **Published Works:** "Kids Acting Against Abuse", illustrated and written booklet, also published in Welcome Home Magazine; **Personal Statement:** "At The Bookstore" is one of my poems I have written and illustrated about children and motherhood. My goal is to have these poems published.

Author: Roseann M. Saltzsieder; **Birthplace:** Trenton, NJ; **Occupation:** Family; **Hobbies:** Life; **Memberships:** C.C.M.O.T.C./ N.J.A.T.M.C./ N.O.M.O.T.C/ P.T.A.; **Spouse's Name:** Lee; **Children:** 3; **Education:** Some College 1997 M.O.T.Y.; **Published Works:** Vacationing With Twins, An Oxymoron; **Personal Statement:** My goal as a writer is to publish articles concerning everyday life through humor. Erma Bombeck is my biggest influence.

Author: Sharon Scheff; **Birthplace:** Farimont, MN; **Occupation:** Secretary; **Hobbies:** Counted cross–stitch, anything crafty, going to auctions; **Spouse's Name:** Anthony; **Children:** 3; **Education:** East Chain H.S.– east chain, MN american computer institute; **Personal Statement:** "As we celebrate" was an anniversary gift for my husband Anthony for our 5th anniversary. It reminds us of the special gift that marriage is.

Author: Nancy Schettig; **Birthplace:** New Brighton, PA; **Occupation:** Leasing agent for Atlas Resources; **Hobbies:** Flower arranging; **Spouse's Name:** Robert Schettig; **Children:** 3; **Grandchildren:** 1; **Education:** High school; **Personal Statement:** My personal view on life is to cherish each day. We can not change who or what we have become, but we can always make improvements.

Author: F. Richard Schneider; **Birthplace:** Chelsea, MI; **Occupation:** Educator; **Hobbies:** Nature, travel and gardening; **Spouse's Name:** Ruth Ann; **Children:** 5; **Grandchildren:** 6; **Education:** Ph D; **Honors:** US Dept of Interior, Outstanding Citizen; **Awards:** Who's Who in World; **Published Works:** In Search of Rainbows

Author: Robin Schwarz; **Birthplace:** Monrovia, CA; **Occupation:** Purchasing assistant; **Hobbies:** Writing, crafts and creative memories photo albums; **Spouse's Name:** Robert Schwarz; **Children:** 3; **Grandchildren:** 3; **Education:** Graduated Northview High School in 1971; **Personal Statement:** A terrific husband, a few wonderful friends and a large loving family are the special influences in my life.

Author: Kathi Serr; **Birthplace:** Sacramento, CA; **Occupation:** DI inspector for an electronics company; **Hobbies:** Writing, 4 wheeling in my husband's Jeepster, reading; **Spouse's Name:** Jim; **Children:** 3; **Education:** Grad Lincoln High, english/ a creative writing/pose at Sierra College, non–fiction writing course through NRI ed center.; **Honors:** Highest honor awards at NRI; **Awards:** Achievement awared at NRI (a sudsidary of McGraw–Hill); **Personal Statement:** My desire to become a writer dates back to when I was a child and found that I could write better than I could speak.

Author: Emma D. Shadrick; **Birthplace:** Sequatchie; **Occupation:** Retired; **Hobbies:** Travel and enjoy baseball, football on TV and in person; **Spouse's Name:** Ben (deceased); **Education:** High School, Some College; **Personal Statement:** Writing poetry is giving your personal expression. I have always had much admiration for Helen Steiner Rice.

Author: Sandra Shelton; **Birthplace:** Nashville, TN; **Occupation:** Bookkeeper; **Hobbies:** Collecting angels, frogs, Barbie dolls; **Spouse's Name:** Danny Shelton; **Children:** 2; **Grandchildren:** 2; **Education:** Graduated Hume Fogg Technical School; **Published Works:** Tennessean Writers Forum (Three Star Winner); **Personal Statement:** I leave my poem "untitled", so every reader will remember it as they will.

Author: Joshua Shipp; **Birthplace:** Rochester, MI; **Occupation:** Student at Arizona State University West; **Hobbies:** Seeing movies, bicycle riding, being with friends and family; **Education:** Working towards my B.A. in communications

Author: Wendy L. Shryock; **Birthplace:** Hammond, IN; **Occupation:** Homemaker; **Hobbies:** Writing, horseback riding; **Spouse's Name:** Duane Shryock; **Children:** 2; **Grandchildren:** 1; **Education:** Graduate of A.P.Brewer High School, Somerville, AL; **Published Works:** A Man With No Name; **Personal Statement:** My goals as a writer to one day become a published novelist. My inspirations, my husband, kids, and my mother who have always shown me support.

Author: Dorothy R. Sirois; **Birthplace:** Texas City, TX; **Occupation:** Hospital linen dept; **Hobbies:** Article and oil painting, crafts; **Children:** 1; **Education:** College of Mainland; **Personal Statement:** I enjoy creating short poems for the fun of it and it is a pleasure to do. Believe in yourself and follow your dreams– be good to yourself. This is for all people including the handicapped and people in all walks of life.

Author: Ralph N. Smiley; **Pen Name:** Smylea; **Birthplace:** Gadsden, AL; **Occupation:** Cook; **Hobbies:** Reading, writing poetry, walking, cycling, swimming, bowling; **Spouse's Name:** Divorced; **Children:** 8; **Grandchildren:** 7; **Education:** Graduated High School, Business College; **Published Works:** Six poems published by National Library of Poetry; **Personal Statement:** To

bring joy or maybe a tear or two, some peace of mind away from a world of strife and crime. Most of all to make people think.

Author: Mark Smith; **Pen Name:** Spinx; **Birthplace:** Mossley, Lancashire; **Occupation:** Unemployed; **Hobbies:** Living and learning; **Grandchildren:** 3; **Education:** Comprehensive; **Personal Statement:** Experience without preference, love without remorse and acceptance of all lives past. Begins the route to a knowledgeable and enlightened path, resulting as, worthwhile life!

Author: Sheila M. Smith; **Birthplace:** Guam, Mariannas Islands; **Occupation:** Steel Foundry Laborer; **Hobbies:** Fishing, reading, writing short stories and poetry; **Memberships:** USWA; **Spouse's Name:** Michael Smith; **Children:** 4+; **Education:** Life; **Honors:** My children, my "extra" kids, my husband, friends, family; **Awards:** The many people who have touched my life; **Published Works:** Reporter, photographer for a local newspaper; **Personal Statement:** I have received life sustaining nourishment from the harvest of the seeds that have touched my life. God bless and keep them all.

Author: Philip L. Smith; **Birthplace:** Crystal Bay, Minn; **Occupation:** Pastor (bi–vocational) landscape gardener; **Hobbies:** Gardening, travel; **Children:** 1; **Education:** University of San Francisco; **Personal Statement:** I believe all thoughts, words, poems are the inspiration given by God.

Author: Cheryl Smith; **Birthplace:** Hagerstown, MD; **Occupation:** Packer in ice cream plant; **Hobbies:** Writing, reading and listening to music; **Education:** High school education; **Awards:** I won the golden poet award in 1988; **Published Works:** Several poems in poetry books; **Personal Statement:** I have been writing poetry since I was a child. My greatestinfluence and who I love and respect is Bob Dylan: a poet, asincere songwriter.

Author: Tammi Kathleen Smith–Santoro; **Birthplace:** Galesburg, IL; **Occupation:** Aspiring Actress; **Hobbies:** Acting, writing, animals and reading; **Spouse's Name:** Nicholas Santoro; **Published Works:** Woman's Own Magazine, Gannett Newspaper; **Personal Statement:** My inspiration for my writing comes from what I see in the world, the worst and most humble, what goes most overlooked.

Author: Pattie G. Snapp; **Pen Name:** Schae Jaxon; **Birthplace:** Sedalia, MO; **Occupation:** Rural carrier associate; **Hobbies:** Volleyball, travel and writing; **Memberships:** Phi Theta Kappa (national honor society); **Spouse's Name:** Tom Snapp; **Children:** 2; **Education:** Graduated Magna Cum Laude from Park College; **Personal Statement:** My biggest dream is to one day write a novel and get it published. My poem being published is also a dream come true!

Author: Amber Snelling; **Pen Name:** Amber Lynn; **Birthplace:** Point Pleasant, NJ; **Occupation:** Production assistant; **Hobbies:** Writing, running; **Education:** Stockton College; **Honors:** Grad with honors in literature; **Awards:** Being noticed by family, those I love and professionals; **Personal Statement:** I write what I feel; I write to escape what I feel, but mostly I write to communicate what I feel to others.

Author: Sharron Spain; **Birthplace:** Walthamstow; **Occupation:** Mother; **Personal Statement:** This poem was written from the heart, it took 5 minutes, after trying to get Social Service and Education to listen to my autistic boy's needs.

Author: Steve Sprigg; **Birthplace:** Kalamazoo, MI; **Occupation:** Software Engineer; **Hobbies:** Computers, acting, singing, writing poetry (of course!); **Education:** College of Wooster; **Personal Statement:** Thoughts of the soul and words of the heart convey more of a person than the tongue can impart.

Author: Tricia Stalion; **Pen Name:** Trey C. Stanfield; **Birthplace:** Miami, AZ; **Occupation:** Student; **Hobbies:** Photography, writing, learning; **Children:** 1; **Education:** Southeastern Oklahoma State Univ, institute of children's literature; **Honors:** President's honor roll, the dean's honor roll; **Published Works:** The Southeastern, The Sherman Democrat; **Personal Statement:** Life revolves around words. Words console confront and con vict us... "On the day of judgment men will account for eve ry idle word spoken". Matthew 12:36.

Author: Valerie J. Sullivan; **Birthplace:** Bruton, Somerset; **Occupation:** Shop Assistant (Supervisor); **Hobbies:** Amateur

Dramatics, dancing; **Spouse's Name:** Derek Bernard Sullivan (deceased); **Children:** 6; **Grandchildren:** 14; **Education:** Bruton County School; **Published Works:** Several Letters; **Personal Statement:** Writing poetry is putting one's thoughts into words.

Author: Domitila R. Tablason; **Birthplace:** Pilar, Camotes, Cebu P.T.; **Occupation:** Retired School Teacher; **Hobbies:** Handicrafts, gardening, sports, music, poetry, homekeeping; **Memberships:** Phil P.S.T.A., CPSTA, Vet Assoc. Senior Citizens; **Spouse's Name:** Vincente Tablason (deceased); **Children:** 9; **Grandchildren:** 30; **Education:** BSEED – Bachelor of Science in Elementary Education; **Honors:** Best Athlete; **Awards:** Teacher of the Year; **Published Works:** Elementary Reading Materials; **Personal Statement:** This serves as an inspiration of my grandchildren who are now in high school and college.

Author: Mary Taylor; **Pen Name:** Mary Taylor; **Birthplace:** Frederick, OK; **Occupation:** Social Worker, Real Estate manager; **Hobbies:** Reading, hiking, crafts interior decorating; **Memberships:** Eagles, D.A.V. Aux, N.A. Asso. Rental Housing of P. C.; **Spouse's Name:** Arch Taylor; **Children:** 5; **Grandchildren:** 6; **Education:** B.S.W. Certified in Child and Family Welfare; **Honors:** Mentioned in "Who's Who in The West", Who's Who in Amer Wom; **Awards:** Many plaques in "Who's Who in Women Executives; **Personal Statement:** I base my writing on events, experiences, goals, feelings,moods, changes, (i.e., disappointments, sadness, gladness, joys, holidays, love, romance, losses, performances and promotions.

Author: Lucille E. Teats; **Birthplace:** Austin, MN; **Occupation:** Resident assistant and nurses aide; **Hobbies:** Reading, writing, playing organ, fishing, hiking; **Spouse's Name:** George A. Teats; **Children:** 2; **Education:** BS elementary education; **Published Works:** Echoes Of Yesterday, The National Library of Poetry; **Personal Statement:** Words are a celebration of life, each individual has a unique way of expressing it.

Author: Veronica Tett; **Pen Name:** A Friend; **Birthplace:** Twickenham; **Hobbies:** Animal care, conservation, writing and gardening; **Spouse's Name:** Frank; **Children:** 4; **Grandchildren:** 4; **Education:** Chiswick Grammar School, West Australian University; **Personal Statement:** Won award at school for reciting "The Listeners" by Walter De La Mere. Always wanted to be involved in poetry ever since that day.

Author: Tonyah Thompson; **Birthplace:** Lawton, OK; **Occupation:** Student; **Spouse's Name:** Russell B Thompson; **Children:** 1; **Education:** B.S.E. Candidate for Spring of 1998: University of Wi – Whitewater; **Honors:** Academic Honors; **Awards:** Acad Recognition from the Minority Teacher Preparation Progr; **Personal Statement:** It is greatly fulfilling to be able to share yourself with others through the writing of poetry.

Author: Jeralyn Toben; **Occupation:** Special ed. trainer; **Hobbies:** Writing, coaching special olympics and travel; **Education:** Three years Bible College; **Awards:** Volunteer of the year for special ed. school; **Personal Statement:** People with special needs have helped me learn more about God's grace than I would ever have learned alone.

Author: Bernadette Tovar; **Birthplace:** El Paso, TX; **Occupation:** English teacher; **Hobbies:** Doll collecting, playing the piano; **Memberships:** Golden key honor society and alpha chi honor society; **Education:** Will graduate May '98 with a BA in english and american lit. from UTEP; **Honors:** Dean's list; **Personal Statement:** Everytime I write a poem, I reveal a piece of my soul...To God be the honor and glory.

Author: Phyllis Tremblay; **Birthplace:** Buffalo, NY; **Occupation:** Homemaker– with some college; **Hobbies:** Needle craft, writing, reading, floral arrngements; **Memberships:** Book clubs; **Spouse's Name:** Lawrence Tremblay; **Children:** 2; **Grandchildren:** 2; **Education:** Graduate from high school, Kensington H.S.; **Honors:** Dramatics; **Awards:** Merit awards; **Published Works:** The Niagara Gazette; **Personal Statement:** I, Phyllis Tremblay, would work very hard to be a well known writer and my goal someday is to write a book. Which of course has to do with life.

Author: Heather Trimble; **Birthplace:** Lancaster, PA; **Occupation:** Store Clerk; **Hobbies:** Hiking, gardening, travel and water sports; **Memberships:** PETA, National Geographic Society; **Education:** Graduated Manhem Central High School; **Honors:** First and second honors; **Awards:** Model United Nations, honors award; **Personal Statement:** Writing poetry is the best way for me to heal and express myself. My favorite writers are: Anne Sexton, Jack Kerouac and Allen Ginsberg.

Author: Wendy Turocy; **Birthplace:** Lodi, OH; **Occupation:** Teacher turned homemaker; **Hobbies:** Writing and crafts; **Spouse's Name:** Kenneth Turocy; **Children:** 1; **Education:** Graduated from the University of Akron; **Personal Statement:** Writing is an extension of one's thoughts, ideas and dreams. All of my life I have wanted to share my world with others.

Author: Sharon Vega; **Birthplace:** Little Rock, AR; **Occupation:** Mother and Homemaker; **Hobbies:** Fishing, crafts, swimming, doll collecting, and writing; **Children:** 4; **Education:** 11th Grade; **Personal Statement:** My goal as a writer is to eventually write a book, and to have it published, along with several other poems of mine.

Author: Elizabeth M. Verbeck; **Birthplace:** Watertown, NY; **Occupation:** Retired; **Hobbies:** Reading, needlework, studying nature; **Memberships:** Friends of Boyd Hill Nature Pk, AARP, Nature Conservancy; **Spouse's Name:** Widow; **Children:** 3; **Grandchildren:** 16; **Education:** High school graduate; **Published Works:** "This Quiet Corner"– a history of boyd hill nature park, St Pete FL, poems in several anthologies; **Personal Statement:** I have written poetry since childhood, and find inspiration in many sources; weather, sorrow, happiness in my life and the lives of friends and relatives. I never sit down and plan to write a poem. They just happen.

Author: Starr Vincnet; **Pen Name:** Starr Appel; **Birthplace:** Maywood, CA; **Occupation:** Jewelry Sales; **Hobbies:** Music; **Memberships:** American Legion Auxiliary; **Spouse's Name:** Bernhard Appel; **Children:** 2; **Grandchildren:** 3; **Education:** Alton Central School Alton H.H. Gr 1–12 Same Bldg.; **Honors:** D.A.R. Awrd–Girl's St Captain Basketball–Athlete of Yr 1968; **Awards:** Queen of School 1968; **Personal Statement:** When we make peace on earth the entrance to heaven is much sweeter.

Author: C. A. Wardell; **Pen Name:** Alvar Wardell; **Birthplace:** Halifax, UK; **Occupation:** Bit of this and that and Publican; **Hobbies:** Wine, rugby, poetry and geraniums; **Spouse's Name:** Deceased; **Children:** 4; **Grandchildren:** 3; **Education:** Military (Royal Military Police); **Personal Statement:** Everything I do! Everything I see! When I drink wine becomes poetry to me.

Author: J. E. Warhurst; **Birthplace:** Fort Payne, AL; **Occupation:** Private investigator; **Hobbies:** Camping, boating, amateur radio; **Memberships:** React internation, forsyth county civil defense; **Spouse's Name:** Ann; **Education:** Graduated Dekalb College

Author: Debbie J. Warren; **Pen Name:** Deb; **Birthplace:** Dublin, GA; **Occupation:** Homemaker; **Hobbies:** Decorating; **Spouse's Name:** Michael E. Warren; **Children:** 2; **Education:** High school diploma and teachers aid college diploma– "int. correspond school"; **Personal Statement:** Back in 1978, my husband and I had a tragic accident. We hit a fertilizer truck, our vehicle was totaled! So was I! After my coma, I waited 10 years to start our family.

Author: Karie Weber; **Birthplace:** Burlington; **Occupation:** Pick–n–save (cashier); **Hobbies:** Poetry writing, writing novels–books; **Education:** Waterford Union High School

Author: Kay Whitaker; **Birthplace:** Tipton, OK; **Occupation:** Journalist; **Hobbies:** Writing, traveling; **Education:** B.A. University of Oklahoma Journalism School; **Honors:** Kappa Tau Alpha, Theta Sigma Phi; **Awards:** National Welfare Foundation scholarship; **Published Works:** Spirit Matters, A book of Poetry; **Personal Statement:** I have been especially influenced by William Wordsworth and Emily Bronte.

Author: Arthur H. White III; **Pen Name:** Art White; **Birthplace:** New Orleans, LA; **Occupation:** Retail store manager; **Hobbies:** Vampires and graveyards; **Personal Statement:** If I leave nothing behind, then I leave nothing to be remembered by. My flesh shall turn to dust but my words live forever!

Author: Michelle L. Whitehead; **Birthplace:** Baltimore, MD; **Occupation:** Correctional Officer; **Hobbies:** Reading, photography and travel; **Education:** Graduated North Harford High School; some college; **Awards:** Short story writing competition (high school); **Published Works:** "Youth", "Say Goodbye" (high school publication); **Personal Statement:** Writing, to me, has always been a "cleansing" of the soul. It is my one true passion and certainly one of my best friends.

Author: Tina Widell; **Birthplace:** Fredric, WI; **Occupation:** Factory Worker; **Hobbies:** Writing poetry and children's stories; **Memberships:** Grace Baptist Church of Grantsburg; **Spouse's Name:** Raymond Widell; **Children:** 3; **Education:** High School Grad; **Awards:** First Place Essay Award 1986; **Published Works:** The Thoughts of a Lonely Tree; **Personal Statement:** Your children are precious gifts and they grow up fast. Spend time with them while they still need you.

Author: Kevin Wilkes; **Birthplace:** Sutton Coldfield, West Mids; **Occupation:** A–level Student; **Hobbies:** Writing, drawing, drama and sports; **Education:** Currently taking English Lit and Drama A–levels; **Personal Statement:** It gives me great satisfaction believing that I may be reaching out to others through my poetry. My inspirations come from the world around me.

Author: Michele H. Wilkinson; **Birthplace:** St Charles, IL; **Occupation:** Full Time Mom (Homemaker); **Hobbies:** Any activity with my family, swimming, gardening, and crafts; **Spouse's Name:** William Wilkinson; **Children:** 2; **Education:** Graduated St Charles High School and took some classes at Glendale Community College; **Personal Statement:** My family is my happiness, my inspiration, my energy, my life. My next goal as a writer is to write a children's book or two.

Author: Marie Williams; **Birthplace:** Michigan; **Occupation:** Retired; **Hobbies:** Crafts, sewing and fishing; **Spouse's Name:** Esta Williams (deceased); **Children:** 7; **Grandchildren:** 24; **Education:** High School; **Personal Statement:** Children, grandchildren, friends and especially Helen Steiner Rice's inspirational poetry has inspired my desire to write poetry.

Author: Beth Willis; **Birthplace:** Chillicothe, OH; **Occupation:** College student; **Hobbies:** Nature walks, travel and writing; **Memberships:** American legion 757 women's auxiliary; **Children:** 1; **Education:** Completed 2 years of University college; **Personal Statement:** I believe that poetry is an escape to the world of fantasy and that it aids me in expressing my hopes and desires.

Author: Patricia L. Wilson; **Birthplace:** Waukegan, IL; **Occupation:** Retired; **Hobbies:** Writings, reading, crafts, sewing, travel; **Spouse's Name:** Richard; **Children:** 3; **Grandchildren:** 2; **Education:** High school; **Personal Statement:** Writings helps me to express what I can't say. It helps to relate to other people and understanding– seeing things more clearly, being on the inside not outside looking in.

Author: B. J. Wood; **Pen Name:** Miss Betty; **Birthplace:** Mannsville, OK; **Occupation:** CEO mfg. firm (Matador Processors Inc.); **Hobbies:** Biking, music, skiing; **Spouse's Name:** Deceased; **Education:** High school –vo tech's and business college (1947); **Honors:** Woman of the yr (blanchard extension homemakers); **Personal Statement:** My sister, Quin Reece, has been an inspiration to me since childhood.

Author: John Woods; **Birthplace:** Joliet, IL; **Occupation:** Full time nursing student; **Hobbies:** Writing, marksmanship; **Spouse's Name:** Sylvia Woods; **Children:** 1; **Education:** 2nd yr college; **Honors:** The national dean's list; **Personal Statement:** For inspiration you only need to look at the ones you love, and who love you. Sometimes family is all we have to see u s through.

Author: Pauline Wright; **Birthplace:** Jamaica; **Hobbies:** Writing songs, poems, enjoying nature and going to church; **Children:** 2; **Education:** Graduate from school in Jamaica; **Personal Statement:** I've been writing songs and poems for awhile.

Author: Gwen Wright; **Birthplace:** Woking Surrey, England; **Occupation:** Retired; **Hobbies:** Writing stories, cooking and art – painting and drawing; **Spouse's Name:** W.B. Wright; **Children:** 5; **Grandchildren:** 8; **Education:** One Year College

Author: Faye B. Wright; **Birthplace:** North Carolina; **Occupation:** Home Maker; **Hobbies:** Bird Watching, hiking, baking; **Spouse's Name:** Howard C Wright; **Children:** 1; **Grandchildren:** 1; **Education:** High School; **Personal Statement:** Nature, God and family, are my inspirations and influences.

Author: Jennie Wysocki; **Birthplace:** Newark, NJ; **Occupation:** Receptionist, reheis inc; **Hobbies:** Writing, reading, music; **Memberships:** Alpha sigma tau national society; **Education:** No. Plainfield HS, Seton Hall University; **Awards:** Editor's choice award, nat'l lib of poetry; **Published Works:** "The Break Of Dawn", nat'l lib of poetry; **Personal Statement:** Talent is not learned or inherited. It is a gift. Only those who recognize this are deserving enough to embrace it.

Author: Timothy Ryan Yeager; **Birthplace:** Fort Thomas; **Occupation:** Bus person/dish tank– Bob Evans; **Hobbies:** Working on puzzles, reading, and learning quotes; **Education:** Currently at Newfort High School; **Personal Statement:** Anyone can write a rhyme, most can speak swiftly, some can even make words that inspire, but only a poet can do all three.

Author: Billy W. Youngblood; **Pen Name:** Billy Youngblood; **Birthplace:** Carthage, TX; **Occupation:** Soldier; **Hobbies:** Singing, song writing, bull riding and writing; **Children:** 2; **Education:** 12th Grade Graduate; **Personal Statement:** I hope my writing becomes as good as Emerson and Twain. At this point and time I'm working on two books.

Author: Susan Yule; **Birthplace:** Dunfermline; **Occupation:** Student; **Hobbies:** Reading, writing stories/poems, drama, cycling; **Memberships:** Dunfermline Children's Heritage Theatre; **Education:** Torryburn Primary School, now Inverkeithing High Sch, Fife; **Personal Statement:** As I am just twelve years old I have not had much experience of life, but I am absorbing – and hope to write more!

Author: Paul Zellermaier; **Birthplace:** Rumania; **Occupation:** Second V Pres Chase Manhattan Bank on Infrastructure Team; **Hobbies:** Chess, programming, poetry; **Memberships:** Too numerous to count; **Spouse's Name:** Margaret; **Children:** 8; **Education:** Brooklyn College, Long Island University; **Honors:** Ed's Choice Award N.L.P., Select to Intn'l Poetry Hall Fame; **Awards:** 54 Awards; **Published Works:** The Burning of a Human Race, 170 poems available to be published; **Personal Statement:** A poem is words of a living dreamer. The words are confine d and concealed in void of space. When transcribed to paper become images that float to life, knowledge and music to others.

Author: Sandra Zobel; **Birthplace:** Moultrie, GA; **Occupation:** Waitress; **Hobbies:** Writing, interior design; **Spouse's Name:** Jeff; **Children:** 3; **Education:** High School; **Personal Statement:** My lifelong goal has been to write fiction. I've alwys en joyed writing and hope to one day have my work published.

APPENDIX

Index
of Poets

This easy-reference index of poets is an alphabetical listing of each author whose poem appears in this anthology. A quick scan of the Poet Index will tell you the full name of every poet featured in the book, followed by a page number on which the poem can be located.

A

Abbate, Robert, 53
Abbott, Anita D., 83
Abraham, K. M., 100
Adkins, Betsey, 117
Aguilar, Alejandra, 258
Al–Harhara, Muna, 283
Albertson, Timothy M., 85
Alcorn, Elise and Ryan, 15
Alden Tisdale, Phebe, 175
Alder, Stephanie, 262
Alderman, J. Gordon, 65
Aldridge, Daisy S., 229
Ali, Shasna, 273
Alire, Morris A., 217
Allen, Susan, 20
Allison, Denise M., 270
Alston, Monica Regina, 46
Alvey, Casey, 301
Alvira, Tina, 141
Amado, Ka'eo, 155
Anasir, Elizabeth, 287
Andersen, Jay, 22
Andersen, Lester V., 277
Anderson, Connie, 85
Anderson, Eva, 105
Anderson, Laura, 55
Anderson, Matthew, 47
Anderson, Patricia, 210, 278
Anderson, Richard, 190
Anderson, Sara M., 229
Anderson, Sara R., 250
Anderson, Sheridan, 150
Andrews, Sara, 236
Andrews, Shelby, 290
Andrus, Barbara, 82
Anlezark, Joyce, 192
Anselmi, Roberta, 6
Antoskiewicz, Gracemary, 137
Aragon, Jr., William G., 248
Arambulo, Jesus J., 98
Arber, S. John, 17
Arbuckle, Annie B., 211
Archer, Joshua Daniel, 279
Armstrong, Laura, 209
Armstrong, Tracy, 42
Arneson, Elaine G., 98
Arnold, Joyce P., 77
Arocho–Fullam, Rose Mary, 52
Arolin, Marianna J., 97
Arriola, FranceAnna, 267
Arthur, Jean M., 293
Ashcroft, Derek, 295
Ashtor, Gila, 104
Atkinson, David, 11
Atkinson, James, 49
Attfield, Erin, 113
Atwood, Alison, 91
Audersch, Anja M., 97

Auen, Debbie, 197
Austin, Patricia, 266
Axt, Sabrina, 260
Ayton, Joseph, 114

B

Bachmeier, Jewel, 245
Backlund, Patricia L., 235
Bader, Debra H., 112
Bailey, Deborah, 228
Bailey, S. M., 230
Bailey, Virginia G., 189
Baker, Chris L., 195
Baker, Christina, 110
Baker, Elizabeth, 230
Bakies, Gretchen, 314
Baladad, Vanessa, 149
Baldwin, Susan, 123
Balloy, Magdalene P., 160
Bamforth, Paula L., 164
Barchuk, Jamie A., 300
Barnes, Ted L., 13
Barnett, Jennifer L., 176
Barnhart, Sunny, 289
Barraza, Vivian, 310
Bartucci, Michele, 217
Bassole–Ouedraogo, Angele, 56
Bateholts, Jason, 178
Bates, Margaret, 269
Bates, Margaret E., 315
Batiste, Kimberly, 292
Baum, Margaret K., 301
Baum, Margaret P., 104
Baumgarten, Stephanie, 233
Bayer, Michele A., 34
Beardsley, Lorie, 176
Beasley, Cadell, 222
Beatty, Tina M., 172
Beck, Mary E., 180
Beck, Tim, 26
Becker, Shirley, 282
Bedard, Morgan, 56
Beliveau, Deborah, 185
Belkin, Nathalie, 53
Bell, Angelia O., 14
Bell, Jane, 315
Bellini, B., 134
Belyeu, Shanna, 177
Benhardt, Bill, 211
Bennett, Rose A., 42
Benz, Barbara B., 64
Berg, Doris, 99
Bergeron, Francine, 229
Berk, Lori Jo, 263
Berman, Lillian, 171
Bernard, Barbara, 280
Berner, U. H., 68
Berrian, Sherrie, 268
Berson, Judith S., 103

Bertalan, Joseph, 36
Bertonazzi, Judy M., 139
Beschi, Martha, 74
Besh, Patricia, 162
Bigard, Sean, 225
Bigelow, Heidi, 227
Bigelow, Rebecca, 217
Billing, Christopher, 18
Bilodeau, Karen, 60
Binder, Barbara, 199
Birdsall, Mildred, 85
Bishop, Daniel, 122
Bishop, L. H., 84
Blackmore, Philip J., 294
Blackstock, Edwinnie C., 106
Blackstock, Jonathan, 162
Blagrove, E., 262
Blair, Nicole M., 203
Blake, Julie, 196
Blake, Nina, 131
Blanck, Michele, 267
Blank, Marilyn J., 241
Blankenship, Irmadene, 155
Blevins, Edward, 161
Block, Pamela, 143
Blue, K. T., 319
Boardman, Jennifer, 172
Bodner, Belva, 215
Boer, Luella M., 23
Boerner, Sheila, 213
Boket, Daphne, 117
Bonham, Joe, 305
Booher, Cindy–Lee, 148
Booth, James, 278
Booth, JoAnita M., 59
Booth, Teresa, 221
Borthwick, Shirley L., 275
Bosher, Joan, 144
Boulay, Margaret, 272
Bouldin, Melissa Gail, 68
Bound, Rebecca, 181
Bowdidge, Sarah, 273
Bowen, Roberta D., 283
Bower, Jamie, 218
Boyce, Denny, 4
Boyd, Paula S., 266
Bradshaw, Chad, 95
Brady, Nancy E., 50
Bragg, J. Lee, 320
Brand, Rebecca, 136
Brandstadter, Beulah C., 148
Brantley, Tiffany, 252
Brantner, Holly F., 157
Breedlove, Keith, 305
Breezee, Amber, 314
Brennan, Siobhan, 286
Brereton, Teresa, 29
Brewer, Twilla Mae, 276
Bridges, Tim R., 196

Bridwell, Johnna, 246
Britt, Jaime, 70
Brochu, Melanie, 245
Brock, Dora, 237
Brogan, John, 233
Brolan, Barbara, 296
Brook–Gibbs, Colm, 263
Brooke, Kerry, 242
Brookes, John, 234
Brooks, Esther Din, 122
Brooks, Helen, 309
Brouse, L. E., 17
Browder, Linda D., 308
Brown, Angela Lei, 152
Brown, Carolyn, 168
Brown, Debbie, 266
Brown, Denise, 210
Brown, Derek, 228
Brown, Florence, 220
Brown, Iris, 147
Brown, Judith, 162
Brown, Julia, 9
Brown, Kate, 296
Brown, Krista, 127
Brown, Kuran Anne, 255
Brown, Luke A., 277
Brown, M., 67
Brown, Nancy L., 275
Brown, Orri D., 243
Brown, Rosina, 14
Brown, Sharon A., 111
Brown, Vevarine I., 288
Browning, G. B., 91
Brubaker, Joshua, 264
Bruce, Melanie, 256
Brumfield, Patricia, 271
Brunell, Roberta, 185
Bryant, Donale, 257
Bryant, Marquetta, 60
Bryant, Nancy Leigh, 199
Bryant, Sharon, 4
Bryant, Sr., John W., 251
Buckman, Julie, 69
Buckman, Ladele M., 317
Burch, John, 120
Burcham, Margaret D., 77
Burgess, Tatiana, 260
Burke, Andrew, 314
Burke, John, 61
Burlbaw, Jason, 136
Burling, Sherrie, 144
Burnett, Stephen, 295
Burns, Laverne E., 24
Burns, Ray, 29
Burns, Sheina, 284
Burns, Stacey, 304
Burrell, Richard Walter, 92
Burris, Chad, 216
Burrows, Marc, 168

Bursik, Nancy, 46
Burton, Cherylle, 201
Burton, Philip Arthur, 182
Butler, Phillip, 308
Bynum, Kevin D., 320

C

Cabibi, Celeste, 186
Cagle, Lisa, 171
Cahill, Ted, 96
Calchi, Diana, 170
Calco, Robert, 35
Caldwell Hooper, Matthew A., 287
Caldwell, Lyndee, 233
Calton, Regina, 251
Cambridge, Glen, 166
Cammaroto, Jessica, 281
Campbell, David W., 165
Campbell, Forrest, 150
Campbell, John K., 273
Canady, Erin, 157
Capansky, Patricia J., 313
Capps Jerome, Mildred, 142
Caraballo, Gladys, 75
Carabin, Leslie–Ann, 73
Carey, Rebecca, 247
Carjile, Flo, 71
Carleton, Courtney, 193
Carlin, Mary Jeanne, 58
Carlock, Bradley, 214
Carlton, Timothy S., 238
Carmon, Sarah A., 79
Carpenter, Aleata, 57
Carpenter–Harnish, Debbie, 121
Carrell, Nicole, 199
Carroll, Amanda, 209
Carroll, Robert A., 270
Carter, Jodie, 67
Carter, Kandice, 299
Case, Diane, 81
Cassidy, J., 293
Castelline, Daniel, 268
Castro, Jewell, 246
Cates, Bob, 187
Catterall, Carrie, 79
Celello, Barbara L., 69
Cesefske, Seena M., 264
Chafin, C. Joy, 172
Chalmers, Michael, 68
Chambers, Monica, 92
Chance, Lou, 257
Chandler, Melva, 249
Chandran, Vidya, 288
Chaney, Linda Jackson, 129
Chaney, Suzanne Elizabeth, 144
Chapman, Debra Anne, 122
Charlton, Robert John, 80
Chenoweth, Andrea Marie, 9

Cherney, Elizabeth A., 280
Chester, Cassie, 9
Chevalier, Darla, 149
Childers, Norma, 280
Chisholm, Jean, 253
Chivers, Christopher, 19
Chokas, Gerald, 60
Christison, Harold L., 226
Christison, Wanda P., 200
Christy, Bill, 304
Churchill, L. A., 19
Cianciotta, Laurie, 33
Clappison, Norah, 275
Clark, Allegra Leigh, 311
Clark, Gina, 265
Clarke, Christian, 118
Coak, Anthony J., 191
Coble, Heather, 211
Cody, Ellen Marie, 27
Cofarella, Theresa L., 206
Coffee, Joyce, 277
Cohen, Philip, 86
Colburn, Carol, 45
Coleman, Keith J., 16
Coleman, Roberta D., 285
Coleman, Veronica, 252
Coles, Ray, 165
Collings, Kim, 79
Collins, Gladys, 200
Collins, Kimberly, 168
Colvin, Eileen M., 260
Colwell, Tomesa, 212
Comadoll, John, 218
Compton, Margaret B., 99
Connell, S., 287
Conto, Beryl T., 124
Conyers, Mary B., 51
Cook, Floyd, 104
Cook, Lonia M., 81
Cook, Wendy, 194
Cooper, Annette, 35
Cooper, Dana M., 300
Cooper, Stuart, 143
Cope, Mavis J., 66
Copestick Moore, Karen, 154
Corbin, Dundi J., 32
Cordon, Amy, 188
Corey, James, 227
Cormell, Marie, 91
Corradino, Ida, 26
Correll, Henrietta, 41
Cosenza, Regina Anne, 55
Costello, Joyce, 114
Cote, Sarah, 146
Covarrubias, Alice, 104
Cowle, Daniel, 87
Cox, Cassie, 312
Cox, Renee, 226
Craig, Brian, 132

Crawford, David A., 97
Crawford, F.S.O., 160
Crawford, Forrest, 153
Crawford, Phillip, 292
Creem, Patricia A., 36
Crellin, Elizabeth M., 196
Crimmins, Maureen, 133
Crispin, JoEllen Dee, 280
Cronin, Jeannette, 76
Cross, Darren, 114
Cross, Margaret D., 200
Cruz, Cherylta C., 230
Cruz, Lillis, 159
Cubitt, Valerie M., 221
Cuevas, Fancy, 190
Culliton, Kaitlyn, 74
Cummins, Ethyle M., 257
Cunningham, Angela V., 177
Cunningham, Rita, 292
Curlett, Katie, 141
Curry Squires, Judy, 185
Custer, Jacquelyn, 259
Cutcher, Hal, 222
Cutler, Gladys, 167

D

D'Adamo, Cynthia, 15
Dahl, Tom, 249
Dahlgren, Martin J., 61
Dalton, Flora, 74
Dalziel, Joanne, 86
Damont, Raymond, 68
Danielle, Wendy, 183
Daniels, Cathy C., 151
Daniels, Evelyn J., 89
DanKenbring, Sarah, 201
Dannemiller, Phyllis, 135
Dartey–Baah, Samuel, 117
Davey, Patricia A., 255
Davidson, Katie S., 64
Davies, Jr., William, 6
Davies, Karen, 15
Davis, Corinna M., 265
Davis, Jonathan C., 145
Davis, Kathryn J., 206
Davis, Pauline, 84
Davis, Ronnisha, 47
Dawson, Mark, 91
Day, Verna E., 106
De Angelo, Jessica, 220
De Decker, George, 159
De Simone, Kim, 44
Deak, Cathy, 284
Dearth–James, Lori, 212
DeBella, Judiann, 241
DeLaurentis, John, 264
DeLisa, Emilia, 10
DeLoatch, Marian S., 30
Demers, Jessie, 216

Deneweth, Marcy S., 73
Denniff, Martha–Claire, 78
Denning, Paula, 93
Dereszynski, Ethan, 164
Derflinger, Judy, 239
Derr, Sharon Rabideau, 93
Devereaux, Karen, 251
Dew, Frances, 181
Diaz, Rachel R., 36
Dib, Marina M. H., 154
DiBenedict, Holly, 218
Dickerson, Ted, 213
Dickinson, Joanne, 147
DiDonato, Lauren, 307
Dieckman, Lauritz, 195
Diehl, C. M., 242
Diekson, Adrian L., 288
Dietrich, Deborah, 31
Dimare, James, 209
Dinsdale, Mary, 76
Dittrich, Kevin, 18
Diveney, Karen K., 253
Dixon, Ruth, 126
Dodge, F. J., 133
Dodok, Jim, 223
Dojee, Jigme, 108
Dolezal, Sandra, 62
Dollard, Mike, 102
Dollarhite, Beverly, 104
Domigan, Rebecca, 236
Donahue, Lynne, 287
Donaldson, Hazel F., 271
Donica, Trish, 138
Dorsey, Amy, 53
Dotson, Clyde, 226
Doty, Dawn, 92
Doty, Susan, 241
Douglas, Scott, 212
Dowell, Petronella, 203
Doyle, Michael R., 245
Doyle, Patrick, 234
Dragan, Joseph, 107
Drake, Pamela L., 85
Drayton, Philip, 101
DuBerry, Kristina DeAnn, 277
Ducke, Colleen, 199
Dudley, Vincent, 274
Duffy, Rosemary, 188
Durnford, Ruth, 110
Dye, Robert, 14
Dyson, Gail, 118

E

Early, James, 88
Easter, Diane, 56
Easter, Heidi, 128
Easterly, Angie, 159
Eberle, Rodney, 227
Ecke, Lee E., 63

Eckert, Michelle, 307
Edwards, C., 73
Edwards, G. Thom, 8
Edwards, Idella, 297
Edwards, Lisa, 46
Edwards, Martha, 211
Edwards, Mary Fitz, 238
Eisner–Thompson, Elizabeth, 278
Elden, Bill, 90
Elkins, Charles A., 289
Ellie, Astrid, 233
Ellis, Marsha G., 232
Ellis, Sherry, 284
Elmore, Kimberly, 33
Elzeni, Amir, 72
Elzey, Brenda, 157
Embury–Parker, Cindy, 108
Emerson, Yvonne, 256
Emery, John Dalton, 198
Epley, Tiffany, 126
Erickson, Carole M., 319
Erickson, Donna M., 51
Estep, Linda E., 305
Estes, Florence E., 125
Estes, Keith M., 187
Eudailey, Molly P., 164
Evans, Dorothy I., 286
Evans, J. Robert, 312
Evans, Louise, 65
Everett, Nancy, 208
Ewing, Suzanah, 265
Ezell, Richard, 160

F

Fallon, Don, 127
Farmer, Karen, 135
Farrah–Pugh, Martina, 96
Fasulo, Jonathan, 65
Fausett, Sarah, 107
Feary, Maisie, 233
Fehervari, Patricia A., 24
Fehner, Barbara, 282
Feldman, Irv, 227
Fender, Martha, 105
Ferraro, Linda, 121
Ferrill, Emily, 10
Ferris, Lawrence, 58
Firth Goddard, Hazel, 310
Fischer, Anita M. F., 189
Fisher, Carol, 116
Fisher, Wanda C., 291
Fiwchuk, Walter, 148
Fleckney, Susan Ann, 12
Fletcher, Velishia, 219
Flinders, Flora, 210
Flood, J. E., 296
Flores, Angel, 203
Flores, Leo J., 309
Flynn, Barbara A., 93

Flynn, Cynthia Ruth, 111
Follansbee, Stella J., 100
Ford Lindsey, Nancy Jo, 174
Ford, Connie G., 293
Forrest, Jenni, 191
Fortmeyer, Cheri A., 123
Foster, Cherylann, 86
Foster, Warren L., 181
Fowler, Sandra, 27
Fowles, Deborah, 15
Frank, Jennifer, 306
Freeland, Samantha P., 159
Freeman, Linda A., 201
Frew, Tammy, 97
Frost, Wendy P., 234
Frum, Lester E., 180
Fry, V. M., 142
Fulkerson, Sue, 278
Fulkroad, Sharon, 178
Full, Loretta K., 280
Fuller, John G., 282
Fuller, Vickie, 95

G

Gabriel, Pat, 301
Gadd, Alice, 275
Gaddy, Warna J., 314
Gair, Michael, 294
Galloso, Jill, 119
Galt, Anna, 67
Gapinski, Amber, 244
Garcia, Amelia, 308
Garcia, Martha, 166
Garcia, Phillip M., 115
Gardner, Gage M., 45
Gardner, Margaret, 94, 297
Garman, Wendy A., 37
Garner, Mike, 146
Garo, Candee, 55
Garrett, Debra E., 249
Garrett, E. E., 133
Garrigan, Patricia, 214
Garton, Jessica, 319
Gastineau, Kim, 256
Gaulke, Sandra, 80
Gaut, Angela, 129
Gauthier, Laura, 134
George, Bernadette, 215
Gertridge, Gillian, 150
Gewirtz, Matthew Dodge, 14
Ghee–Massey, Cynthia, 56
Ghilardi, Marilyn, 126
Gibson, Edwin, 200
Gibson, Elizabeth, 16
Gierczynski, Marlo, 83
Giguere, Patrick, 313
Gilbert, Jane, 218
Gilbert, Tammy, 263
Gillotti, Debbie, 210
Gilmore, Marcia, 317

Gisiora, E. M., 145
Gittens, Lionel J., 220
Gizzi, Michael, 231
Glasscock, Judy K., 119
Glassman, Sandra, 317
Glavinic, Sarah E., 73
Glodgett, Susan, 288
Gnann, Georgia, 122
Goar, David, 95
Good, Michele, 266
Gooday, Carlinda, 279
Goodwin, Joan, 143
Gordon, Serenity, 309
Gordon, Val, 258
Gordy, Amber, 103
Gorman, Elizabeth, 107
Gothard, Sherrye, 32
Gould, E. S., 8
Govar, Mary Lena, 33
Grace, Jeanie M., 245
Grace, Linda F., 106
Grant, Judith, 300
Grassa, Denise, 314
Graves, Melanie K., 55
Gray, Christle, 197
Greco, Carol, 242
Greene, Leslie, 159
Greene, William, 261
Greene–Patton, Laura, 317
Greenwood, Edgar M., 78
Gregoire, Shannon, 255
Gregory, Nancy S., 40
Gregson, Kris, 313
Gresswell, Stan, 118
Greyeyes, Brenda, 62
Gribben, James, 115
Gribbin, Malachy, 76
Griffin, Craig, 229
Grivas, Susan, 234
Gross, Tommie J., 156
Groth, Diane, 100
Grummett, Helen, 224
Guarnaccia, Reina K., 150
Guest, Megan, 17
Guidry, Vanice, 287
Gumpert, Henrietta, 182
Gunzburg–Vitkowsky, Mary, 297
Gustafson, Kathy, 230
Gwin, Robert, 291

H

Hackett, Mathew, 157
Hackworth, Elizabeth, 75
Hagen, Debbie, 251
Hague, Virginia A., 198
Hale, Richard, 113
Haley, Jason, 299
Hall, Olivia, 25
Hall, R. M., 27

Hall, Sheila R., 127
Hallett, Joan M., 114
Hambling, A. Joan, 144
Hamilton, Adam, 292
Hamilton, Judy, 137
Hammel, Virginia, 149
Hammond, Kingsleigh James, 40
Hammond, Scott J., 54
Hancock Rohman, Wanda, 54
Handy, Nixeon Civille, 69
Hannaford, Richard, 155
Hannah, Joan, 305
Hansen, Colleen, 96
Hansen, Joanne, 258
Hansen, Jr., Arne H., 208
Harbison, Alice O., 300
Harden, Jack L., 37
Harding, Pat, 158
Hardy, Beverly J., 73
Hare, Pat, 96
Haren, Tiffany, 201
Hargrave, Heather, 224
Hargrove, Susan, 156
Harper, Charles R., 203
Harper, Julie B., 241
Harr, Kyra A., 314
Harra, Cliffia L., 238
Harris, Carollyn, 259
Harris, Kevin, 247
Harrison, Jenifer, 202
Harse, Elizabeth A., 30
Hart, Christi A., 18
Harte, Derek, 166
Harts, Gail P., 299
Harvey, Robert S., 208
Hasell, Julia L., 315
Hassell, Jr., Frederick A., 319
Hasty, Nina Levorn, 194
Hatcher, Karen, 12
Hathaway, Hope, 310
Hathcock, Wilma, 181
Hatter, Michael, 180
Hatzes, Diane, 177
Hawkins, Paula, 75
Hayes, Joan E., 89
Hayes, Viola V., 210
Hayman, F. G., 297
Hayman, Jacqueline, 273
Haynes, Daniel, 294
Haynes, W., 226
Hays, Harry, 219
Heal, Clare Louise, 170
Hearn, Jr., Charles, 248
Heenan, Amy, 150
Heggan, Danielle, 140
Helmold, Frances, 202
Helms, Dottie, 254
Helton, Valerie, 256

Helton, William, 173
Hemmings, Samantha, 57
Hemstock, Basil, 48
Henderson, Robert, 107
Hendrickson, Jeanie C., 163
Hendrix, Vicki, 224
Henry, Jennifer, 219
Henry, Joseph, 266
Henry, Rhonda A., 63
Herbert, Rita, 163
Herdman, Kathy, 257
Hernandez, Gracie, 137
Hernandez, Margaret L., 293
Hernandez, Sandra, 45
Herrald, Dominick, 297
Hess, Ellen W., 127
Hesse, Tina–Marie, 174
Hethcoat, Martha A., 186
Hewett, Tammy, 176
Hickman, Essie Nicole, 237
Hickman, Pamela J., 256
Hicks, Catherine, 228
Hicks, Dorothy W., 182
Higgins, Debbie, 278
Hilsabeck, Burke, 137
Hinchcliffe, Bess T., 201
Hinz, Thomas, 266
Hipsky, Michelle, 316
Hirayama, Denis K., 76
Hitsman, Marion, 308
Hobbs, Mindy, 211
Hoda, Pearle, 289
Hodge, Nicole M., 237
Hodges, Kelly, 179
Hodges, Rex, 55
Hodges, Tammy, 230
Hoffman, Michelle, 8
Hogg, Gareth M., 63
Hogg, Leeann, 123
Holdgrafer, Edie, 98
Holman, Abby M., 315
Holmes, Carolyn L., 131
Holt, Kimberly G., 133
Holt, Marion, 79
Honomichl, Mary, 204
Hoogterp, Dorothy M., 137
Hope, Andrew, 262
Hopkins, Donald E., 179
Hopkins, Joan A., 31
Horn, Charlotte, 32
Horn, Sue H., 125
Horne, Peter K., 195
Horner, Buford L., 298
Horner, Derrick, 41
Horry, Lorraine, 19
Hostettler, Sarah A., 289
Houchins, Mary I., 244
House, Cheri, 312
House, Kirk K., 316
Howard, Crystal L., 243

Howard, Susan T., 49
Howe, Arlene M., 132
Howell, Cheryl W., 156
Howell, Mary R., 252
Hoyle, Jean H., 260
Hubbard, Holly, 226
Hubbard, Tamara, 285
Huber, Joseph, 172
Hudson, Amy, 250
Hudson, Glen, 304
Hudson, Mary Grace, 100
Huebler, Nancy A., 22
Huening, Adam, 57
Huff, Tammy, 151
Hull, Thelma, 304
Humphreys, Brian, 131
Hunt, Claudine E., 285
Hunt, Stephen D., 101
Hunte, Anetha, 190
Hunter, M., 184
Hunter, Sharon C., 302
Hurrell, Alexandra, 130
Hurst, Christina, 110
Hutson, Frances, 178
Hyde, Wes, 11

I

Iloabuchi, Emmanuel U., 190
Insch, Jack L., 297
Iroegbu, Monica, 257
Iron, Onin–Age, 249
Irvin, Kimberly, 304
Isaac, Julie L., 147
Issa, Walid, 310
Italiano, Judy, 217
Izquierdo, Lorinne, 198

J

Jackson Balay, Jane, 228
Jackson, Michael R., 274
Jackson, Nancy, 274
Jackson, Phyllis E., 128
Jacobs, Dallas, 116
Jacobs, Georgina, 209
Jacobsen, Mary, 213
James, James E., 135
James, R. J., 4
Jameus, Bridget, 217
Janke, Jean, 63
Jaquis, Diane, 72
Jarmon, Karen, 78
Jarzomski, Beth, 4
Jaslanek, Marie, 170
Javed, Naila, 100
Jay, Edward, 115
Jenkins, Vyvyen C., 298
Jenkinson, Philip Michael, 203
Jennings, Cody A., 112
Jensen, Jamie, 272
Jirikowic, Gina, 155
Jobson, Lee, 214

Johannessen, Diane, 61
Johnsen, Trisa I., 31
Johnson, Amanda Jane, 222
Johnson, Barbara, 158
Johnson, Chad, 43
Johnson, M. E., 124
Johnson, Yvonne, 191
Johnston, John, 290
Jones, Aaron, 185
Jones, Anthony P., 160
Jones, J. J., 208
Jones, Jean, 10
Jones, Katherine M., 142
Jones, Latifa, 51
Jones, Stephen L., 110
Jones, T. D., 179
Jones, Tammy D., 179
Jordan, Deirdre, 136
Jordan, Miranda, 215
Jordan, Nicole L., 321
Jorgensen, Cheryl, 271
Joshi, Vishnu P., 68
Joshua, Muriel, 176
Juarez, Epi, 10
Jubak, Matthew R., 44
Julian, Heather, 223
Just, Kathleen, 253

K

Kalota, Anthony M., 205
Kamara, Sharon, 152
Kamler, Dorothy, 280
Karnish, Sara R., 221
Kass, James P., 103
Kaye, Sylvia J., 116
Keane, Kathleen, 281
Keech, Coreen, 75
Keeling, Jr., William H., 145
Keene, Donna M., 102
Kehoe, John, 151
Kehrli–DeDeaux, Amy B., 11
Keill, Kimberly, 130
Keith, Sandy, 186
Kelley, Diane Appling, 223
Kelly, Gregory L., 117
Kelly, Katrina, 174
Kelly, Theresa D., 316
Kemer, Linda, 88
Kemp, Hazel V., 129
Kennedy, Diane, 109
Kennedy, Kerri L., 108
Kennedy, Roberta J., 99
Kennedy, Sheena, 258
Kenny, Louisa, 153
Kent, Stuart J., 267
Ker, Dianne, 293
Kerby, Mary E., 84
Kestenis, Holly, 140
Kester, Kathy, 140
Keyes, Kindell, 239

Keyes, Rebecca, 318
Keys, Betty J., 94
Khmelnitskaya, Yelena, 167
Kiberd, Philip, 197
Kijowski, Donna, 106
Kilby, Marcella M., 198
Kinder, Merle, 189
King, Megan, 218
Kinser, Kathy E., 299
Kinsey, Evelyn, 188
Kinsey, Heather, 85
Kirk, Veronica L., 292
Kirkman, Nellie A., 164
Kister, Anita, 305
Kite, Chad, 291
Kleiman, Connie, 305
Klinge, Peggy J., 244
Klingler, Norm, 42
Klock, Carole, 112
Klos, Alice W., 241
Knight, John W., 6
Knight, Lesley, 169
Knight, Paxton, 154
Knot, Michaela, 260
Knouse, Evelyn M., 94
Knowlton, Linda, 23
Knox, Karissa Anne, 154
Knutson, Richard A., 61
Kolojejchick, Denise, 28
Konsistorum, Eli, 191
Koontz, Kay, 247
Kopack, Pamela Lee, 283
Kosnikowski, Tadeusz T., 44
Kridle, Eric J., 224
Kuhl, Lorene, 166
Kulovitz, Christopher, 153
Kummer, Jenn, 137
Kunz, Gina M., 254
Kurth, Grace Ellen, 82
Kussrow, Tanya, 135
Kuxhausen, Dorothy, 246

L

Labarbera, Coreen, 152
Labescat, Robert, 207
Ladia, Ondray B., 247
Ladner, Allen, 57
LaFerriere, Brenda T., 240
Lafrance, Pierre J., 124
LaFrancis, Monica E., 139
Laing, Phoebe J., 263
Lamb, Emily Victoria, 84
Lamie, Mary E., 82
Landes, Carla, 208
Landini, Amber, 304
Lane, Jessica, 277
Langford, E., 192
Langford, Eva, 181, 195
Langland, Violet, 306
Laroche, Nancyann, 79

Larsen, Michelle, 93
Laughlin, Desiree, 220
Lauretta, Joseph W., 284
Lawlor, Linette, 311
Lawrence, Eileen, 87
Lawrence, Horatio, 221
Lawrence, Mildred Z., 210
Lawson, Penny, 73
Layne, Maria C., 147
Leach, Geraldine, 270
Leach, Renee Lenerville, 72
Leach, Rona, 113
Lee, Dorothy, 101
Lee, Guadalupe, 249
Lee, Kate, 80
Lehr, Jean, 54
Lehr, Marleen Stracener, 158
Leighton, John, 11
Leistra, Nicholas J., 58
Lemonte, Nichole, 265
Leonard, Pamela S., 311
LeRette, Robert A., 131
Lesko, Susan C., 60
Levron, Wilson P., 90
Lewis, Cynthia R., 56
Libuser, Arlene, 222
Lightbody, J. H., 117
Liles, Ashleigh, 306
Lilly, Christine, 254
Lindekugel, Jerrianne, 187
Linden, Amy, 183
Lindenmayer, Arleen J., 173
Linhardt, Kathleen, 16
Lisby, Sherry L., 126
Littlejohn, Barbara, 313
Lodge–Mclachlan, Nicki, 59
Loechel, Betty, 37
Lohrengel, Linda, 194
Long, Melissa, 120
Long, Susan, 26
Longboy, Noel Darion, 139
Lord, Becky, 101
Lovan, Elmer, 243
Lowry, LeeAnne, 170
Lucas, Layne, 316
Luke, Damon E., 88
Lund, Carolene J., 78
Lundmark, Rena, 267
Lunsford, Rebecca Brand, 184
Lutes Fields, Lori, 151
Luttrell, G. Milton, 206
Lynch, Rosemary, 61
Lynn, Irene, 272
LynnHeart, Cheryl, 315
Lyons, Ethyl, 53
Lytle, Gladys E., 55
Lyulkin, Elizabeth, 13

M

Macaden, Ragini, 124

MacDonald, Linda, 128
MacDonald, Marie, 267
MacGregor, J., 57
Macharoni, Valeri A., 158
MacLellan, Amanda, 317
Maclennan, Ian, 286
MacMartin, Lynette R., 197
Maddalena, Sandra, 270
Maddren, David V., 196
Madore, Sherrill, 28
Magie–McKenzie, Judy, 27
Mahoney, Julie, 106
Mahuron, Lisa, 126
Mai, Chau, 10
Malaske, Joyce, 87
Maloch, Anna E., 225
Mann, Annis L., 288
Manning, Adelle, 19
Marasco, Peggy, 61
Marble, Amy, 109
Marceau, Muriel, 303
March, Janice, 188
Marconi, Lily, 290
Marcus, Albert, 23
Marks, Marjorie A., 54
Markwell, Linda Diane, 265
Marquez, Luis, 57
Marshall II, Troy, 138
Marston, Elizabeth, 161
Martin, Inna J., 66
Martin, Pamela, 248
Martin, Wiley, 86
Martinez, Minerva, 177
Marvel Felix, Denna V., 195
Marzano–Sajna, Anna G., 39
Mason, Angela R., 113
Mason, Cherry, 116
Mass, Jason M., 7
Materface, D. R., 148
Matthews, Joan, 119
Matthews, Marilyn S., 105
Maxwell, Charlotte Ellis, 99
Maybury, David, 285
Mayhew, Annie, 113
Mayo, Bloody Feathers, 310
McCalmont, Diane, 81
McCann, Barbara S., 249
McCann, Norma Jean, 69
McCartney, Lois A., 121
McCartney, Pearl, 175
McCaulla, Kelly A., 121
McCollum, Shari, 182
McCommon, Mitchell D., 71
McConville, Kathleen W., 97
McCormack, Mary Ellen, 101
McCormick, Diane D., 38
McCraw, Joan, 214
McCreary, Kristina S., 51
McCroskey, Denise, 33

McCroy, Melaney, 156
McCully, Robert D., 263
McDaniel, James S., 128
McDonald, Kathryn Jean, 167
McElhone, Yvonne, 131
McErlane, Bonnie H., 239
McEvoy, Angela June, 232
McGhee, Sylvia W., 282
McGillis, Felicia Susan, 143
McGlasson, Bryan Keith, 38
McGrail, Edith, 11
McGuire, Inola M., 152
McHugh, Rossana E., 89
McIntosh, Spence, 58
McKay, Athena, 205
McKeller, Mary, 152
McKenzie, Doris, 182
McKissock, Kathleen E., 302
McKnight, Jane, 66
McKnight, Megan, 225
McKune, Arieona R., 112
McLaughlin, Charlotte C., 238
McLemore, Joan, 67
McLendon, Bobbi, 13
McLucas, Patricia L., 271
McManamy, Marion R., 9, 194
McNeil, Mathew, 116
McParland, Micheal, 6
Meadows, Mary Christina, 19
Meagan, Ann–Marie, 47
Meaney, Thelma, 112
Means, Wanda, 84
Mears, Sharina, 291
Medina, Veronica, 162
Meglio, Maria, 131
Melley, Stephanie A., 92
Meloche, Sandy, 72
Melrath, Bernadette, 44
Mendenhall, Ann Hunot, 123
Mendoza, Lolita Arreola, 54
Mercer, Malissa, 246
Meritt, Ann E., 279
Merrell, Phillip, 98
Merry, John, 198
Messer, Kyle E., 169
Messina, Robert, 301
Meyer, James J., 309
Meyers, Vern, 143
Mickel, Chris, 245
Miga, Denise, 155
Mihalik, Bianca, 200
Miller, Betty Lou, 173
Miller, Elizabeth, 300
Miller, Emily, 264
Miller, Jennifer, 207
Miller, Michael, 139
Miller, Michele, 303
Miller, Sharon B., 237
Miller, Tim L., 167

Milligan, Andrena, 192
Mills, Janice, 317
Mills, Michael, 231
Milstein, Jennifer, 205
Milton, Linda, 296
Milward, Sharon, 146
Mimande, Diane L., 134
Ming, Renee R., 78
Minnie, Sandra, 80
Mitchell, Brandy, 216
Mitchell, Mary C., 264
Mitchell, Tracy, 298
Mitchley, Robert L., 240
Mizzell, Barbara J., 255
Mlynski, Melinda, 157
Molex, Jr., Norvell A., 5
Molnar, Krista, 229
Mongrain, Donald G., 196
Monroe, Mandy, 320
Montenegrino, Christina, 60
Montesano, Matt, 147
Montgomery, Shelia, 272
Mook, Curtis M., 216
Mooney, Marissa G., 248
Moore, Alaouise A., 226
Moore, Garland, 205
Moore, John D., 128
Moore, Priscilla McShane, 248
Moore, Thomas, 154
Morales, Theresa, 65
Moran, Barbra, 272
Moran, Michael, 234
Morehead, Marjorie K., 183
Moreno, Rachel, 161
Morgan, Betty, 148
Morgan, Juanita Kay, 206
Morgan, Karen L., 75
Morgan, Stephen, 192
Morgan, Tom, 71
Moritz, Eileen, 313
Morley, Andrea, 161
Morrell, Valerie, 262
Morris, Clover D., 268
Morris–Pierce, Elizabeth, 20
Morrison, Mary Jane, 71
Morrison, Nathaniel Bud, 152
Morton, Suzy, 243
Mosiondz III, Peter, 157
Mosley, Mary, 99
Moss, M. D., 244
Mowat, Diana, 6
Mudger, Sandy, 16
Mueller, Candie, 291
Muellerleile, Michael, 220
Mulcaster, Ruth, 308
Mulchandani, Christina Marie, 193
Mullis, Bobby, 88
Munley, Meggie, 225

Murless, Philip, 219
Murphy, E., 52
Murphy, Lee, 26
Murphy, Martha J., 90
Murphy, Rosie B., 253
Murphy, Ruth Webb, 121
Murray, Darlyn S., 89
Murray, Deborah Ann, 184
Murray, Jan, 258
Murray, Michael J., 18
Murry, Eugenia, 41

N

Naeem, B. J., 70
Napier, Janice, 235
Naylor, Lisa, 259
Negrete, C. C., 156
Neil, Marie E., 296
Nells, Lee, 153
Nelson, Timothy, 214
Nesse, Nicole, 320
Newman, Christian, 191
Newman, Nicole, 98
Newton, B. J., 145
Newton, Geoffrey, 50
Neyman, Vera, 122
Nicholson, Laurie A., 7
Nigh, Danette, 145
Nightingale, Joanna, 82
Noah, Autumn Marie, 149
Noble, Dan, 228
Nolen, Athena, 182
Noriega, Saturnino, 213

O

O'Connor, Robin, 187
O'Dell, Selene S., 287
O'Hara, Doretta, 168
O'Meara, Charles K., 212
Oatley, Jeannette, 190
Odeh, Christopher, 173
Ogburn, Jerry W., 250
Oliver, Barbara W., 132
Olnick, Barbara, 103
Olsen, Ardys M., 179
Olson, Doris M., 171
Olson, Eleanor L., 145
Olson, Laura, 215
Oltmann, Pamala, 279
Olver, Kelly, 319
Orchard, Michael S., 215
Ortega, Margarita, 161
Ortiz, Isabel, 189
Ortiz, Kathy, 48
Ortiz, Maricarda, 197
Osborne, Tara, 62
Osorie, Luis W., 303
Overfield, Ronald L., 35
Owens, Brian, 124

P

Paananen, Katrina, 43
Pagan, Chris, 191
Palmer Lowe, Gwendolyn, 167
Palmer, Mike D., 74
Palmer, Robert A., 34
Palmese, Barbara, 133
Panaccione, Cathy, 232
Papineau, Allison, 229
Parker, Essie B., 159
Parker, Leia, 141
Parks, Ruth A., 86
Parr, Janet L., 95
Parrish, Spring W., 163
Parrish, Winnifred, 132
Pash, Margaret, 115
Pashe, Sheri, 268
Patterson, Ginger Lee, 188
Patterson, Noel, 70
Patterson, Sharon D., 168
Pattni, Sheena, 284
Pauls, Beryl, 195
Paxton, Yvonne, 294
Payton, Brian Michael, 245
Pearson, Rachel, 232
Pearson, Ruth, 308
Pedraza, Cheryl, 253
Peete, Janet H., 146
Pelkey, Karen M., 242
Pelles, Bernice, 90
Pepple, Alexander, 167
Perez, Lauren, 234
Perez, Mitzi N., 193
Perez, Natalie, 124
Perkins, Gordon L., 164
Perkins, Leeann, 204
Perpetua, Diane M., 184
Perritt, Cathy, 219
Pesti, Gary, 282
Peters, Henry, 318
Peters, James, 186
Peters, Ruth C., 219
Peters, Sue, 172
Peterson, Iris A., 261
Petrash, Myska, 186
Petrie, June, 286
Petros, Janice E., 309
Pflug, Robert M., 302
Philipp, Billy, 112
Phillips Ewing, Annie, 146
Phillips, Darrelyn, 45
Phillips, Shirley A., 239
Phipps, Glenda K., 79
Phipps, Tracy, 5
Pickersgill, Dinah, 144
Pickles, Debby, 262
Pielin, Erin K., 125

Pierce, Sandra, 183
Pierce, Sharon M., 306
Pieretti, Gloria, 142
Pike, Nona, 166
Pikus, Adele, 283
Pilch, Donna, 17
Pilkey, Kathy, 286
Pilkington, Patty, 176
Pimentel, Paula M., 34
Piper, Emily Jayne, 67
Pitts, Heather, 207
Ploski, Sally, 36
Ploss, Jim, 12
Pociasek, Stephanie, 37
Poe, Debbie, 25
Pohl, Martha R., 259
Poindexter, Ada Marie, 64
Polasek, Kathleen R., 125
Polikoff, Ron M., 83
Poll, Mary L., 232
Pollestad, Betty Lou, 302
Pomeroy, Roselle, 256
Pond, Patricia G., 111
Pool, Kathy, 59
Pope, Susan E., 235
Portelli, Jon, 48
Portune, Robin Leigh, 13
Poston, Margaret, 189
Potter, Brad, 292
Powells, Michael A., 236
Powers, Mary Lee, 207
Prahl, Lavon, 200
Prasser, Geraldine R., 293
Pratt, Anne–Marie, 134
Pratt, Marguerite, 12
Pratt, T., 12
Prehart–Fourcaud, Lorraine
    Helen, 189
Presland, A., 295
Presley, Dominica, 221
Proia, Carl J., 101
Proietti, Belinda Jean, 123
Pryor, Flynn, 216
Puckett, Lela M., 43
Pugliese, Pamela, 66
Pulliam, Ilse–Dore, 52

Q

Quellette, Donna, 199
Queyquep, Tess, 140
Quinn, Liza, 80

R

Ragsdale, M. E., 63
Rail, Diego, 209
Ramos, Hattie V., 257
Rand, Richard, 163
Randall, George H., 15

Ransom, Dawnita, 307
Raphael–Hall, Shelagh, 225
Rashid, Nancy C., 66
Rasler, Mandy, 119
Rasmussen, Mavis L., 135
Ratcliffe, Patricia, 298
Ravalli, Jennifer, 216
Rawls, Randy, 132
Ray, Peggy, 177
Raymes, Kathi, 184
Reagan, Christopher D., 183
Reece, Ronald L., 213
Reed, Cherie, 303
Rees, D. C., 166
Register, Jayne, 140
Rehill, Ravinder Kaur, 298
Reinhart, Sue, 212
Reinholdt, A. Mae, 119
Reis, Rachel Amanda, 204
Reno, Teresa, 100
Reuther, Laura, 162
Rew–Dixon, Jonathan, 8
Rhynard, Shawna, 202
Richard, Georgia, 202
Richards, Eddie, 160
Richardson, Gloria L., 108
Ricks, Charles Douglas, 41
Riemenschneider, David, 7
Riggins, LaQuanda, 81
Riley, Candy D., 31
Riley, Margaret, 91
Ritch, Cheryl, 49
Ritchie, Cindy L., 129
Rivard, Amber, 280
Rivera, W. R., 160
Rivers, Mozelle W., 271
Roark, Sheila B., 261
Roberson, Geri, 274
Roberts, Tammy Lynn, 223
Robertson Klinger, Velma, 82
Robertson, Eric, 107
Robinson, Debra Lynn, 8
Robinson, Dolly K., 109
Robley, Marjorie H., 192
Robley, Robyn, 138
Robnett, Rick, 178
Rocha, Rafael W., 111
Rochon, Glenn, 265
Rock, Natalie, 22
Rodgers, C., 125
Rodgers, J. B., 301
Rodriguez, Jessyca, 71
Rodriques, Abigail, 90
Roegge, Sara, 9
Roehrick, Vicki Ann, 283
Rogers, Ida, 84

Rogers, Lydia M., 281
Rogers, Shelley, 205
Rolfe, Kevin, 294
Rolling, Yvonne Clement, 251
Rook, Misty Renee, 165
Rooke, David, 295
Roraff, Barbara, 279
Rose, Catherine, 91
Rose, John, 115
Rose, Victoria Denny, 174
Ross, D. I., 4
Ross, Doris, 127
Ross, Enid, 251
Ross, Raymond M., 139
Rosseland, Karen, 268
Rossignol, Chandler, 174
Rouse, Markanne T., 204
Roussel, Gary K., 235
Rowan, Jacqueline, 169
Rudolph, Zoe Murphy, 13
Ruggiero, Michael J., 180
Runnion, Ross, 279
Runyan, Deborah A., 94
Rushton, C., 8
Rushton, Jeff, 60
Rutherford, Elsie, 295
Rutter, Sherry L., 205
Rygh, Danielle M., 193

S

Sadanaga, Amy, 311
Salazar, Rene, 258
Salipek, Stacie, 50
Sallis, Kim D., 320
Salter, Sharon T., 5
Saltzsieder, Roseann M., 232
Salvador, Tara Marie, 172
Salvaggio, Richard Paul, 34
Sams, Dawn, 58
Sanchez, Maureen, 83
Sanders, Joan, 154
Sandy, Myra, 217
Sanginario, Joan M., 153
Santana, Sandra, 111
Santiago, Dawn Marie, 118
Sasso, William E., 151
Saunders, Ronna H., 302
Savage, Amy, 82
Savoury, Edwin, 165
Sawyer, Diane M., 247
Saxon, Joyce I., 168
Scarff, Kenneth, 7
Schaefer, Jennie, 197
Scheff, Sharon, 307
Schettig, Nancy, 63
Scheuermann, Laura M., 275
Schneider, Debbie, 113
Schneider, F. Richard, 318
Schoenbaum, Gregory R., 40
Schuh, Kimberly S., 281

Schultz, John, 5
Schwartz, Mary F., 70
Schwarz, Robin, 77
Scott, May, 164
Scott, Neil, 76
Seaborn, Ida B., 218
Seerattan, Frank, 310
Seibert, Lisa, 173
Seidel, Lillian M., 269
Seitzinger, Ramona, 10
Selby, P. J., 16
Sell, Kim M., 72
Semana, Melissa, 103
Senter, Patricia D., 39
Senter, Wray, 253
Serr, Kathi, 309
Serrano–Gonzalez, Di Maries
  E., 40
Severance, Tonia C., 136
Seymour, Nikki, 48
Shadrick, Emma D., 180
Shady, Helen, 246
Shahan, Jan L., 276
Shankly, G., 7
Shapiro, Rachelle, 198
Shaw, Apikia, 196
Shaw, Lyndsay Jayne, 223
Shaw, Ruth, 225
Shaw, Scott, 177
Shawn, Heath, 204
Shelton, Sandra, 141
Shepherd, Adam, 214
Shipes, Karen, 321
Shipp, Jill G., 187
Shipp, Joshua, 50
Shirey, Hillary, 269
Shirley, Alexandra, 231
Sholly, Myrna, 30
Shore, S. J., 294
Shryock, Wendy L., 118
Shucet, Nicholas G., 95
Sibley, Alene, 71
Siegel, Mina S., 281
Simon, Diane R., 87
Simonson, Megan, 109
Simpson, R., 76
Sippel, Steven, 29
Sirois, Dorothy R., 311
Skinner, J., 81
Slagle, Bonnie L., 126
Slatalla, Joan, 17
Slaughter, Jennifer, 320
Sloan, Jeanette, 275
Sloan, Shana, 224
Smihula, Thomas, 201
Smiley, Ralph N., 185
Smith III, William Henry, 223
Smith, Audrey Nadine, 321
Smith, Beverly J., 236

Smith, Carla J., 290
Smith, Cheryl, 244
Smith, Christina M., 114
Smith, Frances L., 122
Smith, Gail, 151
Smith, Gilbert T., 5
Smith, Gladys M., 95
Smith, Henrietta, 240
Smith, Kevin, 250
Smith, Kimberly, 106
Smith, Margaret A., 290
Smith, Marilyn Faye, 247
Smith, Mark, 92
Smith, Mildred, 206
Smith, Patty, 307
Smith, Philip L., 108
Smith, Sharon, 59
Smith, Sheila M., 87
Smith, Sheryl, 70
Smith, Tammy, 319
Smith–Neil, Sandi, 288
Smith–Santoro, Tammi Kath-
  leen, 25
Snapp, Pattie G., 175
Snead, Olivia S., 184
Sneeringer, Erica, 89
Snell, Sandy A., 39
Snelling, Amber, 169
Sobczak, Laurie, 271
Sobrero, K. L., 209
Soden, Margie A., 181
Sorenson, Jean, 238
Soto, Stephanie, 237
Spain, Sharron, 47
Spears, Rocco C., 306
Spector, Winifred, 194
Spence, Eileen W., 254
Spencer–Smith, Madge, 295
Spinks, K., 12
Spohn, Susan Kay, 77
Spreacker, Anita, 38
Sprigg, Steve, 175
Springston, Geraldine, 85
Squier, Victoria M., 163
St. Peter, Kendra, 43
Stair–Hensley, Patricia, 202
Staley, Anna Belle, 134
Stalion, Tricia, 171
Stallard, Karen, 158
Stallworth, Andrew, 66
Stampley, Joanne, 291
Stark, M. B., 134
Starratt, Fenn Morse, 250
Stavely, Ruth, 87
Steadman, Ron, 135
Stephenson, Natalie, 149
Sterling, Gillian, 74
Stern, Susan R., 169
Stevens, Stevie, 139

Stevens, Verlin H., 203
Stewart, Linda, 281
Stickley, Philip, 14
Stigall, Vicki, 161
Stiles, Mary L., 115
Stovall, Terry D., 276
Strickland, Charles, 173
Strock, Timothy W., 102
Strom, Christina, 74
Strong, Catherine A., 109
Strubberg, Carolyn Marie, 267
Sudol, Eric, 146
Sue, Jacquelene, 252
Suiters, Cloamae, 183
Sullivan, Gladys A., 193
Sullivan, Sarah L., 130
Sullivan, Valerie J., 259
Summers, Robert, 270
Sutherland, Melissa, 208
Sutterfield, Jackie, 264
Sutterfield, Lora, 18
Swackhammer, Nora P., 155
Swanson, James V., 285
Swanson, Rachel, 88
Sweetapple, Jean S., 313
Sykes, Mary E., 224
Szymanski, Michele, 246
Szymecko, Tom, 72

T

Tablason, Domitila R., 90
Tackett, Kristen, 282
Talbot, Tracy, 312
Talley Hynes, Jill, 138
Tamplin, Pamela, 272
Tanksley, Dessie, 49
Tapscott, Brandy, 318
Tarpey, Carla, 118
Tasnier, Margaret, 192
Taubenfeld, Bev, 24
Taylor, Clara F., 239
Taylor, Graham, 254
Taylor, J. L., 273
Taylor, Jeff, 165
Taylor, Lynda, 53
Taylor, Mary, 83
Teats, Lucille E., 250
Tejeda, Pedro, 30
Telschow, Anthony, 243
Templin, David R., 318
Tenney, Christine S., 230
Terwilliger, Jared, 11
Tett, Veronica, 94
Tharp, Glenda Darlene, 194
Thayer Kostenbauder, Sharon,
  64
Thew, Sandy, 110
Thibodeau, Kiley, 307
Thomas Ariyibi, Doris, 52

Thomas, Charlisa, 179
Thomas, Michael W., 105
Thomas, Peggy Wilson, 175
Thompson, Maria S., 236
Thompson, Pam, 185
Thompson, Patricia, 269
Thompson, Robert J., 32
Thompson, Sarah F., 240
Thompson, Shannon, 212
Thompson, Tonyah, 204
Thompson, Veronicka J., 104
Thompson, Victoria, 261
Thompson, Wendy, 5
Thompson-Moser, Deirdre, 315
Thomson, Catherine, 42
Thomson, Evabel, 289
Tidcombe, Steven Paul, 283
Tierney, John, 13
Tijerina, Rebecca, 235
Tillman, Bridgette Denise, 231
Timmons, Brian P., 86
Toben, Jeralyn, 268
Todd, Toni, 290
Toler, Patricia B., 29
Tolley, Doug, 222
Tornstrom, David, 303
Toste, Nina, 22
Touchstone, Jonathan B., 260
Tovar, Bernadette, 202
Townsend, Vickie, 39
Trainor, Chris, 174
Tran, Ben, 255
Treanor, Kristi, 302
Tremblay, Phyllis, 142
Trimble, Heather, 206
Trujillo, Beverly, 25
Tsosie, Donavin, 298
Tsouros, Athina, 242
Tunstall, Troy C., 129
Turner, Gay, 125
Turner, Gloria, 54
Turner, Michael, 96
Turocy, Wendy, 238
Twichell, Rebecca, 169
Tyler, Stephanie, 28

U

Ubbelohde, Paul, 276
Ulreich, Julie M., 62
Ulrich, Jane, 77
Utas, Leah J., 170

V

Valentina, Aljokhina, 62
Van Kirk, Janet M., 109
Van Orman, Sandra S., 188
Vandergriff, Tamarah, 240
Vandersteen, Jennifer, 301

Vannah, Laura K., 263
Vassileva, Vessela, 110
Vega, Sharon, 108
Vela, Estevan, 207
Velasco, Justin, 220
Vennette, Irene E., 147
Verbeck, Elizabeth M., 312
Verdades, Vernon D., 269
Vereen, Jimmy P., 23
Vierck, Jason, 171
Villarreal, Monica, 239
Vincent, Sandra, 65
Vincnet, Starr, 28
Viner, Sharon, 94
Vogel, Eleanor M., 78
Vogel, Jennifer M., 123

W

Wagener, Mary, 69
Wagner, Diane, 233
Wagner, Nigal C., 242
Wainwright, Kim, 252
Waite, Deborah, 58
Walden, Nina, 178
Waldon, Glenda Victoria, 132
Walker, Cheryl, 92
Walker, Erika L., 127
Walker, Virginia L., 187
Wall, Jane, 222
Wallace, Walter, 276
Waller, Pamela, 120
Walmsley, Andrew, 261
Walsh, Nena C., 259
Walsh, Phyllis N., 148
Wampler, Ivan, 17
Wandersee, Wanda, 190
Wapachee, Faith, 231
Wardell, C. A., 69
Warhurst, J. E., 254
Warmann, Carl, 6
Warner, Sherri, 107
Warren, Brenda L., 241
Warren, Debbie J., 207
Watkins, Chris, 299
Watkins, Kimberly, 105
Watkins, Paul W., 303
Watkins, Sheena, 213
Watson, James R., 274
Waugh, Kelly-Ann, 75
Weatherbee, Julia, 64
Webb, Jackie, 300
Webb, John A., 130
Webb, Kenneth E., 120
Weber, Karie, 261
Weber, Lois B., 120
Weems, Carole A., 227
Weese, Joshua G., 64
Weesies, B. J., 237

Weglewski, Tina, 170
Wells, Carmon, 211
Wenzel, Bernice, 14
Werner, Harold, 199
Wertz, Kimberly L., 153
Wesson, Lola W., 273
West, Regina Rena, 70
Westall, Margaret A., 38
Westgate, Judi, 18
Weston, George A., 81
Weyrauch, D. M., 277
Wharton, Amy Grace, 276
Whipple, Leslie E., 98
Whitaker, Kay, 130
Whitaker, M. M., 175
White III, Arthur H., 140
Whitehead, Michelle L., 141
Whitehouse, Christine Mary,
    176
Whitfield, Victoria, 171
Whiting, Martha A., 119
Whittemore, Glenda, 83
Whitten, Kris, 103
Widder, Shareen, 284
Widell, Tina, 312
Wier, Denise, 286
Wigginton, Raven, 138
Wightman, Jo, 19
Wilber, Jennifer, 231
Wilcox, Esther Ruth, 240
Wilcox, T. H., 46
Wilder, Eileen, 59
Wilkes, Kevin, 144
Wilkins, Fern, 236
Wilkins, Janice, 62
Wilkinson, Doreen, 129
Wilkinson, Jeri, 24
Wilkinson, Michele H., 67
Williams, Betty, 150
Williams, Cynthia D., 65
Williams, Elwyn, 15
Williams, Florence, 248
Williams, Heather, 278
Williams, Holly, 228
Williams, Jennie, 35
Williams, Joel, 128
Williams, Lucas, 235
Williams, Marie, 80
Williams, Mark, 142
Williams, Melonia, 244
Williams, Rachel, 121
Williamson, Rose P., 105
Willis, Angela M., 316
Willis, Beth, 163
Willson, Hildegarde, 285
Wilmore, Jr., H. E., 56
Wilshaw, Freda, 114

Wilson, Bethany, 274
Wilson, Jr., Robert, 77
Wilson, Patricia L., 89
Wilson, Rose, 117
Wilson, Valarie, 156
Wingert, Stormey, 102
Winkle, Matthew D., 178
Winslow, Veronica, 227
Wint, Kim, 138
Winter, Ashley, 243
Winter, Tamsin, 99
Wirthlin, Barbara, 68
Wise, Tanya, 289
Wohlman, Kimberli-Ann, 193
Wolfe, Anthony, 281
Wolfe, Sandra, 130
Wolfe, T. R., 143
Wood, B. J., 318
Wood, Betty, 96
Wood, Lincoln E., 269
Wood, R., 221
Woodall, Calvin, 306
Woodham-Irby, Marilyn, 141
Woods Sanders, Laurie, 16
Woods, Deborah, 255
Woods, John, 158
Wray, Cassie D., 88
Wray, Jr., Linford A., 215
Wright, Barbara, 93
Wright, Christina, 102
Wright, Faye B., 59
Wright, Gwen, 262
Wright, Margaret, 311
Wright, Pauline, 186
Wrigley, Francesca, 116
Wynn, Brid, 270
Wysocki, Jennie, 162

Y

Yager, Lacy, 102
Yard, Christina L., 7
Yeager, Timothy Ryan, 252
York, Amy, 299
Young, Josephine Butler, 93
Young, Karen R., 136
Young, Victor J., 149
Youngblood, Billy W., 316
Younger, Ann C., 296
Yowell, Joan, 133
Yule, Susan, 165

Z

Zanetti, Emma M., 180
Zaragoza, Alvin, 97
Zarrella-Schneider, Jeannie,
    120
Zellermaier, Paul, 111
Zettl, Erika, 9
Zobel, Sandra, 136